Feminist Frontiers
Rethinki███████████nder, and Soci█████

Laurel Richardson and Verta Taylor
The Ohio State University

ADDISON-WESLEY PUBLISHING COMPANY

Reading, Massachusetts • Menlo Park, California
London • Amsterdam • Don Mills, Ontario • Sydney

To
Rose Foreman Richardson
Jessica Richardson Phillips
Alice F. Houston
Betty Jo Hudson

Sponsoring Editor: Ron Hill

Production Manager: Robert Duchacek

Editorial Production Services: Comprehensive Graphics

Cover Designer: Richard Hannus

This text was composed in Times Roman by Devlin Graphics, Inc.

Library of Congress Cataloging in Publication Data

Main entry under title:

Feminist frontiers.

  1. Women's studies—United States—Addresses, essays,
lectures. I. Richardson, Laurel Walum. II. Taylor,
Verta A.
HQ1426.F472   1983   305.4′2′0973   82-11396
ISBN 0-201-06197-X

Contents

SECTION FIVE: Institutionalized Violence Against Women   151

Preface

Well-embarked, as we are, in the ninth decade of the twentieth century, we are fortunate to be writing, teaching, and learning at a time when feminist thought is flourishing and deepening, a time of a true regeneration of feminist ideas and scholarly analysis. We are less fortunate, however, to be living and working at a time when the social and political gains of the feminist movement are threatened by powerful conservative interests, on the one hand, and false complacency, on the other.

In the past decade, the scholarly side of the feminist movement has matured. We have seen that a feminist analysis is not simply a list of criticisms detailing the sexism of our institutions. Rather, feminist thought seeks to transform, in fundamentally profound ways, all the old patriarchal ways of seeing, defining, thinking about, and understanding our experiences and the social world. No wonder, then, that the feminist vision has met so much opposition throughout history and that, once again, opposition is renewed.

Feminist ideas can have meaning only within the larger social and political movement organized to put them into practice. We offer this anthology, *Feminist Frontiers: Rethinking Sex, Gender, and Society,* in order to share with our readers materials to aid them in understanding the social and political world they have inherited. The selections and organization of this collection have been predicated on that goal.

We have found in our teaching that although a particular collection of readings may be excellent, the overall coherence of the anthology, the linkages between ideas in one article and ideas in others as well as the relationship of those ideas to a more abstract and unifying conceptual framework is often absent: the students may see the "trees," but they don't recognize that they live in a "forest." We have found this especially problematical in beginning women's studies and gender courses where the backgrounds of the students are so diverse that they lack a common language for analysis. To aid in the acquisition of a shared language and to help place individual readings in a more general context, we have organized this anthology into four parts and have introduced each one with an extensive sociological and feminist theoretical analysis.

The four parts are: "Learning the Culture," an analysis of the role of language, family, education, and sports for socialization into gender; "Maintaining Patriarchy," an analysis of religion, law, science, medicine and violence as institutions of social control; "Sex-Based Inequality," a presentation of stratification issues and the interdependence of inequalities in the political and occupational spheres with those in the domestic sphere; and "Social Change," an analysis of the contemporary women's movement, the issues confronting it in the 1980s, its effects on the interpersonal and institutional spheres, and its future.

The organization of the anthology, therefore, moves the reader from ideas that are more easily apprehended—such as socialization into gender and the maintenance of the social order, to ideas that are more complex—such as the theories of sex-based stratification and social movement theory. The reader is involved in the dialogue between "social order" and "social change," the processes through which androcentrism and patriarchy are perpetuated and maintained, and the processes through which male dominance and female subordination can be altered at the individual, interpersonal and institutional levels.

Selecting the particular articles to include was a difficult task. There was an abundance of excellent articles on certain topics, but a paucity of articles on others. To solve this problem, we established a set of working criteria for choosing the articles and for balancing the entire collection. First, we wanted each article to be well-written and accessible in style and language to the undergraduate; we wanted the article to stimulate the reader's thought and vision. Second, we wanted the selections to explore contemporary theory and issues, to reflect the tremendous growth in depth and understanding of this second generation of scholarship. Third, we wanted the articles to represent the cross-disciplinary nature of gender-research; and fourth, we wanted some of the articles to provide research-models that students could replicate. When we found we could not locate an existing article that met our criteria on a particular topic, we asked colleagues to write or revise an article specifically for this volume. The result, therefore, is an anthology that links well-written and significant articles within a more general sociological and feminist perspective.

This anthology can be used as the major or supplementary text in such courses as the Sociology of Women, Women's Studies, Sex-Roles, and the Psychology of Women. Although the book's organization is similar to that of Richardson's text, *The Dynamics of Sex and Gender: A Sociological Perspective* (Revised Second Edition, New York: Houghton Mifflin, 1981), this anthology can complement other gender texts as well. In addition, because there is a general framework of analysis, this book can be used as a supplementary text in such courses as Introduction to Sociology, Social Problems, Foundations, and Comparative and American Studies.

With the greatest pleasure, finally, we wish to acknowledge the support, skill and help of the many people who have made this volume a reality. First, there are the contributing authors — most of whom we know only through correspondence — but whom we have found to be exceptionally generous, caring and astute individuals. We are appreciative of their contributions. Second, there is the excellent professional staff at Addison-Wesley: we especially thank Ron Hill, our editor, for believing in and supporting this project, and we thank Joan Caratelli, Robert Duchacek, Debra Hunter, and Richard Hannus. We also thank Comprehensive Graphics for their expertise and good will. Third, there are the people in Columbus. Without Connie Gaib, who has kept this project on high gear, our work would have multiplied in hours and "catastrophies." We appreciate not only her incredible organizational and management skills, but her gentle spirit that has infused this project with joy. We are also grateful to Phyllis Gorman for spending endless hours in the library and at the copying machine and for always coming through with support, personal encouragement, and enthusiasm. Sigrid Ehrenberg, Grace Moran, and Virginia Young have also helped immeasurably by juggling their class and work schedules so that the project could proceed. Foremost among those who have contributed to the development of this anthology are students in our Women's Studies classes. Through their questions and responses to articles proposed for inclusion, we have learned a great deal. We also wish to thank the following reviewers, whose suggestions helped us to improve the manuscript: Arlene Eskilson, Lake Forest College, Illinois; Linda Green, Normandale Community College, Minnesota; and Katherine Jensen, University of Wyoming. Finally, special thanks go to those close to us who inspired both the work and the authors. Ernest Lockridge has been steadfast in his belief in and support for the project. Leila Rupp critically reviewed the entire collection at various stages of revision, and offered the friendship and support needed to carry out this project. To all of these, and to the many others who have touched our lives positively, we give our thanks.

Columbus, Ohio   **L. R.**
January, 1983   **V. T.**

General Introduction

Sociological and feminist analysis of sex and gender have matured greatly during the past decade. Scholars from different disciplines have come to recognize that the patterns of differentiation and discrimination between males and females are replicated throughout the social fabric, and that no matter whether one looks at interpersonal, social or macro-institutional relationships, one sees the same thing: male dominance and female subordination. This anthology presents the forms and structures of these sex-based inequalities, and the sources for changing them.

PLAN OF THE BOOK

Four major parts constitute this book, and each is divided into sections. Parts are introduced by a general sociological and feminist analysis, and the specific articles are introduced in the sections.

Part One, "Learning the Culture," introduces the concepts of culture, sex, and gender, as well as normative ideas about the world-taken-for-granted. A selection of articles shows how the primary agents of socialization—verbal and nonverbal language, family, schools, sports, and the mass media—induct the young into an androcentric and patriarchal world.

Introduction of the young into the social world, however, will not ensure the perpetuation of androcentrism. In a complex society such as ours, compliancy and conformity in adults must be maintained if the social order is to persist unchanged. Compliance is achieved through the involvement of institutions such as religion, law, science, medicine; and by the threat or actuality of institutionalized violence. Articles which describe and explain these institutions are included in Part Two, "Maintaining Patriarchy."

Not only are *individuals* socialized into the culture and not only are powerful ideologies existent to keep adults "in line," but there are *structural* bases of sex inequality. In Part Three, "Sex-based Inequality," we examine the ways in which modern industrialized societies are constructed so as to create a world which perpetuates male dominance and female subordination. We discuss and demonstrate how power, wealth, and prestige are differentially distributed to males and females, and how the provinces of "home" and "work" are so intertwined that male superiority becomes, in fact, dependent upon female subordination. Through the articles in this section, the reader is introduced to the theoretical frameworks for understanding the sources of sex-based inequality, and is led to analyze the depth and rigidity of male dominance in those institutions that make sex-based inequality so resistant to change.

Yet, as we know, social and cultural change *has* taken place. In Part Four, "Social and Political Change," we examine the social movement as an agent of change. We discuss the contemporary women's movement in terms of its historical continuity in values and goals, and we present selections that illustrate the diversity of the movement; the issues that it is confronting in the 1980s, both internally and externally (including the anti-feminist backlash); and the impact it has had on individuals, interpersonal relationships, and institutions.

Thus, the four major parts of this anthology lead the reader to an understanding of the processes of gender socialization, the maintenance of patriarchal institutions, the structural bases of sex-based inequalities, and the agents and implications of social and political change.

Learning the Culture

INTRODUCTION

Everyone is born into a *culture—* a *set of shared ideas* about the nature of reality, the nature of right and wrong, *evaluation of what is good and desirable,* and the nature of the good and desirable versus the bad and nondesirable. These ideas are manifested in behaviors and artifacts. As totally dependent infants we are *socialized—* taught the rules, roles and relationships of the social world we will inherit. We exchange our infant hedonism for the love, protection and attention of others; in the process we learn to think, act, and feel as we are "supposed to."

One of the earliest and most deep-seated ideas to which we are socialized is that of gender identity: the *idea* that "I am a boy" or "I am a girl." Because the culture, moreover, has strong ideas about what boys are like and what girls are like, we learn to identify our gender identity (our "boyness" or "girlness") with behaviors and attitudes that are sex-assigned in our culture. Thus, for example, a girl who plays with dolls is viewed as behaving in an appropriate and "feminine" manner and a boy who plays with trucks as appropriate and "masculine." Sometimes consciously and sometimes nonconsciously, children are categorized, differentially responded to and regarded, and encouraged to adopt behaviors and attitudes based on their sex. We raise, in effect, two different kinds of children: boys and girls.

Parents (or surrogate parents) are strong socializing influences in that they provide the first and most deeply experienced socialization experiences. Despite claims to the contrary, parents treat their infant boys and girls differently. Boys have "boy-names," "boy-toys," "boy-room decor," and are played with in more "boy-like" ways than girls. Even if, however, parents monitor their actions in the hope of preventing sexism from affecting their child, their endeavors will not succeed. This is so because *other* socializing influences bear down on the child.

One of the primary socializing influences is in the *language* we acquire. In learning to talk we acquire the thought patterns and communication styles of our culture. Those patterns and styles perpetuate and reinforce differentiation by sex and sex-stereotyping. They are

1

unavoidable. Embedded in the language are such ideas as "women are adjuncts to men" (e.g., the use of the generic "man" or "he"); women's aspirations are and should be different than men's (e.g., "The secretary . . . *she*", "the pilot . . . *he*"); women remain immature and incompetent throughout adult life (e.g., "The girls—office staff—have gone to lunch"); women are defined in terms of their sexual desirability (to men) whereas men are defined in terms of their sexual prowess. (Contrast the meanings of the supposedly equivalent words *spinster* and *bachelor*, *mistress* and *master*, *courtesan* and *courtier*, etc.) As long as we speak the language we have acquired, we are not only speaking but also thinking in sex-stereotyping ways.

As our society becomes more complex, increasingly the mass media have become centralized agents for the transmission of cultural beliefs. The media present sex-stereotypes in their purest and simplest forms. Children spend more time watching television than they spend in school or interacting with their parents and peers. Moreover, children tend to *believe* that what they see on television is an accurate representation of the way the world is and *should* be organized. Although the impact is not as great, other forms of mass media such as comics, newspapers, advertisements, movies and music reiterate the television theme that (white middle-class) males are powerful and prestigious (and should be), and women are subordinate and without esteem.

Added to the socialization through the family and through language (including the mass media), is the educational system. Educational institutions are formally charged with teaching the young. While teaching them reading, writing and arithmetic, however, the schools also imbue them with sexist values. They do this through the pattern of staffing (male principals and custodians, female teachers and food-servers), the curriculum materials, the sex-segregation of sports and activities, and differential *expectations* of boys and girls. No child can avoid this socialization experience.

Through powerful social institutions, then, children learn a culture. The culture they learn is one that views malehood as superior to femalehood; a system that differentially assigns behaviors and attitudes to males and females.

Socialization—whether through the home, the school, language, or the mass media—creates and sustains gender differences. Boys are taught that they will inherit the privileges and prestige of manhood, and girls are taught that they are less socially valuable than boys. Both are expected to view their status as right, moral, and appropriate.

The readings selected for this section, "Learning the Culture," illustrate and explain different aspects of the socialization process, and provide the reader with conceptual frameworks and perspectives for understanding the implications of gender.

Introduction: Language, Images and Ideas

Language—both verbal and nonverbal—affects the way we view ourselves and our relationships, and reflects the values of a society. Our language teaches that males and male-associated behaviors, attitudes and goals are more important and more valuable than females and female-associated behaviors, traits and goals.

In the first selection "'No, Thank You!': A Discourse on Etiquette," Laurel Richardson describes the culturally condoned "courtesies" extended by men to women and explains how they enforce sex-stereotypes and contribute to the perpetuation of a patriarchal system. Mary Brown Parlee in the article "Conversational Politics," reviews some of the research on the ways in which power differences affect speech styles and conversational interactions between males and females. Wendy Martyna in the selection "Beyond the 'He/Man' Approach: The Case for Nonsexist Language," discusses how our verbal language shapes expectations and limits life-opportunities of women.

Embedded in the language are expectations for beauty and sexuality. Not uncommonly do the images of beauty lead women into starvation diets and/or food binges. The selection "Obesity and Desexualization" by Marcia Millman from her book *Such a Pretty Face: Being Fat in America,* describes the cultural images we have of overweight women, and the effects of those images on women and men. Elizabeth Ann James in her poem "I Was the Showgirl, the Nun and the Hooker," presents many of the other cultural images of women. Reading her poem, we visualize the lives of many women, and we see how any individual woman is affected by the lives of other women.

One of the most powerful ways in which lessons are "taught" verbally and nonverbally is through the mass media. Children, for example, *believe* what they see and hear on television; indeed, they tend to believe that television characters and settings are more "real"—and more "right" (the way things are supposed to be)—than the people and places they actually know. The roles assigned to males and females, and the thematic content of the mass media, are explained and described by Gaye Tuchman in "Women's Depiction by the Mass Media." We conclude this section with Ellin Carter's poem, "November Issue," which ironically describes the force of the magazine in one's life.

We cannot emphasize enough the importance of language in both its verbal and nonverbal forms. We are continuously exposed to ideas about images of women as subordinate to men. Moreover, since the language we have acquired and the images we use are so embedded and so omnipresent it is very difficult for us to "break" from that language; to see and describe the world and our experiences in nonsexist ways. Stated another way, the *power* to name—to decide whether, for example, a woman employer is "pushy" or "assertive," "energetic" or a "rate-buster," "cool-headed" or "frigid"—has a major influence on our perception of ourselves and others.

No, Thank You!
A Discourse on Etiquette

Laurel Richardson

Stroll with me, for a block or two, down Fifth Avenue and we shall see what we shall see. Look over there, a woman with an ever-so-slightly petulant expression is waiting in front of Tiffany's while her male companion braves the traffic in pursuit of a taxi. And here, a couple has taken refuge under the awning of the Pierre while she is patiently waiting for him to locate his lighter for her cigarette. Over there, in the G.M. Building restaurant, the waitress has brought the check to a gentleman and his female companion is staring vacantly into space waiting for the financial transaction to be completed. In front of us, the man has taken the woman's arm and his gentle pressures tell her which way to weave through the pedestrian traffic. And here, let us watch more closely. A bustling woman and a leisurely-gaited man carrying a Bonwit box have simultaneously reached the closed office building doors. She stops bustling, steps slightly aside, and waits. He adjusts his package, positions himself, pulls the door open and holds it while she enters. Safely crossing the threshold, she murmurs, "Thank you," and as if on cue, he enters behind her.

We were strolling down Fifth Avenue in New York City. But we could have been on Broad Street in Columbus, Ohio, Mapleton Avenue in Boulder, Colorado, College Road in Claremont, California or Lindy Lane in "As the World Turns." We have been witnessing everyday, everyplace, common social ceremonies between the sexes. Just men and women going about their normal, taken-for-granted ceremonial rituals. At first glance, it does not seem as though we have seen anything remarkable. But it is the very commonness of these rituals which needs to be explained. How is it that persons who have not rehearsed their parts with each other can engage in these rituals without blunder?

We have all learned to abide by a kind of "etiquette" or set of rules governing our conduct. The leisurely-gaited man knows that under the rules of social conduct governing the door ceremony, he is *obliged* to open the door for the bustling woman and the bustling woman *expects* to receive this courtesy. The man lights the cigarette, hails the cab, picks up the restaurant tab, and helps the woman across the street. In each of these performances, the men and women are displaying that they are properly-mannered persons.

But why do we have this *particular* etiquette? Why do men hold doors, light cigarettes, pay for lunches? Manners, despite frequent claims to the contrary, are not simply empty gestures. Rather, they provide the *modus vivendi* by which our cultural values are maintained and our self-images as "males" or "females" are confirmed. As one woman student wrote in a journal she kept for a college class,

> *Tonight I had a date with a gentleman. When I opened the door, he closed it and opened it again. To tell the truth it made me feel good. It's nice to feel like a woman.*

Or, as a male student writes,

> *My courtesies like opening a car door makes women feel feminine and they enjoy this. I enjoy being a gentleman and making them feel this way.*

These students are declaring (without prompting) that the courtesies they extend or receive by virtue of their gender make them *feel* feminine and masculine, respectively. And it is no wonder that they feel that way—for in the door ceremony, the cigarette routine and the bill ritual, we find enacted our cultural stereotypes associated with "masculinity" and "femininity."

First and foremost in this culture to be "masculine" means to have *authority,* to be in charge, in control. Further, it means to be active, independent, efficacious and strong. "Femininity," on the other hand, is associated with protectibility, passivity, dependence and weakness. The distinction between the proper personality traits of properly-mannered males and properly-mannered females pervades the entire door ceremony and every other ritual encounter between the sexes in this culture. The male is in charge, in control of the door-knob, the lighter, the lady's elbow. The male is active and independent; the female *waits,* passive and dependent. By waiting for a service to be done, a cigarette lit, a taxi hailed, a bill discharged or a door to open, she is communicating that she *needs* someone to help her through her daily life.

If she does successfully play her part in each of the ritual ceremonies, if she is indeed well-mannered, she has engaged just those personality traits (frailty, weakness, ineptitude, protectibility, etc.) which our culture associates with "femininity." Of course, she *feels* feminine. And the male, by going through his routines without mishap, has demonstrated such masculine virtues as self-confidence, efficacy, worldliness and power, and naturally enough he *feels* masculine.

These ritual ceremonies between the sexes, then, reaffirm gender identity, the sense of being a "feminine" or "masculine" person. But they do something else, too; they reaffirm basic cultural values.

It is not a cultural accident that the personality traits associated with a *male's* performance in rituals between the sexes are precisely those traits which this culture values the most and considers socially desirable and mentally healthy activity: efficacy, authority, prowess, independence. Nor is it a cultural accident that the personality traits associated with the *female's* performance are exactly those that our culture writes off as immature and childlike: passivity, dependence, weakness, frailty, ineptitude. In a very profound sense, these daily rituals between the sexes become the living testimony of a basic value of this culture: the superiority of men.

Opening a door for a woman because she is a woman—a simple courtesy—is in fact a *political* act which perpetuates the ideology of patriarchy; the superiority of the male. Waiting for the door to be opened just because you are a woman is also a political act and one in which the pleasure of feeling "feminine" is chosen in preference to feeling adult, competent, and autonomous. Acting out the traditional parts in these ritual ceremonies between the sexes certainly ensures that men will feel masculine and that women will feel feminine. It also ensures that women will retain their second-class social citizenship and remain culturally defined as im-

mature, incompetent and childlike. To want "equal pay for equal work" and at the same time to want to be treated "like a lady" are inconsistent and incompatible objectives.

Increasingly, men and women are coming to recognize that the simple courtesies they perform and receive are counter to their goal of equality between the sexes. As one male student wrote in his journal,

> *If women had their heads screwed on right they wouldn't trade doing laundry for me lighting their cigarettes.*

And increasingly as "heads get screwed on right" more and more men and women are acting "ill-mannered," "ungentlemanly" and "unladylike" by refusing to play the parts prescribed for them in these ceremonies. The central value of patriarchy cannot be changed through speeches; but it cannot be maintained if people refuse to go through the daily enactments of this value, which these ceremonial occasions between the sexes represent.

For those interested in equality between the sexes, and first class social citizenship for all members of the society, there is something they *can* do about it. They can respond to persons—not through the etiquette of bondage which they have been taught is "polite"—but through the newly emerging etiquette of *humanism.* Under the humanistic rules of conduct, politeness is not a matter of playing out one's gender role destiny; rather, politeness is a matter of taking into account the *needs* of other people regardless of their sex. One male student with a humanitarian perspective wrote,

> *I had a 15 second encounter with a woman which has left a bad taste in my mouth all day. She had a large stack of papers and I pushed open and held the door for her. I would have done this for a woman or a man. Instead of a thank you I got the coldest, bitterest most glaring stare that went right through me. I resent being seen as a Pig when I was being courteous to her as a* person.

Or as this woman humanitarian reported,

> *I entered the elevator ahead of a football player who lives in my building who had an armful of groceries. I quickly held back the door so he could get on. He was so embarrassed he couldn't even say thank-you.*

In each of these encounters the personhood of those "helped" rather than their sex was taken into account.

Although the helpers acted politely under the rules of a humanistic etiquette, the recipients of their courtesies were uncomfortable. As increasingly numbers of persons choose this humanitarian perspective we might expect an increasing number of ceremonial confrontations, "ill-manners" and embarrassment. But in the long run, if increasing numbers of persons choose this humanitarian etiquette, we might foresee a day when the patriarchal value system disappears and we all—regardless of our sex—can expect to be treated with respect to our needs and dignities. At such time we might even *feel human* rather than masculine or feminine actors in the Etiquette of Bondage.

READING 2

Conversational Politics

Mary Brown Parlee

The Male Conversational Style: Interruptions

Studies of sex as a variable in language have focused on the way conversations among males and among females differ from conversations between males and females. One striking set of findings concerns interruptions—which are violations of the general turn-taking rules. Sociologists Candace West and Donald Zimmerman, whose pioneering work at the University of California at Santa Barbara opened up the topic for scientific investigation, studied conversations in a variety of university settings (including a coffee shop, drugstore, and apartment). After recording and analyzing spontaneous conversations, they found that males interrupt females much more often than they interrupt other males, and more often than females interrupt either males or females. Here is a typical example of male interruptions, taken from the transcript of a conversation about term papers recorded by West and Zimmerman (the brackets indicate points when the man and woman are speaking at the same time):

Reprinted from Mary Brown Parlee, "Conversational Politics," in *Psychology Today* (May, 1979), by permission of Zipf Publishing Company.

Female: How's your paper coming?
Male: All right, I guess. *(pause)* I haven't done much in the past two weeks. *(pause)*
Female: Yeah, know how that
⌈can .⌉. . .
Male: ⌊Hey,⌋ ya got an extra cigarette? *(pause)*
Female: Oh uh sure. *(hands him the pack)*
Like my⌈pa . . .⌉
Male: ⌊How bout⌋a match?
Female: 'Ere you go. Uh like my⌈pa . . .⌉
Male: ⌊Thanks.⌋ *(pause)*
Female: Sure. *(pause)* I was gonna tell you⌈my .⌉. .
Male: ⌊Hey,⌋I'd really like ta talk but I gotta run. See you. *(long pause)*
Female: Yeah.

The patterns of male-female interruptions were similar to those West and Zimmerman had observed in an earlier study between parents and children in a doctor's waiting room. Parents interrupted children much more often than the reverse. Perhaps, the investigators reasoned, they had biased their results by studying only conversations between persons who knew each other; people meeting each other for the first time might be more concerned with being polite, and any interruptions might be more evenly distributed between the sexes.

West and Zimmerman recorded conversations between pairs of previously unacquainted students, once again counting the interruptions in male–male, female–female, and male–female conversations. Concern over politeness apparently does not prevent violations of the turn-taking rules. In laboratory conversations between the sexes, males interrupted females more than females interrupted males. In the male–male and female–female conversations, the researchers frequently found that one partner interrupted the other more than vice versa.

West and Zimmerman argue that interruptions reflect and assert power differences, with the more powerful conversational partner interrupting the less powerful one more frequently. They define power not as an attribute of an individual but as something that is created in an interaction. The person who interrupts is creating and exercising power by violating the other's right to speak. The researchers believe, although they do not yet have data to prove it, that the display of power through interruptions will be found in other relationships besides male–female and parent–child — for example, in conversations between people who differ in race, class, or job status. In their view, such interruptions might be expected to occur even on a first meeting — men might want to make a dominant first impression to set the tone for any future relationship that may occur.

West and Zimmerman's interpretation is similar to one that psychologist Nancy Henley of the University of Massachusetts in Lowell has offered concerning body language. Henley studied couples in outdoor settings such as parks and zoos and found that men touch women more frequently than the reverse. She proposes that touching, when it is not mutual, is a form of body politics: the assertion of power is a significant aspect of the nonverbal message. The nonverbal display of power is particularly important in hierarchical relationships, she argues, because the message can be denied verbally. Body politics thus represents a way in which one group — defined by sex, race, class, job status — can exert control over another.

Sociologist Pamela Fishman has also studied sex differences in male–female conversations, and found that women "work" harder in conversations than men, in the sense that they put more effort into keeping the conversation going even though they have less control over what it is about. She placed tape recorders in the homes of three couples and, with their consent, recorded over 50 hours of naturally occurring conversations. All three couples described themselves as being "liberated" from traditional sex-role stereotypes.

Fishman analyzed the conversations to see how often the men and women introduced topics that "succeeded" (were developed in further conversation between the partners) and how often they raised topics that "failed" (the speaker was unable to get the listener to pursue the subject). She found that topics introduced by men succeeded 96 percent of the time, while topics introduced by women succeeded only 36 percent of the time (even though, overall, women initiated 62 percent of the topics in the conversations).

According to Fishman, the women used a number of strategies to try to increase their chance of success, strategies that men seldom used. Women asked questions (which in our culture demand an answer) nearly three times as often as men did. They often used an introductory attention-getter: "D'ya know what?" or "This is really interesting." As a group, they said "you know" 10 times more often than the men did, with the use of the phrase increasing in individual conversations as the man failed to respond to the topic.

One way men "killed" conversational topics introduced by women was to give a minimal response (*"um"*), sometimes after a pause, when the woman had finished speaking. The minimal response prevents the turn-taking rules from operating smoothly since the topic is not jointly developed. Eventually, a topic receiving only minimal response fails, and the conversation breaks down. By killing topics raised by women, and by having their own topics almost always succeed, men controlled the conversation with little effort, Fishman concluded. Women, on the other hand, not only worked harder to have their own topics succeed, but also regularly took their turns talking about a topic raised by the men.

The following two excerpts (slightly adapted for readability) from dialogues recorded by Fishman illustrate the different treatment given a topic raised by a man compared with the treatment of one raised by a woman. In the first, the man begins by introducing the topic of a newspaper article on Russian gymnast Olga Korbut's visit to then-President Richard Nixon. The woman responds with apparent interest, asking questions:

Male: What do you think your best weight is?
Female: Ninety-five *heheheh*. Oh, I'd say 92.

Male: I saw in the paper where Olga Korbut . . .
Female: Yeah.
Male: . . . went to see Dickie . . .
Female: You're kidding! What for?
Male: I don't know.
Female: I can just imagine what she would go see Dick Nixon for. I don't get it.
Male: I think she's on a tour of the United States.
Female: Has he sat down and talked to her?
Male: *(shows a picture in the paper)*
(conversation continues)

The second full transcript is much longer than the first. In it, the female "worked" for a full five minutes to get a conversation going on an article she is reading. The male responds minimally, and no conversation develops.

Female: I am really offended! That a magazine could publish this book. *(pause, during which male does not respond)* That someone could put together this kind of a book on muckraking sociology. This article I'm reading just *(pause)* just to aggravate myself, I guess, called *"(title of article)"* by Bill London. *(pause, no response from male)* It is the most sexist thing, overtly sexist-racist thing I have read in years.
Male: Why?

Although the male's attention seems to be perking up, he in fact becomes less involved as the female continues to talk about the article. His responses become further apart and less conversational (*"umhum,"* grunts). At the end, it sounds as if she is talking to herself.

Power and Genderlects

Some investigators think another area of sociolinguistic research also supports the idea that women's relative lack of power is reflected in their speech. Linguist Robin Lakoff has suggested that because their social roles are so different, men's and women's speech are almost different enough to be regarded as different dialects ("genderlects"). According to Lakoff, women's language (language used typically but not exclusively by women) has these characteristics:

1. Use of certain words rarely used by men (an example: *mauve*).
2. Use of "empty" adjectives (such as *divine* or *lovely*) that do not have connotations of power.

3. Use of a questioning intonation at the end of a declarative statement (and more frequent use of tag questions as well).
4. Frequent use of modifiers or hedges ("sort of," "kind of," "I guess"). Such qualifiers, like the questioning intonation, decrease the assertiveness in the statement.
5. Intensive use of "so" with an adjective (as in *"so many people"*).
6. Use of hypercorrect grammar and excessively polite speech.

All of these characteristics, Lakoff believes, render women's language expressive and polite rather than direct and informative. It is definitely nonassertive. Lakoff's conclusions were based largely on unsystematic observation and listening. But recent sociolinguistic research has provided evidence that her observations were, by and large, correct.

Cornell linguist Sally McConnell-Ginet has experimental evidence that women do use the diffident declarative (statements with a questioning tone) more often than do men. Her research involved asking men and women on the Cornell campus what the name of a particular building was. Women, she found, would answer with something that sounded like another question ("This is Olin library?") more often than men.

Women, on the average, have been found to be less precise when describing the perceptual properties of a complex scene ("about six books" is a typical phrase); those differences may begin in children as young as four.

Psychologists Faye Crosby and Linda Nyquist, working at Boston University, directly tested Lakoff's hypothesis about the existence of "women's language." They developed a system for scoring speech on all six of the characteristics Lakoff proposed; the summary score could then be used to test whether women use "women's language" more than men do.

Crosby and Nyquist found that "women's language" was more frequently found, in a laboratory setting, in the speech of college women than in that of college men. In another experiment, Crosby and Nyquist studied the speech of police personnel and their clients in conversations at a police station. (Most of the clients came to the station with inquiries of one sort or another.) Crosby and Nyquist found that the clients—males and females—used "women's language more than the police personnel, who were both male and female." They suggest that "women's language" is used by people in particular roles—which tend to be those lacking power. Nothing is inherently female in "women's language."

If men's and women's speech styles are different in systematic ways, what are the social consequences? Recent research by Duke anthropologist William O'Barr suggests that people—male or female—who use the more tentative style of "women's language" are less likely to be believed by a jury. They lack the credibility of someone speaking in the "male" style. For much the same reasons, the British Broadcasting Corporation (BBC) for years prohibited women from reading the news over the air (and only recently broke with this tradition). Thus, speech may not only reflect power differences in the world, it may also create them through a self-fulfilling prophecy. (People who use the diffident declarative do not sound authoritative, therefore they should not be in positions of authority because they will not be believed. No one in positions of authority uses the diffident declarative. And so on.)

Research on how men and women talk to one another is only one example of a larger domain of study that is exploring the way power differences affect speaking styles and conversational interactions. Conversational politics, together with body language and the spoken word, may lie at the heart of the way we maintain roles, relationships, and the feelings that go with them. While researchers don't completely understand why we feel so one down when we're victims of conversational politics, sociolinguistic studies are providing at least the beginnings of some of the answers, don't you think?

READING 3

Beyond the "He/Man" Approach: The Case for Nonsexist Language

Wendy Martyna

Reprinted from Wendy Martyna, "Beyond the 'He/Man' Approach: The Case for Nonsexist Language," in *Signs* 5 (1980): 482–93, by permission of The University of Chicago Press and the author.
This work is dedicated to the memory of Kate De Pierri, who was a contemporary in spirit, energy, and commitment, despite the fifty years between us. Early encouragement, much appreciated, came from Catharine Stimpson, Barrie Thorne, Nancy Henley, Cheris Kramer, and Adrienne Rich. Valuable resources were provided by Mary Ritchie Key, Virginia Valian, Simon Klevansky, Patti Leasure, LeeAnn Slinkard, and the many generous people who are part of the "women-and-language grapevine." I am particularly grateful for the critical readings of earlier drafts by Len Erickson, Herb Clark, Sandra Bem, Leigh Star, and Terri Daly.

Time calls it "Ms-guided,"[1] a syndicated columnist "linguistic lunacy."[2] *TV Guide* wonders what the "women's lib redhots" with "the nutty pronouns" are doing.[3] A clear understanding of the sexist language issue continues to elude the popular press. The medium is not alone in its misunderstanding. This discussion separates

1. Stefan Kanfer, "Sispeak: A Ms-guided Attempt to Change Herstory," *Time* 100 (October 23, 1972): 79.
2. Harriet Van Horne, "Women's Movement Foolishly Assaults the English Language," *Rocky Mountain News* (February 19, 1976), p. 51.
3. "As We See It," *TV Guide* 19 (July 17, 1971): 1.

the strands of argument often tangled in current approaches to the issue, whether these approaches appear in the popular media, academic journals, or feminist publications. The arguments against sexist language have been mistranslated more often than not. Those mistranslations have then been responded to by opponents of language change. Clarifying these, and synthesizing the case against sexist language, can help to offset the continuing, annoying trivialization of this issue, which has constituted a major roadblock on the path toward a language that speaks clearly and fairly of both sexes.

The "he/man" approach to language involves the use of male terms to refer both specifically to males and generically to human beings (*A Man for All Seasons* is specific; "No man is an island" is generic). The he/man approach has received most attention in current debates on sexist language, not only because of its ubiquity but also because of its status as one of the least subtle of sexist forms. In linguistic terms, some have characterized the male as an unmarked, the female as a marked, category. The unmarked category represents both maleness and femaleness, while the marked represents femaleness only.[4] Thus the male in Lionel Tiger's *Men in Groups* excludes the female in Phyllis Chesler's *Women and Madness,* while the male in Thomas Paine's *Rights of Man* is supposed to encompass the female of Mary Wollstonecraft's *Vindication of the Rights of Woman.*

The outlines of the he/man debate are evident in an exchange of letters in the *Harvard Crimson* in 1971. The linguistics faculty of Harvard criticized an attempt by a theology class to eliminate sexist language from its discussions: "The fact that the masculine is the unmarked gender in English . . . is simply a feature of grammar. It is unlikely to be an impediment to change in the patterns of the sexual division of labor towards which our society may wish to evolve. There is really no cause for anxiety or pronoun-envy on the part of those seeking such changes."[5]

Virginia Valian, a psychologist, and Jerrold Katz, a linguist, countered by posing this hypothetical situation: "In culture R the language is such that the pronouns are different according to the color of the people involved, rather than their sex . . . the unmarked pronoun just happens to be the one used for white people. In addition,

the colored people just happen to constitute an oppressed group. Now imagine that this oppressed group begins complaining about the use of the 'white' pronoun to refer to all people. Our linguists presumably then say, "Now, now, there is really no cause for anxiety or pronoun-envy.' It isn't a question of linguistics, but of how the people involved feel."[6] The students' claim: the generic masculine is both ambiguous and discriminatory. The linguists' claim: it is simply a feature of grammar, unrelated to the issue of sex discrimination. The students' counter-response: it is more than a feature of grammar, but a factor which both reflects and maintains societal sexism. This 1971 scenario has been enacted many times in the years since: the cast varies, but the plot and dialogue remain familiar. William James noted three stages a new idea moves through: it is first attacked as absurd; then admitted to be true, but seen as obvious and insignificant; and finally, seen as so important that its adversaries claim they discovered it. If James is correct, then the controversy over sexist language now sits somewhere between stages one and two.

Resistance to Change

Comments on the he/man issue vary in their subtlety. Among the most blatant are personal attacks on those who attack the generic masculine. One columnist describes the editor who had altered his sexist prose as "an ardent Amazonian." He later bursts out: "Women are irrational, all women: when some women threaten to disembowel me unless I say 'personhole-cover,' I am surer even than I was that all women are irrational."[7] Trivializations of the movement for sexist language appear in a wide range of locations, from *Time's* article on "sispeak" to a nationally syndicated columnist's critique of the "libspeak tantrum."[8] This reaction to sexist language appears more striking when contrasted to the popular response to racist language. The U.S. secretary of agriculture, Earl Butz, left office following public outcry over his racist remarks (which the media refused to repeat, "even in this liberated age").[9] Butz's remarks were

4. Herbert H. Clark and Eve V. Clark, *Psychology and Language: An Introduction to Psycholinguistics* (New York: Harcourt Brace Jovanovich, Inc., 1977), p. 524.

5. Harvard Linguistics Faculty, "Pronoun Envy," *Harvard Crimson* (November 16, 1971).

6. Virginia Valian and Jerrold Katz, "The Right to Say 'He,'" *Harvard Crimson* (November 24, 1971).

7. Milton Mayer, "On the Siblinghood of Persons," *Progressive* (September 1975), pp. 20–21.

8. Kanfer.

9. David Felton, "Butz Is Just a 4-Letter Word," *Rolling Stone* (November 18, 1976).

equally sexist, but he apologized only to the black male members of Congress, not the females; and it was his racism, not his sexism, which caused his censure. Public reaction to Billy Carter's "witticisms," often as racist and sexist as Butz's remarks, illustrates this same contrast. Sexist language is popularly treated as a source of humor more often than outrage. Pauli Murray has called this ridicule of women "the psychic counterpart of violence against blacks,"[10] and Naomi Weisstein speaks of this humor as "a weapon in the social arsenal constructed to maintain . . . sex inequalities, . . . showing that women can't be taken seriously."[11] If pronouns are as amusingly insignificant as some consider them to be, we should expect no outcry were the situation reversed, and the female pronoun became the generic. Yet when the female pronoun has been used to refer to both sexes, as in the teaching profession, males have lobbied for use of the male pronoun. They argue that use of "she" is responsible, in part, for their poor public image and low salaries.[12]

Resistance to language change has also involved more sophisticated lines of argument. The first centers on the meaning of "he." The generic masculine does not need replacement, argue some, for "he" can include "she" (or "man" can embrace "woman," as grammar teachers are fond of saying). Frank M. argues this position in a letter to "Dear Abby": "I'm tired of the ignorance of those who insist that the word 'man' applies only to males. My dictionary has several definitions, of which the first two are: 1) human being, person . . . 2) the human race. So why don't we stop all this asinine changing of words?"[13] Jacques Barzun similarly explains: "No one until recently ever saw in the phrase [Madame Chairman] any paradox, incongruity, or oppugnancy between terms. It is consistent with common sense and perfect equity; the 'man' in it denotes either sex."[14]

Others argue that the generic masculine includes both sexes because they intend it to. Anthony Burgess, for example, says that his use of "he" and "man" is neutral, and that it is women who "force chauvinistic sex onto the word."[15]

Yet the question of what "he" and "man" really mean is fully answered neither by turning to dictionary definitions nor by consulting the intentions of their users. Good intentions are not enough, unfortunately, to guarantee that generic meaning will be conveyed. And guided tours through Latin and Old English are not enough to guarantee that the generic masculine is used clearly and fairly today. Further, the denotations found in dictionaries do not always reveal the connotations that "he" and "man" can carry.

Others who resist language change deny neither that sexist language can serve as a symbol of sexist society nor that sexist society needs to be changed. What they do disclaim is that the one has much to do with the other. The need, they say, is to change the sources, rather than the symbols, of sexism in society. Nina Yablok puts forth in rhyme: "If I had my choice, if I had my druthers / I'd take equal rights. Leave equal words to the others."[16] To Stefan Kanfer, the hope for a nonsexist language reveals "a touching, almost mystical trust in words."[17]

Another group, which also tends to support social change, wonders about the very possibility of language change. Robin Lakoff, whose work has encouraged a greater awareness of sexist language, has nevertheless argued that pronouns are "too common, too thoroughly mixed throughout the language, for the speaker to be aware each time he uses them. It is realistic only to hope to change those linguistic uses of which speakers themselves can be made aware, as they use them."[18] Others are deterred by the difficulty, rather than the impossibility, of language change. One writer, referring to "the ugly and awkward 'he or she' forms," says, "They may be only a passing fad, but they offend the traditional eye."[19] Eye trouble is not the only complaint. To William Buckley, the "distortions ring in the ear."[20] This

10. Pauli Murray, testimony, U.S. Congress, House, Special Subcommittee on Education of the Committee on Education and Welfare, *Discrimination against Women,* 91st Cong., 2d sess., 1970, on section 805 of H.R. 16098.
11. Naomi Weisstein, "Why We Aren't Laughing — Anymore," *Ms* 2, no. 5 (November 1973): 49.
12. M. S. Fenner, "After All: Proposal for Unisex Pronoun," *Today's Education* 63 (Summer 1974): 110 ("ne").
13. "Dear Abby," *Los Angeles Times* (August 17, 1976).
14. Jacques Barzun, "A Few Words on a Few Words," *Columbia Forum* (Summer 1974), pp. 17–19.

15. Anthony Burgess, "Dirty Words," *New York Times Magazine* (August 8, 1976).
16. Nina Yablok, "A Woperchild Joins the Arguthing," *New York Times* (March 30, 1977).
17. Kanfer.
18. Robin Lakoff, *Language and Woman's Place* (New York: Harper & Row, 1975).
19. Edward Devol, "The He-She Dilemma Built into the Tongue," *San Francisco Chronicle* (February 13, 1977).
20. William F. Buckley, Jr., "Unsex Me Now," *National Review* (May 28, 1976), p. 583.

pessimism about language change is at least partly due to a misrepresentation of the causes for optimism. A common view seems to be that feminists have failed to take into account the complexities of language change, viewing it as a relatively quick and easy process. In fact, those who advocate nonsexist language do not pretend that change will be quick, easy, or unopposed.

Much resistance to change arises from a confusion over *what* will be changed, as well as *why* there should be change. The widespread worry is that both specific and generic forms of "he" and "man" will be eliminated, should language change go according to feminist plan. Some writers manifest a mania for manipulating each "man" in our language into a "person," and then mentioning the menace such manipulations pose. Russell Baker, for example, would have substituted "person" for "each 'man'" in the previous sentence, as he did in his satire of "Nopersonclature."[21] Despite the many suggestions to the contrary, we do not have to begin language change by renaming NOW the National Organization for Wopeople. The many fears of retitling such works as *Four Horsemen of the Apocalypse* and *A Man for All Seasons* are similarly unfounded: the term "man" as used here is specific, not generic. Sexism, not *sex*, is under attack.

The fear of losing all sex-specific terms in the language has led to the characterization of a nonsexist language as "sexually obscure," "a unisex tongue . . . a dull tongue and a false one," and "a spaying of the language."[22] One member of the California State Assembly opposed a move to replace "assemblyman" with "assembly member." "That takes the masculinity out of it!" he declared.[23] Not only a "sexless" language, but also an ungrammatical one, is dreaded. William Buckley, Jr., is among those refusing to substitute singular "they" for generic "he." Those who issue guidelines for nonsexist language, he says, "want us to validate improper usage." Anyone who uses a singular "they," in Buckley's view, "should not be hired as a professional writer."[24]

Arguments for Change

Those who oppose the generic masculine are concerned with both equal rights *and* equal words. Nonsexist language would not only reflect a move toward a nonsexist ideology; it would also function in itself as one form of social equality. Eliminating the ambiguity and sex exclusiveness of the he/man approach would enable us to communicate more clearly and fairly about the sexes.

The New York State Supreme Court housed a confrontation in 1976 between those who differ on this question of equity. Ellen Cooperman's petition to change her name to "Cooperperson" was denied by the court, on grounds it would set a precedent for other "ludicrous changes (Mannings becoming Peoplings)" and expose the women's movement to ridicule. However, she considered her petition as personally and politically important, arguing that "Cooperman" reflects "the pervasiveness of linguistic male predominance" and is among those factors complicating women's efforts to achieve self-identity.[25] Her view is shared by many others who testify to the importance of the he/man issue. For example, Susan Sontag sees language as "the most intense and stubborn fortress of sexist assumptions," one which "crudely enshrines the ancient bias against women."[26]

The damage the generic masculine has done is itself a strong argument for change. Research has begun to suggest the behavioral implications of sexist language. Sandra Bem and Daryl Bem, for instance, have assessed the impact of sex-biased job advertisements, finding that sex-unbiased advertisements encourage more high school females to apply for male-related jobs.[27] Most of such studies have focused on the psychological impact of broad gender cues. While there are ample data to suggest that manipulating such cues has psychological impact, we have not yet assessed the particular contribution the generic masculine makes in creating these cues. The data on the way the generic "he" encourages a male rather than neutral interpretation, however, suggest that that role is considerable.

Cognitive confusion is another consequence of the

21. Russell Baker, "Nopersonclature," *New York Times* (March 4, 1973).
22. Israel Shenker, "Is It Possible for a Woman to Manhandle the King's English?" *New York Times* (August 29, 1971); E. B. White, as quoted in Blake Green, "A New English: Unbiased or Unsexed?" *San Francisco Chronicle* (October 11, 1974); and Charles McCabe, "Spaying the Language," *San Francisco Chronicle* (May 24, 1977).
23. "Assembly Moves to Desex Its Titles," *Los Angeles Times* (January 14, 1977).
24. Buckley.

25. "Fighting for Her Cooperpersonhood," *Los Angeles Times* (October 24, 1976); and Ellen Cooperperson, "What's in a Name? Sexism," *New York Times* (November 21, 1976).
26. Susan Sontag, "The Third World of Women," *Partisan Review* 40, no. 2 (1973); 186.
27. Sandra Bem and Daryl Bem, "Does Sex-biased Job Advertising 'Aid and Abet' Sex Discrimination?" *Journal of Applied Social Psychology* 3, no. 1 (1973): 6–18.

generic masculine, one particularly relevant for the academic disciplines.[28] Joan Huber, for example, has characterized the use of "he" and "man" as "an exercise in doublethink that muddles sociological discourse." She cites the recent sociology text which proclaims: "The more education an individual attains, the better his occupation is likely to be, and the more money he is likely to earn." The statement is accurate only if the individual is male.[29] The American Anthropological Association is among many scholarly associations to caution its members that use of the generic masculine is "conceptually confusing."[30] Ambiguity results when generic and specific meanings are not easily separable; exclusion results when context prohibits a generic interpretation. Watch what context does to the supposedly generic "he" used by Paul Meehl to describe this hypothetical researcher: "He" produces a long list of publications but little contribution to the enduring body of knowledge, and "his true position is that of a potent-but-sterile intellectual rake, who leaves in his merry wake a long train of ravished maidens, but no viable scientific offspring."[31]

Context, many say, should be sufficient to decide whether a specific or generic meaning of "he" and "man" is intended. Yet my empirical explorations demonstrate that, even in a clearly generic context (e.g., "When someone is near a hospital, he should be quiet"), "he" is ambiguous, allowing both specific and generic interpretations to be drawn.[32] My research does not argue that "he" *cannot* function generically, but that it allows both specific and generic interpretation, even in a context which should force a generic inference. Moreover, our encounters with "he" rarely take place in clearly generic contexts. In educational materials, for instance, the sex-specific "he"

appears five to ten times for every single generic "he."[33] The generic masculine thus appears amidst a profusion of references to specific males. Based on this predominantly sex-specific usage, our best guess when encountering a "he" is that it will not contain an implicit "she."

Startled laughter often greets such sentences as "Menstrual pain accounts for an enormous loss of manpower hours," or "Man, being a mammal, breast-feeds his young." We do a double take when hearing of the gynecologist who was awarded a medical award for "service to his fellowman." C. S. Lewis captures the importance of these reactions: "In ordinary language the sense of a word . . . normally excludes all others from the mind. . . . The proof of this is that the sudden intrusion of any irrelevant sense is funny. It is funny because it is unexpected. There is a semantic explosion because the two meanings rush together from a great distance; one of them was not in our consciousness at all till that moment. If it had been, there would be no detonation."[34] To avoid this "semantic explosion," we are cautioned by writers' manuals to avoid a generic "he" when the issue of sex "is present and pointed," as in "The pool is open to both men and women, but everyone must bring his or her own towel."[35] Similarly, we avoid a generic "he" when the female meaning is predominant. An investigation of psychology textbooks found that hypothetical professors, physicians, and psychologists were referred to as "he," while hypothetical nurses, teachers, and librarians were "she."[36] If "he" includes "she"—if "man" embraces "woman"—why these shifts to the female pronoun?

Empirical explorations of how we comprehend the generic masculine also indicate its sex exclusiveness. My studies of pronoun usage show striking sex differences in both the use and understanding of the generic masculine. Females use "he" less often than do males, and turn more frequently to alternatives such as "he or she" and "they."

28. Mary Beard observed in 1946, "For hundreds of years the use of the word 'man' has troubled critical scholars, careful translators, and lawyers. Difficulties occur whenever and wherever it is important for truth-seeking purposes to know what is being talked about and the context gives no intimation of [what] 'man' means" (Mary Beard, *Woman as Force in History* [New York: Macmillan Publishing Co., 1946], p. 59).

29. Joan Huber, "On the Generic Use of Male Pronouns," *American Sociologist* 11 (May 1976): 89.

30. American Anthropological Association, *Newsletter* (January 1974), p. 12.

31. Paul Meehl, "Theory Testing in Physics: A Methodological Paradox," *Philosophy of Science* 34 (1967): 103–15.

32. Wendy Martyna, "Using and Understanding the Generic Masculine: A Social-psychological Approach" (Ph.D. diss., Stanford University, 1978).

33. Carol Tittle, Karen McCarthy, and Jane Steckler, *Women and Educational Testing* (Princeton, N.J.: Educational Testing Service, 1974); and Alma Graham, "The Making of a Nonsexist Dictionary," *Ms* 2 (December 1973): 12–16.

34. C. S. Lewis, *Studies in Words* (Cambridge: Cambridge University Press, 1960), p. 11.

35. Theodore Bernstein, *The Careful Writer: A Modern Guide to English Usage* (New York: Atheneum Publishers, 1965), p. 351.

36. American Psychological Association Task Force on Issues of Sexual Bias in Graduate Education, "Guidelines for Nonsexist Use of Language," *American Psychologist* 30, no. 6 (June 1975): 682–84.

Males have an easier time imagining themselves as members of the category referenced by generic "he." Seven times as many males as females say they see themselves in response to sex-neutral sentences referring to a "person" or "human being." In general, males appear to be using and understanding "he" in its specific more often than in its generic sense. Females both avoid the use of "he" and respond to its use with a more generic than specific interpretation. For females to do otherwise would be to encourage self-exclusion.[37]

The confusion and exclusion caused by the generic masculine have striking social implications. Although one legal scholar notes the "useful function" ambiguity can perform, "by virtue of its lack of precision,"[38] the ambiguity of "he" and "man" is far from useful for those who are included by inference only. A member of the Canadian Parliament, Simma Holt, challenged the equity of the Federal Interpretation Act, which reads: "Words importing male persons include female persons and corporations." Holt was reassured that the act creates no injustice, for females are explicitly included within the definition of the generic masculine. Doubting that assurance, Marguerite Ritchie surveyed some 200 years of Canadian law and discovered that the ambiguity of the generic masculine has allowed judges to include or exclude women, depending on the climate of the times and their own personal biases. As she concludes: "Wherever any statute or regulation is drafted in terms of the male, a woman has no guarantee that it confers on her any rights at all."[39] Legal controversy over the generic masculine has arisen in the United States as well, involving, for example:

Administration of a scholarship fund set up for "worthy and ambitious young men";[40]
dispute over a Kiwanis Club admission of women, despite bylaws specifying "men" as members;[41]

the appeal of a murder conviction in which the self-defense instructions to the jury were phrased in the generic masculine, thus "leaving the jury with the impression that the objective standard to be applied is that applicable to an altercation between two men";[42]
and
sex-biased application of the legal notion of "a reasonable man."[43]

Prospects for Language Change

Language change may be difficult, but it is not impossible. Some prominent individuals, for example, have made striking changes in their language use. Millions were listening when Harry Reasoner apologized for referring, on a previous broadcast, to the "men" of the Judiciary Committee. In response to the many objections he had received, he not only apologized but also asked indulgence for future language offenses he might inadvertently commit.[44] A variety of government agencies, feminist groups, professional associations, religious organizations, educational institutions, publishing firms, and media institutions have also endorsed language change, issuing guidelines or passing regulations concerning sexist language.[45] Initial empirical studies suggest considerable language changes among university faculty and politicians.[46]

The strongest argument for the possibility of

37. Wendy Martyna, "What Does 'He' Mean—Use of the Generic Masculine," *Journal of Communication* 28, no. 1 (Winter 1978): 131–38; and Wendy Martyna, "Using and Understanding the Generic Masculine" (paper presented at the Ninth World Congress of Sociology, Uppsala, Sweden, August 1978).
38. Ovid Lewis, "Law, Language and Communication," *Case Western Reserve Law Review* 23 (1972): 316.
39. Marguerite Ritchie, "Alice through the Statutes," *McGill Law Journal* 21 (Winter 1975): 702.
40. Frederick Cusick, "Law Students Win Their Case—against a Will," *Daily Hampshire (Northampton, Mass.) Gazette* (March 1, 1975).
41. B. W. O'Hearn, "N.Y. Kiwanis Club Admits First Woman," *Middletown Connecticut Press* (January 23, 1974).

42. State of Washington v. Yvonne Wanrow, Supreme Court of Washington 559 Pacific Report, 2d ser., 1977, pp. 548–59.
43. Ronald K. L. Collins, "Language, History, and the Legal Process: A Profile of the 'Reasonable Man,'" *Camden Law Journal* 8, no. 2 (Winter 1977): 312, 323.
44. Jean Ward, "Attacking the King's English: Implications for Journalism in the Feminist Critiques," *Journalism Quarterly* 52 (Winter 1975): 699–705.
45. For example, American Psychological Association, "Guidelines for Nonsexist Language in APA Journals," *Publication Manual Change Sheet 2* (Washington, D.C.: American Psychological Association, 1977); Scott, Foresman & Co., *Guidelines for Improving the Image of Women in Textbooks* (Glenview, Ill.: Scott, Foresman & Co., 1974); Macmillan Publishing Co., *Guidelines for Creating Positive Sexual and Racial Images in Educational Materials* (New York: Macmillan Publishing Co., 1975); and "Assembly Panel Acts to Rid Laws of Sexism," *New York Times* (February 19, 1976).
46. Barbara Bate, "Nonsexist Language Use in Transition," *Journal of Communication* 28, no. 1 (Winter 1978): 139–49; and Sandra Purnell, "Politically Speaking, Do Women Exist?" *Journal of Communication* 28, no. 1 (Winter 1978): 150–56.

language change is that substantial numbers of language users have already managed to construct detours around generic "he" and "man." Ann Bodine[47] surveys instances of socially motivated language change in England, Sweden, and Russia; Paul Friedrich[48] investigates the Russian example in detail, exploring how pronominal change resulted from a growing concern for social equality.

Many guidelines for nonsexist language encourage either the replacement of the generic masculine with sex-inclusive or sex-neutral forms or rewriting to avoid the need for a single pronoun or noun.[49] "They" has long been in use as an alternative to "he"; Bodine claims that "despite almost two centuries of vigorous attempts to analyze and regulate it out of existence, singular 'they' is alive and well."[50] Research on pronoun use confirms Bodine's observation.[51] Maija Blaubergs and Barbara Bate have both categorized the many proposed alternatives to sexist language forms.[52] The two main ones are sex-inclusive forms (such as "he or she" and "women and men") and sex-neutral terms (such as "chairperson" and "humanity"). Since 1970, several new pronouns, including "tey," "co," "na," and "E," have been suggested.[53] The difficulty of changing the language must also be contrasted with the difficulty of *not* changing. The awkwardness that may result from the "he or she" construction may be less troublesome than the ambiguity and sex exclusiveness of the he/man approach, and even that awkwardness will eventually decline.

Why the persistent misrepresentation and misunderstanding of the sexist language issue?[54] The simplest explanation is antifeminism, yet this by itself is not enough. Why should this issue remain a source of ridicule when other feminist claims have come to be treated seriously? Why do some feminists, both female and male, consider the fight for "equal words" to be a misdirection of energy? There seems to be a general cultural reluctance to acknowledge the power of language in our lives, an insistence that language is of symbolic rather than actual importance. We chant in childhood, "Sticks and stones can break my bones, but words can never hurt me," yet we carry the psychological scars from words long after the bruises and scrapes have healed. We may still be in the midst of a cultural reaction against early preoccupation with the magical power of words.

The importance of this kind of "magic" was suggested by the Sapir/Whorf hypothesis, which states that language can determine our thought and behavior patterns and that different languages can shape different world views.[55] It is usually assumed that feminist argument is grounded in the Sapir/Whorf hypothesis. Michael Schneider and Karen Foss worry that "feminists inadvertently have helped to perpetuate and diffuse an outdated, oversimplified, and basically inaccurate view of the relationship between thought and language."[56] In its strongly stated form, this hypothesis has seen little empirical support and strong theoretical criticism since its formulation in the 1920s and 1930s. Yet it has come to be generally accepted in its moderate version: that language may influence, rather than determine, thought and behavior patterns. The moderate version of the Sapir/Whorf hypothesis is reflected in the feminist move for nonsexist language. The issue is not what *can* be said about the sexes, but what can be *most easily* and *most*

47. Ann Bodine, "Androcentrism in Prescriptive Grammar: Singular 'They,' Sex-indefinite 'He' and 'He or She,'" *Language in Society* 4 (August 1975): 129–46.

48. Paul Friedrich, "Social Context and Semantic Feature: The Russian Pronominal Usage," in *Directions in Sociolinguistics,* ed. J. Gumperz and D. Hymes (New York: Holt, Rinehart & Winston, 1972).

49. An example of such guidelines: McGraw-Hill Book Co., *Guidelines for Equal Treatment of the Sexes* (New York: McGraw-Hill Book Co., 1974).

50. Bodine, pp. 129–46.

51. Martyna, "What Does 'He' Mean — Use of the Generic Masculine"; and D. Terence Langendoen, *Essentials of English Grammar* (New York: Holt, Rinehart & Winston, 1970).

52. Maija Blaubergs, "Changing the Sexist Language: The Theory behind the Practice," *Psychology of Women Quarterly* 2, no. 3 (Spring 1978): 244–61; and Bate.

53. Casey Miller and Kate Swift, "De-Sexing the English Language," *Ms* 1 (Spring 1972): 7 ("tey"); Mary Orovan, "Humanizing English," mimeographed (Hackensack, N.J.: Mary Orovan, 1971) ("co"); June Arnold, *The Cook and the Carpenter* (Houston, Tex.: Daughters Publishing Co., 1975) ("na"); Fenner ("ne"); and Donald G. MacKay, "Birth of a Word," manuscript, Department of Psychology, University of California at Los Angeles ("E").

54. Nonsexist language change has also been ridiculed. See, e.g., "Of Men and Wopersons," *New York Times* (April 12, 1975); "Dr. Spock Treats His Gender Problem," *San Francisco Chronicle* (April 5, 1976); and "Dr. Spock Tells Why He No Longer Sings in Praise of Hims," *New York Times* (October 13, 1973).

55. Benjamin Whorf, *Language, Thought and Reality: Essays of Benjamin Whorf,* ed. J. B. Carrol (Cambridge, Mass.: M.I.T. Press, 1956).

56. Michael Schneider and Karen Foss, "Thought, Sex, and Language: The Sapir/Whorf Hypothesis in the American Women's Movement," *Bulletin: Women's Studies in Communication* 1, no. 1 (1977): 3.

clearly said, given the constraints of the he/man approach and other forms of sexist language.

What can be done to resolve the controversy over sexist language? A dual strategy, involving both research and action, can be most effective in accelerating the language changes already in progress. The many research projects, articles, and course offerings described in *Women and Language News,* a national newsletter, reflect the increasing interdisciplinary and international interest in language and sexism.[57] These theoretical and empirical approaches contribute to our understanding of the nature and consequences of sexist language and lend a credibility to feminist claims. Such approaches need to be translated into other persuasive forms. Pressure on government agencies and the media, for example, can involve letter-writing campaigns, public advertisements, popularization of research results, workshops for those with power to effect language change, and organized demands for guidelines and regulations encouraging nonsexist language use.

Despite the misinterpretation of the sexist language controversy, the movement toward nonsexist language has begun. That movement has been slowed by confusion. Increased clarity can help us be more effective in crafting future changes. Edward Sapir was aware of the psychological implications of language. "All in all," he claimed, "it is not too much to say that one of the really important functions of language is to be constantly declaring to society the psychological place held by all of its members."[58] The goal of those of us who argue for language change is to revise the character of that declaration, so that our language comes to suggest the equal humanity of *all* its users.

57. *Women and Language News* (Stanford, Calif.: Stanford University, Department of Linguistics), various issues, 1976–78.

58. Edward Sapir, *Selected Writings of Edward Sapir in Language, Culture, and Personality,* ed. David Mandelbaum (Berkeley: University of California Press, 1963).

READING 4

Obesity and Desexualization

Marcia Millman

For women, the association of obesity with asexuality largely stems from the assumption that fat women have chosen not to make their bodies attractive, chosen to be unfeminine, to avoid sexuality and sexual relations. The image of keeping men away with a "wall of fat" is a popular expression of this psychological interpretation of obesity. In this the media offer assistance. Typically the media caricature fat women as loud, clumsy, hostile, aggressive, and undelicate. But the physical bulk of fat women need not have acquired this image. In other societies or historical periods, a fleshy woman has often been viewed as sensual, graceful, sexual, and particularly feminine. The recent four-hundredth anniversary of the painter Rubens was the occasion for art critics to note that Western art between about 1500 and 1900 idealized the rotund woman and treated her as opulent and erotic.[1]

Since 1900 our society has progressively regarded

1. Anne Hollander, "When Fat Was in Fashion," *The New York Times Magazine,* October 23, 1977, p. 36.

fleshiness as unsexy. The reason is complex. In part, being thin is increasingly equated with wealth and "class." Being thin is a kind of inconspicuous consumption that distinguishes the rich at a time when most poor people can more easily afford to be fat than thin. Since idealized sex objects are modeled partly on class-associated images, this is surely a factor. For a man to have a thin woman on his arm is a sign of his own worth, and a woman increases her market value by being slender. Fat women are either accorded a nonsexual status in this system, or else (and less publicly) are granted a degraded "lower-class" kind of animal sexuality.

In some cases the association of asexuality with obesity is created as much by the individual herself as it is imposed by the outside world. Joan Bauer, a physicist, reflects on this problem:

My husband, David, is a mathematician. He is a victim in all of this. He has always felt that I'm a beautiful woman. He's always been attracted to me personally and sexually. He doesn't like it that I weigh 250 but he doesn't bother me about it. He'd rather I weighed 170 but mostly he'd rather I didn't hate myself and spend all of my energy agonizing about dieting. He loves me and he'd rather I weighed less than more but it isn't a big deal to him. He's the victim of my cutting off sexuality because I feel so unattractive and elephant-like that how could any elephant like me be interested in sex. He has to put up not only with my being fat but also with my becoming asexual as my way of coping with being fat.

One clue to understanding why obesity is treated as a violation of sex roles is suggested by the popular imagery linking being fat with an autoerotic and/or self-indulgent disposition. Overweight women are suspected of feeding and taking care of themselves, giving pleasure to their own bodies rather than stimulating, pleasing, feeding, and nurturing others. Fat men are correspondingly viewed as passive, vulnerable, soft, and self-indulgent, as if they had failed in a male obligation to be aggressive and achievement-oriented. In the stereotype the fat woman substitutes food for sex, she nurtures herself as if she were a baby, she substitutes a private fantasy life for mature engagement with the real world.

If fat women are considered "out of the running" with reference to men, curiously enough, so are fat men. They are treated as withdrawn from the competition between men; it is as though they have joined the world of

women. And since men are valued more than women, in the cases of both fat men and women, it is one's position vis-à-vis men that is considered the test of value.

The suspicion associating obesity with an antisocial or self-centered nature is exacerbated by the fact that many fat women prefer to eat in private. They are ashamed and discomfited at how others see them. Thus eating becomes even more a private, secret, forbidden act, symbolizing the individual's withdrawal from the social world and its obligations. One of the most common stories told by fat women is of their furtive visits to the refrigerator at night after everyone else has gone to sleep. The association of obesity with secrecy, darkness, self-gratification, and social withdrawal rather than service to or engagement with others is consistent with the overall image of obesity as a violation of women's social obligations:

*I always thought that people knew that the reason I was fat was because I didn't have a man. Being fat was a clear signal that I was home masturbating with my box of cookies. Being fat was the sign that no one else could gratify me and so I turned to food. (*Ellin, *Autobiography)*

In my mind I associated my mother's weight with her cruelty and with being overbearing and non-nurturant and masculine. (Shirley Kaufman, a clinical psychologist)

In keeping with the demand that women nurture others rather than themselves, Joan Bauer relates how eating becomes the one thing she can do to replenish herself when she is drained by effort to perform in the traditional female role and in her professional life:

Indulgent is a crucial word. I view eating as a safety valve. I go home from here at four in the afternoon. I've been carrying tremendous pressure trying to move from student to faculty, trying to be a peer overnight to people who were my authority figures, trying to be everything that everyone wants, to be the first woman this and first woman that, to be the only scientist around here involved in political work against nuclear proliferation, to be the only woman who wants to work part time, to be the student's best friend, the feminist, to do a damn good job in the classroom and get started on new research.

I go home and try to be home enough for my two kids, who need attention, and my husband feels abandoned, and I'm trying to cook dinner—that's when I eat. It's very clear to me that eating is a way of coping with the multiple pressures of a life that feels like it's just got to fly apart at the seams—where if one thing gets out of line it will bring the whole thing tumbling down in a crisis. With that kind of pressure—I feel this is the one place I can be indulgent and I do not make myself exercise control over food. When I need to diet or fast, it's clear that the shifting of control into this realm which is the one place I've always given myself freedom to be—not really psychically but behaviorally—just about drives me up the wall.

I would sometimes stand in my kitchen with tears on my face and I would say, "I can't stand these kids, and if I can't eat right this minute I'm gonna go crazy." And then I eat or have a fight with my husband and say I just can't do any more. I can't be all these things to all these people. I can't do all these things right. I've got to eat. So eating does provide me with the one area where I allow myself to be indulgent and out of control when I'm trying to keep ninety-seven balls in the air. I'm taking care of everyone else and food takes care of me.

The kids are taking out of me, the students are taking out of me, David wants this, my parents want that. I'm trying to be a good neighbor and a good daughter and a good parent and a good wife and a good teacher and a good scholar and a good friend and the one thing that will take care of me is food.

Being the one who gives to everyone is a significant part of being a woman. It certainly is the way my mother was. This is the one way I'm continuous with her. Even though my relationship with my husband is different from the relationship between my parents, and David does much more than my father did at home, I still feel like I give, give, give.

I think occasionally that my abilities are apparently so great that, if I were freed of the constraints of this role conflict, what could I do?

For example, I once had an opportunity to do key work on a very exciting research project that had vital importance in my field. It was during a period when David and I were separated and I had one child, and my first feeling was, "I can't do it, and I'm really pissed I can't do it." And then we worked out a way where my parents and David together took care of Mark for six weeks and I was

not a mother for those six weeks. He was physically gone. And I worked twenty hours a day, and I was exhilarated, and it was fantastic not to be worried all the time that I was working about whether I ought to be home and whether the kid had an ear infection or whether I ought to be at the PTA meeting and whether I was a bad mother to be gone—all those things that drain inner energy. I just worked like a man would work. Like a super-ambitious, really talented man would work. It was very freeing to be absolutely single-focused. The main experience I have of womanness is to be constantly divided—constantly trying to do the splits across nineteen floating logs on a rapidly moving river and keep myself from falling in the water.

I sometimes have the image in my mind that my husband is like a child and I have three children that are always taking from me. I feel like I am the strong, stable earth mother. I am the giver, the nurturer of last resort. If everyone else goes to hell ultimately I am the one, no matter how bad I feel, to give. I will pull myself together and give what needs to be given. No matter what happens—no matter how angry or tired or hurt. As the nurturer you keep on asking about other people's needs and try to respond to them, and you don't just throw in the towel and say, "Okay, someone else take care of me." I'm the one who will keep going, doing what has to be done. If that means suppressing my own needs and feelings, then I will. And that's when I eat.

Obesity in a woman violates conventional sexuality not only through association with self-absorption and autoeroticism but also because largeness equals masculinity. The fat woman may be seen not only as asexual but as androgynous. One woman I spoke with recalled overhearing a child who, confused by her large size, asked her mother "Is that a man or a woman?" The imputation of androgyny has an interesting biological correlate: with extreme weight deviations in either direction, hormones often act to develop secondary sexual characteristics of the opposite sex. Thus one of the most sensitive concerns of very fat women is the fact that they sometimes develop considerable facial hair and cease to menstruate.

One woman who weighed over 300 pounds had developed a full beard and had to shave her face every morning. Only her boyfriend knew this secret, but it contributed to her sense of shame and furtiveness. It is interesting to note that at the low end of the weight spectrum as well, women may stop menstruating and develop body hair in places unusual for women. Fat men correspondingly develop an appearance that is feminine.

At an OA [Overeaters Anonymous] meeting, one man described hitting rock-bottom when a child approached him on the beach and screamed, "Look, Mommy! That man has boobies just like you!" Developing breasts for a man is as devastating as growing a beard for a woman—even worse, since breasts cannot be shaved.

In *Grand Obese,* a novel about an enormously fat family, the obese son is attacked and stripped by neighborhood boys who point and jeer at his diminutive genitals. In his terror, his testicles have ascended and his penis has shrunk and retracted into a "dark pink button trembling against the padded mound of sandy hair."[2] However extreme, the example reflects the popular image of the diminished appearance of the fat man's genitals in comparison with his bulk.

The "femininity" requirement affects overweight women. But it is also essential to remember that many thin and average-weight women are deeply affected as well. Many dread the thought of getting fat. Some even *view* themselves as fat when they are not because of their deep anxiety about their desirability as women.

The account that follows comes from a woman who is now of a very slender but unremarkable build. As she explains, when she was young she approached an extreme condition of thinness bordering on anorexia nervosa, an increasingly common syndrome in which young women literally starve themselves into critical illness and even death. In the following story, Lois Cowell retrospectively wonders whether the quest for thinness is not actually a kind of caricature, a self-mockery of the experience of being a woman, since it dramatically demonstrates the physical discomfort, self-denial, and self-sacrifice required in the conventional female role.

I grew up in South Africa in a religious Christian family. In South Africa white middle-class women have servants and spend all their time being manicured, permed, and putting on cosmetics.

My mother was very concerned about the way her children looked. At the time I became anorexic I must have felt a lot of conflict between being like my mother—a mother—and having a career. I

---

2. Cesar Rotondi, *Grand Obese* (New York: St. Martin's Press, 1979), p. 48.

remember a woman once said to me, "Career women are selfish." I was twenty-seven at the time and not getting married and wanting a career. I wanted to run a boutique.

I had been very thin all my life; in fact, I had tried to gain weight. They used to call me Flea in school. Then I went to London and started to gain weight, and I didn't mind at all. When I returned to South Africa I must have weighed 120 pounds, whereas before I weighed 100 or 110. I never got fat—I never weighed more than 120. But just after I opened my own boutique in South Africa an old boyfriend of mine came into the store and said, "God, you're fat," and so I decided I would go on a diet, and what I did was I stopped eating. I would go all day, working like crazy, and at midnight I would have my first meal—a snack—because I never kept any food in the house so I wouldn't eat. I had a roommate then, so I would eat her food at midnight. If I were starving, I would actually binge and then I'd make myself vomit or take diuretics or laxatives. I used to weigh myself every day and do all this exercise. I'd swim. I'd walk up to the fourth floor where I lived. I'd walk to work up a steep hill instead of taking my car. I went to an exercise gymnasium for an hour every day. I was so thin, 103 pounds, and still I considered myself fat. I reached a point at 103 pounds where I stopped losing weight, but I still considered myself overweight or thought that my thighs were out of proportion. During the winter I would go back to 125 and then I'd starve myself back to 103 again. When I was dieting I would have short black-outs from not eating. I felt myself fat throughout all of this—even when I weighed 103.

I ran a boutique and thin was in—Twiggy was the model. All of my friends and I were competing on diets to see who could lose the most. I stopped menstruating shortly after my first starvation in 1967 and didn't start to menstruate again until 1971. I saw a gynecologist and he told me this sometimes happens when people get so thin.

I was a little afraid that I was going to turn into a man—that I was changing my sex. I would examine my chin and my upper lip for hair.

I didn't realize that I had anorexia nervosa until recently when I was in a class and someone talked about it and I realized this had happened to me. I wrote down my gut reaction to the whole thing. Here it is:

"Ninety percent of those who suffer from anorexia nervosa are women. Why? Anorexia nervosa is a slow and painful form of suicide. It requires such characteristics as self-control, determination, and willpower. It also requires self-hatred and masochism, and women have been trained through all of recorded history to hate themselves. Remember the story of the Garden of Eden . . . women should be getting pleasure from pain. From fairy stories in childhood, we learn that a woman who is not beautiful or so passive as to be half dead (like Sleeping Beauty) is to be hated. She is ugly, wicked, evil, and is generally punished for having autonomy and power.

"She is banished from the kingdom, or, fate worse than death, fails to catch a husband, the handsome prince. The process of grooming oneself to please the handsome prince is inevitably painful. Think of eyebrow-plucking, sleeping in curlers, having one's nose fixed. The pain, of course, teaches an important lesson: no price is too great, no process too repulsive, no operation too painful for the woman who would be beautiful. The tolerance of pain and the romanticization of that tolerance begins here, in preadolescence, in socialization. In fact every aspect of our socialization unites to convince us that we are dirty and smelly, inferior, and weak, the weaker sex. In a materialist world we are man's property like his cars and ships which are also given the female gender. Therefore a man can do with us as he will. To earn his love we must obey him . . . and please him. There the message is that as a female you will never be loved, wanted, respected, or admired unless you change yourself, and this process inevitably involves pain.

"In this climate, then, is anorexia nervosa bred—the condition in which a person participates in her own slow death. This destructive experience commences innocently enough. One strips off one's clothes and stands in front of a mirror to examine whether or not one is overweight. For a man, this method is probably sensible. For a woman, however, the criteria cannot be those of health and strength, for she must inevitably compare the body she sees in the mirror to those images of women the media bombards her with. If the time is the 1960s she must compare herself with Twiggy, and if the 1970s with Farrah Fawcett-

Majors. Therefore, dieting for women generally has nothing to do with health and strength and everything to do with appearance. For men, the norms are flexible.

"Let me recount my own experiences with anorexia nervosa. I am now aware that I was at that time—about ten years ago—not trying to kill all of myself but only to eliminate in myself that large part of me that identified as woman. For according to Jung we all have both male and female identities. I developed my male tendencies toward aggression and ruthlessness and ambition, running a successful business with male detachment. I was, until my body became too weak for any sex drive to exist, a sexual masochist, having sex with men who were my inferiors and then begging them to hurt and debase me. Through the use of clothing and cosmetics I made myself and other women into caricatures of womanhood. As the owner of a boutique I had the power to do this. I also rejected my mother, thus rejecting in me the person who identified with her. Finally I succeeded in killing off the woman in me and ovulation and menses ceased. . . ."

It is often observed that to achieve a position of commanding authority and power in situations conventionally reserved for men, a woman must display stereotypically masculine behavior or renounce her claims to "femininity." Some feel, for example, that being fat made it possible for a woman—Sarah Caldwell—to conduct at the Metropolitan Opera. Her bulk made her more like a man in others' eyes and therefore more acceptable to others in a position of power:

"If she'd been a babe," says one musician, "we'd have walked right over her." Miss Caldwell's success may, in other words, have a great deal to do with her figure. There is something monumental about her. One senses instinctively that this is a formidable creature, one who will prove as immovable and as irresistible as a military tank, one whom it will be extremely dangerous to cross.[3]

For many women, life seems to demand a choice between being successful in love and sex or being successful

3. Robert Jones, "Walking into the Fire: Sarah Caldwell Comes to the Met," *Opera News,* vol. 40, no. 14 (February 14, 1976): 11–12.

in work. One woman I interviewed, Claire Stewart, now runs a successful employment counseling agency. She spoke of how being 20 pounds overweight as an adolescent allowed her to escape from some of the constraints of being female:

> Since they were having financial problems, my father didn't want me to go to college. He wanted my four brothers to go to college but he wanted me to get thin and become an airline stewardess. When my father told me to get thin and become a stewardess I associated being thin with having everything happen the way my parents wanted it, and then my life would be all over. I knew if I were thin I'd be married to a naval officer and have three kids and play bridge all day.
>
> Because I was fat and I wanted to go to college I had to find a way to save money and pay for it myself. So being fat really saved my life because it made it possible for me to become independent.
>
> One thing that saved me during all the years my father told me how unattractive I was was that people told me I was smart and that I had a pretty face. I clung to that. If I had internalized everything my father said, I would have committed suicide. Even though my present reality was not great, I had high hopes. Even now, that's still left over from childhood in my life — I cling to being smart. I never had any doubt that I was bright and I've also always been artistic. When I was twelve years old I made money by selling Christmas decorations I made to stores. When I was nineteen I ran my own gallery.
>
> When you're fat you have your own little world — you have to develop other talents. If I had been thin when I was a teenager and in my early twenties I would never have developed the way I did.
>
> I was in a lot of misery when I was a teenager. I felt I should be a cheerleader but in retrospect the people I associated with because I was unattractive were a lot more important and valuable than the friends I would have had if I were a cheerleader.
>
> I feel completely self-reliant and able to make a good living and talented in many areas. I think being fat allowed me to put off choices I wasn't able to make when I was younger — I feel I had to wait until I was thin to make the right choices about men. I still feel that but I am trying not to because

> now it's a way of not making the relationships I have really count.

As Claire Stewart suggests, there is a bind — being fat brings both the pain of failing in the conventional female role and protection from some of its dangers and constraints in both work and relationships. Nevertheless, fat women are ultimately at a great disadvantage. Their personal stories tip the balance heavily toward the painful consequences. Even a woman who is remarkably successful in work will have her problems, as Joan Bauer, the physicist, poignantly observes:

> I was president of various organizations in high school, including a large social-service organization. When I was elected president they had their formal ceremonial transition of officers at a big dance and I went to be ceremonially inducted, and then I went home right after the ceremony. I had to have a formal gown to go to this damn thing and then go home because I didn't have a date. The ceremony shouldn't have been at a dance — it's stupid that it was, but at the time I felt stupid.

We are left, finally, with a paradox. Since obesity is viewed as rebellion or default in conventional notions of femininity, being fat provides women with certain consolations (for example, being able to nurture themselves) and protections (for example, from being tempted to sacrifice work careers for love). But except in rare cases, the failure in the conventional female role is still deeply upsetting to the individual, and like Joan Bauer, many fat women with successful careers remain insecure and miserable:

> Well, I have plenty of success in male-associated areas, but I would trade it for being a sexually attractive woman. I'm hooked to the most superficial things and need sexual confirmation in a way that's really sad. A woman who's truly beautiful in men's eyes can walk away from the pain and the ridiculousness of sex-stereotyping in that area much more freely than I can. Someone who is vulnerable in stereotypic roles will cling to them longest because of the forever unsatisfied need to be confirmed. . . . I take all the work success for granted. I've always been good at work. What I'd give my right arm for is to be good at what I'm not good at — at being a sexually attractive woman.

Even in cases of less extreme conflict, the wish to remove oneself from men is usually only partial. By turning the desire not to be in the running into a physical handicap the individual can maintain the belief that she is the rejected rather than the rejector.

> *Being fat has been a way of insulating me from having to deal with men, and it works. I know that objectively being 20 pounds overweight doesn't matter that much, and I'm probably just as attractive as I'd be if I lost 20 pounds, but it's in my mind—it's a way of punishing myself.*
>
> *The times I've felt like a fat person had to do with men and my relationship to them—not with food.*
>
> *And yet, even when I'm fat I still take care of myself in other ways—I still take baths, get haircuts and buy nice clothes. There's a woman who works with me in my office who is not only overweight but has stringy hair and she doesn't take baths. So I stop being sexual to some degree when I am fat, but I don't take it to the extreme. I still take care of myself. It's puzzling to me why I would do all these little things like get a good haircut and wear nice clothes when I stay fat. It's a kind of approach-avoidance to men.* (Claire Stewart)

If obesity indeed signifies a rebellion against conventional female sex roles, then surely this rebellion is unconscious or conflicted, not fully embraced. Most fat women feel self-hatred, shame, and a sense of failure. If a rebellious element motivates obesity, the woman frequently punishes herself for it with guilt and self-defeat. In rejecting the standards of conventional attractiveness without a clear sense of purpose, fat people make themselves more and not less vulnerable to the judgments of society.

READING 5

I Was the Showgirl, the Nun, and the Hooker

Reading For November Noons Program
By The Women's Poetry Workshop, Columbus, Ohio
At The Art League Gallery

Elizabeth Ann James

When they unstrap me from the electro-
    shock table
When I see the red eyes of the firing squad

between the slits of the hangman's black
    stocking
I'll tell them
Jesus I sang

I was the showgirl, the nun, and the hooker

I stood behind the dimestore counter and sold
    rhinestone jewelry

Reprinted from Elizabeth Ann James, "I Was the Showgirl, the Nun, and the Hooker," in *Righting,* ed. Margaret Honton (Argus Press, 1977), by permission of the author. Copyright 1977 by Elizabeth Ann James.

I danced Ravel's waltz in a white ballet skirt

I was the magic drink girl at the Kahiki

I dressed like the cover on Brides' magazine

I traded my foodstamps
               for a drink of Johnny Walker

A police dog devoured my fatherless baby

   I walked the line because you were mine

   I was a Lady, a chick, a broad

   I relied on Nathan B. Detroit
                  and Emily Dickinson
   I was Embraceable Me and Evil Woman

   I said Good Morning Funny Face
   I love you

   I murdered my children
   and stuffed them in garbage bags

I wore Windsong and Arpege and Skinny Dip

I slept all night in Central Park
in a stolen navy jacket

I wrote a paper that said Shakespeare
was cool about women

I painted faces on store mannequins

   I watched Citizen Kane
   and understood about the sled named
      Rosebud

   I left letters in the snow
   on my husband's grave
   and I felt the snow
   on Garbo's face
   when she stepped off the train
   in Anna Karenina

   I died in the snow . . .

On the third day
I dissolved into a river
which ran into a Harlem reservoir,
and sprayed out of a fire hydrant in El Barrio
where the Puerto Rican kids
splashed in my rainbows . . .

      I arose toward the popsicle sun
      and filtered down as snow
                        over a barn
            where a cat was having kittens
      and melted under a milk cow's breath

I ascended into heaven once again . . .

Saint Bernadette dressed as a cocktail waitress
asked me, "Where you from?"

I said I'm Elizabeth Ann
      I come from Winesburg, and Port Au
         Prince,
      and Mobile, and Grovers Corners and
      Raintree County

And Zelda Fitzgerald
tied a ballet shoe ribbon around my neck
and Billie Holiday
dabbed me behind the ears
with gardenia perfume, and stuffed the pocket
   of my nightie with Egyptian cigarettes

And I descended in a balloon decorated
         with Emma Goldman's likeness
      and was left in a basket on the steps
      of the convent of Our Lady of Unwed Actresses
      at Frenchtown Ohio
         where I was reborn
in the year when the nuns
and the hookers
         wrote poems

Women's Depiction by the Mass Media

Gaye Tuchman

So angry at the blatant sexism of the mass media as to be blinded, students of the media's presentation of women have been more politically sophisticated than theoretically sound. In part, their research has been crippled by dependence upon the academic study of mass communications, a field hardly known for its intellectual vigor, but one whose problems must be understood in order to see why research on women and the media is theoretically stalled.

The American Study of the Mass Media

In the years following World War II, the media grew exponentially. So did study of the media. Perhaps because the media associated with the "mass" were insistently differentiated from high culture and intellectual substance, no academic field was willing to give such study a home. Instead, just as interdisciplinary teams of social scientists had cooperated during the war to study propaganda, they now cooperated to study the mass media. Perhaps defensively, the field became ponderously "scientific." To demonstrate that the media constituted an intellectually valid subject, researchers embraced the sophisticated techniques of modern social science and simultaneously hired themselves out as media consultants. Working for both Madison Avenue and the media conglomerates, they were asked to supply practical answers to seemingly practical questions.[1] Perhaps this emphasis upon the applications of research also helped to divert the field from the battles about ideas that characterize the study of high culture. Consider Harold Lasswell's suggestion that the proper study of the media was "who said

what to whom in what channel with what effect."[2] Rather than being interpreted as a theoretical question about, say, the mass media as myth and the origin and impact of myth (topics of great concern in the study of both high culture and anthropology), Lasswell's dictum was interpreted by media researchers as a practical/technical query. A sentence that now parades as a theory, it has been used to divide the field into separate areas of research that talk past each other.

Virtually every word in Lasswell's original sentence has been transformed into a subfield with a separate name and separate theory. Studies about "who" tend to be either social-psychological examinations of communicators' traits or sociological studies identified as institutional analyses.[3] "What," too often investigated atheoretically, but sometimes given a rich historical treatment, usually appears as a statistical compendium.[4] "Whom" and "what effect" are wedded in both laboratory experiments and correlational studies that, in the last decade, discuss role theory and psychological modeling.[5] "In what channel" is used to separate studies of news from studies of entertainment, the local press from the national press, long-playing records from television. Mostly, though, in the last ten years, Lasswell's dictum has been collapsed into a three-step model applied to successive topics. As

Reprinted from Gaye Tuchman, "Women's Depiction by the Mass Media," in *Signs,* 4 (1979): 528–42, by permission of The University of Chicago Press.

1. Stuart Ewen offers a very early example in *Captains of Consciousness: Advertising and the Social Roots of the Consumer Culture* (New York: McGraw-Hill, 1976), p. 160.

2. Harold Lasswell, "The Structure and Function of Communication in Society," in *The Communication of Ideas,* ed. Lyman Bryson (New York: Harper & Bros., 1948), pp. 37–51.
3. Such as John W. Johnstone et al., *The News People: A Sociological Portrait of American Journalists and Their Work* (Urbana: University of Illinois Press, 1976); and Judith Gelfman, *Women in Television News* (New York: Columbia University Press, 1976).
4. Leo Lowenthal, "The Triumph of Mass Idols," in *Literature, Popular Culture and Society* (1944; reprint ed., Englewood Cliffs, N.J.: Spectrum, 1961), is historically rich. Melvin DeFleur, "Occupational Roles as Portrayed on Television," *Public Opinion Quarterly* 28 (Spring 1964): 57–74, is more typical but extremely useful.
5. Many are reviewed in R. Liebert, J. Neale, and E. Davidson, *The Early Window: The Effects of Television on Children and Youth* (New York: Pergamon Press, 1973).

public concern and funding have turned from one aspect of the media to another, there have been (1) some studies of communicators' traits and several of mass media organizations; (2) a series of content analyses about violence, race, and, most recently, gender; and (3) experiments and surveys about the "violent" antisocial effects of the media, the prosocial effects, the effects of racial stereotypes in the media upon black and white children's attitudes toward race, and, finally, the impact of the media on the development of gender behavior and attitudes. The theoretical model used for the study of media violence has simply been applied to race and gender.

Recent Work on Women

An issue tackled by the nascent women's movement was the relationship between images of women in the mass media and social roles. Betty Friedan based *The Feminine Mystique* in part on a content analysis of women's magazines.[6] As early as 1967 some consciousness-raising groups sought to excise media stereotypes from their collective understanding of gender roles and stratification. During this same period other women, seeking concrete feminist projects and influenced by concern for children's development, examined materials aimed at youngsters.[7]

Needless to say, all these activities assumed that images of women in the mass media have some sort of detrimental impact upon both individual consciousness and collective social life. That tenet permeates feminist actions, such as the challenge to WRC-TV's license mounted by the National Organization for Women, journalistic commentaries, and academic research.[8] To cite but one indicator of this common belief, Friedman comments that only twelve of the 1,018 items included in her annotated bibliography of sex-role stereotyping in the media defend sexist portrayals of women.[9]

Practical, like the field from which it derives, recent work on the media has tried to locate facts with which to flesh out a quasi-political attack on sexism in the media, its origins and impact. The argument ordering those facts

explicitly concerns "who," "what," and "with what effect" and is also implicit in Friedan's book, the NOW challenge to WRC-TV, journalistic work, and reviews of the existing literature by Busby, Janus, the U.S. Commission on Civil Rights, and myself.[10] It assumes a direct correspondence among media organizations, their content, and the everyday world. It states:

1. Few women hold positions of power in media organizations, and so:
2. The content of the media distorts women's status in the social world. The media do not present women who are viable role models, and therefore:
3. The media's deleterious role models, when internalized, prevent and impede female accomplishments. They also encourage both women and men to define women in terms of men (as sex objects) or in the context of the family (as wives and mothers.)[11]

6. Betty Friedan, *The Feminine Mystique* (New York: Dell Books, 1963).

7. Several articles on sexism in children's books appear in the Fall 1969 issue of *Women: A Journal of Liberation.* Contributions by collectives include Women on Words and Images, *Dick and Jane as Victims: Sex Stereotypes in Children's Readers,* 1972 (available from P.O. Box 2163, Princeton, N.J. 08540).

8. National Organization for Women (National Capitol Area Chapter), *Women in the Wasteland Fight Back* (Washington, D.C.: NOW, 1972).

9. Leslie J. Friedman, *Sex Role Stereotyping in the Mass Media: An Annotated Bibliography* (New York: Garland Press, 1977), p. xv. An annotated bibliography on television is Helen Franzwa, "The Image of Women in Television: An Annotated Bibliography," in *Hearth and Home: Images of Women in the Mass Media,* ed. Gaye Tuchman, Arlene Kaplan Daniels, and James Benét (New York: Oxford University Press, 1978), pp. 272–99. *Media Report to Women* (ed. Donna Allen, 3306 Ross Place, N.W., Washington, D.C., 20008) discusses both journalistic and academic works as they appear, as well as political and legal actions.

10. Linda Busby, "Sex-Role Research on the Mass Media," *Journal of Communication* 25, no. 4 (1975): 107–31; Noreene Janus, "Research on Sex Roles in the Mass Media," *Insurgent Sociologist* 7 (Summer 1977): 19–31; U.S. Commission on Civil Rights, *Window Dressing on the Set* (Washington, D.C.: Government Printing Office, 1977); and Gaye Tuchman, "Introduction: The Symbolic Annihilation of Women by the Mass Media," in Tuchman et al. Useful references may also be found in Maurine Beasley and Sheila Silver, *Women in Media: A Documentary Source Book* (Washington, D.C.: Women's Institute for Freedom of the Press, 1977); Marion Marzolf, *Up from the Footnote: A History of Women Journalists* (New York: Hastings House, 1977); and Matilda Butler and William Paisley, *Women and the Mass Media: A Sourcebook* (New York: Human Sciences Press, 1979).

11. These ideas are found in U.S. Commission on Civil Rights (n. 10 above); and Gaye Tuchman, "The Impact of Mass Media Stereotypes upon the Employment of Women," in *Women in a Full Employment Economy: A Compendium Prepared for the Use of the Joint Economic Committee of Congress* (Washington, D.C.: Government Printing Office, 1977), pp 247–68. (The latter is a version of Tuchman's intro. in Tuchman et al.) They are also expressed in Josephine King and Mary Scott, eds., *Is This Your Life? Images of Women in the Mass Media* (London: Virago, 1977); and Kathryn Weibel, *Mirror, Mirror: Images of Women Reflected in Popular Culture* (New York: Doubleday Anchor, 1977).

Although politically useful, this argument is mired in a naive literalness and propounds a theory of a vulgar and odd mimesis,[12] that is, reality really will mirror the media. Consider the core of the argument: The media distort women's status in the social world and do not present viable role models.

The Content of the Media

The descriptive facts seem straightforward: Since 1954, there has been relatively little change in the presentation of women according to the available statistical indicators.[13] Then as now, only about 45 percent of the people presented on television have been women; about 20 percent of those shown as members of the labor force have been women. Men are shown as aggressors, women as victims. Symbolically subservient, policewomen who have been knocked to the floor by a bad guy are pulled from the floor by a good guy; in both cases, women are on the floor in relationship to men. Twenty-five years ago, as today, women on television were concentrated in the ghetto of situation comedy. They are and were, as the U.S. Commission on Civil Rights put it, "window dressing on the set."

That similarity between past and present is found elsewhere in the media. In the 1950s as now, the lives of women in women's magazine fiction have been defined in terms of men — husbands, lovers, or the chasm of male absence.[14] Ads continue to portray women in the home and men outside it, although there are no systematic statistical comparisons of ads from twenty-five years ago with those of today.[15] Voiceovers continue to be dominated by men; fewer than 10 percent use women's voices to announce station breaks, upcoming programs, and where to buy a product.[16]

To be sure, there appear to be some differences between yesterday's and today's media, particularly with regard to minorities. However, minority women, about 2.9 percent of the people on television, are concentrated in family-centered situation comedies.[17] But at least they now appear on television; in the early 1960s, the regular presence of a black woman on a prime-time show contributed to its cancellation. However, mere presence does not suffice. Lemon points out that on some shows men dominated women so much that the regular appearance of a female co-star seemed to increase white male dominance.[18] Presence also enables the reiteration of stereotypes: Dominance patterns in interactions on prime-time television contrast the "black matriarch" with the less forceful position of the white woman within her family. And, the mass media so assume male superiority that men even give more advice about personal entanglements on the soap operas than women do.[19] This finding seems particularly significant, because the soap operas come closer to presenting a pseudoegalitarian world than other television programs and most other media.

Too frequently, the term used to characterize these findings is "distortion." Both political and pejorative, the term itself seems to transmute the literary theory of realism. However, the idea that a literature reflects its society is transformed into the statement that the media should reflect society and the charge that contemporary media do not properly reflect the position of women. Citing demography and data on the labor force and on family structure, and contrasting the presentation of men with that of women,[20] studies imply there should be a direct, discernible correspondence between the depiction of women in the media and contemporary life. By political references to our culture's normative expectations that news should transcend distortion, the dominant models of women's presentation in the media suggest that entertainment *should* also be a veridical reproduction of social life, an accurate representation, Proust's *Remembrance of Things Past* as CBS's "You Were There."

However, the very underrepresentation of women, including their stereotypic portrayal, may symbolically capture the position of women in American society — their

---

12. A term suggested by Catharine Stimpson (personal communication).

13. Summarized in U.S. Commission on Civil Rights, pp. 4–27.

14. See Helen Franzwa, "Women in Fact and Fiction," *Journal of Communication* 24, no. 2 (1972): 104–9; "Female Roles in Women's Magazine Fiction, 1940–1970," in *Woman: Dependent or Independent Variable*, ed. R. K. Unger and F. L. Denmark (New York: Psychological Dimensions, 1975).

15. See the summary of this literature by Busby, as well as A. J. Silverstein and R. Silverstein, "The Portrayal of Women in Television Advertising," *FCC Bar Journal* 1 (1974): 71–98; and Charles Winick, Lorne G. Williamson, Stuart Chusmir, and Mariann P. Winick, *Children's Television Commercials: A Content Analysis* (New York: Praeger Publishers, 1973). See also the Winter 1978 issue of the *Journal of Communication*.

16. This generalization includes voiceovers on public television. See Caroline Isber and Muriel Cantor, *Report of the Task Force on Women in Public Broadcasting* (New York: Corporation for Public Broadcasting, 1975).

17. U.S. Commission on Civil Rights, p. 28.

18. Judith Lemon, "Dominant or Dominated? Women on Prime-Time Television," in Tuchman et al., pp. 51–68.

19. Joseph Turow, "Advising and Ordering: Daytime, Prime-time," *Journal of Communication* 24, no. 2 (1974): 138–41.

20. Two examples are Tuchman, "The Impact of Mass Media Stereotypes," and U.S. Commission on Civil Rights.

real lack of power. It bespeaks their "symbolic annihilation" by the media. For, according to Gerbner, just as representation in the media signifies social existence, so too underrepresentation and (by extension) trivialization and condemnation indicate symbolic annihilation.[21]

Gerbner's concept is more politically sensitive than the cry of distortion. Interacting with their environment, social movements seek fresh tactics to gain new or modified goals, and their environment, including the media, may seek to repel, consolidate, or coopt those efforts. Gerbner sees the gross statistical similarities between today's and yesterday's media as indicators of the media's espousal of the politics of cultural resistance.[22] Rather than keeping pace with, say, the increased participation of women in the labor force, the media discredit, isolate, and undercut: They discuss "women's libbers," present issues of liberation on shows distasteful to a general audience, and muddy the distinction between women's liberation and sexual liberation. Ever alert and energetic, they transform and absorb dissent.

Yet, although the idea of symbolic annihilation seems to be a theoretical advance, it too has been used to advocate a naively literal notion of mimesis.

Why the Media Are Sexist

There are two dominant explanations of the media's sexism: women's position in media organizations, and the socioeconomic organization of the media. The first both cites the wrong evidence and ignores pertinent existing evidence.[23] The second assumes that the media will change essentially as the status of women improves.[24]

Some researchers have announced or implied that the media offer a deleterious portrait of women because few women hold positions of responsibility within the media.[25] Most of the data thought to support this explanation concern television stations and the networks. Following a spurt of hiring women around 1970, the increase in women holding administrative positions at television stations has fallen off. Although it is difficult to determine, because the forms designed by the Federal Communications Commission permit a minority woman to be counted twice, women and minorities seem to have similar patterns of authority: Both tend to be in such dead-end jobs as affirmative action officer, to be marginal to the organizational chart, and to be primarily supervising other women and minorities. Evidence of discrimination in hiring and promotion was strong enough for women employees to have won lawsuits or achieved substantial out-of-court settlements from each of the three television networks.

None of this evidence indicates that discrimination in employment leads to the symbolic annihilation of women. As Cantor points out, these data mostly pertain to television stations, but decisions about programming are dominated by the networks, and the programs themselves are made by production companies which are technically independent of the networks.[26] Furthermore, sensitivity to affirmative action and a concern with how women are presented do not necessarily indicate that a corporation is free of sexism. The Public Broadcasting Corporation charged Isber and Cantor to prepare a report on its personnel and programs, which revealed an insistent definition of women as a special interest group and a consistent display of sex stereotypes.[27] Yet the corporation did not significantly change its policies. Equally important, the content and staffing characteristic of other media indicate that women frequently create "sexist" content.

Consider journalists. Using survey data, Phillips finds that women's judgments about general news resemble those of men.[28] Merritt and Gross affirm that female editors of women's pages have virtually the same priorities

---

21. George Gerbner, "Violence in Television Drama: Trends and Symbolic Functions," in *Media Content and Control: Television and Social Behavior,* ed. George C. Comstock and Eli A. Rubinstein (Washington, D.C.: Government Printing Office, 1972), 28–187. The extension is developed in Tuchman, "The Symbolic Annihilation of Women."

22. George Gerbner, "The Dynamics of Cultural Resistance," in Tuchman et al.

23. This material is reviewed by Muriel Cantor, "Will More Women Make a Difference? A Sociological Perspective on Employment and Portrayal in Television," prepared for Telecommunications Policy Research Conference (Arlie, Virginia, May 11, 1978) and available from the author (Department of Sociology, American University, Washington, D.C.)

24. This criticism is raised by Janus (see n. 10 above) of the "reflection hypothesis" developed in Tuchman, "Symbolic Annihilation of Women."

25. This notion is implicit in U.S. Commission on Civil Rights (see n. 10), which also serves as the main source for statements in this paragraph. The United Church of Christ publishes annual analyses of employment at television stations.

26. See n. 23.

27. See Isber and Cantor; and Muriel Cantor, "Where Are the Women in Public Broadcasting?" in Tuchman et al.

28. E. Barbara Phillips, "The Artists of Everyday Life: Journalists, Their Craft and Their Consciousness" (Ph.D. diss., Syracuse University, 1975).

and preferences as their male counterparts.[29] According to Orwant and Cantor's study of journalism students, women seem to have the same stereotypes of women as men do. Although these women students are interested in politics, not the traditional content of the women's pages, they believe that they are unusual and that other women are interested in the traditional fare.[30] In part the maintenance of stereotypes derives from the culture (an unfortunately diffuse explanation), in part from professionalism. Even when women do see a topic differently from men, professionalism limits the possible presentations and defuses radical critiques.[31] More generally, it is difficult for women employees to resist ideas and attitudes associated with success in their profession, even if those ideas disparage women, for sexism, like racism, is best understood as an institutional, not a personal, phenomenon.[32]

The second explanation for media sexism, the socioeconomic organization of the media, appears to be more sensitive to institutional issues. For instance, it records that professionalism serves organizational interests in both journalism and entertainment. One observational study finds that both male and female members of a talk show may elicit sexist comments from celebrities in the preinterview preparatory to the network show; both may seek to defuse expressions of feminism in order to appease stations airing their program, much as they also seek to blunt other radical critiques.[33] For television writers, professionalism includes not offending the networks. And, the development of professionalism in the media is associated with the growth of the media as complex and capitalist bureaucracies. It is also probable that professional procedures encourage male domination; such topics as housework may, for instance, be dismissed as unimportant, uninteresting, unentertaining (unless

handled incompetently, as was done sometimes on the old "I Love Lucy" show).

Elsewhere, I have argued that the symbolic annihilation of women associated with professionalism serves the economic interests of media profiting from advertising and of advertising itself.[34] Radio, television, newspapers, and magazines all seek to deliver as many consumers as possible to advertisers. Like advertisers, they speak the language of "markets," viewing aggregated individuals called "groups" as "potential markets" for specific products. Which messages are formed depends on the market sought. More common in American homes than bathrooms, television demands larger audiences than more specialized media, and so may be more traditional. For instance, Saturday morning children's television programs have been designed specifically to please advertisers: Time slots bought for companies advertising boys' toys are filled with gender-specific programs purposely different from those designed to deliver little girls to companies advertising dolls or toy stoves.[35] More specialized media, such as women's magazines, consider the specific interests and attitudes of those in their market, such as what appeals to college-educated women between the ages of twenty-five and forty, and may introduce less traditional ideas—if they deem it financially wise to do so.

That different media are responsive to different groups also implies that the content of some media changes more quickly than that of others. As we have seen, the conventional statistical indicators find little change in the portrayal of women by television in the last twenty-five years. (Of course, the indicators are not sensitive to the current use of the words "pregnancy" and "rape," terms that were taboo in the 1950s.) However, there has been some change in how women's magazines present women. Today they show a "gentle support" for the women's movement, mainly by recognizing that most women face the dual tasks of paid employment and housework. Short stories appear to be entering the "majority culture" represented by "male magazines": Like

29. Sharyne Merritt and Harriet Gross, "Women's Page/Life Style Editors: Does Sex Make a Difference?" *Journalism Quarterly,* vol. 55 (August 1978).
30. Jack E. Orwant and Muriel Cantor, "How Sex Stereotyping Affects Perceptions of News Preferences," *Journalism Quarterly* 54 (Spring 1977): 99–108, 139.
31. Gaye Tuchman, "The Topic of the Women's Movement," in *Making News: A Study in the Construction of Knowledge* (New York: Free Press, 1978).
32. Especially when they are a relatively small proportion of those in the profession; see Rosabeth Moss Kanter, *Men and Women of the Corporation* (New York: Basic Books, 1977).
33. Gaye Tuchman, "Assembling a Television Talk Show," in *The TV Establishment: Programming for Power and Profit,* ed. Gaye Tuchman (Englewood Cliffs, N.J.: Prentice-Hall Spectrum, 1974).

34. Tuchman, "The Symbolic Annihilation of Women." The argument omits film. Since the invention of the *auteur* theory of film, most analyses have had the flavor of literary criticism and film has been treated as though it were high culture. See, e.g., Joan Mellen, *Women and Their Sexuality in the New Film* (New York: Horizons Press, 1974).
35. Muriel Cantor, "Producing Television for Children," in Tuchman, ed., *The TV Establishment.* But one should not infer that the media "give *people* what they *do* want," since they are also creating a sense of what markets with specific demographic characteristics *should* want.

those in *Esquire,* fictional stories in the *Ladies' Home Journal* are tending toward downbeat endings.[36]

But are these changes significant? Studying the depiction of Jackie Kennedy Onassis by magazines catering to different social classes, Lopate learns that sex-role stereotyping is pervasive. By viewing Jackie as a Rorschach ink blot, Lopate[37] finds some variations in the published image of women—but those are class variations around the theme of female dependence, passivity, and male dominance, updated versions of patterns discussed by both Flora and Franzwa.

Clearly, considering present content to be variations on past themes minimizes any changes. Doing this also discredits the notion that the media respond to the changing interests of their markets; it charges that some researchers are too anxious to locate differences when they may be dealing with reincarnations. Janus insists that even new patterns in the gross statistical indicators of symbolic annihilation might represent new twists in the bourgeois oppression of women rather than "real" social change.[38] Ehrenreich puts it more gracefully: "Today's New Woman is the Cosmo Girl with her shirt buttoned and the heavy black eye-liner tastefully removed. Unlike the Cosmo girl, she doesn't want to work for the boss, date the boss, or even marry the boss: she wants to be the boss. And, in this respect, the New Woman—like Wonder Woman . . . and other new models of feminine *machisma*—has a certain feminist appeal."[39] But,

Ehrenreich continues, that appeal undermines feminism by identifying achievement with the economically successful "gray-suited upwardly mobile corporate woman" and by insisting that any determined and talented woman can make it. The cult of the New Woman subverts the tenet that sexism is an institutionalized phenomenon and simultaneously depicts woman in the image of man—woman as compleat corporate bureaucrat. Seemingly urging women to identify with the drive for upward mobility, and so extending the dominant-class hegemony to women, the media announce: Every woman should aim for both her own achievement of upward mobility and a rewarding marriage as the joined essence of a satisfying life.

Rather than negating the notion that the socio-economic organization of the media determines the image of women, the radical view that Ehrenreich helps to voice extends it. It argues that both past and present images uphold woman's role as individual and family consumer. Charlie's Angels parade *machisma;* they also flaunt conspicuous consumption. Finally, radical analysis adds, the ideological hegemony of the media is a *means not to know:* It obscures the actual distribution of women in the labor force; it encourages the women's markets to believe "you've come a long long way" (by smoking cigarettes and so breaking old taboos); it prevents women from realizing how their roles as consumers contribute to the maintenance of advanced capitalism.[40] Such statements, of course, presuppose that the media have a significant effect on consumers. In part these statements, like those of less radical feminists, draw on conventional studies of media effects when they propose the New Woman as role model. In part they mesh with some of the newer and more promising theories.

The Effects of the Media

No area of mass media research is as confused as the study of effects. Psychological theories, which sometimes parade as sociology, compete to explain the influence of the media on individuals. That those individuals are sometimes studied as groups—the college educated versus the high school educated—or studied in groups does not mitigate the refusal to analyze the impact of media on social structure. Two main theories have pervaded the

36. See Sheila Silver, "Then and Now—Content Analysis of *McCall's* magazine" (paper presented at the annual meetings of Association for Education in Journalism, College Park, Maryland, August 1976 [also available through School of Journalism, University of Maryland]); and Margaret Davis, "The *Ladies' Home Journal* and *Esquire:* A Comparison," manuscript (Stanford, Calif.: Stanford University, Department of Sociology, 1976). The development of minority literature is discussed in Elaine Showalter, *A Literature of Their Own* (Princeton, N.J.: Princeton University Press, 1977). On women's magazines, see also Matilda Butler and William Paisley, "Magazine Coverage of Women's Rights," *Journal of Communication* 28 (Winter 1978): 183–86; and Jennie Farley, "Women's Magazines and the ERA: Friend or Foe?" *Journal of Communication* 28 (Winter 1978): 187–92.
37. Carol Lopate, "Jackie!" in Tuchman et al.; Cornelia Flora, "The Passive Female: Her Comparative Image by Class and Culture in Women's Magazine Fiction," *Journal of Marriage and the Family* 33 (August 1971): 435–44; Franzwa, "Female Roles in Women's Magazine Fiction, 1940-1970" (see n. 14 above).
38. Janus.
39. Barbara Ehrenreich, "Combat in the Media Zone," *Seven Days* (March 10, 1978), reprinted in *Against the Grain,* no. 11 (June–July 1978), p. 3.

40. Dorothy Smith, "The Ideological Practice of Sociology," *Catalyst* 8 (1974): 39–54, analyzes ideology as a means "not to know."

study of effects: stimulus-response and limited effects.[41] Sometimes called the hypodermic needle theory, because it supposedly claims that an injection of media fare produces a specific outcome, stimulus-response has now been essentially rejected. It could never show that a specific message inevitably produced a specific effect. In contrast, the theory of limited effects argues that the influence of specific messages is inevitably mediated by such social variables as age, social class, religion, ethnicity, and education. These mediating variables are also invoked by uses and gratifications research which looks to see what people say they get out of the media. This research has yet to demonstrate any linkage between what people say and recognizable effects. Instead it has established that individuals of varying psychological and social characteristics claim slightly different uses and gratifications and that different media serve different functions.

Modeling theory, an extension of the concept of role model, also invokes mediating variables. Familiar to those who followed the debate on whether televised violence had a harmful effect on children, modeling theory has more recently been applied to the impact of the media's vision of women. Using both laboratory experiments and surveys, academic researchers have established that (1) boys and girls pay particular attention to children of their own gender performing gender-typed tasks; (2) they can reproduce these tasks; (3) sex-stereotyped content prompts from children traditional responses about women's roles; (4) content contradicting dominant stereotypes prompts less traditional views; and (5) the more television girls watch, the more traditional are their attitudes and aspirations.[42] Although the statistical strength and significance of these generalizations varies with the mediating factors, some girls do appear to use the images of women in the mass media as role models. Yet, were a national commission to weigh the evidence, its conclusion would probably resemble that of the Surgeon General's Advisory Committee on television violence: For some children, under some circumstances, televised sex-role stereotypes may be harmful to optimal personal development.

This statement is weak, not because of the technical inadequacies of current social science methods, but rather because of the theoretical shallowness of this field's empirical approach. For instance, neither role modeling nor the more general limited-effects theory has taken into account Piagetian research on the cognitive development of children. Only recently have we learned that young children do not understand the conceptual distinction between a program and a commercial.[43] Does their lack of understanding mean that we should talk about stages in the development of media skills as we analyze stages in the development of language skills and a sense of time and space? Equally important, does the child's confusion of program and commercial create a "community of discourse" that presupposes consumerism and takes it for granted?[44] The answer to this question is important to the study of women's depiction because of the twentieth century's identification of the woman as consumer for the family and the use of that role to maintain women's subjugation.[45] Researchers, developing the concept of a community of discourse, are turning away from the theory of limited effects. What becomes important is not the mediating factor of religion or social class but rather that individuals of all religions, political predilections, and social classes can discuss Johnny Carson, Wonder Woman, Mary Tyler Moore, *Time* magazine, and *Playboy*. A community of discourse is comparable to a language: It integrates and controls; it provides common elements for strangers to use when they meet and creates strictures for what can be noticed or said. Viewing the media as a community of discourse may enable a new understanding of both women's presentation by the media and the impact of the media on society.

41. "Limited effects" is proposed in Joseph Klapper, *The Effects of the Mass Media* (New York: Free Press, 1960), and criticized in Sidney Kraus and Dennis Davis, *The Effects of Mass Communication on Political Behavior* (University Park: Pennsylvania State University Press, 1976). Uses and gratifications research is both explained and criticized in Jay Blumler and Elihu Katz, eds., *The Uses of Mass Communications Annual Review of Communications Research,* (Beverly Hills, Calif.: Sage Publications, 1974), vol. 3. For a summary of modeling theory, see Liebert et al.
42. See references in Tuchman et al.; U.S. Commission of Civil Rights; and Aimee Dorr Leifer, "Socialization Processes in the Family" (paper presented at Prix Jeunesse Seminar, Munich, June 1975).

43. See Scott Ward, D. B. Wackman, and Ellen Wartella, *Consumer Socialization: An Information Processing Approach to Consumer Learning* (Beverly Hills, Calif.: Sage Publications, 1978); and National Science Foundation, *Research Applied to National Needs, Research on the Effect of Television Advertising on Children. A Review of the Literature and Recommendations for Future Research* (Washington, D.C.: Government Printing Office, 1978).
44. On the "community of discourse," see David Chaney, "Communication and Community," *Working Papers in Sociology,* no. 12 (University of Durham, England, 1977).
45. See Ewen; and Mary P. Ryan, *Womanhood in America* (New York: Franklin Watts, 1975).

New Approaches and Possibilities

For some years now, anthropologists have been writing about frames, "the principles of organization which govern events—at least social ones—and our subjective involvement in them." Frames organize "strips, . . . an arbitrary slice or cut from the stream of on-going activity."[46] Goffman uses frame analysis to show how media (books and theater) and forms of sociality (games, pretense, play) organize and reproduce experience. Particularly noteworthy is his work on play and on photographs, including his concrete analysis of how photographs articulate social behavior.[47] He reminds us, for instance, that when a man and a woman demonstrate affection by mock combat—the man pretending to threaten, the woman to cower—they reproduce male dominance. One might add that when such relationships are portrayed in the media, they provide a vocabulary of interaction. The media may then also be read as "ensembles of texts" in which both meaning and structure are encapsulated.[48] Such a reading should prevent the too literal invocation of symbolic annihilation and mimesis. Instead, it might encourage examining more complex topics such as which aspects of gender relationships may be displayed in comedy and which in action/adventure, how rape can be handled in either a half-hour comedy format or a longer drama, how men and women display seriousness, concern, grief. It may force explication and interpretation of the subtleties we all know how to reproduce.

By viewing the media as frames providing ensembles of texts, we may also advance our understanding of women's position in society. Elsewhere, I have suggested that it is profitable to discard the idea of image, the term used to discuss the media's depiction of women, and to discuss the media and their contents as myths—ways of seeing the world that resonate with the conscious mind and the unconscious passions and that are embedded in,

expressive of, and reproductive of social organization.[49] The essay demonstrated that news, the area of the media in which our culture most insistently demands a veridical reproduction and decries distortion, simultaneously defuses radical critiques of American life and reinforces existing patterns of political and social power. The entertainment media may also generate myths, not images: Their myths may also absorb attempts to introduce radical change. Gerbner and Gross suggest that television functions like religion (another frame and ensemble of texts).[50] Worth and Gross remind us of the power of background information, through the pictorial merger of ground and figure.[51] Bauman compares television to the medieval church, distributing essentially the same message to all social classes at essentially the same time in a one-directional flow of information.[52]

By observing women's depiction as myth, whether in semiextended form (entertainment) or vignette (news or advertising), we may come to know how myth and the community of discourse are part of the professional and organizational procedures governing the media. Historical work, supplementing Ewen's research on ads and Ryan's, Cowan's, and Vanek's discussions of consumerism and the shift in women's roles, is also needed.[53] We need to know how the *machisma* New Woman came to supersede the strident "women's libber" who seemed to have replaced the strung-out hippie. We need to understand what Maude Findlay has in common with Lucy Ricardo, Mary Richards with Our Miss Brooks, Wonder Woman with Lois Lane—and how they all differ from one another.

By explicating the frames inherent in the media, we should know much more about the media's effect: The structure of frames, like the structure of language use,

46. Erving Goffman, *Frame Analysis* (Philadelphia: University of Pennsylvania Press, 1974), pp. 9, 10. See also Gregory Bateson, "A Theory of Play and Phantasy," in *Steps to an Ecology of Mind* (New York: Ballantine Books, 1972).
47. Erving Goffman, "Gender Advertisements," *Studies in the Anthropology of Visual Communication,* vol. 3 (Fall 1976); Erving Goffman, "The Arrangement between the Sexes," *Theory and Society* 4 (Fall 1977): 301–32.
48. Clifford Geertz, *The Interpretation of Cultures* (New York: Harper Colophon, 1973), p. 452.

49. Gaye Tuchman, "Television News and the Metaphor of Myth," *Studies in the Anthropology of Visual Communication,* vol. 4 (Summer 1978), and n. 31 above.
50. George Gerbner and Larry Gross. "Living with Television: The Violence Profile," *Journal of Communication* 26 (Summer 1976): 172–201.
51. Sol Worth and Larry Gross, "Symbolic Strategies," *Journal of Communication* 24 (Autumn 1974): 27–39.
52. Zygmunt Baumann, "A Note on Mass Communication: On Infrastructure," in *Sociology of Mass Communication,* ed. Denis McQuail (Baltimore: Penguin Books, 1972).
53. Ewen; Ryan; Ruth Cowan, "The Industrial Revolution in the Home: Household Technology and Social Change in the 20th Century," *Technology and Culture* 17 (January 1976): 1–23; Joann Vanek, *Married Women and the Work Day: Time Trends* (Baltimore: Johns Hopkins Press, in press).

may contain its own questions and forced responses, its own "Guess what?"/"what?"[54] If this approach works for understanding the depiction of women, as it seems to work for understanding the production of news, the field of women's studies will have instructed mass media researchers how both to rebuild their enterprise and to escape the limitations of intellectual error. And we will have identified how some of the practices common to the media organizations and taken for granted by professions subjugate women. Once analyzed, they can be more forcefully attacked.

54. Pam M. Fishman, "Interaction: The Work Women Do," *Social Problems* 25 (April 1978): 397–406.

READING 7

November Issue

Ellin Carter

Harvard nutrition expert's
calorie-control diet plan
   do I want this magazine
pretty afghans to keep you cozy
   that preys upon my needs

16 best hair styles
   insecurities

elegant decorating ideas
at do-it-yourself prices
   incapacities

everything-in-a-dish party meals
   loneliness

fabulous food gifts
   dullest yearnings

how to shape and tone your body
   innermost fears

10 at-home tests to guard your health
   I seem to be buying it

Reprinted from Ellin Carter "November Issue." Reprinted by permission of the author.

Introduction: Early Socialization

We begin our lives in families, and they have strong socializing impacts on our expectations for ourselves as males and females. Our earliest socialization takes place in the home through interactions with parents or parent surrogates. Although parents may claim to raise their children free of gender-stereotyping, there is not much evidence to support those claims.

Letty Cottin Pogrebin, in the first selection "The Secret Fear That Keeps Us From Raising Free Children," discusses the fear many parents have that if allowed "sex-role" freedom their children will become homosexual—and presents evidence that shows their fear is groundless. Alexis Tyrrell in her poem " Galatea and How She Grew," describes a particular socialization experience in learning to be a " little lady."

The third selection, excerpts from Adrienne Rich's book, *Of Woman Born: Motherhood as Experience and Institution*, explores ways in which the institution of motherhood and the experience of motherhood historically, and in the present, have been and are currently being shaped by patriarchal values and interests. The extent to which we take for granted that girls will some day be mothers is illustrated in the short excerpt from " Ideology and Reality: Sexuality and Women's Status in the Oneida Community" by Louis J. Kern. In that community, indoctrination toward motherhood was seen as destructive. Ellen Goodman, in the selection " Must Women Operate Family Switchboard" describes a particular way in which mothers teach daughters to interpret the actions of males and to act as conciliators. Susan Griffin's "The Anatomy Lesson," a prose poem, describes the physiological consequences of "mothering" on a woman.

Fathers, also, have an impact on sons and daughters. In the selection " Fathers: The Men in Our Lives," by Judith Arcana from her book, *Our Mother's Daughters* (Shameless Hussy Press: 1978), Arcana analyzes the impact of fathers on daughters and on the relationship between mothers and daughters, and describes how androcentric (male-centered) assumptions are inculcated through familial interactions. Franz Kafka's "Letter to His Father," illustrates further the depth of those assumptions. In the selection "Incest: Whose Reality, Whose Theory," Sandra Butler challenges psychoanalytical and psychological explanations of incest, reviews recent research, and offers a feminist and power-analysis explanation that does not blame the victim.

The gender socialization of children takes place not only in the home; educational and sports systems also play a major role. Barrie Thorne in "An Analysis of Gender and Social Groupings" (an excerpt from her paper, "Gender. . . How Is It Best Conceptualized?"), describes how children are sorted—and sort themselves—into gender groups, and how children use their gender to control others. Janet Lever in " Sex Differences in the Complexity of Children's Play and Games" explores further the impact of peers on children's socialization, and the effects that children's games may have on the development of social skills in boys and girls. The limits of male-to-male interaction in sports is illustrated in the newspaper article, "A Handshake Will Do."

We conclude this section with a set of "Guidelines" for evaluating sexism in elementary school readers and mathematics textbooks, because not only do children learn reading and arithmetic in the schools—they learn that males and females are differentially evaluated.

The Secret Fear That Keeps Us From Raising Free Children

Letty Cottin Pogrebin

In the 19th century when women of all races began their drive for the vote, what was the argument most often used against them?

That voting was a masculine concern, and that therefore women who attempted it would become (or already were) "mannish," "unwomanly," and "unnatural." In short, sexually suspect.

In the 20th century when young men objected to the rationale for the American military presence in Vietnam, what was the argument most used to discredit their protest?

That refusing a masculine enterprise like war made them "like a woman," "soft," "scared," and therefore sexually suspect.

It's time we faced head-on the most powerful argument that authoritarian forces in any society use to keep people — male or female — in line: the idea that you are not born with gender but must earn it, and thus the threat that if you don't follow orders you will not be a "real man" or "real woman."

Even those of us who have long since stopped worrying about this conformity for ourselves may find that our own deepest conditioning takes over in the emotional landscape inhabited by our children and our feelings about child-rearing. It is this conditioning that the right wing plays on to prevent change, no matter how life-enhancing. And it is these fears that sometimes inhibit pro-child attitudes in the most well-intentioned parents; the fear

1. that sex roles determine sexuality;
2. that specific ingredients *make* a child homosexual; and
3. that homosexuality is one of the worst things that can happen.

Assumption 1: Sex Roles Determine Sexuality

It was inevitable that the cult of sex differences would lead us to the familiar romantic bromide — *opposites attract*. Most people truly believe that the more "masculine" you are, the more you'll love and be loved by females, and the more "feminine" you are, the more you'll love and be loved by males.

If you believe this quid pro quo, you will systematically raise your daughters and sons differently so that they become magnets for their "opposites," and you will fear that resistance to stereotyped sex roles might distort their behavior in bed as adults.

Clever, this patriarchy. In return for conformity, it promises a "normal" sex life for our children. But it can't deliver on that promise, because all available evidence proves that *sex role does not determine sexual orientation*.

During the last decade thousands of homosexual men and women have "come out" from behind their "straight" disguises, and we discovered that except for choice of sex partner, they look and act so much the same as everyone else that as sexologist Dr. Wainright Churchill put it, "they may not be identified as homosexuals even by experts." Most female and male homosexuals have tried heterosexual intercourse; many have been married and have children; and sometimes they are remarkable only for being so *unlike* the "gay" stereotype.

Take a quintessential "man's man," David Kopay — six feet one, 205 pounds, 10-year veteran of pro football. "I was the typical jock," writes Kopay in his autobiography (*The David Kopay Story;* Bantam). "I was tough. I was successful. And all the time I knew I preferred sex with men."

And great beauties, such as Maria Schneider, the sex bomb of "Last Tango in Paris"; "feminine-looking" women, married women, mothers of many children have, for centuries, had lesbian love affairs with one another, disproving the opposites-attract theory with a vengeance, and reminding us again that sex roles do not determine sexuality.

Assumption 2: Specific Ingredients
Make a Child Homosexual

Although no one knows what causes homosexuality, there is no shortage of theories on the subject. Sociobiologists and other behavioral scientists pursue the idea that "genetic loading" can create a predisposition toward homosexuality, a theory that will remain far-fetched until researchers find many sets of identical twins both members of which became homosexual although reared separately.

Proponents of *hormone theory* have tried to find a definitive connection between testosterone level and homosexual orientation. However, various biochemical studies of the last decade show directly contradictory results, and even when hormonal differences are found, no one knows whether hormones cause the homosexuality, or the homosexual activities cause the hormone production.

The biochemical "explorers," like the geneticists, perpetuate the idea that homosexuals are a different species with a hormonal disturbance that chemistry might "cure." So far, attempts to alter sexual orientation with doses of hormones have only succeeded in increasing the *amount* of sex drive, not in changing its direction.

The *conditioned-response theory* holds that sexual orientation depends not on biology or "instincts" but on learning from experience, from the same reward-and-punishment process as any other acquired behavior, and from sexual trigger mechanisms, such as pictures, music, or certain memories, that set off homosexual or heterosexual responses the way the bell set off Pavlov's dog salivating.

The conditioning theory, logical as far as it goes, leads us down several blind alleys. Why might one child experience a certain kind of stroking as pleasurable when a same-sex friend does it but *more* pleasurable when a friend of the other sex does it, while another child feels the reverse? Why do some children "learn" to overcome the effects of a frightening early sexual experience, while others may be hurt by it forever, and still others "learn" to merge pain with pleasure?

Doesn't cultural pressure itself "teach" children to avoid a particular sexual response, no matter what the body has learned to like? Otherwise, how do millions of adolescents move from masturbation to homosexual experimentation—often the *only* interpersonal sexual pleasure they have known—to heterosexuality?

Perhaps the conditioned-response theory can explain the man who has felt homosexual since childhood, but how does it account for the woman who, after 20 years as

an orgasmic, exclusive heterosexual, had a lesbian encounter and found she didn't have to "learn" to like it?

One research psychiatrist reminds us that we don't yet understand the basic mechanism of sexual arousal in the human central nervous system, and until we do, questions about homosexual or heterosexual arousal are entirely premature.

Psychoanalytic theory, the most steadfast and intimidating of all the causation theories, is the one that "blames" homosexuality on the family. To challenge it, we must begin at the beginning.

In 1905, Sigmund Freud declared that human beings are innately *bisexual* at birth and their early psychosexual experiences tip the scales one way or the other.

To ensure a heterosexual outcome, the child is supposed to identify with the same-sex parent, to "kill them off" so to speak, as an object of sexual interest. For example, a girl's psychodynamic is "I become like Mother, therefore I no longer desire Mother; I desire Father, but I can't have him so I desire those who are like him."

If instead the girl identifies with the other-sex parent ("I become like Father"), he is killed off as object choice ("therefore I do not desire Father"), and the girl will be a lesbian ("I desire Mother or those who are like her"). For the boy, obviously, the same psychodynamic is true in reverse.

According to this theory, female homosexuality derives mainly from too much *hostility* toward the mother for passing on her inferior genital equipment. The lesbian girl identifies with Father and compensates for her hatred of the inferior mother by loving women, while rejecting "femininity" (meaning passivity, masochism, inferiority) for herself.

Male homosexuality derives mainly from too much *attachment* to the mother; *i.e.,* a Momma's Boy can't be a woman's man.

Although many contemporary psychologists now believe otherwise, and despite the fact that Freud's views are unsupported by objective evidence, it is his ideas that millions of lay people have accepted—the view that human beings grow "healthy" by the Oedipal resolution: fearing and thus respecting one parent (Dad) and disdaining the other (Mom). Since our parents stand as our first models of male and female, this primal fear and disdain tends to form a paradigm for lifelong sexual enmity, suspicion, betrayal, and rejection.

Father is supposed to represent reality and Mother is associated with infant dependency. In order to gain their independence, both girls and boys must form an alliance with Father against Mother. Politically, this translates to male supremacy ("alliance with Father") and cultural misogyny ("against Mother"). Psychologically, the message is conform or you might turn out "queer."

The hitch is, as we've noted, that sex role and sexual orientation have been shown to be totally unrelated. Modern practitioners may know this, but since they have not loudly and publicly revised psychoanalytic theories on homosexuality, they are in effect supporting the old lies. What's more, their silence leaves unchallenged these contradictions within psychoanalytic theory itself:

- A human *instinct* by definition, should be the same for everyone, everywhere; yet in societies where sex stereotypes do not exist, the supposedly instinctual Oedipal psychodrama doesn't exist either.
- If the castration complex, the fear of losing the penis, is the founding element of "masculinity," how is it that Dr. Robert Stoller, professor of psychiatry at UCLA Medical School, found boys who were born without penises believed themselves boys anyway?
- How do we account for millions of children who become heterosexual though raised in father-absent homes? How do these mothers arouse fear and respect in the boy and the requisite penis envy in the girl?
- Why do batteries of psychological tests *fail to show any significant difference* between lesbians and heterosexuals on the psychological criteria that are supposed to "cause" female homosexuality?
- How can one say that male homosexuals identify with Mother and take on "feminine" ways, when mothers of homosexuals are supposedly "masculine," dominant, and aggressive?
- If a woman's compensation for her missing penis is a baby boy, then of course she'll overprotect her son as a hedge against a *second* castration—losing him. It's a cruel tautology to posit motherhood in these terms and, at the same time, to hold Mother responsible for overprotection of the one treasure she's supposedly spent her whole life seeking.
- Could it be that girls and women envy the *privileges* that accrue to people whose distinguishing feature happens to be the penis, without envying the penis?
- Freud declared the "vaginal orgasm" to be the diploma of heterosexual maturity, yet in *Human Sexual Response,* William Masters and Virginia Johnson have proved the clitoris to be the physiological source of all female orgasms. Why require a girl to unlearn

clitoral pleasure when in every other instance Freud believed that "urges dissipate when they become satisfied"? Is it because the clitoral orgasm is active, not receptive; because it doesn't require a penis and it doesn't result in procreation? Was the promotion of the "vaginal orgasm" patriarchy's way of keeping females passive, male-connected, and frequently pregnant?

We could devote pages and pages to poking holes in psychoanalytic theory, but these final points should do the trick: studies show that the classic "homosexual-inducing" family produces plenty of "straight" children; other kinds of families raise both heterosexual and homosexual siblings under the same roof; and totally "straight" family constellations rear homosexual kids.

And so, all speculations have been found wanting, and we are left with one indisputable fact: *no one knows what causes homosexuality.*

Assumption 3: Homosexuality Is One of the Worst Things That Can Happen to Anyone

Studies show that the majority of American people want homosexuality "cured." Yet the facts—when this volatile subject can be viewed factually—prove that homosexuality is neither uncommon, abnormal, nor harmful to its practitioners or anyone else.

When the "naturalness" of heterosexuality is claimed via examples in the animal kingdom, one can point to recorded observations of homosexuality among seagulls, cows, mares, sows, primates, and many other mammals. But more important, among humans, "there is probably no culture from which homosexuality has not been reported," according to Drs. Clellan Ford and Frank Beach in *Patterns of Sexual Behavior* (Harper). And no matter what moral or legal prohibitions have been devised through the ages, none has ever eliminated homosexuality. In fact, the incidence of homosexuality is greater in countries that forbid it than in those that don't. With all the fluctuations of public morality, many sources confirm that 10 percent of the entire population consider themselves exclusively homosexual at any given place and time.

Aside from choosing to love members of their own sex, lesbians and homosexual males have been found no different from heterosexuals in gender identity or self-esteem, in drinking, drug use, suicide rates, relationships with parents and friends, and general life satisfaction.

One study actually found lower rates of depression among lesbians; another study measured higher competence and intellectual efficiency; still another found more lesbians (87 percent) than heterosexual women (18 percent) experienced orgasm "almost always"; and two important recent reports revealed that homosexuals seem clearly far *less* likely than heterosexuals to commit child abuse or other sexual crimes. In short, many homosexuals "could very well serve as models of social comportment and psychological maturity." And yet, parents feel obliged to protect their children from it.

Why?

In a word, *homophobia*—fear and intolerance of homosexuality. Despite the facts just enumerated, millions still believe homosexuality *is* the worst thing. In one study, nearly half of the college students questioned labeled it more deviant than murder and drug addiction. Others reveal their homophobia by sitting an average of 10 inches further away from an interviewer of the same sex wearing a "gay and proud" button than from an interviewer wearing no button. Another group said they wouldn't be able to form a close friendship with a gay person.

In a society that works as hard as ours does to convince everyone that Boys are Better, homosexual taunts, whether "sissy" or "faggot" say *nonboy*. In pure form, the worst insult one boy can scream at another is "you girl!" That curse is the coming home to roost of the cult of sex differences. Indeed, sexism and homophobia go hand in hand. The homophobic male *needs* sharp sex-role boundaries to help him avoid transgressing to the "other side." His terror is that he is not different enough from the "opposite" sex, and that his "masculine" facade may not always protect him from the "femininity" within himself that he learned as a boy to hate and repress. Among men, homophobia is rooted in contempt for everything female.

A homophobic man cannot love a woman with abandon, for he might reveal his vulnerability; he cannot adore and nurture his children because being around babies is "sissy" and child care is "women's work." According to his perverse logic, making women pregnant is "masculine," but making children happy is a betrayal of manhood. One man complained that his child wouldn't shake hands and was getting too old for father-son kissing. How old was "too old"? Three.

Homophobia, the malevolent enforcer of sex-role behavior, is the enemy of children because it doesn't care about children; it cares about conformity, differences, and divisions.

If women seem to be less threatened by homosexuality than men and less obsessed with latent homosexual impulses, it's because the process of "becoming" a woman is considered less arduous for the female and less important to society than the process of "proving" one's manhood. "Masculinity" once won is not to be lost. But a girl needn't guard against losing that which is of little value.

Like male homosexuals, the lesbian doesn't need the other sex for physical gratification. But the lesbian's crime goes beyond sex: she doesn't need men at all. Accordingly, despite the relative unimportance of female sexuality, lesbianism is seen as a hostile alternative to heterosexual marriage, family, and patriarchal survival.

Before children have the vaguest idea about who or what is a homosexual, they learn that homosexuality is something frightening, horrid, and nasty. They become homophobic long before they understand what it is they fear. They learn that "What are you, a sissy?" is the fastest way to coerce a boy into self-destructive exploits.

While homophobia cannot prevent homosexuality, its power to destroy female assertiveness and male sensitivity is boundless. For children who, for whatever reason, would have been homosexual no matter what, homophobia only adds external cruelty to their internal feelings of alienation. And for those who become the taunters, the ones who mock and harass "queers," homophobia is a clue to a disturbed sense of self.

It's all so painful. And so unnecessary. Eliminate sex-role stereotypes and you eliminate homophobia. Eliminate homophobia and you eliminate the power of words to wound and the power of stigma to mold a person into something she or he was never meant to be. So here's my best advice on the subject: *Don't worry how to raise a heterosexual child; worry about how not to be a homophobic parent.*

Galatea and How She Grew

Alexis Tyrrell

Teachers complained. Relatives, too.
  "We can't understand her."
Father, agreeing, ordered elocution
lessons, the year I turned seven.

Miss Teasdale in purple long gown,
eyelids violeted, lips oranged,
smelling of show-biz, enun-
ciated clearly:
    Do not miss a trill or
    'm' you 'n' or behind
    your knees a prickly
    swit-swat with the quill
    end of my feather fan.
And:
    My dear litle chickabouttobe,
    word-talk is just the start.
    Time now for you to learn
    the delicious part.
        sit down on a chair by
        feeling it with the back

of your calf never ever
once taking your eyes off
your charming gentlemanfriend
who will certainly be there
if you remember to cross
your legs at the ankles
knee against knee spine
straight nose high upended
palm on thighs five inches
from your panty line
Picture Pretty.

    Walk toe-heel, toe-heel,
    toe-heel, sugar hips swaying,
    swaying like the dance of
    my fan. Smile on being smiled
    to, cry on cue, use your eyes
    as butterfly wings, flutter,
    flutter
Little Beauty.

Relatives rejoiced. Teachers, too.
Father agreed.
  "We can understand her now."
Only I was incomprehensible to me.

Of Woman Born

Adrienne Rich

I

Motherhood—unmentioned in the histories of conquest and serfdom, wars and treaties, exploration and imperialism—has a history, it has an ideology, it is more fundamental than tribalism or nationalism. My individual, seemingly private pains as a mother, the individual, seemingly private pains of the mothers around me and before me, whatever our class or color, the regulation of women's reproductive power by men in every totalitarian system and every socialist revolution, the legal and technical control by men of contraception, fertility, abortion, obstetrics, gynecology, and extrauterine reproductive experiments—all are essential to the patriarchal system, as is the negative or suspect status of women who are not mothers.

Throughout patriarchal mythology, dream-symbolism, theology, language, two ideas flow side by side: one, that the female body is impure, corrupt, the site of discharges, bleedings, dangerous to masculinity, a source of moral and physical contamination, "the devil's gateway." On the other hand, as mother the woman is beneficent, sacred, pure, asexual, nourishing; and the physical potential for motherhood—that same body with its bleedings and mysteries—is her single destiny and justification in life. These two ideas have become deeply internalized in women, even in the most independent of us, those who seem to lead the freest lives.

In order to maintain two such notions, each in its contradictory purity, the masculine imagination has had to divide women, to see us, and force us to see ourselves, as polarized into good or evil, fertile or barren, pure or impure. The asexual Victorian angel-wife and the Victorian prostitute were institutions created by this double thinking, which had nothing to do with women's actual sensuality and everything to do with the male's subjective experience of women. The political and economic expediency of this kind of thinking is most unashamedly and dramatically to be found where sexism and racism become one. The social historian A. W. Calhoun describes the encouragement of the rape of black women by the sons of white planters, in a deliberate effort to produce more mulatto slaves, mulattos being considered more valuable. He quotes two mid-nineteenth-century southern writers on the subject of women:

> *"The heaviest part of the white racial burden in slavery was the African woman of strong sex instincts and devoid of a sexual conscience, at the white man's door, in the white man's dwelling."* . . . *"Under the institution of slavery, the attack against the integrity of white civilization was made by the insidious influence of the lascivious hybrid woman at the point of weakest resistance. In the uncompromising purity of the white mother and wife of the upper classes lay the one assurance of the future purity of the race."*[1]

The motherhood created by rape is not only degraded; the raped woman is turned into the criminal, the *attacker*. But who brought the black woman to the white man's door, whose absence of a sexual conscience produced the financially profitable mulatto children? Is it asked whether the "pure" white mother and wife was not also raped by the white planter, since she was assumed to be devoid of "strong sexual instinct?" In the American South, as elsewhere, it was economically necessary that children be produced; the mothers, black and white, were a means to this end.

Neither the "pure" nor the "lascivious" woman, neither the so-called mistress nor the slave woman, neither the woman praised for reducing herself to a brood animal nor the woman scorned and penalized as an "old maid" or a "dyke," has had any real autonomy or selfhood to gain from this subversion of the female body (and hence of the

Reprinted from Adrienne Rich, *Of Woman Born: Motherhood as Experience and Institution* (New York: Norton Publishers, 1976), by permission of the publisher and the author.

female mind). Yet, because short-term advantages are often the only ones visible to the powerless, we, too, have played our parts in continuing this subversion.

• • •

The institution of motherhood is not identical with bearing and caring for children, any more than the institution of heterosexuality is identical with intimacy and sexual love. Both create the prescriptions and the conditions in which choices are made or blocked; they are not "reality" but they have shaped the circumstances of our lives. The new scholars of women's history have begun to discover that, in any case, the social institutions and prescriptions for behavior created by men have not necessarily accounted for the real lives of women. Yet any institution which expresses itself so universally ends by profoundly affecting our experience, even the language we use to describe it. The experience of maternity and the experience of sexuality have both been channeled to serve male interests; behavior which threatens the institutions, such as illegitimacy, abortion, lesbianism, is considered deviant or criminal.

Institutionalized heterosexuality told women for centuries that we were dangerous, unchaste, the embodiment of carnal lust; then that we were "not passionate," frigid, sexually passive; today it prescribes the "sensuous," "sexually liberated" woman in the West, the dedicated revolutionary ascetic in China; and everywhere it denies the reality of women's love for women. Institutionalized motherhood demands of women maternal "instinct" rather than intelligence, selflessness rather than self-realization, relation to others rather than the creation of self. Motherhood is "sacred" so long as its offspring are "legitimate" — that is, as long as the child bears the name of a father who legally controls the mother. It is "woman's highest and holiest mission," according to a socialist tract of 1914;[2] and a racist southern historian of 1910 tells us that "woman is the embodied home, and the home is the basis of all institutions, the buttress of society."[3]

A more recent version of the argument comes from the British critic Stuart Hampshire, who equates the "liberated woman" of today with Ibsen's panic-driven, suicidal heroine Hedda Gabler (who also refuses motherhood), in the following melancholy prophecy:

An entirely enlightened mind, just recently conscious of its strength and under-employed, finally corrodes and bleaches all the material of which respect is made — observances, memories of a shared past, moral resolutions for the future: no stain of

weak and ordinary sentiment will remain, no differentiation of feeling and therefore no point of attachment. Why carry on the family, and therefore why carry on the race? Only a feminine skepticism, newly aroused, can be so totally subversive.[4]

Patriarchy would seem to require, not only that women shall assume the major burden of pain and self-denial for the furtherance of the species, but that a majority of that species — women — shall remain essentially unquestioning and unenlightened. On this "underemployment" of female consciousness depend the morality and the emotional life of the human family. Like his predecessors of fifty and a hundred and more years ago, Hampshire sees society as threatened when women begin to choose the terms of their lives. Patriarchy could not survive without motherhood and heterosexuality in their institutional forms; therefore they have to be treated as axioms, as "nature" itself, not open to question except where, from time to time and place to place, "alternate life-styles" for certain individuals are tolerated.

The "sacred calling" (motherhood) has had, of course, an altogether pragmatic reality. In the American colonies an ordinary family consisted of from twelve to twenty-five children. An "old maid," who might be all of twenty-five years of age, was treated with reproach if not derision; she had no way of surviving economically, and was usually compelled to board with her kin and help with the household and children.[5] No other "calling" was open to her. An English working-woman whose childhood was lived in the 1850s and 1860s writes that "I was my mother's seventh child, and seven more were born after me — fourteen in all — which made my mother a perfect slave. Generally speaking, she was either expecting a baby to be born or had one at the breast. At the time there were eight of us the eldest was not big enough to get ready to go to school without help."[6] Under American slavery,

. . . it was common for planters to command women and girls to have children. On a Carolina plantation of about 100 slaves the owner threatened to flog all of the women because they did not breed. They told him they could not while they had to work in the rice ditches (in one or two feet of water). After swearing and threatening he told them to tell the overseer's wife when they got in that way and he would put them on the land to work.[7]

Both the white pioneer mother and the black female slave, worked daily as a fully productive part of the economy. Black women often worked the fields with their children strapped to their backs. Historically, women have borne and raised children while doing their share of necessary productive labor, as a matter of course. Yet by the nineteenth century the voices rise against the idea of the "working mother," and in praise of "the mother at home." These voices reach a crescendo just as technology begins to reduce the sheer level of physical hardship in general, and as the size of families begins to decline. In the last century and a half, the idea of full-time, exclusive motherhood takes root, and the "home" becomes a religious obsession.

By the 1830s, in America, the male institutional voice (in this case that of the American Tract Society) was intoning:

> *Mothers have as powerful an influence over the welfare of future generations,* as all other earthly causes combined. . . . *When our land is filled with pious and patriotic mothers, then will it be filled with virtuous and patriotic men. The world's redeeming influence, under the blessing of the Holy Spirit, must come from a mother's lips.* She who was first in the transgression, must yet be the principal earthly instrument in the restoration. *It is maternal influence, after all, which must be the great agent in the hands of God, in bringing back our guilty race to duty and happiness.* (Emphasis mine.)

The mother bears the weight of Eve's transgression (is, thus, the first offender, the polluted one, the polluter) yet precisely because of this she is expected to carry the burden of male salvation. Lest she fail, there are horrible examples to warn her:

> *It was the mother of Byron who laid the foundation of his preeminence in guilt. . . . If the crimes of the poet deserve the execration of the world, the world cannot forget that it was the mother who fostered in his youthful heart those passions which made the son a curse to his fellow-man.*[8]

But female voices, also, swell the chorus. Maria McIntosh, in 1850, describes the ideal wife and mother:

> *Her husband cannot look on her . . . without reading in the serene expression of her face, the Divine beatitude, "Blessed are the pure in heart." Her children revere her as the earthly type of perfect*

love. They learn even more from her example than from her precept, that they are to live, not in themselves, but to their fellow-creatures, and to the God in them. . . . She has taught them to love their country and devote themselves to its advancement . . .[9]

Certainly the mother serves the interests of patriarchy: she exemplifies in one person religion, social conscience, and nationalism. Institutional motherhood revives and renews all other institutions.

The nineteenth-century "mother at home" seems, however, to have suffered from certain familiar evil traits, such as ill-temper.

> *. . . can a mother expect to govern her child when she cannot govern herself? . . . She must learn to control herself, to subdue her own passions; she must set her children an example of meekness and of equanimity. . . . Let a mother feel grieved, and manifest her grief when her child does wrong; let her, with calmness and reflection, use the discipline which the case requires; but never let her manifest irritated feeling, or give utterance to an angry expression.*[10]

This from the male expert. *The Mother's Book* (1831), by Lydia Maria Child, advises:

> *Do you say it is impossible always to govern one's feelings? There is one method, a never-failing one — prayer. . . . You will say, perhaps, that you have not leisure to pray every time your temper is provoked, or your heart is grieved. — It requires no time. — The inward ejaculation of "Lord, help me to overcome this temptation" may be made in any place and amid any employments; and, if uttered in humble sincerity, the voice that said to the raging waters, "Peace! Be still!" will restore quiet to your troubled soul.*[11]

Such advice to mothers gives us some sense of how female anger in general has been perceived. In *Little Women,* Marmee tells Jo, the daughter with an "Apollyon" of a "temper":

> *I am angry nearly every day of my life, Jo; but I have learned not to show it; and I still hope to learn not to feel it, though it may take me another forty years to do so.*[12]

I recall similar indoctrination in my own girlhood: my "temper" was a dark, wicked blotch in me, not a response to events in the outer world. My childhood anger was often alluded to as a "tantrum," by which I understood the adult world to mean some kind of possession, as by a devil. Later, as a young mother, I remember feeling guilt that my explosions of anger were a "bad example" for my children, as if they, too, should be taught that "temper" is a defect of character, having nothing to do with what happens in the world outside one's flaming skin. Mother-love is supposed to be continuous, unconditional. Love and anger cannot coexist. Female anger threatens the institution of motherhood.

The nineteenth- and twentieth-century ideal of the mother and children immured together in the home, the specialization of motherhood for women, the separation of the home from the "man's world" of wage-earning, struggle, ambition, aggression, power, of the "domestic" from the "public" or the "political"—all this is a late-arrived development in human history. But the force both of the ideal and of the reality is so great that, clearly, it serves no single, simple purpose.

How did this notion begin? And what purpose does it serve?

From earliest settled life until the growth of factories as centers of production, the home was not a refuge, a place for leisure and retreat from the cruelty of the "outside world"; it was a part of the world, a center of work, a subsistence unit. In it women, men, and children as early as they were able, carried on an endless, seasonal activity of raising, preparing, and processing food, processing skins, reeds, clay, dyes, fats, herbs, producing textiles and clothing, brewing, making soap and candles, doctoring and nursing, passing on these skills and crafts to younger people. A woman was rarely if ever alone with nothing but the needs of a child or children to see to. Women and children were part of an actively busy social cluster. Work was hard, laborious, often physically exhausting, but it was diversified and usually communal. Mortality from childbirth and pregnancy and the loss of infant lives was extremely high, the lifespan of women brief, and it would be naive to romanticize an existence constantly threatened by malnutrition, famine, and disease. But motherhood and the keeping of the home as a private refuge were not, could not be, the central occupation of women, nor were mother and child circumscribed into an isolated relationship.

• • •

The physical and psychic weight of responsibility on the woman with children is by far the heaviest of social bur-

dens. It cannot be compared with slavery or sweated labor because the emotional bonds between a woman and her children make her vulnerable in ways which the forced laborer does not know; he can hate and fear his boss or master, loathe the toil; dream of revolt or of becoming a boss; the woman with children is a prey to far more complicated, subversive feelings. Love and anger *can* exist concurrently; anger at the conditions of motherhood can become translated into anger at the child, along with the fear that we are not "loving"; grief at all we cannot do for our children in a society so inadequate to meet human needs becomes translated into guilt and self-laceration. This "powerless responsibility" as one group of women has termed it, is a heavier burden even than providing a living—which so many mothers have done, and do, simultaneously with mothering—because it is recognized in some quarters, at least, that economic forces, political oppression, lie behind poverty and unemployment; but the mother's very character, her status as a woman, are in question if she has "failed" her children.

Whatever the known facts,* it is still assumed that the mother is "with the child." It is she, finally, who is held accountable for her children's health, the clothes they wear, their behavior at school, their intelligence and general development. Even when she is the sole provider for a fatherless family, she and no one else bears the guilt for a child who must spend the day in a shoddy nursery or an abusive school system. Even when she herself is trying to cope with an environment beyond her control—malnutrition, rats, lead-paint poisoning, the drug traffic, racism—in the eyes of society the mother *is* the child's environment. The worker can unionize, go out on strike; mothers are divided from each other in homes, tied to their children by compassionate bonds; our wildcat strikes have most often taken the form of physical or mental breakdown.

For mothers, the privatization of the home has meant not only an increase in powerlessness, but a desperate loneliness. A group of East London women talked with Hannah Gavron of the difference between trying to raise children in a street of row houses and in the new high-rise flats of postwar London: the loss of neighborhood, of stoop life, of a common pavement where children could

---

*Twenty-six million children of wage-earning mothers, 8 million in female-headed households in the United States by the mid-1970s (Alice Rossi, "Children and Work in the Lives of Women," a paper delivered at the University of Arizona, February 7, 1976).

be watched at play by many pairs of eyes. In Cambridge, Massachusetts in the 1950s, some married graduate students lived in housing built on the plan of the "lane" or row-house street, where children played in a common court, a mother could deliver her child to a neighbor for an hour, children filtered in and out of each others' houses, and mothers, too, enjoyed a casual, unscheduled companionship with each other. With the next step upward in academic status, came the move to the suburbs, to the smaller, then the larger, private house, the isolation of "the home" from other homes increasing with the husband's material success. The working-class mothers in their new flats and the academic wives in their new affluence all lost something: they became, to a more extreme degree, house-bound, isolated women.

Lee Sanders Comer, a British Marxist-feminist, reiterates the classic Marxist critique of the nuclear family — the small, privatized unit of a woman, a man, and their children. In this division of labor the man is the chief or the sole wage-earner, and the woman's role is that of housewife, mother, consumer of goods, and emotional support of men and children. The "family" really means "the mother," who carries the major share of child-rearing, and who also absorbs the frustrations and rage her husband may bring home from work (often in the form of domestic violence). Her own anger becomes illegitimate, since her job is to provide him with the compassion and comfort he needs at home in order to return daily to the factory or the mine pit. Comer sees this division of labor as demanded by capitalism. But why should capitalism *in and of itself* require that women specialize in this role of emotional salvager, or that women and never men rear children and take care of the home? How much does this really have to do with capitalism, and how much with the system which, as Eli Zaretsky points out, predated capitalism and has survived under socialism — patriarchy?[13]

The dependency of the male child on a woman in the first place, the spectacle of women producing new life from their bodies, milk from their breasts, the *necessity* of women for men — emotionally and as reproducers of life — these are elements we must recognize in any attempt to change the institutions that have germinated from them. Under patriarchal socialism we find the institution of motherhood revised and reformed in certain ways which permit women to serve (as we have actually served through most of our history) *both* as the producers and nurturers of children *and* as the full-time workers demanded by a developing economy. Child-care centers, youth camps, schools, facilitate but do not truly radicalize

the familiar "double role" of working women; in no socialist country does the breakdown of the division of labor extend to bringing large numbers of men into child-care. Under Marxist or Maoist socialism, both motherhood and heterosexuality are still institutionalized; heterosexual marriage and the family are still viewed as the "normal" situation for human beings and the building-blocks of the new society. Lesbianism is announced to be nonexistent in China, while in Cuba homosexuals are treated as political criminals. Birth control may or may not be available to women, depending on economic, military, and demographic pressures; in China women are pressured to become experimental subjects for new methods of birth control "for the revolution."[14] There is nothing revolutionary whatsoever about the control of women's bodies by men. The woman's body is the terrain on which patriarchy is erected.

II

It is hard to write about my own mother. Whatever I do write, it is my story I am telling, my version of the past. If she were to tell her own story other landscapes would be revealed. But in my landscape or hers, there would be old, smoldering patches of deep-burning anger. Before her marriage, she had trained seriously for years both as a concert pianist and a composer. Born in a southern town, mothered by a strong, frustrated woman, she had won a scholarship to study with the director at the Peabody Conservatory in Baltimore, and by teaching at girls' schools had earned her way to further study in New York, Paris, and Vienna. From the age of sixteen, she had been a young belle, who could have married at any time, but she also possessed unusual talent, determination, and independence for her time and place. She read — and reads — widely and wrote — as her journals from my childhood and her letters of today reveal — with grace and pungency.

She married my father after a ten years' engagement during which he finished his medical training and began to establish himself in academic medicine. Once married, she gave up the possibility of a concert career, though for some years she went on composing, and she is still a skilled and dedicated pianist. My father, brilliant, ambitious, possessed by his own drive, assumed that she would give her life over to the enhancement of his. She would manage his household with the formality and grace becoming to a medical professor's wife, though on a limited budget; she would "keep up" her music, though there was no question of letting her composing and practice conflict with her duties as a wife and mother. She was supposed to bear him two children, a boy and a girl. She had to keep her household books to the last penny—I still can see the big blue-gray ledgers, inscribed in her clear, strong hand; she marketed by streetcar, and later, when they could afford a car, she drove my father to and from his laboratory or lectures, often awaiting him for hours. She raised two children, and taught us all our lessons, including music. (Neither of us was sent to school until the fourth grade.) I am sure that she was made to feel responsible for all our imperfections.

My father, like the transcendentalist Bronson Alcott, believed that he (or rather, his wife) could raise children according to his unique moral and intellectual plan, thus proving to the world the values of enlightened, unorthodox child-rearing. I believe that my mother, like Abigail Alcott, at first genuinely and enthusiastically embraced the experiment, and only later found that in carrying out my father's intense, perfectionist program, she was in conflict with her deep instincts as a mother. Like Abigail Alcott, too, she must have found that while ideas might be unfolded by her husband, their daily, hourly practice was going to be up to her. ("'Mr. A. aids me in general principles, but nobody can aid me in the detail,' she mourned. . . . Moreover her husband's views kept her constantly wondering if she were doing a good job. 'Am I doing what is right? Am I doing enough? Am I doing too much?'" The appearance of "temper" and "will" in Louisa, the second Alcott daughter, was blamed by her father on her inheritance from her mother.[15]) Under the institution of motherhood, the mother is the first to blame if theory proves unworkable in practice, or if anything whatsoever goes wrong. But even earlier, my mother had failed at one part of the plan: she had not produced a son.

For years, I felt my mother had chosen my father over me, had sacrificed me to his needs and theories. When my first child was born, I was barely in communication with my parents. I had been fighting my father for my right to an emotional life and a selfhood beyond his needs and theories. We were all at a draw. Emerging from the fear, exhaustion, and alienation of my first childbirth, I could not admit even to myself that I wanted my mother, let alone tell her how much I wanted her. When she visited me in the hospital neither of us could uncoil the obscure lashings of feeling that darkened the room, the tangled thread running backward to where she had labored for three days to give birth to me, and I was not a son. Now, twenty-six years later, I lay in a contagious hospital with my allergy, my skin covered with a mysterious rash, my lips and eyelids swollen, my body bruised and sutured, and, in a cot beside my bed, slept the perfect, golden, male child I had brought forth. How could I have interpreted her feelings when I could not begin to decipher my own? My body had spoken all too eloquently, but it was, medically, just my body. I wanted her to mother me again, to hold my baby in her arms as she had once held me; but that baby was also a gauntlet flung down: *my son*. Part of me longed to offer him for her blessing; part of me wanted to hold him up as a badge of victory in our tragic, unnecessary rivalry as women.

But I was only at the beginning. I know now as I could not possibly know then, that among the tangle of feelings between us, in that crucial yet unreal meeting, was her guilt. Soon I would begin to understand the full weight and burden of maternal guilt, that daily, nightly, hourly, *Am I doing what is right? Am I doing enough? Am I doing too much?* The institution of motherhood finds all mothers more or less guilty of having failed their children; and my mother, in particular, had been expected to help create, according to my father's plan, a perfect daughter. This "perfect" daughter, though gratifyingly precocious, had early been given to tics and tantrums, had become permanently lame from arthritis at twenty-two; she had finally resisted her father's Victorian paternalism, his seductive charm and controlling cruelty, had married a divorced graduate student, had begun to write "modern," "obscure," "pessimistic" poetry, lacking the fluent sweetness of Tennyson, had had the final temerity to get pregnant and bring a living baby into the world. She had ceased to be the demure and precocious child or the poetic, seducible adolescent. Something, in my father's view, had gone terribly wrong. I can imagine that whatever else my mother felt (and I know that part of her *was* mutely on my side) she also was made to feel blame. Beneath the "numbness" that she has since told me she experienced at that time, I can imagine the guilt of Everymother, because I have known it myself.

But I did not know it yet. And it is difficult for me to write of my mother now, because I have known it too well. I struggle to describe what it felt like to be her daughter, but I find myself divided, slipping under her skin; a part of me identifies too much with her. I know deep reservoirs of anger toward her still exist: the anger of a four-year-old locked in the closet (my father's orders, but my mother carried them out) for childish misbehavior; the anger of a six-year-old kept too long at piano practice (again, at his insistence, but it was she who gave the lessons) till I developed a series of facial tics. (As a mother I know what a child's facial tic is—a lancet of guilt and pain running through one's own body.) And I still feel the anger of a daughter, pregnant, wanting my mother desperately and feeling she had gone over to the enemy.

And I know there must be deep reservoirs of anger in her; every mother has known overwhelming, unacceptable anger at her children. When I think of the conditions under which my mother became a mother, the impossible expectations, my father's distaste for pregnant women, his hatred of all that he could not control, my anger at her dissolves into grief and anger *for* her, and then dissolves back again into anger at her: the ancient, unpurged anger of the child.

My mother lives today as an independent woman, which she was always meant to be. She is a much-loved, much-admired grandmother, an explorer in new realms; she lives in the present and future, not the past. I no longer have fantasies—they are the unhealed child's fantasies, I think—of some infinitely healing conversation with her, in which we could show all our wounds, transcend the pain we have shared as mother and daughter, say everything at last. But in writing these pages, I am admitting, at least, how important her existence is and has been for me.

For it was too simple, early in the new twentieth-century wave of feminism, for us to analyze our mothers' oppression, to understand "rationally"—and correctly—why our mothers did not teach us to be Amazons, why they bound our feet or simply left us. It was accurate and even radical, that analysis; and yet, like all politics narrowly interpreted, it assumed that consciousness knows everything. There was, is, in most of us, a girl-child still longing for a woman's nurture, tenderness, and approval, a woman's power exerted in our defense, a woman's smell and touch and voice, a woman's strong arms around us in moments of fear and pain. Any of us would have longed for a mother who had chosen, in Christabel Pankhurst's words, that "reckoning the cost [of her suffragist activism] in advance, Mother prepared to pay it, for women's sake."[16] It was not enough to *understand* our mothers; more than ever, in the effort to touch our own strength as women, we *needed* them. The cry of that female child in us need not be shameful or regressive; it is the germ of our desire to create a world in which strong mothers and strong daughters will be a matter of course.

We need to understand this double vision or we shall never understand ourselves. Many of us were mothered in ways we cannot yet even perceive; we only know that our mothers were in some incalculable way on our side. But if a mother had deserted us, by dying, or putting us up for adoption, or because life had driven her into alcohol or drugs, chronic depression or madness, if she had been forced to leave us with indifferent, uncaring strangers in order to earn our food money, because institutional motherhood makes no provision for the wage-earning mother; if she had tried to be a "good mother" according to the demands of the institution and had thereby turned into an anxious, worrying, puritanical keeper of our virginity; or if she had simply left us because she needed to live without a child—whatever our rational forgiveness, whatever the individual mother's love and strength, the child in us, the small female who grew up in a male-controlled world, still feels, at moments, wildly unmothered. When we can confront and unravel this paradox, this contradiction, face to the utmost in ourselves the groping passion of that little girl lost, we can begin to transmute it, and the blind anger and bitterness that have repetitiously erupted among women trying to build a movement together can be alchemized. Before sisterhood, there was the knowledge—transitory, fragmented, perhaps, but original and crucial—of mother-and-daughterhood.

Endnotes

1. Arthur W. Calhoun, *A Social History of the American Family from Colonial Times to the Present* (Cleveland: 1917). See also Gerda Lerner, *Black Women in White America: A Documentary History* (New York: Vintage, 1973), pp. 149–50 ff.
2. John Spargo, *Socialism and Motherhood* (New York: 1914).
3. Benjamin F. Riley, *White Man's Burden* (Birmingham, Ala.: 1910), p. 131.
4. Stuart Hampshire, review of Elizabeth Hardwick's *Seduction and Betrayal, New York Review of Books,* June 27, 1975, p. 21.
5. Arthur W. Calhoun, *A Social History of the American Family from Colonial Times to the Present* (Cleveland: 1917), I: 67, 87. Julia C. Spruill, *Women's Life and Work in the Southern Colonies* (New York: Norton, 1972), pp. 137–39; first published 1938.
6. Margaret Llewelyn Davies, ed., *Life as We Have Known It* (New York: Norton, 1975), p. 1; first published 1931 by the Hogarth Press, London.
7. Calhoun, *op. cit.,* II: 244.
8. Rev. John S. Abbott, *The Mother at Home, or The*

Principles of Maternal Duty (New York: American Tract Society, 1833); this book was a best-seller in its time.

9. Maria J. McIntosh, *Woman in America: Her Work and Her Reward* (New York: Appleton, 1850).

10. Abbott, *op. cit.*, pp. 62–64.

11. Lydia Maria Child, *The Mother's Book* (Boston: 1831), p. 5.

12. Louisa May Alcott, *Little Women* (New York: A. L. Burt, 1911), p. 68.

13. Lee Sanders Comer, "Functions of the Family under Capitalism," pamphlet reprinted by the New York Radical Feminists, 1974. Eli Zaretsky, "Capitalism, the Family, and Personal Life," *Socialist Revolution,* January–June 1973, p. 69.

14. Carl Djerassi, "Some Observations on Current Fertility Control in China," *The China Quarterly,* No. 57 (January–March 1974), pp. 40–60.

15. Charles Strickland, "A Transcendentalist Father: The Child-Rearing Practices of Bronson Alcott," *History of Childhood Quarterly: The Journal of Psycho-History,* Vol. 1, No. 1 (Summer 1973), pp. 23, 32.

16. Midge Mackenzie, ed., *Shoulder to Shoulder* (New York: Knopf, 1975), p. 28.

READING 11

Ideology and Reality: Sexuality and Women's Status in the Oneida Community

Louis J. Kern

In 1851 the utopian community at Oneida, New York, undertook a vigorous campaign to destroy what was called "philoprogenitiveness"—women's feelings of maternal love for their children. To root out maternal instincts among the second generation of Oneida women, young girls were chastized for talking to their dolls "as though they were living children" and were required to participate in a dramatic rite of absolution—the destruction by fire of all dolls in the community. A participant described the ceremony:

> . . . we all formed a circle around the large stove, each girl carrying on her arm her long-cherished favorite, and marching in time to a song; as we came opposite the stove-door, we threw our dolls into the angry-looking flames, and saw them perish before our eyes

Next the girls were required to sign a testimonial identifying the maternal spirit evident in their love for their dolls with the natural temptation of women to express feelings of "special affection." The testimonial concluded with the following oath:

> We think this doll spirit that seduces us from a Community spirit in regard to helping the family and that prevents us from being in earnest to get an education is the same spirit that seduces women to allow themselves to be so taken up with their children that they have no time to attend to Christ and get an education for heaven

Like the "special affection" which they symbolized, dolls were forever banned from the Oneida community.

Reprinted from Louis J. Kern, "Ideology and Reality: Sexuality and Women's Status in the Oneida Community" in *Radical History Review.* Reprinted by permission of the author. Copyright 1979 by Louis J. Kern.

Must Women Operate Family Switchboard?

Ellen Goodman

BOSTON—The little girl doesn't understand.

A boy in her first-grade class has selected her as his recess quarry. All week he has pursued her, capturing her scarf, circling her with it, threatening to tie her up.

The look on her face as she tells us the story is puzzled and upset. She has brought home similar tales of playground encounters since Monday and laid them across the dinner table.

My friend, who is her mother, and amused by it all, explains again to the little girl, "That's because he likes you." But she still doesn't understand.

Finally, the mother turns to me, because I have been through it before, seen the tears of another first grader, offered the same explanations. "Tell her," says the mother in frustration.

I begin to form the analysis in my mind. I will tell her how the boy wants attention, doesn't know how to ask for it, only knows how to grab for it, confuses aggression with affection.

Suddenly I stop.

I hear an odd echo from the words inside my head. What is it? An echo of a hundred generations of women interpreting males to their daughters? An echo of a hundred generations of women teaching their daughters the fine art of understanding human behavior?

All at once I find myself reluctant to pass on that legacy. I am wary of teaching this little girl the way to analyze. I am not so sure we should raise more girls to be cultural interpreters for men, for families.

I look at my friend. This woman is admirably skilled in the task of transmitting one person's ideas and feelings to another. Indeed, she operates the switchboard of her family life.

The people in her home communicate with each other through her. She delivers peace messages from one child to another; softens ultimatums from father to son;

explains the daughter to her father. Under her constant monitoring, communication lines are kept open; one person stays plugged into the next.

Sometimes I wonder whether she has kept all these people together or kept them apart. Does she make it easier for them to understand each other, or does she stand between them, holding all the wires in her hands?

Last week, I watched Katherine Hepburn play the same role magnificently in "On Golden Pond." She placed herself between the angry, acerbic, viciously amusing husband—Henry Fonda—and the world. She was his buffer and his interpreter—to gas station attendants, the postman, their daughter.

"He wasn't yelling at you," she tells the boy who comes to live with them. "He was yelling at life. Sometimes you have to look hard at a person and remember he's doing the best he can—just trying to find his way, like you."

Her caring was wondrous, inspiring, full of energy and love. But it was only when the boy confronted the old man, dialing directly, shortcutting the switchboard, that the man changed.

In Gail Godwin's new novel, "A Mother and Two Daughters," there is another aging mother, still negotiating between her two "children" who are turning 40. She is like the woman in many of our autobiographies—the mother or grandmother—behind the scenes.

How many families only know each other through such women? Some mothers, like the one in this movie and this book, have been forced to occupy the stormy fulcrum of family life. Others have chosen to be the power broker of human relationships. Some keep people at peace. Others keep them at bay. Sometimes the endless interpretation, especially of men by women, keeps couples together. Other times, it keeps men from explaining themselves.

I know it is a skill to be able to understand and analyze one person's motives and psyche to another. It requires time, attention and emotional dexterity to run these switchboards. Yet it also can overload the operator

Reprinted from Ellen Goodman, "Must Women Operate Family Switchboard?" in the *Columbus Citizen Journal,* 1982. Reprinted by permission of the author.

and cripple the people from talking across their own private lines.

Today, I feel peculiarly unwilling to explain the first-grade boy to the first-grade girl, peculiarly unwilling to initiate a six-year-old into this cult of communication.

I offer only friendship and sympathy. Those are things she doesn't have to struggle to understand.

READING 13

The Anatomy Lesson

Susan Griffin

The medical student is overcome with feeling. She vomits when she ought to be lifting the corpse's arm, breaking it against the stiffening of death. She associates her own body with the coldness of this one, trembles before it. No measure is taken to relieve her fear. No one asks her to describe it or to sing it out. No ceremony exists to reveal it. She is told instead she must learn to move about the human body without feeling. She must leave feeling behind. No one wonders if there might have been a use for that feeling—it is discarded before it is examined. She shall never know about death. The anatomy lesson becomes lifeless. And now this probing of the dead body gives her no help against her fear of death. Yet, isn't that why she wanted to see the body, despite her loathing, despite her fear, because of the fear itself, the feeling.

From the body of the old woman we can tell you something of the life she lived. We know that she spent much of her life on her knees. (Fluid in the bursa in front of her kneecap.) *We say she must have often been fatigued, that her hands were often in water.* (Traces of calcium, traces of unspoken anger, swelling in the middle joints of her fingers.) *We see white ridges, scars from old injuries; we see redness in her skin.* (That her hands were often in water; that there must have been pain.) *We can tell you she bore several children. We see the white marks on her belly, the looseness of the skin, the wideness of her hips, that her womb has dropped.* (Stretching in the tissue behind the womb.) *We can see that she fed her children, that her breasts are long and flat, that there are white marks at the edges, a darker color of the nipple. We know that she carried weights too heavy for her back.* (Curvature of the spine. Aching.) *From the look of certain muscles in her back, her legs, we can tell you something of her childhood, of what she did not do.* (Of the running, of the climbing, of the kicking, of the movements she did not make.) *And from her lungs we can tell you what she held back, that she was forbidden to shout, that she learned to breathe shallowly. We can say that we think she must have held her breath. From the size of the holes in her ears, we know they were put there in her childhood. That she wore earrings most of her life. From the pallor of her skin, we can say that her face was often covered. From her feet, that her shoes were too small* (toes bent back on themselves), *that she was often on her feet* (swelling, ligaments of the arch broken down). *We can guess that she rarely sat through a meal.* (Tissue of the colon inflamed.) *We can catalogue her being: tissue, fiber, bloodstream, cell, the shape of her experience to the least moment, skin, hair, try to see what she saw, to imagine what she felt, clitoris, vulva, womb, all we can tell you that despite each injury she survived. That she lived to an old age.* (On all the parts of her body we see the years.) *By the body of this old woman we are hushed. We are awed. We know that it was in her body that we began. And now we say that it is from her body that we learn. That we see our past. We say, from the body of the old woman, we can tell you something of the lives we lived.*

Fathers: The Men in Our Lives

Judith Arcana

Contemporary American society continues to define both women and children as property belonging to the husband-father. Thus, a daughter is her father's chattel twice over. The father-as-owner's purpose is served by facilitating his daughter's socialization. His role is to maintain the present order. He is supposed to protect his daughter, support her until she marries, and oversee her training as a woman through the agency of his wife and whatever schooling he sees fit.

The folklore of father/daughter relations also asserts that there is a fondness, an affection, a doting and even covetous attitude on the part of fathers toward daughters; this is the acknowledged emotional stance which describes intimacy between the two. In fact, most fathers seem to have very little to do with their daughters. Sixty-nine percent of the fathers in this study took no active role in raising their daughters, and many of them were barely present. Their supposed protection and affection are remote; our fathers certainly are not present in our daily lives to the extent that our mothers are. Daughters interviewed said:

He was the man. A provider. We were his girls, both my mother and me. It didn't have to be said; it was right there, that he was taking care of his girls. He loved the fact that we were both his girls. He didn't want a boy for anything. He loved it.

My dad went away mostly to work, the harvest, any kind of work. This was during the depression. When he wasn't working my mother would say he was "chasing the honey pot and the butter tree." He was away from home a lot.

Nonetheless, daughters consider their fathers "special." Not only do we see that men are powerful and dominant, but that our fathers are particularly so. Daughters are supposed to hero-worship their fathers, idolize them, fear them if necessary, but to assume an automatic measure of respect. We are schooled in daughterly respect and admiration by our mothers, and their training is enhanced by fairy tales and legends.

From fairy tales to contemporary TV programs is no noticeable jump, for all the daddies from Ozzie Nelson through "Father Knows Best" to Archie Bunker are patriarchs just the same. Wise or foolish, they are the kings of their respective households. We see them as romantic figures, even in their negative aspects.

Frequently our mothers buttress this romantic image of our fathers. If they do criticize the father, it is rarely straightforward, and often not in his presence. If they eschew criticism and follow the traditional mode, they often go out of their way to create or shore up the superior position of the father. My mother always presented my father, to my brothers and myself, as the ultimate arbiter of truth and judgment. When my own child was born, I had the opportunity to actually see this process worked out. Even in my son's infancy, his grandmother would give him up to her husband, saying as she did so, "Go to your Papa; all the children love Papa." By the time the boy could walk and talk, he readily understood, from her own words as well as other social cues, that Grandma wasn't as interesting as Papa; perhaps when he was older, he would "appreciate" her. When we discussed this self-effacement, my mother told me "the same thing happened with my mother; none of the grandchildren would go to her until they were much older; they always loved my dad." She had learned the technique from her mother.

The socialization process that creates the parental pair of good father and self-effacing mother is reflected in the population of my interview group. For instance, though only 31 percent of us had contact with our fathers that could be construed as their "raising" us, 48 percent of us preferred our fathers to our mothers as we grew up.

Reprinted from Judith Arcana "Fathers: The Men in Our Lives," in *Our Mothers' Daughters* Berkeley, CA: (Shameless Hussy Press, 1979) by permission of the author and the publisher, Judith Arcana.

They always kidded me that I was his favorite child, and I was daddy's girl. I would sneak in the car and go off with him. I was like his sidekick. I respect and love him; there are times when I do get scared that I love him more than I do my mother. I sympathize with him in a funny way.

When I think about being little I can remember running up and jumping into my father's arms, and I can't remember doing that with my mother. I know that I was held by her but I can't remember it.

I show a preference for my father actually because I can't talk to him. I will always bend over backwards to try to talk to him about things in the news and all the things that he's interested in but he ignores me continually no matter what I do. So I've always tried to show a preference for him outwardly, because mothers, they just love you; they don't care.

Some of us prefer our fathers to such an extent that we give our lives to them. Daughters are expected to marry, but there is still a tradition which decrees that there be one daughter who takes care of her father, who remains single to assume her mother's role as it becomes necessary, or who marries only when her father dies.

A number of daughters in this study expressed such devotion to their fathers:

I guess I loved him very much because I used to feel that if my father hadn't died—you know he died when I was 17 or 18—I would never marry; I would never marry because I never would have left him.

He wanted to be taken care of until he died. He got it, I didn't marry until I was 38. I didn't marry until after he died.

I was tied to him because I felt a lot of responsibility for his welfare. He would say that if I left him he would kill himself; he was going to drink himself to death. When I got it together to break off with him, he would try it sometimes on the few occasions we would be together. He would say, "I'm a lonely old man; come and stay with me; be my little girl." But I was able to escape the guilt when I got a better attitude about myself, and understood the sexual aspects of our relationship.

Though we are not all so devoted, and, in fact, may have serious problems with our fathers or actually dislike them, the majority of us excuse them, make allowances

for them, deny those aspects of the relationship which don't fit the social stereotype of father–daughter relations. It is this attitude about our fathers which we transfer to other men, usually husbands, when we are adults. We have learned that despite their failings or even their absence, we must give them our affection and service. There were fathers in the study who beat their daughters (7 percent), were alcoholic (12 percent), or were harsh disciplinarians, in addition to those already mentioned who ignored their daughters or shared no interests with them. Yet their daughters usually continued to seek their affection, continued to express "love" for them.

It takes nothing in the way of research to understand that many relationships between adult women and men fit this same description. Thus, many women learn that they ought not expect comradeship, tenderness, or sociability from men. We actually excuse our fathers for behavior we condemn in our mothers, female friends, or even, sometimes, other men. We pity them, rationalize their faults, see their flaws as being caused by other people—their parents or our mothers. We accept behavior from them that is unacceptable, and we call this acceptance "love."

He said to me once, "Some women never get married and you're one of those women." [laugh] I don't know whether it was because he wanted me to stay at home with them all the time, or whether he thought I was way too smart to be satisfied with the men in that small rural community, but he just thought I would never marry. He loved me very much and still does.

He calls me up all the time, and we have a real wonderful trust. But every time I accomplish anything now on my own, whether in music or in photography, he gets deeply offended.

There are many of us who could not see that our fathers were not returning all the out-of-proportion affection we lavished on them. (Of course there were fathers who did—despite their training in the male role—manage to be affectionate with us, to relate to us with some warmth and human commitment.) Those of us who were truly "daddy's girl" have continued to prefer our fathers into adulthood, or have only begun to diminish that preference with feminist consciousness.

My father always seemed superior to my mother. By the time I was an adolescent and had begun to be severely critical of my mother, I perceived the difference between them in intellectual and political terms. I thought my mother was empty-headed and boring; my father was well-read and always abreast of current happenings in the world. Even my mother's years as a competent and powerful PTA executive seemed to me trivial; I called her and the other workers "PTA Ladies." My father appeared to be always in command of his emotions. My mother and I were beneath him in this respect, and control over personal feelings was given high priority in my family. I remember my father saying to me as I sprawled on my bed, sobbing uncontrollably (often after a screaming fight with my mother), "When you can control yourself, we can talk about this . . ." He would sit there on the edge of my bed, waiting for me to stop "being emotional." To this day, his quiet demeanor and reticence to engage on an emotional level often allow him to escape notice in family discussions, and excuse him from criticism—whereas my mother is an easy target, since her behavior and psychology fit so well the popular negative stereotype of older women whose children are grown and gone. Moreover, because she does engage, fight back, and challenge my argument, she is far more visible than he. In becoming conscious of the way my father operates, I can see that as an American businessman he is as much a patriarch as his father, a political philosopher, and his grandfather, a peasant rabbi. The style, to be sure, has changed. The family attitude has always been that he operates in a democratic fashion, reflecting his intelligence and decency. All of us—my two brothers, my mother, and I—acknowledged his power and position in the same subtle way he wielded it; no blatant show of authority was necessary. In my adolescence I would brag about him, and put down my mother, by saying, "My mother yells all the time but my father never has to raise his voice. All he has to do is give that look, and I know I've done something really bad."

Many of the other "daddy's girls" in the study have had similar experiences. Not only did 39 percent of the interview daughters state that they preferred their fathers, and demonstrate that preference as they spoke, but another 9 percent who said either that they preferred their mothers or that they preferred neither parent *also* actually preferred their fathers, as their interviews revealed. Most of us are women who identified with our fathers, were known within the family to be like our fathers, looked like them, and followed their interests and habits. Where this is not the case, it is those "masculine" aspects of our fathers that have attracted us to them. We prefer reading newspapers to romance magazines, want to do carpentry or mechanical work, like to consider ourselves independent. Positive aspects of these choices derive not only

from the activities themselves, in which we may well have genuine and serious interest, but also from their high (male) status, their connection to male power. We do not choose to associate ourselves with our mothers, with the "feminine" sphere of interests and activities, even if we feel an affinity for or a fascination with such work, because it has such low status. Sometimes it is even enough just to hang out with our fathers, to pal around with them when we are girls, to avoid the stigma of the female role.

Some of the fathers actively encouraged their daughters to identify with them, competing with the mothers in doing so. Others didn't encourage it openly, but continued to foster the close tie in covert ways.

In direct opposition to the classically defined competing pairs of mothers and daughters are those who collaborate consistently to outwit, outmaneuver, or simply leave out the father. These fathers were frequently present in the home, and functioning "correctly" in the nuclear family, but were considered to be of no consequence by both their wives and daughters. In some cases, the mother and daughter both felt and verbalized that they had a special relationship from which the father, and perhaps other children, were excluded. In other situations, the daughter, in rejecting her father, is affirming not only what her mother perceives as her father's insignificance, but her mother's superiority as well. Some daughters are well aware of the chances their mothers take for them in spending "too much" time, affection, or money on the daughter or in approving behavior the father would disapprove. Not so often as this, but often enough to note, daughters knew that their mothers were risking their own security to defend the daughter against the father, verbally or physically in violent confrontations.

I was too much the footstamper, and "I want my way," and my mother would back me up on it. It was not only an emotional or disciplinary alignment between my mother and me. It was economic. He usually thought, "Well, she knows what's best for the kids"—so he'd let her spend the money she said she needed for us.

Once when my father was very ill, and I was bitterly resentful, I said to him, "You haven't done anything. Ma does everything." He smacked me good, and I crept under the bed and never said anything else. He did do some good things; I don't mean to intimate that he was a bad father, but I had a real passion for my mother.

Among those of us who've not formed a bond of this type with our mothers—the majority of daughters, to be sure—there is still some anger smoldering under our constant acceptance and allowance, the "excusing" of our fathers. Most of it is indignation based upon ethics and morals, upon our hurt feelings, our realization that our fathers are not the models of perfection we'd been led to believe; but much of the anger we feel, the criticism we make, is based upon our recognition of our mothers' oppression. Far more daughters than the social stereotypes would suggest are women who see their father's treatment of their mothers as unacceptable. This step is one we all must take so that we may regard our mothers as equals and understand that our fathers are wielders of power that we and our mothers have never shared.

READING 15

Letter to His Father

Franz Kafka

What was always incomprehensible to me was your total lack of feeling for the suffering and shame you could inflict on me with your words and judgements. It was as though you had no notion of your power.

Reprinted from Franz Kafka "Letter to His Father," in *Letter to His Father* (New York: Schocken Books, 1974).

How terrible for me was, for instance, that: "I'll tear you apart like a fish." It was also terrible when you ran around the table, shouting, grabbing at one, obviously not really trying to grab, yet pretending to, and Mother (in the end) had to rescue one, as it seemed. Once again one had, so it seemed to the child, remained alive through your mercy and bore one's life henceforth as an undeserved gift from you.

Incest: Whose Reality, Whose Theory

Sandra Butler

While I was gathering material for my book,
Conspiracy of Silence: The Trauma of Incest, *I
read the incest literature exhaustively. Most of it
was disquieting to me, but I held my doubts in
abeyance until I had an opportunity to speak with
professionals across the country who saw and
treated incest. My expectations of clarity and
understanding remained unfulfilled. Although a
language has indeed begun to develop across the
country and we are now beginning to talk about the
sexual abuse of children, in 1977 this was not
the case. I found a silence from the professionals, a
need to assure me that "that" didn't happen in their
communities. I was also assured, "Try across
town . . . or across the tracks . . ." or someplace
where "they" lived and "it" probably occurred with
much regularity. I did not find that to be true when
I began to speak with women who had been
assaulted as children or children who had reported
their own assaults. It was in returning to the sounds
of the lived experience that I began to discover the
truth of these women rather than that of those who
studied and described them.*

This piece attempts to look at the theory and the
reality of incestuous assault; they are not the same. I am
going to juxtapose the experience against the words of the
theorists so that we can, as feminists, begin to understand
the woman-blaming, misogyny and excuses at the foundation of the writing about incest.

The legal definitions and consequences of incest vary
widely from state to state. The laws are inconsistent and
rarely used to prosecute. In California, the penalty for incest is sixteen months to two or three years in state prison.

In other states, the penalties range from a small fine to
twenty and thirty years imprisonment.

Because of inconsistencies in the law, I have formulated the following definition to encompass a range of
abuses: Incestuous assault is any manual, oral or genital
sexual contact or other explicitly sexual behavior that an
adult family member imposes on a child by exploiting the
child's vulnerability and powerlessness. The vulnerability
of the child stems from specific lack of information about
the unacceptability of the behavior because of her early
state of psychological and psychosexual development.
Her powerlessness stems from the inability to say "no" to
an adult member of her family.

Incestuous assault is a reality in the lives of children
of all races and classes. The only constant is that aggressors are overwhelmingly male and the victims are
nearly always female.

Incestuous assault is like rape in that it is still viewed
as a "sex" crime, most of the offenders are male and victims experience similar feelings of humiliation, fear,
powerlessness and self-blame. But it is the differences that
augment the suffering caused by this form of assault. One
difference is that in an incestuous assault, there is always a
close if not primary relationship between the offender and
the victim. Second, the incestuous assault is not one-time
"only" but continues for a long period during which it increases in sexual specificity. Third, the child is less likely
to report the violation since her family is at stake and is
more likely to be disbelieved if she does.

These differences point out the importance of understanding the family as the system in which incestuous
assault occurs. At the same time, it is important to
remember that families do not sexually abuse children,
men do.

There is an urgent need for a feminist analysis of
families and particularly families in which sexual violence
occurs. We need to look closely at power in the family,
who has it and why. Power can be translated through

Reprinted from Sandra Butler "Incest: Whose Reality, Whose
Theory," in *Aegis: Magazine on Ending Violence Against
Women* (Summer/Autumn, 1980), P.O. Box 21033, Washing-
ton, D.C., by permission of the publisher and the author.

choice and we need to look at how those choices are exercised. Do women and children have the power to say "yes" when they do not have equal power to say "no"?

The issue of men's power in the family is rarely integrated in a non-feminist analysis of incest. Men have, at least in their homes if nowhere else, the power and the options that power affords them. Men who have little or no prestige or status in the larger world still have the ability to control the events and the people in their "castles." When prevailing social theory on incest begins to approach this aspect of male power, it turns away.

Non-feminist theorists do not move to look at male power in the family, but instead study sexual violence within the context of the family as a psychological unit. This analysis began during the 1960s when incest was first defined as a "transaction which protects and maintains the family from disintegration. It is a symptom of family dysfunction and utilized as a tension-reducing device."[1] According to Dr. Graves, "It's easier for the man to admit the problem if it's presented in terms of family dynamics. He's the one on the defensive and seeing it as a family problem will help him open up."[2] Incest is no longer seen as something which happens to a victim, but rather a sophisticated interplay between two victims within the context of the family.

Typically, the description of the family in which incestuous assault occurs is as follows: father rarely has a criminal record, has a good and steady work history, tends to be domineering and tyrannical and unable to deal well with adult women. He views his wife as rejecting and threatening. His wife is described as needy, insecure both in her own sense of self-worth and her "femininity," less interested in sex than her husband, immature and in need of approval. Is that family unfamiliar to any of us?

The theory that incestuous assaults occur when families become dysfunctional serves to excuse the offender. To assign to each family member a role in causing the incestuous assault is to imply that whatever happens to women and children in our homes can be traced back to something that is our fault. The promise held out to us by family systems theorists is that once we figure out as mothers and as children what we have done wrong, our victimization will stop. Men will simply stop hunting our flesh for reassurance of their power over us and their need for reminders of their sexual strength.

I suggest that incestuous assault is not an unnatural acting out of a particular configuration of family interaction or personality types but is simply further along on the continuum of societally condoned male behaviors. We must recognize incestuous assault as culturally and politically sanctioned violence against women and children.

Although it is necessary to look at individual psychopathology and psychosexual development as well as at ways in which the family system provides a context for sexual violence, we must also see incestuous assault as part of an established social structure built with stones engraved:

- children are the property of their parents and families
- blood is thicker than water
- men are kings in their castles
- a sexually successful man is a "ladykiller"
- the "little" woman stands loyally and firmly behind her man.

This conclusion is strenuously avoided throughout the literature on incest. In its place are psychological interpretations which bear little resemblance to reality and which serve to justify the abuser's actions and further maintain women's powerlessness.

The Child

One of the earliest canons in the writing on incestuous assault is the assertion that children are not to be believed. To this day, this is the premise from which most non-feminist professionals begin. The most frequent model for training in mental health agencies is that of disbelief and assumed manipulation. Staff have been repeatedly trained with a variation on the following: "Don't believe them. Always try to think about why they are telling you what they are saying. What's in it for them and what do they expect to get from you as a result?"

The need to disbelieve has its origins in Freud's need to deny what he was hearing about his male associates from their daughters who were clients of his. Freud preferred to turn things around and focus his attention on the child's fantasies rather than on the adult's predatory behavior. Many clinicians still are taught that children want genitally specific contact with the adults in their immediate environment, fantasize it, and when angry may even make it up to punish the male figure.

In reality, from reports I've gathered, children go to great lengths to lie in order to assure us that incestuous assaults do *not* happen. I have never known a child who said she was assaulted who "made it up," but I do know of many who do not tell anyone until early adolescence or when they have a feeling of enough power to survive outside the protection of the family. By the time they tell us, either directly or more often by "acting out" behaviors such as running away, drug addiction, alcoholism, or suicide attempts, we find it easier to scrutinize the symptomatic behaviors rather than to believe the underlying reality that caused enough pain and rage to precipitate such extreme behavior.

Besides accusing children of making up stories, many who have written about incestuous assault begin with the view that it is the child who is the source of the blame, responsibility and seduction of the adult. In some instances, she is the "active seducer rather than the one innocently seduced."[3] Some children are "passive participants who seldom complain or resist"[4] and yet others "avoid guilt feelings by denying their enjoyment in the sexual experience."[5] These children not only instigated the incest, according to these writers, but even if they didn't, it was seen as proof that they were seductive by "their acquiescence and albeit masked pleasure."[6]

These assumptions are based on the observation that incestuous assault rarely begins with threats of physical harm or corporal abuse. Overlooked is the more subtle coercion of bribes, gifts or misrepresentation of moral standards. The child has no reason to feel threatened by an adult in her family and will assume that what the adult is telling her to do is all right. That is, after all, the training we give our children. They respond to an adult whose love is important to them by denying their own reality and perceptions. Women remembering such experiences thirty years later, still remember it felt "funny." One woman told me, "What your Daddy tells you to do can't be wrong. So you start to think that it's you that's wrong for feeling funny about it."

The fondling and touching, often gentle and nonthreatening, gradually progress to specific genital contact and intercourse during a period of years. As the sexual activity escalates, the child makes an adaptive response in order to survive in her family environment. Her response is to endure her own victimization in silence, to keep the family intact.

Some youngsters feel further torn because they may be enjoying the only form of love and attention that is offered in their family and the special position it offers them. The child is caught in the knot of being hugely powerful — the one who holds the key to the secret — and yet completely powerless to do anything to stop it from continuing. In a few instances where women felt some closeness and enjoyment during the incestuous assault, remembering back, they consistently said it was "their fault" for letting it happen, their responsibility and badness. It becomes a double betrayal. One at the hands of their assailant and the other at the response of their bodies.

Most youngsters fail to report the abuse to others due to the fear that they will be blamed, or that no one will believe them. They are sure they will be punished, rejected, and even abandoned for bringing shame upon the family. It is, after all, the only family they have and assailants often warn repeatedly of the "trouble" that will result from their telling. The trouble is often vague and amorphous with intimations of dissolution of the family, jail for the man, and beatings by the mother. In other instances, the threats are more specific. Many women remembered being threatened with brutal violence against them, their mothers, their friends, anyone they might choose to confide in in the hope of ending the relationship. There is an endless parade of horrifying possibilities marched before the child, who most often responds with silence and repression.

How, then, can one researcher claim that, in his sample of 54 girls who were involved in incestuous relationships between the ages of 9–14, 46 of them had made "acceptable adaptations."[7] No definition of acceptable is noted.

This conclusion is repeated by other studies which state that incest prior to puberty causes no "long term damage to the child."[8] The terms "acceptable" and "damage" are most often defined (if at all) in terms of the adult woman's sexual response in a monogamous heterosexual model. If an adult woman who was sexually victimized as a child is "frigid," "promiscuous," or lesbian, — all seen as sexual maladaptations — the incestuous assault is seen to have had a deleterious effect on her natural development as a woman. When these young girls grow into women who marry and, as wives, remain silent, such behavior is seen as an appropriate model for women's mental health and no "damage" is believed to have resulted.

The effects of incestuous assault are multiple and not measurable by these crude and disrespectful indicators. They are lasting, though they need not be permanent. They are, however, a consistent source of pain because there are very few interventions that are successful, caring, believing and healing. Most of our responses still compound the trauma and pain of the child and the rest of the family as well.

We are learning that women who were assaulted as children find it extremely difficult to enter a relationship based on trust and intimacy. There is often a fearful expectation of repeated rejection, fears of vulnerability and openness, and an inability to acknowledge their own power.

One woman I spoke with was married to a man she valued and with whom she was struggling to create a relationship based on friendship, trust, and caring. She told me, "Sometimes when he wants to do certain things sexually I just can't. They are the same things my father forced me to do when I was small. I know it's not the same and I know he loves me, but when I say 'no,' part of me feels like that little girl finally grown strong who is able to say the 'no' I couldn't say all those years ago. The other part of me feels guilty that I am saying 'no' to the wrong person and I really love my husband and am making him suffer for my own history."

This woman and many others I spoke with have little self-esteem, self-worth, and perspective on how arduous and lonely their struggle is and how sadly unnecessary it is to hold themselves responsible.

Besides the many professionals who respond with disbelief or blame, there are also those who tell us that the trauma may come not from the experience itself but from an uptight and puritanical society that cannot allow uninterrupted a tender and loving rite of passage without causing trouble and interfering.

Dr. Wardell Pomeroy writes in *Forum* magazine that he has known many cases of father–daughter incest which illustrate that this kind of relationship can be positive as well as negative. He reports that "incest between adults and younger children can also prove to be a satisfying and enriching experience."[9] James Ramey, Professor of Psychiatry, writes in the "SIECUS" newsletter that incest is a matter of "personal morality"[10] and that the laws concerning it are "overly harsh."[11]

The male interpretation appears to suggest that incest doesn't happen at all and we make it up. Or, if it does happen, however rarely and to lower-class people, then it was because we were seductive and wanted it and we are to blame. And finally, that even if it does happen frequently and we were not seductive and encouraging, it is something that is a pleasurable experience and an enriching part of our growth into womanhood.

The Mother

Most researchers view both the mother and the child as similarly responsible. The mother's assumed culpability is based on the following questions, "How can the incest continue without her knowledge? Why doesn't she do something about it?" These questions the experts proceed to answer as follows:

Mother is defined as the "cornerstone in the pathological family system."[12] Father is aided and abetted in his liaison by the "conscious or unconscious seduction by his daughter and by his wife's collusion."[13] She is "frigid, hostile and unloving."[14] Even when she does not sexually deny her husband, she is unable to respond and frustrates him."[15]

Another scholar suggests that incest begins when the "father and daughter felt abandoned because of the birth of a baby or the wife's developing some outside interests."[16] Additionally, mothers promote incest by "frustrating their husbands sexually or symbolically deserting them and encouraging their daughters to assume mothering functions."[17]

These interpretations are grounded in the premise that mothers are responsible for maintaining the family unit in a state of balance and equilibrium. This logic suggests that if she withdraws from that role by choice or necessity, then all that happens within the family unit is her fault. If she decides to get a job to augment the family income; if she is giving birth to another, often unplanned child; if she returns to school or develops outside interests; if she masks the pain of her life with too much alcohol; if she is invalided emotionally or physically; her daughters, usually the eldest, will often assume her function in the family. That includes cooking, cleaning and caring for the younger children and providing the attention the "head of the family" requires.

If incestuous assault should occur as an outgrowth of any of these alterations of "appropriate" family roles, the mother is held responsible. Why the father does not assume the wife's maternal role when she withdraws or is incapacitated seems to be ignored by these theorists. Instead, the man feels his "first right is to receive the services which his wife formerly provided, sometimes including sexual services."[18]

In contrast to these approaches, feminist scholar Dr. Judith Herman encapsulates the mothers' painful message to their daughters: "Your father first, you second. It is dangerous to fight back, for if I lose him, I lose everything. For my own survival I must leave you to your own devices. I cannot defend you and if necessary I will sacrifice you to your father."[19]

In a forthcoming book, Dr. Herman compassionately describes many mothers in incest families as "disabled." Untreated depression, alcoholism, psychosis, and repeated involuntary childbearing are cited by Dr. Herman. Fear, loss, isolation, and anger at being abandoned and powerless are the underpinning of most of these women's lives and those dimensions are rarely, if at all, mentioned in the literature.

After the secret has been disclosed, children feel more betrayed by their mother's inability to protect them than from their father's assault. Although feelings of disappointment and even contempt for fathers are reported, it is still easier to be angry at one who does not have power rather than at the legal and actual perpetrator.

It is important for us to understand that by viewing incestuous dynamics in this way, that is, holding a woman responsible for her husband's assault on her child, we are doubly punishing a woman for her pain, her powerlessness, and her passivity and, furthermore, intimating that none of this would have happened had she fulfilled her responsibilities.

Let us suppose that the mother is withdrawn, disabled, and cannot provide good role-modeling for her daughter. Can we not conclude that her behavior is symptomatic of the oppression of women in this culture? If women are so robbed of power and strength that a mother feels she is unable to prevent her husband's assault on her daughter, then we need to look at women's oppression as a direct cause of incestuous assault. In some cases, a woman who was an incest victim herself may feel as powerless to stop her husband's assault on her daughter as she was to stop her father's assault on herself years before.

The Father

I have reviewed how the children and the mothers are portrayed. Now let us look at the aggressors. They were described during the 1940s and 1950s as uniquely pathological, culturally different and rare, when they were mentioned at all. They were the men caught in the criminal justice process, whose lives were studied by the agencies that provided services to them and their families. These were therefore men in poor and fragmented families in the ghettoes of our cities. Or they were tyrannical men heading isolated rural families. The pictures of these men and the extrapolations drawn from their lives remain in much of the literature today. "These men were seen against a backdrop of deprivation and a need to appear as a strong patriarch while uncertain of their masculine identity."[20]

Nowadays, the incestuous male is described in more sympathetic psychological language. One factor often taken into account is the "sexual maladjustment and estrangement between the husband and the wife" coupled with the male's "poor impulse control."[21] Since these males were of normal intelligence and acceptable occupational and social adjustment, incarcerated men who were studied were described as "fully exploiting their position as the authoritarian head of the home, also acting in many ways like a caricature of an adolescent."[22]

Incestuous males are often described as being overwhelmed by a maelstrom of unmet needs: emotional, psychological, physical, and sexual. They are experiencing stress from one or a combination of job-related, mid-life related, economically related or sexually related pressures. These stresses are considered to be exacerbated by their wives' collusion and their children's compliance and inability to protect themselves. The man is a "psychological child in the physical guise of an adult."[23] Men who receive very little love and nurturing from their mothers ". . . become symbiotic personalities and want someone to satisfy their needs as adults"[24] and are presumably motivated because they had "mothers who were overtly seductive or overly attentive."[25]

In a startling new piece of analysis, emphasis is placed on going beyond the need to "blame" and urging renewed application of "compassion,"[26] undoubtedly to be applied directly to the male offender. We are now to understand that these men are emotionally troubled and incest is not something that happens *to* a victim but rather something that happens *between two* victims, circling back to the suggestion that these men have been victimized by poor parenting (read "mothering").

The researcher whose analysis this is points out that incarcerating the abuser may "leave the family destitute."[27] Additionally there are suggestions in the recent literature that incest should be decriminalized: "Incarceration causes both economic and psychological hardship to the family."[28]

Lucy Berliner, a victim advocate experienced in sexual abuse cases, observed, "When was the last time we heard anyone voice those concerns about a bank robber or a car thief? Why are we concerned about the economic hardships when it involves incestuous assault?" Why, indeed?

Once again, our work, our images as women, our reality is being defined by males and male-defined clinicians, scholars and theorists. There *is* a "conspiracy of silence" and as feminists, we must break our part of the silence by speaking the truth of our lives and experiences so that the theory, the funding, the clinicians, and the criminal justice personnel will be made to respond to us with clarity, respect, and immediacy.

Fear, isolation, and secrecy are the underpinnings of powerlessness. We need to speak, to break the silences between our lives, to listen and to provide compassionate alternatives for the women and children brave and strong enough to speak out. Listening, believing, caring are the first steps for us to take to hear the sounds and shapes of each other's lives, each other's pain. Then we can begin to develop *our* theory, *our* analysis, *our* interventions in a way that reflects our lives and validates our experiences as women.

Bibliography

1. Cormier, B. M., Kennedy, M., Sangowicz, J., "Psychodynamics of Father–Daughter Incest," *Canadian Psychiatric Association Journal,* 7 (1962), 203.
2. Dr. Graves, Richard, cited in *Sexuality Today* newsletter, August 27, 1979.
3. Bender, L., and Blau, A., "The Reaction of Children to Sexual Relations with Adults," *American Journal of Orthopsychiatry,* 7 (1937), 500–18.
4. Sarles, R. M. "Incest: Symposium on Behavioral Pediatrics," *Pediatric Clinics of North America,* 22 (1975), 108.
5. Weiner, J. B., "Father–Daughter Incest," *Psychiatric Quarterly,* 36: 1132–38.
6. Bender, L. et al., *ibid.*
7. Rasmussen, A. "The Importance of Sexual Attacks on Children Less than 14 Years of Age for the Development of Mental Disease and Character Anomalies," *Acta Psychiatric Neurology,* 9 (1934), 351–434.
8. Sarles, R. M., *ibid.*
9. Pomeroy, Wardell, B., "A New Look at Incest," *Forum,* November 1976.
10. Ramey, James W., "Dealing With The Last Taboo," *SIECUS Report,* Vol VII, No. 5, (May, 1979).
11. *Ibid.*
12. Lustig, N., Dreser, J., Spellman, S. and Murray, T., "Incest: A Family Group Survival Pattern," *Archives of General Psychiatry,* 14 (1966), 31–40.
13. Henderson, D.J., "Incest: A Synthesis of Data," *Canadian Psychiatric Association Journal.* 17 (1972), 299.
14. Cormier, B. M., et al., *ibid.*
15. *Ibid.*
16. Henderson, D. J. *ibid.*
17. *Ibid.*
18. Herman, J., and Hirschman, L. "Father–Daughter Incest," *Signs: Journal of Women in Culture and Society* (Summer 1977).
19. *Ibid.*
20. Lustig, N. et al., *ibid.*
21. Summitt, R., and Kryso, J. "Sexual Abuse of Children; A Clinical Spectrum." *American Journal of Orthopsychiatry* (1978), 1237–1251.
22. Cormier, B. M., *ibid.*
23. Groth, N., Burgess, A., Holmstrom, L. and Sgroi, S., *Sexual Assault of Children and Adolescents.* (Lexington, Mass.: Lexington Books, D.C. Heath and Co.)
24. *Ibid.*
25. Lustig, N. et al., *ibid.*
26. Rosenfeld, A., "Incest: The Victim–Perpetrator Model," Submitted for Publication. (Dr. Rosenfeld is Assistant Professor of Psychiatry and Director of Child Psychiatry Training at the Dept. of Psychiatry at Stanford University. Reprints are available from him directly.)
27. *Ibid.*
28. Cooper, Ingrid, "Decriminalization of Incest – New Legal/Clinical Approaches," *McGill Clinic in Forensic Psychiatry* (June 1977).

An Analysis of Gender and Social Groupings

Barrie Thorne

In the elementary school, children often sorted themselves, or were sorted by teachers, along lines of gender. Groups which formed for play and classroom activities were typically of the same sex, with taboos against cross-sex touch and easeful cross-sex talk. The children chose their own arrangement of desks in the classroom, and with the exception of one girl who for part of the year sat with the boys, it was a spatial moiety system — boys on the left, girls on the right. In the lunchroom, all but a few of the girls routinely sat at one long table, and most of the boys from the class sat at the other. The boys most often found near "female space" — those who sat closest to the girls' area in the classroom and music room, and who occasionally sat at the girls' table in the cafeteria — were the ones at the bottom of the male hierarchy: the two non-bilingual Chicanos and a "loner" boy who was terrified of sports and aggressive encounters. The girls who more often traveled in the boys' world, sitting at their cafeteria table or playing soccer and baseball with them, had fairly high status with the other girls. In short, the sexes were in an asymmetrical relationship; it was seen as contaminating for boys to be near girls' space, but girls who moved within the boys' world did not lose status. Arrangements in space mapped out class, race, and gender dominance and some of their complex interrelationships (a topic, by the way, which the sex difference and role approaches tend to neglect).

On the playground there were stable female enclaves — the two jungle gym areas, and male enclaves — the large field used for baseball, soccer and football; basketball courts; and skateboard area. The boys controlled much more space than did the girls, a pattern Lever (1976) also found for children this age. In other areas, such as the handball courts, there was more mixing of the sexes, but often in ritualized ways, as in group chasing: boys chasing girls, girls chasing boys, with a cross-sex dyad emerging from two larger, roaming same-sex troupes, for a short chase witnessed by the groups; all this in a pattern of advancing and retreating, challenging and reacting.

In that overall context it was meaningful to speak of a girls' world, with inner subdivisions and rankings, and a boys' world, also internally divided and ranked. Seen from the perspective of gender and the composition of groups and encounters, the daily round of activities in the school followed what Goffman (1977) calls a "with-then-apart rhythm." He notes that this pattern is generally present in our society, with the presence of special single-sex places like bathrooms, beauty parlors, bars, locker rooms. The "segregative punctuation of the day's round," Goffman observes, reaffirms separate gender subcultures in the face of contact between the sexes.

The following kinds of questions — posed ethnographically for varied situations, institutions, ages, social classes, ethnic contexts — would help us develop a more rooted and sociological understanding of gender: How does gender enter into group formation? Who makes gender relevant in a given situation, and how? (The teacher sometimes sorted the children by gender, as when she set up spelling bees or math contests with girls vs. boys.) How do all-female, all-male, and mixed-sex groups compare, in subcultures, structures, patterns of communication? How do female and male collectivities interrelate? What is the experience of individuals who travel in worlds predominantly of the other sex? How do cross-sex bonds take shape and relate to same-sex bonds in the daily rounds of groups and individuals? By what rituals, processes, forms of social organization and conflict, do "with-then-apart rhythms" get enacted? How does all of this relate to sexual inequality? Note that these sorts of questions do not emerge if one understands gender as an individual attribute or as a role.

Social Situations: The Variable Salience of Gender

A related line of inquiry concerns the variable salience of gender in different situations. This phenomenon is especially neglected by the sex difference approach, which assumes that gender is an attribute of the individual, immutable and always present, like one's nose. To be sure, individuals continuously display gender (e.g., through dress and speech) and are categorized by others as female or male, and gender forms a basic core of identity. All these processes are important to study. But gender is more prominent in some situations than others, may wax and wane in visibility in an encounter, and may be verbally invoked on some occasions and not others.

Beliefs about sex differences, and our system of placing—and socially creating—all humans in the gender categories female or male (Kessler & McKenna, 1978) provide symbolic materials which are drawn upon in specific encounters. Carole Joffe's observations in a nursery school first led me to think about gender as an idiom invoked for other purposes, in this case to impose one's will over others. According to Joffe (1971: 472) in the nursery school there was little systematic articulation of the rights of males and females, but

> . . .on a more sporadic basis the simple fact of sex difference itself would occasionally be invoked as an attempt at behavior control. Under the appropriate conditions, e.g., an encounter between persons of both sexes, one of the parties would sometimes point to the fact of sex difference as an attempt to justify his actions. The following is an example of this use of sex categories as an 'ideology of control':
>
> C. and two other girls are playing on top of a large structure in the yard. A. (male) comes over and C. screams, 'Girls only!' to which A. screams back, 'No, boys only!'

I observed situations of this kind in the elementary school. Gender was sometimes invoked in efforts to control others, and to include or exclude them. The following example from my fieldnotes illustrates the complex way in which gender may enter into social situations:

> A group of fourth-grade girls had established a lively activity in a corner of the playground. One of them, the 'baby-catcher,' commanded six others, 'the babies,' to 'lie down and go to sleep.' One by one the 'babies' would disobey and try to escape, and the 'baby-catcher' would try to catch them and pin them down, yelling with mock anger and frustration. Several times she threatened, 'Your momma's at work and I'm gonna call her,' and made a pretend telephone call by a tree. All the while, a row of three boys watched, with enraptured expressions, sitting on a bench about five feet away. At one point, one boy said to the others, loud enough for the girls to hear, 'If they scratch us, we can hit them,' an invitation to interaction which the girls heard, but ignored. Later several of the girls began to taunt the boys, 'Boys can babysit!' Soon after, the bell rang, and as the children began to head for the school building, one of the girls chased one of the boys for a few feet.

This sequence involved sex segregation, with boys acting as an audience for the girls' play, which was anchored in a female subculture. "We/they" talk and the explicit mentioning of gender ("Boys can babysit!") affirmed gender boundaries. The situation also involved cross-sex antagonism, and ritual interaction (the chasing) between a girl and a boy. In this example, it is clear that the sexes are distinct social groups, and that gender is a symbolic resource, drawn upon and made relevant in a variety of ways. In other situations in the school—as when a mixed-sex group did an art project, sharing a pot of paste—gender was less salient to the patterns of interaction.

The analysis of gender as a system of relationships provides a needed context for understanding sex similarities and differences. As Chodorow (1979:67) observes, studies of sex difference tend to assume that women and men are qualitatively and permanently different, rather than understanding gender as "processual, reflexive, and constructed." (Also see Rosaldo, 1980.)

References

Chodorow, Nancy. 1978. *The Reproduction of Mothering.* Berkeley: University of California Press.

Goffman, Erving. 1961. *Encounters.* New York: Bobbs-Merrill.

————. 1977. "The Arrangement Between the Sexes," *Theory and Society* 4: 301–331.

Joffe, Carole. 1971. "Sex Role Socialization and the Nursery School: As the Twig is Bent." *Journal of Marriage and the Family* 33: 467–475.

Kessler, Suzanne J. & Wendy McKenna. 1978. *Gender:*

An Ethnomethodological Approach. New York: John Wiley & Sons.

Lever, Janet. 1976. "Sex Differences in the Games Children Play," *Social Problems* 23 (4): 479–488.

Rosaldo, M. Z. 1980. "The Use and Abuse of Anthropology: Reflections on Feminism and Cross-Cultural Understanding," *Signs* 5: 389–417.

READING 18

Sex Differences in the Complexity of Children's Play and Games

Janet Lever

The cognitive development theorists in psychology, most notably Jean Piaget, have traced the growth in knowledge and perceptions through the various stages of childhood. To date, little has been done to chart the parallel development of interpersonal skills needed as the child moves from the egocentric orientation of the family to the community of children found in the school. George Herbert Mead (1934) initiated this line of thought with his classic essay on the child's learning to regard the "self as object" and "take the role of the other." Unfortunately, few have followed Mead's example.

Significantly, both Mead and Piaget recognized the rich learning environment provided in play. Mead credits the child's shift from aimless play to the realm of structured games as a crucial step in the development of role taking. Piaget (1965), through a close study of the game of marbles, meticulously explains how children develop moral values while they play rule-bounded games. Aside

from Mead and Piaget, little attention has been paid to the world of play and games in the study of childhood socialization.[1]

This study follows in the Mead and Piaget tradition by focusing on play and games as situations in which crucial learning takes place, but it goes beyond Mead's and Piaget's work in three important ways. First, Mead and Piaget each rests his analysis on a single game, whereas this study is based on a wide range of play and game activities. Second, both Mead and Piaget ignore sex differences in play. Mead's solitary example is the boy's game of baseball, but he does not tell us how girls, who are less familiar with team play, learn the same role-taking lessons. Piaget mentions, almost as an afterthought, that he did not find a single girls' game that has as elaborate an organization of rules as the boys' game of marbles, but he too fails to draw out the implications of his observation. A central concern of this study is to explore sex differences in the organization of children's play

Reprinted from Janet Lever, "Sex Differences in the Complexity of Children's Play and Games," in *The American Sociological Review,* 43(1978):pp. 471–483; by permission of the publisher and the author.

---

1. Among others who have recognized the importance of play in childhood socialization are Roberts and Sutton-Smith, 1962; Stone, 1971; Bruner et al., 1976.

and to speculate on the sources as well as the potential effects of those differences.

Third, the paper highlights a specific dimension of play hitherto disregarded, namely, the *complexity* of the learning experience. I shall define complexity in more detail below, but it includes many of those attributes associated with the emergence of modern industrial society, such as division of labor, differentiation, heterogeneity, and rationalization (Simmel, 1955; Tonnies, 1955; Durkheim, 1893; Weber, 1967; Parsons and Smelser, 1956). My basic thesis is that the play activities of boys are more complex than those of girls, resulting in sex differences in the development of social skills potentially useful in childhood and later life.

Methodology

A variety of methods was used to gather as much data as possible in one year, 1972. In total, 181 fifth-grade children, aged 10 and 11, were studied. Half were from a suburban school and the other half from two city schools in Connecticut. The entire fifth grade of each school was included in the study. Three schools were selected whose student populations were predominantly white and middle-class—a choice made deliberately because of the possibility that race and class distinctions would confound the picture at this stage of exploratory research.

Four techniques of data collection were employed: observation of schoolyards, semistructured interviews, written questionnaires, and a diary record of leisure activities. The diary was a simple instrument used to document where the children had actually spent their time for the period of one week. Each morning, under the direction of the researcher, the children filled out a short form on which they described (1) what they had done the previous day after school, (2) who they did it with, (3) where the activity took place, and (4) how long it had lasted. Half the diaries were collected in the winter and half in the spring. The questionnaire, designed to elicit how children spend their time away from school, also was administered by me inside the classroom. I conducted semistructured interviews with one-third of the sample. Some were done in order to help design the questionnaire and diary; others were done later to help interpret the results. I gathered observational data while watching children's play activity during recess, physical education classes, and after school.[2]

---

2. See Lever (1974:65–108) for a detailed description of the methodology.

Measuring Complexity

In common usage, the word "complex" means something that is made up of a combination of elements. Sociologists similarly have applied the term to describe the amount of functional differentiation in any social unit, from a small group or a large organization, to society as a whole. Based on the ideal type of complex organization, regardless of the scale of the collectivity, there is general agreement that increases in any of the following six attributes constitute greater complexity (Etzioni, 1969; Blau and Schoenherr, 1971):

1. division of labor based on specialization of roles;
2. interdependence between individual members;
3. size of the membership;
4. explicitness of the group goals;
5. number and specificity of impersonal rules; and
6. action of members as a unified collective.

Borrowing from the work of some contemporary students of games (Roberts et al., 1959; Redl et al., 1971; Avedon, 1971; Eifermann, 1972), I developed operational definitions for these six dimensions of complexity as they apply to the structure of play and games:

1. Role Differentiation. For the purposes of this study, activities are to be considered low in role differentiation if the same behavior is required or expected from all players. For example, in the game of checkers, each player is equipped with the same number of pieces and is expected to move them in accordance with the same rules. Role differentiation is to be scored medium if one player has more power and acts differently from the undifferentiated group of other players. This describes all central-person games such as tag and hide-and-seek. An activity is to be scored high on role differentiation if three or more distinct game roles are present. For example, in the game of baseball, the pitcher has a different task to perform than the shortstop whose task is different from the center fielder and so on.

2. Player Interdependence. An activity is to be judged low on the dimension of interdependence of players when the performance of one player does not immediately and significantly affect the performance of other players. For example, in the game of darts, one person's score does not interfere with the next player's score for the round. On the other hand, in the game of tennis, each player's move greatly affects the other's so that game has high interdependence of players.

3. Size of Play Group. This is a simple count of the number of players engaged in an activity. In this analysis, a group of three or fewer children is considered low on this dimension of complexity.

4. Explicitness of Goals. The explicitness of goals is found in the distinction between play and games. *Play* is defined as a cooperative interaction that has no stated goal, no end point, and no winners; formal *games,* in contrast, are competitive interactions, aimed at achieving a recognized goal (e.g., touchdown; checkmate). Goals may involve tests of physical or mental skills, or both. Formal games have a predetermined end point (e.g., when one opponent reaches a specified number of points; end of ninth inning) that is simultaneous with the declaration of a winner or winners. The same basic activity may be either play or games. For example, riding bikes is play; racing bikes is a game.

5. Number and Specificity of Rules. Sometimes the word "rule" is broadly used to refer to norms or customs. Here the term is used in a narrower sense and refers to explicit rules which (a) are known to all players before the game begins, (b) are constant from one game situation to the next, and (c) carry sanctions for their violation. Play as defined above never has rules, whereas games always are governed by them. But games do vary by the number and specificity of their rules. Some games, like tag and hide-and-seek, have only a few rules; other games, like baseball and monopoly, have numerous well-established rules.

6. Team Formation. A team is a group of players working collectively toward a common goal. Play, as defined above, is never structured by teams. Games, on the other hand, are to be divided into those requiring team formation when played with three or more persons and those prohibiting or excluding team formation. Within the category of games with team formation are included both those games where teammates play relatively undifferentiated roles, as in tug-of-war or relay races, and those that require coordination between teammates playing differentiated positions, as in baseball.

In order to test the hypothesis that boys' play and games are more complex in structure, I examine closely the type and frequency of the play activities of both sexes as they occur in public and private places. The evidence for private play is in the diary data, reporting after school and weekend play. Diary data are important because they reflect a large number of incidents, a wide range of activities, and a free choice of both games and playmates. The evidence for public play, based on observational data collected mostly during recess and gym periods, reveals the rich texture of the play world, replete with dialogue that helps the researcher understand the meanings children attribute to different play forms.

Diary Data

The diary responses reflect activities played inside or around the home in the hours after school. From over two thousand diary entries, 895 cases of social play were isolated for this analysis.[3] They represented 136 distinct play activities which were then scored by the author and three independent coders.[4] The operational definitions of the six dimensions of complexity were presented to the coders, along with descriptions of play activities derived from the children's interviews. The activities were then rated along each of the six dimensions. All games were given ratings based on the children's own reports of how a game is played most typically at the fifth grade level.[5]

Table 1 presents the basic data. To develop an overall complexity score, five of the dimensions were dichoto-

---

3. There were 2,141 activities recorded in the children's diaries. Five hundred eight entries were eliminated from this analysis because they were descriptions of nonplay activities like attending church services, doing homework or household chores, or going to the doctor. Another 527 items were eliminated because they reflected pastimes rather than actual play. This category included: watching television; reading books, comics or newspapers; going to the movies; going for an auto ride; and talking on the telephone. Television viewing, by far, accounts for most of the entries in this category. Of the remaining 1,106 play activities, 211 were not included because they were instances of the child's playing alone rather than in the company of others. Because the complexity dimensions reflect interpersonal skills, pastimes and solitary play are not relevant. However, it should be noted that there was no sex difference in the number of leisure hours spent with the television (15 to 20 hours/week) or playing alone (about 20% of all play).
4. The coders included the headmistress of a private elementary school who previously had taught fifth graders for over a decade, a graduate student who had been a camp counselor for ten-year-olds for several years, and an assistant professor of sociology. Overall, the judges agreed on over 90% of the items coded.
5. Such reports were especially needed because separate groups of children may play the same game somewhat differently, while even the same children do not necessarily play a game in identical fashion from one occasion to the next. It is also important to note that children modify adult games, so that a game like pool, which has complicated rules for adults, usually is played according to simple rules by children.

TABLE 1
Coding and Complexity Scores of the Most Frequently Listed Diary Activities

	Girls	*Boys*	*Total*
Type I: Complexity Score = 0			
one role (0); low interdependence (0); play (0)			
no rules (0); no teams (0).			
1. listen to records (g) 11. exploring woods (b)			
2. listen to radio (g) 12. hiking (g)			
3. drawing (g) 13. horseback riding (g)			
4. painting (g) 14. grooming horses (g)			
5. work with clay (g) 15. take a walk (g)			
6. build things (b) 16. jump roofs (b)			
7. ice skating (g) 17. climb trees (b)			
8. roller skating (g) 18. sled ride (b)			
9. bike riding 19. launch rockets (b)			
10. mini-biking (b) 20. fly kites (b)			
Type I:	42%	27%	34%
	(179)	(126)	(305)
Type II: Complexity Score = 1			
A. one role (0); high interdependence (1); play (0);			
no rules (0); no teams (0).			
21. cheerlead practice (g) 23. dancing (g)			
22. singing (g) 24. catch (b)	(13)	(14)	(27)
B. one role (0); low interdependence (0); game (1);			
few rules (0); no teams (0).			
25. bowling (g) 28. paddle pool (b)			
26. skittle bowl (b) 29. race electric	(17)	(42)	(59)
27. pool (b) cars (b)			
Type II:	7%	12%	10%
	(30)	(56)	(86)
Type III: Complexity Score = 2			
A. two or more roles (1); high interdependence (1);			
play (0); no rules (0); no teams (0).			
30. dolls (g) 32. jumprope (g)			
31. indoor fantasy (g) 33. outdoor fantasy (b)			
(e.g., school, house) (e.g., Army, FBI,			
Batman)	(72)	(19)	(91)
B. two roles (1); low interdependence (0); game (1);			
few rules (0); no teams (0).			
34. tag, chase (g) 36. kick the can (b)			
35. hide-and-seek (g)	(38)	(23)	(61)
C. one role (0); high interdependence (1); game (1);			
few rules (0); no teams (0).			
37. simple card games (g) 38. 2-square;	(21)	(29)	(50)
4-square			
Type III:	31%	15%	22.5%
	(131)	(71)	(202)

Coding and Complexity Scores of the Most Frequently Listed Diary Activities

			Girls	*Boys*	*Total*
Type IV: Complexity Score = 3					
one role (0); high interdependence (1); game (1); many rules (1); no teams (0).					
39. chess (b)	41. board games (g)				
40. checkers (b)	(e.g., Monopoly, Parchesi)				
		Type IV:	8%	15%	12%
			(35)	(70)	(105)
***Type V:** Complexity Score = 4					
one role (0); high interdependence (1); game (1); many rules (1); team formation (1).					
		Type V:	2%	1%	1.5%
			(9)	(5)	(14)
Type VI: Complexity Score = 5					
two or more roles (1); high interdependence (1); game (1); many rules (1); team formation (1).					
42. football (b)	46. soccer (b)				
43. ice hockey (b)	47. kickball (g)				
44. baseball (b)	48. punch ball (b)				
45. basketball (b)		Type VI:	10%	30%	20%
			(43)	(140)	(183)
		Total Social Play:	100%	100%	100%
			(427)	(468)	(895)

*Infrequently played activities, exemplified by Newcombe (g) and Capture the Flag (b).

mized and assigned either a low or high value (0,1).[6] (The sixth dimension, size of group, varied from one play situation to the next and was tabulated independently.) The five dichotomous attributes yield thirty-two possible combinations; however, only nine occurred empirically. In Table 1 they are organized from lowest to highest complexity (scores from 0 to 5). Only the forty-eight activities that appeared in the diaries ten or more times are used to exemplify this scoring procedure, but all social play activities, even those less frequently mentioned, are included in the tabulations.[7] By age ten, play activities are generally

6. To justify linking the six dimensions, a factor analysis was run on the 136 activities. There was only one factor present, and all six dimensions were a part of it (the lowest degree of communality was .60); I have referred to this single factor as "complexity." While it may be argued that some dimensions add more complexity than others, the absence of guidelines encourages equal weighting at this time.
7. See Lever (1974:394–7) for a complete list of games recorded in the children's diaries.

known to be sex segregated. The "g" or "b" after each activity in Table 1 indicates whether it is played predominantly by girls or boys; the absence of a letter implies that the sexes engage in the activity with roughly equal frequency.

Table 1 yields two important findings. First, it shows the great variety regarding levels of complexity in the games played by children of similar age. Mead and Piaget, by focusing on only a single game, could not show the range of experiences available within the play world. Fully a third of the activities were low on all the measured dimensions of complexity. Another fifth were high on all. Children exposed to one or the other of these types of play are likely to be learning very different skills. Second, if we can agree that games provide differential learning environments, then we must assume differential effects for boys and girls. Boys experience three times as many games at the highest level of complexity and over twice as many boys' activities are located in the top half of the complexity scale.[8]

Table 2 views the data from a different perspective by showing the sex distribution separately for each of the six dimensions. Although greater complexity in boys' activities is demonstrated for all six, the major finding of Table 2 is seen on the fourth dimension, explicitness of goals. Sixty-five percent of boys' activities were competitive games compared to only 37% of girls' activities. In other words, *girls played more* while *boys gamed more*. This difference is not merely a function of boys' playing more team sports. Only 140 of the 305 games played by boys were team sports. Eliminating team sports for both sexes, we would still find 54% of the boys' activities and 30% of the girls' activities competitively structured. Sedentary games, like chess and electric race cars, are as important as sport in reflecting boys' greater competitiveness.

Nor is it the case when girls do participate in competitive games that they experience the same level of complexity as their male peers. The games girls play have fewer rules, and less often require the formation of teams.[9] In summary, the data from children's diaries show strongly that boys, far more often than girls, experience high levels of complexity in their play and games.

Observational Data

Observations of children at play during recess, gym classes, and after school also indicate very distinct play patterns for boys and girls. As in the diary data, boys' activities were found to be more complex. The following descriptions of a few selected play activities illustrate the way in which each of the dimensions of complexity is ex-

---

8. Because some children reported more activities than others, there is the possibility that these results, based on activities as the units of analysis, reflect the extreme scores of a few individuals and are not representative of the sample as a whole. To guard against such misinterpretation, I made the individuals the units of analysis. To do so, I used the same dichotomization and point system displayed in Table 1 and added the sixth dimension, size of play group, as it appeared in each of the 895 entries. Once each activity could be given a complexity score (now zero to six), an average complexity score could be ascertained for each child based on the entire week's social play report. Seventy percent of the boys, compared with 36% of the girls, had average complexity scores of 3.0 or higher—a fact which further sustains the hypothesis.

9. Fifty-one percent of the games girls play (n = 158) contain many rules, compared with 69% of the boys' games (n = 305). Looking only at games with three or more participants, we note that boys played 26% more games which called for team formation.

TABLE 2

Sex Differences on the Six Dimensions of Complexity in Play and Games

Dimensions of complexity	Girls	Boys
1. Number of roles	18%	32%
(3 or more roles)	(427)	(468)
2. Interdependence of players	46%	57%
(high interdependence)	(427)	(468)
3. Size of play group	35%	45%
(4 or more persons)	(427)	(468)
4. Explicitness of goals	37%	65%
(game structure)	(427)	(468)
5. Number of rules	19%	45%
(many rules)	(427)	(468)
6. Team formation	12%	31%
(teams required)	(427)	(468)

pressed. Greater attention is given to girls' games as they are less familiar to adults. Some implications of differential organization of play are suggested, but their elaboration awaits the discussion section.

1. Role Differentiation. The largest category of girls' public activity was the same as their private activity, namely, single-role play. These were cooperative activities with both or all parties doing basically the same thing such as riding bikes, roller skating, or ice skating. A minority of girls' activities were competitive games. Observing recess periods for a year, I saw only one instance of a spontaneously organized team sport, namely, kickball. The activities that appeared most regularly during recess were the traditional girls' games, like hopscotch, which are turn-taking games with only one game role present at a given time. Each player, in specified sequential order, attempts to accomplish the same task as all other players. A few turn-taking games have two distinct roles: for example, in jumprope there is the role of rope turner and that of rope jumper. The other girls' games I observed frequently at recess were central-person games, the most popular being tag, spud, and Mother May I. These games also have only two roles—the "it" and the "others." Power is usually ascribed in these games through "dipping rules" like "odd-man-out."

Boys at this age have largely stopped playing central-person games except as fillers; for example, they might play tag while waiting for a bus or after so many team members have been called home to dinner that their previous game has disintegrated. The great majority of observed games were team sports with their multiple roles. Besides distinctions based on positions and assigned tasks, there were also distinctions in power between team captains and their subordinates. Sometimes the leaders were appointed by teachers, but more often the children elected their captains according to achievement criteria.[10] After school especially, I observed boys in single role activities, some noncompetitive, like flying kites and climbing trees, but most competitive like tennis, foot races, or one-on-one basketball.

2. Player Interdependence.   There are many types of player interdependence: (1) interdependence of action between members of a single group; (2) interdependent decision-making between single opponents; (3) simultaneous interdependence of action with one's own teammates and an opposing group of teammates.

Very little interdependence was required of those girls engaged in single role play; coaction rather than interaction is required of the participants. Also, little interdependence was required of those playing turn-taking games. Even though the latter activity is competitive, the style of competition is indirect, with each player acting independently of the others. That is, one competes against a figurative "scoreboard" (Player A $\rightarrow$ norm $\leftarrow$ Player B). Participation in such games is routinized and occurs successively or after the previous player's failure; that is, opponents do not compete simultaneously. Interdependent decision-making is not necessary in turn-taking games of physical skill as it may be in some of the popular board games.

When girls do play interdependently, they tend to do so in a cooperative context where there is interdependence of action between members of a single group. This type of interaction is best exemplified (but rarely observed) in the creation of private fantasy scenarios. One public example occurred when seven girls from one school took the initiative to write, produce, and act out a play they called "Hippie Cinderella." They stayed indoors at recess and rehearsed almost daily for three weeks in preparation for presentation to the entire fifth-grade class.

When boys compete as individuals, they are more likely to be engaged in direct, face-to-face confrontations (Player A $\rightleftharpoons$ Player B). Interdependent decision-making between single opponents is necessary in games like tennis or one-on-one basketball that combine strategy with physical skill. More often, boys compete as members of teams and must simultaneously coordinate their actions with those of their teammates while taking into account the action and strategies of their opponents. Boys interviewed expressed finding gratification in acting as representatives of a collectivity; the approval or disapproval of one's teammates accentuates the importance of contributing to a group victory.

3. Size of Play Group.   Observations made during recess periods showed boys playing in much larger groups than girls to a far greater extent than appeared in the diary data. Boys typically were involved in team sports which require a large number of participants for proper play. Boys in all three schools could play daily, depending on the season, in ongoing basketball, football, or baseball games involving ten to twenty-five or more persons. Girls were rarely observed playing in groups as large as ten persons; on those occasions, they were engaged in cooperative circle songs that seemed to emerge spontaneously, grow, and almost as quickly disintegrate. More often, girls participated in activities like tag, hopscotch, or jumprope, which can be played properly with as few as two or three participants and seldom involve more than five or six. In fact, too many players are considered to detract rather than enhance the fun because it means fewer turns, with longer waits between turns. Indeed, Eifermann (1968), after cataloging over 2,000 children's games, observed that most girls' games, like hopscotch and jacks, can be played alone, whereas the great majority of boys' games need two or more players.

4. Explicitness of Goals.   In the recess yards, I more often saw girls playing cooperatively and boys playing competitively. Some girls engaged in conversation more than they did in play (see Lever, 1976:481). Others, like those who initiated the circle songs and dances, preferred action governed by ritual rather than rules. For example, the largest and most enthusiastic group of girls witnessed during the year of research was involved in a circle chant called "Dr. Knickerbocker Number Nine." Twenty-four

---

10. In response to the interview question, "Who are the fifth-grade leaders?" the boys in all three schools answered that the best athletes/team organizers rightly held that position. In contrast, most girls hesitated with the question, then named persons who had power, but credited their aggression rather than particular valued skills. They equated giving directives with assertiveness and gave that behavior negative labels like "bossy" or "big mouth." Some openly stated that leaders acted less than ladylike and were not envied for their power. Attitudes that underlie Kanter's (1977:201) "mean and bossy woman boss" stereotype obviously are set at a very young age.

girls repeated the chant and body motions in an outer circle, while one girl in the center spun around with eyes closed. She then stopped, with arm extended, pointing out someone from the outer circle to join her. The ritual chant began again while the new arrival spun around; this procedure continued until nine persons had been chosen in similar random fashion to form the inner circle. Then the ninth person remained in the circle's center while the others resumed their original positions and the cycle would begin anew.

Although this activity appeared monotonous to the observer because it allowed the participants little chance to exercise physical or mental skills, these ten-year-olds were clearly enjoying themselves. Shouts of glee were heard from the circle's center when a friend had been chosen to join them. Indeed, a girl could gauge her popularity by the loudness of these shouts. For some the activity may provide an opportunity to reaffirm self-esteem without suffering any of the achievement pressures of team sports.

Even when girls engaged in presumably competitive games, they typically avoided setting precise goals. In two schools, I observed girls playing "Under the Moon," a popular form of jumprope. The first person hops in and jumps once, in any fashion of her choosing, and then hops out. She then enters again and does two jumps, usually though not necessarily, different from the first. She increases her jumps by an increment of one until she has jumped ten times. Her turn over, she then becomes a rope turner. There was no competition exhibited between players. They participated for the fun of the turn, not to win. Even if the jumper trips the rope, she is allowed to complete her turn. If the jumper competes, it is with herself, as she alone determines whether to attempt an easy jump or a more difficult one.

The point is that girls sometimes take activities in which a comparison of relative achievement is structurally possible (and sometimes normatively expected) and transform them into noncompetitive play. Girls are satisfied to keep their play loosely structured. For example, in the game of jacks, girls can say before beginning, "The first to finish 'double bounces' is the winner." More often, however, they just play until they are bored with the game. Players may or may not verbalize "you won," and recognize who has advanced the most number of steps. Boys grant much more importance to being proclaimed the winner; they virtually always structure their games, be it one-on-one or full team basketball, so that the outcomes will be clear and definite.

5. Number and Specificity of Rules.   This investigator also observed, reminiscent of Piaget, that boys' games more often have an elaborate organization of rules. Girls' turn-taking games progress in identical order from one situation to the next; prescriptions are minimal, dictating what must be done in order to advance. Given the structure of these games, disputes are not likely to occur. "Hogging" is impossible when participation is determined by turn-taking; nor can fouls occur when competition is indirect. Sports games, on the other hand, are governed by a broad set of rules covering a wide variety of situations, some common and others rare. Areas of ambiguity which demand rule elaboration and adjudication are built into these games. Kohlberg (1964) refines Piaget's thesis by arguing that children learn the greatest respect for rules when they can be used to reduce dissonance in ambiguous situations.[11]

Because girls play cooperatively more than competitively, they have less experience with rules per se, so we should expect them to have a lesser consciousness of rules than boys. On one of those rare occasions when boys and girls could be watched playing the same games, there was striking evidence for a sex difference in rule sensitivity. A gym teacher introduced a game called "Newcombe," a simplified variation of volleyball, in which the principal rule is that the ball must be passed three times before being returned to the other side of the net. Although the game was new to all, the boys did not once forget the "3-pass" rule; the girls forgot it on over half the volleys.

6. Team Formation.   Team formation can be seen as a dimension of complexity because it indicates simultaneously structured relationships of cooperation and conflict. In turn-taking games, girls compete within a single group as independent players, each one against all others. Boys compete between groups, acting interdependently as members of a team. Team formation is required in all of their favorite sports: baseball, football, basketball, hockey, and soccer. Only a few girls in each school regularly joined the boys in their team sports; conversely, only a few boys in each school avoided the sports games. Questionnaire data support these observations. Most boys reported regular participation in neighborhood sports games. In addition, at the time of the study 68% said they belonged to some adult-supervised teams, with a full schedule of practice and league games. In fact, some

---

11. See Lever (1976:482–3) for a description of sex differences in the handling of quarrelling in games.

of these fifth graders were already involved in interstate competitions.

The after-school sports program illustrates boys' greater commitment to team competition. Twenty girls from the third, fourth, and fifth grades elected captains who chose teams for Newcombe games. Only seven of those girls returned the following week. In contrast, after-school basketball attracted so many boys that the fifth graders were given their own day. The teacher called roll for the next two weeks and noted that every boy had returned to play again.

Thus observational data, like the diary data, support the basic hypothesis that boys' play activities are more complex in structure than those of girls. Boys' play more frequently involves specialization of roles, interdependence of players, explicit group goals, and larger group membership, numerous rules, and team divisions. This conclusion holds for activities in public as well as in private. It suggests a markedly different set of socialization experiences for members of each sex.

Discussion

Sources of the Sex Difference

What is it that produces these distinct play patterns for boys and girls? The answer is mostly historical and cultural and holds true for much of Europe as well as the United States. While the rise of recreational physical activities in the late nineteenth century was enjoyed by women and men alike, the organized team sports which flourished at the same time were limited to participation by males (Paxson, 1917). The combined beliefs in the masculine nature of sport and the physiological inferiority of females led early twentieth century educators to lobby for competitive athletics for boys while restricting the physical education of girls to gymnastic exercises and dance. The emphasis on competitive athletics for males was reinforced by the view that sport served as a training ground for future soldiers ("the battle of Waterloo was won on the playing fields of Eton") and by the growing interest in spectator sports in which the dominant performers were young men (Cozens and Stumpf, 1953). Despite some outstanding individual female athletes in golf, tennis, and track and field, there was no development of interest in women's team sports. This situation is only now beginning to change.

Evidence generated in connection with Title IX of the Education Amendments Acts shows the extraordinary sex difference with respect to the allocation of funds for athletic programs from the primary grades through college. In 1969 the Syracuse New York School board allocated $90,000 for boys' extracurricular sports compared to $200 for girls' sports. In rural Pennsylvania, the Fairfield area school district set its 1972-73 budget at a ratio of 40:1 in favor of male athletes whose interscholastic competition begins in earnest by fifth grade. Even at Vassar, where sports for women are given great attention, the boys' athletic budget was double that of girls, although they comprised only one-third of the student body (Gilbert and Williamson, 1973).

Of course, it is not only the schools that encourage boys' and restrict girls' athletic participation. Parents act as the conveyor belts for cultural norms, and it is no less the case for norms pertaining to sport. Male children are quick to learn that their demonstrations of athletic skill earn the attention and praise of adults. Many fathers show more emotion and enthusiasm for professional sports than anything else. Girls at young ages may not be actively discouraged from sports participation, but they are told that they are "tomboys" which is understood to be a deviant label. In the recent Little League debate, psychologists, parents, and coaches voiced their concern for the masculinization of female athletes, and the possible damage to young male egos when girls defeat boys in public (Michener, 1976). This cultural legacy is still with us, even though we now appear to be on the verge of radical change.

Historical analysis of children's games confirms that boys are playing more team sports now than ever before. Equally important, boys have drifted away from loosely structured play towards more formally organized competitive games (Sutton-Smith and Rosenberg, 1971). Evidence presented here supports this picture. It appears that the growing cultural emphasis on sports and winning has carried over to nonphysical activities and made them more competitive, and that, to date, it has had this effect to a far greater extent for boys than for girls.

Consequences of the Sex Differences

Boys' games provide a valuable learning environment. It is reasonable to expect that the following social skills will be cultivated on the playground: the ability to deal with diversity in memberships where each person is performing a special task: the ability to coordinate actions and maintain cohesiveness among group members; the ability to cope with a set of impersonal rules; and the ability to work for collective as well as personal goals.

Team sports furnish the most frequent opportunity to sharpen these social skills. One could elaborate on the lessons learned. The rule structure encourages strategic thinking. Team sports also imply experience with clear-cut leadership positions, usually based on universalistic criteria. The group rewards the individual who has improved valued skills, a practice which further enhances a sense of confidence based on achievement. Furthermore, through team sports as well as individual matches, boys learn to deal with interpersonal competition in a forthright manner. Boys experience face-to-face confrontations — often opposing a close friend — and must learn to depersonalize the attack. They must practice self-control and sportsmanship; in fact, some of the boys in this study described the greatest lesson in team sports as learning to "keep your cool."

Girls' play and games are very different. They are mostly spontaneous, imaginative, and free of structure or rules. Turn-taking activities like jumprope may be played without setting explicit goals. Girls have far less experience with interpersonal competition. The style of their competition is indirect, rather than face to face, individual rather than team affiliated. Leadership roles are either missing or randomly filled.

Perhaps more important, girls' play occurs in small groups. These girls report preferring the company of a single best friend to a group of four or more.[12] Often girls mimic primary human relationships instead of playing formal games, or they engage in conversation rather than play anything at all. In either case, there are probable benefits for their affective and verbal development. In Meadian terms, it may be that boys develop the ability to take the role of the *generalized other* while girls develop empathy skills to take the role of the *particular other*.

That the sexes develop different social skills in childhood due to their play patterns is logical conjecture; that those social skills might carry over and influence their adult behavior is pure speculation. Indeed, the weight of evidence indicates that life experiences are vast and varied; much can happen to intervene and change the patterns set during childhood. Still, there is so much continuity between boys' play patterns and adult male roles

that we must consider whether games serve a particular socializing function.

This idea is now popular. In a recent best seller on managerial leaders, Maccoby (1976) describes the 250 executives he studied as gamesmen who organize teams, look for a challenge, and play to win. The same social skills may be equally helpful in lower level bureaucratic jobs or other settings, like trade unions and work crews, where complexity of organization is also found. One need not endorse the world of organizations, bureaucracy, sharp competition, and hierarchy to recognize it as an integral part of modern industrial society.

The unfortunate fact is that we do not know what effect playing games might have on later life. We do not know, for example, whether the minority of women who have succeeded in bureaucratic settings are more likely to have played complex games. A recent study offers a modicum of supporting data. Hennig and Jardim (1977) portray their small sample of twenty-five women in top management positions as former tomboys. It is also the case that elite boarding schools and women's colleges, many of which stress team sports, have been credited with producing a large portion of this nation's female leaders. I would not want to argue that competitive team sports are the only place to learn useful organizational skills. Surely, the skills in question can be learned in nonplay settings in both childhood and adulthood. Nevertheless, it can be argued that complex games are an early and effective training ground from which girls traditionally have been excluded.

Conclusion

Children's socialization is assumed to have consequences for their later lives. Sociologists have looked to the family and the school as the primary socializing agents. In contrast, this analysis focused on the peer group as the agent of socialization, children's play as the activity of socialization, and social skills as the product of socialization. The data presented here reaffirm Mead's and Piaget's message that during play children develop numerous social skills that enable them to enjoy group membership in a community of peers.

The data also demonstrate that some games, when analyzed structurally, provide a highly complex experience for their young players while others do not. By itself, the notion of complexity adds to our appreciation of games as important early training grounds. However, the evidence of differential exposure to complex games leads

---

12. It is important to note that, according to their questionnaire responses, the minority of thirty girls who reported playing complex games during the diary week also indicated a preference for larger friendship groups. The fact that the sex difference in size of friendship cliques disappears when controlling for complexity of game experience is one indication of the importance of this classification scheme.

to the conclusion that not all children will learn the same lessons. Here the approach to play and games differs dramatically from that of Mead and Piaget who presumed social and moral development as a normal part of the growth process and, therefore, did not make problematic the different experience of boys and girls. One implication of this research is that boys' greater exposure to complex games may give them an advantage in occupational milieus that share structural features with those games. At the very least, the striking similarity between the formula for success in team sports and in modern organizations should encourage researchers to give serious attention to play patterns and their consequences.

References

Avedon, Elliott M.
  1971 "The structure elements of games." Pp. 419–26 in Elliott M. Avedon and Brian Sutton-Smith (eds.). The Study of Games. New York: Wiley.
Blau, Peter and R. A. Schoenherr
  1971 The Structure of Organizations. New York: Basic Books.
Bruner, J. S., A. Jolly, and K. Sylva
  1976 Play: Its Role in Development and Evolution. New York: Penguin.
Cozens, Frederick and Florence Stumpf
  1953 Sports in American Life. Chicago: University of Chicago Press.
Durkheim, Emile
  [1893] The Division of Labor in Society. New York: Free
  1964 Press.
Eifermann, Rivka
  1968 "School children's games." Final Report, Contract No. OE-6-21-010. Department of Health, Education and Welfare; Office of Education, Bureau of Research. Unpublished paper.
  1972 "Free social play: a guide to directed playing." Unpublished paper.
Etzioni, Amitai
  1969 A Sociological Reader on Complex Organization. New York: Holt.
Gilbert, Bill and Nancy Williamson
  1973 "Sport is unfair to women." *Sports Illustrated* 38 (May 28):88–98.
Hennig, Margaret and Ann Jardim
  1977 The Managerial Woman. New York: Doubleday.
Kanter, Rosabeth Moss
  1977 Men and Women of the Corporation. New York: Basic Books.
Kohlberg, Lawrence
  1964 "Development of moral character and moral ideology." Pp. 383–431 in M. L. Hoffman and L. W. Hoffman (eds.), Review of Child Development Research, Vol. 1. New York: Russell Sage.
Lever, Janet
  1974 Games Children Play: Sex Differences and the Development of Role Skills. Ph.D. dissertation, Department of Sociology, Yale University.
  1976 "Sex differences in the games children play." Social Problems 23:478–87.
Maccoby, Michael
  1976 The Gamesman. New York: Simon and Schuster.
Mead, George Herbert
  1934 Mind, Self, and Society. Chicago: University of Chicago Press.
Michener, James A.
  1976 Sports in America. New York: Random House.
Parsons, Talcott and Neil J. Smelser
  1956 Economy and Society: A Study in the Integration of Economic and Social Theory. London: Routledge.
Paxson, Frederic L.
  1917 "The rise of sport." Mississippi Valley Historical Review 4:144–68.
Piaget, Jean
  1965 The Moral Judgment of the Child. New York: Free Press.
Redl, F., P. Gump, and B. Sutton-Smith
  1971 "The dimensions of games." Pp. 408–18 in Elliott M. Avedon and Brian Sutton-Smith (eds.), The Study of Games. New York: Wiley.
Roberts, John M., M. J. Arth, and R. R. Bush
  1959 "Games in culture." American Anthropologist 61:597–605.
Roberts, John M. and Brian Sutton-Smith
  1962 "Child training and game involvement." Ethnology 1:166–85.
Simmel, Georg
  1955 The Web of Group Affiliations. Trans. by Reinhard Bendix. New York: Free Press.
Stone, Gregory P.
  1971 "The play of little children." Pp. 4–17 in R. E. Herron and Brian Sutton-Smith (eds.), Child's Play. New York: Wiley.
Sutton-Smith, B. and B. Rosenberg
  1971 "Sixty years of historical change in the game preference of American children." Pp. 18–50 in R. E. Herron and B. Sutton-Smith (eds.), Child's Play. New York: Wiley.
Tonnies, Ferdinand
  1955 Community and Association. Trans. by Charles P. Loomis. London: Routledge.
Weber, Max
  1967 From Max Weber: Essays in Sociology. Trans. and ed. by H. H. Gerth and C. Wright Mills. New York: Oxford University Press.

A Handshake Will Do

The International Football Federation in Zurich told soccer players Tuesday to act like men and stop hugging and kissing each other after scoring goals.

The Federation called on national soccer associations to take disciplinary measures against "unmanly behavior."

"The exultant outbursts of several players at once

Reprinted from "A Handshake Will Do," compiled from staff and wire reports, The Ohio State *Lantern,* November 17, 1980.

jumping on top of each other, kissing and embracing is really excessive and inappropriate and should be banned from the football pitch," the Federation said in its September Bulletin.

Supporting a call for sanctions made by its technical committee, the Federation said jubilation over a goal should be limited to congratulation by the team captain.

It conceded that top players get a lot of bonus money for scoring goals but said they should all the same be "reminded" to behave like adults.

Guidelines for Evaluation of Elementary Textbooks

Elementary Reading Textbooks

The following is a set of guidelines to be used in evaluating sex-role stereotyping and sexism as they appear

Reprinted from Laurel Richardson, "Guidelines for Evaluation of Elementary Textbooks," in "Teaching/Learning Gender for Elementary and Secondary Schools," by permission.

in elementary readers. To use these guidelines count the number of stories or characters falling into each category. "Male" and "female" are used to refer to both child and adult.

1. Characters in stories	Male	Female
A. Stories centered around child	_____	_____
B. Stories with adult main characters	_____	_____
C. Biographies	_____	_____
D. Animal stories giving sex of character	_____	_____
E. Folk fantasy stories centered around main character	_____	_____
F. Child engaged in active play	_____	_____
G. Child engaged in quiet activity	_____	_____

2. Family Life	Number of Stories
A. Single parent families with mother or father as parent	_____
B. Working mother	_____
1. Sole support of family	_____
2. Both parents working	_____
C. Single career woman	_____
D. Father helping with domestic chores	_____
E. Homemaking tasks done by woman	_____
1. Creative or intellectual —ex. reading or keeping budget	_____
2. Drudgery and routine—ex. washing dishes, cleaning	_____

3. Illustrations	Number of Stories
A. Boy pictured as doing something	_____
B. Girl passively watching activity	_____
C. Mother doing routine household chores	_____
D. Mother wearing apron, symbolizing kitchen chores (include animals)	_____
E. Female clothing	
1. Dresses	_____
2. Slacks	_____

4. Occupations

List the occupations of both men and women that are mentioned in the book. These could then be compared for the variety of occupations available, the number of stereotyped "manly" or "womanly" jobs, number of women helping men do more important jobs, number of jobs involving service to others, number of professional jobs.

Male	*Female*

The previous guidelines will help decide if a book's overall tone is sexist or gives an equal representation of male and female. However, much can also be learned by studying the personalities and character traits of persons in the book. For example, a book may have an equal number of boys and girls. But if an analysis made of their character traits reveals that the boys all have stereotype "masculine" personalities, then this book has not eliminated sexism. Use this guideline for a deeper look into how men and women are portrayed in reading books.

5. Character traits and personalities

	Male	*Female*
A. Exhibits creativity, ingenuity, and resourcefulness	_____	_____
B. Takes initiative and shows leadership	_____	_____
C. Exhibits helplessness and needs protection	_____	_____
D. Has timid, docile, dependent, passive personality	_____	_____
E. Has dominant, aggressive personality	_____	_____
F. Exhibits physical strength, bravery, heroism	_____	_____
G. Has high degree of problem-solving ability, logical thinking	_____	_____
H. Engages in competition	_____	_____
I. Gives up easily	_____	_____

J. Engages in adventure, exploration and imaginative play	_____	_____
K. Lacks competence in tasks and has mishaps and accidents	_____	_____
L. Inhibits or squelches activities planned by others	_____	_____

Mathematics Textbooks

These guidelines are for the purpose of evaluating both elementary and secondary mathematics texts. There are two places where stereotyping shows most clearly in elementary, junior high and lower-level secondary texts. These are in the illustrations and in the "word problems". Notice if the items bought or used in "word problems" — or the activities the problem centers around — conform to typical stereotypes of sex-roles.

	Male	*Female*
1. Illustrations		
A. Number of times a child or adult shown working problem	_____	_____
B. Number of times adult shown in occupation using mathematics	_____	_____
C. Number of times child or adult used in illustration for "word problem"	_____	_____
2. Word Problems		
A. Number of times problems say person saved money	_____	_____
B. Number of times problems say person spent money	_____	_____
C. Number of times person named as income producer	_____	_____
D. Number of times person named in occupation	_____	_____
E. Number of times problems say person earned money	_____	_____

F. Number of times person
    mentioned in athletics   _____   _____

G. Number of times
    mathematician referred
    to as "he"   _____   _____

H. Number of actual
    mathematicians named
    in book   _____   _____

I. Number of times male
    (female) used in word
    problems   _____   _____

3. List items purchased by persons
    in word problems as bought by:

               Male | *Female*

PART TWO

Maintaining Patriarchy

INTRODUCTION

Socialization of the young, as we have seen, is a powerful force directed toward creating sex-differences and sex-inequalities. If maintaining the culture's ideology and social institutions depended only upon the inculcation of values, attitudes and behaviors in children, the task of maintaining the status quo would be easy for those who embrace traditionalism. However, in one important sense socialization is never completed: adults, especially in complex societies, continue to have new experiences and new ideas; that is, they are constantly "desocialized" and "resocialized." Change and growth within an individual is a *continuing* process: heretical thoughts, atypical experiences and system-altering activities are not only possible but probable. Society requires, however, that the adults be kept in line—not only so that they will appropriately socialize the young, but also so that they will fulfill their own mandated social roles.

Because the potential for non-traditionalism is strong in societies such as ours, *authority structures* are activated to maintain the traditional culture. These structures are of several kinds, the primary ones being religious, legal and scientific.

Religion carries *moral authority*. To violate religious precepts risks exclusion from the community of believers "here and now" as well as "then and there" into eternity. The legal system codifies norms and values and carries the *authority of the state*. To break the law risks social sanctions, punishment, and the loss of privileges. The sciences carry with them empirical truth or *pragmatic authority*. To disagree with scientific findings or to act in ways deemed scientifically inappropriate is to risk being labeled ignorant, irrational or perverse, and to be subject to pity or ridicule. Thus to disagree with the primary lessons from religion, law, and the sciences can result in ostracism and/or incarceration.

Not surprisingly, the force of authority in regard to sex and gender is toward traditionalism. The major religions differentiate and discriminate between the sexes and hold that certain activities and behaviors are appropriate for men, others for women. For example, in many denominations the ordination of women is still withheld; in others where it is permitted, actual church leadership positions are withheld. The limited role of women in the church is thought to be divinely sanctioned.

The legal system is predicated on ancient assumptions regarding the differences between the sexes, including the assumptions that women are childlike and in need of protection; that men are the natural protectors of women; that husband and wife become "one" under the law, and that "one" is the husband; and the belief in a double standard of morality based on biological deterministic arguments. These assumptions become solidified as law and have negative and discriminatory consequences for both men and women.

The social, biological and psychological sciences often non-consciously borrow the ideological presumptions of their culture and repackage them as scientific truths and facts. So, for example, the assumption that women *should* want to be mothers becomes the basis for psychological and sociological theories of motherhood, as well as the basis for medical, clinical and social work practices. Women who choose not to mother are viewed as deviants, social problems, and immature. Correlatively, men who choose not to compete for financial success and sexual prowess, are viewed as misfits, losers, and in need of counseling.

Even as authority structures can function to maintain the status quo, however, they can also function as agents of social change. For not only do these ideas and institutions restrain, they also can be catalysts for social reform. Adults who work and think within these institutions are continually desocialized and resocialized, and they use their new ideas to help change the very institutions in which they work. These reformists and revolutionaries can and do create *alternative paradigms* that modify, and in some cases radicalize, the existing authority structures. Because adults continue to find justification or solace from religion or law or science for their nontraditional beliefs and behaviors, these alternative paradigms provide a source of legitimation and comfort whose importance cannot be minimized.

In addition to the institutions of religion, law and science (including medicine), there are a number of institutionalized practices that so severely limit the lives of women that they must be addressed separately: These are the institutionalized practices of violence, including the threat of violence. Some of these practices—such as clitoridectomies and infibulation (genital multilation) and snuff films (pornographic flicks where the woman is *really* murdered at the end)—are nearly unspeakable; others, such as harassment on the street, may be proposed as "harmless," but are not. For whether one considers rape, street harassment, spouse-abuse or other such practices, the dynamic is the same: women live under the threat of violence—and violence is always, and has always been, the ultimate weapon of social control.

Introduction: Religion and the Law

The supposed separation of "church" and "state" is belied by the close intertwining of religious ideas and the legal system. Most of our laws that differentiate and discriminate between the sexes are, in fact, based on biblical assumptions about the nature of men and the nature of women.

The first selection, "Introduction to the New Woman's Bible" by Elizabeth Cady Stanton, an activist in the Women's Suffrage Movement, was written in 1896. Stanton, in that introduction, addresses some of the major ways in which the Bible perpetuates male-superiority and privilege. The second selection, "Uncle Arthur's Bedtime Stories: A Content Analysis of Sex-Stereotyping" by Karen Schwartz, analyzes how religious stories for young children sustain inequality between males and females.

Carol P. Christ in "Heretics and Outsiders: The Struggle Over Female Power in Western Religion," provides an historical analysis of the processes in Judaic-Christianity through which female religious symbols became heretical.

The close relationship between religion and the law in terms of the roles and responsibilities of husband and wife is seen in the fourth selection, "The Traditional Marriage Contract" by Lenore Weitzman, et al. One of the consequences of the intertwining of the legal and the religious is the difficulty that the Equal Rights Amendment (the "ERA") has faced. Sonia Johnson describes her experiences as a devout Mormon who supported the Equal Rights Amendment, in the article "The Woman Who Talked Back to God—And Didn't Get Zapped."

The Woman's Bible

**Elizabeth Cady Stanton
and the Revising Committee**

Introduction

From the inauguration of the movement for woman's emancipation the Bible has been used to hold her in the "divinely ordained sphere," prescribed in the Old and New Testaments.

The canon and civil law; church and state; priests and legislators; all political parties and religious denominations have alike taught that woman was made after man, of man, and for man, an inferior being, subject to man. Creeds, codes, Scriptures and statutes, are all based on this idea. The fashions, forms, ceremonies and customs of society, church ordinances and discipline all grow out of this idea.

Of the old English common law, responsible for woman's civil and political status, Lord Brougham said, "it is a disgrace to the civilization and Christianity of the Nineteenth Century." Of the canon law, which is responsible for woman's status in the church, Charles Kingsley said, "this will never be a good world for women until the last remnant of the canon law is swept from the face of the earth."

The Bible teaches that woman brought sin and death into the world, that she precipitated the fall of the race, that she was arraigned before the judgment seat of Heaven, tried, condemned and sentenced. Marriage for her was to be a condition of bondage, maternity a period of suffering and anguish, and in silence and subjection, she was to play the role of a dependent on man's bounty for all her material wants, and for all the information she might desire on the vital questions of the hour, she was commanded to ask her husband at home. Here is the Bible position of woman briefly summed up.

Those who have the divine insight to translate, transpose and transfigure this mournful object of pity into an exalted, dignified personage, worthy our worship as the mother of the race, are to be congratulated as having a share of the occult mystic power of the eastern Mahatmas.

The plain English to the ordinary mind admits of no such liberal interpretation. The unvarnished texts speak for themselves. The canon law, church ordinances and Scriptures, are homogeneous, and all reflect the same spirit and sentiments.

These familiar texts are quoted by clergymen in their pulpits, by statesmen in the halls of legislation, by lawyers in the courts, and are echoed by the press of all civilized nations, and accepted by woman herself as "The Word of God." So perverted is the religious element in her nature, that with faith and works she is the chief support of the church and clergy; the very powers that make her emancipation impossible. When, in the early part of the Nineteenth Century, women began to protest against their civil and political degradation, they were referred to the Bible for an answer. When they protested against their unequal position in the church, they were referred to the Bible for an answer.

This led to a general and critical study of the Scriptures. Some, having made a fetish of these books and believing them to be the veritable "Word of God," with liberal translations, interpretations, allegories and symbols, glossed over the most objectionable features of the various books and clung to them as divinely inspired. Others, seeing the family resemblance between the Mosaic code, the canon law, and the old English common law, came to the conclusion that all alike emanated from the same source; wholly human in their origin and inspired by the natural love of domination in the historians. Others, bewildered with their doubts and fears, came to no conclusion. While their clergymen told them on the one hand, that they owed all the blessings and freedom they enjoyed to the Bible, on the other, they said it clearly marked out their circumscribed sphere of action: that the demands for political and civil rights were irreligious, dangerous to the stability of the home, the state and the

Reprinted from Elizabeth Cady Stanton and the Revising Committee, "New Women's Bible: Introduction," in *The Woman's Bible* (Seattle, WA: Coalition on Women and Religion, 4759 15th Avenue), by permission of the publisher.

church. Clerical appeals were circulated from time to time conjuring members of their churches to take no part in the anti-slavery or woman suffrage movements, as they were infidel in their tendencies, undermining the very foundations of society. No wonder the majority of women stood still, and with bowed heads, accepted the situation.

Listening to the varied opinions of women, I have long thought it would be interesting and profitable to get them clearly stated in book form. To this end six years ago I proposed to a committee of women to issue a Woman's Bible, that we might have women's commentaries on women's position in the Old and New Testaments. It was agreed on by several leading women in England and America and the work was begun, but from various causes it has been delayed, until now the idea is received with renewed enthusiasm, and a large committee has been formed, and we hope to complete the work within a year.

The only points in which I differ from all ecclesiastical teaching is that I do not believe that any man ever saw or talked with God, I do not believe that God inspired the Mosaic code, or told the historians what they say he did about woman, for all the religions on the face of the earth degrade her, and so long as woman accepts the position that they assign her, her emancipation is impossible. Whatever the Bible may be made to do in Hebrew or Greek, in plain English it does not exalt and dignify woman. My standpoint for criticism is the revised edition of 1888. I will so far honor the revising committee of wise men who have given us the best exegesis they can according to their ability, although Disraeli said the last one before he died contained 150,000 blunders in the Hebrew, and 7,000 in the Greek.

But the verbal criticism in regard to woman's position amounts to little. The spirit is the same in all periods and languages, hostile to her as an equal.

There are some general principles in the holy books of all religions that teach love, charity, liberty, justice and equality for all the human family; there are many grand and beautiful passages, the golden rule has been echoed and re-echoed around the world. There are lofty examples of good and true men and women, all worthy our acceptance and imitation whose lustre cannot be dimmed by the false sentiments and vicious characters bound up in the same volume. The Bible cannot be accepted or rejected as a whole, its teachings are varied and its lessons differ widely from each other. In criticising the peccadilloes of Sarah, Rebecca and Rachel, we would not shadow the virtues of Deborah, Huldah and Vashti. In criticising the Mosaic code we would not question the wisdom of the golden rule and the fifth Commandment. Again the church claims special consecration for its cathedrals and priesthood, parts of these aristocratic churches are too holy for women to enter, boys were early introduced into the choirs for this reason, woman singing in an obscure corner closely veiled. A few of the more democratic denominations accord women some privileges, but invidious discriminations of sex are found in all religious organizations, and the most bitter outspoken enemies of woman are found among clergymen and bishops of the Protestant religion.*

The canon law, the Scriptures, the creeds and codes and church discipline of the leading religions bear the impress of fallible man, and not of our ideal great first cause, "the Spirit of all Good" that set the universe of matter and mind in motion, and by immutable law holds the land, the sea, the planets, revolving round the great centre of light and heat, each in its own elliptic, with millions of stars in harmony all singing together, the glory of creation forever and ever.

---

*See the address of Bishop Doane, June 7th, 1895, in the closing exercises of St. Agnes School, Albany.

Uncle Arthur's Bedtime Stories:
A Content Analysis of Sex-Stereotyping

Karen Schwartz

In 1928 Arthur S. Maxwell published his 10-volume *Uncle Arthur's Bedtime Stories.* Since then the books have been issued an additional eight times with the latest being in 1964. Through pictures and words, these stories teach young children Biblical values, but on a more subtle level, the books also depict the stereotypes taught to young boys and girls. In essence, the stories and illustrations have not changed since first publication in 1928. These books are still very popular today and are sold by religious bookstores and publishing houses. Order forms are also placed along with appropriate advertising, in pediatrician and children's dentists' offices. The influence of Uncle Arthur's stories has been widespread because the stories cross denominational lines and are endorsed and advertised by people of varied faiths. The stories are aimed at preschoolers and young elementary children.

I think it is time for the church to take a look at the stereotypes taught to young children brought up in religious backgrounds. For the purposes of this article, I have examined story titles, main characters, pictures and verbal content of Volumes One, Two, Three and Four.

A look at the content page gives the discerning reader the first clue to the contents within. In Volume One there are thirty-nine stories listed. Of these, eighteen titles refer specifically to either boys or girls, nine to boys and nine to girls; however, the titles themselves differentiate between boys and girls along sex-stereotypical lines. Compare "Wilfred's Secret" to "Dreamy Dora" and "Joe's Quarter" to "Little Miss 'Tisn't" or "How Tommy Opened the Windows of Heaven" to "Little Miss Grumblestone." Of the thirty-five titles listed in Volume Two, twelve refer specifically to boys and only five to girls. Again different gender connotations are presented. Compare "Two Brave Firemen" and "Jimmie to the Rescue" to "Jane's Pet" and "Amy's Gift." The first two titles imply excitement and ac-

tion while the latter titles are of a passive nature. Also compare "Two Lucky Boys" to "The Little Girl Who Went to Sleep." In Volume Four only six of the thirty-seven titles refer to males and four to females, but again differences are seen. Compare "Tom's Thoughtfulness" to "Mary's Sacrifice." Two of the titles mention parents but compare "How Lazy Laurie Became Mother's Helper" to "Daddy's Discovery." Although the majority of the titles in this volume are neutral referring either to animals or inanimate objects, those titles that refer specifically to the sexes tend to uphold positive qualities assigned to males and negative qualities to females.

In summary then, titles of stories in the volumes examined suggest that girls are inactive and possessed by undesirable traits, whereas boys are active and blessed with positive virtues.

The volumes comprising *Uncle Arthur's Bedtime Stories* contain many illustrations, which also convey stereotypes. For example, the inside front cover of each volume features children in different settings of play and work. Volume One shows children enjoying a summer day in the country. There are eighteen boys in the scene compared to only nine girls. The boys are engaged in active play, like swimming, walking on a fence, playing in a tree house, sailing a toy boat in the creek, and playing leap frog. The boys are all dressed in jeans and sports shirts. On the other hand, all the girls are wearing dresses and playing passively. Two girls are picking flowers and two others are watching a boy walk on top of a fence. One girl is swinging on a tree swing, and one is riding a horse but holding on to the waist of a boy straddled in front of her. The most active girl is chasing a butterfly, but the boy with her is using the net to catch the creature.

Volume Two shows children on a playground at school. Again, the girls are all attired in dresses and the boys are dressed in casual clothes for rough playing. In this scene, there are twenty-five boys shown and eighteen girls plus one female adult, probably the teacher. Eight of

Reprinted from Karen Schwartz, "Uncle Arthur's Bedtime Stories," by permission of the author.

the girls are standing on the playground watching the other children play. Five girls are jumping rope and the others are sliding down the slide and playing on the teeter-totter. The boys in comparison are running, playing soccer, baseball, leap frog, marbles, and several are wrestling.

In Volume Four, although the sex balance is more equal (10 girls, 11 boys), sex-stereotyping in clothing styles and kinds of activity persists. Boys are dressed casually; girls in dresses. The boys are shown swimming in a lake, painting birdhouses, building a model boat, mowing the lawn, assembling a kite, and building a soap-box racer and a dog house. The girls are shown playing the piano, sweeping the living room carpet, sewing doll dresses, making stuffed animals, painting flowers on a vase, and making an afghan. Pets are shown in these scenes, dogs with the boys and cats with the girls. Once again, the boys are shown in action-oriented tasks generally occurring out of doors while the girls are all shown engaged in indoor activities of a more passive, quiet nature. In brief, the illustrations are consistent with society's social expectations for boys and girls.

In addition to the cover leaf illustrations, each volume contains many illustrations for each story. Since each volume is similar in style and content, I shall provide a detailed analysis of only one, namely, Volume One. Looking at all the illustrations in that volume and counting how many boys and girls are depicted, there are one hundred boys shown and only forty-eight girls, or a ratio of 2:1. Again, the girls all wear dresses, even at play, and the boys are dressed in more rugged clothes. The behaviors depicted are also indicative of sex role stereotypes. Girls are seen setting the table, playing with dolls, sneakily stealing a bite of a forbidden cake, writing letters, asking help from a policeman, and crying. Boys, on the other hand, are shown playing with trucks, cars, and balls, running, looking for treasure, helping girls, raking leaves, and finding constellations in the sky. Mothers are shown shopping, cooking and caring for children. Fathers are shown fighting fires, disciplining children, working on a ship, and reading the paper in an easy chair. Like the titles of the stories, the illustrations continue to show boys displaying more activity, and activity which is more highly valued in society.

Perhaps, it can be argued that although the story titles and illustrations are sex-stereotyped, the actual stories are not. To explore this question, I analyzed the story lines based on sex of major character, and then, the content of the stories.

Using Volume Two, I found that of the thirty-five stories contained in it, boys were the main characters in twenty-four of the stories and girls in only eleven of the stories. Story lines differed for the main characters by sex. One little girl had to be saved from drowning by a dog. Another girl was grumbly and disobedient and had to learn to be different. Another girl gave her best doll to a less fortunate girl. In contrast, one boy and his father built a model plane together. Two other boys put out a grass fire while another boy saved his sister by throwing water on her burning dress. Another boy learned not to be a "crybaby" and instead became mother's helper and was rewarded with a little car for him to ride in. Another boy saved a little girl from drowning in a stormy lake. Again, the story lines for boys depicted action; unacceptable behavior for boys, like crying, was soon eliminated and rewarded with a masculine prize—a car. The stories concerning girls dealt more with maintaining positive relationships with others than with action. The lessons girls learned were how to be caring for others, like mothers care for children.

The actual content of stories in Volume Four was examined to determine what stereotypes were being advanced in the text of the stories. In general, the purpose of the stories is to teach morals, such as honesty, kindness, love, forgiveness, obedience and love for God. Each story was read to see if phrases and contexts stereotyped boys and girls. A few examples are illustrative of the stereotyping within those stories.

"Teresina" opens with two girls mending doll clothes. The conversation is as follows:

"Oh, this wretched needle!" exclaimed Dorothy. "It simply won't thread."

"Never mind," said Sylvia, sewing away gaily, "think of Christmas, when all the dresses will be finished, and we can take Marguerita and Roxana out in their new carriage."[1]

In "A Little Child Shall Lead Them," a little girl is upset at her mother for burning an old Christmas card she wanted to keep. Her brother, who is two years older, takes on the job of teaching his sister not to disobey mother. The conversation is as follows:

"Margaret," said Donald, "you must be a good girl and go fast asleep."

---

1. Arthur S. Maxwell, "Teresina," in *Uncle Arthur's Bedtime Stories.* Vol. 4. (Washington, D.C.: Review and Herald Publishing Association, 1964), p. 9.

"I can't go to sleep," said Margaret. "I've been so naughty, and I don't want Mamma to spank me any more."

"Yes, dearie," said Donald, with sympathy and wisdom beyond his years, "you have been very naughty, and it made me feel so sad and ill inside, . . ."[2]

In this story, as in others, the boy imparts some of his wisdom to the erring female.

"Rosalind's Medicine" tells about a girl who lives with her parents on a mission station in Africa. In order to lessen the severity of malaria, she has to take quinine, a bitter-tasting medicine. The following takes place between the little girl and her mother:

. . . Rosalind did not want the quinine. She disliked it so much she thought she would rather have the malaria than take the horrid stuff.

Mother begged and implored her to take it, but in vain. You know the scene that so often takes place when a little girl is asked to take some nasty

medicine! *Well, that is just what happened then. Rosalind was obstinate.*[3]

In general, the text of the stories, like the titles, pictures and main characters, show little girls displaying behaviors and attitudes less valued by society. There are exceptions when little boys display wrong behavior and have to be shown the error of their ways, but it is more apt to be a girl than a boy.

I realize that these stories were written in 1928 when few questioned the ways girls and boys were depicted in stories. I also realize that the stories are used primarily to teach morals. But I question the way the morals are taught by favoring boys over girls. There is no equality or equity in these stories. Since subtle teachings are often more potent than overt teaching, the underlying meanings of these stories are forcefully passed on to young children both in words and pictures. Fifty-one years later, these stories are still highly valued by religious educators. I think it is time for the church to examine all the principles taught to children, overt as well as subtle teachings. I think it is time to write new stories: Aunt Sojourner's Bedtime Stories.

---

2. Arthur S. Maxwell, "A Little Child Shall Lead Them," op cit., p. 22.

3. Arthur S. Maxwell, "Rosalind's Medicine," p. 64.

Heretics and Outsiders: The Struggle Over Female Power in Western Religion

Carol P. Christ

I approach this topic as one who views herself as an outsider to the canons and traditions of the West. It is no secret that the "great works" of the Western tradition are written from a male-centered perspective in which the experiences specific to women are ignored, suppressed, or treated only in relation to the interests of men.

The *Iliad* is a case in point. Its major dramatic conflict between Achilles and Agamemnon generates Achilles' "metaphysical dilemma" of whether to seek honor and live a short but glorious life, or to refuse honor and live long but unmemorably. Critics rarely note that both the dramatic conflict and the metaphysical dilemma are generated by an argument between two men over one of the most precious spoils of war, the "spear captive" Briseis. Briseis is a raped woman, a victim of the wars of men, yet her tragedy is treated simply as the occasion for the conflicts of men. How can I find myself in such a tradition without losing my identity as a woman?

This sense of myself as outsider has led me to question many conventional pieties about canons and traditions, particularly the largely unexamined premise that the so-called "great works" have become central and authoritative primarily because they express the struggles and aspirations of humanity in a compelling and beautiful way.

Biblical scholar James Sanders, for example, expresses such a view when he says that his book *Torah and Canon* is a "quest *for the essence of the power of life the Bible demonstrably has.* This power is evident not only in the Bible's remarkable survival for over 2,500 years," he writes, "but in its function as the vehicle of survival to the communities whose identities and life-styles issue from

their adherence to it."[1] Sanders apparently assumes that canonical works survive because of an intrinsic vision which commends itself to the hearts and minds of communities. Certainly the Bible has had a compelling power for some in the West; I only note that this view is deceptively one-sided. Sanders does not ask to what extent the survival of the Bible might also be due to political struggles, including slander and repression of rival traditions. Nor does he ask for whom Biblical tradition is a power of life, and for whom, perhaps, a power of death.

It is precisely this mundane question which I wish to address here. My first point is simple, obvious, and often overlooked: *the existence of a canon or a canonical tradition implies the existence of outsiders and heretics.* Now the consequences of being outside a canonical tradition (in the West at least) are as follows: texts outside the canon are slandered, often suppressed, sometimes destroyed; groups existing outside canonical authority are often declared heretical; adherents of heretical groups are often persecuted, sometimes killed.

My second point is an hypothesis which I will explore through the discussion of three historic struggles between the proponents of the traditions which became canonical and those whom they declared to be outsiders and heretics. This hypothesis is as follows: myths suppressed by the canonical tradition often contained powerful female symbolism; the texts or traditions transmitting this symbolism may often have had a special appeal for women because they offered greater opportunities for the expression of female power; and the persons persecuted by the canonical tradition may have been disproportionately female.

I will explore this hypothesis by examining some intriguing evidence concerning the struggles between the

Reprinted from Carol P. Christ, "Heretics and Outsiders: The Struggle Over Female Power in Western Religion," in *Soundings*, vol. 61, no. 3, by permission of the publisher and the author.

1. (Philadelphia: Fortress Press, 1974), x.

proponents of views which became canonical and persons whom they identified as outsiders and heretics. Instances of such struggles will be drawn from ancient Hebrew religion, early Christianity, and the middle Christian period. The juxtaposition of these three periods presents a disturbing pattern of suppression of female symbolism and power by the traditions which became canonical in the West.

I do not wish to belabor the feminist criticism of Western religion as male-centered in its specific teachings on the place of women in family, church, and society, and in its core symbolism of divinity. Rather, I wish to examine the apologetic argument which states that the male symbolisms and hierarchies of the Jewish and Christian religions were a spontaneous and natural development given their historical contexts. I will argue to the contrary that the Jewish and Christian traditions were not passive with regard to their environments. At crucial points proponents of the canonical traditions engaged in ideological struggles with competing religious traditions in the course of which female symbolism and female power were actively suppressed.

The historical arguments which I make here are more difficult to document than the familiar charges of sexism in Western religion. Because histories of Western religion do not usually ask how Western religion came to be male-centered, there is no body of secondary scholarship to which to appeal. Moreover, the practitioners of defeated religious traditions have been slandered as idol worshippers, whores, and worse in the official texts of the canonical tradition, and few scholars have been willing to challenge this official view. Finally, the texts of competing religious traditions were often destroyed by the canonical groups, for example, in the burning of the library at Alexandria and the book burnings of the middle Christian period. Because the evidence on which a clear picture of the outsiders and heretics in Western tradition could be constructed is too often nonexistent or not adequately interpreted by scholarship, the argument of this paper will have to be somewhat more hypothetical than I could wish.

The interest of non-canonical groups in female power and female symbols is no longer hypothetical in the contemporary period, however. In the traditions being developed by some of today's most conspicuous outsiders and heretics, the women in the women's spirituality movement and the feminist witches, there is a resurgence of interest in female power and female symbolism. In a final section of this paper I will briefly discuss this new development in contemporary religious consciousness,

particularly as it bears on the relation of canon and anti-canon.

The Suppression of the Goddess in Ancient Hebrew Religion

According to a widely held view, the official religion of ancient Israel was largely a monotheistic worship of one God, Yahweh. The Hebrew people held to their monotheistic tradition against the temptations presented by the polytheistic traditions of neighboring peoples, because monotheism was ethically and religiously superior to polytheism. Only rarely did the people of Israel succumb to polytheistic practices, referred to as "Baalism," "fetishism" (often synonymous with goddess worship), and "cult prostitution." The prophets criticized these "excesses" and "aberrations" of faith and returned the people to monotheism. Recent scholarship and archaeological discoveries have challenged this interpretive paradigm. Scholars have discovered that the religion of the Hebrew people was more pluralistic than the monotheistic paradigm indicates, and that the religion of the Canaanites was not mere fetishism and idolatry. Nonetheless the paradigm of a dominant Yahwistic monotheism remains a major interpretive scheme through which the history of Biblical religion is taught.[2]

---

2. Bernard W. Anderson's widely used text, *Understanding the Old Testament,* Second Edition (Englewood Cliffs: Prentice Hall, Inc., 1966) typifies the problem created when the new evidence about Canaanite religion is discussed within the old paradigm of dominant monotheism. Anderson takes account of the latest historical and archeological evidence. However, the narrative structure of *Understanding the Old Testament* follows the Yahwistic narrative line, from exodus covenant with Yahweh at Sinai (chs. 1 and 2) to struggle between faith and culture (ch. 4) to prophetic criticism (ch. 7) to renewal of covenant (chs. 12–14), etc. Within the chapter on Canaanite religion, Anderson improves on previous scholarship, "In many respects, this (the religion portrayed in the Ras Shamra texts) was a highly developed, sophisticated religion, far ahead of the belief in local fertility spirits which scholars once thought to have been (104)." Yet Anderson's discussion of Canaanite religion is set within a chapter in which the narrative line stresses "the great dangers and temptations of life in Canaan" (100), a Yahwistic interpretation which Anderson adopts without acknowledging that he is presenting a Yahwistic viewpoint which may have been a minority opinion in Israel at the time of settlement in Canaan. A work on the religion of the Hebrew people not biased by the Yahwistic viewpoint would not speak of Canaanite religion as a "temptation," but rather as a plausible "solution" to the problems engendered by the settlement.

In his book, *Palestinian Parties and Politics Which Shaped the Old Testament,*[3] Morton Smith questioned the standard paradigm of biblical religion. He argued that widespread adherence to monotheism in ancient Israel was a fiction created by ultimately victorious "Yahweh alone" groups which established control of Israelite religion after the Babylonian exile. These "Yahweh alone" groups edited and rewrote the texts which became the biblical canon to make them conform to their view that the worship of Yahweh alone was the true religion of ancient Israel and Judah from the beginning and that worship of gods and goddesses other than Yahweh constituted heretical deviation. According to Smith the dominant groups in ancient Israel and Judah were polytheistic, worshipping several gods and goddesses, including Baal, Anath, Asherah, El, and others, alongside Yahweh. The defining characteristic of ancient Hebrew religion was worship of Yahweh, but not worship of Yahweh only.

Mythologist Raphael Patai's work, *The Hebrew Goddess,*[4] complements Smith's work. Patai also argues that goddess worship was prevalent in the official religions of ancient Israel and Judah. He cites the books of I and II Kings as one record of struggles between worshippers of Yahweh and worshippers of other gods and goddesses. Though these books were edited to slander the worshippers of gods and goddesses other than Yahweh as followers after "abomination," they acknowledge the widespread occurrence of polytheism and goddess worship in the biblical period, not only among the populace, but in the official state cults. According to Patai's count the goddess Asherah was worshipped in the temple of Solomon in Jerusalem for 236 of its 370 years of existence. In the Northern Kingdom Asherah was consistently worshipped in the capital city of Samaria from the time of Jezebel. Even if these precise figures are rendered problematic by the recognition that they may be the product of partisan editorship, as Smith suggests they are, the general picture of polytheistic worship in both kingdoms must be accepted. This picture is further supported by the discovery of female figures in archaeological digs at sites connected with worship in ancient Israel and Judah.

Based on the evidence brought forth by Smith and Patai, we might reverse the conventional notion of ancient Hebrew religion, and speak instead of a dominant tradition of polytheism and goddess worship in the official

cult, which was broken only occasionally by the victories of Yahweh alone groups.

It should be stressed that the struggles between the Yahweh alone groups and the others were not mere ideological battles. They were political struggles in which force was often used. Exodus records that the Levites ordained themselves for the service of Yahweh by murdering 3000 worshippers of the golden calf (Exodus 32:25–29).[5] After Elijah's victory over Elisha 450 prophets of Baal were killed (I Kings 18:40).[6] Jehu killed the worshippers of Baal in the house of Baal in order to solidify his ascension to the throne following the slaying of Jezebel (II Kings 10:18–30).

Clearly the struggles between the Yahweh alone groups and the other groups were not simple struggles between women worshippers of the goddess and men worshippers of Yahweh. Men and women were involved in both the worship of Yahweh and the worship of gods and goddesses other than Yahweh. And the polytheistic groups were not exclusively devoted to the goddess. Still we may note that one consequence of the suppression of polytheism by the Yahweh alone groups was the elimination of goddess worship. And we may ask whether women may have been particularly attracted to the worship of the goddess as an expression of female power. There is some evidence to suggest that this may have been the case.

In the books of I and II Kings and I and II Chronicles the worship of the goddess in the cult sites is often blamed on the influence of foreign queens, wives of the kings. Jezebel is the most notorious example. Now it is possible that the queens worshipped the goddess because they were foreign, not because they were women. And it is also possible, though unlikely, that the misogynist biblical editors attributed everything they considered evil to the influence of women, but that women were not in fact central figures in the institution and defense of goddess worship. Nonetheless it is intriguing to speculate that foreign

---

3. (New York: Columbia University Press, 1971).

4. (New York: KTAV, 1967). See especially pp. 42–43, 50, 58–61.

---

5. The "J" or Yahwistic source in Exodus, which records the political-religious murders of the worshippers of the golden calf in the pre-settlement period, may not be historically reliable. Still it reflects a pattern of murder of opponents of Yahwism which the "J" editors wished to legitimate by reading it back into the pre-settlement period.

6. The precise figures may not be historical but the pattern of suppression of competing religious groups through murder probably is. Also note that I Kings 18:19 mentions that Elijah called 450 prophets of Baal and 400 prophets of Asherah, but the test is waged only with the prophets of Baal for some reason that the text leaves unexplained.

and native women, like the queens of Israel and Judah, were attracted to the worship of the goddess as a symbol for female power. The murder of Jezebel (II Kings 9:30–37) would then have been a political attack on the religion of the goddess.[7] And the prohibitions at the time of the second Temple against Israelite men taking foreign wives would have been part of an attempt finally to suppress goddess worship and polytheism since women who had been reared in goddess worshipping traditions would not easily give up the symbol of female power.

The book of Jeremiah offers further evidence in support of the view that women were especially devoted to the goddess. In Jeremiah the following words are put in the mouth of "all the people":

As for the word that you have spoken to us in the name of Yahweh—we shall not listen to you. But we shall do everything as we said: we shall burn incense to the Queen of Heaven, and shall pour her libations as we used to do, we, our fathers, our kings, and our princes, in the cities of Judah and in the streets of Jerusalem. For then we had plenty of food, and we all were well and saw no evil.

To these words the women added:

Is it we alone who burn incense to the Queen of Heaven and pour her libations? Is it without our husbands that we make her cakes in her image and that we pour her libations? (44:15–17)

Though the passage indicates that all the people participated in the worship of the Queen of Heaven, it also suggests that women performed many of the acts related to the cult and that women may have been viewed as the instigators or special devotees of goddess worship.

Women's attraction to goddess worship may not have been only a symbolic preference. In *When God Was A Woman* Merlin Stone brings together a great deal of evidence in support of her view that the status of women was higher in matrilineal goddess worshipping cultures than it was in patrilineal Israel and Judah. In Egypt the woman was often head of the family, while in Babylon the wife could acquire property, take legal action and make contracts.[8] In Israel and Judah these rights were curtailed.

These lines of evidence point to the conclusion that the Bible was shaped by politically victorious Yahweh alone groups whose victory had the effect (if not the intent) of slandering and prohibiting goddess worship, declaring the religious inclinations of many women to be outside the tradition and depriving women of many of the rights which they had had in goddess worshipping cultures. If this conclusion is correct, then we must ask whose "power of life" the Biblical tradition expressed, and we must entertain the conclusion that it was not women's.

Suppression of the Gnostic "Heretics"

The victory of Christianity signaled the suppression of goddess worship in the ancient world. The temples of the goddess at Aphaca, Eleusis, Rome, Ephesus, Athens, and elsewhere were forcibly closed in the fourth and fifth centuries C.E. This was the end of public goddess worship in the Christian West. However, it is not the struggle between Christianity and other religions over female symbolism and female power which I wish to consider here. Rather I wish to consider a suppression of female symbolism and power which occurred *within* the Christian tradition in the struggles which led to the formation of the Christian canon.

A study of the religion of the gnostic Christians suggests that the question of female symbolism and power was also a significant factor in their struggle with those who became orthodox Christians. In fact, if we are to believe the recent Vatican declaration denying the priesthood to women, the ordination of women by the gnostics was one of the reasons the orthodox church suppressed them. "A few heretical sects in the first century, especially Gnostic ones, entrusted the priestly ministry to women," the Vatican statement reports, and "this innovation was immediately noted and condemned by the fathers."[9]

A common paradigm used to interpret early Christian history assumes that the early Christian communities which grew up after the death of Jesus were founded by Peter and Paul and the other male disciples, and that there was a fairly smooth transition between these groups and the early orthodox Church. If they are mentioned at all, the gnostics are viewed as libertine heretics who denied the central Christian doctrine of the unity of the

---

7. See Merlin Stone, *When God Was A Woman* (New York: The Dial Press, 1976), 57–58.
8. Ibid., esp. 30–61, and Roland de Vaux, *Ancient Israel*, Vol. I, *Social Institutions* (New York: McGraw-Hill Book Company, 1965), 39–40.

---

9. "Excerpts from Vatican's Declaration Affirming Prohibition on Women Priests," *New York Times* (January 28, 1977), 8.

spirit and the flesh, and whose factionalizing influence was rightly suppressed by the Church Fathers. So widespread is this view, that "gnosticism" has become a pejorative theological shorthand for any antinomian spiritualizing tendency.

As recent discoveries of gnostic gospels have proved, this conventional view is more polemical than factual. Early Christianity seems to have been far more plural than is generally recognized. Both the gnostic Christians and those groups which later declared themselves orthodox and canonical had their own gospels and claimed to be followers of the religion of Jesus Christ. Only after political struggles did some groups emerge victorious and declare the others heretical.

Elaine Pagels' recent study[10] offers convincing evidence that the gnostic Christian groups provided more avenues for the expression of female symbolism and female power than did their orthodox Christian opponents. Gnostic Christian groups, as Pagels describes them, abounded in female imagery of God. The Valentinians, for example, imaged the divine as a Dyad consisting of two elements, on the one hand, the Ineffable, the Source, the Primal Father, and on the other, the Silence, the Mother of All Things. Other gnostics viewed the Holy Spirit as a divine Mother, and still others characterized the female element in God as the Holy Wisdom, following Hebrew traditions of Wisdom as the companion of God.

Were the gnostics declared heretical primarily because they employed female symbolism? Pagels rejects this conclusion as simplistic. However, among the "scandals" the victorious Christian groups claimed to find in the heretics, she notes the often repeated charge that they allowed women authority in their communities. Gnostic works like the *Gospel of Mary* provide further evidence of a political struggle between female and male disciples of Jesus over the issue of female leadership. In the *Gospel of Mary,* Peter objects to Mary's claim to have received a special revelation from Jesus and he is rebuked by Levi who says, "Peter you are always irascible. You object to the women as our enemies do. Surely the Lord knew her very well, and indeed loved her more than us. . . ." Mary is then allowed to speak with authority of the revelation Jesus entrusted to her.[11]

From this evidence Pagels concludes that, whether or not it was the primary cause, one of the effects of the condemnation of the gnostics by the canonical tradition was that female symbolism and leadership were suppressed.

This evidence from the early Christian era suggests that the suppression of female symbolism and power was one of the results of the political struggles which led to the establishment of the Christian canon, a pattern similar to that which seems to have occurred in the establishment of the Hebrew canon. Again we must ask whose "power of life" the victorious tradition reflected. Perhaps women found themselves better represented by the traditions which were declared heretical.

Witch Persecution in the Middle Christian Period

The story of the suppression of female symbolism and female power by the canonical traditions of the West could be continued through a discussion of other "heretical" movements which surfaced within Christianity.[12] But I will instead focus on a conflict between the tradition and the outsiders in which the suppression of female power was carried out in particularly violent fashion, the witch persecution of the middle Christian period.

As with the goddess worshippers and the gnostics, the canonical view of the witches has impeded unbiased treatment of their practices and beliefs. It is commonly thought that witches worshipped the devil in bizarre rites in which children were sacrificed and that participants engaged in perverse sexual practices.

This view is the product of Christian polemic such as that found in *The Malleus Maleficarum,* but it has also influenced two standard paradigms used in scholarship concerning witchcraft. On the one side the "ultraconservative" scholars accept the charges of the

---

10. "What Became of God the Mother? Conflicting Images of God in Early Christianity," *Signs,* 2/2 (Winter, 1976), 293–303, esp. 295, 299, 300–301.
11. Ibid., 300–301.

---

12. Gnosticism is not the only heretical movement which provided greater outlets for female power than canonical tradition. Elisabeth Schüssler Fiorenza notes that women had authority and leading positions in Montanism, Gnosticism, Manichaeism, Donatism, Priscillianism, Messalianism, and Pelagianism, and that they were found among the bishops and priests of the Quintillians, "Feminist Theology as a Critical Theology of Liberation," *Theological Studies,* 36/4 (December, 1975), 618. See also Robert E. Lerner, *The Heresy of the Free Spirit in the Later Middle Ages* (University of California Press, 1972), 228–30, and Gottfried Koch, *Frauenfrage und Ketzertum im Mittelalter* (Berlin, 1962), both cited by Anne Driver in "Materials Not Included in the Canon of Religious Studies: A Neolithic Goddess Cult," 6 (unpublished).

persecutors that witchcraft was an anti-Christian rite inspired by the devil. On the other side the "liberal rationalists" view witchcraft as the creation of the witch persecutors and deny the historic reality of witch practice.[13] A third and different view is reflected in the much disputed hypothesis of Margaret Murray that witchcraft was a survival of the pagan religions of Western Europe. Murray's work has been widely challenged by scholars but her general theory has recently been defended by Mircea Eliade, a leading historian of religions.

Unfortunately less is known about witch practice and belief than about the religions of the goddess worshippers and the gnostics. After the forced closing of their temples and the suppression of their priesthoods and priestesshoods in the early Christian period, European pagan traditions survived only in folk custom and in secret societies, and were communicated orally. The major written documents concerning witch practice and belief are the trial documents, and writings and decrees of Christian theologians and Church councils, which are biased. Thus the picture of witchcraft presented here will have to be somewhat hypothetical.

Though scholars disagree about what witchcraft was, except for the ultraconservatives, they agree that many of the charges against the witches were fabricated by their persecutors. It is further agreed by all that large numbers of people were killed as witches between the years 1400 and 1700 as a result of persecutions carried out in the name of the Catholic and Protestant faiths. Estimates of the numbers killed range from 100,000 to 9,000,000 or more, with some scholars settling on 1,000,000 as a reasonably *conservative* estimate,[14] staggering numbers considering the smaller population of Europe at the time. Though scholars are also agreed that women figured disproportionately among those persecuted as witches, few have asked why this was so.[15]

Often portrayed as resulting from peasant hysteria, the witch persecutions were in fact instigated by an educated elite who saw themselves as defenders of canonical tradition. In 1484 Pope Innocent issued a bull[16] which made official the Church's intention to persecute witches. Two Dominican theologians, Heinrich Kramer and James Sprenger were the authors of *The Malleus Maleficarum,*[17] which became the classic text for witch "hammering." Kramer and Sprenger argue that women are more attracted to witchcraft than men, providing arguments from scripture and tradition to support their view. In answer to the question, "Why is it that women are chiefly addicted to evil superstitions?" they assert that women are more credulous and light-minded, more impressionable, and more given to gossip than men. But the most compelling reason "is that a woman is more carnal than a man, as is clear from her many carnal abominations." Or as they sum it up, "All witchcraft comes from carnal lust which in women is insatiable."[18] The crimes of the witches which Kramer and Sprenger find most objectionable are related to women's alleged sexual nature, including copulating with devils, obstructing the act of generation, making the male organ disappear, and offering newborn children to the devil. Other crimes Sprenger and Kramer allege against witches can be interpreted as species of folk magic, folk medicine, and folk psychology, including methods of preventing conception, procuring abortion, harming animals or crops, producing hail, and predicting the future through a variety of means.

The preoccupation of Sprenger and Kramer with crimes relating to female sexuality, female control over the birth process, and male impotence suggest that the witch persecutions were an attempt to suppress a form of female power which was threatening to the male authorities of church and state.

The question is, what sort of female power did witchcraft represent? Was it simply female sexuality which threatened the witch persecutors, or was witchcraft a competing religious system in which female symbolism and female power were recognized to a greater extent than they were in Christianity? A conclusive answer to this question cannot be obtained at present, but a number of lines of evidence suggest that the witch persecutions may fit into the pattern of suppression of female symbolism and female power which was hypothesized for the periods in which the Hebrew and Christian canons were formed.

---

13. Mircea Eliade divides scholarship on witchcraft into the two groups discussed here. See his "Some Observations on European Witchcraft," *History of Religions,* 14/3 (February, 1975), 150–51. He notes that the ultraconservative view is also held by some modern occultists and Luciferians.

14. Rosemary Ruether, *New Woman/New Earth: Sexist Ideologies and Human Liberation* (New York: Seabury Press, 1975), 111.

15. See, e.g., Margaret Murray, *The Witch-Cult in Western Europe* (Oxford: Oxford University Press, 1971), 255–70, and Ruether, 89.

16. See Heinrich Kramer and James Sprenger, *The Malleus Maleficarum,* translated with an introduction and notes by Montague Summers (New York: Dover Publications, 1971), xliii–xlv.

17. Ibid., esp. 41, 44, 47, 54–61, 66, 80–82, 144–50.

18. Ibid., 44, 47.

Two recent feminist interpretations, which fall into the liberal-rationalist camp, offer intriguing interpretations of the nature of the female power which was suppressed. Barbara Ehrenreich and Dierdre English in their study, *Witches, Nurses, and Midwives,*[19] suggest that many of those persecuted as witches were country doctors, midwives, and herbalists, women who delivered babies, cured the sick, and of course had patients who died. Ehrenreich and English argue that women healers were persecuted because their power over life and death challenged the Church's claim that God and his male deputies, the priests, held all power over life and death. This hypothesis is supported by those portions of the *Malleus* which specifically accuse midwives of using witchcraft to control conception and produce abortion.

In "Why Witches Were Women"[20] Mary Nelson proposes a plausible explanation of some of the more scandalous charges against the witches. The common allegation that witches took away men's generative powers, killed infants, and publicly indulged their sexual lust were projections, she believes, of men's fear of a type of female power which had some basis in social reality. According to Nelson, the years of witch persecution were periods of massive social displacement and poverty, bringing about increases in the numbers of prostitutes (women who publicly indulged sexual lust) and making it necessary to limit family size. Moreover, the most common methods of birth control may have been *coitus interruptus* (women who took away men's generative power) and infanticide of female babies (women who killed infants). Poor women's only ways of surviving the poverty produced by social disruption may have led to their persecution.

In 1921 Margaret Murray[21] challenged both the Christian and the rationalist views of witchcraft and proposed the then startling thesis that witchcraft was a pagan religion and that the persecution of witches was part of a religious war. While many of the details of Murray's view of witch religion have been challenged, her basic hypothesis that witchcraft was a pagan survival has been supported by such scholars of religion as Mircea Eliade[22] and Rosemary Ruether.

Briefly, Murray's hypothesis, deduced from coherences she discovered in the testimony given at witch trials, is that witchcraft in Western Europe was an organized religion with a fairly uniform set of symbols, rituals and social structures. The witches worshipped a deity who could be incarnate as a male figure (Janus or Dianus), a female figure (Diana), or an animal. The deity personified natural energy and was associated with fertility. Witches met in covens of thirteen and their major celebrations were on May Eve and November Eve. Women had access to leadership positions in the covens.

Rosemary Ruether[23] disputes Murray's theory that witchcraft was an organized religion at the time of the persecutions. She believes that Christianity had already succeeded in destroying the official cults and priesthoods or priestesshoods of pagan religions by the middle Christian period. What survived, Ruether believes, was folk religion, that stratum of religion which belongs to village daily life, the rituals of home and farming life which people carry on by themselves. It included group celebrations such as dances and festivals at planting and harvest times, folk magic, and folk superstition. Ruether believes that women were the primary cultivators of folk magic, or the use of charms, spells, and herbal remedies for curing. According to Ruether, those persecuted as witches were female charismatics, inheritors of traditions of folk religion and the powers derived from it.

In my opinion the theories of witches as midwives and healers should not be set over against the theories of witches as inheritors and transmitters of folk religion, for in these traditions, religion, medicine, and magic probably were not clearly distinguished. If the more spectacular charges of the witch persecutors (copulation with the devil, sacrifice of children) are discounted, a remarkably coherent picture of the practices of the witches can be suggested. Witches were wise and powerful women, practitioners of folk religion, magic, and medicine, whose knowledge of charms, spells, and herbal lore brought them to the bedside at times of birth, illness, and death. The wise woman was summoned at the crises of the life cycle *before* the priest; she delivered the baby, while the priest was called upon later to perform baptism. She was the first to be called upon to cure illness or treat the dying, while the priest was called in after all other remedies had failed, to administer the last rites. Moreover, if the wise woman had knowledge of herbs which could aid or prevent conception or cause abortion, she had a power over

19. *A History of Women Healers,* Second Edition (Old Westbury: The Feminist Press; 1973).
20. Published in Jo Freeman, ed., *Women: A Feminist Perspective* (Palo Alto: Mayfield Publishing Company, 1975), 335-50.
21. *The Witch-Cult in Western Europe,* op.cit.
22. Eliade, op.cit. Eliade discusses evidence which shows how pagan religious groups gradually came to incorporate practices alleged of them by their persecutors.

23. *New Woman/New Earth,* 89-114.

the life process which clearly was superior to that of the priest, and which according to official theology made her a rival of God himself. If, moreover, she appealed to pagan deities, some of them probably female, in the performance of divinations or blessings and spells used to promote healing and ward off evil, then it is not difficult to see why she was persecuted by an insecure and misogynist Church which could not tolerate rival power, especially the power of women.

Though the evidence concerning witchcraft is inconclusive due to the lack of direct verification from the free testimony or written texts of witches, the lines of evidence cited here suggest that witch persecution followed the pattern of suppression of female symbolism and female power which seems to have occurred in the formative periods of the Hebrew and Christian traditions.

A Methodological Note

This examination of three instances of conflict between the proponents of traditions which were or became canonical and the outsiders or heretics suggests that one of the issues at stake in the definition and defense of canonical tradition in the West was the suppression of female symbolism and power.

Given the persistence of this pattern in the history of the Western tradition, we must ask why scholarship has not been more vigorous in exploring it. The answer to this question seems to be that even the so-called objective traditions of scholarship in the university are not entirely free from certain biases of the canonical tradition. Specifically, the scholarly tradition has largely accepted three canonical views: (1) the ethical and religious superiority of monotheism to polytheism; (2) the inferiority of religious traditions in which sexuality and fertility are central concerns, and the equation of female symbolism with sexuality and fertility; and (3) the importance of maintaining order, and the interpretation of challenges to authorities as antinomian and therefore bad. In addition the androcentrism of the scholarly tradition, which renders questions about women, female power, or female symbolism trivial and uninteresting because it accepts the subordinate status of women as a given, has blinded scholars to the fascinating history of the suppression of female power and symbolism by the traditions they study. But since an examination of androcentric and other biases in the *scholarly* tradition[24] could form the subject of another paper, I will not pursue it here.

---

24. See Rita Gross, "Methodological Remarks on the Study of Women and Religion: Review, Criticism, and Redefinition," in Judith Plaskow and Joan Arnold Romero, eds., *Women and Religion,* Revised Edition (Missoula, Montana: AAR and Scholars' Press, 1974), 153–65; also see Valerie Saiving, "Androcentrism in Religious Studies," *Journal of Religion,* 56/2 (April, 1976), 177–96.

The Traditional Marriage Contract

Lenore J. Weitzman, Carol M. Dixon, Joyce Adair Bird, Neil McGinn, Dena M. Robertson

Although they may not realize it (and they may not like it), when two people marry they are legally committing themselves to a series of duties, rights, and obligations imposed by law (Weitzman, 1974). This "marriage contract" is unlike most contracts people enter: its provisions are unwritten, its penalties are unspecified, and the terms of the contract are typically unknown to the "contracting" parties. While its provisions will be enforced by the courts, no state gives the parties the opportunity to read the terms of their marriage contract, nor does any state ask them if they are willing to assume the duties, rights, and obligations it specifies. Nor are the parties allowed to modify the provisions of the contract, or to substitute alternate but mutually acceptable provisions. It is simply assumed that everyone who gets married will want to (or will have to) abide by the state-imposed contract known as legal marriage.

What are the obligations of traditional legal marriage? While the details vary from state to state, and a complete answer is clearly beyond the scope of this paper (but see Weitzman, 1978), the four essential provisions are as follows.

First, *the husband is the head of the household.* Today, when a woman marries she still loses her independent legal identity. For example, the law assumes that she will take her husband's surname. Although she is no longer technically forced to in many states, administrative regulations governing drivers' licenses and voting registration often harass the woman who, for personal or professional reasons, chooses not to relinquish her birthname

when she marries. The married woman is also supposed to assume her husband's domicile, his legal residence, which determines a number of rights and duties, such as where she must vote, register a car, and pay taxes. Thus, she may lose the privilege of paying taxes (at a lower rate) in her home state, or may suddenly be charged tuition at the state university she was attending free of charge as a resident if she marries a man whose legal residence is in another state.

The second provision of the traditional marriage contract is that *the husband is responsible for family support.* Family law assumes a clear division of roles within the family; the husband has the duty to support his wife, and the wife has a duty to provide her husband with services in the home. All states, even those with community property systems, place the prime burden of family support on the husband; he is to provide necessities for both his wife and his children.

One effect of placing the primary support obligation on men is to further reinforce the husband's position as head of the household and, more specifically, his authority over family finances. The obligation is a mixed blessing for both the husband and the wife. The husband is given power at the price of the pressures and responsibility of carrying a potentially crippling burden. The wife is given support at the price of limiting her economic capacity (and self-image), for the law assumes that she will always be economically dependent on a man (Kay, 1974).

It is important to note that the spousal support obligations of the husband are rarely enforced in an ongoing marriage because the courts have been reluctant to interfere with "family privacy." In fact, as Krauskopf and Thomas (1974) note, there is no legal action that a wife can bring to require the husband to provide adequate support for herself and the children, unless she is willing to leave him and set up a separate household. The wife is

Reprinted from Lenore J. Weitzman, Carol M. Dixon, Joyce Adair Bird, Neil McGinn, Dena M. Robertson, "The Traditional Marriage Contract," from "Contracts for Intimate Relationships," in *"Confronting the Issues: Marriage, the Family and Sex Roles,* ed. Kenneth Kammeyer (Boston: Allyn and Bacon, 1980) with permission. Copyright 1978 by Lenore J. Weitzman.

not entitled to an allowance, to any control over family finances, or to make a claim against the husband's income or property. As head of the household, the husband determines how much of his funds shall be spent for the family. The courts will not undermine his authority.

Third, traditional legal marriage makes *the wife responsible for domestic services.* As we have already noted, legal marriage assigns specific roles to both the husband and wife. The man exchanges financial support for his wife's service as a companion, housewife, and mother. Because a husband is *entitled* to the benefit of his wife's labor, the courts have refused to honor contracts in which a husband agrees to pay his wife for her domestic services because "one of the terms of the contract of marriage is that the wife's services will be performed without compensation" (Rucci v. Rucci, 1962).

The law's assumption that a wife "owes" her domestic services to her husband thereby undermines the economic value of the wife's work in the home. It also allows the law to disregard the importance of the wife's labor in building the family wealth and property. Although the wife's traditional work of homemaking and child rearing contribute significantly to the family's economic welfare by making it possible for the husband to earn income and amass property during the marriage (Levy, 1968), the law in most states does not give the homemaker any property rights during the marriage.

In the 42 states with common law property systems, all of the husband's earnings and property are his alone. Although these states give the wife the same right to *her* own income, the wife's obligations in the home either restrict her opportunities to earn her own income or restrict her from earning an income comparable to her husband's. For example, in over half the families with small children, the husband earns all the funds; if he titles the family home and bank accounts in his name, they are his alone. The common law presumes that all household goods which do not have documentary title are the husband's property (Krauskopf, 1977: 96).

Thus, the woman who has contributed to the growth of her husband's business, career, property, or income during the marriage generally finds that her contribution to the partnership is unrecognized in law. Upon dissolution the partnership is treated as a one-man business, and she does not get a fair share for her half of the effort (Weitzman, 1975). For example, in a recent Illinois case (Norris v. Norris, 1974) a farming couple who started out their marriage with nothing acquired considerable net worth in 20 years, but at the termination of the marriage the wife received only her personal belongings and clothing.

In contrast, eight states in the United States have a community property system.[1] These states treat marriage as an equal partnership. They recognize the importance of the wife's contribution to the family and to anything her husband earns. In community property states the wife legally owns half of her husband's property (and vice versa). She may use her share during marriage—and must be awarded it upon divorce.

The fourth provision of the legal marriage contract makes *the wife responsible for child care.* The state-imposed marriage contract places almost total responsibility for child care, both during marriage and after dissolution, upon the wife.

Although the legal view of women as the natural and proper caretaker of the young has resulted in great deference to mothers in some areas (for example, women are awarded custody of their children in over 90% of the divorce cases), they have often been given a double-edged benefit. For when women alone assume the social role of caretaker of the children after divorce, they also end up assuming all the financial costs of child support as well. (Although the law continues to place the primary responsibility for postdivorce child support on the husband, husbands have notoriously low rates of compliance with support orders, and the women, as the custodial parents, are often left to bear the costs of raising their children alone.) In addition, the legal assumption that women alone can rear the children has also been used to justify discrimination against women in other areas such as employment and jury service.

From the husband's perspective, the woman-as-caretaker assumption may be seen as a benefit when it leads to less than rigorous efforts to enforce child support orders, but the law also serves as a disincentive to men who would like to play a more active role in raising their children. Furthermore, it may deprive fathers who want custody of their children of an equal chance of obtaining it after divorce.

The traditional marriage contract, with its rigidly prescribed roles for husbands and wives, is inconsistent with the emergence of more egalitarian family patterns. More women (and men) are rejecting the traditional assumption of a husband-headed hierarchical family with domestic and child care roles assigned exclusively to women.

---

1. Arizona, California, Idaho, Louisiana, Nevada, New Mexico, Texas, and Washington.

In the context of the women's liberation movement and changing norms about family roles, more couples are becoming interested in alternatives to traditional legal marriage. One possible route to a less sex-based system of family law is through legislative changes such as Equal Rights Amendments to the federal and state constitutions. Another possibility, which is especially attractive to couples who do not want to wait for the law to change, is to circumvent the law by writing a contract.

References

American Law Institute (1932) Restatement of Contracts.

Fleishmann, K. (1974) "Marriage by contract: defining the terms of relationships." Family Law Q.: 27–49.

Kay, H. H. (1974) Sex Based Discrimination in Family Law. MN: West.

Krauskopf, J. M. (1977) "Partnership marriage: legal reforms needed," in J. R. Chapman and M. Gates (eds.) Women into Wives: The Legal and Economic Impact of Marriage. Beverly Hills, CA: Sage.

———— and R. C. Thomas (1974) "Partnership marriage: the solution to an ineffective and inequitable law of support." Ohio State Law J. 35:558–600.

Levy, R. (1968) Uniform Marriage and Divorce Legislation: A Preliminary Analysis. Chicago: Aldine.

Weitzman, L. J. (1978) The Marriage Contract. Englewood Cliffs, NJ: Prentice-Hall.

———— (1975) "To love, honor and obey? Traditional legal marriage and alternative family forms." Family Coordinator (October): 531–548.

———— (1974) "Legal regulation of marriage: tradition and change." Calif. Law Rev. 62:1169–1288.

Wells, J. G. (1976) "A critical look at personal marriage contracts." Family Coordinator (January): 33–38.

READING 25

The Woman Who Talked Back to God and Didn't Get Zapped!

Sonia Johnson

Not long after we settled in Virginia, which was—and at the time of this writing still is—a very, very unratified state, I began hearing about the Equal Rights Amendment. The place I heard about it was church, and everything I heard was bad.

This disturbed me. Not because I cared about the ERA—I didn't even know what it was for a long while—but because I found that hearing politics discussed

Reprinted from Sonia Johnson, "The Woman Who Talked Back to God and Didn't Get Zapped!", in *From Housewife to Heretic,* (New York: Doubleday, 1981); by permission of the publisher. Copyright 1981 by Sonia Johnson, Ltd.

so much in our most sacred church services interfered with my feelings of reverence and worship. It was disorienting to me for sacrament meeting to change suddenly, right in the middle, from a religious meeting to a precinct meeting. And, too, I liked the *name* of the amendment. I couldn't help feeling uneasy that the church was opposing something with a name as beautiful as the *Equal Rights* Amendment.

I would like to have forgotten about it, frankly, because in being driven by the church's vehemence to study, and growing more and more positive about the ERA as I studied, I was also growing more and more miserable: guilty about not being able to agree with the

Brethren (as we call the leaders of the church) and seriously perplexed about why they had taken such an obvious anti-human rights stand.

But the political excitement, talk, and activity in the church only intensified, until I was in serious emotional distress. So I was pleased when, in the spring of 1978, it was announced that our stake president (roughly equivalent to a Catholic bishop) was coming to explain the church's opposition to the ERA. I didn't know this stake president—he was new—but I was impressed by his credentials. Not just that he was a local church authority, which always impressed me in those days, but that he had, some years before, been the project director of the Army's jet propulsion laboratory for the manned exploration to the moon!

So I rushed home and called my friends Hazel and Ron, who were also suffering about the church's anti-ERA stance. *"Finally,* we're going to hear something intelligent on the other side of this issue!"

The next Sunday night when he got up to speak, nine of us pro-ERA Mormons (in a group of 20 or 30 of the other kind) sat hoping that he would help us understand why our church, the Church of Jesus Christ, had taken what seemed to us such an *un*-Christlike stand. But he wasn't halfway through his first sentence before he had murdered that hope.

He had not, he informed us, prepared anything to say that night. And while he was on his way to the church, he had begun to get a little nervous about this ("I should think so!" I whispered to my husband Rick). In the midst of his growing alarm, he suddenly remembered someone's telling him there was an article about the ERA in the latest *Pageant* magazine. So when a 7–11 store miraculously appeared on the horizon, he dashed in, bought a *Pageant* and, while we were having our opening song and prayer, read that article. Now, he announced triumphantly, he was ready to talk to us about the ERA.

This confession, which he seemed to regard as charming, dumbfounded me, and a fury like none I'd ever felt before anywhere for anyone—to say nothing of in church and for a church official—began to boil up inside me.

Looking incredulously at his bland, empty, smiling face, I knew the answer to the biblical question: "Which of you, if your child asked for bread, would give her a stone?" The answer was, "My church leaders." We had come hungering and thirsting for help, for a reason to believe that the leaders of our church were inspired, for a reason not to have to become renegades. We had come asking for thoughtful answers, for good sense, for concern, for comfort. And he had given us a stone. We had brought him our pain and our longing to believe, and he had given us *Pageant.*

Like all other leaders of the church with whom I have spoken or whose words I have read or heard since, he obviously considered women's issues so trivial, so peripheral, that he did not feel any need to inform himself about them before going forth to teach and work against them. In his infinite ignorance and insensitivity and lack of love, the project director of the manned exploration of the moon stood before us as a true representative of the leaders of our church. It was a heart-stopping revelation. I began to be in serious spiritual pain.

Then he made his second critical mistake with me: he read the short and beautiful text of the Equal Rights Amendment. *Equality of rights under the law shall not be denied or abridged by the United States or by any state on account of sex.* When he read those words in that hostile room that night, they took hold of my heart like a great warm fist and have not let go for one single second, waking or sleeping, since.

After he had converted me heart and soul to the Equal Rights Amendment, the project director began to read the letter from the first presidency of the church explaining their opposition. It began with a reminder of how the men of the church have always loved us. Although I had heard that rhetoric for 42 years, until that night I had refused to hear how condescending, how patronizing that language is. I realized that the women of the church would never write a letter to the men telling them how much we loved them. We simply are not in a position to—what? *matronize?*—them like that.

The letter went on to say how Mormon women have always been held in an exalted position. I knew instantly what the Women's Movement was all about. It hit me like a 10-ton truck. It was the largest lump of pain I had ever been handed at one time, and I found myself concentrating during the remainder of that meeting simply to survive it.

I was such a mass of emotions when I left that meeting that I am surprised I didn't atomize on the spot. I felt betrayed. I felt ashamed and humiliated that I, who should have known better, had been so easily duped for so long. And I felt a fury that I had never dreamed possible. But most of all I felt an incredible sorrow. Sorrow for the lives women have lived for as long as we have record, sorrow for my grandmothers' lives, my mother's, my own.

On the way home I turned to Rick and said, finally,

what I had been resisting saying for a long time. "I am a feminist. In fact, I am a *radical* feminist!" I didn't even know what that meant, but I knew that at my very root—which is the meaning of "radical"—I was changed, that I would never be the same, nor would I wish to be.

When Rick and I reached home that night, I was ready to explode with emotion, and needing to, and no longer afraid to. I went over to the room above the garage, locked myself in, and let God have it.

I told him what I thought of a supreme being who had made women so full, so rich, so talented and intelligent, so eager for experience and so able to profit by it, and then put us in a little box, placed the lid on tightly, and said, "Now stay there, honey!" I told him that was the most vicious, the ugliest, and ultimately the most evil act I could conceive of, and that if I could get hold of him I would kill him.

I know this is shocking. But I was coming to grips with the ugliest, most insidious and damaging aspect of my enculturation. In our patriarchal world, we are all taught—whether we like to think we are or not—that God, being male, values maleness much more than he values femaleness. God will stand behind the men; he will uphold them in all they do because he and they—being men and having frequent, very male, very important, business dealings—know what they know, a large part of which is that women must be made to understand that females are forever outside their charmed circle, forever consigned to the fringes of opportunity and power. I had been taught as we all have, not in so many words but nonetheless forcefully, that in order to propitiate God, women must propitiate men. After all, God won't like us if we don't please those nearest his heart, if we don't treat his cronies well.

For two solid hours I raged at God at the top of my lungs, screaming and sobbing. I think you must understand that this was quite unlike my usual parlance with God. I have a naturally quiet voice and am not given to raising it in anger, to say nothing of screaming. In addition, I grew up in a family where God was much respected (by my father) and much loved (by my mother). From my earliest years I had tried to establish the same close, loving relationship with heaven that my mother had. I saw what comfort and strength she found in prayer, and though I did not understand then why she needed it, that it is one of women's only possible recourses in misogynist society, I determined to have it also. And so, despite the serious handicap of envisioning God as the Old Testament tyrant, which is the way he is portrayed in Mormon

scripture and worshiped in the church, I had come to love and trust him because I loved and trusted my mother. And I had also read the scriptures, and knew that people who did not respect God got zapped. There is a lot of zapping in the Old Testament (and in the Book of Mormon). I respected that kind of power.

But that night I didn't care if I *did* get zapped. I figured I didn't have anything to lose—that I *had* been zapped, that all women have been zapped; and I even felt that it might be a relief to be hit by a bolt of something. How was I going to go from day to day knowing what I knew, seeing so clearly? But nothing happened except that my frenzy continued and my horror spilled out into the night.

The only frustration I felt through the whole wild scene was that my vocabulary was not potent enough for the job. I had led such a sheltered existence that I just did not have the appropriate verbal ammunition; when the best you can do is, "You rotten old rascal!" or "You son of a gun!" it leaves a lot to be desired. But I made up in volume what I lacked in vocabulary, and fought God with all the might of my accumulated pain and rage and sorrow.

When my vocal cords and lungs finally gave out and I found myself reduced to an exhausted perspiration- and tear-soaked heap, I discovered to my amazement that I felt wonderful—absolutely euphoric. I even got the fanciful impression that up in heaven there was general jubilation at my coming of age, that my friends there were saying to me, "Well, Sonia, it took you long enough! Forty-two years and you're just figuring it out! But we don't mean to scold. Congratulations on coming around at last. And now don't waste any more time. Get busy and do something for women!"

I would, I silently promised, but first I had to do something for myself. Because I thought of myself foremost as a religious person, for the next few months I concentrated on coming to terms with heaven. First I decided to continue to believe in the existence of a supreme being, because I wanted to. That is all any of us does—chooses to believe or not to believe. I chose to believe.

But I could no longer choose to believe in the God of the Old Testament, which is the God of the Mormons—very patriarchal (male hierarchical), very firm and easily angered; more stern than smiling, more just than merciful, more punitive than loving. To keep God and to learn to trust again, that was the first requisite of my revolution. Gradually, stroke by stroke, I redrew deity, piece by piece I reorganized heaven, because I wanted neither to give them up nor to fight against them. I had been in close communication with them all my life, and I had found comfort there.

In the days that had followed the night of the project director, I had made several critical discoveries, one of which was that I was not going to be zapped. At least not by God. (Nowadays women in my audience sometimes insist, "Well, I never felt that I was going to be zapped." And I can only answer that I know for a certainty that out there in the New Right, as we call it, out there where the Moral Majority lives, where the Mormons and other fundamentalist religionists keep patriarchy sacred on their altars, women *do* fear that they will be zapped. I know because I have been there.) I began to understand that God is not going to punish women for thinking, for questioning, for seeing through the myths that bind us, for being angry about what so richly deserves our anger, for going forth boldly to fight against the injustices that have been visited upon us so casually and so cruelly for so long. I began to understand that women are, in fact, going to be blessed and strengthened and comforted for this. I began to understand that we are going to be made joyful.

I say "began to understand" these things because this knowledge came and went; it would not stay put. It took several more profoundly revolutionizing experiences to make this truth firmly mine and to help me stop feeling automatically that when I displeased the men of the church I also displeased God.

I also made the totally un-unique discovery one day that men had made God in their own image to keep control of women. Why then could not women reorganize heaven and remake God in a way that would empower everyone?

Thinking about this, I remembered Mother in Heaven, the divine being to whom Mormon doctrine attests (and who was put there, appropriately enough, by a female prophet — probably when the men were away at some Old Boys' meeting). Remembered, sought her, and found her. And loved her. Oh, how I loved and continue to love her! As I gradually reinstated her in her rightful position in my new heaven as equal in power and glory to Father — not in subordination, as the churchmen so wishfully think (and won't they be surprised!) — I began to feel a wholeness and a personal power that transcended any happiness I had ever known. With Mother on her throne as a model for me in heaven, I felt wonderful. I felt wonderful knowing that femaleness is as divine, as desirable, as powerful as maleness. "No wonder men have

felt so great for so long!" I marveled. "No wonder they have loved having a male God!" It felt marvelous to be able to identify with God. I felt like the ancient Celtic warrior Boadicea, deeply and contentedly strong. Nothing seemed impossible. I was eager for experience, open to everything. I look forward with calm and cheerful anticipation to all the battles that lie ahead. I am a warrior in the time of women warriors; the longing for justice is the sword I carry, the love of womankind my shield.

In July of that year, we marched, one hundred thousand of us, for an extension of time to ratify the Equal Rights Amendment. About 20 of us marched under the Mormons for ERA banner — and no one who saw that banner ever forgot it. As the *New York Times* joked shortly after my excommunication, "Mormons for ERA? Isn't that a little like astronauts for a flat earth?" We were a contradiction in terms, and people shook their heads disbelievingly.

When the extension bill passed the United States House of Representatives and went over to the Senate, Senator Birch Bayh asked his staff to get a religious panel together for hearings in the Senate Subcommittee on Constitutional Rights. Someone on Senator Bayh's staff remembered our banner and decided to find one of us Mormon "astronauts" to take part in the hearing. I was the one they called. At the time I was only a baby feminist, about three and a half months old.

I accepted the assignment to testify. Rick and the children were away while I was writing my testimony. The house was very still. I began to notice my heart beating. Generally my heart beats along without any recognition, but it was beating so hard I could see my blouse jump. "As if I were frightened," I smiled to myself, bemused. My breathing seemed irregular. Worst of all, I could not sleep. As soon as I would doze off, some vague dream, some half-image as of a gun at my head about to go off or a knife in my ribs would shock me rigidly upright with my pulse sounding in my ears like feet pounding down an empty street, my whole body shaking with terror and slippery with perspiration.

Since the first flickerings of this inexplicable fear, I had tried to pray about it. I would, of course, have prayed about the hearing anyway, fear or not. But I found that when I knelt, I could not collect my thoughts. And I felt foolish for being so afraid. "It's only a five-minute testimony, and you *read* it," I reminded myself. I was accustomed to teaching mature university students. Why was I so afraid of this?

Finally, I had finished writing the testimony except

for the last paragraph. The rest of it consisted largely of quotations from my great Mormon foremothers of the late 19th century, who not only fought for suffrage, but who with all their souls wanted equal rights under the law as well. Their early magazine, the *Woman's Exponent,* is full of rhetoric about women's rights that today's Mormon women would find shockingly radical, and for which, if they were to utter or write it, they would be looked upon with grave suspicion.

They are venerable women, our Mormon mothers—real saints. And coming from them, the ideas in my testimony had the force of their known piety and of their honored position in the present-day church. After all, *I,* Sonia Johnson, was not saying it. Emmeline B. Wells was. *I* wasn't saying it, Lucinda Dalton was. How could anyone fault *them*? I wanted to remind the church of the humanitarian and liberal roots it was repudiating by opposing women's rights in this century. I wanted to remind Mormon women, my sisters, of what strength and courage and conviction our mothers had.

When I had nearly finished the writing of the testimony, I felt a great desire to end it well, so I decided to try once more to offer up a bona fide, honest-to-goodness prayer, a coherent prayer. I knelt by the couch in my library, shut my eyes, and said simply, "Dear parents, help me." Hearing a rustling, I opened my eyes, and there around the three sides of the room, with their heads about six inches from the ceiling, stood a throng of women in old-fashioned dress. Not like a photograph or a tableau, but moving slightly. They were the women whose words I had been reading all week with gratitude and love—my foremothers. They did not speak to me, but I heard their message clearly and ringingly in my mind: "Don't be afraid. This work has to be done. It is hard, but it is our work too, and we are helping you all we can. Have courage. Know we are with you. And don't be afraid."

I felt surrounded and lifted up by loving arms. Nothing like that had ever happened to me before. I am willing to entertain any reasonable explanation of this event that leaves the feelings of love and support and necessity intact. Perhaps all the caring of these marvelous women, all their suffering and sacrifice, all their long years of labor for women's happiness, all the passion behind all the bone-breaking work, perhaps all that simply does not disappear off the earth with their physical bodies. And perhaps sometimes when we are especially sensitive to it and in need of it, we flip some spiritual switch and there it is, waiting to encourage and lift us.

When I rose from my knees that afternoon, I was not afraid any more. The dread and recurring panic were gone, and I have never felt them since. I went directly to my desk and wrote the final paragraph: "We [Mormons for ERA] believe that what our early sisters would have wanted, what they would be working for if they were here today, what constitutes the whole loaf with which they would be contented, is ratification of the Equal Rights Amendment."

I did not just believe it; I knew it.

The Friday morning of the hearing, the long, gracefully winding stairs to the chamber were already double-lined with waiting people, a good many of them anti-ERA Mormons who met my homemade "Mormon for ERA" button with hostile eyes. I shivered at the unaccustomed coldness that was to become the customary Mormon response to me, and climbed to the head of the line to be with the other members of the panel.

Through the entire experience, from the time I walked into the room until I walked out again, Birch Bayh treated me with extraordinary gentleness and concern. I am sure he could see how inexperienced I was in such matters, how naïve and vulnerable. Senator Orrin G. Hatch of Utah, a Mormon and one of the subcommittee members, made his entrance to the packed house flanked by two young male assistants. Senator Bayh's assistants were both young women.

Before I spoke, I was trembling so that without looking directly at it, I could see my skirt dancing across my knees. But when my turn came, I suddenly felt very calm and strong. It was eerily quiet in the room as I read.

When I finished, the audience—at least what must have been much of it—exploded in applause so loud and so sudden that I almost leaped off my chair. For the briefest, most absurd instant, I thought I had been shot.

Senator Bayh, grinning from ear to ear, rapped on the table for silence. The committee members prepared to ask us questions, and my heart started knocking about in my chest again.

Senator Bayh, being the chairman, led off. When he came to me, he asked, "Ms. Johnson, what percentage of the people within the Mormon church share your views, do you believe?"

"There has been no scientific effort or study," I answered. "We know of many people like ourselves. We hear from them daily, but we have done no polls."

Then he asked with concern whether or not I would find myself in trouble with the church because of my position on the ERA. I told him I hoped not. "So do I," he replied. Senator Hatch quickly leaned over and said, "Oh, I'm sure she won't!"

When Senator Hatch spoke to me, his voice changed. He put on his churchman's voice for me—unctuous, condescending; I was not alone in hearing it. Several people asked me afterward whether I had noticed. Indeed I had, and had said to myself incredulously at the time, "For heaven's sake, Sonia. Do you mean to say that men in the church have been speaking to you like that for forty-two years and *you've never noticed it*?"

While this revelation was maddening, it also gave me unique power. The Senator became a known quantity. Hatch, being the sort of patriarchal male who tends to view women as so much alike that one approach will work for all, prepared to assert in his usually successful ways his innate male superiority.

This faulty judgment gives women the upper hand when dealing with patriarchs, because such men usually have not developed alternative strategies, and are left defenseless and foolish when their stereotypes fail them—as they are increasingly failing them.

"Mrs. Johnson," he intoned down his shiny Boy Scout nose, "you must admit that nearly one hundred percent of Mormon women oppose the Equal Rights Amendment." (Here's where the Relief Society sisters from Hatch's ward and stake applauded and stamped.)

When the tumult subsided, I replied, "Oh, my goodness, I don't have to admit that. It simply isn't true."

When one has just spoken in one's churchman's voice, one does not expect to be answered back like that, and Hatch, chagrined, began his serious work of intimidation and humiliation. Ironically, however, the harder he worked, the more ruffled he himself became and the calmer I felt. We began to have a delightfully brisk dialogue—at least, *I* enjoyed it:

Hatch: I notice in your letter to the legislature that you had twenty women listed.
Johnson: There were not just women on that list. . . . The point here is that numbers of adherents have never proved an issue true or false. You yourself belong to a church of only three million members which purports to be the only true church in the world. That is a pretty precarious position. I am accustomed to being one of the few and right.
Hatch: I notice you are very self-confident that you are right and everybody else is wrong. I would have to admit that the majority can be wrong, but on the other hand I have also seen the minority wrong many times.

You may well be wrong here, as confident as you are.
Johnson: You may very well be wrong, as confident as you are.
Hatch: That is true, and I am very confident. As a matter of fact, I am very confident that I am right.
Johnson: And so am I.

During this interchange, Hatch began to show signs of ego wear. Repeatedly pulling at his tie, tugging at his sleeves, leaning across the table as if he were preparing to spring at me, he had fended off pleas from his aides who knelt at either side of him (imagine taking oneself so seriously as to have an aide kneeling at one's either side!), and paid no heed to a note from Senator Bayh who was becoming progressively more alarmed as the Utah Senator's control visibly and swiftly disintegrated.

Finally, the struggling Senator lost his composure altogether. It was wonderful. I wish everyone who has worked long hours and years for human rights for women could have been there to see it.

He began innocuously enough. You couldn't have foreseen that he was about to push Mormons for ERA to a national scale. In my journal, I have recorded his words like this:

"It's implied by your testimony that you're more intelligent than other Mormon women, and that if they were all as intelligent as you, they would all support the Equal Rights Amendment." And then he banged his fist on the table in angry emphasis and shouted, "Now that's an insult to my wife!"

The audience inhaled as one. Ahhh! And everyone woke up, including reporters from the Associated Press and United Press International who had been snoozing over in the corner during the boring religious stuff. Suddenly they were thrusting microphones under our noses, carrying TV cameras out of the marble halls and next day, all across the country, newspapers carried articles with headlines such as: "Mormon Senator and Mormon Woman Spar"; "Utah Senator and Mormon Woman Clash at Hearing on ERA." My favorite was: "Mormon Family Feud on Senate Floor."

People magazine published a very condensed version, and Hatch objected in a letter to the editor that the reporter had not checked his facts. The magazine editors asked the writer to check the story out, and this is what he sent back to them:

"It's hard to believe that Hatch would want to challenge Sonia Johnson's account of their meeting at the Senate ERA-extension hearing, August 4, 1978. According to three eyewitnesses and the transcript of the proceedings, Sonia's version and our reporting were right on target. By all accounts, Hatch fumed at Johnson through much of her testimony and blew up several times during the question-and-answer period that followed."

When I walked out of the hearing room into the foyer, the anti-ERA Mormon women surrounded me at once. From the outset, I have known it is fruitless to try to convince members of my church of the correctness of the Equal Rights Amendment, fruitless because Mormons who are anti-ERA are anti-ERA not because of the demerits of the amendment, but primarily because the president of the church—who, good members believe, is a prophet as Moses and Isaiah were—has taken a very firm anti-ERA stance. And though Mormons are repulsed by the word "infallible," its being such a papist concept, they nevertheless believe that God will not allow the prophet and president of the Mormon church to make a mistake. They therefore believe in the infallibility of the prophet, while strongly denying belief in infallibility.

The Mormon anti-ERA women who besieged me afterward felt that I should not have made "it" a Mormon issue, and I replied that the *church* had made it a Mormon issue by choosing to publish their opposition widely.

We received many responses to my testimony. Perhaps the image of greatest terror crawled from the psyche of Hartman Rector, one of the General Authorities of the church: "In order to attempt to get the male somewhere near even, the Heavenly Father gave him the Priesthood or directing authority for the Church and home. Without this bequeath, the male would be so far below the female in power and influence that there would be little or no purpose for his existence in fact [sic] would probably be eaten by the female as is the case with the black widow spider."

When I testified before the subcommittee, the church had only succeeded in making me a feminist. And although the pain of being a woman in a church that was fighting women's rights was deepening every day, threatening to invade my whole life, I still thought I could be a good Mormon and a good feminist at the same time.

It took repeated beatings of my unbelieving head against the solid rock of chauvinism, and an excommunication, to teach me the impossibility of that combination.

Women cannot serve two masters at once who are urgently beaming antithetical orders, though I know many who are trying to do just that—compromising, adjusting, rationalizing, excusing, apologizing for the men and for men's system. I understand perfectly why they do this, having done it myself for years. But it is psychologically unhealthful and in the long run spiritually disastrous for both sexes. Either we believe in patriarchy—the rule of men over women—or we believe in equality. We cannot believe in both at once. Neither can we with impunity choose not to choose which one we believe in. To remain in indecision, and perhaps thus to have our cake and eat it too, erodes great chunks of our identity, along with great chunks of our integrity.

For the 17 years preceding my feminist awakening in 1978, I was living a sort of half-life, in half-light, a grayish, half-awake limbo of neither clouds nor sunlight, a gray, same numbness. Because I was not allowing myself to feel the pain of oppression, and was in fact actively denying it, I was unable to feel emotions on the other side of the continuum either.

I accomplished this great reductionist feat by lowering the threshold of my awareness, allowing very little stimuli into my consciousness for fear of inadvertently letting in the scary things. Those first 17 years of my marriage lie like a flat gray canvas in my mind. I feel bereft of memories, because I am bereft, as if I have had amnesia. But I do not mean to imply that I was miserable; I was contented.

Feminism called upon me to have the courage to grow up, to discover and exercise my womanly strength, to be unafraid of pain—and the pain is immeasurable—knowing that fully experienced, it makes joy fully possible. If a friend were to ask me today who I am, I would answer unhesitatingly, "I am Sonia—woman, human being, glad to be alive, loving every second of it. I was dead and am alive. I had wandered far from home and have at last found my way home again."

Introduction: Science and Medicine

The biological, psychological and social sciences have held a number of unexamined assumptions that perpetuate gender-inequalities. Those assumptions are often translated into the practices of the medical doctor, clinical psychologist and social worker.

The depth and rigidity of gender assumptions is illustrated in the selection "Sex Change Operations: The Last Bulwark of the Double Standard," by Margrit Eichler from her book, *The Double Standard: A Feminist Critique of the Social Sciences* (St. Martin's Press: 1979). She argues that the desire for sex change operations is not located in the physiology or even the psychology of the transsexual, but in the *social* practices which inculcate such rigid definitions of appropriate behavior for males and females that individuals choose to mutilate their bodies, change their sex, rather than behave in ways they view as inappropriate for their gender; and medical doctors choose to view these operations as "right" and "moral." Suzanne Hyers in her brief account "(Not Just) Another Day at the Gynecologist" describes the sexual assumptions of her doctor, including his lack of knowledge of female sexuality. Two short comments about doctors follow, the first excerpted from Charlotte Perkins Gilman's *The Yellow Wallpaper* and the second from Piers Paul Read's narrative *Alive: The Story of the Andes Survivors.*

The consequences of scientific theory, including contemporary socio-logical theory on parenting and the medical practices of childbirth, are described by Alice Rossi in the selection "A Biosocial Perspective on Parenting." Rossi finds much lacking in obstetrical philosophy and practice. Gary Selden in "Frailty, Thy Name's Been Changed: What Sports Medicine Is Discovering about Women's Bodies" describes the positive consequences of athletics for women, and the effects of the new style of coaching and training—which no longer assumes that women are weak and frail—on women's health and sport skills. Some traditional expecta-tions for women are ironically depicted in the selection, "Exercises for Men," from the Willamette Bridge / Liberation News Service.

Science, in addition to being a "way of knowing" which has conse-quences for the medical profession, is a *social* institution. Norms and values govern how, for example, scientists interact with one another; who is allowed entry into the scientific field and who is credited with discovery. Ruth Hubbard in the selection "Reflections on the Story of the

Double Helix" describes the concrete experiences of one woman, Rosalind Franklin, whose research was central to the discovery of DNA but who remained unheralded and Nobel prizeless. The full impact of science as a male-imperium is critically examined by Susan Griffin in the selection "Women and Nature: The Roaring Inside Her," from her book with the same title (Harper and Row: 1978). Griffin challenges the legitimacy of science-as-practiced, and through metaphor, illustrates how the ideology of patriarchy is manifested in science such that women and nature are both defined as objects to be subjected to male control.

Sex Change Operations:
The Last Bulwark of the Double Standard

Margrit Eichler

Sex change operations have become increasingly frequent over the past decade. The fact that modern societies are willing to allocate a portion of their scarce resource of highly trained medical personnel and highly sophisticated and expensive medical instruments for such operations suggests a complete acceptance of sex role ideology and therefore an extreme intolerance of sexual ambiguity.

In conventional psychology, people distinguish between people who have a 'sex-appropriate gender identity' and those who have a confused gender identity, or exhibit a 'gender dysphoria syndrome' (Meyer, 1974). Within the last decade, the treatment of people with gender dysphoria, that is, people who believe that they have the wrong-sexed body for their 'real' self, has increasingly been through sex change operations, more commonly referred to in the literature as 'sex reassignment surgery.'

Sex reassignment surgery has as its goal to make a man as much as is anatomically possible similar to a woman, although it can never make a woman out of a man. The intention of the surgery is to make it possible for the erstwhile male to live as much as possible like a woman, and to be accepted as a woman by his (now her) friends and acquaintances. Vice versa, the surgery aims to make a woman as much as is anatomically possible similar to a man, although, again, it can never make a man out of a woman. Again, the surgery is considered successful if the erstwhile woman is accepted and treated as a man by her (now his) friends and acquaintances. In general, sex reassignment surgery is a costly and long process, and the final surgery which gives it its name is only, if responsibly done, the last step in a several years' process of 'changing one's sex'—namely, living in the mode of a member of the opposite sex.

Reprinted from Margrit Eichler, "Sex Change Operations: The Last Bulwark of the Double Standard," in *The Double Standard,* (St. Martin's Press, 1980), by permission of the original publisher, Croom and Helms, London, England, St. Martin's Press, and the author. Copyright 1980 by Margrit Eichler.

As a rule, transsexualism for a man who wants to become a woman involves, first, hormone treatment, which increases his breast development, effectively sterilises him, and decreases his facial hair growth. A second step would be electrolysis of his facial hair, of his breast hair and, if necessary, of other parts. After the second hair removal, the hair is usually permanently removed. Sometimes a hair transplant to alter his hair line at the forehead and/or a nose operation are performed. Sometimes breast implants are made to increase his breast size beyond the increase that is due to the hormonal treatment. At this point the patient is often expected to live as a woman for a minimum of six months, and, if possible, for several years. Physicians seem to vary greatly in this requirement, but most seem to be more willing to perform the ultimate sex reassignment surgery the longer the patient has already lived as a member of the sex which he wishes to join. The next step, then, is the removal of the penis and the testes and, lastly, the construction of an artificial vagina (vaginoplasty), with which the person is actually capable of having sexual intercourse, assuming the role of the woman, sometimes to such a degree that her partner is unaware of the fact that the person used to be an anatomical male.

For female-to-male transsexuals, the process is even more complicated. As with male-to-female transsexuals, the first medical step is usually hormone treatments. The androgens tend to lower the voice, and to stimulate facial hair growth. After a prolonged period of time, they also effectively sterilise the erstwhile woman, and periods cease, just as the man with a great influx of estrogens becomes incapable of ejaculation. The next step would be the surgical removal of the breasts, and preceding or succeeding it a hysterectomy (removal of the uterus). This is about as far as many female-to-male transsexuals can go, although there is, by now, a technology which allows the construction of a penis (phalloplasty). The construction of a penis by surgical means is more complicated than the removal of the male sex organs and the construction of an artificial vagina: female-to-male transsexuals can receive a penile construction and an implant of simulated testes which look like male genitals, but the penis cannot get erect, and, of course, cannot ejaculate since there are no functioning testes, and often it cannot even be used for urination. For sexual intercourse it seems to be useless (with the exception of one case that has been reported). The surgical changes are, therefore, of an even more cosmetic nature (since still less functional than the artificial vagina) than those of the male-to-female transsexual.

As can be seen, the whole process is by necessity painful, physically as well as emotionally, and expensive. Persons undergoing sex reassignment surgery need to possess a great deal of determination in order to obtain the desired treatments and operations. Nevertheless, there is no doubt that the incidence of these sex reassignment surgeries has greatly increased over the past few years. Money and Wolff (1973) estimated that in 1971 there were around 300 post-operative transsexuals in the United States, and in 1976 Feinbloom estimated that there were about 2,000 post-operative transsexuals in the USA. Overall, Pauly (1974a, p. 493) estimates the prevalence of male transsexualism as 1:100,000 and of female transsexualism as 1:130,000 of the general population. The lower female transsexualism rate may simply be a function of the fact that female-to-male sex reassignment surgery is even more complicated and expensive than male-to-female sex reassignment surgery, and that male transsexualism has received more publicity through some famous cases such as Christine Jorgenson and Jan Morris. Were the possibility of female-to-male surgery better known, more people might request it.

The generic term that is utilised to describe a person who wishes to live as a member of the other sex is 'transsexual.' In the last years, the term has been utilised to designate all those people who seek (but do not necessarily obtain) a sex change operation. The ratio of patients receiving surgery and those requesting it has been estimated as 1:9 (Bentler, 1976, p. 577). The usage of calling all patients requesting surgery transsexual has been criticised by Meyer (1974) as being too vague, and he proposes to call transsexual only those people who have actually managed to live as members of the other sex. It is common to distinguish between post-operative and pre-operative transsexuals. This, to me, seems a very questionable custom, since it assumes that all 'pre-operative' transsexuals will, some day, become post-operative, which is not the case. More important, it stresses the surgical aspect of transsexualism rather than the cultural aspect by implying that transsexualism culminates in sex reassignment surgery, and that a form of transsexualism which involves living as a member of the opposite sex without surgery is simply a step to having surgery performed. If nothing else, it indicates the mechanical nature of the way in which gender dysphoria is regarded among the clinical experts.

Related to, but not synonymous with, transsexualism are transvestism and homosexuality. Transvestism involves an acceptance of oneself as a man, but the overwhelming urge occasionally to dress as and behave like a woman. (There are also female transvestites, but they are less frequently written about and commented upon, except when their transvestism is a prelude to transsexualism, probably because it is vastly more socially acceptable for a woman to dress as a man than it is for a man to dress as a woman. A female transvestite is, therefore, less of a deviant than a male transvestite.) Transvestites may achieve such proficiency in cross-dressing that people do not notice anything strange when they pass them dressed as women.

Transsexuals tend to be homosexual in so far as they tend to prefer sexual contacts with a member of the sex to which they belong physically. Since they believe themselves to be people trapped in an anatomically wrong body, this desire is not subjectively experienced as homosexuality, but as heterosexuality, and consequently, a male-to-female transsexual is likely to prefer a man who is not a self-defined homosexual and a female-to-male transsexual is likely to prefer a woman who is not a self-defined lesbian as sexual partners.

This is a brief description of the background information on sex change operations and related phenomena, such as transvestism. What is so very interesting in these phenomena is the underlying overwhelming sexual dimorphism that becomes obvious when reading the literature. My major thesis here is that transsexual patients have an excessively narrow image of what constitutes 'sex-appropriate' behavior, which is reflected in the attitudes of the attending clinicians (psychologists, therapists and medical doctors) and the family of origin of the patient. Were the notions of masculinity and femininity less rigid, sex change operations should be unnecessary. Rather than identify somebody with a 'gender identity problem' as sick, we could define a society which insists on raising boys and girls in a clearly differentiated manner as sick. What should be treated as a *social* pathology is treated as if it were normal and when it manifests its effect in individuals it is treated as an *individual* pathology, and is 'corrected,' rather than any attempts being made to combat the issue at its root: the oppressive (non-human) definition of sex roles, and the lack of recognition of intermediate sexes in Western society and, apparently, Westernised Eastern society, if one can make such a statement on the basis of a few isolated cases.

Sexual Dimorphism in Transsexuality

Masculinity-Femininity in the Transsexual Patient
Anatomically, contrary to the prevailing notion, the sexes are not 'opposites.' In many ways we are biologically similar; for example, both males and females have so-called male and female hormones, but the proportions are different for the sexes. Besides the external and internal accessory sexual organs all else is shared between the sexes, although the distributions are, statistically speaking, different.

As far as physical traits are concerned, it is possible to differentiate between different physical characteristics, for example, pitch of voice—at the statistical level—between males and females, but the difference is one of range rather than an absolute difference. As far as character traits are concerned (e.g., gentleness, dependence, emotionality for women; roughness, independence, and non-emotionality for men) we can identify sex stereotypes (as Bem has done for the construction of the Bem Sex-Role Inventory [hereafter BSRI]) and we can observe statistical distributions which point toward differences in the distribution of behavior traits (e.g., greater verbal ability of girls and greater physical aggressiveness of boys). All people encompass in themselves some elements that are stereotypically ascribed to the other sex, and most people seem not to worry about that. However, when we read the accounts of transvestites and transsexuals, we are struck by the very rigid and sharp distinction that is drawn between so-called feminine and masculine attributes, and, more significantly, by the perceived inappropriateness of engaging in behaviors that are seen as being fitting for the other sex.

Jan Morris (1975), for example, in her description of the years of her changeover from male to 'female,' makes very clear statements as to what she expects a man and a woman to be. She notes that '. . . my own notion of the female principle was one of gentleness as against force, forgiveness rather than punishment, give more than take, helping more than leading' (p. 12); '. . . though my body

often yearned to give, to yield, to open itself, the machine was wrong' (p. 24). Contrast this with her description of a journalist colleague while Jan was still James Morris.

> *Though I never heard evil spoken of him by a living soul, still we were antipathetic from the start. 'How marvelous it must be,' I once remarked to him by way of small talk, apropos of his great height, 'to be able to command every room you enter.' 'I do not want,' he replied in his most reproving liberal style, 'to command anything at all'—an unfortunate response, though he could not know it,* to one whose ideals of manhood had been molded by military patterns, and who liked a man to be in charge of things. *(p. 75, second emphasis added)*

Rather, therefore, than permit it to be legitimate for a man to be gentle, give rather than take, help rather than lead or command, Morris perceives of these character traits as only legitimate for a woman (instead of clearly human)—these yearnings that he himself had, were, therefore, for himself illegitimate. He accepts a sexual dimorphism which strictly separates the sexes in terms of character traits, thus trying to live up to an inhuman masculine image, which, after a while, proves to be too much for him. A similar picture emerges from other descriptions (e.g., in Meyer, 1974) and is particularly obvious, also, in transvestites.

In one transvestite club which has recently been studied, the men come for one evening a week to dress up as females, and they go, cross-dressed, to outings. Typically, a man would have selected a female name for himself that would be used exclusively while he was dressed as a female, and that is referred to as his 'sister.' For reasons of keeping their everyday identity secret, only first names are used, and members would know each other by both names, the 'brother' and 'sister' names. If a person did not bring his suitcase with clothes, he might say that he did not bring his sister along, but that he might do so next week. Reading the accounts of these transvestites who appear in ultra-feminine apparel, with make-up, typically feminine clothes (rather than, for instance, blue jeans and a shirt), wigs, nylons, etc., it becomes apparent that they uphold a likewise ultra-masculine appearance when they are not 'dressed' (as females). Feinbloom (1976, p. 126) comments:

> *These men are visually perfect examples of 'compartmentalized' deviance. For the most part, their cross-dressing is carefully delimited in time and*

place and hidden from the rest of their lives. Their appearance, occupations, avocations, etc., outside their dressing, are strictly masculine. For example, most are balding or keep their hair very short. They dress conservatively and appropriately. They walk and talk in a masculine way, from the way they cross their legs to the way they hold their cigarettes. Their jobs and hobbies are 'accounts' insofar as they are frequently very 'masculine' in quality. The reinforced message, as I said before, is that any man who races sportscars, parachute jumps, looks so much like a man, is an army sergeant or a top-level computer analyst could not possibly be a 'pansy' or a 'deviant.'

If it were personally and socially acceptable for these men to wear clothes with ruffles, bright colors and soft materials (as was, for instance, customary in the Middle Ages) and to show their softer and gentler and more dependent side in everyday life, it is an open question whether they would still feel the need to assume, temporarily but regularly, the outer appearance of a member of the other sex.

Sexual Dimorphism in the Family of Origin of Transsexuals

The etiology of transsexualism has not been determined. The only thing that seems clear is that social factors play an extremely important role, and that biological factors are, at the very most, contributing towards predisposing a person to become a transsexual, and that possibly they play no role at all.

Bentler (1976) has recently attempted to isolate the possible developmental basis of male (male-to-female) transsexualism. Of 22 possible causes for male transsexualism which he enumerates, two are clearly biological in character (prenatal feminisation of the brain and inborn temperament to fussiness and unresponsiveness), one may be either biological or socially determined (low activity and energy level) and the rest are all social variables (presence of weak and non-nurturant father, learning of negative attitudes toward sexual organs, absence of consistent, effective rewards for sex role stereotyped behaviors and interests, learning not to look at females as sex objects, perceived difficulties with masculine work roles, development of a self-concept as different from other boys, etc.).

Clearly, possible explanations of transsexualism are at an early stage. Just as clearly, if people would delineate

less sharply between males and females than they do at present, many of the suspected causes would simply cease to exist. The desire to be a member of the opposite sex presupposes very clear and mutually exclusive notions as to what each sex is like.

It is impressive to read some of the accounts of the manner in which parents distinguish between what is proper for a boy and what is proper for a girl. In one reported instance a family had two male-to-female transsexuals. During one of the interviews, the mother was asked:

Dr S: When you would buy them gifts for Christmas or birthdays, what would you get them when they were 2 or 3 years old?
Mother: I liked to buy them dolls. I like dolls. You know, *dressing* dolls I like. But I buy a little car.
T: Oh yeah. She used to buy us cars. She said she liked dolls. She wanted to buy us dolls but she bought us cars.
Dr S: Where did you get the dolls from?
T: My cousin's.
Dr S: When they were little, you would buy them boys' toys?
Mother: Yes. Sometimes they would play, but they would play with dolls. They like to play with dolls, and I say, 'NO!' (Stoller and Baker, 1973, p. 327, emphases in the original)

On the other hand, it seems impossible at this point of time to weigh the familial influences against other social pressures. Since these transsexuals are from a culture which is highly sex-stereotyped and very conscious of 'sex-appropriate' behavior, some children who had yearnings to behave in a 'sex-inappropriate' manner may have simply found it impossible to overcome the feeling of inappropriateness, and may have thereby been pushed to imagine themselves as members of the other sex who happen to be endowed with the wrong body.

Whatever the role of the family may be, one thing seems certain: clinicians who are attending transsexuals need to believe strongly in 'gender differentiation' in order to be willing to offer their services to transsexuals who request them.

Sexual Dimorphism in Attending Clinicians

The prevailing clinical view of transsexuals, transvestites and homosexuals is that they have a gender identity problem, that they have chosen improper sex objects (homosexuality) and that they behave, in a general way, in a gender-inappropriate manner. Indeed, a diagnosis of a gender identity problem is a prerequisite for obtaining sex reassignment surgery. The factor on which surgery seems to hinge is whether or not the patient is judged to have a primary identification as a member of the opposite sex.

It warrants a moment's reflection that the reason for which sex reassignment surgery is performed is gender confusion, and not sex confusion. In other words, the patients are all clearly aware what their anatomical sex is. There is absolutely no 'confusion' on this issue. The only 'confusion' is their refusal to behave in the manner that is socially prescribed for their sex.

Clinicians need to believe fairly strongly in the appropriateness of 'sex-appropriate behavior' and a 'proper gender identity' in order to be able to justify, to themselves and others, the removal of physiologically perfectly normal and healthy sex organs in substantial numbers of patients. Clinicians involved with transsexuals—at least those who perform sex reassignment surgery—must not only accept the present sex structure, but must passionately believe in its essential rightness.

There are different ways in which accounts can be read. So far, we have used accounts of transsexuals in order to extract information about the femininity-masculinity attitudes of the patients and their families. However, the same reports (when written by clinicians) can be used to extract not the problems of the patients, but the prejudices of clinicians. One example is particularly striking which is reported by Money, since it reveals at least as much about the clinician's concern with sex role behavior and gender identity (and the malleability of the human character) as about any problems that the patient may have. It is especially interesting to examine this example because Money is one of the earliest authors who previously had advanced the thesis that humans are psychosexually undifferentiated at birth (Money 1963, p. 39). According to Money, Hampson and Hampson (1955, p. 316)'. . . sexuality is undifferentiated at birth and . . . becomes differentiated as masculine or feminine in the course of the various experiences of growing up.' These conclusions are based on studies of people with inconsistent sex attributes (hermaphrodites) and, in general, the investigators found that infants can be successfully raised—irrespective of their biological sex—in either sex. In this particular example, the raising of a genetic male as a female is reported.

The case is one of identical male twin brothers, one of whom lost his penis through an accident at the age of seven months. Consequently, Money advised the parents to raise this child as a female:

I gave them advice and counseling on the future prognosis and management of their new daughter, based on experiences with similar reassignments in hermaphroditic babies. In particular, they were given confidence that their child can be expected to differentiate a female gender identity, in agreement with her sex of rearing. (Money, 1975, p. 67)

By the age of nine years (the age when this case was reported), the two identical (genetically male) twins showed two clearly differentiated personalities, with different dress preferences, different attitudes towards cleanliness, very different toy preferences, different duties around the house which were willingly performed, and generally a sharply differentiated behavior structure. Money is very laudatory of the successful efforts of the mother to raise this child as a girl, and reports in positive terms on the mother's activities in these regards, e.g., 'in pointing out the specifics of the female and male adult reproductive roles,' and 'their other different roles, such as wife and husband or financial supporter of the family and caretaker of children and house' (p. 69).

Regarding domestic activities, such as work in the kitchen and house traditionally seen as part of the female's role, the mother reported that her daughter copies her in trying to help her tidying and cleaning up the kitchen, while the boy could not care less about it. She encourages her daughter when she helps her in the housework. (Money, 1975, pp. 69–70)

Through systematically applying a double standard (by differentially rewarding identical behavior—e.g., the mother encourages the daughter when she helps her in the housework, but presumably she does not encourage the son) and with the expert guidance of the clinician two different sex identities of anatomically identical people are constructed. The result of the process is likely to be two more adults who will consider it fitting for the 'nature' of a woman to take care of house and children, and fitting for the 'nature' of a man to be the breadwinner of a family. The assisting clinician obviously perceives this as the appropriate role division, and actively furthers this outcome. Considering that the girl is anatomically a boy, this case graphically illustrates—perhaps clearer than other cases of transsexualism, because we are here dealing with an involuntary transsexual—the completely arbitrary nature of our sex identity which is thereby shown not to be related to the presence of internal and/or external sex organs, counter to the claims of many psychologists.

In another study, Green (1976) compares 60 boys characterised by 'extensive cross-gender behavior' who are seen as potential future transsexuals, and therefore of a pathological inclination. They were so identified if on a 'never, occasionally, or frequently trichotomy' they 'at least occasionally cross-dressed, role-played as a female, preferred girls' toys and games, related better to girls, avoided rough-and-tumble play, and were called "sissy" by their peer group.' Instead of viewing a situation in which games are rigidly divided by sex, in which boys and girls are supposed not to like to play with each other, etc., as a case of social pathology, children who refuse to participate in this form of social sickness are seen as being individually pathological. It is striking that the discussion of transsexual pathology concerns almost exclusively gender identity rather than sex identity. Patients do not have a confused image about their sexual organs, although they display a strongly negative view of their own sex organs since these symbolise to them at the anatomical level the restrictions that they think they must accept at the personality level. Clinicians further this interpretation by themselves subscribing to a sexual dimorphism at the psychic level.

An alternative route would be not to attempt to convince these people to behave in a 'gender-appropriate manner,' but to try to get them to accept themselves as men or women, boys or girls who happen to have tastes that are similar to those of many (but not all) members of the other sex rather than to those of many (but not all) members of their own sex. Such an effort may possibly be too late for patients who seek sex reassignment surgery, and in that sense one cannot fault clinicians if they do not succeed in fostering a more positive self-image which includes an acceptance of one's sex organs without any attempt to conform to rigid sex roles. However, this does not alter the fact that individual transsexuals are casualties of an overly rigid sex role differentiation, and that clinicians who perform sex reassignment surgery help to maintain this overly rigid sexual dimorphism which is restrictive to every human being, whether female, male, or transsexual.

There is also some evidence of a scientific double standard on the part of clinicians, i.e., a differential interpretation of data according to the sex of the actor. Stoller and Baker (1973, p. 326), for example, when discussing the background of a male-to-female transsexual, note that he took some pride in getting away from his overly protective mother. 'When she [previously he] left the house, it was not to express masculine independence but was simply a rebellion against her mother's demands for housekeeping and for just staying in the house.' The action reported upon is asexual, but the interpretation offered is sexual.

Sexual dimorphism implies that one does not socially accept the presence of persons who are neither unambiguously male nor female, although in nature such people do exist, and in previous times at least some limited recognition was accorded to them.

Eunuchs and Intersexes

Biological sex is determined in different ways: chromosomal sex, gonadal sex, internal accessory organs, external genital appearance. In addition, the assigned sex and gender role may be consistent or inconsistent with the other determinants of sex (Rosenberg and Sutton-Smith, 1972, p. 31). In most people, all four biological determinants of sex and the assigned sex and rearing coincide, so that we have persons who are both in anatomy and in behavior unambiguously male or female. However, sometimes the determinants of sex are inconsistent with each other, and then we have cases of hermaphrodism, or mixed sex. The occurrence of different types of hermaphrodism has been estimated to be: for true hermaphrodites (with both male and female sex organs) very rare, for pseudomales 1 out of every 2,000, for pseudofemales also 1 out of every 2,000, for male pseudohermaphrodites 1 out of every 2,000, and for female pseudohermaphrodites 1 out of every 50,000 (*Encyclopedia Britannica*, 1973, vol. 11, p. 432). Inconsistent sex therefore, is in any given population not a very frequent phenomenon; but at a world level, it is not an uncommon condition, either. In Western societies we regard these people with inconsistent sex variables as abnormal and we attempt to rear them unambiguously as either male or female, although this is inconsistent with their true 'intersex,' since contemporary Western society has no social category for intersexes.

This has not always been the case. In some primitive societies, we find a social category for people who are neither female nor male but something else, for example, men who behave like women, or women who behave like men, etc. (Other primitive societies, however, would kill infants if they seemed somehow 'abnormal.') A fair bit has been written about people with an intersex status (for a discussion, see Martin and Voorhies, 1975, pp. 84–107), especially about the berdache, but Stoller (1976, pp. 537–8) suggests that

> *Although the subject has caught the attention of anthropologists and psychiatrists, this may be more for its oddity than frequency. Reviewing the anthropological literature, one cannot judge how many people like this existed at any time. My impression is that it was rare, so much so that whenever an anthropologist heard of such a person, a report was filed. The whole subject is mushy. And now it is too late to know.*

Whatever the frequency — or rarity — of social inter-sexes may have been, it seems certain that quite a number of peoples recognise more than two sexes, and that these cultures were not threatened by men who wanted to live like women and women who wanted to live like men. For instance, Evans-Pritchard (1945) describes the case of Nyaluthni, a woman among the Nuer (a semi-nomadic nilotic tribe) who was rich and barren and purchased for herself two wives. The wives bore her two children by Dinka men who did not live in Nyaluthni's homestead but frequently visited it, stayed there for one or several nights, and hoed her gardens. She chose them as the genitors of her children because they were known to be hard-working gardeners. Her children

> *address her as* gwa, *'father,' and not as* ma, *'mother.' She is a woman of outstanding character, with fine features, and always well-dressed. She is very competent and runs her homestead like a man. If her wives are lazy or disobedient she beats them. They treat her with the respect due to a husband and place meals before her with the same ceremony as they would employ to a male husband. She speaks of them as 'my wives.' She directs the business of the Kraal and homestead with the skill of an experienced herdsman and householder and stands no interference in matters pertaining to cattle, even from her initiated son. (Evans-Pritchard, 1945, pp. 31-2).*

This is the case of a woman who has been socially defined as a man. There are two contemporary reported instances in which non-operative transsexuals are apparently fully accepted within their own culture: among contemporary American Indians and in Vietnam. In spite of being socially accepted within their own culture, these people expressed the wish for sex reassignment surgery, which is probably due to the influence of Westernised America on their own culture.

In the first of these instances, Stoller (1976) reports of two contemporary male Indians who desired surgery. Neither one reported any ridicule from his peers or parents for his propensity to live as a female, and at least one of them had obtained a very high status within his tribe as the best basketweaver and dressmaker of the tribe. The other case is about 'Mimi,' another male-to-female (non-operative) transsexual in Vietnam. Mimi had been arrested as a prostitute by the police and was discovered to be a man only at the time of the routine gynecological examination, at which point he was suspected to be a draft dodger and was sent to the army induction center. He wanted to go to the United States for a sex change operation, but was apparently doing well in Vietnam as he was, and seemed to be relatively well-to-do. The authors reporting on this latter case distinguish between three distinct cultural attitudes towards transsexuals in contemporary Vietnam:

> *First, it provides an institutionalized transsexual role with high status and power in the society, perhaps in some ways similar to the Koniag culture and the Chuckchee shaman. Second, there is a tolerant attitude with low prestige but not social ostracism, perhaps similar to the Zuni 'la-mana.' This tolerance is extended to pre-pubertal children but appears to be considerably less for adults. Finally, westernized Vietnam appears similar to the United States in its strong societal disapproval of the marginal role for the transsexual. (Heiman and Le, 1975, pp. 93-4)*

Not only does Western society not award an official — and even less a high and powerful — status to people who behave in a 'sex-inappropriate' manner, we also socially deny the existence of people who — since birth or later in life — have changed in some aspect of their sexuality, such as through castration. It used to be the case that in a number of societies, being a eunuch (castrated male) was a recognised sexual status, which was often combined with a powerful political status. Eunuchs tended to be considered as good political advisers, since they were thought to be more likely to be loyal to the ruling dynasty because of their incapacity to sire children. Accordingly, eunuchs were used as political advisers in a number of empires, such as in China during the Chou period, and under the Han, T'ang, Ming and Sung emperors. The Achaeminid Persians employed political eunuchs, as did some Roman emperors and most of the emperors of Byzantium. Many of the patriarchs of Constantinople were eunuchs (*Encyclopedia Britannica,* 1973, vol. 8, p. 822). The Italians used to castrate boys in order to train them as adult sopranos. Without wishing to suggest that it is a recommendable practice to castrate boys (for whatever reason), I simply wish to point out that castrated males were in the past socially recognised as castrated males, whereas today they are likely to be treated as females, as was the twin who lost his penis as reported by Money (1975).

As a little side observation, it is interesting to note that while we have a historical name for castrated males (namely eunuch) we have no corresponding name for castrated females (women with hysterectomies), possibly because the changes in appearance are not as observable.

The Last Bulwark of the Double Standard

At present, the prevailing sex roles are under attack. At the social level, this manifests itself in collective movements, such as the women's liberation movement and the total woman movement as a backlash, the men's liberation movement and the National Organization for Men as a backlash, the gay liberation movement and the anti-homosexual movement (in the United States spearheaded by Anita Bryant) as a backlash. At the individual level, this is likely to result in more problems for some individuals who feel threatened by the gradual change in sex roles that is occurring. For others, it opens up options which have not been previously available to the same degree. Although changes in sex roles tend to be discussed in terms of female liberation, a change in the role of one sex necessitates a change in the role of the other. Widening of options—for members of both sexes—is as frightening to some as it is exhilarating to others.

While sex roles have been increasingly under attack, sex change operations have also become increasingly popular during the past few years. Historical reviews (e.g., Pauly, 1974a and 1974b, and Bullough, 1975) report only sparse information on older transsexuals. According to Pauly (1974b, p.520) the 'legitimization of sex reassignment surgery is vastly superior to that which existed only a few years ago.' The increase in numbers and medical legitimization of sex reassignment surgery is partially a reflection of the increase in technological expertise

for performing such operations, and the fact that only when the availability of such operations is known will people request it. On the other hand, sex change operations seem to have achieved some modicum of respectability which would indicate a change in the attitudes among physicians.

From a strictly physiological viewpoint, we must designate sex change operations as bodily mutilation—the willful destruction of physically healthy portions of the body for purely social reasons. What is absolutely stunning to me is the fact that, when asked, transsexuals do not seek this form of bodily mutilation primarily for sexual reasons (which seems to me the only conceivable justification) but for social reasons, as the completion of a process of transformation into a member of the other sex. And yet, the transformation can never truly take place, even if phalloplasty and vaginoplasty were vastly improved.

In the follow-up study of 42 male-to-female postoperative transsexuals, the transsexuals were asked to rank nine possible alternatives for 'your basic motivations for getting your sex changed.' The primary reason that was given was 'to make my body more like my mind, as a woman,' over such alternatives as the wearing of pretty clothing, being less aggressive, avoiding masculine expectations, having sex with a male, eliminating the male self through amputation of the penis, competing with another female, and winning the love of a parent. When the transsexuals were asked, after surgery, 'Which have you found to be more important and satisfying, your life as a female (able to have sex with males) or your social role as a woman in society?' the averages clearly showed that for the subjects surgery was important for non-sexual reasons (Bentler, 1976, p.569).

Seeking a sex change operation presupposes that the individual concerned considers him/herself incapable of achieving the goals that he or she has within the given body. This implies a mechanical identification of certain behavior and character traits with one's anatomy which is so strong that people are willing to have their bodies mutilated in order to decrease the differential between their preferred behavior and the restriction that they see as being set on this behavior through their bodies. Performing the operation implies that the physicians agree that the perceived discrepancy is a real discrepancy—that indeed the behaviors and traits displayed are appropriate for a member of the other sex only. Patient and doctor thus jointly reinforce the idea that behavior and character traits are legitimately determined by one's body, in the face of the evidence that suggests that our sex identity is imposed on a sexually largely or entirely undifferentiated character structure, and that, therefore, sex identity is a social rather than a biological product.

The rationale for sex reassignment surgery seems to be based on a circular logic which goes like this. Sex determines character. This is natural. Therefore, cases in which biological sex does not result in the expected sex identities are unnatural. Consequently, we need to change the biological sex (i.e., nature) in order to uphold the principle that biological sex determines one's character.

Transsexuals are people who suffer so deeply from the sex structure that they are willing to endure terrible pain and loneliness in order to reduce their suffering. This group of people would — potentially — be the most potent group of people pressing for changes in the sex structure, because their aversion to their 'sex-appropriate' roles is apparently insurmountable. By declaring them, by surgical fiat, as members of the other sex, this change potential is diverted and becomes as conservative as it could have been revolutionary. Each situation is individualized, rather than being recognized as the result of a social pathology, and the social pathology has overcome one more threat to its continued well-being.

Jan Morris (1975, p. 192), who underwent sex reassignment surgery, addressed this issue as follows:

Is mine only a transient phenomenon, between the dogmatism of the last century, when men were men and women were ladies, and the eclecticism of the next, when citizens will be free to live in the gender role they prefer? Will people read of our pilgrimage to Casablanca, a hundred years hence, as we might read of the search for the philosopher's Stone, or Simeon Stylites on his pillar?

I hope so. For every transsexual who grasps that prize, identity, ten, perhaps a hundred discover it to be only a mirage in the end, so that their latter quandary is hardly less terrible than their first.

Once we recognize the social pathology which creates the discussed individual pathologies, we must recognize the call of clinicians such as Pauly's (1974b, p. 522) that 'Parents ought to be more aware of the need to positively reinforce all infants for those gender characteristics which are consistent with their biological identity' as an attempt to ensure the continuing existence of the preconditions from which the problems with which these clinicians are concerned arise.

Endnotes

1. As noted in the introduction, many people distinguish between gender and sex, with sex referring to biological and gender to social differences between the sexes. Having tried for a while to use this terminology, I have since given it up as confusing. As a rule, I only use the term 'sex.' In this chapter, however, I shall use the term 'gender' when I am discussing authors who use the term.
2. In a more recent paper, Bem (1977) concurs with the suggestion that the BSRI ought to be scored so as to yield four rather than three distinct groups, namely masculine (high masculine, low feminine scores), feminine (high feminine, low masculine scores), androgynous (high masculine and low feminine scores) and undifferentiated (low masculine and low feminine scores). Although this introduces a variation into the operationalization of androgyny, it does not alter the basic problem underlying androgyny scores.

References

Bem, Sandra L. 'The Measurement of Psychological Androgyny,' *Journal of Clinical Psychology,* vol. 42, no. 2 (1974), pp. 155–62.

Bem, Sandra L. 'On the Utility of Alternative Procedures for Assessing Psychological Androgyny,' *Journal of Consulting and Clinical Psychology,* vol. 45, no. 2 (1977), pp. 166–205.

Bentler, Peter M. 'A Typology of Transsexualism: Gender Identity Theory and Data,' *Archives of Sexual Behavior,* vol. 5, no. 6 (1976), pp. 567–83.

Bullough, Vern L. 'Transsexualism in History,' *Archives of Sexual Behavior,* vol. 4, no. 5 (1975), pp. 561–71.

Decision Marketing Research Ltd. *Women in Canada* (Ottawa, Office of the Coordinator, Status of Women, 2nd ed., 1976).

Eichler, Margrit, 'Power, Dependency, Love and the Sexual Division of Labour. A Critique of the Decision-Making Approach to Family Power and an Alternative Approach' (unpublished paper).

Encyclopedia Britannica, vols. 8 and 11 (1973 ed.).

Evans-Pritchard, E.E. *Some Aspects of Marriage and the Family among the Nuer* (The Rhodes-Livingstone Papers no. 11) (Livingstone, Northern Rhodesia, The Rhodes Livingstone Institute, 1945).

Feinbloom, Deborah Heller. *Transvestites and Transsexuals* (USA, Delacorte Press/Seymour Lawrence, 1976).

Green, Richard, 'One-Hundred Ten Feminine and Masculine Boys: Behavioral Contrasts and Demographic

Similarities,' *Archives of Sexual Behavior,* vol. 5, no. 5 (1976), pp. 425–46.

Heiman, Elliott M. and Cao Van Le. 'Transsexualism in Vietnam,' *Archives of Sexual Behavior,* vol. 4, no. 1 (1975), pp. 89–95.

Holter, Harriet. *Sex Roles and Social Structure* (Oslo, Bergen, Tromso, Universitetsforlaget, 1970).

Hore, B. D., F. V. Nicolle and J. S. Calnan. 'Male Transsexualism: Two Cases in a Single Family,' *Archives of Sexual Behavior,* pp. 317–31.

Laurie, Bonnie. 'An Assessment of Sex-Role Learning in Kindergarten Children: Experimental Application of a Toy Test with Direct Reinforcement of Sex-Typed and of Androgenous Behaviour' (unpublished MA thesis, Dept. of Educational Theory, University of Toronto, 1977).

Martin, M. Kay and Barbara Voorhies. *Female of the Species* (Toronto, Methuen, 1975).

Meyer, Jon K. 'Clinical Variants Among Applicants for Sex Reassignment,' *Archives of Sexual Behavior,* vol. 3, no. 6 (1974), pp. 527–58.

Money, John. 'Development Differentiation of Femininity and Masculinity Compared,' in *Man and Civilization: The Potential of Woman* (New York, McGraw-Hill, 1963), pp. 51–65.

Money, John. 'Ablatio Penis: Normal Male Infant Sex-Reassigned as a Girl,' *Archives of Sexual Behavior,* vol. 4, no. 1 (1975), pp. 65–71.

Money, John and Anke A. Ehrhardt. *Man and Woman, Boy and Girl* (New York: New American Library, 1974).

Money, John, J. L. Hampson and J. G. Hampson, 'An Examination of some Basic Sexual Concepts: The Evidence of Human Hermaphroditism' *Bulletin of the Johns Hopkins Hospital,* vol. 97 (1955), pp. 301–19.

Money, John and George Wolff. 'Sex Reassignment: Male to Female to Male,' *Archives of Sexual Behavior,* vol. 2, no. 3, (1973), pp. 245–50.

Morris, Jan. *Conundrum* (New York, Signet Books, 1975).

Pauly, Ira B. 'Female Transsexualism: Part 1,' *Archives of Sexual Behavior,* vol. 3, no. 5 (1974a) pp. 487–507.

Pauly, Ira B. 'Female Transsexualism: Part II,' *Archives of Sexual Behavior,* vol. 3, no. 6 (1974b) pp. 509–26.

Rosenberg, B. G. and Brian Sutton-Smith. *Sex and Identity* (New York, Holt, Rinehart and Winston, 1972).

Sawyer, Jack. 'On Male Liberation,' in Deborah S. David and Robert Brannon (eds.), *The Forty-Nine Percent Majority: The Male Sex Role* (Reading, Mass., Addison-Wesley Publ. Co., 1976), pp. 287–90.

Stoller, Robert, 'Etiological Factors in Female Transsexualism: A First Approximation', *Archives of Sexual Behavior,* vol. 2, no. 1 (1972), pp. 47–64.

Stoller, Robert J. 'Two Feminized Male American Indians,' *Archives of Sexual Behavior,* vol. 5, no. 6 (1976) pp. 529–38.

Stoller, Robert J. and Howard J. Baker. 'Two Male Transsexuals in One Family,' *Archives of Sexual Behavior,* vol. 2, no. 4 (1973), pp. 323–8.

Swift, Jonathan. *Gulliver's Travels* (New York, Airmont Books, 1963).

(Not Just) Another Day at the Gynecologist

Suzanne Hyers

My doctor is a man, fiftyish, with a heavy accent; Austrian, I think. I've been seeing him for about four years. He doesn't really appear to be at ease with my body, seeming almost shy. During the breast exam, for example, he always raises his head and shuts his eyes a bit while rolling my breast in his two hands, reminding me of a fortune teller with her crystal ball. I'm usually charmed by his awkwardness. He also gives me gynecological exams, referring always to my sex partner(s) as "he." I've never corrected him. Until now.

Last week we went through the same routine, but during our requisite, impersonal discussion (*"Are you sure you don't want birth control pills?"*), I corrected the pronouns he used. He assumed I had made an error and continued. I corrected him again and he just looked at me.

"That's right. I sleep with women." (*Long pause.*) Again, "I'm with women. I don't go out with men. I go to bed with women, a woman." He sat down.

"What exactly do you do?" he asked. (*My turn to pause, spitting out nervous laughter.*)

"What do you mean 'what do we do'? What do *you* do? It's not all that different." (*I lied.*)

He thought about that for a while and said, "I don't understand how one of you plays boy without a penis."

Wishing desperately for, but just as desperately lacking, the wit of Dorothy Parker after being handed such a line, I could only (*with a smile recognizing that this is what is meant by 'the real world'*) look him in the eye and say, "We don't try to play boy."

"Then what exactly do you do?" he said. I began to get impatient.

"Well, what do *you* do when you don't have intercourse with your wife?" His face was a total blank. Another long pause. "Well, there's the whole area of oral sex, for example." Again, his face was a total blank—as must be, I began to think, his sex life. He sat with his head down for a while, looked up at me a few times, and said, 'man-to-man',

"I knew a homosexual once. In the war. POW camp. He always went to young boys. I never really knew what they did. I never asked."

He asked if there were anything else he could do for me; he said it was good seeing me again. And, for the first time, he shook my hand, thanking me for answering his questions.

(*I hope his wife thanks me.*)

Reprinted from Suzanne Hyers, "(Not Just) Another Day at the Gynecologist," by permission of the author.

The Yellow Wallpaper

Charlotte Perkins Gilman

John [my husband] is a physician, and *perhaps*—(I would not say it to a living soul, of course, but this is dead

Reprinted from Charlotte Perkins Gilman, *The Yellow Wallpaper,* (Boston: Small, Maynard, 1899).

paper and a great relief to my mind)—*perhaps* that is one reason I do not get well faster. . . .

There comes John, and I must put this away,—he hates to have me write a word.

Alive: The Story of the Andes Survivors

Piers Paul Read

Psychological testing had revealed him as a boy with violent instincts, a fact that had at least partly determined

Reprinted from Piers Paul Read, *Alive: The Story of the Andes Survivors* (Philadelphia: Lippincott, 1974).

the choice of both rugby and medical study for him; the demanding physical contest and the practice of surgery, it was thought, would help to channel his aggressive tendencies.

A Biosocial Perspective on Parenting

Alice S. Rossi

Contemporary Research on Variant Marriage and Family Forms

A very diverse set of groups now shares the common view that the nuclear family and monogamous marriage are oppressive, sexist, "bourgeois," and sick. Exponents of sexual liberation, self-actualization, socialism, humanism, gay liberation, existentialism, and certain segments of feminism have joined hands in a general denunciation of the stereotyped "traditional nuclear family," although rarely defining what they mean. One infers, however, that they usually refer to a legal marriage between a man and a woman who share a household with their legitimate offspring, with the male as the breadwinner and the female as a homemaker.[1] "Variant" or "experimental" families and marriages would then include a wide array of forms, from cohabitant heterosexual couples, multilateral marriages, single-parent households, dual-career couples with or without children to families traditional in everything except consensual participation in co-marital, swinging, or swapping sexual relationships outside the marriage. This is a wide assortment indeed, and interestingly the "traditional" category has been counted at something less than a third of the actual families in the United States simply by regarding the criterion of an employed wife as being sufficient to classify a family as a variant form.[2] By doing this, of course, the researcher also artificially exaggerates the degree to which genuinely variant marriage and family forms are prevalent in our society.

But there is a further interesting characteristic of this literature. Although the titles of publications on alternate-family forms almost always refer to "families," in fact the works themselves focus almost exclusively on the adult relationship between men and women, in and out of, or in

addition to, marriage. They rarely concern themselves with children, parenting, or parent-child relations. For example, the special 1972 issue of *The Family Coordinator* consists of fifteen articles published under the title "Variant Marriage Styles and Family Forms." A simple line-count content analysis, however, reveals the following (converting the line count to estimated pages): *only 5 percent of the total 123 full-text pages in this issue deal with any aspect of parenting, child care, or the parent-child relationship.* Marriage and the male-female relationship are receiving the central attention in this new genre of family sociology, not family systems or the birth and rearing of children.

The implicit premise in much of this literature is the right of the individual to an expanded freedom in the pursuit of private sexual pleasure: I want what I want when I want it. Thus Smith and Smith variously refer to monogamous marriage as "sexual monopoly," "a form of emotional and sexual malnutrition," and a "condition of sexual deprivation."[3] Variant families, Cogswell summarizes, are entered into not with an expectation of permanence, as traditional nuclear families are, but with "the expectation that relationships will continue only so long as they serve the mutual benefit of the members."[4] A similar note is struck in Lorber's claim that "a feminist goal is total freedom of choice in sex partners throughout one's life."[5]

There are several problems posed by these views of family relations that are often revealed in the actual experiences of men and women who are currently experimenting with new forms of marriage and family relations. The sexual liberationist clearly rejects the traditional double standard; what is not clear is whether the new single standard will be modeled after what has been the male pattern, the female pattern, or some amalgam of the two. A close reading of the literature on contemporary sexual practices and on the attitudes of the young suggests the

Reprinted from Alice Rossi, "A Biosocial Perspective on Parenting," in *Daedalus,* Journal of the American Academy of Arts and Sciences, vol. 106, no. 2 (1977) Boston, Massachusetts, by permission of the publisher and the author.

model is a male pattern: early initiation, sexual diversity, physical play through casual sex. In studies of adolescent attitudes toward sexuality, it has been found that adolescents are coming to regard sex as a "good way to get acquainted," a means to *develop* rather than to *express* couple intimacy. At the same time, extremely large gender differences still exist among the holders of such attitudes, with men two to three times more apt than women their own age to endorse the more casual attitude to sexuality.[6] The literature on co-marital sex shows that, in three out of four cases, it is the husband who initiates the seeking of other sex partners, participation tends to last about six months, the wives tend to be homemakers with neither jobs nor community involvements, and the couples are very careful to keep their sexual activities a secret from their children.[7] Sexual liberation, then, seems to mean that increasing numbers of women are now following male initiatives in a more elaborate, multi-partner sexual script.

A second issue concerns the pressure toward widening the circle of sexual partners that is implicit in the notion of expanded freedom of private sexual pleasure. If no sex is to take place under the new ideological "cult of mutual desire," there necessarily must be either a considerable decline in the frequency of sex or access to more than one partner, since any marital relationship that includes two busy people with busy lives will be frequently out of phase in sexual desire. It is but a short step to the view that spouse swapping or co-marital sex is precisely what contemporary marriages need to remain intact, healthy, and self-actualizing for both partners. For a married woman not to enjoy sex with men other than her husband, or, in some quarters, not to be bisexual is to be out of step with the times — an old-fashioned spouse or a poor feminist. The message seems to be that to be faithful, possessive, exclusively heterosexual, and able to postpone gratification are signs of immaturity and oppression. Smith and Smith argue that the ". . . conquest of sexual jealousy . . . could be the greatest advance in human relations since the advent of common law or the initiation of democratic processes. The increased frequency and incidence of swinging and swapping . . . could then be viewed . . . as [presaging] a new era in sexual and interpersonal relationships."[8]

A third issue concerns the implications of ego indulgence and immediate gratification for parenthood. What is the analogue of sexual liberation here? Can women or men be parents only when they want to be or only when their children want to be parented? One would assume that any awareness of the developmental needs of children, or of the emotional attachment of parents to them, would require an answer of "no." But this is not the case in the new family sociology. The following quotation advocating communal families illustrates explicitly what is implicit in much of this literature: "By always having some children in our unit, we will be able to assume parental roles when and for as long as we want. . . . Our children will have an advantage [in that] from the adults they can select their own parents, brothers, sisters, friends. . . . Our social ties will not be forced nor strained by the mandates of kinship and marital obligation."[9] Here the image is clear: in the post-nuclear-family era, the adult can turn parenthood on and off and exchange children as well as sexual partners.

In more serious studies by observers, there are hints of difficulties and strains arising when such an ideology is put into practice. In Kanter's studies of urban middle-class communes,[10] she points to a tendency to view children as miniature adults, free to establish relationships with adults other than their parents in the communal household. But since notions of discipline and tolerance of children vary among adults, Kanter reports a considerable amount of confusion among the four-to-twelve-year-old children she interviewed, as a consequence of what she calls the "Cinderella effect" (rapid demands or corrections by a number of unrelated adults to the same child at the same time). There is also evidence that the sharing of children creates emotional difficulties for many parents, particularly the mothers of the children, until eventually parents tend to reserve for themselves the right to protect and punish their children. The researchers note that very rarely did a mother allow a male communal member to invoke sanctions with her children, and even when he did, it was clear that he was acting for the mother through some form of delegated authority.[11]

Berger's work on communal families[12] also reveals stress in child-rearing. Communal ideology is extended to children through the notion of equality defined as identity, so that the children are viewed as "autonomous human beings, equal to adults."[13] Berger cites one mother who aptly caught the dilemma of this ideology in action: "What I wanted was a baby; but a kid, that's something else." Having a baby, particularly by a natural birth in a communal household, is a great occasion of collective celebration: it is organic, earthy, beautiful. Besides, babies represent human potential unspoiled by the corrupting influence of repressive institutions. But rearing a child involves obligations for which commune members are not prepared, since it means future orientation, planning, and some status distinctions between adults, who have knowledge, and children, who do not. This cuts across the communal view that tends to "regard themselves as kids, their lives as unsettled, their futures uncertain."[14] Despite the ideology, Berger notes that infants and knee babies are almost universally in the charge of their mothers, and that whatever sharing takes place of children from two to four is largely confined to the group of mothers with young children; only children over five are supervised by other adults, and then with some of the difficulties Kanter noted.

The power of ideology is well illustrated in Rothchild and Wolf's recent book on children of counterculture parents.[15] The report provides an overall portrait of children almost uniformly neglected, deprived, and tormented; many are uneducated, disorganized, and disturbed; a pervasive boredom and lack of joy and serious problems of mal- or undernourishment were prevalent. After such a sad portrait, it comes as a shock to find the authors concluding that the communes are a success in child-rearing because they have done away with materialism and competitiveness. In reality, the counterculture parents are obviously trying to rear children without having to be bothered by them, a profile strikingly similar to the earlier one by Berger.

Just as the sexual script, so the parenting script in the new family sociology seems to be modeled on what has been a male pattern of relating to children, in which men turn their fathering on and off to suit themselves or their appointments for business or sexual pleasure. The authors and dramatists of both the mating and parenting scripts in the new perspectives on the family are just as heavily male as the older schools of thought about the modern family, if not in the generic sense, then in the sense that parenting is viewed from a distance, as an appendage to, or consequence of, mating, rather than the focus of family systems and individual lives. It is not at all clear what the gains will be for either women or children in this version of human liberation.[16]

The Articulation of Mating and Parenting in a Biosocial Perspective

Western societies have long had a split image of woman — the temptress Eve and the saintly Mary — that symbolized the polarity between sex (bad) and maternity (good) in Christian theology. Until the twentieth century,

Eve for the most part remained outside the family as the loose woman, mistress, prostitute. More recently, she has come indoors to reign as the sensuous wife Eve bonded tenuously to the nurturant mother Mary. In the nineteen-seventies, the variant-marriage literature extols a good Eve who makes it both at home and away from home, while Mary recedes into an anti-natalist shadow, a reverse split-image, but still a split-image: what was good is now bad, what was bad is now good. In sociological terms, recreative sex has contemporary ascendance over procreative sex and parenting.

Beneath this cultural scenario, however, are intimate connections between sexuality and maternalism in the female of the species that Western society has not reckoned with. Indeed, it could be argued that the full weight of Western history has inserted a wedge between sex and maternalism so successfully that women themselves and the scientists who have studied their bodies and social roles have seldom seen the intimate connections between them. Yet the evidence is there in female reproductive physiology, thinly covered by a masculine lens that projects male fantasy onto female functions.

A good starting place to observe such fantasy is the initial coming together of sperm and ovum. Ever since Leeuwenhoek first saw sperm under the microscope, great significance has been attached to the fact that sperm are equipped with motile flagella, and it was assumed that the locomotive ability of the sperm fully explained their journey from the vagina through the cervix and uterus to the oviduct for the encounter with the ovum. This notion persists even today in scientific publications, to say nothing of more literary examples.[17] Rorvik describes the seven-inch journey through the birth canal and womb to the waiting egg as equivalent to a 500-mile upstream swim for a salmon, and comments with admiration that they often make the hazardous journey in under an hour, "more than earning their title as the most powerful and rapid living creatures on earth."[18] The image is clear: powerful active sperm and a passive ovum awaiting its arrival and penetration, male sexual imagery structuring the very act of conception. In fact, the transport through the female system is much too rapid to be accounted for purely by the locomotive ability of the sperm. Furthermore, completely inert substances such as dead sperm and even particles of India ink reach the oviducts as rapidly as live sperm do.[19]

What, then, does transport the sperm? The stimulus comes from the impact of sexual stimulation upon the female, which by neural impulses to the hypothalamus stimulates the posterior pituitary to release oxytocin, which in turn produces uterine contractions that propel the sperm on their way.[20] Nor can the sperm immediately penetrate the ovum, for, once in the oviduct, it takes several hours of what physiologists call "capacitation" before the sperm acquires the ability to penetrate the ovum,[21] so there is not even much point to the notion of a competitive race to be the first to reach the ovum—another male fantasy.

Interestingly, oxytocin is a hormone that is a clear link between sexuality and maternalism: it stimulates the uterine contractions that help the sperm on their way to the oviduct; at high levels it produces the stronger contractions of childbirth; and it causes nipple erection during either nursing or loveplay. Whether the sucking is by an infant or a lover, oxytocin acts upon the basket cells around the alveoli, causing them to constrict, and in the case of nursing, to squeeze out the milk in the phenomenon known as "milk let-down."[22]

The interconnection between sexuality and maternalism makes good evolutionary sense. By providing some erotogenic pleasure to the mother of a newborn baby, there is greater assurance that the child will be nursed and the uterus restored to pre-pregnancy status. The fact that the clitoris is not in the birth canal contributes to sensual pleasure in the immediate post-birth period of greatest infant fragility. Pregnancy and childbirth in turn improve the gratification women derive from coital orgasm, since orgasmic intensity is directly related to the degree of pelvic vasocongestion, and vasocongestion increases with each subsequent pregnancy.[23] On either score, then, human female physiology both contributes to the personal sexual gratification of women and assures their continued cooperation in species survival.[24]

There is some evidence from both physiological and anthropological research of the connection between sexual attitudes and childbirth experiences. Grimm[25] and Newton[26] report a coherent syndrome of good sexual adjustment and low incidence of nausea during pregnancy, easier and shorter labor, desire for and success at nursing, and preference for natural childbirth. Mead and Newton[27] report that childbirth is remarkably short and painless in a society with relaxed sexual attitudes, such as that of the South American Siriono, where birth is an easy, public event controlled by the mother herself, but that it is a prolonged painful process among the Cuna in Panama who prevent young girls from learning about either coitus or childbirth until the final stages of the marriage ceremony. Western societies have historically approximated the Cuna to a greater extent than the Siriono.

Contemporary writers reveal more than they intend when they distinguish between recreative and procreative sex. In the "beyond monogamy" literature, this distinction is typically the starting point in discussions of the advantages of an "open" marriage, swinging, or spouse swapping, which are premised on fully effective contraceptives: sexual freedom is possible because no pregnancy will follow from the multiple sex encounters a woman may have in a given month, and, should one occur, there is always the back-up of an abortion. By the same token, however, pregnancies which are wanted or permitted to come to term are assumed to be legitimate ones in the context of a "primary" relationship. Even when birth is a joyful public event in a communal household or in an Israeli kibbutz, where the child will be reared largely in the children's houses, there is apparently as strong a mother-infant bond as in the American nuclear family. Thus proponents of experimental family forms continue to link parenting to either marriage or a stable "primary" relationship. It is questionable whether the single mothers who head the households that include eight million children under eighteen retain responsibility for their children because they are "stuck with the kids" simply as a result of cultural pressure, as some current family critics claim. It is more likely that the emotional ties to the children are more important to the mothers than to the fathers. It is probably still the case that the vast majority of women can have ex-spouses but not ex-children.[28]

As pregnancies become increasingly intentional and freely chosen, and less often the unintended consequences of the pursuit of sexual pleasure, this fundamental salience of the mother-child relationship may become stronger, not weaker, than it has been in the past. Infants may respond to anyone who provides stable loving caretaking, but the predisposition to respond to the child may be much greater on the part of the mother than the father, a reflection of the underlying dual orientation of the female to both mate and child, a heritage that links mating and parenting more closely for females than males, and one rooted in both mammalian physiology and human culture. If a society wishes to create shared parental roles, it must either accept the high probability that the mother-infant relationship will continue to have greater emotional depth than the father-infant relationship, or institutionalize the means for providing men with compensatory exposure and training in infant and child care in order to close the gap produced by the physiological experience of pregnancy, birth, and nursing. Without such compensatory training of males, females will show added dimensions of intensity to their bonds with children.

Obstetric Management of Childbirth

Since the biological sciences, medicine, and clinical psychiatry have been more closely associated with one another than sociology and psychology have been to any of them, one might think that obstetric management of childbirth would reflect an awareness of female physiology in the psychological experience it provides for the woman during pregnancy and birth and the impact it may have upon the bonding of mother and newborn. There is no evidence that this has been the case. In fact, there is hardly an instance in human life in industrial societies that has shown so great a degree of technological interference with a natural process than American obstetric management of pregnancy and birth. In the past fifty years, spontaneous birth in a familiar setting has been replaced by medically managed deliveries, and, as noted earlier, breast feeding has been largely replaced by bottle feeding.

Until very recently, obstetric practice received very little criticism in the United States, despite the fact that many aspects of obstetric management have warranted it—to name just some of them: heavy reliance on anesthetics which produces drugged babies prone to respiratory distress and apathetic response at birth, the use of instruments which risk brain damage and newborn trauma, obstetric insistence on horizontal delivery tables which prolong second-stage labor because the body is not working with but against gravity, foot stirrups which stretch the perineal tissue so that physicians feel justified in performing routine episiotomies that would otherwise be unnecessary in most cases, premature cutting of the umbilical cord which robs the newborn of up to a quarter of its blood supply and prolongs the third stage of labor because the placenta remains engorged, and, perhaps most important from a psychological perspective, the use of general anesthesia which cheats the mother of consciousness at the moment of birth, at precisely the point when hormonal levels and the euphoria of accomplishment could contribute to a positive experience for the woman and a deep attachment between mother and child.[29] A search of the literature yields no studies which contrast the early attachment of the mother and infant when the mother was fully conscious at the birth with that when the mother was anesthetized, but, in several well-designed studies, Klaus and his associates have found that the earlier the contact of a mother with her newborn and the longer that contact, the greater the mother-child attachment at the end of the first month.[30] Kennell reports the persistence of such early-contact effects at the end of the first year of the child's life.[31] In this critical area, the medical field may have grossly exaggerated the degree of difference between human mothers and other primate mothers, for numerous studies have found that separation of the mother and infant at birth produces impairment in their relationship and in the development of the young.[32] From the point of view of the health and well-being of the newborn, American babies are cheated of a good start in life: the Apgar scores[33] of infants born in home settings with midwife attendants in poor sections of Appalachia show healthier babies than those born in private obstetric practice in many hospitals in wealthy suburbs. In the Netherlands where birth is managed in as natural a way as possible, babies show markedly better Apgar scores of physical well-being at birth than American babies do.[34]

It is surprising that so little research has been done on the impact of pregnancy upon women from the point of view of the impact of medical management of pregnancy and birth.[35] A flood of literature can be found on the relation between hormones and behavior,[36] but little has been done to extend our understanding of the impact of the sharply elevated hormonal levels during pregnancy and what their contribution may be to attachment behavior, particularly when women have, or do not have, first contact with their babies during the post-birth hours when hormonal levels are still high. We already know of fluctuations in estrogen and progesterone levels during the female menstrual cycle and the mood and behavioral correlates of those fluctuations,[37] yet the fact that estrogen levels show a tenfold increase and progesterone a hundredfold increase during pregnancy has not stimulated comparable research.[38]

Studies of this sort are important also, of course, for their implications regarding the often unanticipated impact of pregnancy and birth upon young women. A more sociological perspective is also needed, one that deals with the distortion of the natural process involved in the medical management of birth. In medical literature, the model of pregnancy is apt to be couched in terms of intrapsychic forces within the woman—e.g., that pregnancy involves a "regression" to childhood as the mother identifies with the fetus (and hence provides a rationale for patient infantilization by obstetricians?). But pregnancy and birth take place in a social context, and they clearly demonstrate the impact of technocratic management to the detriment of women and their babies. Most recently, the use of fetal-monitoring equipment during the early stages of labor has provided an unprecedented amount of information on the course of labor. Physicians were so ill-prepared for it that a steady increase in Caesarian deliveries has resulted in hospitals using such equipment, suggesting yet another new pressure in the direction of technological takeover of a natural process.

Parlee[39] and Rossi[40] have suggested that one reason for post-partum distress among women may be the isolation in which women find themselves when they return with their babies from the hospital. This, too, is a radical departure from the experience of the species in our long history. In earlier stages of human history, mothers moved in a world crowded with supportive kin who supplemented their care of infants, a situation in sharp contrast to the experience of most American women today. Not only is the natural process interfered with through medical distortion of spontaneous birth, the mother separated from the baby for most of the critical first days of life, the infant fed on a rigid hospital schedule, and kept in a brightly lit and noisy nursery, but then the mother is sent home with her infant to cope as well as she can totally on her own. If she breaks down under this strange regimen, she is regarded as incompetent to handle "normal" female responsibilities.

Social scientists who have been concerned with the transition to parenthood in American families have been puzzled by the fact that post-partum depression increases with the parity of the birth. Sociological expectations had been that a first birth would represent more of a "crisis" than later births, since it is a "new" experience and an important transition in family structure. In fact, it is multiparous women who show greater emotional stress,[41] perhaps because of the shorter intervals between births that have become common in Western societies only in relatively recent human history. In the larger framework of human evolution, breast-feeding imposed its own control on the spacing of births, for lactation together with physical activity and a low sugar and carbohydrate diet kept body fat low enough to prevent ovulation and hence to assure a child spacing of three or more years, the number depending on the cultural norms that governed the duration of breast-feeding.[42] With our enriched diets, lactation no longer serves as a good ovulatory inhibitor.[43]

Jane Lancaster[44] has pointed out that the modern practice of deliberately timing births close together may be an aberration from desirable practice and a key factor in the stress many women experience in coping with their young.

By neglecting the biosocial dimension of human life, American society may set the stage for unprecedented stress in the lives of young mothers and an impoverishment of the quality of their relationship with their children. A second child who is born when the first child is under two years of age is not only taxing on the mother's physical and emotional stamina, but whatever support system of kin and friends the mother has is more apt to consider her "experienced" in mothering by the second birth and consequently to give her less, rather than more, assistance. In the absence of any adequate empirical investigation of the effects of family size,[45] birth spacing, and the presence or absence of supplementary aid in the care of the child, no scientific guidelines exist by which women who wish to make informed decisions can space their pregnancies. The ability to plan pregnancies by contraceptives is a partial achievement at best, if it is not coupled with some notion of what optimal spacing is. The anticipated drop in family size implied by the current low-fertility plans of young women does not settle the issue, because the spacing between two births may be as brief in a two-child as in a four-child family.

One final aspect of the pregnancy issue may be of even greater significance in the future, as more women work through the months of pregnancy. In light of the Supreme Court ruling in November, 1975,[46] that mandatory laying-off by the employer of women during the last three months of pregnancy and the first six weeks following childbirth is in violation of the Fourteenth Amendment, the practice of working throughout pregnancy may increase in future years. This is not purely a legal or women's-rights issue, for a correct assessment of its implications calls for knowledge we do not yet possess. We need to know two things: what the effects of stress during pregnancy are for the healthy development of the fetus, and what the effects of working environments are upon the health of the pregnant woman and the fetus. The latter issue is of growing concern in light of Hunt's estimate that more fetuses are in the American workplace now than there were children in our mines and factories in the whole history of American child labor.[47] Yet no large-scale investigations have been undertaken of the potential influence on the fetus of the vast array of chemicals and synthetics among which many women now work.

Second, some evidence has been found that psychological stress in the mother may be transmitted to the fetus prenatally. Ferreira[48] found that the infants of high-stress mothers show more irritability, crying, irregular bowel movements, etc., than infants of low-stress mothers, behavior that is as clear on the first day after birth as it is on the fifth—a significant point because, in the hospital involved, mothers have no contact with their infants for the first twenty-four hours after birth, and consequently observations of the baby on the first day clearly took place before any mother-infant contact. The study suggests, therefore, that prenatal environment includes more than simply food intake from the mother; it embraces the mother's attitudes and expectations concerning the child, in a process that probably involves the emotional state of the mother and its effects upon maternal body chemistry and, from there, on the nervous system of the fetus. Some women may find that withdrawal from their customary activities during pregnancy is conducive to anxiety, while others may find continuing their customary activities has that effect. Here again, we need to know more about the social circumstances and the personal characteristics that affect anxiety levels in women during pregnancy, so that guidelines might be developed to assist them in deciding whether to continue full-time employment, adopt a part-time schedule, or withdraw altogether, according to their susceptibilities to stress.

Children and Work

In the long evolution of the human species, women have always engaged in productive labor along with childbearing and -rearing. Hence women in industrial societies are not departing radically from the past when they combine child-rearing and employment. All women work, and they always have—sometimes as producers of goods and services on the land and in the household, sometimes for wages in the marketplace. The questions now are where women work during pregnancy, how adequate the support system is that provides assistance to mothers of very young children, and what the best conditions are for the healthy development of the preschool child. In this last section, attention will focus on these aspects of early child development.

That it is a critical subject is suggested by the sharp increase in the past decade in the employment of mothers with at least one child under three years of age, for such women show a labor-force participation rate that has more than quadrupled in the past decade. It is widely ex-

pected that the trend toward employment among mothers of very young children will accelerate in future years, so that urgent questions of child care will continue to be with us.[49] Unfortunately, the rationale for child-care programs in the past has been the needs of the economy or the needs of the mother, not the needs of children. Public programs have been developed to encourage women to enter the labor force in wartime or to attract women to industries in regions with an inadequate labor supply.[50] Recent efforts to fund day care have been similarly motivated: to permit, or coerce, welfare mothers to support themselves, or to compensate for inadequate care of the child in impoverished homes. Feminist efforts have been similarly focused on the needs of women, with child care justified as a necessary means to permit participation by women in the labor force at a rate and a level of job commitment equal to that of men.

As a consequence, little has yet been done to disturb the idea that under the best of all circumstances, the best place for young children is in the home under the mother's care. Even as innovative and dedicated a child-care researcher as Bettye Caldwell reports[51] the difficulty with which she struggled to rid herself of the concept of child "care" as a substitute or supplement to maternal care, and to use instead the concept of a "supportive environment" for optimal growth in the child. It was a big step for Caldwell to move from the idea of caring for a child in a custodial sense or as compensation for an impoverished home to the idea of a growth center as a kind of third parent that could contribute creatively to the child's development in ways the best home could not provide. American attitudes toward child care have a long way to go before they reach the level of Swedish appreciation of the preschool years as a developmental stage when contact both with peers and with trained personnel can make vital contributions to healthy child development.

Once this shift in perspective does take place, it becomes possible to compare the family home with a growth center in a new light. Much has been made of the isolation of the young mother with preschool children in the suburban home, cut off from her former life, isolated from adult stimulation. By the same token, such a household is an isolating hothouse for young children, too, cutting them off from easy access to other children of their own age. Birth-order effects may be attributed to the pecking order that is built into the structure of the sibling set in the small-family household, a hierarchy of an invidious sort: at the top, the oldest child—bigger, smarter, stronger, bossier, an aristocrat with the ego-blustering that sometimes goes with that status; at the bottom, the youngest child—smaller, weaker, less knowledgeable—incompetent compared to the older siblings and turning to cuteness and attention-seeking as a result. In the past, when larger groups of adults and children provided the context within which children were reared, this pecking order did not occur. We have already noted that close child-spacing is a phenomenon of quite recent development. Close spacing between children may also have stimulated far more sibling rivalry than existed in the past: the birth of a sibling may be felt far more keenly as displacement when a child is between one and four years of age than it is when the child is older. Indeed, precisely because women have little support from other women, care of the newborn can in fact so preoccupy a mother that neither her time nor her energy is sufficient for the slightly older child. In other words, there may be a social reality behind the subjective sense of displacement in the three-year-old following the birth of a younger sibling. By contrast, when five years intervene between births, the older children have already reached an age at which peers from neighborhood and kindergarten reduce their dependence on their mothers. They are also old enough to help the mother, serving as assistant in home and baby care that makes the mother/older-child relationship an alliance. The result can well be less emotional and physical fatigue for the mother, a forward step in the growth of skills and independence in the older child, and warmth, rather than rivalry, in the sibling relationship.

In the modern circumstance, growth centers in which young children regularly spend part of each day may help to teach humility to the oldest child and self-confidence to the youngest. It can also be viewed as a means of shifting back toward a more natural way of life for both women and children.[52] Multi-family households, in which the sexual and parenting lines of the nuclear families remain intact but which include overlapping and shared living space, would similarly provide children with access to peers and parents with built-in support systems for alternating child care, coping more easily with family emergencies, and easing the combination of work and family responsibilities carried by both male and female household members.

Endnotes

1. B. E. Cogswell and M. B. Sussman, "Changing Family and Marriage Forms: Complications for Human Service Systems," *The Family Coordinator,* 21:4 (1972), pp. 505–16.

2. *Ibid.,* p. 507.

3. J. R. Smith and L. G. Smith, eds., *Beyond Monogamy: Recent Studies in Sexual Alternatives in Marriage* (Baltimore, 1974).

4. B. E. Cogswell, "Variant Family Forms and Life Styles: Rejection of the Traditional Nuclear Family," *The Family Coordinator,* 24:4 (1975), p. 401.

5. J. Lorber, "Beyond Equality of the Sexes: The Question of the Children," *The Family Coordinator,* 24:4 (1975), p. 465.

6. A recent example of this large gender difference was found in the attitudes of freshmen entering college in the fall of 1975: two-thirds of the male, but only one-third of the female, freshmen in this national sample agreed with the view that sex was all right even if the couple have known each other only a very short time. See American Council on Education, *The American Freshman: National Norms for Fall 1975* (Washington, D.C., 1976). In a study by Sorensen of 13- to 19-year-old adolescents, two-thirds of the males but only one-fifth of the females thought sex was "all right with someone known only for a few hours." See P. Sorensen, *Adolescent Sexuality in Contemporary America* (New York, 1973).

7. J. R. Smith and L. G. Smith (cited in earlier section of this article).

8. *Ibid.,* p. 38.

9. R. Thamm, *Beyond Marriage and the Nuclear Family* (San Francisco, 1975), p. 124.

10. R. M. Kanter, D. Jaffe, and D. K. Weisberg, "Coupling, Parenting and the Presence of Others: Intimate Relationships in Communal Households," *The Family Coordinator,* 24:4 (1975), pp. 433–52.

11. *Ibid.,* p. 447.

12. B. Berger, B. Hackett, and R. M. Millar, "The Communal Family," *The Family Coordinator,* 21:4 (1972), pp. 419–28.

13. *Ibid.,* p. 422.

14. *Ibid.,* p. 427.

15. J. Rothchild and S. B. Wolf, *The Children of the Counterculture* (New York, 1976).

16. Rather than a variant family form to replace the nuclear family in the future, it may be that the phenomenon of communal households will eventually develop into a form of half-way house between leave-taking from the parental home in late adolescence and the final establishment of a family with the birth of a child. Marciano sees communes as analogous to monastic retreat houses—places for renewal, self-integration, and new experiences during a phase of life—rather than as a permanent pattern for most adults. See T. D. Marciano, "Variant Family Forms in a World Perspective," *The Family Coordinator,* 24:4 (1975), pp. 407–20. The emergence of the pattern

itself may be a function not simply of the "alternate culture" of the nineteen-sixties but also of changes in the role-set sequence of late adolescence. Prolonged education and residential segregation on campuses mean a long period of exposure exclusively to peers and the encouragement of egocentrism in the absence of adult responsibilities. This pattern may have contributed to the development of the communal residence as an intermediary between the completion of school and the assumption of adult responsibilities. It may also reflect the demographic composition of young people in college in the sixties and seventies, since these cohorts were born in the late forties and fifties, when the number of children in American families was relatively high, and these cohorts therefore contain a much larger proportion of middle- and later-born children than did previous cohorts. The more social, gregarious characteristics associated with middle- and last-born birth-order positions may have contributed to the attractions of communal living. This possibility could be checked by ascertaining the birth-order distribution of communal residents compared to non-communal control samples of comparable age-sex groups in the population.

17. For example, Norman Mailer has a fantasy of sperm slung across a "few inches of eternity — his measure, his meaning, his vision of a future male." See N. Mailer, *The Prisoner of Sex* (Boston, 1971), pp. 197–98.

18. D. M. Rorvik, *Brave New Baby: Promise and Peril of the Biological Revolution* (New York, 1971).

19. A. V. Nalbandov (cited in earlier section of this article), pp. 106–7; 225–26.

20. It is interesting to note that the amount of oxytocin released increases with the increased sexual excitation in the female and is greater still if female orgasm is attained. It is also the case that uterine contractility is greater during the follicular and ovulatory phases than it is during the luteal phase of the menstrual cycle. See R. Berde, *Recent Progress in Oxytocin Research* (Springfield, Illinois, 1959).

21. This makes very dubious the theory that the smaller-headed, long-tailed Y sperm is apt to reach and penetrate the ovum before the heavier X female sperm, as Shettles and McCary have argued in suggesting procedures for determining the sex of the child or accounting for the very high sex ratio at conception. See D. M. Rorvik (cited above, note 18); and J. L. McCary, *Human Sexuality* (New York, 1967). A period of capacitation prior to penetration makes less important the speed with which sperm reaches the oviducts.

22. R. Berde (cited above, note 20).

23. M. M. Sherfey, "The Evolution and Nature of Female Sexuality in Relation to Psychoanalytic Theory," *Journal of the American Psychoanalytic Association,* 14:1 (1966), pp. 28–128.

24. Provide a woman with a rocking chair, and the faraway look of pleasure one often sees among nursing mothers is much closer to the sensual Eve than to the saintly Mary. Many American women never experience this fusion, however: persuaded by their culture to share men's dissociation of sexuality from maternalism, they may react negatively to the sensual component of nursing and give it up very early on. Yet a culturally permissible association between sexuality and lactation stimulates maternal milk supply, as shown by Campbell and Petersen's finding of a positive correlation between the amount of milk ejected and the degree of sexual arousal. B. Campbell and W. E. Petersen, "Milk Let-Down and Orgasm in the Human Female," *Human Biology,* 25 (1953), pp. 165–68.

25. E. E. Grimm, "Women's Attitudes and Reactions to Childbearing," in G. D. Goldman and D. S. Milman, eds; *Modern Woman: Her Psychology and Sexuality* (Springfield, Illinois, 1969), pp. 129–51.

26. N. Newton, "Interrelationships between Sexual Responsiveness, Birth and Breast Feeding," in J. Zubin and J. Money, eds., *Contemporary Sexual Behavior* (Baltimore, 1973), pp. 77–98.

27. M. Mead and N. Newton, "Cultural Patterning of Perinatal Behavior," in S. A. Richardson, and A. F. Guttmacher, eds., *Childbearing: Its Social and Psychological Aspects* (Baltimore, 1967); and N. Newton, (cited above, note 26).

28. By contrast, the relations of divorced men to their children suggests much less close emotional bonds. Hetherington reports an initial post-divorce increase in contact between fathers and their children, but by a year or so later, the contact declines and the father-child relationship is about what it was before the divorce. E. M. Hetherington, M. Cox, and R. Cox, "Beyond Father Absence: Conceptualization of Effects of Divorce" (unpublished paper, 1975). This does not mean, however, that change is not taking place. Under the influence both of desire and of pressure from their wives, many young men are attempting to establish closer emotional and social ties to their young children. Should these marriages fail, the fathers may continue to show closer ties with their children than previous cohorts of divorced men. Indeed, there are growing numbers of divorces in which child custody is granted to the fathers. How extensive this pattern will become in the future and whether paternal investment and attachment to children will approximate that of maternal attachment are open questions at this point. The author's prediction is that the gap may narrow, but not close, unless males

receive compensatory training for parenthood far in excess of anything now envisaged.

29. See S. Arms, *Immaculate Deception: A New Look at Women and Childbirth in America* (Boston, 1975); D. Haire, "The Cultural Warping of Childbirth," *I.C.E.A. News* (Milwaukee, 1972); and N. Newton, "Emotions of Pregnancy," *Clinical Obstetrics and Gynecology,* 6:3 (1963), pp. 639–68.

30. M. H. Klaus *et al.* (cited in earlier section of this article).

31. J. H. Kennell in a discussion of early human interaction at the Third Annual Conference on Psychosomatic Obstetrics and Gynecology, Philadelphia, 1975, cited in M. A. Parlee, "Psychological Aspects of Menstruation, Childbirth, and Menopause: An Overview with Suggestions for Further Research," paper given at a conference on New Directions for Research on Women, Madison, Wisconsin, May 31–June 2, 1975 (mimeographed).

32. C. Kaufman and L. A. Rosenblum, "The Reaction to Separation in Infant Monkeys: Anaclitic Depression and Conservation-Withdrawal," *Psychosomatic Medicine,* 29:6 (1967), pp. 648–75.

33. Apgar scores are 10-point scores based on the skin color, breathing/crying, activity, and pulse of the infant at birth.

34. D. Haire (cited above, note 29).

35. V. Larsen, "Stresses of the Childbearing Years," *American Journal of Public Health,* 56 (1966), pp. 32–36. Unique for its time, Larsen asked women directly about the stresses they experienced in connection with pregnancy and birth. She reports that a large percentage of the stress and difficulty women remember in connection with birth had to do with hospital routines, the delivery itself, and the restrictions imposed on them during their hospital stay.

36. M. Ferin, F. Halberg, M. Richart, and R. L. Vande Wiele, *Biorhythms and Human Reproduction* (New York, 1974).

37. H. Persky, in Friedman (cited in earlier section of this article).

38. There is some evidence from animal research that this is a fruitful area to explore. See J. Terkel and J. S. Rosenblatt, "Maternal Behavior Induced by Maternal Blood Plasma Injected into Virgin Rats," *Journal of Comparative and Physiological Psychology,* 65 (1968), pp. 479–82. Terkel and Rosenblatt found a factor in the blood of rats within forty-eight hours after birth which, when given to virgin rats, quickly stimulated maternal behavior. Animals treated with estradiol, progesterone, and prolactin become responsive to pups by the second day after receiving the hormones. See H. Moltz, M. Lubin, M. Leon, and M. Numan, "Hormonal Induction of Maternal Behavior in the Ovariectomized Rat," *Physiology and Behavior,* 5 (1970), pp. 1373–77. The capacity for maternal-response behavior may well be present without these added boosts of hormones, but the endocrines do seem to activate, or speed up the activation of, maternal behavior. Since the extraordinarily high levels of hormonal secretion during pregnancy drop very quickly after birth, they may play a role in intensely activating maternal behavior only if the infant is seen, held, and nursed very shortly after birth, something typical obstetric practice in American hospital settings rarely permits, even in natural-childbirth cases.

39. M. A. Parlee (cited above, note 31).

40. A. S. Rossi, "Transition to Parenthood," *Journal of Marriage and Family,* 30:1 (1968), pp. 26–39.

41. M. B. Cohen, "Personal Identity and Sexual Identity," *Psychiatry,* 29:1 (1966), pp. 1–14.

42. In their research among the !Kung Bushmen in Africa, Lee and Devore have shown the critical role played by diet and breast-feeding patterns for change in fertility rates. Among nomadic Bushmen, an average birth spacing of 3.8 years is a consequence of unusually active lives among women, coupled with a low sugar and carbohydrate diet; together with breast-feeding, this profile does not permit the critical volume of fat to be regained for about three years after a baby is born. Such lactation-related infertility does not work very well among sedentary Bushmen because their enriched diets lead to faster fat gain, with the result that birth spacing drops to every two years, i.e., very like settled agriculturalists in peasant societies. In innumerable African societies today, the real threat of both population excess and impoverishment of health among babies is the adaptation of the Western pattern of bottle-feeding babies and the changed content of maternal diets. See D. Dumont, "The Limitations of Human Population: A Natural History," *Science,* 187 (February 28, 1975), pp. 713–21.

43. Perez and his associates investigated the relationship between breast-feeding and first ovulation after childbirth. They found some postponement of ovulation when women nursed their infants with no supplementary feeding for the first nine postpartum weeks, but thereafter the chances of ovulation increased despite the continuation of full nursing. See A. Perez, P. Vela, G. S. Masnick and R. G. Potter, "First Ovulation after Childbirth: The Effect of Breastfeeding," *American Journal of Obstetrics and Gynecology,* 144:8 (1972), pp. 1041–47. Masnick has warned that adequate research on the relationship between nursing and the resumption of ovulation is yet to be done. G. S. Masnick, "Biosocial Aspects of Breastfeeding," A.A.A.S. Symposium, Boston,

February 18–24, 1976 (mimeographed).

44. Lancaster, personal communication.

45. Although there has been a great deal of research on family size, there has been little on the effect of child spacing on maternal psychological health, the quality of parent-child relations, or the impact on the parental marriage, particularly with adequate controls to exclude the impact of choice and accident in closely timed births, long-term goals of the parents, etc. For examples of research and thinking about the impact of close child-spacing see J. D. Wray, "Population Pressure on Families: Family Size and Child Spacing," in National Academy of Sciences, *Rapid Population Growth* (Baltimore, 1971), pp. 403–61; and H. T. Christensen, "Children in the Family: The Relationship of Number and Spacing to Marital Success," *Journal of Marriage and Family,* 30 (1968), pp. 283–89. Clausen reports that in the longitudinal data at the Institute of Human Development in California, mothers with three or more children closely spaced recalled the early years of their motherhood as a period of extreme exhaustion and discouragement. See J. A. Clausen and S. R. Clausen, "The Effects of Family Size on Parents and Children," in J. T. Fawcett, ed., *Psychological Perspectives on Population* (New York, 1972).

46. American Civil Liberties Union, *Civil Liberties,* 310 (January, 1976), p. 1.

47. V. Hunt, "Reproduction and Work," *Signs: Journal of Women in Culture and Society,* 1:2 (1975), pp. 543–52.

48. A. J. Ferreira, "The Pregnant Woman's Emotional Attitude and Its Reflection on the Newborn," *Journal of Orthopsychiatry,* 30 (1960), pp. 553–61.

49. Most children of employed women continue to be cared for in private homes, either their own or someone else's, and by relatives more often than by non-relatives. Among the relatives the husband tops the list, followed by the child's grandmother, older sibling, or aunt. A survey of day-care facilities in 1970 found that only 1.3 million children of working women are supervised in either licensed or unlicensed facilities. See Westinghouse Learning Corporation-Westat Research Inc., *Day Care Survey, 1970: Summary Report and Basic Analysis* (Washington, D.C., 1971). This is a small number of children provided for, but it is in fact a doubling of the total licensed day-care facilities by 1973 compared with a comprehensive child-care survey in 1965. See Women's Bureau, *Child Care Arrangements of Working Mothers in the United States,* U.S. Department of Labor, Children's Bureau Publication No. 461 (Washington, D.C., United States Printing Office, 1968).

50. V. Kerr, "One Step Forward — Two Steps Back: Child Care's Long American History," in P. Roby, ed., *Child Care — Who Cares: Foreign and Domestic Infant and Early Childhood Development Policies* (New York, 1973), pp. 151–71.

51. B. Caldwell, "Infant Day Care — The Outcast Gains Respectability," *ibid.,* pp. 20–36.

52. It should be noted that, in recent years, there has been a drift in East European countries away from day-care centers for children less than three years old. Not only is such care extremely expensive — the younger the child is, the more costly its care — but there have been rumblings that all is not well in terms of the very young child's welfare in such group-care institutions. Some Czechoslovak researchers have suggested that the under-three child's nervous system cannot take the noise and bustle of being with others his own age all day. After a lively national debate on this issue, the Czechs have moved away from group care for the youngest age group toward foster care in private homes and long-leave policies for employed mothers. See H. Scott, *Does Socialism Liberate Women? Experiences from Eastern Europe* (Boston, 1974). In Tiger and Shepher's recent book on the kibbutz, it is difficult to get behind the author's gleeful pouncing on any shred that can be taken as evidence of renewed familism among kibbutz women in order to tell if they have any evidence that the youngest children in the kibbutz fare less well in children's houses than do older children. The authors merely report the mothers' desires for more contact with their children, without specifying the age of the children to which they are referring. See L. Tiger and J. Shepher, *Women in the Kibbutz* (New York, 1975).

Frailty, Thy Name's Been Changed: What Sports Medicine Is Discovering About Women's Bodies

Gary Selden

The young woman studies the television screen as if she were seeing herself through a microscope—and in a way she is. High-speed movie cameras have filmed her running stride from front and back, both sides, and above. Pressure plates sensitive enough to weigh an ant have electronically charted the forces on each square centimeter of her footsoles during their instant of contact with the earth. The angle of each joint in her limbs has been calculated at each phase of her movements, along with every gram of effort that each muscle contributes. Now she is watching her fluid motion displayed as a pattern of stick figures on a computer terminal, and she can see, in a way impossible by videotape or any other means, a tiny flaw that detracts from her near-perfect physical efficiency.

She is Evelyn Ashford, fourth in the 1976 Olympic 100-meter dash and perhaps the best American woman sprinter. Like many other champions, she came to Coto Research Center of Coto de Caza, California, 50 miles from Los Angeles, for computerized biomechanical analysis (CBA). Directed by Gideon Ariel, Ph.D., Coto and its parent company, CBA, Inc., of Amherst, Massachusetts, have added 20 or 30 yards to golfers' drives, improved football placekickers' accuracy to 98 percent, and developed a new straight-legged shot-putting style that has been used to set records. Tennis players now have a chance to emulate Martina Navratilova's awesome forehand—by turning into the stroke and thus using their whole body's momentum instead of just the shoulder and arm—thanks to Ariel's imaginative union of sweat and silicon chips.

CBA is one of many inventions that are turning sports medicine (the science of preventing or treating injuries and improving athletic performance) into a technological glamour specialty. The arthroscope ("joint scanner"), a stainless-steel tube containing a micro-TV camera, lets surgeons work through a quarter-inch incision instead of opening up a whole knee or elbow; it has shortened recovery time for many operations from months to days. Transcutaneous electrical nerve stimulators can be strapped over a minor muscle strain to let athletes compete without favoring the ache and thus inviting further injury. A pair of "inflatable hip boots" fight post-workout fatigue by rhythmically pumping blood out of the leg veins, where it tends to collect after exertion, laden with metabolic waste products.

Benefits from some of these machines already are sifting down from world-class to recreational athletes. Ashford found that, like most women, she runs a bit "like a duck," with too much hip sway due to the female's wider-angled thighbone attachments to the pelvis. Computer analysis of this problem should help her run more efficiently by bringing her feet closer to the midline. Like CBA's tennis hints, any improved technique will become the common property of all runners.

Another machine with potential to aid all athletes, the electromyograph (which measures muscle tension by sensors wired to the body), is being used to chart the muscle interaction of gymnasts. These records then are used as templates to guide others. Eventually, radio sensors derived from spaceflight telemetry will be able to record a champion's movements unencumbered by two dozen wires; likewise, the novice, with the same sensors taped to her body, could find out instantly how each move differs from prerecorded muscle tapes of, say, Nadia Comaneci.

Such immediate feedback is already available with computerized resistance training. Developed by Dr. Ariel and his associates, this technique employs a computerized exercise machine. As it monitors muscle tension, fatigue, work load, force, and speed, the computer automatically adjusts the load to your capability at that moment. It's like having a personal coach who won't push you past your limit but won't let you fake it for an instant. This device is not on the market yet, but Wilson Sporting Goods just bought the patent on one design, and in a few years the machine should be standard equipment—not only in health clubs, but even in home gyms, since the computer chip that does all the work will be very cheap to produce.

Along with training technology, injury treatment has come a long way from the days when amateur women found it hard to get the best care because it was assumed they weren't as serious about sport as men. Take the case of Virginia, a researcher in psychoanalytic linguistics. She began running in her early thirties, overjoyed to have found an outlet for her competitive spirit: "Even when I was a terrific swimmer as a teenager, I was always channeled into water ballet and life-guarding. It was great to run *against* somebody in a race, or even against my own times in training." She suffered a series of injuries—severe sprains, knee and hip pain, recurrent shin splints (tiny tears in the front calf muscle fiber), and broken ankles—but her doctors tried many new forms of therapy that enabled her to keep running. They gave her whirlpool baths, electrotherapy to speed muscle healing, flexible casts to allow some exercise during recuperation, corrective exercises, and orthotics (custom-molded plastic shoe inserts) to correct her "foot plant"—but they never suggested she give up the sport she loves. "I can't imagine not running," she says, "but I'm sure that if I hadn't had support from these wonderful doctors, I would have gotten discouraged and quit. And I wouldn't be as happy a person as I am now."

Sports medicine's main value to women, however, probably has been in basic physiology, not repair or technology. Coming of age in the great fitness boom of the last decade, the young science grew up with the feminist movement and the mass entry of women into athletics. Therefore, although some myths linger from the era when doctors said running would make the womb fall out, most sports physicians are remarkably free of bias against active women. As Title IX of the 1972 Education Amendments Act mandated equal facilities in federally aided schools, physiologists were publishing research quashing the old fears. At the same time, the genetic differences that do exist between male and female athletes came into clearer focus. As a result, women have begun to get instruction specifically adapted to their needs. So women

have benefited even more than men from sports medicine's rapid growth, and its practitioners invariably count their share in the new ideal of athletic womanhood among their proudest accomplishments.

One of the main fears laid to rest was the idea that women are too frail, that they get hurt more than men, especially in contact sports. The rash of injuries as large numbers of women first took up sports in the early 1970s was due to women's poor physical condition, says Dorothy Harris, M.D., sports psychologist with the United States Olympic Committee and coordinator of a graduate program in sports psychology at Pennsylvania State University. "Once better medical attention, facilities, and coaching became available to women, the injuries became sports-specific rather than sex-specific."

Women were found to have few needs for protective clothing different from men's. Breast bruises turned out to be much less common than expected, even in rugby or boxing, and there is no known relation between them and cancer, as had been feared. Most women who wear more than an A-cup need a sport bra, especially for running. Some doctors still say the bouncing that occurs without a good bra will contribute to a falling bustline. But pathologist and marathoner Joan Ullyot, M.D., in her new book, *Running Free* (Putnam's), authoritatively states the emerging consensus that special support is needed only for comfort: "So-called ligaments that can be stretched irreparably are merely bands of fibrous tissue that do not offer any 'support.' Indeed, the breasts are supported mainly by their own content of glands and fat. 'Sagging' occurs because of age and hormonal changes, which reduce this supportive filling. Sports are not the culprit." Unfortunately, not all the bras have been tested by athletes themselves, so a lot of shopping around may be needed to find one that offers enough support with no hooks or inside seams to chafe. Ullyot recommends Danskin, Jogbra, or Sears, but new designs appear continually.

The only other protection specifically needed by women is in water skiing—a rubber strip or panty to cover the perineum. In case of a fall, this will prevent the rare but dangerous chance of a forceful douche that can tear vaginal tissue or enter the uterus and Fallopian tubes, causing inflammation and possible sterility. Otherwise, anatomy protects the female's genitals better than the male's. (In fact, some elementary schools have tried to even up this disparity by making the girls wear cups in coed sports like ice hockey, to give them the same awkward discomfort as the boys.)

Menstruation also has proved to be little hindrance to

athletes, although some women do perform below par on certain days. Olympic records have been set by menstruating women. Exercise generally makes for less painful periods, as well as easier childbirth. One reaction of their reproductive system has given many women a needless scare. During intense training, some stop menstruating for a few months to a few years. This most often happens in women with lean bodies whose fat content drops below 18 percent, although many with much less fat menstruate normally. The exact causes are unknown. Stress and nervousness generated by competition may also affect a woman's periods. But the important thing to remember is that missing menses is not harmful and does not presage sterility. In fact many women have gotten pregnant by assuming they were not ovulating when their periods stopped. (Dr. Ullyot believes that regular menstruation may be abnormal, developed only in the last few thousand years as humans became a sedentary species.)

Sports physiology has revealed that women athletes have a few nutritional needs different from men's, but only one is cause for concern. In general, a woman needs less food than a man of equal weight; she has more accessible calories to burn in the same activity because of the thicker layer of fat under her skin. This fat gives her a larger reserve energy supply for endurance contests, so she is less dependent on carbohydrate loading—filling up on starch to build up stores of glycogen fuel in the muscles. The insulating fat also makes a woman's slightly lower body temperature more stable than a man's. She relies less on sweating to dissipate heat; therefore she retains fluid and salts better and doesn't need to drink as much during exertion. As a result of this difference, a woman tends to perform better in cold but has less tolerance of heat than a man of equal size.

A woman's main nutritional problem is that, while menstruating, she is likely to suffer iron-deficiency anemia. Females need twice as much iron as males, and IUDs often increase the need by causing heavier bleeding. Iron depletion is one of the most common culprits when women athletes get "stalled" or overtired during training. Many physicians routinely suggest iron supplements for all active women, because they may have low iron levels in bone marrow even if blood iron levels are normal.

Sports medicine also has put our knowledge of the hormone-related differences in physique on a scientific basis. Schools are beginning to accept the fact, as stated by Dr. Elizabeth Coryllos who chaired a 1979 seminar on girl athletes, that, "before puberty there is no real reason for anything but coed sports." Around age 11, girls often have a slight edge in size and strength because of their earlier onset of puberty. After about 13, the average greater size and strength of boys, and their greater proportion of muscle to fat, dictate separate teams for many sports so that girls' participation is not limited to the exceptional ones who can compete evenly with the boys. On the other hand, the preponderance of estrogen over androgen makes girls, on the average, more flexible. As Dr. Coryllos puts it, "The female is essentially a thoroughbred; the male is a quarter horse." This average distinction suggests slightly different warm-ups for the two sexes: males need to concentrate on stretching and limbering up, while females can benefit from more vigorous movements to mobilize strength.

The main structural differences due to hormones are the wider hips of the woman and the broader shoulders of the man. Their implications for performance are well known—the male's advantage in throwing and running, the females in wrestling's leg holds. The woman's lower center of gravity also means that, size being equal, she's harder to tackle in football; in skiing she tends to fall on her back, while the man falls on his face. Dr. Coryllos, a skier herself, therefore suggests "his 'n' her" ski boots—hers with a raised heel, his with a raised toe.

The wider hips may also mean that the outer part of a woman's front thigh muscle (quadriceps) pulls her kneecap more to the side than does a man's making her more susceptible to *chondromalacia patellae* (runner's knee). Fortunately, this problem now can be corrected in most cases without surgery, using orthotics and exercises to strengthen the inner quadriceps. This predisposition, however, means that women need to be more careful about squatting than men do. Many doctors say "No knee bends" and recommend that, in playing the catcher's position in softball or baseball, women should kneel on one knee instead. Gabriel Mirkin, M.D., a pioneer in orthotics and coauthor of *The Sportsmedicine Book* (Little, Brown), goes further: "Women should catch in a chair. That's ridiculous, of course, but really, for the sake of their knees, they shouldn't catch at all."

Recent research suggests that hormonal differences actually may create different muscles in men and women. All muscle tissue is a mixture of fast-twitch (FT) and slow-twitch (ST) fibers. FT fibers burn primarily glycogen as fuel without benefit of oxygen, and are most efficient in quick bursts of power. Some studies suggest that they predominate in sprinters and weight lifters. ST fibers burn fat as well as glycogen and depend on a steady oxygen supply, reaching their maximum efficiency in sustained efforts like

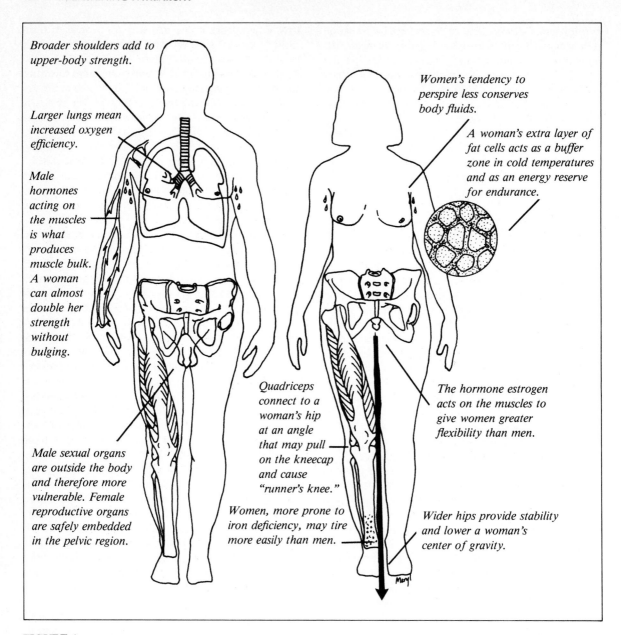

Broader shoulders add to upper-body strength.

Larger lungs mean increased oxygen efficiency.

Male hormones acting on the muscles is what produces muscle bulk. A woman can almost double her strength without bulging.

Male sexual organs are outside the body and therefore more vulnerable. Female reproductive organs are safely embedded in the pelvic region.

Quadriceps connect to a woman's hip at an angle that may pull on the kneecap and cause "runner's knee."

Women, more prone to iron deficiency, may tire more easily than men.

Women's tendency to perspire less conserves body fluids.

A woman's extra layer of fat cells acts as a buffer zone in cold temperatures and as an energy reserve for endurance.

The hormone estrogen acts on the muscles to give women greater flexibility than men.

Wider hips provide stability and lower a woman's center of gravity.

FIGURE 1

marathons. Some work suggests that FT fibers predominate in men, while women average a greater proportion of ST fibers, which combine with their higher percentage of body fat for a large natural advantage in endurance. This conclusion is still controversial, however, and it is certain that there is more variation among individuals of each sex than the average difference, if any, between the sexes.

The last statement, in fact, applies to every aspect of athletic activity, and it is perhaps the single most important finding of sports medicine. Many female athletes today are working out with weights—dead lifts of 400 pounds, for example—that many men could never hope to lift no matter how hard they might train. United States Olympic volleyball teams no longer have men's and women's programs, only "a program." Sports medicine has finally taught us what should have been obvious all along: athletic training must be geared to the individual, not the sex. For example, Dr. Ariel, in cautioning against blanket application of his work with Evelyn Ashford, notes that the great 1960s' sprint star Wilma Rudolph had a hip structure, and therefore a stride, closer to the male stereotype than the female.

Sports science continues to show that many of the "genetic" differences are really fostered by culture, just as women's greater tendency toward shin splints is due to wearing high heels. We are learning that "innate weaknesses" often disappear with equal opportunity. Man's greater oxygen efficiency in running had always been ascribed to his larger lungs and the denser concentration of hemoglobin in his blood. Now we know that woman's slower metabolic rate, as well as better coaching, makes up some of this difference, while training that calls upon woman's ability to "run on her fat" tips the scales further in her favor the longer the distance. These facts have been proved, notes Christine E. Haycock, M.D., associate professor of surgery at the New Jersey Medical School in Newark, by study of several 50- and 500-mile races which women have not only finished but won,

hours ahead of exhausted men.

As to other capabilities, it has long been known that, due to lower androgen levels, the average woman can increase her strength by 50 to 75 percent before her muscles start to grow big enough to "scare" people. Now, some research indicates that lifelong exercise can slightly alter the hormone balance itself, even to the point of increasing growth by delaying puberty, giving women greater size and strength without affecting sexual characteristics. Some physiologists are even starting to think that, pound for pound, women are potentially *stronger* than men, since weight-lifting records show that lighter people tend to be more powerful in proportion to weight.

Sports medicine even may help to change the identification of sport with machismo. Dr. Harris observes: "For males insecure in their masculinity, the first place to go was sports. The idea is, 'As long as you stay in your place, I'm assured of mine.' On the other hand, women in sport had to be pretty well glued together to incur the kind of stigma involved." By exposing as a sham the ancient taboo that sports masculinize females, the new athletic science has encouraged millions of women to make the most of their abilities. As Dr. Mirkin simply puts it: "You find out that muscles aren't ugly in women; they're pretty."

Sudden freedom from woman's physical straitjacket has made hers the most exciting side of athletics today. Men are already fairly close to their limits; women have scarcely begun to imagine theirs. "That's why so many male coaches like to coach females now," says Dr. Ariel, "because it's so easy to get quick results."

The beauty of the science is that knowledge derived from and for the top performers automatically helps every jogger and weekend tennis player get more out of her sport. As Dr. Ariel emphasizes: "Before, you trained for two years and then you said, 'Well, maybe I did it wrong.'" Sports medicine is one technology helping women do it right, right from the start.

Exercises for Men

Willamette Bridge/Liberation News Service

1. Sit down in a straight chair. Cross your legs at the ankles and keep your knees pressed together. Try to do this while you're having a conversation with someone, but pay attention at all times to keeping your knees pressed tightly together.

2. Bend down to pick up an object from the floor. Each time you bend remember to bend your knees so that your rear end doesn't stick up, and place one hand on your shirt-front to hold it to your chest. This exercise simulates the experience of a woman in a short, low-necked dress bending over.

3. Run a short distance, keeping your knees together. You'll find you have to take short, high steps if you run this way. Women have been taught it is unfeminine to run like a man with long, free strides. See how far you get running this way for 30 seconds.

Reprinted from Willamette Bridge/Liberation News Service, "Exercises for Men," in *The Radical Therapist* (forerunner of *State and Mind*), December–January 1971, by permission of the publisher, New Directions in Psychology, Inc., The State and Mind Collective, P.O. Box 89, Somerville, MA 02143.

4. *Sit comfortably on the floor. Imagine that you are wearing a dress and that everyone in the room wants to see your underwear. Arrange your legs so that no one can see. Sit like this for a long time without changing your position.*

5. *Walk down a city street. Pay a lot of attention to your clothing: make sure your pants are zipped, shirt tucked in, buttons done. Look straight ahead. Every time a man walks past you, avert your eyes and make your face expressionless. Most women learn to go through this act each time we leave our houses. It's a way to avoid at least some of the encounters we've all had with strange men who decided we looked available.*

6. *Walk around with your stomach pulled in tight, your shoulders thrown back, and your chest thrust out. Pay attention to keeping this posture at all times. Notice how it changes your breathing. Try to speak loudly and aggressively in this posture.*

Reflections on the Story of the Double Helix

Ruth Hubbard

1. Autobiographical

Though I was born in Austria and think of myself as a European, I came to the United States in 1938 and attended high school and college in pre-Second World War and wartime America. I first returned to Europe (or what non-British people have the temerity to call Europe) when I re-crossed the Atlantic to England in 1948. At that time I came to London, the post-war London of rationing, queuing, bomb-sites; of a spirit of victory over bombs and missiles (familiarly known as doodle-bugs); of a labor government that had been elected by a strong majority and was introducing a National Health Service to become a model for the rest of the world. It was a drab and dowdy London, drizzly and foggy and cold; a happy and optimistic London, full of well-fed and cared-for children, the country's special pride and concern; the London I fell in love with, and the London a young English chemist, named Rosalind Franklin, gladly exchanged for Paris—at least for a time.

I worked there for more than a year, then came back to the United States for my PhD. But in 1950, I was back in Europe for the summer, this time at the Carlsberg Laboratory in Copenhagen, where the Carlsberg brewery rationed each of us to only six bottles of beer (or soda water) a day. When I visited the laboratory of the biochemist, Hermann Kalckar, before returning to America in the fall, I found him all excited because two bright young phage workers were about to come to him from Max Delbrück's laboratory at Cal. Tech.: Gunther Stent and Jim Watson. Watson has written about his Copenhagen period in *The Double Helix*.[1]

When I returned to Copenhagen in 1952, on fellowship for a year, Watson had moved to Cambridge, England. He hadn't accomplished much in Copenhagen other than accompany Kalckar and others to Naples for the spring. What he was doing in Cambridge we found out in April 1953, when he and Francis Crick published their immediately famous paper in *Nature* that proposed the double helical model of DNA.[2] Five weeks after the appearance of this paper, on that rainy June day in 1953, when the London streets were a dense crowd of people, come to see Elizabeth crowned Queen of England, I found myself quite by accident in the Cavendish Laboratory in Cambridge, listening to Francis Crick expound on their exciting new DNA structure. I did not meet Watson until he came to Harvard a year or two later. We became friends, and remained friends until quite recently, when disagreements over the story of Rosalind Franklin and the controversy surrounding the recombinant DNA technology stretched our relationship beyond the breaking point.

My years of scientific apprenticeship and intercontinental wandering therefore overlap Watson's. We spent our scientific adolescence at the same time and in similar places. When I read *The Double Helix,* I recognized attitudes, friends, and sights. When I first read it in manuscript, I liked it tremendously. I felt that it described scientific work 'like it is.' I knew nothing of Rosalind Franklin, had not met her or even heard of her (to remember, that is), and such was my state of integration into male-dominated science that I noticed nothing wrong. (Let me say at once that many others, who also didn't know Franklin, were a good deal more alert than I to the outrageous sexism of Watson's descriptions of her as a woman and as a scientist.)

I first became aware of the scandal surrounding the Watson–Crick model of the double helix when a friend, herself a crystallographer, gave me the manuscript of Anne Sayre's book about Rosalind Franklin.[3] I read it and was appalled. I have since checked many of Sayre's facts and spoken with a number of Franklin's friends and

Reprinted from Ruth Hubbard, "Reflections on the Story of the Double Helix," in *Women's Studies International Quarterly,* 2 (1979), Reprinted by permission of the publisher, Pergamon Press, Inc., and the author.

acquaintances. I have summarized my impressions in a review I wrote of Anne Sayre's book and will recapitulate some of them here.[4]

2. Philosophical

The art historian, Ernst Gombrich, has quoted one of his colleagues as saying 'that all pictures owe more to other pictures than they do to nature.'[5] And so it is with science. Nature, of course, is in there; but the primary linkages are with the science that has gone before. In a way that is only to say that like art, science is a product of the human imagination, and like art, to be acceptable and have meaning, it has to be comprehensible in terms of our experience of the real world and of the accepted interpretations of it. When the imagination becomes freewheeling and loses all linkages with the real world, or rather, with the world that we accept as real, we call it diseased or insane. But in the activity of making science (and science of course is *made*; it isn't 'out there') we abstract from what Alan Watts has aptly referred to as the 'seamless unity of nature' those things that we notice and therefore pull out of the continuum. 'Things,' he has said, 'are the measuring units of thought just as pounds are the measuring units of weighing.'[6] And just as the enumeration of the pounds in a rock or the inches in a log are only a one-dimensional description of these objects, so the 'things' or 'facts' we use to signify and describe our experience of nature are but discrete fragments of its total reality. When we translate these units of thought and experience — facts and things — into words, we delimit and trim them even further; because, as Watts point out, 'The fundamental realities are the relations . . . in which facts [or things] are the terms or limits . . .' So, if the world consists of an infinitely intertwining web of relationships, which our sensations and thought processes sort into things and facts, and which we delimit still further by the process of naming, science raises these stages of abstraction (or, more correctly, of concretization or reification) yet another notch. For a further selection is made when scientists turn 'facts of nature' into 'facts of science.'

Scientists don't just hold up a mirror to nature. They use something more in the nature of a coarse sieve through which drop all the things that they either don't notice or those that they take to be irrelevant to the inquiry at hand. The real intellectual labor of scientists consists of constructing a coherent picture of the world from what they sift out of it as noteworthy and significant. Anthropologists use two interesting terms for the process that they engage in when they enter a foreign culture and try to formulate its laws: *backgrounding* and *foregrounding*. By these words, they denote the often unconscious activity of allowing certain things and habits and events to merge with the background of the unnoticed or the 'unnoteworthy,' while pulling others into the foreground where they command attention and have to be dealt with. And I would argue that a similar process occurs in the natural sciences. Scientists make juxtapositions and construct relationships out of the 'facts' into which they sort or delimit the complex web of interdigitating relationships that constitutes the real world. To extend Watts's image, we can say that scientists transform the seamless unity of nature into a carefully patterned patchwork quilt. And it is important to be aware of the elements of both patchwork and patterning: for both involve choices that are far from arbitrary.

But the way in which the patches are selected — the unconscious decisions on what remains background and what gets pulled into the foreground — and the way in which they are stitched together, are determined only in part by the explicit postulates and rules of the 'scientific method.' For they, as well as our total selective mind-set are social products that depend on who we are and where and when. Our scientific reality, then, like all reality, is a social construct — by which I don't mean to say that I am an eighteenth-century idealist and believe that there is nothing out there. I am quite sure that there is something out there, but I believe that what we see out there and our interpretation of it, depend on the larger social context that determines what we actively notice and accept as real.

We learn to see the world while we are infants and young children, and we do it by a process that requires patient guidance from all the adults around us. By the time we are educated, which literally means 'led out of' or 'away from' (from whom? our selves?), we end up so transformed that we have no way of remembering how we saw the world when it truly was our own, when we were tiny children and hadn't yet been taught what the world is 'really' like. In fact, the very act of language acquisition in young children in part is precisely this kind of teaching of the important social, and therefore verbal, distinctions and categories. When a child has been corrected often enough that 'this is a doggy and not a kitty,' s/he has not only learned two words, but s/he has also learned that there are two different kinds of domestic animals with fur and a tail, and that it is important for an educated, grown-up person to know them apart. And when a child learns much subtler distinctions, such as 'no, dear, this is a boy, not a girl,' the very subtlety, coupled with the insistence that the distinction be made correctly and every time, convey a profound social message. In another culture or in another natural setting, this kind of emphasis may be put on different textures of snow or on the different sounds made by water. It just depends on what is important in life and in one's particular setting.

What I am trying to say is that the most profound and significant concepts are often internalized quite without our knowing it, and usually only people who are, for some reason, marginal to the prevailing belief system — radicals of some sort, or women — are even tempted to become conscious of the process and to question the results. That, of course, is what 'consciousness raising' is about.

3. Sociological

The story I am focusing on has to do with styles of work in science, with what one considers important in it, and with the ways women and men live in scientific laboratories.

The first question I want to ask is: why was DNA 'the most golden of all molecules,'[7] the most important molecule in biology — the molecule that a bright and ambitious young biologist, a former Quiz Kid, named James Dewey Watson, might reasonably decide at age 19 to be the key to understanding what life is, as well as, perhaps not incidentally, to his own success? For Watson made a very conscious choice.[8]

I would like to suggest that perhaps a less individualistic society, one that cared less about the traits, accomplishments and successes of *individuals,* might also care less about how these are passed on from parents to their very own, individual offsprings. Such a society and the people in it might find many aspects of biology more interesting than heredity, genes, and hence (in a reductionist science) ultimately DNA. To appreciate this point it is useful to read the literature of the early and mid-nineteenth century, when there was no proper genetic theory — such as the novels of Dickens or George Eliot and the scientific writings of Darwin's cousin, Francis Galton. In a book entitled, *Hereditary Genius,* for example, Galton sets himself the task of understanding why it is that as one reads down the roster of the best students at Cambridge University, one keeps coming up with the same surnames in generation after generation. And the answer he gives is that the factors that make for these successes must be

inherited biologically. (However, he fails to notice that they are inherited only in the male line.)

It seems clear that, beginning with the period of the American and French Revolutions, the meritocratic philosophy of Euro-American liberalism, combined with the unwillingness of the ruling classes to share their power, made it mandatory that the men from the educated, upper classes find biological 'reasons' why they were ruling the world.

That is one point. But I would also suggest that even in a highly competitive and individualistic society, we would never expect that we could answer the question, what is life, by studying genes, had we not accepted Descartes' definition of organism as machine. It is this that leads us to expect to answer such questions as what life is, by taking living organisms apart into smaller and smaller units — to reduce them to chemistry and physics — even though the attributes of 'life' or 'living' be lost in the process. Nor might we expect to learn how genes work from studying molecular genetics, the branch of biochemistry that its founders have called 'molecular biology,' so implying in the very name that DNA is the only important molecule in biology.

I emphasize this because Watson has written that he and Francis Crick, quite separately and long before they knew each other, were led to their keen interest in genes and DNA by reading Schrödinger's *What is Life?*[9] This little book, published by one of the great physicists toward the end of the Second World War, drew the attention of many physicists to biology. For at the war's end many physicists were disappointed with what had become of the physics that at the turn of the century had produced the far-reaching generalizations of relativity, quantum theory, complementarity, uncertainty. By 1945, physicists had generated two atom bombs that had been dropped on people. Furthermore intellectually, at least in the view of some physicists, physics was beginning to degenerate into a queuing up in front of bigger and bigger machines so as to produce smaller and smaller particles. Many bright physicists were looking for more interesting and meaningful problems and some of them were excited by Schrödinger's promise of the gene as the new frontier.

It is worth realizing that in the story of the double helix, the only main actor who had been trained as a biologist was Jim Watson. The others were physicists or chemists. Moreover, Max Delbrück, on whose ideas Schrödinger based much of his discussion of the gene, was promising not only that life would ultimately be understood by reducing it to physics (not chemistry:

Delbrück didn't like chemistry), but that in the process new physical laws were likely to emerge. This was one of the attractions that brought Delbrück himself in, and it may have brought in some of the other physicists as well. Watson has written that one reason he decided to work for his PhD with Salvador Luria was because Luria had worked with Delbrück and they were close friends.[8] And indeed his association with Luria quickly brought him into contact with Delbrück.

In the event, learning the structure of DNA has brought no new physical laws, nor do we know what life 'is.' But we have learned a lot about the biochemistry and structure of those big molecules, the proteins and nucleic acids, that occur by and large only in living organisms. If we ask further, whether the elucidation of the structure of the double helix has introduced a new paradigm into biology and produced a revolution in our way of thinking about organisms, I would say that it has not. On the contrary, the discovery of the double helix and everything that has since happened in molecular biology, lie squarely within the dual paradigm of organism (1) as machine, and (2) as a machine that will be understood better and better as we come to understand the workings of its smaller and smaller parts.

Before getting into the scientific part of the story in more detail, it is worth asking what we can learn from Watson's *Double Helix* about the way science is done, and particularly, about the roles women and men play in the scientific enterprise. This is not a trivial question because the book *was* a best seller and still is required reading for many high school students. So let us look at the way he introduces the four principal characters in his story: himself, Francis Crick, Maurice Wilkins and Rosalind Franklin. (Watson also lists Linus Pauling as a main player, but he comes in quite late in the book and is never rounded out like the others, who enter the scene in the first half dozen pages.)

We meet Watson already in the Introduction, climbing in the Swiss Alps with a fellow scientist, and being hailed by a scientific acquaintance from London as 'Honest Jim,' the phrase he originally intended to use as the title for his book. (It is my memory that he didn't because of the similarity to the title of Kingsley Amis's *Lucky Jim*.) Crick enters in the first sentence ('I have never seen Francis Crick in a modest mood . . .') and by the fourth, is likened to Rutherford and Bohr. For Wilkins we have to wait till the second chapter (only three pages further on) where we learn that 'At this time [fall of 1951] molecular work on DNA in England was, for all

practical purposes, the personal property of Maurice Wilkins, a bachelor who worked in London at King's College. Like Francis [Crick], Maurice had been a physicist and also used X-ray diffraction as his principal tool of research . . .'

So at once the stage is set with our three male principals: Watson a bit frivolous and problematic (though clearly extraordinary: after all he is the one who is writing); Crick loud, ebullient, and brilliant; Wilkins serious and a bit musty. The latter qualities are emphasized within another paragraph by the statement that 'Maurice continually frustrated Francis by never seeming enthusiastic enough about DNA.' At the end of this paragraph Franklin makes her entrance: 'Moreover it was increasingly difficult to take Maurice's mind off his assistant, Rosalind Franklin.' And we must pause at once to understand that Franklin was *not* Wilkins's 'assistant'; that their appointments were independent, equivalent and both in the laboratory headed by John (later, Sir John) Randall, the professor at King's. Furthermore, though Franklin was a newcomer to this laboratory in which Wilkins had been for some time, she was invited to come because she knew *more* than Wilkins about X-ray diffraction, and had been led to believe that she would be working there on her own. But let us go on with Watson's description:

> '*Not that he was at all in love with Rosy, as we called her from a distance. Just the opposite . . . . Maurice, a beginner in X-ray diffraction work,* wanted some professional help *and hoped that Rosy, a trained crystallographer (incidentally, she was not that), could speed up* his *research. Rosy, however, did not see the situation this way. She claimed that she had been given DNA for her own problem and would not think of herself as Maurice's assistant'* (my parentheses and [emphasis]).

Then follows a discussion of her lack of femininity and her unattractiveness, her hair, clothes and grooming. It ends with the statement that 'Clearly Rosy had to go or *be put in her place*. The former was obviously preferable because, given her belligerent moods, it would be very difficult for Maurice to *maintain a dominant position that would allow him to think unhindered* about DNA' (my italics).

These passages speak for themselves. The only factual correction that needs to be made is Sayre's insistence that no one—neither family nor friends—ever addressed Franklin as Rosy; that this is part of the stage-set in which this dowdy (she happened not to be that), petulant, uppity blue-stocking claimed as her own, work that rightfully belonged to a serious, albeit somewhat stodgy, and of course male, scientist. As the story goes on, this picture is embroidered and amplified. And what we learn from the entire book is that real science—good science—is something that is done by men, indeed very bright and ambitious men, who relate to women in two ways: if they are beautiful and charming, women offer a delightful escape from important and serious concerns, such as finding the key to what life is. But women can also be a damned nuisance: particularly if they aren't sufficiently helpful and submissive technicians and, worse yet, if they try to be scientists and follow their own ideas. In that case, they can stem progress and even stop science dead.

I want to digress for a moment because I think it is worth asking whether Watson is unique in this aspect of his description of science. And for comparison, I want to look at two earlier stories that describe science and scientists: Sinclair Lewis's *Arrowsmith* and C. P. Snow's *The Search*. Written respectively in the 1920s and 30s, these books are very different from *The Double Helix* in that they picture scientists as highly idealistic and dedicated to the search for Knowledge and Truth, and with much less interest in worldly honors and success than does Watson. The protagonists have an eye much less on the main chance than has Honest Jim. In fact, when the hero of C. P. Snow's novel recognizes that he has begun to do his science for the sake of the status and worldly success that it will bring him, he promptly decides that he'd better get out and quick. And Arrowsmith, of course, ends up doing his research in a small laboratory off in the woods and away from worldly distractions.

But both books agree with Watson's description of the roles of women. In them, too, women exist to nurture and sustain the hard-working scientist and to offer *him* (and I don't ever use male pronouns generically) much needed relief from *his* serious work. In that capacity women have major roles in both novels and are well-rounded characters, significant and strong. When they leave or die, they are sorely missed by the male scientist-heroes. But the three times in *Arrowsmith* that Lewis mentions professional women, it is to scoff. Once, while Arrowsmith is still in medical school, female colleagues are mentioned, but only as 'virginal and unhappy coeds.' Another time they are 'emotional and frightened'; the third, they 'shudder' as the male professor, the great scientist in the book, injects a virulent strain of bacteria into a guinea pig.

C. P. Snow is even more interesting, for there are several strong, important women in his book. But if a visitor from outer space were to read *The Search* there is only one point at which she/he/it could discover that women also can be scientists. Not that there is a female scientist in the book; but at one point, the hero counsels one of his more frivolous friends, for whom seducing women is a significant avocation, but who has now decided to make it in academic science. He warns him that the one thing he mustn't do is to go around seducing professors' wives. His friend retorts gratefully, 'I promise, Arthur, not a scientist's wife. Not one. Not even a woman scientist.' And that's the only mention of women scientists in a lengthy novel about British X-ray crystallographers, a group that is unusual among scientists for counting many distinguished females among its members.

So we are in the customary bind, where when women actively participate in a field that is not stereotypically female—and not in their accepted roles as cleaning women, technicians, secretaries and wives—they are either maligned, or ignored and written out of the story.

4. Scientific

I shall now try to evaluate Rosalind Franklin's contribution to the elucidation of the structure of the double helix. I am using as sources things that she and others have published. Listings of the main references are available in Robert Olby's *The Path to the Double Helix,*[10] in Anne Sayre's book and in my review of it.

I shall begin in 1951 when Wilkins had been given a sample of DNA with which he and a graduate student, named R. G. Gosling, had taken a first, quite good X-ray diffraction picture. He showed this to Watson when they met in Naples that spring. Watson got excited. And since he was not enthusiastic about his situation in Copenhagen, he decided to move to Cambridge, England and learn something about X-ray crystallography in order to work on the structure of DNA. There, in the fall of 1951 he met Francis Crick who, though already 35, was working for his PhD at the Cavendish Laboratory. (Watson was 23 and already had his doctorate.) Crick and Watson have recalled that as soon as they started talking together, they were struck by the similarity in each other's ways of thinking about biology. Both believed the structure of DNA to be the most important thing to work on and wanted to do something about it. Unfortunately Crick, who knew about X-ray crystallography, was still involved with the work for his thesis. So Watson had to learn quickly.

Wilkins, as we have seen, at this time was working on DNA at King's in London. His chief, Professor Randall, had invited Rosalind Franklin, who was an expert in X-ray analysis, to come and build up the X-ray diffraction unit there. Franklin had spent the preceding years in Paris doing the X-ray analysis of three-dimensional forms of carbon and wanted to turn her attention to biological substances. She therefore was glad to accept a research fellowship in Randall's biophysics unit and came there in January 1951.

Wilkins was away when Franklin arrived and her work was underway by the time he returned. What each of them thought their official relationship to the other was meant to be is not clear; but Sayre writes that they took an instant dislike to each other and never were able to get along. Perhaps this is the time to ask whether Franklin or Wilkins were just plain difficult. Watson would have us believe that Franklin was. My own inquiries suggest that she was argumentative and at times overdefensive and prickly; but she established successful collaborations with her colleagues in Paris, with Gosling at King's, and after she left King's with Aron Klug and others at Birkbeck College in London. Similarly Wilkins has collaborated with many people. So Sayre is probably right in believing that this was an unfortunate collision of two very different, and apparently incompatible, temperaments. No doubt it was also exacerbated by antiquated sexist practices at King's, that excluded Franklin from the easy sociabilities of morning coffee and afternoon tea with her male colleagues, since they were served in separate and unequal combination rooms. (Why, we ask with Virginia Woolf, do the women always get boiled beef and prunes, while the men feast on partridges and wine?) But whatever the reasons, almost immediately tension ran high between Franklin and Wilkins.

Franklin began by building a high resolution X-ray camera to use for studying the structure of DNA with Gosling. Wilkins worked on DNA with A. R. Stokes, and there apparently was little communication between the two pairs, even though they were housed in the same laboratory. Within a few months of her arrival, Franklin discovered that, depending on the water content, DNA forms two kinds of fibers with quite different X-ray diffraction patterns. She called the dry form **A**, and the wet form **B**, and decided to begin her structural analysis by working up the **A** pattern because it showed more detail, and to go on to the **B** pattern in due course. In retrospect, this proved to be a misjudgment, but one that made sense at the time.

In November 1951, when Watson had been about 6 weeks in Cambridge and as yet knew very little about X-ray diffraction, he went to King's to hear a seminar in which Franklin talked about her work on DNA. In *The Double Helix* he tells us that he did not take notes, speculated about Franklin's looks, misunderstood or misremembered a good deal of what she said and communicated his recollections to Crick the next day. Crick got intrigued, started making some calculations, and on this basis the two of them quickly built their first model of DNA. They promptly invited the group from King's to come and see it. Rosalind Franklin immediately pointed out that the data she had presented made the model highly unlikely and saw no reason to involve herself further with such idle speculations.

This encounter had a variety of important consequences. For one thing, Sir Lawrence Bragg, who headed the Cavendish Laboratory, instructed Watson and Crick not to work any further on DNA, since the King's group was working on it. But there were also subtler consequences for Watson and Franklin. Watson had been shown up by a woman, and one whom he liked to think of as Wilkins's 'technician.' Franklin, on the other hand, seems to have decided that Watson was a clown and to stop taking him seriously. After all he had sat through her talk and then gone off and built a model that was highly speculative and almost certainly nonsense. That was not her idea of how one did science. She saw no reason to depart from her projected course of X-ray analysis in order to engage in similar games of model building.

Watson and Crick, on the other hand, were obsessed by the realization that Linus Pauling and his colleagues at the California Institute of Technology had recently cracked the structure of proteins by the careful and imaginative construction of three-dimensional models. However, there is an important difference between the Pauling group's model building and Watson's and Crick's: prior to building their models, the group at Cal. Tech. had systematically investigated the structures of all the component building blocks and had established a large body of information regarding their possible configurations, bond lengths and bond angles. Watson and Crick, on the other hand, hardly knew what some of the units looked like out of which they were trying to build DNA. In the summer of 1952, Erwin Chargaff, one of the pioneers in nucleic acid chemistry, found them ignorant even of the chemical formulas of the so-called 'purine' and 'pyrimidine bases' that compose DNA. And some 6 months later Jerry Donohue, another chemist, pointed out to them that these bases can assume two different forms, of which one is considerably more likely than the other.

Late in 1952, Watson and Crick heard rumors that Pauling thought he had deciphered the structure of DNA and was writing a paper about it. Through Pauling's son, Peter, they got a copy of the manuscript, quickly noticed that Pauling had made a rather basic mistake, and with that, decided that all bets were off. If Pauling was going after DNA, then it no longer 'belonged' to King's; so why shouldn't they work on it, too?

It was about this time that Wilkins showed Watson Franklin's best X-ray diffraction picture of the wet (**B**) form of DNA, which clearly showed it to be helical. Meanwhile their Cambridge colleague, Max Perutz, gave Crick and Watson a copy of a privileged report to the Medical Research Council, in which Franklin had summarized her most recent findings including the spacings of the critical reflections on the X-ray diffraction pattern of the DNA fibers. Any model of DNA had to account for these spacings and for their relative intensities. So, seeing themselves in a race against Pauling and with Franklin's new data against which to check plausible models, Watson and Crick went into a frenzy of model building. Within a few weeks they arrived at the now famous structure, wrote it up, and sent the manuscript to Wilkins.

This was the first indication Wilkins had that Watson and Crick had gone back to working on DNA. Both he and Franklin immediately accepted the essential correctness of the structure, and on April 25, 1953 there appeared in *Nature* the dramatic triad of papers. The first, by Watson and Crick, described the structure; the second and third, by Wilkins and Stokes, and by Franklin and Gosling, offered supporting X-ray evidence. The papers made a big splash and Watson and Crick were instantly famous.

Franklin never knew that the crucial features of her 'supporting' evidence were in their hands before they began to construct their model. At the time, she was in the process of moving from King's, which she hated, to Bernal's laboratory at Birkbeck College. There she remained, doing distinguished work on the structure of tobacco mosaic virus, until virtually the day she died of cancer in 1958, at the age of 37.

Watson, Crick and Wilkins shared the Nobel Prize in 1962; and the matter probably would have ended there had Watson not published *The Double Helix* in 1968. Until then no one knew the precise sequence of events, and hence the role that Franklin's data—unbeknownst to her—had played in guiding Watson's and Crick's formulation of the DNA structure.

Before continuing with our story, it will help to summarize the main features of the Watson-Crick model. The model pictures DNA as two ribbons, each of which consists of a long, invariant, alternating sequence of sugar (deoxyribose) and phosphate molecules: -sugar-phosphate-sugar-phosphate-. The ribbons have a polarity that allows one to tell one end from the other. Two of them, running in opposite directions (i.e., head to tail), are wound into a double helix. The two ribbons are connected at regular intervals by horizontal rungs, each of which is formed by a pair of flat discs (the purine and pyrimidine bases). There are four different bases in DNA: adenine (A), guanine (G), thymine (T) and cytosine (C). Two of them are large (the purines, A and G), and two smaller (the pyrimidines, T and C). To fit properly inside the helix, A must pair with T, and G with C. This feature of the model incorporates observations of Erwin Chargaff and his colleagues at Columbia University, who showed several years earlier that DNAs from different organisms contain different proportions of the bases, but that in all DNAs the amounts of A and T always are equal, as are the amounts of G and C.

Watson likens the DNA structure to 'a spiral staircase with the base pairs forming the steps.' The helix can be very long and there can be many thousands of base pairs in a DNA molecule. In this simple, elegant structure the two base pairs therefore can be arranged in an almost infinite number of different sequences and can form a very large number of different DNAs. (This wide diversity is an essential biological requirement if the millions of different genes that code for millions of different characteristics of all the different kinds of organisms are simply different variants of DNA sequences.) That this diversity can be drawn out of such a simple basic structure is one of the features that won the model its immediate and wide acceptance.

The *Nature* paper specified all the critical dimensions, such as helical pitch, the diameter of the helix, and the number of turns between repeats along the helix. All these were obtained from Franklin's data, though this is nowhere acknowledged. Furthermore, it was Franklin who had insisted as early as 1951 that the sugar-phosphate backbone had to be on the outside of the fiber with the bases pointing inward, since that was the most reasonable way to explain why DNA fibers readily take up water. She had also suggested that the bases were probably held together by hydrogen bonds. Both these features became part of the Watson–Crick model, though this also is not acknowledged in the *Nature* paper. In a long, follow-up paper that Crick and Watson sent to the *Proceedings of the Royal Society* of London in the latter part of the summer, they wrote: 'We have only considered such structures as would fit the preliminary X-ray data of Wilkins, Franklin and their co-workers. Our search has so far yielded only one suitable structure.'[11] So here they say it, but this fuller account is rarely referred to or read; and it, too, does not state that they had had access to Franklin's privileged report, including her calculations. Their achievement was considerable, no matter what. Though *all* the data they used had been the work of others (Franklin, Wilkins, Chargaff, plus Donohue's suggestion about base structures), Crick and Watson were the ones who saw how to fit them together and come up with the structure. They would have been no worse off had they acknowledged this.

It is therefore interesting to see what they did acknowledge. The *Nature* paper says:

> "*We are much indebted to Dr. Jerry Donohue for constant advice and criticism, especially on interatomic distances. We have also been stimulated by a knowledge of the* general nature *of the unpublished experimental results and ideas of Dr. M. F. H. Wilkins, Dr. R. E. Franklin and their co-workers at King's College, London' (my [emphasis]).*

The *Royal Society* paper ends:

> '*We are most indebted to Dr. M. F. H. Wilkins both for informing us of unpublished experimental observations and for the benefit of numerous discussions. We are also grateful to Dr. J. Donohue for constant advice on the problems of tautomerism and van der Waals contacts, and to Professor A. R. Todd, FRS, for advice on chemical matters, and for allowing us access to unpublished work.*'

There follows a remarkable final paragraph in which 'One of us (J.D.W.) wishes in addition to acknowledge' respectively 'hospitality', 'encouragement' and general indebtedness to Sir Lawrence Bragg, J. C. Kendrew, M. F. Perutz and S. E. Luria—all of them important and powerful men, and then or future Nobel Laureates. But not a word about Franklin.

5. Some Final Thoughts

I want to repeat that I don't think that Watson's treatment of Franklin in the book is idiosyncratic. Perhaps a bit exaggerated; but not that unusual. Seeing a woman work in a laboratory, he is not alone in assuming that she must be somebody's technician. People walking into my office or calling on the phone, often ask me for Professor Hubbard, confident in the assumption that the Professor must be male. Furthermore, as late as 1970, so 2 years after the publication of *The Double Helix*, Linus Pauling, who has good reasons of his own to be leery of the scurrilous innuendos in the book, refers to Franklin's work as 'Wilkins' X-ray photographs . . .'[12] Indeed as I write this I see in the *New York Times* (April 9, 1978) an article about last year's Nobel Laureate, Rosalyn Yalow, that repeatedly suggests that in the work for which she won the Prize the real, imaginative thinking was done by her male colleague, Berson, while Yalow shook the test tubes.

A question that is often asked is how 'close' Franklin was to solving the DNA structure. Obviously there is no good answer. She was proceeding systematically and making good progress. She was intent on exhausting the possibilities of traditional X-ray analysis before getting involved in model building, which seems to have appeared to her a highly speculative approach. There is little doubt that had she been able to continue working on DNA, she could have solved the structure. But Franklin had decided to move to Birkbeck, because she hated her situation at King's and Sayre tells us that this had necessitated a promise 'to stop thinking about DNA entirely' (to which she commented quite appropriately, 'But how could I stop thinking?'). So probably it is historically correct to say—if such speculation can be called history—that she would not have solved the structure. Whether and how much the fact that Watson was breathing down her and Wilkins' necks exacerbated the situation at King's no one will ever know.

We must be clear about the fact that at the point at which Watson and Crick began their second (and successful) bout of model building, a number of important things had been learned about DNA: (1) Wilkins and Stokes, and Franklin and Gosling had shown that it was helical (at least in the **B** form); (2) Franklin's conclusion that the sugar–phosphate backbone lies on the outside meant that the bases must be fitted into a regular, repeating pattern *inside* the helix; (3) her X-ray data supplied the critical parameters against which to test possible models; (4) Chargaff's rules regarding the equivalence of

A and T and of G and C set further limits. With all these constraints to guide the search, the structure was bound to be solved before long.

It is sometimes said that Watson's and Crick's race for the double helix and its celebration in Watson's best-selling book have lowered the moral tone of science and escalated its frenetic competitiveness, particularly in 'molecular biology.' I am skeptical. As I see it, science reached its *man*hood during the heyday of industrial capitalism when competition was hailed as the road to success in a system that was claimed to be meritocratic. Western scientists operate with the explicit assumption that competition sorts the chaff from the wheat and that genuine ability is what determines competitive success, not accidents of birth, entrepreneurial skills and/or ruthlessness. During the 25 years since the discovery of the double helix, the number of young people entering science has increased greatly, but the number of available top positions has not. I attribute the deterioration in the social relationships and mores—the enormous competitiveness and secretiveness that poison the contemporary scene for many aspiring young (and not so young) scientists—on this larger social context more than on the 'winner takes all' morality, exemplified in Watson's race for the Nobel; which is not to deny that the overwhelming success of this race and the power and prestige it quickly brought the till then quite obscure Watson and Crick, probably helped give it respectability.

In this connection, it should not go unnoticed that Sir Lawrence Bragg, who less than 2 years earlier had summarily warned Watson and Crick off DNA, was far from disapproving when they 'won' DNA for Cambridge (which, not incidentally, was still smarting from the 'loss' of protein structure to Linus Pauling). Bragg even went further and wrote the Foreword to *The Double Helix*—a decided coup for Watson in the face of vociferous disapproval of the manuscript by many of its characters, including Crick who threatened to sue. In this Foreword, Bragg expresses 'deep satisfaction' at the 'due recognition . . . given to the long, patient investigation by Wilkins at King's College (London) as well as to the brilliant and rapid final solution by Crick and Watson at Cambridge' by the Nobel Committee's decision to split the prize between them; but not a word about Franklin.

So, the standard of morality certainly is low; but I am not sure that this is new. I have recently looked into the origins of my own field of visual pigment biochemistry, which dates back 100 years, and find there a situation that also is very bad. Being the nineteenth century, of course,

it involves only men. In this instance, a discovery by an apparently very modest, young scientist immediately turned into a race with a much older, more established and powerful one. The young man shortly was dead from tuberculosis; the older one continued with the work and entirely overshadowed him.[13]

A final point: at the masthead of his concluding chapter in *The Path to the Double Helix,* Olby has two quotations, one from Crick, the other from Michael Polanyi, a philosopher of science who began his career as a physical chemist. Crick's quotation begins: 'The ultimate aim of the modern movement in biology is in fact to explain *all* biology in terms of physics and chemistry.' And the rest of it expands on this reductionist paradigm and ends: 'It is the realization that our knowledge on the atomic level is secure which has led to the great influx of physicists and chemists into biology.'[14] Placed right up against this, Polanyi's quote begins: 'The universal topography of atomic particles . . . which, according to Laplace, offers us a universal knowledge of all things is seen to contain hardly any knowledge that is of interest.' It ends by extending this recognition to biology: 'But now the analysis of the hierarchy of living things shows that to reduce this hierarchy to ultimate particulars is to wipe out our very sight of it. Such analysis proves this ideal to be false and destructive.'[15]

Such is the parting of the roads that we confront in biology. The reductionists call the synthesists pessimistic; the holists call the reductionists blind, and even destructive and dangerous. Nothing illustrates the dichotomy more clearly than the current controversy over recombinant DNA. For this technology is a practical application of the reductionist view, that sees nothing improper in regarding living organisms, such as the lowly colon bacillus, *E. coli,* as convenient chemical tools; and that sees no danger in teaching these bacteria in the wink of an eye a molecular vocabulary that other, 'higher' organisms have taken eons to learn—and eons during which there has been an opportunity for many trials and many fatal errors. This is the side on which Watson, Crick and most of the other 'molecular biologists' line up. On the other side are people who see the organic world as much more than the sum of its parts; who believe that connections and process cannot be understood by isolating things or events; who distrust oversimplifications, and in Chargaff's words, hate 'to see *E. coli* impersonating nature. The difference in talents is really too great.'[16]

It is not pessimistic to recognize that in the real world everything is connected with everything else; that 'isolated variables' are figments of a miseducated imagination. 'To light a candle is to cast a shadow,' writes Ursula LeGuin in *A Wizard of Earthsea*. This does not mean that we should abandon all attempts at analysis and at science. But it means that we must keep our perspective on what they can tell us. We cannot expect the science of atoms and molecules to unveil what life is.

References

1. Watson, J. D. 1968, 1969. *The Double Helix.* Atheneum Publishers, Mentor Paperback, New York.
2. Watson, J. D. and Crick F. H. C. 1953. A structure for deoxyribose nucleic acid. *Nature* **171**, 737–738.
3. Sayre, A. 1975. *Rosalind Franklin and DNA.* W. W. Norton and Co., New York.
4. Hubbard, R. 1976. *Rosalind Franklin and DNA* (Book Review). *Signs* **2**, 229–237.
5. Gombrich, E. H. 1963. Meditations on a hobby horse or the roots of artistic form. In: *Meditations on a Hobby Horse and Other Essays on the Theory of Art.* Phaidon Press, London.
6. Watts, A. W. 1958, 1970. *Nature, Man and Woman.* Pantheon Books, Vintage Books, New York.
7. Watson, J. D. 1969. *The Double Helix, op. cit.,* p. 21.
8. Watson, J. D. 1966. Growing up in the phage group. In: Cairns, J., Stent, G. S. and Watson, J. D. eds. *Phage and the Origins of Molecular Biology.* Cold Spring Harbor Laboratory of Quantitative Biology, Cold Spring Harbor, LI.
9. Schrödinger, E. 1944. *What is Life?* Cambridge University Press, London.
10. Olby, R. 1974. *The Path to the Double Helix.* Macmillan Co., London.
11. Crick, F. H. C. and Watson, J. D. 1954. The complementary structure of deoxyribonucleic acid. *Proc. R. Soc.* **A223**, 80–96.
12. Pauling, L. 1970. Fifty years of progress in structural chemistry and molecular biology. *Daedalus, Boston, Mass.* **99**, 988–1014.
13. Hubbard, R. 1977. Preface to the English translations of Boll's on the anatomy and physiology of the retina and of Kühne's chemical processes in the retina. *Vision Res.* **17**, 1247–1248.
14. Crick, F. H. C. 1966. *Of Molecules and Men,* pp. 10, 14 as quoted in Olby, p. 425.
15. Polanyi, M. 1968. Life's irreducible structure. *Science* **160**, 1308–1312, as quoted in Olby, p. 425.
16. Chargaff, E. 1974. Building the Tower of Babble. *Nature* **248**, 776–779.

READING 34

Women and Nature: The Roaring Inside Her

Susan Griffin

A simple thought runs through this writing: that is that the predominant civilization of the West, this patriarchy, has always regarded and treated women and nature in the same way. We are less than human men, in the regard of patriarchy, less intelligent, less spiritual, less rational. And under the sway of this regard, the fathers have decided that we cannot decide for ourselves (and, yes, that we are even dangerous when, by chance or struggle, we break free of their control). And so patriarchy accepts our existence as legitimate only when we are subjected to male power, a power in the word which objectifies us, both women and nature, and a power in the act which dominates us.

Women and Nature: The Roaring Inside Her is a record of this relation of patriarchy to woman and nature, and in the telling of this record the metaphors by which nature is so often compared to or personified by a woman, and with which women are revealed as more a part of nature, or closer to the earth than men, are used to a different purpose, because now the old story is retold by a woman and so turns around to face its origins.

The book [*Women and Nature: The Roaring Inside Her,* from which this article is excerpted] begins in a parody of the objective voice—I call it the voice of patriarchy—that voice which rarely uses pronouns as the subject of any sentence and thus utters sentences and phrases such as, "It is decided . . ." or "it is declared . . ." or "it is discovered that . . ." In this voice a history of scientific opinion about the nature of matter (or ultimately the nature of nature) is traced and woven in chronologically with a history of opinions (from Saints, philosophers, poets and psychoanalysts) about the nature of woman.

Slowly in the midst of this "objective" unravelling of history another voice, faint and muffled, begins to appear. This is the object herself, the dominated one speaking out, and in the course of the book, her voice becomes stronger, but that is the dramatic plot of the story: now, in this book, woman and nature, formerly shamed by our mutual association, become allies, assume a voice and question the inquisitors (I shall not reveal who wins).

1382
Thomas Brawardine, in *Treatise on the Proportions of Velocities in Moving Bodies,* proposes a mathematical law of dynamics universally valid for all changes in velocity.

1431
Joan of Arc, age 22, "placed high on the fire so the flames would reach her slowly," dies.
She is asked why she wears male costume.

1468
Pope defines witchcraft as *crimen exceptum,* removing all legal limits to torture.

1482
Leonardo da Vinci moves to Milan and begins his notebooks on hydraulics, mechanics, anatomy: he paints the *Madonna on the Rocks. Does she see the body of Saint Michael, they ask her? Did he come to her naked?*

1500–1525
1000 witches are burned every year in the diocese of Como.

1543
Vesalius publishes *De Humani Corporis Fabria.*

1543
Copernicus publishes *De Revolutionibus Orbium Celestium. She is asked if she is in a state of grace. She is asked if Saint Margaret speaks English.*

1571
Johannes Kepler is born.

1572
Augustus Pious issues *Consultationes Saxionicae,* stating that a good witch must be burned because she has made a pact with the Devil. *She confesses that she falsely pretended to have revelations from God and his angels, from St. Catherine and St. Margaret.*

1585
Witch-burnings in two villages leave one female inhabitant each.

1589
Francis Bacon is made clerk of the Star Chamber.
He says that nature herself must be examined.

1581–1591
Nine hundred witches are burned in Lorraine.
That nature must be bound into service, he persuades.

1600
Gilberte publishes *De Magnete.*

1603
William Harvey serves as physician to King James I and assists at the examination of the witches.

1609
Galileo, on hearing a rumor of the invention of a glass magnifying distant objects, constructs a telescope. *It is urged that nature must be hounded in her wanderings before leading her and driving her.*

1609
Kepler publishes *Astronomica Nova.*

1609
The whole population of Navarre is declared witches.
He says that the Earth should be put on the rack and tortured for her secrets.

1615
William Harvey lectures on the circulation of the blood at the Royal College of Physicians.

1607–1618
William Harvey assists at the examination of witches.

1619
Kepler publishes his third law, *Harmonies Mundi*.
She is asked if she signed the Devil's book. She is asked if the Devil had a body. She is asked who she chose to be an incubus.

1622
Francis Bacon publishes *Natural Experimental History for the Foundation of Philosophy*.

1622–1623
Johann George II, Prince Bishop, builds a house for the trying of witches at Bamberg, where 600 burn.

1628
158 witches are burned at Würzburg.

1637
Descartes publishes *Discours de la Methode*.
She is asked what oath she made. What finger she was forced to raise. Where she made a union with her incubus. What food she ate at the sabbat. What music was played, what dances were danced. What Devil's marks were on her body. Who are the children on whom she cast spells; what animals bewitched. How she was able to fly through the air.

1638
Galileo publishes *Two New Sciences*.

1640
Carbon dioxide is obtained by **Helmont**.

1644
Descartes publishes *Principia Philosophiae*.

1670
Rouen witch trials are held.
She confesses that every Monday the Devil lay with her for fornication. She confesses that when he copulated with her she felt intense pain. She confesses that after having intercourse with the Devil she married her daughter to him.

1666
Newton procures "a triangular glass prism to try the celebrated phenomena of colors."

1706
Newton publishes *Opticks*.

1726
Newton publishes *Principia*.

1738
Dean of Faculty of Law at Rostock demands that witches be extirpated by fire and sword.

1745
In witch trial at Lyon, five are sentenced to death.

1749
Sister Maria Renanata is burned.

1775
Anna Maria Schnagel is executed for witchcraft.
She confesses that she passed through a keyhole of a door. That she became a cat and then a horse. She confesses that she made a pact with the Devil, that she asked for the Devil's help. She confesses that she was carried through the air in a moment.

Show Horses

The Bit

> #### The Book of Common Prayer
> *"Be ye not like to horses and mules which have no understanding: whose mouths must be held up with bit and bridle, lest they fall upon thee."*

The right thumb of the rider holds the center of the bridle in front of the horse's face and above her head so that the bit is in front of the horse's mouth. The right hand is placed under the horse's jaw. If the horse does not open her mouth when the bit touches her teeth, if she clenches her teeth, the rider presses his left forefinger on the toothless bars of the lower jaw which will make the horse open her mouth and accept the bit. The thicker the bit the milder its effect on the mouth of the horse. The bit should neither pull up the corners of the mouth nor touch the teeth. The nose-band must be tight but not so tight that the horse cannot breathe. And she must be able to accept tidbits from the rider's hand. The throat latch however should be fastened loosely.

Nature

> #### Captain Elwyn Hartley Edwards, From Paddock to Saddle
> *"[The Horse] is by Nature a very lazy animal whose idea of heaven is an enormous field of lush grass in which he can graze undisturbed until his belly is full, and after a pleasant doze can start filling himself up all over again."*

> #### Emily Post, Etiquette
> *"A perfect hostess in a household with servants gives the impression that she has nothing whatever*

to do with household arrangements, which apparently run themselves. In a servantless household, she has the cleaning, marketing and as much cooking as possible done in advance, so that an absolute minimum of her time is spent on these chores while her guests are with her."

It is the horse's extreme sensitivity to pain, especially in the mouth but also all over her body which allows the rider to control her with the pressure of his own weight, the movements of his legs, and with the aid of the bit, the bridle and the rein, the riding whip, long whip and the spur.

It is the timorous nature of the animal coupled with this sensitivity that allows her to be trained. The horse is not aggressive; her only defense is to flee. Therefore the horse reacts to pain by running away from the pain. If the rider stands at the horse's head and taps her flank with a long whip, the horse will move away from the discomfort.

In addition the horse has a prodigious memory, is a social animal, has a desire to please and a need for security, and all these qualities are used in her training. Her faults are nervousness, laziness and an excitability that is at times unpredictable.

As One

Alois Podhajsky,
The Riding Teacher
"The onlooker should have the impression that two creatures are fused together, one thinking, the other executing the thoughts."

The rider loves his horse. He dreams of her at night. He sees her sometimes in a fury of wildness, her excitable frenzies pouring over his body in waves; his head tossing becomes her head, a silky black mane on the pillows, large nostrils flaring, the long neck flailing back and forth throwing the sheets to the floor, hoofs kicking at the walls, and one eye, wild staring, unknowing, hurtling now, seven hundred pounds, crashing through the wall, galloping blood bright at the teeth where the bit has been torn away, a white frothy sweat, running through the dark night, all night: he is not the rider but the horse, riding, riding, riding. But in the morning she is calm. She is his mare. He speaks softly to her. She is supple. She responds quickly to his least movement. They have developed a silent language. If he presses with his left thigh, a subtle movement, imperceptible to the onlooker, she moves immediately to the right, her feet graceful, her

head high, executing with exquisite grace his barely whispered will. It is as if she reads his mind and peacefully lets his thoughts enter and guide her body. They are beautiful together, seemingly effortless, artful, her back seems part of his ass, her legs are his legs, they ride as one.

The Stable

Captain Elwyn Hartley Edwards,
From Paddock to Saddle
". . . the stable and the return to it after work is the greatest reward we can give our horse."

When does the horse first know that the rider has left her side? Even when his weight is no longer on her back, his hand may be connected to her mouth, by the rein, by the bit. And even when his hand is off the rein, his eyes may be upon her. When can she be certain he is gone? Does she listen to his footsteps as they recede? Then, does she remember? Does she remember that she has a tongue, that she can push it between her teeth and over her lips? Does she feel a sense of dread as she lets it out? Does she feel a sense of shame, apart from the rider, when she rolls on her back? Is this a private ecstasy? Is she in fear of being discovered? Does she dread and not give this dread a name? Does she love the dark privacy of her stall? The smell of hay newly laid, the food that is brought every day at the same precise hours, always fresh, always familiar. Never changed. Does she love even the sound of the stable door as it opens to let her in and closes behind her, the sound of the chain on her halter as it is run through the manger ring? And when she is led out, finally, to the riding school or the track, even at her moment of triumph, even after she has waited for this, as the flowers are put over her silky neck, does she dream of the stable? Does she dream of returning?

Love

Andreas Capellanus,
The Art of Courtly Love
"Love gets its name (amor) from the word for hook (amus) which means to capture or to be captured."

Though she loves her stable because of the comfort, because she can always count on it to be there, because it is her private world and it is where she rests and is fed, she waits there. It is in the stable that she waits for her rider. It is only when her rider appears that she leaves her stable, that she moves. She loves to please her rider. It is her rider who rubs her flanks, who carries bits of food in the white flesh of his palm, who speaks to her softly, kindly. It is her rider who has trained all her movements, her rider who tells her what she must do from one moment to the next. Her rider who possesses a secret knowledge of a series of memorable movements whose purpose she cannot decipher, a knowledge above her capacity to understand, her rider who knows how to produce food and pleasure, for she is so entirely stupid and helpless that she cannot even feed herself without his aid, let alone know what or where to go, to do. The horse has no wish for freedom. She awaits the occasional visits of her master who day after day seems more powerful, more wise, taking on a majesty the horse would never dream of for herself. When he is in her presence, her thoughts are riveted on him. She likes no one else to ride her. Is this not love the horse is feeling? But she is mute. The rider has named her and so he must also name her feeling. He decides that she loves him.

The Zoological Garden

> *Cris Williamson,*
> *Wild Things*
> *"Wild, wild things can turn on you*
> *And you got to set them free."*

In the cage is the lion. She paces with her memories. Her body is a record of her past. As she moves back and forth, one may see it all: the lean frame, the muscular legs, the paw enclosing long sharp claws, the astonishing speed of her response. She was born in this garden. She has never in her life stretched those legs. Never darted further than 20 yards at a time. Only once did she use her claws. Only once did she feel them sink into flesh. And it was her keeper's flesh. Her keeper whom she loves, who feeds her, who would never dream of harming her, who protects her. Who in his mercy forgave her mad attack, saying this was in her nature, to be cruel at a whim, to try to kill what she loves. He had come into her cage as he usually did early in the morning to change her water, always at the same time of day, in the same manner, speaking softly to her, careful to make no sudden movement, keeping his distance, when suddenly she sank down, deep down into herself, the way wild animals do before they spring, and then she had risen on all her strong legs, and swiped him in one long, powerful, graceful movement across the arm. How lucky for her he survived the blow. The keeper and his friends shot her with a gun to make her sleep. Through her half-open lids she

knew they made movements around her. They fed her with tubes. They observed her. They wrote comments in notebooks. And finally they rendered a judgment. She was normal. She was a normal wild beast, whose power is dangerous, whose anger can kill, they had said. Be more careful of her, they advised. Allow her less excitement. Perhaps let her exercise more. She understood none of this. She understood only the look of fear in her keeper's eyes. And now she paces. Paces as if she were angry, as if she were on the edge of frenzy. The spectators imagine she is going through the movements of the hunt, or that she is readying her body for survival. But she knows no life outside the garden. She has no notion of anger over what she could have been, or might be. No idea of rebellion.

It is only her body that knows of these things, moving her, daily, hourly, back and forth, back and forth, before the bars of her cage.

Naming

Behind naming, beneath words, is something else. An existence named, unnamed, unnamable. We give the grass a name, and earth a name. We say grass and earth are separate. We know this because we can pull the grass free of the earth and see its separate roots—but when the grass is free, it dies. We say the inarticulate have no souls. We say the cow's eye has no existence outside of ourselves, that the red wing of the blackbird has no thought, the roe of the salmon no feeling, because we cannot name these. Yet for our own lives we grieve all that cannot be spoken, that there is no name for, repeating for ourselves the names of things which surround what cannot be named. We say Heron and Loon, Coot and Killdeer, Snipe and Sandpiper, Gull and Hawk, Eagle and Osprey, Pigeon and Dove, Oriole, Meadowlark, Sparrow. We say Red Admiral and Painted Lady, Morning Cloak and Question Mark. Baltimore and Checkerspot, Buckeye, Monarch, Viceroy, Mayfly, Stonefly Cicada, Leafhopper and Earwig, we say Sea Urchin and Sand Dollar, Starfish and Sandworm. We say mucous membrane, uterus, cervix, ligament, vagina and hymen, labia, orifice, artery, vessel, spine and heart. We say skin, blood, breast, nipple, taste, nostril, green, eye, hair, we say vulva, hood, clitoris, belly, foot, knee, elbow, pit, nail, thumb, we say tongue, teeth, toe, ear, we say ear and voice and touch and taste and we say again love, breast and beautiful and vulva, saying clitoris, saying belly, saying toes and soft saying ear, saying ear, saying ear, ear and hood and hood and green and all that we say we are saying around that which cannot be said, cannot be spoken. But in a moment that which is behind naming makes itself known. Hand and breast know each one to the other. Wood in the table knows clay in the bowl. Air knows grass knows water knows mud knows beetle knows frost knows sunlight knows the shape of the earth knows death knows not dying. And all this knowledge is in the souls of everything, behind naming, before speaking, beneath words.

The Lion in the Den of the Prophets

She swaggers in. They are terrifying in their white hairlessness. She waits. She watches. She does not move. She is measuring their moves. And they are measuring her. Cautiously one takes a bit of her fur. He cuts it free from her. He examines it. Another numbers her feet, her teeth, the length and width of her body. She yawns. They announce she is alive. They wonder what she will do if they enclose her in the room with them. One of them shuts the door. She backs her way toward the closed doorway and then roars. "Be still," the men say. She continues to roar. "Why does she roar?" they ask. The roaring must be inside her, they conclude. They decide they must see the roaring inside her. They approach her in a group, six at her two front legs and six at her two back legs. They are trying to put her to sleep. She swings at one of the men. His own blood runs over him. "Why did she do that?" the men question. She has no soul, they conclude, she does not know right from wrong. "Be still," they shout at her. "Be humble, trust us," they demand. "We have souls," they proclaim. "We know what is right," they approach her with their medicine, "for you." She does not understand language. She devours them.

Introduction: Institutionalized Violence Against Women

Violence against women is institutionalized in many societies and in many different ways. The extent of the practices, combined with the fact that the threat of violence is qualitatively different from, for example, the threat of ridicule or social sanctioning, require that violence against women be addressed as yet another institution of social control.

Violence as proof of "masculine" identity, and aggression as proof of sexuality, are described by R. Wayne Eisenhart in the selection "You Can't Hack It Little Girl: A Discussion of the Covert Psychological Agenda of Modern Combat Training." This article reveals not only how misogyny (hatred of women) and violence toward women are inculcated through military training, but also how a man's sexuality is repressed and numbed, and replaced with the urge to "kill somebody."

In the article "Rape: The All-American Crime," by Susan Griffin, the relationship between sexuality and violence is examined. Griffin argues that the attitudes toward "normal" heterosexual intercourse—women passive, men active—within the context of a structurally unequal power relationship, have created a world in which rape is but one end of the continuum. The taken-for-grantedness that "women want it/ask for it" is exposed in an interview conducted by James F. Skipper, Jr. and William L. McWhorter with a convicted rapist, entitled "A Rapist Gets Caught in the Act." This selection, as well as the following two brief readings—"I Make No Apology" and "Judge Faces Recall"—illustrate many of the analytical points made by Griffin.

Less extreme, but still classified as violence because of the fear they engender in women, are the practices of sexual harassment. The selection "Myths and Facts About Sexual Harassment" is taken from *Fighting Sexual Harassment: An Advocacy Handbook* written by the staff of Alliance Against Sexual Coercion. It reviews the myths—based on incorrect biological assumptions—which condone harassment in the workplace and ensure that women who are harassed feel guilty and responsible, rather than violated. Each myth is countered with the facts about this type of violence.

Harassment takes place not only in work settings but in many public places—coffee-shops, bus stops, laundromats, streets. Cheryl Bernard and Edit Schlaffer in the selection "The Man in the Street: Why He Harasses," interviewed men who harassed them. They report that the male's ego is aggrandized through the harassment; and, although a "minor sex offender," he is nevertheless "an accomplice in the more massive forms of violence against women."

Violence against women in terms of physical abuse and wife-battering is, also, institutionalized. We include an article from *Response* titled "Premarital Violence: Battering on College Campuses," which details the extent of physical abuse experienced by women in dating relationships.

Finally, we include some cross-cultural materials to illustrate that violence against women appears in many different forms in many different societies. Societally endorsed mutilation of women to meet male standards of beauty and eroticism is discussed in the selection "Gynocide: Chinese Footbinding," by Andrea Dworkin from her book *Women Hating* (E. P. Dutton: 1974). As Dworkin argues, in order to be attractive to men, millions of Chinese women have been brutalized. Although women's feet are no longer bound in China, female infanticide has become a relatively frequent practice as indicated in the news clipping, "Chinese Are Killing Newborn Girls at a High Rate."

Anne Sostrom's poem, "It's Custom, Simply Custom," was inspired by a recent newspaper account of the burning of an Indian woman by her new in-laws because her marriage dowry was judged inadequate. Mary Daly's "Indian Suttee: The Ultimate Consummation of Marriage" from her book *Gyn-Ecology* describes the (now outlawed) East Indian practice of burning a widow after her husband's death. Both of these selections help us to recognize that the most extreme violences against women are all-of-a-piece with those that seem to be minor, and that each culture has its own form of institutionalized violence.

We conclude this section with an article by Robin Morgan and Gloria Steinem, "The International Crime of Genital Mutilation." This article is difficult to read, for it describes practices that are extraordinarily painful, both physically and emotionally.

You Can't Hack It Little Girl:
A Discussion of the Covert Psychological
Agenda of Modern Combat Training

R. Wayne Eisenhart

What I seek to accomplish with this article is to share and articulate as well as possible an experience common to thousands of American young men. This experience must be better understood for it is exacting a high toll in suffering. According to statistics from the Emergency Ministry for Veterans Services of the National Council of Churches (1971), over 49,000 Vietnam veterans have died since discharge and return to civilian life, primarily as a result of suicides, drug overdoses, and vehicular accidents, etc. I wish to explore the roots of this national tragedy and in so doing must look to military basic training. The observations presented here represent three years of personal experience, one year of clinical experience dealing with veterans in a crisis intervention clinic, one year of study of the available literature, and two years as a peer counselor and street organizer in a veterans' self-help project, The Flower of the Dragon, Inc. The lack of hard data concerning these processes allows one only to make generalized observations of recurring patterns of behavior and discuss possible origins. The need for further research is obvious.

My central thesis is that the nature of military basic training which sought to prepare America's young men for the most difficult of her wars was ineffective—in that it did not provide instruction pertinent to the accomplishment of the designated mission—and it was brutal, and that this inept and brutal training created intense emotional conflicts. These conflicts were exacerbated by the frustrating nature of the Vietnam War and later provided the basis of debilitating emotional stresses. Millions of American men have been shaped by the process of mili-

tary basic training. It is crucial therefore to more fully understand the dynamics of a social institution which has so affected the lives of a great portion of our society.

This discussion will center primarily upon the nature and dynamics of Marine Corps basic training. While Marine Corps basic training has the added catalyst of physical violence in the conditioning process, it appears that the psychological agenda of basic training in all the services is the same. The processes are only more clearly etched and blatant in the Marine Corps.

The Boot Camp Experience

The overt purpose of training at Parris Island, South Carolina and San Diego, California is to produce superbly conditioned and disciplined men who will obey the orders of their superiors without question and will contribute to the unexcelled combat record of the Corps. As they go into the Marine Corps young men are told that they will learn discipline and that they will become men, they will develop confidence, pride, masculinity, and will become part of a glorious military unit. However, the means by which this is accomplished must be examined.

The psychological experiences of basic training may be understood as having three interlocking components: the acceptance of psychological control, the equation of masculine identity with military performance, and the equation of the entire military mission with raw aggression. The experiences of basic training contribute to each of these transformations of behavior and attitude. Change in one area serves to promote change in another.

Psychological Control

Psychological control may be defined as that state of mind in which an individual remains passive or behaves

Reprinted from R. Wayne Eisenhart, "You Can't Hack It Little Girl: A Discussion of the Covert Psychological Agenda of Modern Combat Training," in the *Journal of Social Issues,* vol. 31, no. 4 (1975), pp. 13–23, by permission of the publisher and the author.

only in a prescribed fashion in the face of acute stress. Kelman (1973), considering how men may become powerless to resist violence, even violence directed at themselves, speaks of three interrelated processes: authorization, routinization, and dehumanization. In this case, authorization meant not challenging specific actions; one could not challenge the overall authority of the drill instructor or the military. Daily conditioning and structuring of activities led one to a state of resigned routinization, and the continual structured effort to degrade and shape the individual's self-image formed the basis of dehumanization. The achievement of psychological control in Marine Corps boot camp was aided greatly by the threat of physical violence. One had to remain utterly passive in the face of physical and verbal abuse or suffer continuing degradation, exercise to the point of exhaustion, and physical violence sufficient to maintain passivity. The recruit learned that instant unquestioning obedience to authority was insufficient to avoid physical violence. If one did his job to the best of his ability and kept his mouth shut, he still was beaten and terrorized — until a certain "blank look" in his eyes, signifying the achievement of psychological control, was achieved.

Sexual Identity and Military Function

Whenever I failed any task or performed poorly, I was physically assaulted. At the same time the drill instructor screamed in my face something like, "You can't hack it, you goddamned faggot." The means by which the military socialization process forged this link between an individual's sexuality and his military mission was proportional in intensity to the resistance encountered. Rituals coupled with ever escalating violence were the predominant mode.

While in basic training we were issued M-14 rifles. The breech of the weapon is closed by a bolt which is continually pushed forward by a large spring with considerable force. One night three men who had been censured for ineffectiveness in their assigned tasks were called forward in front of the assembled platoon, ordered to insert their penises into the breeches of their weapons, close the bolt, and run the length of the squad bay singing the Marine Corps Hymn. This violent ritual ended as the drill instructor left and the three men sank to the floor, penises still clamped into their weapons. We helped them remove the rifles and guided them to their beds. There was considerable bleeding as the men cupped their wounded penises with their hands, curled into balls, and cried.

Promotion of Aggression

As control is achieved and sexual identity is threatened and linked with the military function, it is also made clear that the military function is aggression. The primary lesson of boot camp, towards which all behavior was shaped, was to seek dominance. The mission was always "close with the enemy and destroy him." To fail at this, as at all else, was nonmasculine. Aggression and the seeking of dominance were equated with masculinity. Recruits were brutalized, frustrated, and cajoled to a flash point of high tension. They were often stunned by the depths of violence erupting from within themselves. Only on these occasions of violent aggressive outbursts did the drill instructor cease his endless litany of "you dirty faggot" and "can't hack it, little girls?" In several outbursts I utterly ravaged men. In one instance during hand to hand combat training, I choked a man into submission while biting and gashing his face. Although I was shocked by my behavior, the drill instructor gleefully reaffirmed my masculinity in front of the platoon, saying that I was a lot more of a man than he had previously imagined. Aggressiveness was also promoted by the constant reminder that one would soon be in combat and facing instant death if not aggressive. On the bayonet field we were told upon our last lesson: "The next time you are in a bayonet fight, one of you will die and that will be the one who is not aggressive enough."

Accomplishment of mission, violence, and aggressiveness became equated with masculinity. We were continually reminded that we were soon to be in Vietnam and in combat. The best way to stay alive was to learn the training, be aggressive, and accomplish the designated mission (close and destroy). In other words, effectiveness and aggressiveness became a means of protecting our lives as well as our masculine self-image. Noneffectiveness and nonaggressiveness were a clear and present danger. The group ritual as a means to inculcate these belief systems is illustrated by the following incident:

> In boot camp one recruit had a good deal of difficulty keeping up with the rigorous physical regime. He was a bright, intelligent young man who had volunteered, yet lacked the composite aggressive tendencies thought to comprise manhood. He was slender and light complexioned, not effeminate by civilian standards, but he was considered so in boot camp. He was continually harassed and called "girl" and "faggot." We, his fellow recruits, began to accept the stereotyping of him as effeminate.

In the midst of a particularly grueling run, when Pvt. Green began to drop out, we were ordered to run circles around him. Two men from the formation attempted to carry him along. His eyes were glazed and there was white foam all around his mouth. He was beyond exhaustion. He fell again as the entire formation of 80 men continued to run circles around him. Four men ran from the formation and kicked and beat him in an attempt to make him run. He stumbled forward and fell. Again he was pummelled. Finally four men literally carried him on their shoulders to the base area where we expected to rest. We were then told, "No goddamn bunch of little girl faggots who can't run seven miles as a unit will get a rest." We were ordered to do strenuous calisthenics. The weak "effeminate" individual who had caused the additional exercises was made to lead us without participating, counting cadence while we sweated. The tension crackled in the air, curses were hurled, and threats made. As we were made to exercise for another full hour we became so exhausted that stomachs began to cramp and men vomited. Pvt. Green was made to laugh at us as he counted cadence.

The DI looked at Green and said, "You're a weak no-good-for-nothing queer," then turning to the glowering platoon, "As long as there are faggots in this outfit who can't hack it, you're all going to suffer." As he turned to go into the duty hut he sneered, "Unless you women get with the program, straighten out the queers, and grow some balls of your own, you best give your soul to God because your ass is mine and so is your mother's on visiting day." With a roar 60–70 enraged men engulfed Green, knocking him to the ground and kicking and beating him. He was picked up and passed over the heads of the roaring densely-packed mob. His eyes were wide with terror; the mob beyond reason. Green was tossed and beaten in the air for about five minutes and then literally hurled onto a concrete wash rack where he sprawled, dazed and bleeding.

A young recruit had almost been beaten to death in a carefully orchestrated ritual of exorcism. The three components of the covert agenda of modern basic training are combined in interlocking supportive fashion in such violent rituals as this. In Pvt. Green were invested those qualities most antithetical to the military ethos. The sexuality of the men was closely tied to the success or failure of the unit. Masculinity was affirmed through completion of the military function. The identity of the group coalesced against Green, and he and the qualities he represented literally were cast out of the group ethos.

The linking of the military function with sexual identity, the exacerbation and promotion of violence and aggression, and the repeatedly hammered ideal of seeking dominance at all costs, had produced in the recruits a well-honed emotional edge. We were out to "kill them gooks," as many and as soon as possible.

Racism

The terms "gook" and "slope" were continually used by training personnel as well as in written material and movies. Although the racism instilled in boot camp was directed towards Asians, it also increased black-white tensions. A black marine cannot help but be reminded of the racism inherent in the structure when he hears a white marine say, "We're gonna kill the *yellow* bastards." We did not question or challenge this racism as it made it considerably more comfortable to denigrate our potential enemies while learning how to kill. However, if one considers the black vs. white race riots that have plagued the military in the United States, Germany, Vietnam, and even aboard ships, this would appear to be a highly questionable, short-sighted tactic.

Cultural Insensitivity

There was little or no effort made to orient marines to Vietnamese culture. During the training process there was a conspicuous lack of trenchant information and that which was available and presented was done so in desultory fashion. This is in contrast to World War II and the Korean War during which soldiers were inundated with lectures, books, and pamphlets concerning friend and foe alike. It seems a tactical error of significant import to inculcate racism and cultural insensitivity during the training process of a war for which the objective is the allegiance of the population (rather than territory) and in which enemy and ally are racially indistinguishable.

On the last day of training before leaving for Vietnam we were ushered into a clearing where a staff sergeant stood holding a rabbit. He stroked and petted it. As soon as we were all seated, with no word of explanation, he crushed its head with a rock and proceeded to actually skin and disembowel the animal with his bare hands and teeth while showering the entrails on us. As we left the clearing he stood there with fur all around his mouth and blood running down his throat. The intended message was that one was going into a war and civilization and all its emotional vestiges must be left behind. One must be violent and unmerciful. "Kill gooks." This type of training seems ill-suited to the intricacies of the agrarian revolution that was the Vietnam situation.

Conjecture

In my view the training was ineffective. However, it could be argued that perhaps these men were being trained quite effectively for the job which they were going to be asked to do. Conjecture could be made that the underlying concealed mission was not to kill the soldiers of the North Vietnamese Army (NVA) and the Viet Cong (VC), nor to win the hearts and minds of the population. Perhaps the mission was to kill many civilians, terrorize the remainder, and drive them away from the arms of the VC/NVA into relatively safe refugee camps and cities. The Vietnam War was basically an agrarian revolution. Guerilla warfare has been compared to fish in a pond, in which the pond is the population and the free swimming fish are the guerillas. The guerilla moves freely amongst the population and is dependent on it for supplies and information. Political allegiance (hearts and minds) is the means to victory. Territorial objectives are of little consequence. The American response to this situation, in reality, appears to have been to drain the pond.

> If the direct application of mechanical and conventional power takes place on such a large scale as to produce a massive migration from countryside to city, the basic assumptions underlying the Maoist doctrine of revolutionary war no longer operate. The Maoist rural revolution is undercut by the American Sponsored urban revolution. (Huntington, 1968, p. 650)

Such a heavy job would perhaps require numb, dehumanized, and brutal men. Perhaps the training process served very well to prepare men for terrorism and systematic brutality upon civilians. What appears to have been seemingly irrational and ineffective training may in fact have produced the sort of army needed to serve unacknowledged and politically unacceptable purposes.

The Vietnam Experience

Vietnam provided insurmountable difficulties for the traditionally trained American. There were no territorial objectives, the enemy refused to engage, and there was a tremendous reliance on fire power. Once contact was made the unit pulled back and fire missions were called in. The effect was the elimination of the traditional job of infantry, close and destroy. This is most significant considering the fine emotional edge honed on the men for close combat, killing, and aggressive behavior.

The Enforcement of Passivity

Americans soon learned through a variety of means that aggressive behavior would not ensure victory or even survival. Booby traps, snipers, and ambushes took their toll of those who sought to move aggressively. Nor did killing necessarily achieve the desired result. Killing villagers promoted the VC/NVA cause. Greater control was often achieved by less aggressive means. The VC/NVA were able to use what had heretofore been considered passive means for aggressive ends, while the Americans discovered that aggressive means entailed more danger. Running, hiding, and refusing to fight were the traditionally passive modes. The VC/NVA used these means aggressively to fight only on their terms, not the Americans'. Thus to run or hide was no longer a passive act, it was a prelude to aggression — aggression at the expense of the Americans. Passivity, as significant as that was, was forced on the Americans.

Tension and Lack of Meaning

The level of tension in Vietnam was high for support troops as well as for infantry. There was a gnawing cold fear of unknown and unexpected violence and danger. Thus rear echelon troops in Vietnam experienced some of the same emotional conflicts as the infantry. An all-pervading climate of fear and absurdity prevailed. A great many young Americans bled and died in Vietnam, carried 50–60 pound packs in 120-degree temperatures through rough terrain and rice paddies, fought pitched battles, and participated in the macabre ritual of stacking bodies for body counts. In the midst of all this, officers dined quietly on steak and lobster, attended by beautiful young waitresses, while the men had to endure constant petty indignities and harassment. Lifton describes it well:

> The predominant emotional tone is one of all encompassing absurdity and moral inversion. The absurdity has to do with a sense of being alien and profoundly lost, yet at the same time locked into a situation as meaningless and unreal as it is deadly . . . the men were adrift in an environment not only strange and hostile, but offering no honorable encounter, no warrior grandeur. (1973)

The individual was unable to integrate the reality of the situation into the frame of reference provided by military training and instilled with brutal intensity. A traditionally trained soldier who experienced Vietnam became disoriented and experienced what may be described as cognitive dissonance—trained for aggression, he had to accept passivity.

Homecoming

Returning home, Vietnam veterans wander alone through a maze of questions concerning emotion, aggression, masculinity, guilt, love, and sexuality. Often, years after discharge, impacted rage and intense guilt become locked into patterns of antisocial, self-destructive behavior.

Self-Help Projects

It is because of the inability of Vietnam veterans to receive adequate counseling for what they perceive as their unique problems that Vietnam veterans' self-help projects have sprung up across the United States. I initiated one such project, Flower of the Dragon, Inc., while working with my colleague, Peter Cameron, as mental health interns for the Sonoma County Mental Health Department. Discovering the unique stresses and problems which affected Vietnam veterans, we served as catalyst for the development of a much larger and more substantial organization, speaking to all the needs of the veteran.

Impacted Sexuality and the Potential for Violence

The violence potential of Vietnam veterans is perhaps the most crucial issue for society. Lifton (1973) differentiates between three specific forms of violence potential. The first of these is the "habit of violence," as inculcated by military training. The second centers around a feeling of being "fucked over," by being asked to fight in such an ambiguous situation as Vietnam and by the nature of the treatment received upon return at the hands of the society that sent them to war. The third form is that of a reaction against peer group, family, and society's indifference to the veteran's experience. It is a rage at being rebuffed in the attempt to explain your experiences, or at sharing your world and experiences and then being cruelly rebuked. There is, however, a fourth and I feel vastly more consequential potential for violence that rises out of the Vietnam experience. The training process created intense emotional conflicts generated by the formation of a male role that required two things: a constant proving of adequacy and a prohibition of intimacy. The means to

prove adequacy (dominance and aggression) were not to be found in Vietnam. The result was a nonviable male role conception and concomitantly what might be termed an *impacted sexuality*.

The sexuality of Vietnam veterans was systematically assaulted and shaped in training. They then underwent a chronic stress event denying them the means to express their masculinity in the manner which had so recently been intensively and brutally instilled. Sexual dysfunction, deterioration of self-image, and a lack of viable means to express masculinity resulted. A frustrated sexuality became linked with violence and aggression. One young veteran I have worked with became completely impotent three years after discharge. Unable to maintain an erection during the last three attempts at intercourse, he was afraid to try again. At this time he purchased a weapon, a pistol, and began brandishing and discharging it. His sexuality was blocked by a frustrated idealized male role which could not tolerate intimacy. The means to affirm manhood was through face to face combat, aggressive behavior, and the seeking of dominance.

In those individuals who have sufficient control not to act out, the problem may be one of violent intrusive imagery. Shatan (Note 1) speaks of the "paranoid position of combat being inculcated during the training process." This is a constant fear of being harmed by someone and a constant elimination of real or fantasized adversaries in order to maintain a feeling of adequacy and security. My personal experience directly validates this. Since I was not exposed to much combat in Vietnam, I can only conclude that this process originated for me in basic training.

Perhaps this can best be articulated if I share some observations concerning my own intrusive imagery. Generally these take the form of daydreams. They consist of brief very violent eye-gouging, throat-ripping fantasies revealing an underlying hypermasculine ideal. There is usually a woman involved and I am always dominant and inordinately violent in defeating some adversary. These brief images leave me with a feeling of power and supermasculinity. I usually find that my muscles tense during such imagery. I have made a further observation: These images increase in frequency and intensity during periods of sexual deprivation. I feel irritable, restless, and filled with much energy.

As a civilian, one generally attempts to create a more authentic masculine self-image that cannot help but be influenced by the military experience. Constantly in social and sexual relationships I have found myself trying to be "heavy," feeling at times foolishly as if I were a caricature of myself. I have striven constantly to achieve dominance. In the past more so than now, I felt insecure sexually and had a very low tolerance for feeling threatened. Occasional outbursts of violence have shamed and frightened me. This all has cost me dearly in social relationships.

Returning from a chronic stress event, one looks carefully at weakness as it is a threat to life, limb, and sexual identity. Many Vietnam veterans report repressing their weak, emotional, and homosexual feelings, which are equated with each other. However, sexual components cannot be repressed differentially. The result is a sexuality repressed or numbed in its entirety and one that must constantly be proven adequate. Many Vietnam veterans that I have worked with report sexual frustration, a fear of intimacy, and strong urges to "kill somebody." The frustration of the belief system and the nonviability of the role model offered in training have, it appears, often created an impacted sexuality.

Conclusion

In conclusion, I wish to assert that the foregoing must not be viewed as abstract intellectualism. Behind the theory and language is pain. We are speaking of young men whose world view was violently disoriented and whose sexual identity brutally and systematically assaulted. They were further disoriented by a war for which they were ill-prepared and, subsequently, they have been cast adrift in an indifferent, often hostile, society.

Vietnam veterans' self-help projects such as the Flower of the Dragon are attempting to fill a need not being met by social or clinical psychology. Research and hard data are needed. More important, human concern and the energy of committed caring professionals will be required to deal with this very important social issue.

Reference Notes

1. Shatan C. *Bogus manhood, bogus honor: Surrender and transfiguration in the United States Marine Corps.* Paper presented at the meeting of the American Orthopsychiatric Association, San Francisco, April 1974.

References

Emergency Ministry for Veterans Services. *The church and the returning veteran.* New York: National Council of Churches, 1971.

Huntington, S. P. Squaring the error. *Foreign Affairs,* July 1968.

Kelman, H. C. Violence without moral restraint: Reflections on the dehumanization of victims and victimizers. *Journal of Social Issues,* 1973, 29(4), 25–61.

Lifton, R. J. *Home from the war.* New York: Simon & Schuster, 1973.

Rape: The All-American Crime

Susan Griffin

I

I have never been free of the fear of rape. From a very early age I, like most women, have thought of rape as part of my natural environment—something to be feared and prayed against like fire or lightning. I never asked why men raped; I simply thought it one of the many mysteries of human nature.

I was, however, curious enough about the violent side of humanity to read every crime magazine I was able to ferret away from my grandfather. Each issue featured at least one "sex crime," with pictures of a victim, usually in a pearl necklace, and of the ditch or the orchard where her body was found. I was never certain why the victims were always women, nor what the motives of the murderer were, but I did guess that the world was not a safe place for women. I observed that my grandmother was meticulous about locks, and quick to draw the shades before anyone removed so much as a shoe. I sensed that danger lurked outside.

At the age of eight, my suspicions were confirmed. My grandmother took me to the back of the house where the men wouldn't hear, and told me that strange men wanted to do harm to little girls. I learned not to walk on dark streets, not to talk to strangers, or get into strange cars, to lock doors, and to be modest. She never explained why a man would want to harm a little girl, and I never asked.

If I thought for a while that my grandmother's fears were imaginary, the illusion was brief. That year, on the way home from school, a schoolmate a few years older than I tried to rape me. Later, in an obscure aisle of the local library (while I was reading *Freddy the Pig*) I turned

to discover a man exposing himself. Then, the friendly man around the corner was arrested for child molesting.

My initiation to sexuality was typical. Every woman has similar stories to tell—the first man who attacked her may have been a neighbor, a family friend, an uncle, her doctor, or perhaps her own father. And women who grow up in New York City always have tales about the subway.

But though rape and the fear of rape are a daily part of every woman's consciousness, the subject is so rarely discussed by that unofficial staff of male intellectuals (who write the books which study seemingly every other form of male activity) that one begins to suspect a conspiracy of silence. And indeed, the obscurity of rape in print exists in marked contrast to the frequency of rape in reality, for *forcible rape is the most frequently committed violent crime in America today*. The Federal Bureau of Investigation classes three crimes as violent: murder, aggravated assault and forcible rape. In 1968, 31,060 rapes were *reported*. According to the FBI and independent criminologists, however, to approach accuracy this figure must be multiplied by at least a factor of ten to compensate for the fact that most rapes are not reported; when these compensatory mathematics are used, there are more rapes committed than aggravated assaults and homicides.

When I asked Berkeley, California's Police Inspector in charge of rape investigation if he knew why men rape women, he replied that he had not spoken with "these people and delved into what really makes them tick, because that really isn't my job. . . ." However, when I asked him how a woman might prevent being raped, he was not so reticent, "I wouldn't advise any female to go walking around alone at night . . . and she should lock her car at all times." The Inspector illustrated his warning with a grisly story about a man who lay in wait for women in the back seats of their cars, while they were shopping in

Reprinted from Susan Griffin, "Rape: The All-American Crime," in *The Politics of Rape* by Susan Griffin. Reprinted (New York: Harper & Row, 1979), by permission of the publisher and the author. Copyright 1971.

a local supermarket. This man eventually murdered one of his rape victims. "Always lock your car," the Inspector repeated, and then added, without a hint of irony, "Of course, you don't have to be paranoid about this type of thing."

The Inspector wondered why I wanted to write about rape. Like most men he did not understand the urgency of the topic, for, after all, men are not raped. But like most women I had spent considerable time speculating on the true nature of the rapist. When I was very young, my image of the "sexual offender" was a nightmarish amalgamation of the bogey man and Captain Hook: he wore a black cape, and he cackled. As I matured, so did my image of the rapist. Born into the psychoanalytic age, I tried to "understand" the rapist. Rape, I came to believe, was only one of many unfortunate evils produced by sexual repression. Reasoning by tautology, I concluded that any man who would rape a woman must be out of his mind.

Yet, though the theory that rapists are insane is a popular one, this belief has no basis in fact. According to Professor Menachem Amir's study of 646 rape cases in Philadelphia, *Patterns in Forcible Rape,* men who rape are not abnormal. Amir writes, "Studies indicate that sex offenders do not constitute a unique or psychopathological type; nor are they as a group invariably more disturbed than the control groups to which they are compared." Alan Taylor, a parole officer who has worked with rapists in the prison facilities at San Luis Obispo, California, stated the question in plainer language, "Those men were the most normal men there. They had a lot of hang-ups, but they were the same hang-ups as men walking out on the street."

Another canon in the apologetics of rape is that, if it were not for learned social controls, all men would rape. Rape is held to be natural behavior, and not to rape must be learned. But in truth rape is not universal to the human species. Moreover, studies of rape in our culture reveal that, far from being impulsive behavior, most rape is planned. Professor Amir's study reveals that in cases of group rape (the "gangbang" of masculine slang) 90 percent of the rapes were planned; in pair rapes, 83 percent of the rapes were planned; and in single rapes, 58 percent were planned. These figures should significantly discredit the image of the rapist as a man who is suddenly overcome by sexual needs society does not allow him to fulfill.

Far from the social control of rape being learned, comparisons with other cultures lead one to suspect that, in our society, it is rape itself that is learned. (The fact that rape is against the law should not be considered proof that rape is not in fact encouraged as part of our culture.)

This culture's concept of rape as an illegal, but still understandable, form of behavior is not a universal one. In her study *Sex and Temperament,* Margaret Mead describes a society that does not share our views. The Arapesh do not ". . . have any conception of the male nature that might make rape understandable to them." Indeed our interpretation of rape is a product of our conception of the nature of male sexuality. A common retort to the question, why don't women rape men, is the myth that men have greater sexual needs, that their sexuality is more urgent than women's. And it is the nature of human beings to want to live up to what is expected of them.

And this same culture which expects aggression from the male expects passivity from the female. Conveniently, the companion myth about the nature of female sexuality is that all women secretly want to be raped. Lurking beneath her modest female exterior is a subconscious desire to be ravished. The following description of a stag movie, written by Brenda Starr in Los Angeles' underground paper, *Everywoman,* typifies this male fantasy. The movie "showed a woman in her underclothes reading on her bed. She is interrupted by a rapist with a knife. He immediately wins her over with his charm and they get busy sucking and fucking." An advertisement in the *Berkeley Barb* reads, "Now as all women know from their daydreams, rape has a lot of advantages. Best of all it's so simple. No preparation necessary, no planning ahead of time, no wondering if you should or shouldn't; just whang! bang!" Thanks to Masters and Johnson even the scientific canon recognizes that for the female, "whang! bang!" can scarcely be described as pleasurable.

Still, the male psyche persists in believing that, protestations and struggles to the contrary, deep inside her mysterious feminine soul, the female victim has wished for her own fate. A young woman who was raped by the husband of a friend said that days after the incident the man returned to her home, pounded on the door and screamed to her, "Jane, Jane. You loved it. You know you loved it."

The theory that women like being raped extends itself by deduction into the proposition that most or much of rape is provoked by the victim. But this too is only myth. Though provocation, considered a mitigating factor in a court of law, may consist of only "a gesture," according to the Federal Commission on Crimes of Violence, only 4 percent of reported rapes involved any precipitative behavior by the woman.

The notion that rape is enjoyed by the victim is also convenient for the man who, though he would not commit forcible rape, enjoys the idea of its existence, as if rape confirms that enormous sexual potency which he secretly knows to be his own. It is for the pleasure of the armchair rapist that detailed accounts of violent rapes exist in the media. Indeed, many men appear to take sexual pleasure from nearly all forms of violence. Whatever the motivation, male sexuality and violence in our culture seem to be inseparable. James Bond alternately whips out his revolver and his cock, and though there is no known connection between the skills of gun-fighting and love-making, pacifism seems suspiciously effeminate.

In a recent fictional treatment of the Manson case, Frank Conroy writes of his vicarious titillation when describing the murders to his wife:

"Every single person there was killed." She didn't move.

"It sounds like there was torture," I said. As the words left my mouth I knew there was no need to say them to frighten her into believing that she needed me for protection.

The pleasure he feels as his wife's protector is inextricably mixed with pleasure in the violence itself. Conroy writes, "I was excited by the killings, as one is excited by catastrophe on a grand scale, as one is alert to pre-echoes of unknown changes, hints of unrevealed secrets, rumblings of chaos. . . ."

The attraction of the male in our culture to violence and death is a tradition Manson and his admirers are carrying on with tireless avidity (even presuming Manson's innocence, he dreams of the purification of fire and destruction). It was Malraux in his *Anti-Memoirs* who said that, for the male, facing death was *the* illuminating experience analogous to childbirth for the female. Certainly our culture does glorify war and shroud the agonies of the gun-fighter in veils of mystery.

And in the spectrum of male behavior, rape, the perfect combination of sex and violence, is the penultimate act. Erotic pleasure cannot be separated from culture, and in our culture male eroticism is wedded to power. Not only should a man be taller and stronger than a female in the perfect lovematch, but he must also demonstrate his superior strength in gestures of dominance which are perceived as amorous. Though the law attempts to make a clear division between rape and sexual intercourse, in fact the courts find it difficult to distinguish between a case where the decision to copulate was mutual and one where a man forced himself upon his partner.

The scenario is even further complicated by the expectation that, not only does a woman mean "yes" when she says "no," but that a really decent woman ought to begin by saying "no," and then be led down the primrose path to acquiescence. Ovid, the author of Western Civilization's most celebrated sex-manual, makes this expectation perfectly clear:

. . . and when I beg you to say "yes," say "no."
Then let me lie outside your bolted door. . . . So love grows strong. . . .

That the basic elements of rape are involved in all heterosexual relationships may explain why men often identify with the offender in this crime. But to regard the rapist as the victim, a man driven by his inherent sexual needs to take what will not be given him, reveals a basic ignorance of sexual politics. For in our culture heterosexual love finds an erotic expression through male dominance and female submission. A man who derives pleasure from raping a woman clearly must enjoy force and dominance as much or more than the simple pleasures of the flesh. Coitus cannot be experienced in isolation. The weather, the state of the nation, the level of sugar in the blood—all will affect a man's ability to achieve orgasm. If a man can achieve sexual pleasure after terrorizing and humiliating the object of his passion, and in fact while inflicting pain upon her, one must assume he derives pleasure directly from terrorizing, humiliating and harming a woman. According to Amir's study of forcible rape, on a statistical average the man who has been convicted of rape was found to have a normal sexual personality, tending to be different from the normal, well-adjusted male only in having a greater tendency to express violence and rage.

And if the professional rapist is to be separated from the average dominant heterosexual, it may be mainly a quantitative difference. For the existence of rape as an index to masculinity is not entirely metaphorical. Though this measure of masculinity seems to be more publicly exhibited among "bad boys" or aging bikers who practice sexual initiation through group rape, in fact, "good boys" engage in the same rites to prove their manhood. In Stockton, a small town in California which epitomizes silent-majority America, a bachelor party was given last summer for a young man about to be married. A woman was hired to dance "topless" for the amusement of the guests. At the high point of the evening the bridegroom-to-be dragged the woman into a bedroom. No move was made by any of his companions to stop what was clearly going to be an attempted rape. Far from it. As the woman described, "I tried to keep him away—told him of my Herpes Genitalis, et cetera, but he couldn't face the guys if he didn't screw me." After the bridegroom had finished raping the woman and returned with her to the party, far from chastizing him, his friends heckled the woman and covered her with wine.

It was fortunate for the dancer that the bridegroom's friends did not follow him into the bedroom for, though one might suppose that in group rape, since the victim is outnumbered, less force would be inflicted on her, in fact, Amir's studies indicate, "the most excessive degrees of violence occurred in group rape." Far from discouraging violence, the presence of other men may in fact encourage sadism, and even cause the behavior. In an unpublished study of group rape by Gilbert Geis and Duncan Chappell, the authors refer to a study by W. H. Blanchard which relates, "The leader of the male group . . . apparently precipitated and maintained the activity, despite misgivings, because of a need to fulfill the role that the other two men had assigned to him. 'I was scared when it began to happen,' he says. 'I wanted to leave but I didn't want to say it to the other guys—you know—that I was scared.'"

Thus it becomes clear that not only does our culture teach men the rudiments of rape, but society, or more specifically other men, encourage the practice of it.

II

Every man I meet wants to protect me. Can't figure out what from.

Mae West

If a male society rewards aggressive, domineering sexual behavior, it contains within itself a sexual schizophrenia. For the masculine man is also expected to prove his mettle as a protector of women. To the naive eye, this dichotomy implies that men fall into one of two categories: those who rape and those who protect. In fact, life does not prove so simple. In a study euphemistically entitled "Sex Aggression by College Men," it was discovered that men who believe in a double standard of morality for men and women, who in fact believe most fervently in the ultimate value of virginity, are more liable to commit "this aggressive variety of sexual exploitation."

(At this point in our narrative it should come as no

surprise that Sir Thomas Malory, creator of that classic tale of chivalry, *The Knights of the Round Table,* was himself arrested and found guilty for repeated incidents of rape.)

In the system of chivalry, men protect women against men. This is not unlike the protection relationship which the mafia established with small businesses in the early part of this century. Indeed, chivalry is an age-old protection racket which depends for its existence on rape.

According to the male mythology which defines and perpetuates rape, it is an animal instinct inherent in the male. The story goes that sometime in our pre-historical past, the male, more hirsute and burly than today's counterparts, roamed about an uncivilized landscape until he found a desirable female. (Oddly enough, this female is *not* pictured as more muscular than the modern woman.) Her mate does not bother with courtship. He simply grabs her by the hair and drags her to the closest cave. Presumably, one of the major advantages of modern civilization for the female has been the civilizing of the male. We call it chivalry.

But women do not get chivalry for free. According to the logic of sexual politics, we too have to civilize our behavior. (Enter chastity. Enter virginity. Enter monogamy.) For the female, civilized behavior means chastity before marriage and faithfulness within it. Chivalrous behavior in the male is supposed to protect that chastity from involuntary defilement. The fly in the ointment of this otherwise peaceful system is the fallen woman. She does not behave. And therefore she does not deserve protection. Or, to use another argument, a major tenet of the same value system: what has once been defiled cannot again be violated. One begins to suspect that it is the behavior of the fallen woman, and not that of the male, that civilization aims to control.

The assumption that a woman who does not respect the double standard deserves whatever she gets (or at the very least "asks for it") operates in the courts today. While in some states a man's previous rape convictions are not considered admissible evidence, the sexual reputation of the rape victim is considered a crucial element of the facts upon which the court must decide innocence or guilt.

The court's respect for the double standard manifested itself particularly clearly in the case of the People v. Jerry Plotkin. Mr. Plotkin, a 36-year-old jeweler, was tried for rape last spring in a San Francisco Superior Court. According to the woman who brought the charges, Plotkin, along with three other men, forced her at gunpoint to enter a car one night in October 1970. She was taken to Mr. Plotkin's fashionable apartment where he and the three other men first raped her and then, in the delicate language of the *San Francisco Chronicle,* "subjected her to perverted sex acts." She was, she said, set free in the morning with the warning that she would be killed if she spoke to anyone about the event. She did report the incident to the police who then searched Plotkin's apartment and discovered a long list of names of women. Her name was on the list and had been crossed out.

In addition to the woman's account of her abduction and rape, the prosecution submitted four of Plotkin's address books containing the names of hundreds of women. Plotkin claimed he did not know all of the women since some of the names had been given to him by friends and he had not yet called on them. Several women, however, did testify in court that Plotkin had, to cite the *Chronicle,* "lured them up to his apartment under one pretext or another, and forced his sexual attentions on them."

Plotkin's defense rested on two premises. First, through his own testimony Plotkin established a reputation for himself as a sexual libertine who frequently picked up girls in bars and took them to his house where sexual relations often took place. He was the Playboy. He claimed that the accusation of rape, therefore, was false—this incident had simply been one of many casual sexual relationships, the victim one of many playmates. The second premise of the defense was that his accuser was also a sexual libertine. However, the picture created of the young woman (fully 13 years younger than Plotkin) was not akin to the light-hearted, gay-bachelor image projected by the defendant. On the contrary, the day after the defense cross-examined the woman, the *Chronicle* printed a story headlined, "Grueling Day For Rape Case Victim." (A leaflet passed out by women in front of the courtroom was more succinct, "rape was committed by four men in a private apartment in October; on Thursday, it was done by a judge and a lawyer in a public courtroom.")

Through skillful questioning fraught with innuendo, Plotkin's defense attorney James Martin MacInnis portrayed the young woman as a licentious opportunist and unfit mother. MacInnis began by asking the young woman (then employed as a secretary) whether or not it was true that she was "familiar with liquor" and had worked as a "cocktail waitress." The young woman replied (the *Chronicle* wrote "admitted") that she had worked once or twice as a cocktail waitress. The attorney

then asked if she had worked as a secretary in the financial district but had "left that employment after it was discovered that you had sexual intercourse on a couch in the office." The woman replied, "That is a lie. I left because I didn't like working in a one-girl office. It was too lonely." Then the defense asked if, while working as an attendant at a health club, "you were accused of having a sexual affair with a man?" Again the woman denied the story, "I was never accused of that."

Plotkin's attorney then sought to establish that his client's accuser was living with a married man. She responded that the man was separated from his wife. Finally he told the court that she had "spent the night" with another man who lived in the same building.

At this point in the testimony the woman asked Plotkin's defense attorney, "Am I on trial? . . . It is embarrassing and personal to admit these things to all these people. . . . I did not commit a crime. I am a human being." The lawyer, true to the chivalry of his class, apologized and immediately resumed questioning her, turning his attention to her children. (She is divorced, and the children at the time of the trial were in a foster home.) "Isn't it true that your two children have a sex game in which one gets on top of another and they—" "That is a lie!" the young woman interrupted him. She ended her testimony by explaining "They are wonderful children. They are not perverted."

The jury, divided in favor of acquittal ten to two, asked the court stenographer to read the woman's testimony back to them. After this reading, the Superior Court acquitted the defendant of both the charges of rape and kidnapping.

According to the double standard a woman who has had sexual intercourse out of wedlock cannot be raped. Rape is not only a crime of aggression against the body; it is a transgression against chastity as defined by men. When a woman is forced into a sexual relationship, she has, according to the male ethos, been violated. But she is also defiled if she does not behave according to the double standard, by maintaining her chastity, or confining her sexual activities to a monogamous relationship.

One should not assume, however, that a woman can avoid the possibility of rape simply by behaving. Though myth would have it that mainly "bad girls" are raped, this theory has no basis in fact. Available statistics would lead one to believe that a safer course is promiscuity. In a study of rape done in the District of Columbia, it was found that 82 percent of the rape victims had a "good reputation." Even the Police Inspector's advice to stay off the streets is rather useless, for almost half of reported rapes occur in the home of the victim and are committed by a man she has never before seen. Like indiscriminate terrorism, rape can happen to any woman, and few women are ever without this knowledge.

But the courts and the police, both dominated by white males, continue to suspect the rape victim, *sui generis,* of provoking or asking for her own assault. According to Amir's study, the police tend to believe that a woman without a good reputation cannot be raped. The rape victim is usually submitted to countless questions about her own sexual mores and behavior by the police investigator. This preoccupation is partially justified by the legal requirements for prosecution in a rape case. The rape victim must have been penetrated, and she must have made it clear to her assailant that she did not want penetration (unless of course she is unconscious). A refusal to accompany a man to some isolated place to allow him to touch her does not in the eyes of the court, constitute rape. She must have said "no" at the crucial genital moment. And the rape victim, to qualify as such, must also have put up a physical struggle—unless she can prove that to do so would have been to endanger her life.

But the zealous interest the police frequently exhibit in the physical details of a rape case is only partially explained by the requirements of the court. A woman who was raped in Berkeley was asked to tell the story of her rape four different times "right out in the street," while her assailant was escaping. She was then required to submit to a pelvic examination to prove that penetration had taken place. Later, she was taken to the police station where she was asked the same questions again: "Were you forced?" "Did he penetrate?" "Are you sure your life was in danger and you had no other choice?" This woman had been pulled off the street by a man who held a 10-inch knife at her throat and forcibly raped her. She was raped at midnight and was not able to return to her home until five in the morning. Police contacted her twice again in the next week, once by telephone at two in the morning and once at four in the morning. In her words, "The rape was probably the least traumatic incident of the whole evening. If I'm ever raped again, . . . I wouldn't report it to the police because of all the degradation. . . ."

If white women are subjected to unnecessary and often hostile questioning after having been raped, third-world women are often not believed at all. According to the white male ethos (which is not only sexist but racist), third-world women are defined from birth as "impure." Thus the white male is provided with a pool of women

who are fair game for sexual imperialism. Third-world women frequently do not report rape and for good reason. When blues singer Billie Holliday was 10 years old, she was taken off to a local house by a neighbor and raped. Her mother brought the police to rescue her, and she was taken to the local police station crying and bleeding:

> When we got there, instead of treating me and Mom like somebody who called the cops for help, they treated me like I'd killed somebody. . . . I guess they had me figured for having enticed this old goat into the whorehouse. . . . All I know for sure is they threw me into a cell . . . a fat white matron . . . saw I was still bleeding, she felt sorry for me and gave me a couple glasses of milk. But nobody else did anything for me except give me filthy looks and snicker to themselves.
>
> After a couple of days in a cell they dragged me into a court. Mr. Dick got sentenced to five years. They sentenced me to a Catholic institution.

Clearly the white man's chivalry is aimed only to protect the chastity of "his" women.

As a final irony, that same system of sexual values from which chivalry is derived has also provided womankind with an unwritten code of behavior, called femininity, which makes a feminine woman the perfect victim of sexual aggression. If being chaste does not ward off the possibility of assault, being feminine certainly increases the chances that it will succeed. To be submissive is to defer to masculine strength; is to lack muscular development or any interest in defending oneself; is to let doors be opened, to have one's arm held when crossing the street. To be feminine is to wear shoes which make it difficult to run; skirts which inhibit one's stride; underclothes which inhibit the circulation. Is it not an intriguing observation that those very clothes which are thought to be flattering to the female and attractive to the male are those which make it impossible for a woman to defend herself against aggression?

Each girl as she grows into womanhood is taught fear. Fear is the form in which the female internalizes both chivalry and the double standard. Since, biologically speaking, women in fact have the same if not greater potential for sexual expression as do men, the woman who is taught that she must behave differently from a man must also learn to distrust her own carnality. She must deny her own feelings and learn not to act from them. She fears herself. This is the essence of passivity, and of course, a woman's passivity is not simply sexual but functions to cripple her from self-expression in every area of her life.

Passivity itself prevents a woman from ever considering her own potential for self-defense and forces her to look to men for protection. The woman is taught fear, but this time fear of the other; and yet her only relief from this fear is to seek out the other. Moreover, the passive woman is taught to regard herself as impotent, unable to act, unable even to perceive, in no way self-sufficient, and, finally, as the object and not the subject of human behavior. It is in this sense that a woman is deprived of the status of a human being. She is not free to be.

III

Since Ibsen's Nora slammed the door on her patriarchal husband, woman's attempt to be free has been more or less fashionable. In this 19th century portrait of a woman leaving her marriage, Nora tells her husband, "Our home has been nothing but a playroom. I have been your doll-wife just as at home I was papa's doll-child." And, at least on the stage, "The Doll's House" crumbled, leaving audiences with hope for the fate of the modern woman. And today, as in the past, womankind has not lacked examples of liberated women to emulate: Emma Goldman, Greta Garbo and Isadora Duncan all denounced marriage and the double standard, and believed their right to freedom included sexual independence; but still their example has not affected the lives of millions of women who continue to marry, divorce and remarry, living out their lives dependent on the status and economic power of men. Patriarchy still holds the average woman prisoner not because she lacks the courage of an Isadora Duncan, but because the material conditions of her life prevent her from being anything but an object.

In the *Elementary Structures of Kinship*, Claude Levi-Strauss gives to marriage this universal description, "It is always a system of exchange that we find at the origin of the rules of marriage." In this system of exchange, a woman is the "most precious possession." Levi-Strauss continues that the custom of including women as booty in the marketplace is still so general that "a whole volume would not be sufficient to enumerate instances of it." Levi-Strauss makes it clear that he does not exclude Western Civilization from his definition of "universal" and cites examples from modern wedding ceremonies. (The marriage ceremony is still one in which the husband and wife become one, and "that one is the husband.")

The legal proscription against rape reflects this possessory view of women. An article in the 1952–53 *Yale Law Journal* describes the legal rationale behind laws against rape: "In our society sexual taboos, often enacted into law, buttress a system of monogamy based upon the law of 'free bargaining' of the potential spouses. Within this process the woman's power to withhold or grant sexual access is an important bargaining weapon." Presumably then, laws against rape are intended to protect the right of a woman, not for physical self-determination, but for physical "bargaining." The article goes on to explain explicitly why the preservation of the bodies of women is important to men:

> *The consent standard in our society does more than protect a significant item of social currency for women; it fosters, and is in turn bolstered by, a masculine pride in the exclusive possession of a sexual object. The consent of a woman to sexual intercourse awards the man a privilege of bodily access, a personal "prize" whose value is enhanced by sole ownership. An additional reason for the man's condemnation of rape may be found in the threat to his status from a decrease in the "value" of his sexual possession which would result from forcible violation.*

The passage concludes by making clear whose interest the law is designed to protect. "The man responds to this undercutting of his status as *possessor* of the girl with hostility toward the rapist; no other restitution device is available. The law of rape provides an orderly outlet for his vengeance." Presumably the female victim in any case will have been sufficiently socialized so as not to consciously feel any strong need for vengeance. If she does feel this need, society does not speak to it.

The laws against rape exist to protect rights of the male as possessor of the female body, and not the right of the female over her own body. Even without this enlightening passage from the *Yale Law Review,* the laws themselves are clear: In no state can a man be accused of raping his wife. How can any man steal what already belongs to him? It is in the sense of rape as theft of another man's property that Kate Millett writes, "Traditionally rape has been viewed as an offense one male commits against another—a matter of abusing his woman." In raping another man's woman, a man may aggrandize his own manhood and concurrently reduce that of another man. Thus a man's honor is not subject directly to rape, but only indirectly, through "his" woman.

If the basic social unit is the family, in which the woman is a possession of her husband, the superstructure of society is a male hierarchy, in which men dominate other men (or patriarchal families dominate other patriarchal families). And it is no small irony that, while the very social fabric of our male-dominated culture denies women equal access to political, economic and legal power, the literature, myth and humor of our culture depicts women not only as the power behind the throne, but the real source of the oppression of men. The religious version of this fairy tale blames Eve for both carnality and eating of the tree of knowledge, at the same time making her gullible to the obvious devices of a serpent. Adam, of course, is merely the trusting victim of love. Certainly this is a biased story. But no more biased than the one television audiences receive today from the latest slick comedians. Through a media which is owned by men, censored by a State dominated by men, all the evils of this social system which make a man's life unpleasant are blamed upon "the wife." The theory is: were it not for the female who waits and plots to "trap" the male into marriage, modern man would be able to achieve Olympian freedom. She is made the scapegoat for a system which is in fact run by men.

Nowhere is this more clear than in the white racist use of the concept of white womanhood. The white male's open rape of black women, coupled with his overweening concern for the chastity and protection of his wife and daughters, represents an extreme of sexist and racist hypocrisy. While on the one hand she was held up as the standard for purity and virtue, on the other the Southern white woman was never asked if she wanted to be on a pedestal, and in fact any deviance from the male-defined standards for white womanhood was treated severely. (It is a powerful commentary on American racism that the historical role of Blacks as slaves, and thus possessions without power, has robbed black women of legal and economic protection through marriage. Thus black women in Southern society and in the ghettoes of the North have long been easy game for white rapists.) The fear that black men would rape white women was, and is, classic paranoia. Quoting from Ann Breen's unpublished study of racism and sexism in the South *"The New South: White Man's Country,"* Frederick Douglass legitimately points out that, had the black man wished to rape white women, he had ample opportunity to do so during the civil war when white women, the wives, sisters, daughters and mothers of the rebels, were left in the care of Blacks. But yet not a single act of rape was committed during this time. The Ku Klux Klan, who tarred and feathered black men and lynched them in the honor of the purity of white womanhood, also applied tar and feathers to a Southern white woman accused of bigamy, which leads one to suspect that Southern white men were not so much outraged at the violation of the woman as a person, in the few instances where rape was actually committed by black men, but at the violation of his property rights. In the situation where a black man was found to be having sexual relations with a white woman, the white woman could exercise skin-privilege, and claim that she had been raped, in which case the black man was lynched. But if she did not claim rape, she herself was subject to lynching.

In constructing the myth of white womanhood so as to justify the lynching and oppression of black men and women, the white male has created a convenient symbol of his own power which has resulted in black hostility toward the white "bitch," accompanied by an unreasonable fear on the part of many white women of the black rapist. Moreover, it is not surprising that after being told for two centuries that he wants to rape white women, occasionally a black man does actually commit that act. But it is crucial to note that the frequency of this practice is outrageously exaggerated in the white mythos. Ninety percent of reported rape is intra- not inter-racial.

In *Soul on Ice,* Eldridge Cleaver has described the mixing of a rage against white power with the internalized sexism of a black man raping a white woman. "Somehow I arrived at the conclusion that, as a matter of principle, it was of paramount importance for me to have an antagonistic, ruthless attitude toward white women. . . . Rape was an insurrectionary act. It delighted me that I was defying and trampling upon the white man's law, upon his system of values and that I was defiling his women — and this point, I believe, was the most satisfying to me because I was very resentful over the historical fact of how the white man has used the black woman." Thus a black man uses white women to take out his rage against white men. But in fact, whenever a rape of a white woman by a black man does take place, it is again the white man who benefits. First, the act itself terrorizes the white woman and makes her more dependent on the white male for protection. Then, if the woman prosecutes her attacker, the white man is afforded legal opportunity to exercise overt racism. Of course, the knowledge of the rape helps to perpetuate two myths which are beneficial to white male rule — the bestiality of the black man and the desirability of white women. Finally, the white man surely benefits because he himself is not the object of attack — he has been allowed to stay in power.

Indeed, the existence of rape in any form is beneficial to the ruling class of white males. For rape is a kind of terrorism which severely limits the freedom of women and makes women dependent on men. Moreover, in the act of rape, the rage that one man may harbor toward another higher in the male hierarchy can be deflected toward a female scapegoat. For every man there is always someone lower on the social scale on whom he can take out his aggressions. And this is any woman alive.

This oppressive attitude towards women finds its institutionalization in the traditional family. For it is assumed that a man "wears the pants" in his family—he exercises the option of rule whenever he so chooses. Not that he makes all the decisions—clearly women make most of the important day-to-day decisions in a family. But when a conflict of interest arises, it is the man's interest which will prevail. His word, in itself, is more powerful. He lords it over his wife in the same way his boss lords it over him, so that the very process of exercising his power becomes as important an act as obtaining whatever it is his power can get for him. This notion of power is key to the male ego in this culture, for the two acceptable measures of masculinity are a man's power over women and his power over other men. A man may boast to his friends that "I have 20 men working for me." It is also aggrandizement of his ego if he has the financial power to clothe his wife in furs and jewels. And, if a man lacks the wherewithal to acquire such power, he can always express his rage through equally masculine activities—rape and theft. Since male society defines the female as a possession, it is not surprising that the felony most often committed together with rape is theft. As the following classic tale of rape points out, the elements of theft, violence and forced sexual relations merge into an indistinguishable whole.

The woman who told this story was acquainted with the man who tried to rape her. When the man learned that she was going to be staying alone for the weekend, he began early in the day a polite campaign to get her to go out with him. When she continued to refuse his request, his chivalrous mask dropped away:

I had locked all the doors because I was afraid, and I don't know how he got in; it was probably through the screen door. When I woke up, he was shaking my leg. His eyes were red, and I knew he had been drinking or smoking. I thought I would try to talk my way out of it. He started by saying that he wanted to sleep with me, and then he got angrier and angrier, until he started to say, "I want pussy," "I want pussy." Then, I got scared and tried to push him away. That's when he started to force himself on me. It was awful. It was the most humiliating, terrible feeling. He was forcing my legs apart and ripping my clothes off. And it was painful. I did fight him—he was slightly drunk and I was able to keep him away. I had taken judo a few years back, but I was afraid to throw a chop for fear that he'd kill me. I could see he was getting more and more violent. I was thinking wildly of some way to get out of this alive, and then I said to him, "Do you want money. I'll give you money." We had money but I was also thinking that if I got to the back room I could telephone the police—as if the police would have even helped. It was a stupid thing to think of because obviously he would follow me. And he did. When he saw me pick up the phone, he tried to tie the cord around my neck. I screamed at him that I did have the money in another room, that I was going to call the police because I was scared, but that I would never tell anybody what happened. It would be an absolute secret. He said, okay, and I went to get the money. But when he got it, all of a sudden he got this crazy look in his eye and he said to me, "Now I'm going to kill you." Then I started saying my prayers. I knew there was nothing I could do. He started to hit me—I still wasn't sure if he wanted to rape me at this point—or just to kill me. He was hurting me, but hadn't yet gotten me into a strangle-hold because he was still drunk and off balance. Somehow we pushed into the kitchen where I kept looking at this big knife. But I didn't pick it up. Somehow, no matter how much I hated him at that moment, I still couldn't imagine putting the knife in his flesh, and then I was afraid he would grab it and stick it into me. Then he was hitting me again and somehow we pushed through the back door of the kitchen and onto the porch steps. We fell down the steps and that's when he started to strangle me. He was on top of me. He just went on and on until finally I lost consciousness. I did scream, though my screams sounded like whispers to me. But what happened was that a cab driver happened by and frightened him away. The cab driver revived me—I was out only a minute at the most. And then I ran across the street and I grabbed the woman who was our neighbor and screamed at her, "Am I alive? Am I still alive?"

Rape is an act of aggression in which the victim is denied her self-determination. It is an act of violence which, if not actually followed by beatings or murder, nevertheless always carries with it the threat of death. And finally, rape is a form of mass terrorism, for the victims of rape are chosen indiscriminately, but the propagandists for male supremacy broadcast that it is women who cause rape by being unchaste or in the wrong place at the wrong time — in essence, by behaving as though they were free.

The threat of rape is used to deny women employment. (In California, the Berkeley Public Library, until pushed by the Federal Employment Practices Commission, refused to hire female shelvers because of perverted men in the stacks.) The fear of rape keeps women off the streets at night. Keeps women at home. Keeps women passive and modest for fear that they be thought provocative.

It is part of human dignity to be able to defend oneself, and women are learning. Some women have learned karate; some to shoot guns. And yet we will not be free until the threat of rape and the atmosphere of violence is ended, and to end that the nature of male behavior must change.

But rape is not an isolated act that can be rooted out from patriarchy without ending patriarchy itself. The same men and power structure who victimize women are engaged in the act of raping Vietnam, raping black people and the very earth we live upon. Rape is a classic act of domination where, in the words of Kate Millett, "the emotions of hatred, contempt, and the desire to break or violate personality," take place. This breaking of the personality characterizes modern life itself. No simple reforms can eliminate rape. As the symbolic expression of the white male hierarchy, rape is the quintessential act of our civilization, one which, Valerie Solanis warns, is in danger of "humping itself to death."

READING 37

A Rapist Gets Caught in the Act

As told to James K. Skipper, Jr. and William L. McWhorter

Interviewer: Can you tell me something about yourself?

Respondent: Sure, why not. I am 32 years old. I am 5 feet 7 inches tall and I weigh 165 pounds. I drive a truck for a living and make pretty good money. I got an old lady and two nice kids. One is 12 a nice girl and a boy almost 9 now. What else is there to say? Oh, yes, I am not dumb. I got a high school diploma. I never got arrested for nothing before, not even a

Reprinted from James K. Skipper and William L. McWhorter, "A Rapist Gets Caught in the Act," in *Deviance: Voices from the Margin* (Belmont, CA: Wadsworth, 1981), by permission of Wadsworth Publishing Company.

parking violation. What else do you want to know? Yes, I love my wife and I loved my father and mother. Isn't that what you are supposed to say? Well, in my case it is true except for my father. I did not know him very well because he left my mother when I was about four and we never saw him again. I don't think she cared whether she saw him again or not. She never went looking. I guess she figured he didn't have anything she wanted anyway. She never wanted to talk about him much and there wasn't anything for me to talk about. I didn't know enough about him to miss him.

Interviewer: Do you remember anything else about your father?

Respondent: Not really. I guess he had a lot of odd jobs like store clerk, repair man. I think he worked in a mail room once, but was not what you would call a mailman. I mean he did not deliver mail. Mom said he liked to collect coins. That's all I can remember. Like I said he left when I was about 4 maybe it was 5. It does not matter. Anyway I never hated the guy if that's what you are trying to get at. How can you hate someone you don't even remember? You can't blame him for what I did.

Interviewer: What was your relationship with your mother?

Respondent: What do you mean what was my relationship with my mother? I never screwed her if that's what you mean. For Christ sake what type of guy do you think I am? Sure I fucked some women in my time whether they liked it or not, but your own mother that is disgusting. My God man, what do you take me for?

Interviewer: I am sorry, you misunderstood me. I meant how did you get along with your mother. Did you have a happy family life?

Respondent: Oh, I see what you mean. Well it is like this. I loved my mother a lot I really did. She was always good to me and gave me all the things she could afford. She was a waitress at a fancy type restaurant. You know the type where you got to have money and class or you don't get in the door. She worked at night and did not get in until late. I was always asleep when she got home. That's after I was in school. I don't remember before that. She used to get up early and see me off to school and then give me an early dinner before she went to work. I was on my own most of the time since I was about 7. But I didn't mind. I could find things to do for myself. We didn't live in a real bad neighborhood and besides she used to give me money. I always had more money than the other kids to do things. We always used to spend Sundays together and do things like going to movies, out to dinner. Things like that. I always liked to have Sundays with her until I was about 15. Then I didn't like to do it any more. I had better things to do by then. You know what I mean? Now I kind of miss them. She died in a car crash about a year after I got married. It really came as a shock. I had not seen her much after I got married. Then I got this phone call at work that she had been killed in a head-on collision.

It was right here in town. The police said the cars couldn't been going more than 35, but it was enough to kill both drivers. I really felt bad about it. After all she had done for me, she deserved something better. Anyway, you can't blame her either for what I have done. It couldn't be her. It was all just me.

Interviewer: What do you think was the cause of your conduct?

Respondent: Well if you mean my wife you are crazy. I have had a normal sexual life with my wife. We have two kids don't we? I am normal in every respect. I have never beat my wife or my kids. I have fooled around a little in my day but nothing serious. You get me? I take my women one at a time. That way nothing gets serious. It does not interfere with your life. At least not until now it has not. My wife never knew nothing.

Interviewer: You mean your wife was not aware of your affairs with other women?

Respondent: Now there you go again. I didn't say I had affairs with other women did I? That's not right. What I meant was sometimes you just have the urge to go out and fuck the living shit out of some broad. You don't have to like them. You don't have to want to ever see them again. You just get the urge to go out and fuck one of them. It does not matter who they are or what they look like. You just want to do it. It has nothing to do with loving your wife. Once it is over it is over. Anyway I suppose it is normal for a guy to want to do that once or twice a year. I think most women expect it.

Interviewer: You mean women would not consider it a case of rape?

Respondent: Hell no, Hell no. I mean most women like to get their box battered as much as a man likes to get his balls off. They want to be grabbed and taken hard. It makes them feel like a woman. I know that to be a fact. And what's more you feel more like a man when you do it that way. This time I just got unlucky and got a cold-hearted bitch. That's the only difference.

Interviewer: Could you describe the circumstances of your present offense?

Respondent: OK I guess so. There really is not much to tell though. I got up one morning. It was a hot day in August. I had not got much sleep the night before. I felt kind of mean and ugly. My wife was nagging again. The kids were getting on my nerves even before I got out of the house. I had trouble starting the truck and I was late to work. The boss did not like that much, I could tell he didn't. But he did not yell at me or nothing. He just told me to get going and make up the time as best I could. I tried but I got stuck in traffic and it got later and later. By lunch time I was so far behind I was not going to make all my deliveries by 5:00 no matter what I did. I stopped at this little diner and had a few beers. I did not feel like eating at all. Then I thought by God what you need is a good piece. That ought to fix you up good. Just go out and grab yourself a broad. Hell I was not going to make my deliveries anyway. It was after 2:00 by then. So I got me back in the truck and started cruising around looking. About an hour went by and nothing. I thought oh God don't let this be my unlucky day. Then I saw this woman standing alone at a bus stop. She was not much to look at. Skinny as a rail, about 40 years old I would say. I pulled up and asked her if she could give me directions to County Line Road. She told me the way right off. But I pretended not to understand. After she told me again and I said I still did not get it, I asked her if she would like to get in the truck and show me. I knew she must be going in that general direction because that is the way the bus was going. She hesitated for a moment and looked to see if the bus was coming. It was not. She said, "Well I suppose it would be OK. You look like a nice enough kid, but I am not going quite that far." Right then I figured I had her. So I says, "Hop in." She does and we are on our way. I know a good place just outside of town down a side road where there is an old abandoned barn. It is not far from the road, but you can't see it from the road and sound does not carry from it very well. I have been there before. I figure it is safe. We get to talking real nice. I start thinking about how I am going to grab her. We miss her stop and she doesn't even seem to know. Finally she realizes it and says, "You missed my stop! You missed my stop! You even missed County Line Road." I apologized and play dumb and say I didn't know we had passed them. I stop the truck and start to turn around and then I say, "Wait a minute. We are just a couple of miles from another of my deliveries. Would you mind if we just drove a little farther down this road?" She agrees if it will not take long. I assure her it won't and we are on our way again. Before you know it we are at my safe place. I grab a couple of packages out of the back and start toward the trees to the barn. I stop and say, "Hey I hate to leave you alone in the car. Why don't you walk with me to the house? It is just through the trees." She thinks that is a good idea and we start out. We get about 200 feet from the barn through the trees and she sees it is no farm house and says, "I am going back." I grab her by the arm and she starts fighting and screaming. I figure I got a real loony this time I am never going to make it to the barn. It might as well be right here on the ground. I tell her to be quiet and quit fighting. She won't stop so I slug her one and that takes most of the steam out of her and she falls down and starts groaning. I figure let her groan. Nobody is going to hear that. I plop down on her and start to get her dress off and in the meantime I get my cock out. I may have got my cock close to her, but I sure never got it in let alone come. The last thing I remember is a big crash on my head. It felt like the whole world came down on my head. I remember waking up and thinking lord my God that must have been the biggest come I ever had. I remember them picking me up and taking me to a police car. I can't move my hands they are cuffed. I don't know what the hell happened to me. It was not until much later until I figure it out. You know what happened?

Interviewer: No I do not. Please tell me what happened.

Respondent: Well it was like this. There was some Goddamn 19-year-old kid fucking his broad in the barn. They hear the goings on outside and instead of getting scared and running away the cocksucker sneaks up behind me and crowns me on the head with a quart beer bottle. No wonder I went out like a light. The son of a bitch never gave me a chance to explain. And he had been doing the same thing! If I had caught him in the barn I sure as hell would not have tried to break his head. I would let him alone. Anyway he called the police on his C.B. I never did find out where he had his car hid. I sure never saw it. Well I did not have a leg to stand on. The woman was half naked and had a cut lip and black eye. My cock was out, and there were two witnesses. She claimed rape and I swear I never got in her. But all the evidence looked against me. This is the first time for me. I have pushed a few women around before when I got the urge and fucked them. But I never hurt them and they never said nothing about it. I don't think this woman would have either if that prick had not hit me over the head. What right did he have to do that? I never did nothing to him. I never saw him before. I guess I just got unlucky.

"I Make No Apology"

To Whom It May Concern — Which I'm sure is no one of any importance

I don't believe in petitions.
I don't believe in the feminist movement.
I don't even believe in authority.
Since joining the intramural football team known as THE STATUTORY RAPISTS during their second year of regular play, I have felt that the name lacked intelligence and creativity. However disgusting I find such a label I do, however, strongly believe in the concept behind it and as a member of the male species I feel that it has been both my perogative and my pleasure. Recognizing that I can not speak for my team and my team captain, and realizing what little loss there is, I can only say that some of us will play under no other name.

I make no apology.

Quarterback of THE STATUTORY RAPISTS

Reprinted from "I Make No Apology," anonymous letter by the Quarterback of the Statutory Rapists, Football Team of the College of Law, The Ohio State University, Columbus, Ohio.

Judge Faces Recall

Columbus Citizen-Journal

A citizens group in Lancaster, Wis., said Tuesday it will circulate petitions seeking the ouster of a circuit judge who called a 5-year-old sexual assault victim an "unusually sexually promiscuous young lady."

Diane Barton said her ouster group has decided "it was an irresponsible thing to say this child was promiscuous."

Mrs. Barton said she expected the petitions to be ready for distribution next week in the group's quest to force a recall election of Judge William Reinecke. Reinecke contended his remarks were taken out of context.

Reinecke made the remark in sentencing Ralph Snod-grass, 24, to 90 days in a work-release program for sexually assaulting the 5-year-old daughter of the woman with whom he was living.

The judge observed the girl was "an unusually sexually promiscuous young lady" and Snodgrass "did not know enough to refuse. No way do I believe Mr. Snodgrass initiated sexual contact."

The hired hand said he was sleeping and the girl climbed on top of him. The girl later was found to have been sexually assaulted.

The judge said he was simply trying to show that the girl, not really knowing what she was doing, was the aggressor.

Reprinted from the *Columbus Citizen-Journal*, 20 January 1982.

"The Man in the Street": Why He Harasses

Cheryl Bernard and Edit Schlaffer

"It is a violation of my natural external freedom, not to be able to go where I please, and to experience other restrictions of this kind . . . Even though the body and life are something external, just like property, nevertheless my personality is wounded by such experiences, because my most immediate identity rests in my body."

Hegel
Texte Zur Philosophischen Propaedeutik

"I am standing at Wittenbergplatz waiting for the light to turn green, in my left hand I am carrying a bag filled with groceries . . . behind me I sense the approach of two men and turn my head, at that moment the man on my left reaches for my hair which falls to my shoulders colored with henna, he runs his fingers through my hair experimentally and says to his friend: great hair . . . An ordinary everyday experience for the colonized in a city of the First World."

Verena Stefan
Haeutungen

By the time we are in our twenties we have become accustomed to the laws of the street. The abrupt but regular interruptions of our daily movements have become familiar, we have acquired the habit of overhearing comments, we are graceful at dodging straying hands, we have the skill of a general in making rapid strategic evaluations, we can usually tell at a glance whether that group of young men leaning against a car door might use physical intimidation or just jokes, whispered comments, laughter, whether it's worth crossing over to the other side

of the street or enough to act nonchalant and cultivate deafness. It's no longer frightening, just annoying, sometimes jolting when one is called abruptly out of a train of thought or a moment of absentmindedness. One gets used to it.

Is all of this normal, inevitable? It was a question I had stopped asking myself by the time I spent a year abroad at the university in Beirut. In the dorm I shared a room with Widad from Bahrein, an 18-year-old who wanted to be a teacher. At home, Widad always wrapped an abaya around her jeans and T-shirt when she went out of the house, and to Widad, the behavior of men on the street was news. Not yet hardened by long experience, Widad spent her first week in Beirut in tears. Sobbing with anger and confusion, she would report on the insulting and unbelievable things that had been said to her, the grabbing, the pushing, the comments, the aggressive looks, the smacking lips, the hissing in her ear. The abaya, she would conclude, has nothing to do with women. In Bahrein we wear it because of the men, someday maybe we won't have to but right now, this is how they are, and who can stand it? The final outcome, I am sorry to report, was not that Widad became hardened and militant, schooled in the martial arts and an example to us all, but that she was instrumental in organizing a group of Bahreini men, so that for the rest of the academic year the women from Bahrein moved through the city like a convoy flanked by a string of guards ready to fight at the sign of a covetous glance.

For the American women, this was an occasion to think again about the kind of world we have learned to accept as normal. On public streets, we plan our routes and our timing as if we were passing through a mine field. We are touched, harassed, commented upon in a stream of constant small-scale assaults, and in a culture which values privacy and anonymity in crowds these intimacies are considered inevitable. Secretly, women like it, popular opinion believes, and posters of men whistling after a

Reprinted from Cheryl Bernard and Edit Schlaffer, "The Man in the Street: Why He Harasses," by permission of the authors.

woman are thought by advertising agencies to sell their product. Besides, popular opinion goes on to explain, women provoke it, with their fashions, their manner of walking, their behavior. These are familiar arguments; we hear them whenever the subject of violence against women comes up. There are few facts to hold up against them. Stamped as trivial, the harassment of women has received no attention from sociology, and cities that regulate almost everything from bicycles and dogs to the use of roller skates in order to keep the traffic moving have no ordinances or rules to guarantee women the right to free passage.

What kinds of men harass women, what do they think they are doing, how do women feel about it? Diaries and essays by women, and reports from other times and cultures, give some very sketchy information. For a more systematic picture, we observed the behavior of men in four cities (Berlin, Los Angeles, Rome and Vienna) over the period of a year, allowing for differences in season, time of day and part of town. Interviews with women provided information on how the victims feel. Some of the results were surprising, and some were depressingly predictable.

That the behavior of the "man on the street" has received so little attention is odd, because it captures in quintessential, almost primordial form the combination of the ordinary and the bizarre which we have learned to regard as normal. The "man on the street" is a synonym for everyone, which in our society means every man. The behavior he casually accords to randomly passing women he has never seen before serves to identify him as a member of the ruling group, to whom the streets and the society belong. And at the same time this behavior, looked at with an analytic eye, is very peculiar. The anthropologist from outer space, that popular device for viewing the world with a bit more perspective, would be very astonished to find adult males moaning, jumping, whistling, singing, honking, winking, contorting face and body, hissing obscenities, laughing hysterically and mumbling hoarse endearments to perfect strangers without apparent provocation. However odd, though, these single and seemingly irrational instances add up to a pattern, and the pattern spells intimidation.

Women are assigned, in this interaction, an inevitably passive part. They have a number of available responses, but their response makes little difference. A woman can ignore what she sees or hears, she can reply, she can curse, keep walking, stop, try for a disarming smile, get angry, start a discussion. What she does has little influence. A friendly answer may stop the man, or it may encourage him to further intimacies; threats and curses may silence him, or they may prompt genuine aggression. The language itself puts us at a permanent disadvantage; it is hard to exchange serious insults without using sexual put-downs that invariably go against women. And passers-by, far from supporting a woman who defends herself, will shed their former indifference to disapprove of feminine vulgarity.

It is commonly supposed that certain countries and cultures display this behavior more than others; the Mediterranean cultures, particularly, are assumed to be swarming with papagallos dedicated to the female foreign tourist. In fact, this form of male behavior is distributed quite evenly across the continents, races and generations. The nationalist author Qasim Amin deplored the harassment of the heavily veiled Egyptian women at the turn of the century and in fact attributed masculine aggression to the veil. As a sign of women's inferior status, he argued, it encouraged men to treat them with disrespect and take liberties. This interpretation comes very close to the truth. Like other forms of sexual violence, harassment has little to do with the individual woman and nothing to do with sex; the issue is power.

Whether you wear a slit skirt or are covered from head to foot in a black chador, the message is not that you are attractive enough to make a man lose his self-control, but that the public realm belongs to him and you are there by his permission as long as you follow his rules, and as long as you remember your place. Badr-al-Moluk Bamdad[1] recalls in her book on growing up in Iran that there was no way for a woman to win this game: if, in the opinion of any passing male, one's veil was not wrapped with sufficient modesty, one could be insulted, reprimanded and threatened, while if obediently covered one would be followed and taunted by boys and young men shouting that one looked like a "black crow or an inkwell."

Harassment of women is timeless, but the notion that women really like it and feel flattered is a refinement that has been added more recently. Women's own accounts have always shown a clear awareness of the essential hostility implied by these male attentions, even when they didn't put that awareness into the context of any more general picture of sexist structures. Descriptions have been handed down to us from many different sources. Evelyn Scott, an American woman who later was

1. *Women's Emancipation in Iran,* N.Y. 1977.

to become a successful author, spent the year of 1916 in Brazil with her lover. They were poor, she was pregnant. In her diary, she wrote that, in Rio, "something objectionable always occurred" when she went outdoors unaccompanied. "Perhaps it is because I am only 20 years old," she wrote. "Perhaps it is because I am shabbily dressed. I know perfectly well that I am not particularly pretty. Inwardly shrinking and cold with an obscure fear, I make it a point to look very directly at all the men who speak to me. I want to shame them by the straightforwardness of my gaze. Perhaps I am ridiculous. If I could consider sex more factually and with less mystical solemnity I might find amusement in the stupidity of these individuals who can't be so sinister after all."[2]

Anger and an "obscure fear" are the most common responses of women, and those feelings are all the greater when the situation seems too intimidating to allow a reply. Pretending to have heard nothing, looking away, hoping the men will get bored and stop or will be too busy with the woman walking in front of you to attend to you are calculations that increase the impact of the experience. A 22-year-old law student remembered one pivotal incident in her life: "I was 17, and just walking around downtown with my friend Marie. Two men started talking to us, making jokes and telling us to come with them. They grabbed our arms and tried to pull us along. Marie got angry and told them to let us go. The men pushed her against a building and started shaking her and saying she was unfriendly and stuck up and should watch out. Finally they left. It was afternoon and there were a lot of people around, but nobody said anything. At the time I learned from that that it was better to ignore men who talked to you like that. If you act like you don't care, they usually let you go without any trouble. I don't think that's a very good conclusion to draw, but I still don't know how to act in situations like that without getting into trouble."

What is going on in the minds of the men who do this? Not much, judging from their difficulties in articulating their intentions. We interviewed 60 men, choosing a range of age groups out of those who addressed us on the street. (Incidentally, this was the only female response we found that genuinely and predictably disarms the harassing male, so if you want to transform a lewdly smirking man into a politely confused one within a matter

of seconds you need only pull a mimeographed questionnaire out of your bag and inform him that he is part of a research project. This method, however, is rather time-consuming.) Pressed for an explanation of their behavior, most of the men initially played it down. Boredom and a feeling of youthful camaraderie that came over them when discussing women with other men emerged as the most frequent feelings prompting harassment. The notion that women disliked this and felt infringed upon in their freedom of movement was a novel one for most men, not because they had another image of the woman's response but because they had never given it any thought at all. Only a minority, around 15%, explicitly set out to anger or humiliate their victims. This is the same group that employs graphic sexual commentary and threats. Other forms of antagonism often become mixed up with the sexual. Some migrant laborers or construction workers insult not so much the woman as the snobbish privileged class she symbolizes to them. Another minority of men believes with firm conviction that women enjoy receiving their attention. One 45-year-old construction worker portrayed himself as a kind of benefactor to womanhood and claimed to specialize in older and less attractive women to whom, he was sure, his display of sexual interest was certain to be the highlight in an otherwise drab and joyless existence. A significant group of men, around 20%, said that they would not engage in this behavior when alone, but only in the company of male friends. This supports the explanation that the harassment of women is a form of male bonding, of demonstrating solidarity and joint power.

The symbolic nature of the behavior is its most important attribute. A surprising finding was that harassment declines in the late evening and during the night, and that men are then more likely to display the kind of behavior typical of the avoidance usually shown to strangers in public or crowded situations: averting one's eyes, accelerating the pace of walking to keep a distance, etc. At first glance, this finding is surprising. It would seem that harassment would be even more effective at night, even more intimidating to the woman. Probably, this is precisely the reason it declines during the night; on a deserted street, it would be *too* effective. The woman, not merely annoyed or unnerved but genuinely alarmed, may well be driven to an "extreme" response (such as calling for help) that the good citizen would not like to have to explain. In the daytime, he takes no such risk. The age, education and income of the man make little difference; in their street behavior, they revert to a primordially

---

2. *Revelations, Diaries of Women,* Mary Jane Moffat/Charlotte Painter eds., Vintage Press, N.Y. 1974, p. 100.

uniform condition across the lines of class and genera-tion. Younger men tend to be more aggressive, and older men to lower their voices and whisper hastily as they pass you. Some areas are exempt altogether: small villages, where all the inhabitants know each other, and residential suburban areas.

The genuinely *public* world is the main arena for harassment. The street, as a place where strangers en-counter each other, is also the place where societies have always taken care to clearly mark the lines of order and status. It is on the streets that members of subordinate groups have to wear special clothing or identifying marks, that they must salute, take off their hat or jump down from the sidewalk to make way for the members of the superior group. Harassment is a way of ensuring that women will not feel at ease, that they will remember their role as sexual beings available to men and not consider themselves equal citizens participating in public life. But the ritual of harassment does more than that. By its seem-ing harmlessness and triviality, it blurs the borders of women's right to personal integrity, and encourages men who would never commit a violent crime against a strange woman to participate in minor transgressions against her right to move freely, to choose which interactions to par-ticipate in and which people to communicate with. By making of the "man on the street," the average man, a minor sex offender, it also makes him an accomplice in the more massive forms of violence against women.

READING 41

Myths and Facts about Sexual Harassment

AASC Staff: Rags Brophy, Ann Eliopulos, Alice Friedman, Beth Johnson, Freada Klein, Margaret Lazarus, Anne Lopes, Denise Wells, Nancy Wilber

An elaborate series of myths supports all forms of violence against women. These myths, often based on false assumptions about men's and women's "natural" biological make-up, ensure that women who encounter violence against themselves feel guilty rather than violated. Women are therefore less likely to speak up or to take action to eliminate harassment. The following myths, reflecting current attitudes, serve in particular to perpetuate sexual harassment at the workplace.

Reprinted from "Myths and Facts About Sexual Harassment," in *Aegis,* September/October, 1979, pp. 22–26, a publication of the Alliance against Sexual Coercion, P. O. Box 1, Cam-bridge, MA 02130, with permission.

MYTH: Sexual harassment is not a serious social problem and it affects only a few women.

FACT: In a 1976 survey in *Redbook Magazine,* 88 percent of the 9,000 respondents reported that they had experienced one or more forms of unwanted sexual ad-vances on the job.

FACT: Women suffer from sexual harassment re-gardless of their appearance, age, race, marital status, oc-cupation, or socio-economic class.

MYTH: If women don't speak up about sexual harassment, then it's not happening.

FACT: Women don't report about sexual harassment because they feel isolated, guilty, scared of losing their jobs.

FACT: We can begin to eliminate sexual harassment at the workplace only when we share and understand our experiences. If we remain silent, workplace harassment will continue to be seen as a personal problem rather than as a social issue. These two myths will operate until so many women speak up about sexual harassment that our society can no longer pretend it doesn't happen.

MYTH: Women invite sexual harassment by their behavior and/or dress.

FACT: As with rape, sexual harassment is not a sexually motivated act. It is an assertion of hostility and/or power expressed in a sexual manner. Sexual harassment is not women's fault in any way.

FACT: Often women are expected to act or dress seductively both to get and keep their jobs.

MYTH: Only women in certain occupations are likely to be sexually harassed.

FACT: Waitresses, flight attendants, and secretaries are not the only victims of sexual harassment. Women who work in factories, at professional jobs—and all kinds of jobs—consistently report this problem. Students, clients of professionals (doctors, dentists, therapists, etc.) domestic workers, and babysitters also suffer sexual harassment and abuse.

MYTH: Black women are exposed to sexual activity at an early age, are more sensuous and are not as upset by harassment.

MYTH: Asian women are more submissive than other women and would be less likely to be offended by sexual harassment.

FACT: These are patently racist assumptions, and constitute another example of blaming the victim rather than the harasser.

MYTH: It is harmless to harass women verbally on the job or to pinch or pat them. Women who object have no sense of humor.

FACT: Harassment on the job is humiliating and degrading. It undermines a woman's job performance—and often threatens her economic livelihood. Women victimized by sexual harassment suffer emotionally and physically. We should not be prepared to endure degradation with a smile.

MYTH: A firm "no" is enough to discourage any man's sexual advances.

FACT: Because people believe women say no when they really mean yes, men often dismiss women's resistance. Men's greater physical, economic and social power enables them to override the firmest "no." It should not be women's responsibility to ensure that sexual harassment doesn't happen.

MYTH: Women who remain in a job where they are sexually harassed are masochistic—or are really enjoying it.

FACT: Women's lower socio-economic position in the U.S. means that many are unable to quit their jobs or find new employment.

MYTH: Only bosses are in a position to harass women at the workplace.

FACT: Co-workers and clients can also harass women at the workplace. Clients threaten to withdraw their business. Co-workers make work intolerable. Both complain to the boss—or already have the boss's support.

MYTH: If women can't handle the pressure of the working world, they should stay home.

FACT: Women work out of economic necessity. Staying home is not an option for most working women. Nor—as we know from current publicity on wife abuse—is staying home a protection against sexual harassment.

MYTH: Women make false charges of sexual harassment.

FACT: Women who speak out against harassment meet with negative reactions, ranging from disbelief and ridicule to loss of job. Women have little to gain from false charges.

MYTH: Women sleep their way to "the top" and other positions of power in the workforce.

FACT: Very few women hold positions of power. For those isolated cases where women have tried to engage in sexual activity to gain promotions, evidence shows that it ultimately works against their advancement. This myth works against a woman who gives in to sexual pressure, because she is then mistrusted by fellow workers.

MYTH: Only certain men harass women at work.

FACT: All types of men, in all occupations—whether or not they hold positions of power—have been reported as harassers.

MYTH: There are adequate procedures to take care of men who seriously assault or threaten women at work.

FACT: Society continues to view sexual harassment from a double standard. While the sexual harassers are tolerated—boys will be boys—the women victims bear the brunt of the blame. Personnel managers, union represen-tatives, human rights agencies, courts, and legislators reflect these discriminatory attitudes. Women who seek assistance from these sources to stop sexual harassment are frequently placing themselves at risk of humiliating in-difference, ridicule, or even further sexual insinuation and harassment. Nevertheless, it is important to use these channels where possible.

READING 42

Premarital Violence:
Battering on College Campuses

Editor, *Response*

Experts on family violence have called the marriage license a "hitting license," but according to three recent studies in Minnesota, Arizona, and Oregon, plenty of couples slap, kick, and punch each other without it. The studies, which queried students at three universities about violence in their dating relationships, found that physical abuse occurs in at least one out of every five collegiate relationships.

At St. John's University in Minnesota, James Makepeace, a professor of sociology, questioned 202 freshman and sophomore students in the spring of 1979 and found that 21.2 percent had been abused or had inflicted abuse in a premarital relationship at least once, and that most victims of abuse were women. An addi-tional 61.5 percent of the students had friends who were involved in violent relationships. Of the students who had been abused, 4 percent said they were assaulted with closed fists and 1 percent said they were strangled, choked, or had a weapon used against them. A total of 13 percent of the students said they had been pushed, while 12.9 percent said they were slapped, and 4 percent were punched.

"Although the percentages of the students who have experienced the more serious forms of violence may seem small, the students actually suggest a significant social problem," Makepeace states in his study. "If the 4 percent incidence of assault with closed fists is typical, then 800 students on a 20,000 student campus would have experi-enced this form of violence."

The violent incidents in the Minnesota study were most often sparked by sexual jealousy, disagreements over drinking, and anger over sexual denial. Makepeace speculates that much of the violence in premarital rela-tionships derives from a lack of rules or limits in these relationships. "The adolescent world is gray—not black and white as it once was," Makepeace commented in an interview.

According to the study, which was published in the January 1981 issue of *Family Relations,* abused students rarely seek help. Only 5 percent of the battered students identified by the study called the police. "Violence among young unmarried couples may be even more under-reported than spouse abuse," Makepeace stated, "because

Reprinted from "Premarital Violence: Battering on College Campuses," in *Response*, vol. 4, no. 6, by permission of the Center for Women's Policy Studies, 2000 P Street NW, Suite 508, Washington, D.C. 20036.

young people view their world as a closed system, apart from adults. Even if they are being abused, calling the police is ratting on a peer to an adult, and that is unacceptable."

At Oregon State University, almost a fourth of 355 students surveyed reported that they were involved in violent relationships with their boyfriends or girlfriends, according to Rodney M. Cate of the University's Family Life Department. Over half of those students revealed that they had remained in the violent relationship.

"We were surprised by the high incidence of abuse and also by the number of students who believed violence helps a relationship," Cate commented in an interview. Of the 53 percent who remained in abusive relationships, 37 percent said their relationships improved with abuse, 41 percent said the relationships did not change, and 22 percent believed that their relationships became worse after the first abusive incident.

"The idea 'he wouldn't hit me if he didn't love me' seems to be operating among abusive college couples," Cate suggested. "Of our respondents, 29 percent viewed abuse as signifying love while only 8 percent considered abuse as an expression of hate."

Rodney Cate and June Henton, authors of the study, are currently interviewing high school students to determine when violence in dating relationships begins.

In another study of premarital violence on college campuses, Mary Riege Laner, a sociologist at Arizona State University, found that over 60 percent of 371 students questioned in the fall of 1980 had been either a victim or perpetrator of abuse in a dating relationship. A total of 46 percent of the students who reported abuse said they were pushed or shoved, 19 percent were punched or kicked, and 21 percent were pushed to the floor. Students who were abused as children were more likely to report an abusive premarital relationship than students who did not have violent childhoods, according to the study.

The study concludes that physical abuse is more likely to occur in serious rather than casual dating relationships. Laner theorizes that violence occurs more often between serious courting couples because they, like married couples, have a greater presumed range of interests and activities, greater intensity of involvement, an implied right to influence one another, and an extensive knowledge of one another's social biographies which include vulnerabilities and fears that can be used for purposes of attack. While these characteristics by themselves do not lead to violence, when added to a tolerance of violent behavior fostered in childhood and sexism in the relationship, the situation is ripe for abuse, according to Laner.

"Our culture accepts violence in all its institutions—including marriage, courtship, and child-rearing," Laner commented. "We're taught to accept violence from those who say they love us—so violence comes to connote a depth of feeling. Until we can reduce our acceptance of violence as a means to an end, abuse in intimate relationships will continue to be a serious problem."

READING 43

Gynocide: Chinese Footbinding

Andrea Dworkin

Footbinding Event

Instructions Before Reading Chapter
  1. Find a piece of cloth 10 feet long and 2 inches wide
  2. Find a pair of children's shoes

3. Bend all toes except the big one under and into the sole of the foot. Wrap the cloth around these toes and then around the heel. Bring the heel and toes as close together as possible. Wrap the full length of the cloth as tightly as possible
4. Squeeze foot into children's shoes
5. Walk
6. Imagine that you are 5 years old
7. Imagine being like this for the rest of your life

The origins of Chinese footbinding, as of Chinese thought in general, belong to that amorphous entity called antiquity. The 10th century marks the beginning of the physical, intellectual, and spiritual dehumanization of women in China through the institution of footbinding. That institution itself, the implicit belief in its necessity and beauty, and the rigor with which it was practiced lasted another 10 centuries. There were sporadic attempts at emancipating the foot—some artists, intellectuals, and women in positions of power were the proverbial drop in the bucket. Those attempts, modest as they were, were doomed to failure: footbinding was a political institution which reflected and perpetuated the sociological and psychological inferiority of women; footbinding cemented women to a certain sphere, with a certain function— women were sexual objects and breeders. Footbinding was mass attitude, mass culture—it was the key reality in a way of life lived by real women—10 centuries times that many millions of them.

It is generally thought that footbinding originated as an innovation among the dancers of the Imperial harem. Sometime between the 9th and 11th centuries, Emperor Li Yu ordered a favorite ballerina to achieve the "pointed look." The fairy tale reads like this:

Li Yu had a favored palace concubine named Lovely Maiden who was a slender-waisted beauty and a gifted dancer. He had a six-foot high lotus constructed for her out of gold; it was decorated lavishly with pearls and had a carmine lotus carpet in the center. Lovely Maiden was ordered to bind her feet with white silk cloth to make the tips look like the points of a moon sickle. She then danced in the center of the lotus, whirling about like a rising cloud.[1]

From this original event, the bound foot received the euphemism "Golden Lotus," though it is clear that Lovely Maiden's feet were bound loosely—she could still dance.

A later essayist, a true foot gourmand, described 58 varieties of the human lotus, each one graded on a 9-point scale. For example:

Type: Lotus petal, New moon, Harmonious bow, Bamboo shoot, Water chestnut
Specifications: plumpness, softness, fineness
Rank: Divine Quality (A-1), perfectly plump, soft and fine
Wondrous Quality (A-2), weak and slender
Immortal Quality (A-3), straight-boned, independent
Precious Article (B-1), peacocklike, too wide, disproportioned
Pure Article (B-2), gooselike, too long and thin
Seductive Article (B-3), fleshy, short, wide, round (the disadvantage of this foot was that its owner *could* withstand a blowing wind)
Excessive Article (C-1), narrow but insufficiently pointed
Ordinary Article (C-2), plump and common
False Article (C-3), monkeylike large heel (could climb)

The distinctions only emphasize that footbinding was a rather hazardous operation. To break the bones involved or to modify the pressure of the bindings irregularly had embarrassing consequences—no girl could bear the ridicule involved in being called a "large-footed Demon" and the shame of being unable to marry.

Even the possessor of an A-1 Golden Lotus could not rest on her laurels—she had to observe scrupulously the taboo-ridden etiquette of bound femininity: (1) do not walk with toes pointed upwards; (2) do not stand with heels seemingly suspended in midair; (3) do not move skirt when sitting; (4) do not move feet when lying down. The same essayist concludes his treatise with this most sensible advice (directed to the gentlemen of course):

Do not remove the bindings to look at her bare feet, but be satisfied with its external appearance. Enjoy the outward impression, for if you remove the shoes and bindings the aesthetic feeling will be destroyed forever.[2]

Indeed. The real feet looked like this: (See figure 1)

The physical process which created this foot is described by Howard S. Levy in *Chinese Footbinding: The History of a Curious Erotic Custom:*

The success or failure of footbinding depended on skillful application of a bandage around each foot.

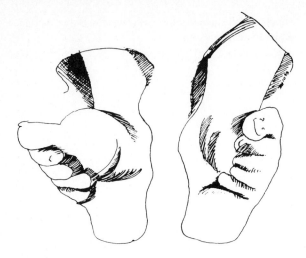

FIGURE 1   *(Feet: 3 to 4 inches in length)"*

The bandage, about two inches wide and ten feet long, was wrapped in the following way. One end was placed on the inside of the instep, and from there it was carried over the small toes so as to force the toes in and towards the sole. The large toe was left unbound. The bandage was then wrapped around the heel so forcefully that heel and toes were drawn closer together. The process was then repeated from the beginning until the entire bandage had been applied. The foot of the young child was subjected to a coercive and unremitting pressure, for the object was not merely to confine the foot but to make the toes bend under and into the sole and bring the heel and sole as close together as physically possible.[3]

A Christian missionary observed:

The flesh often became putrescent during the binding and portions sloughed off from the sole; sometimes one or more toes dropped off.[4]

An elderly Chinese woman, as late as 1934, remembered vividly her childhood experience:

Born into an old-fashioned family at P'ing-hsi, I was inflicted with the pain of footbinding when I was seven years old. I was an active child who liked to jump about, but from then on my free and optimistic nature vanished. Elder Sister endured the process from six to eight years of age [this means

that it took Elder Sister two years to attain the 3-inch foot]. It was in the first lunar month of my seventh year that my ears were pierced and fitted with gold earrings. I was told that a girl had to suffer twice, through ear piercing and footbinding. Binding started in the second lunar month; mother consulted references in order to select an auspicious day for it. I wept and hid in a neighbor's home, but Mother found me, scolded me, and dragged me home. She shut the bedroom door, boiled water, and from a box withdrew binding, shoes, knife, needle and thread. I begged for a one-day postponement, but Mother refused: "Today is a lucky day," she said. "If bound today, your feet will never hurt; if bound tomorrow they will." She washed and placed alum on my feet and cut the toenails. She then bent my toes toward the plantar with a binding cloth ten feet long and two inches wide, doing the right foot first and then the left. She finished binding and ordered me to walk, but when I did the pain proved unbearable.

That night, Mother wouldn't let me remove the shoes. My feet felt on fire and I couldn't sleep; Mother struck me for crying. On the following days, I tried to hide but was forced to walk on my feet. Mother hit me on my hands and feet for resisting. Beatings and curses were my lot for covertly loosening the wrappings. The feet were washed and rebound after three or four days, with alum added. After several months, all toes but the big one were pressed against the inner surface. Whenever I ate fish or freshly killed meat, my feet would swell, and the pus would drip. Mother criticized me for placing pressure on the heel in walking, saying that my feet would never assume a pretty shape. Mother would remove the bindings and wipe the blood and pus which dripped from my feet. She told me that only with the removal of the flesh could my feet become slender. If I mistakenly punctured a sore, the blood gushed like a stream. My somewhat fleshy big toes were bound with small pieces of cloth and forced upwards, to assume a new-moon shape.

Every two weeks, I changed to new shoes. Each new pair was one- to two-tenths of an inch smaller than the previous one. The shoes were unyielding, and it took pressure to get into them. Though I wanted to sit passively by the K'ang, Mother forced me to move around. After changing more than ten pairs of shoes, my feet were reduced to a little over four inches. I had been in binding for a month when my younger sister started; when no one was around, we would weep together. In summer, my feet smelled offensively because of pus and blood; in winter, my feet felt cold because of lack of circulation and hurt if they got too near the K'ang and were struck by warm air currents. Four of the toes were curled in like so many dead caterpillars; no outsider would ever have believed that they belonged to a human being. It took two years to achieve the three-inch model. My toenails pressed against the flesh like thin paper. The heavily-creased plantar couldn't be scratched when it itched or soothed when it ached. My shanks were thin, my feet became humped, ugly, and odiferous; how I envied the natural-footed![5]

Bound feet were crippled and excruciatingly painful. The woman was actually "walking" on the outside of toes which had been bent under into the sole of the foot. The heel and instep of the foot resembled the sole and heel of a high-heeled boot. Hard callouses formed; toenails grew into the skin; the feet were pus-filled and bloody; circulation was virtually stopped. The footbound woman hobbled along, leaning on a cane, against a wall, against a servant. To keep her balance she took very short steps. She was actually falling with every step and catching herself with the next. Walking required tremendous exertion.

Footbinding also distorted the natural lines of the female body. It caused the thighs and buttocks, which were always in a state of tension, to become somewhat swollen (which men called "voluptuous"). A curious belief developed among Chinese men that footbinding produced a most useful alteration of the vagina. A Chinese diplomat explained:

The smaller the woman's foot, the more wondrous become the folds of the vagina. (There was the saying: the smaller the feet, the more intense the sex urge.) Therefore marriages in Ta-t'ung (where binding is most effective) often take place earlier than elsewhere. Women in other districts can produce these folds artificially, but the only way is by footbinding, which concentrates development in this one place. There consequently develop layer after layer (of folds within the vagina); those who have personally experienced this (in sexual intercourse) feel a supernatural exaltation. So the system of footbinding was not really oppressive.[6]

Medical authorities confirm that physiologically footbinding had no effect whatsoever on the vagina, although it did distort the direction of the pelvis. The belief in the wondrous folds of the vagina of footbound woman was pure mass delusion, a projection of lust onto the feet, buttocks, and vagina of the crippled female. Needless to say, the diplomat's rationale for finding footbinding "not really oppressive" confused his "supernatural exaltation" with her misery and mutilation.

Bound feet, the same myth continues, "made the buttocks more sensual, [and] concentrated life-giving vapors on the upper part of the body, making the face more attractive."[7] If, due to a breakdown in the flow of these "life-giving vapors," an ugly woman was footbound and still ugly, she need not despair, for an A-1 Golden Lotus could compensate for a C-3 face and figure.

But to return to herstory, how did our Chinese ballerina become the millions of women stretched over 10 centuries? The transition from palace dancer to population at large can be seen as part of a class dynamic. The emperor sets the style, the nobility copies it, and the lower classes climbing ever upward do their best to emulate it. The upper class bound the feet of their ladies with the utmost severity. The Lady, unable to walk, remained properly invisible in her boudoir, an ornament, weak and small, a testimony to the wealth and privilege of the man who could afford to keep her—to keep her idle. Doing no manual labor, she did not need her feet either. Only on the rarest of occasions was she allowed outside of the incarcerating walls of her home, and then only in a sedan chair behind heavy curtains. The lower a woman's class, the less could such idleness be supported: the larger the feet. The women who had to work for the economic survival of the family still had bound feet, but the bindings were looser, the feet bigger—after all, she had to be able to walk, even if slowly and with little balance.

Footbinding was a visible brand. *Footbinding did not emphasize the differences between men and women—it created them,* and they were then perpetuated in the name of morality. Footbinding functioned as the Cerberus of morality and ensured female chastity in a nation of women who literally could not "run around." Fidelity, and the legitimacy of children, could be reckoned on.

The minds of footbound women were as contracted as their feet. Daughters were taught to cook, supervise the household, and embroider shoes for the Golden Lotus. Intellectual and physical restriction had the usual male justification. Women were perverse and sinful, lewd and lascivious, if left to develop naturally. The Chinese believed that being born a woman was payment for evils committed in a previous life. Footbinding was designed to spare a woman the disaster of another such incarnation.

Marriage and family are the twin pillars of all patriarchal cultures. Bound feet, in China, were the twin pillars of these twin pillars. Here we have the joining together of politics and morality, coupled to produce their inevitable offspring—the oppression of women based on totalitarian standards of beauty and a rampant sexual fascism. In arranging a marriage, a male's parents inquired first about the prospective bride's feet, then about her face. Those were her human, recognizable qualities. During the process of footbinding, mothers consoled their daughters by conjuring up the luscious marriage possibilities dependent on the beauty of the bound foot. Concubines for the Imperial harem were selected at tiny-foot festivals (forerunners of Miss America pageants). Rows upon rows of women sat on benches with their feet outstretched while audience and judges went along the aisles and commented on the size, shape and decoration of foot and shoes. No one, however, was ever allowed to touch the merchandise. Women looked forward to these festivals, since they were allowed out of the house.

The sexual aesthetics, literally the art of love, of the bound foot was complex. The sexual attraction of the foot was based on its concealment and the mystery surrounding its development and care. The bindings were unwrapped and the feet were washed in the woman's boudoir, in the strictest privacy. The frequency of bathing varied from once a week to once a year. Perfumes of various fragrances and alum were used during and after washing, and various kinds of surgery were performed on the callouses and nails. The physical process of washing helped restore circulation. The mummy was unwrapped, touched up, and put back to sleep with more preservatives added. The rest of the body was never washed at the same time as the feet, for fear that one would become a pig in the next life. Well-bred women were supposed to die of shame if men observed them washing their feet. The foot consisted, after all, of smelly, rotted flesh. This was naturally not pleasing to the intruding male, a violation of his aesthetic sensibility.

The art of the shoes was basic to the sexual aesthetics of the bound foot. Untold hours, days, months went into the embroidery of shoes. There were shoes for all occasions, shoes of different colors, shoes to hobble in, shoes to go to bed in, shoes for special occasions like birthdays, marriages, funerals, shoes which denoted age. Red was the favored color for bed shoes because it accentuated the whiteness of the skin of the calves and thighs. A marriageable daughter made about 12 pairs of shoes as a part of her dowry. She presented two specially made pairs to her mother-in-law and father-in-law. When she entered her husband's home for the first time, her feet were immediately examined by the whole family, neither praise nor sarcasm being withheld.

There was also the art of the gait, the art of sitting, the art of standing, the art of lying down, the art of adjusting the skirt, the art of every movement which involves feet. Beauty was the way feet looked and how they moved. Certain feet were better than other feet, more beautiful. Perfect three-inch form and utter uselessness were the distinguishing marks of the aristocratic foot. These concepts of beauty and status defined women: as ornaments, as sexual playthings, as sexual constructs. The perfect construct, even in China, was naturally the prostitute.

The natural-footed woman generated horror and repulsion in China. She was anathema, and all the forces of insult and contempt were used to obliterate her. Men said about bound feet and natural feet:

> A tiny foot is proof of feminine goodness. . . .
>
> Women who don't bind their feet, look like men, for the tiny foot serves to show the differentiation. . . .
>
> The tiny foot is soft and, when rubbed, leads to great excitement. . . .
>
> The graceful walk gives the beholder mixed feelings of compassion and pity. . . .
>
> Natural feet are heavy and ponderous as they get into bed, but tiny feet lightly steal under the coverlets. . . .
>
> The large-footed woman is careless about adornment, but the tiny-footed frequently wash and apply a variety of perfumed fragrances, enchanting all who come into their presence. . . .
>
> The natural foot looks much less aesthetic in walking. . . .
>
> Everyone welcomes the tiny foot, regarding its smallness as precious. . . .
>
> Men formerly so craved it that its possessor achieved harmonious matrimony. . . .
>
> Because of its diminutiveness, it gives rise to a variety of sensual pleasures and love feelings. . . .[8]

Thin, small, curved, soft, fragrant, weak, easily inflamed, passive to the point of being almost inanimate—this was footbound woman. Her bindings created extraordinary vaginal folds; isolation in the bedroom increased her sexual desire; playing with the shriveled, crippled foot increased everyone's desire. Even the imagery of the names of various types of foot suggest, on the one hand, feminine passivity (lotuses, lilies, bamboo shoots, water chestnuts) and, on the other hand, male independence, strength, and mobility (lotus boats, large-footed crows, monkey foot). It was unacceptable for a woman to have those male qualities denoted by large feet. This fact conjures up an earlier assertion: footbinding did not formalize existing differences between men and women—it created them. One sex became male by virtue of having made the other sex some thing, something other, something completely polar to itself, something called female. In 1915, a satirical essay in defense of footbinding, written by a Chinese male, emphasized this:

> The bound foot is the condition of a life of dignity for man, of contentment for woman. Let me make this clear. I am a Chinese fairly typical of my class. I pored too much over classic texts in my youth and dimmed my eyes, narrowed my chest, crooked my back. My memory is not strong, and in an old civilization there is a vast deal to learn before you can know anything. Accordingly among scholars I cut a poor figure. I am timid, and my voice plays me false in gatherings of men. But to my footbound wife, confined for life to her house except when I bear her in my arms to her palanquin, my stride is heroic, my voice is that of a roaring lion, my wisdom is of the sages. To her I am the world; I am life itself.[9]

Chinese men, it is clear, stood tall and strong on women's tiny feet.

The so-called art of footbinding was the process of taking the human foot, using it as though it were insensible matter, molding it into an inhuman form. Footbinding was the "art" of making living matter insensible, inanimate. We are obviously not dealing here with art at all, but with fetishism, with sexual psychosis. This fetish became the primary content of sexual experience for an entire culture for 1,000 years. The manipulation of the tiny foot was an indispensable prelude to all sexual experience. Manuals were written elaborating various techniques for holding and rubbing the Golden Lotus. Smelling the feet, chewing them, licking them, sucking them, all were sexually charged experiences. A woman with tiny feet was supposedly more easily maneuvered

around in bed and this was no small advantage. Theft of shoes was commonplace. Women were forced to sew their shoes directly onto their bindings. Stolen shoes might be returned soaked in semen. Prostitutes would show their naked feet for a high price (there weren't many streetwalkers in China). Drinking games using cups placed in the shoes of prostitutes or courtesans were favorite pastimes. Tiny-footed prostitutes took special names like Moon Immortal, Red Treasure, Golden Pearl. No less numerous were the euphemisms for feet, shoes, and bindings. Some men went to prostitutes to wash the tiny foot and eat its dirt, or to drink tea made from the washing water. Others wanted their penises manipulated by the feet. Superstition also had its place—there was a belief in the curative powers of the water in which tiny feet were washed.

Lastly, footbinding was the soil in which sadism could grow and go unchecked—in which simple cruelty could transcend itself, without much effort, into atrocity. These are some typical horror stories of those times:

> A stepmother or aunt in binding the child's foot was usually much harsher than the natural mother would have been. An old man was described who delighted in seeing his daughters weep as the binding was tightly applied. . . . In one household, everyone had to bind. The main wife and concubines bound to the smallest degree, once morning and evening, and once before retiring. The husband and first wife strictly carried out foot inspections and whipped those guilty of having let the binding become loose. The sleeping shoes were so painfully small that the women had to ask the master to rub them in order to bring relief. Another rich man would flog his concubines on their tiny feet, one after another, until the blood flowed.[10]
> . . . about 1931 . . . bound-foot women unable to flee had been taken captive. The bandits, angered because of their captives' weak way of walking and inability to keep in file, forced the women to remove the bindings and socks and run about barefoot. They cried out in pain and were unable to move on in spite of the beatings. Each of the bandits grabbed a woman and forced her to dance about on a wide field covered with sharp rocks. The harshest treatment was meted out to prostitutes. Nails were driven through their hands and feet; they cried aloud for several days before expiring. One form of torture was to tie up a woman so that

*her legs dangled in midair and place bricks around
each toe, increasing the weight until the toes
straightened out and eventually dropped off.*[11]

End of Footbinding Event

One asks the same questions again and again, over a
period of years, in the course of a lifetime. The questions
have to do with people and what they do—the how and
the why of it. How could the Germans have murdered
6,000,000 Jews, used their skins for lampshades, taken
the gold out of their teeth? How could white people have
bought and sold black people, hanged them and castrated
them? How could "Americans" have slaughtered the Indian nations, stolen the land, spread famine and disease?
How can the Indochina genocide continue, day after day,
year after year? How is it possible? Why does it happen?

As a woman, one is forced to ask another series of
hard questions: Why, everywhere, the oppression of
women throughout recorded history? How could the Inquisitors torture and burn women as witches? How could
men idealize the bound feet of crippled women? How and
why?

The bound foot existed for 1,000 years. In what
terms, using what measure, could one calculate the enor-
mity of the crime, the dimensions of the transgression, the
amount of cruelty and pain inherent in that 1,000-year
herstory? In what terms, using what vocabulary, could
one penetrate to the meaning, to the reality, of that
1,000-year herstory?

Here one race did not war with another to acquire
food, or land, or civil power; one nation did not fight
with another in the interest of survival, real or imagined;
one group of people in a fever pitch of hysteria did not
destroy another. None of the traditional explanations or
justifications for brutality between or among peoples applies to this situation. On the contrary, here one sex
mutilated (enslaved) the other in the interest of the *art* of
sex, male-female *harmony*, role-definition, beauty.

Consider the magnitude of the crime.

Millions of women, over a period of 1,000 years,
were brutally crippled, mutilated, in the name of erotica.

Millions of human beings, over a period of 1,000
years, were brutally crippled, mutilated, in the name of
beauty.

Millions of men, over a period of 1,000 years, reveled
in love-making devoted to the worship of the bound foot.

Millions of men, over a period of 1,000 years, worshiped and adored the bound foot.

Millions of mothers, over a period of 1,000 years,
brutally crippled and mutilated their daughters for the
sake of a secure marriage.

Millions of mothers, over a period of 1,000 years,
brutally crippled and mutilated their daughters in the
name of beauty.

But this thousand-year period is only the tip of an
awesome, fearful iceberg: an extreme and visible expression of romantic attitudes, processes, and values organically rooted in all cultures, then and now. It demonstrates
that man's love for woman, his sexual adoration of her,
his human definition of her, his delight and pleasure in
her, require her negation: physical crippling and psychological lobotomy. That is the very nature of romantic
love, which is the love based on polar role definitions,
manifest in herstory as well as in fiction—he glories in her
agony, he adores her deformity, he annihilates her
freedom, he will have her as sex object, even if he must
destroy the bones in her feet to do it. Brutality, sadism,
and oppression emerge as the substantive core of the
romantic ethos. That ethos is the warp and woof of
culture as we know it.

Women should be beautiful. All repositories of
cultural wisdom from King Solomon to King Hefner
agree: women should be beautiful. It is the reverence for
female beauty which informs the romantic ethos, gives it
its energy and justification. Beauty is transformed into
that golden ideal, Beauty—rapturous and abstract.
Women must be beautiful and Woman is Beauty.

Notions of beauty always incorporate the whole of a
given societal structure, are crystallizations of its values.
A society with a well-defined aristocracy will have aristocratic standards of beauty. In Western "democracy" notions of beauty are "democratic": even if a woman is not
born beautiful, she can make herself *attractive*.

The argument is not simply that some women are not
beautiful, therefore it is not fair to judge women on the
basis of physical beauty; or that men are not judged on
that basis, therefore women also should not be judged on
that basis; or that men should look for character in
women; or that our standards of beauty are too parochial
in and of themselves; or even that judging women according to their conformity to a standard of beauty serves to
make them into products, chattels, differing from the
farmer's favorite cow only in terms of literal form. The
issue at stake is different, and crucial. Standards of beauty
describe in precise terms the relationship that an individual will have to her own body. They prescribe her mobility, spontaneity, posture, gait, the uses to which she can

put her body. *They define precisely the dimensions of her physical freedom.* And, of course, the relationship between physical freedom and psychological development, intellectual possibility, and creative potential is an umbilical one.

In our culture, not one part of a woman's body is left untouched, unaltered. No feature or extremity is spared the art, or pain, of improvement. Hair is dyed, lacquered, straightened, permanented; eyebrows are plucked, penciled, dyed; eyes are lined, mascaraed, shadowed; lashes are curled, or false — from head to toe, every feature of a woman's face, every section of her body, is subject to modification, alteration. This alteration is an ongoing, repetitive process. It is vital to the economy, the major substance of male-female role differentiation, the most immediate physical and psychological reality of being a woman. From the age of 11 or 12 until she dies, a woman will spend a large part of her time, money, and energy on binding, plucking, painting, and deodorizing herself. It is commonly and wrongly said that male transvestites through the use of makeup and costuming caricature the women they would become, but any real knowledge of the romantic ethos makes clear that these men have penetrated to the core experience of being a woman, a romanticized construct.

The technology of beauty, and the message it carries, is handed down from mother to daughter. Mother teaches daughter to apply lipstick, to shave under her arms, to bind her breasts, to wear a girdle and high-heeled shoes. Mother teaches daughter concomitantly her role, her appropriate behavior, her place. Mother teaches daughter, necessarily, the psychology which defines womanhood: a woman must be beautiful, in order to please the amorphous and amorous Him. What we have called the romantic ethos operates as vividly in 20th-century America and Europe as it did in 10th-century China.

This cultural transfer of technology, role, and psychology virtually affects the emotive relationship between mother and daughter. It contributes substantially to the ambivalent love-hate dynamics of that relationship. What must the Chinese daughter/child have felt toward the mother who bound her feet? What does any daughter/child feel toward the mother who forces her to do painful things to her own body? The mother takes on the role of enforcer: she uses seduction, command, all manner of force to coerce the daughter to conform to the demands of the culture. It is because this role becomes her dominant role in the mother-daughter relationship that tensions and difficulties between mothers and daughters

are so often unresolvable. The daughter who rejects the cultural norms enforced by the mother is forced to a basic rejection of her own mother, a recognition of the hatred and resentment she felt toward that mother, an alienation from mother and society so extreme that her own womanhood is denied by both. The daughter who internalizes those values and endorses those same processes is bound to repeat the teaching she was taught — her anger and resentment remain subterranean, channeled against her own female offspring as well as her mother.

Pain is an essential part of the grooming process, and that is not accidental. Plucking the eyebrows, shaving under the arms, wearing a girdle, learning to walk in high-heeled shoes, having one's nose fixed, straightening or curling one's hair — these things *hurt*. The pain, of course, teaches an important lesson: no price is too great, no process too repulsive, no operation too painful for the woman who would be beautiful. *The tolerance of pain and the romanticization of that tolerance begins here,* in preadolescence, in socialization, and serves to prepare women for lives of childbearing, self-abnegation, and husband-pleasing. The adolescent experience of the "pain of being a woman" casts the feminine psyche into a masochistic mold and forces the adolescent to conform to a self-image which bases itself on mutilation of the body, pain happily suffered, and restricted physical mobility. It creates the masochistic personalities generally found in adult women: subservient, materialistic (since all value is placed on the body and its ornamentation), intellectually restricted, creatively impoverished. It forces women to be a sex of lesser accomplishment, weaker, as underdeveloped as any backward nation. Indeed, the effects of that prescribed relationship between women and their bodies are so extreme, so deep, so extensive, that scarcely any area of human possibility is left untouched by it.

Men, of course, like a woman who "takes care of herself." The male response to the woman who is made-up and bound is a learned fetish, societal in its dimensions. One need only refer to the male idealization of the bound foot and say that the same dynamic is operating here. Romance based on role differentiation, superiority based on a culturally determined and rigidly enforced inferiority, shame and guilt and fear of women and sex itself: all necessitate the perpetuation of these oppressive grooming imperatives.

The meaning of this analysis of the romantic ethos surely is clear. A first step in the process of liberation (women from their oppression, men from the unfreedom of their fetishism) is the radical redefining of the relation-

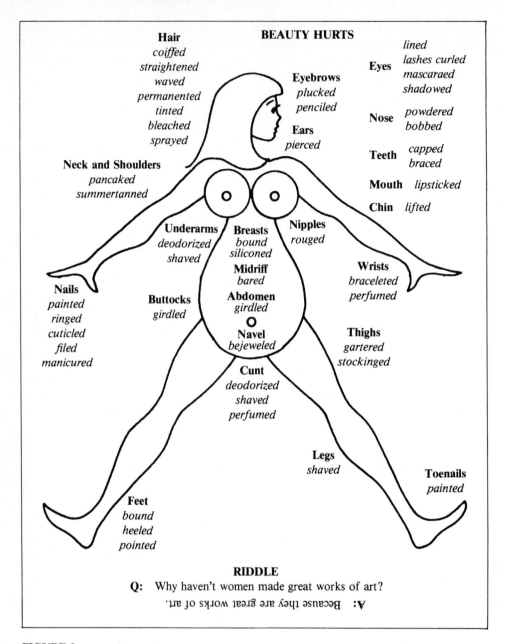

BEAUTY HURTS

Hair
coiffed
straightened
waved
permanented
tinted
bleached
sprayed

Eyebrows
plucked
penciled

Ears
pierced

Eyes
lined
lashes curled
mascaraed
shadowed

Nose
powdered
bobbed

Teeth
capped
braced

Mouth   *lipsticked*

Chin   *lifted*

Neck and Shoulders
pancaked
summertanned

Underarms
deodorized
shaved

Breasts
bound
siliconed

Nipples
rouged

Midriff
bared

Abdomen
girdled

Navel
bejeweled

Wrists
braceleted
perfumed

Nails
painted
ringed
cuticled
filed
manicured

Buttocks
girdled

Cunt
deodorized
shaved
perfumed

Thighs
gartered
stockinged

Legs
shaved

Toenails
painted

Feet
bound
heeled
pointed

RIDDLE

Q: Why haven't women made great works of art?

A: Because they are great works of art.

FIGURE 2

ship between women and their bodies. The body must be freed, liberated, quite literally: from paint and girdles and all varieties of crap. Women must stop mutilating their bodies and start living in them. Perhaps the notion of beauty which will then organically emerge will be truly democratic and demonstrate a respect for human life in its infinite, and most honorable, variety.

Endnotes

1. Howard S. Levy, *Chinese Footbinding: The History of a Curious Erotic Custom* (New York: W. Rawls, 1966), p. 39. Mr. Levy's book is the primary source for all the factual, historical information in this chapter.
2. Ibid., p. 112.
3. Ibid., pp. 25–26.
4. Ibid., p. 26.
5. Ibid., pp. 26–28.
6. Ibid., p. 141.
7. Ibid.
8. Ibid., p. 182.
9. Ibid., p. 89.
10. Ibid., p. 144.
11. Ibid., pp. 144–45.

READING 44

Chinese Are Killing Newborn Girls at High Rate

PEKING (UPI)—Chinese peasants are killing newborn girls at such a high rate that the nation's balance between males and females could be upset, an official publication said yesterday.

The China Youth News newspaper said female babies were being drowned or abandoned in the streets at such a rate that in 20 years Chinese men may have trouble finding women to marry.

In a study of rural communes, the report said three out of every five babies were boys. Because of reports of widespread killing and abandonment of unwanted female babies, the male to female ratio could be artificially damaged, it said.

"Is there anything on earth more heinous than this?" the report said.

Reprinted from the *Columbus Citizen-Journal,* 11 November 1982.

China's tough birth control policy allows only one child per couple in urban areas and a maximum of two in the countryside without the risk of economic penalties and, in extreme cases, forced abortions.

For young couples clinging to "feudalistic thinking" that favors men over women, the pressure is to have a son even if it means killing a female baby born first, the newspaper said.

The Chinese traditionally believe a son can provide more labor as he grows up, take better care of his parents when they retire and carry on the family name.

A daughter often is viewed as a financial burden who eventually would change her name once married and care for her in-laws first.

Statistics of communes already indicate an imbalance in the sex ratio in the last two years because of the infanticide, China Youth News said.

"In two decades, if this phenomenon goes unchecked, there will appear a serious social problem in which a large group of men will be unable to find spouses."

"The law governing human development and propagation requires the rough balance between men and women in society," it said.

Men presently outnumber women 51 percent to 49 percent with 106 men to every 100 women in the nation of more than 1 billion people, according to census results announced last month.

The newspaper stressed the current marriage law demands both sons and daughters care for their parents and said in many cases the daughters provide better comfort and support.

READING 45

It's Custom, Simply Custom

Anne Sostrom

*"Women are not for burning," chanted 150
demonstrators last weekend outside the home of a
New Delhi family accused of fatally burning a
young bride . . . over the issue of dowry.*
                                        May 1979

*The Torah prefers
stones
and reason,
the British
poisoned tea,
American guns.
(How can we then object?)*

*In New Delhi
fathers set the dowry—
one modern bride,
one motor scooter,
one television set,*

*one refrigerator, $2,500,
and her grandmother's jewelry—
to wear like ribbons on
her sari.
The fathers agreed.*

*His mother stood
circled by cold
marble stairs
and smiled at the
gold coins
the bride's mother placed
in his outstretched palm,
thinking of goods to come,
wondering what bargain her
husband struck.*

*Her mother bathed her in myrrh
rubbing her young brown skin soft
and pliable,
instructing her—
voice husky, lump in throat—
to lie still, obedient
while her new husband tore
her body open, blood*

oozing down her leg,
she listening
to his triumphant breathing
in the hot, damp night.

Her sister-in-law splashed cold
kerosene
down her yellow sari
as she watched Sadat sign
peace treaties on TV,
and her mother-in-law dropped
the match,

smiling,
slowly counting their disappointments
with her dowry
until her screams brought
servants to put out the fire.

She talked through blistered lips
to a bored policeman,
the doctor bathing
flesh that crumbled
like burned toast
And then she died.

READING 46

Indian Suttee: The Ultimate Consummation of Marriage

Mary Daly

Lynn Caine, Widow
"Widow" is a harsh and hurtful word. It comes
from the Sanskrit and it means "empty." . . . I
resent what the term has come to mean. I am alive,
I am part of the world.

The Indian rite of *suttee,* or widow-burning, might at first appear totally alien to contemporary Western society, where widows are not ceremoniously burned alive on the funeral pyres of their husbands.* Closer examination unveils its connectedness with "our" rituals. Moreover, the very attempt to examine the ritual and its social context through the resources of Western scholarship demonstrates this connectedness. For the scholars who produced these resources exhibit by their very language their complicity in the same social order which was/is the radical source of such rites of female sacrifice.

* Although *suttee* was legally banned in 1829, and despite the existence of other legal reforms, it should not be imagined that the lot of most Indian women has changed dramatically since then, or since the publication of Katherine Mayo's *Mother India* in 1927. The situation of most widows is pitiable. An article in an Indian paper, the *Sunday Standard,* May 11, 1975, described the wretched existence of the 7,000 widows of the town of Brindaban, "the living spectres whose life has been eroded by another's death." These poverty-stricken women with shaved heads and with a single white cloth draped over their bare bodies are forced every morning to chant praise (*"Hare Rama, Hare Rama, Rama Rama, Hare Hare, Hare Krishna"* . . . ad nauseam) for four hours in order to get a small bowl of rice. In mid-afternoon they must chant for four more hours in order to receive the price of a glass of tea. A not unusual case is that of a sixty-nine-year-old widow who was married at the age of nine and widowed at eleven, and has been waiting ever since for the "day of deliverance." Surveys carried out by an Indian Committee on the Status of Women revealed that a large percentage of the Indian population still approves of such oppression of widows.

The Hindu rite of *suttee* spared widows from the temptations of impurity by forcing them to "immolate themselves," that is, to be burned alive, on the funeral pyres of their husbands. This ritual sacrifice must be understood within its social context. Since their religion forbade remarriage and at the same time taught that the husband's death was the fault of the widow (because of her sins in a previous incarnation if not in this one), everyone was free to despise and mistreat her for the rest of her life. Since it was a common practice for men of fifty, sixty, or seventy years of age to marry child-brides, the quantitative surplus of such unmarriageable widows boggles the imagination. Lest we allow our minds to be carried away with astronomic numerical calculations, we should realize that this ritual was largely confined to the upper caste, although there was a tendency to spread downward. We should also realize that in some cases—particularly if the widow was an extremely young child before her husband's unfortunate (for her) death—there was the option of turning to a life of prostitution, which would entail premature death from venereal disease.[1] This, however, would be her only possible escape from persecution by in-laws, sons, and other relatives. As a prostitute, of course, she would be held responsible for the spread of more moral and physical impurity.

If the general situation of widowhood in India was not a sufficient inducement for the woman of higher caste to throw herself gratefully and ceremoniously into the fire, she was often pushed and poked in with long stakes after having been bathed, ritually attired, and drugged out of her mind.[2] In case these facts should interfere with our clear misunderstanding of the situation, Webster's invites us to re-*cover* women's history with the following definition of *suttee:* "the act or custom of a Hindu woman *willingly* cremating herself or being cremated on the funeral pyre of her husband as an indication of her *devotion* to him [emphases mine]." It is thought-provoking to consider the reality behind the term *devotion,* for indeed a wife must have shown signs of extraordinarily slavish devotion during her husband's lifetime, since her very life

depended upon her husband's state of health. A thirteen-year-old wife might well be concerned over the health of her sixty-year-old husband.

Joseph Campbell discusses *suttee* as the Hindu form of the widely practiced "custom" of sending the family or part of it "into the other world along with the chief member."[3] The time-honored practice of "human sacrifice," sometimes taking the form of live burial, was common also in other cultures, for example in ancient Egypt. Campbell notes that Professor George Reisner excavated an immense necropolis in Nubia, an Egyptian province, and found, without exception, "a pattern of burial with human sacrifice—specifically, female sacrifice: of the wife and, in the more opulent tombs, the entire harem, together with the attendants."[4] After citing Reisner's descriptions of female skeletons, which indicated that the victims had died hideous deaths from suffocation, Campbell writes:

In spite of these signs of suffering and even panic in the actual moment of the pain of suffocation, we should certainly not think of the mental state and experience of these individuals after any model of our own more or less imaginable reactions to such a fate. For these sacrifices were not properly, in fact, individuals at all; that is to say, they were not particular beings, distinguished from a class or group by virtue of any sense or realization of a personal, individual destiny or responsibility.[5]

I have not [emphasized] any of the words in this citation because it seemed necessary to stress *every* word. It is impossible to make any adequate comment.

At first, *suttee* was restricted to the wives of princes and warriors, but as one scholar (Benjamin Walker) deceptively puts it, "in course of time *the widows* of weavers, masons, barbers and others of lower caste *adopted the practice* [emphases mine]."[6] The use of the active voice here suggests that the widows actively sought out, enforced, and accepted this "practice." Apparently without any sense of inconsistency the same author supplies evidence that relatives forced widows to the pyre. He describes a case reported in 1796, in which a widow escaped from the pyre during the night in the rain. A

1. See Katherine Mayo, *Mother India* (New York: Blue Ribbon Books, 1927), esp. pp. 81–89, 51–62.
2. See P. Thomas, *Indian Women through the Ages* (New York: Asia Publishing Company, 1964), p. 263. This author describes the situation in muslim India of widows who tried to escape cremation, writing that "to prevent her escape, she was usually surrounded by men armed with sticks who goaded her on to her destination by physical force."

3. Joseph Campbell, *The Masks of God: Oriental Mythology* (New York: Viking Press, 1962), p. 62.
4. Ibid., p. 60.
5. Ibid., p. 65.
6. Benjamin Walker, *The Hindu World: An Encyclopedic Survey of Hinduism,* 2 vols., (New York: Praeger, 1968), Vol. II, p. 461.

search was made and she was dragged from her hiding place. Walker concludes the story of this woman who "adopted the practice" as follows:

> She pleaded to be spared but her own son insisted that she throw herself on the pile as he would lose caste and suffer everlasting humiliation. When she still refused, the son with the help of some others present bound her hands and feet and hurled her into the blaze.[7]

The same author gives information about the numerical escalation of *suttee:*

> Among the Rājputs and other warrior nations of

northern India, the observance of suttee took on staggering proportions, since wives and concubines immolated themselves *by the hundred. It became customary not only for wives but for mistresses, sisters, mothers, sisters-in-law and other near female relatives and retainers* to burn themselves along with their deceased master. With Rājputs it evolved into the terrible rite of *jauhar which took place in times of war or great peril* in order to save the honour of the womenfolk of the clan *[emphases mine].*[8]

Again the victims, through grammatical sleight of hand, are made to appear as the agents of their own destruction.

---

7. Ibid., p. 464.

---

8. Ibid., pp. 462–63.

READING 47

The International Crime of Genital Mutilation

Robin Morgan and Gloria Steinem

As you read this, an estimated 30 million women in the world are suffering the results of genital mutilation. The main varieties of this extensive custom are:

1. Sunna "circumcision," or removal of the prepuce and/or tip of the clitoris;
2. Clitoridectomy, or the excision of the entire clitoris (both prepuce and glans), plus the adjacent parts of the labia minora;

3. Infibulation (from the Latin *fibula,* or clasp); that is, the removal of the entire clitoris, the labia minora, and the labia majora—plus the joining of the scraped sides of the vulva across the vagina, where they are secured with thorns or sewn with catgut or thread. A small opening is preserved by inserting a sliver of wood (commonly a matchstick) into the wound during the healing process, thus allowing passage of urine and menstrual blood. An infibulated woman must be cut open to permit intercourse, and cut further to permit childbirth. Often, she is closed up again after delivery, and thus may be subject to such procedures repeatedly during her reproductive life.

The age at which these ritual sexual mutilations are performed varies with the type of procedure and local tradition. A female may undergo some such rite as early as the eighth day after birth, or at puberty, or after she herself has borne children. In most areas, however, the ritual is carried out when the child is between the ages of three and eight, and she may be considered unclean, improper, or unmarriageable if it is not done.

To readers for whom such customs come as horrifying news, it is vital that we immediately recognize the connection between these patriarchal practices and our own. They are different in scope, but not in kind. Not only have American and European women experienced the psychic clitoridectomy that was legitimized by Freud,* but Western 19th-century medical texts also proclaim surgical mutilation an accepted treatment for "nymphomania," "hysteria," masturbation, and other nonconforming behavior. Indeed, there are women living in the United States and Europe today who have suffered this form (as well as other, more familiar forms) of gynophobic, medically unnecessary, mutilating surgery.

As a general practice and precondition of marriage, however, some researchers cite recent evidence for genital mutilation in areas as diverse as Australia, Brazil, Malaya, Pakistan, and among the "Skoptsi" Christian sect in the Soviet Union. In El Salvador, it is still not uncommon for a mother to carve the sign of the cross with a razor blade on the clitoris of her little girl to "make her a better worker and keep her from getting ideas" ("Upheaval in El Salvador," *Ms.,* January, 1980). But international health authorities find the most extensive evidence of such customs on the African continent and the Arabian peninsula. The majority of mutilations take place without anesthetic at home (in the city or village), but many are now performed in hospitals as approved procedures. Nor are these rites limited to one religion; they are practiced by some Islamic peoples, some Coptic Christians, members of various indigenous tribal religions, some Catholics and Protestants, and some Fellasha, an ancient Jewish sect living in the Ethiopian highlands.

The form most common on the African continent is clitoridectomy, which is practiced in more than 26 countries from the Horn of Africa and the Red Sea across to the Atlantic coast, and from Egypt in the North to

Mozambique in the South, also including Botswana and Lesotho. According to Awa Thiam, the Senegalese writer, clitoridectomy—in the form of either complete excision or the more "moderate" Sunna variant—also can be found in the two Yemens, Saudi Arabia, Iraq, Jordan, Syria, and Southern Algeria. Infibulation appears to be fairly standard in the whole of the Horn—Somalia, most of Ethiopia, the Sudan (despite legislation prohibiting it in 1946), Kenya, Nigeria, Mali, Upper Volta, and parts of the Ivory Coast. Many ethnic groups have local versions: some cauterize the clitoris with fire or rub a special kind of nettle across the organs in order to destroy nerve endings; some stanch the flow of blood with compounds made of herbs, milk, honey, and sometimes ashes or animal droppings.

The health consequences of such practices include primary fatalities due to shock, hemorrhage, or septicemia, and such later complications as genital malformation, delayed menarche, dyspareunia (pain suffered during intercourse), chronic pelvic complications, incontinence, calcification deposits in the vaginal walls, recto-vaginal fistulas, vulval cysts and abscesses, recurrent urinary retention and infection, scarring and keloid formation, infertility, and an entire array of obstetric complications—plus increased probability of injury to the fetus (by infection) during pregnancy, and to the infant during birth. Psychological responses among women range from temporary trauma and permanent frigidity to psychoses. A high rate of mortality is suspected by health officials, although there are few fatality records available, due to the informality or secrecy surrounding the custom in many areas.

Although such practices are frequently described as "female circumcision," the degree of damage is not comparable to the far more minor circumcision of males. Certainly, the two procedures are related: both are widely practiced without medical necessity and are extreme proofs of subservience to patriarchal authority—whether tribal, religious, or cultural—over all sexual and reproductive capacity. But there the parallel stops. Clitoridectomy is more analogous to penisectomy than to circumcision: the clitoris has as many nerve endings as the penis. But male circumcision does not destroy its victim's capacity for sexual pleasure; indeed, some justify the practice as increasing it. The misnomer "female circumcision" seems to stem from conscious or unconscious political motives: to make it appear that women are merely experiencing something men also undergo—no more, no less.

Politics are also evident in the attribution of this

---

* S. Freud, *Sexuality and the Psychology of Love:* "The elimination of clitoral sexuality is a necessary precondition for the development of femininity."

custom. The Sudanese name for infibulation credits it to Egypt ("Pharaonic circumcision"), while the Egyptians call the same operation "Sudanese circumcision." The more moderate "Sunna circumcision" was supposedly recommended by the Prophet Muhammed, who is said to have counseled, "Reduce, but don't destroy," thus reforming—and legitimizing—the ritual. That version was termed "Sunna," or traditional, perhaps in an attempt to placate strict traditionalists—although such rituals are mentioned nowhere in the Koran; a fact Islamic women who oppose this mutilation cite in their arguments.

The overt justifications for genital mutilation are as contradictory as are theories about its origins. Explanations include custom, religion, family honor, cleanliness, protection against spells, initiation, insurance of virginity at marriage, and prevention of female promiscuity by physically reducing—or terrorizing women out of—sexual desire; this last especially in polygamous cultures. (On the other hand, the fact that some women in the Middle East who are prostitutes also have been clitoridectomized is cited as proof that it *doesn't* reduce pleasure—as if women became prostitutes out of desire.)

A superstition is a practice or belief justified by simultaneous and utterly opposing sets of arguments. Thus, a frequently given reason for sexual mutilation is that it makes a woman more fertile—yet in 1978, Dr. R.T. Ravenholt, then Director of the United States Agency for International Development's Population Bureau, failed to oppose it on the ground that it was a *contraceptive* method, claiming that "because it is aimed at reducing female sex desire, [clitoridectomy/infibulation] undoubtedly has fertility control as part of its motivation." In fact, the pain of intercourse often leads mutilated women to seek pregnancy as a temporary relief from sexual demands.

In some cultures the justification is even less obscure. Myths of the Mossi of Upper Volta, and the Dogon and Bambaras of Mali, clearly express the fear of an initially hermaphroditic human nature and of women's sexuality: the clitoris is considered a dangerous organ, fatal to a man if brought into contact with his penis.

Similarly, in 19th-century London, Dr. Isaac Baker Brown justified scissoring off the clitoris as a cure for such various ills as insomnia, sterility, and "unhappy marriages." In 1859, Dr. Charles Meigs recommended application of a nitrate of silver solution to the clitoris of female children who masturbated. Until 1925 in the United States, a medical association called the Orificial

Surgery Society offered surgical training in clitoridectomy and infibulation "because of the vast amount of sickness and suffering which could be saved the gentler sex. . . ." Such operations (and justifications) occurred as recently as the 1940s in the United States.

During the 1970s, clitoral "relocation"—termed "Love Surgery"—entered some medical practice. As late as 1979, the feminist news service *Her Say* carried the story of Dr. James Burt, an Ohio gynecologist who offered a $1,500 "Mark Two" operation, which involved vaginal reconstruction in order to "make the clitoris more accessible to direct penile stimulation."

Whatever the supposed justifications, we can explore the real reasons only within the societal context: control of women's bodies as the means of reproduction, and resulting fear of the independent power of women's sexuality—both motives enforced by socioeconomic rewards and punishments.

If marriage is the primary means of economic survival for a woman, then whatever will make her more marriageable becomes desirable. If a bride who lacks virginity literally risks death or renunciation on her wedding night, then a chastity belt forged of her own flesh is a gesture of parental concern. If the tribal role of clitoridectomist or midwife who performs such mutilations is the sole position of honor, power, or even independent livelihood available to women, then the "token women" who perform such rites will fight to preserve them. If those who organize the ceremonies of excision (sometimes whole families by inherited prerogative) have the right, as they do in some cultures, to "adopt" the excised children to work in their fields for two or three years, then such families have a considerable economic motive for perpetuating the custom. If Western male gynecologists also believed women's independent sexuality to be dangerous and unnatural, then surgery was justified to remove its cause. If a modern gynecologist still presumes that men may not be willing to learn how to find or stimulate the clitoris for female pleasure, then he will think it natural to move the clitoris closer to the customary site of penile pleasure.

Illogical responses can be carried to new depths by bureaucrats. The White House and its concern for "human rights," the various desks of the U.S. State Department, and such agencies as the United Nations International Children's Fund and the World Health Organization—all in the recent past have expressed reluctance to interfere with "social and cultural attitudes" regarding female genital mutilation. This sensitivity has been markedly absent on other issues—for example, campaigns to disseminate vaccines or vitamins despite resistance from local traditionalists.

Clearly, "culture" is that which affects women while "politics" affects men, and human rights statements do not include those needed by the female majority of humanity. Some international agencies take a reformist position—that clitoridectomy and/or infibulation should be done in hospitals under hygienic conditions and proper medical supervision. Feminist groups and such respected organizations as Terre des Hommes, the (ironically named) Swiss-based international agency dedicated to the protection of children, repeatedly have urged a strengthening of this position to one condemning the practice outright.*

The situation is further complicated by the understandable suspicion on the part of many African and Arab governments and individuals that Western interest in the matter is motivated not by humanitarian concerns but by a racist or neocolonialist desire to eradicate indigenous cultures. In fact, as Jomo Kenyatta, Kenya's first president, noted in his book, *Facing Mount Kenya,* the key mobilization of many forces for Kenyan independence from the British was in direct response to attempts by Church of Scotland missionaries in 1929 to suppress clitoridectomy. Patriarchal authorities, whether tribal *or* imperial, have always considered as central to their freedom or power the right to define what is done with women. But past campaigns against female mutilation, conducted for whatever ambiguous or even deplorable reasons, need not preclude new approaches that might be more effective because they would be sensitive to the cultures involved and, most important, supportive of the *women* affected, and in response to *their* leadership.

Precisely such an initiative began in February, 1979, at a historic meeting in Khartoum, Sudan, attended by delegates (including physicians, midwives, and health officials) from 10 African and Arab nations, and supported by many who could not attend. Initiated by the WHO Regional Office for the Eastern Mediterranean with the assistance of the Sudanese Government, this meeting was cautiously called a seminar on "Traditional Practices Affecting the Health of Women and Children"—such practices as child marriage and nutritional taboos during

pregnancy and lactation, but also including genital mutilation. Four recommendations resulted:**

- Adoption of clear national policies for the abolition of "female circumcision."
- Establishment of national commissions to coordinate activities, including the enactment of abolition legislation.
- Intensification of general education on the dangers and undesirability of the practice.
- Intensification of education programs for birth attendants, midwives, healers, and other practitioners of traditional medicine, with a view to enlisting their support.

Later in 1979, a UN conference held in Lusaka, Zambia—one of the series of regional preparatory meetings for the UN's 1980 world conference for women—also dealt with the subject. Adopting a resolution sponsored by Edna Adan Ismail of Somalia, the meeting condemned female mutilation and called on all women's organizations *in the countries concerned* "to mobilize information and health education campaigns on the harmful medical and social consequences of the practices."

It is also true, however, that genital mutilation is not always cited as a priority by women in developing countries: starvation, general health, agricultural and industrial development may take precedence. Yet the Khartoum and Lusaka meetings showed clearly that many women—and men of conscience—throughout the African and Arab countries have for a long time been actively opposing clitoridectomy and infibulation. Such groups as the Voltaic Women's Federation and the Somali Women's Democratic Organization, and such individuals as Dr. Fatima Abdul Mahmoud, Minister of Social Affairs of the Sudan, Mehani Saleh of the Aden Ministry of Health, Awa Thiam of Senegal, and Esther Ogunmodede, the crusading journalist of Nigeria, have been campaigning in different ways against genital mutilation—and with little international support. In fact, according to Fran P. Hosken, a feminist who for years has been trying to mobilize American and international consciousness on this issue, "international and UN agencies, as well as charitable and church groups and family-

---

* In November, 1979, UNICEF's regional directors discussed the subject at length and for the first time, and "female excision"—also for the first time—was among the issues raised in a special report on women in the development process presented to UNICEF's executive board meeting in May, 1980.

** The Khartoum Report was forwarded to the Secretariat of the World Conference for the UN Decade for Women, which met in Copenhagen, July, 1980.

planning organizations working in Africa, have engaged in a 'conspiracy of silence.' . . . As a result, those Africans who are working for change in their own countries have been completely isolated or ignored."

Now, victims and witnesses are beginning to be heard as they speak personally about the suffering inflicted — whether in a village hut, a modern apartment, or a sterile operating room — by genital mutilation; suffering that may continue for a lifetime. Their voices are unforgettable. It's long past time that we heard them, and understood what is being done — to them, and to all of us. It's time that we began to act — *with* them, the most immediate victims, and in the shared interest of women as a people.

PART THREE

Sex-Based Inequality

INTRODUCTION

All known societies have *stratification systems;* that is, systems for categorizing and ranking individuals and groups in terms of the extent to which they possess characteristics that are highly valued by the society. Members can be differentiated either on the basis of *ascribed* characteristics (those that befall individuals regardless of their efforts; such as sex, race, age, and family background), or on the basis of *achieved* characteristics (those attained by individuals because of their own efforts; such as education, occupation, and marital status). However, no matter which criteria are used to evaluate people, social stratification functions to ensure that those persons with characteristics more highly valued by a particular society will be given superior access to whatever rewards and scarce resources the society has to offer; and, conversely, that those with less valued characteristics will be deprived of these advantages. Social stratification is, in essence, society's institutionalized pattern of social inequality.

When sex is a fundamental basis for social stratification – when the distribution of society's scarce goods and services is profoundly related to, if not determined by, whether one is male or female – then sex-based inequality exists. Most scholars agree that sex-based inequality is a fundamental and universal feature of all social life. Indeed, no society exists that does not assume that men and women are "different" in a variety of ways, and that it is these "differences" that account for and necessitate women's subordinate position in the society. True, considerable diversity can be found in the specific roles performed by men and women in various cultures throughout the world; however, in most societies the roles assigned to men, whatever they may be, are generally more highly valued than those assigned to women.

To understand how male domination is perpetuated and why it is so resistant to change, the readings up to now have focused primarily on the ways in which women and men are inducted into the stratification system at the *individual* level. We have seen how, through socialization, society's folklore, and the lessons taught by all its institutions, women and men are taught to know their place; in effect, to accept the legitimacy of their limited role options and the differentiated rewards attached to their performance. What we seek to examine in the forthcoming section are the *structural* bases of sex-based inequality. We shall be looking at the ways in which modern industrialized societies are constructed so as to create a social world which perpetuates male dominance and female subordination.

Like other forms of social inequality, sex-based inequality can generally be viewed as arising from an unequal distribution of rights to control three kinds of valued commodities; *power,* or the ability to carry out one's will despite opposition; *prestige,* or the ability to command respect, honor, and deference; and *wealth,* or economic and material compensation. Because these commodities—or rewards—are closely and reciprocally linked, sex-based inequality perpetuates itself through a kind of built-in feedback process. Quite obviously, those who are more highly situated are more likely to be in control of the distribution of these scarce rewards. Such control, in turn, further reinforces and heightens their dominance. In American society, as in other industrialized societies, power, prestige, and wealth belong to those who control the distribution of resources outside the home; that is, in the extradomestic institutions of work and politics. The assignment of *extradomestic* tasks to men and *domestic* tasks to women—or the ideology that "woman's place is in the home"—is, therefore, one of the primary means by which men have achieved and maintained greater dominance. When women enter the extradomestic arena, moreover, they are channeled into occupations that involve doing the "domestic" work of the society. In 1980, more than 50 percent of women held occupations that are consistent with prevailing American cultural definitions of "femininity," such as elementary school teacher, nurse, secretary, stenographer, bookkeeper, waitress, and household worker. These are jobs that do not confer the right to distribute scarce and valued goods and resources. To unravel the complex structural basis of sex-based inequality requires, then, that we examine the interplay between what scholars have traditionally called the private or domestic sphere, and the public or extradomestic sphere of social life.

In this section we shall illustrate how the structures of major institutions—work, politics, and family life—are formed and informed by the ideology of patriarchy and the practices of androcentrism. Furthermore, we shall see how these institutions are linked to one another in such a way that male superiority becomes in fact dependent upon female subordination. For example, the sexual division of labor in the traditional family benefits men because it gives them access to the non-salaried domestic services of women, such as cooking, cleaning, and child-rearing. This social arrangement, at the same time, weakens women's position in the labor force and provides justification for segregating or slotting women into low-paying, seasonal and "fringe" occupations with little opportunity for advancement. Occupational sex-segregation, in turn, functions not only to keep women dependent on men and marriage for economic support, but to ensure higher wages for men. In addition, by providing a class of easily exploitable female laborers, occupational sex-segregation increases profits—thereby serving the larger economic system of capitalism.

In short, we have reached the point in our analysis where we must take into account the full and awesome reality of the power of social institutions and the ways in which they are intricately interrelated to serve and to perpetuate the interests of the powerful. The subordination of women persists because those who control the distribution of resources perpetuate sex-based inequality in every sphere of social life. It is in their interest to do so.

Introduction: Explanations and Origins

Over the past decade, scholars have struggled to understand why sex-based stratification is so ubiquitous. Their explanations fall into two basic schools of thought: the *biogenetic* and the *biocultural*. The biogenetic argument holds that the behaviors of men and women are rooted in biological and genetic factors; such as the differences in hormonal patterns, physical size, intelligence, temperament, propensity to "bond" with members of the same sex, capacity to rear children, aggressiveness, capacity to lead, etc. Whether they view these differences as innate or as a natural outgrowth of human evolution, biogeneticists contend that sex-based inequality and the natural superiority of the male are inevitable, immutable, and necessary for the survival of the species. For the biogeneticist, the sexual division of labor in human societies is rooted, then, in the sexual determination to be found in all species; from ants to felines to deer to primates.

The second school of thought, the biocultural approach, bases its position on a growing body of historical and anthropological research that points to wide variations in gender-based behavior and in the sexual division of labor among different societies throughout time. Bioculturalists contend that the diversity of cultural adaptations to biological differences in the sexes is so great that biological determinants, such as heredity and species survival, do not sufficiently explain universal male dominance. They argue that one of the reasons that the superiority of males appears so inevitable is that in all types of societies—capitalist and communist, democratic and authoritarian, industrial and preindustrial—a cultural idea or belief has arisen to justify and to perpetuate sex-based stratification systems that entitle men to greater power, prestige and wealth. This ideology is patriarchalism. Why it arose in the first place is difficult to answer, but social scientists have long understood that it is common for groups to propagate beliefs that aggrandize themselves, and it is equally common for the subordinate group to accept the dominant group's definition as natural and inevitable. The important point is that ideas are culturally produced and, therefore, are always subject to revision. If, however, we are to refute the inevitability of male dominance, we must understand the structures through which it is perpetuated. The biocultural perspective holds that it is within the context of universal social stratification, or institutionalized social inequality, that sex-based inequality occurs and can be understood.

Lila Leibowitz in "'Universals' and Male Dominance Among Primates: A Critical Examination" looks at various assumptions of traditional primatology and the more recent ideas of sociobiology, and discusses how the actual social arrangements of primates, in fact, contradict the idea that there are "primatological" explanations for the relationships between men and women, including the division of labor.

While traditional social science theories of stratification generally link women's subordination to society's economic structure (paid labor), Nona Glazer's review essay "Housework" examines how gender differences in family roles contribute to the subordinate status of women. Glazer believes that it is the domestic division of labor which assigns women responsibility for housework that ensures and perpetuates male dominance. She concludes that in order to understand the structural basis of women's subordination we must examine women's position in the home as housewives, and the general disparagement of housework, as factors which are linked to and support the larger social and political economy of capitalism.

In the next article, "Compulsory Heterosexuality and Lesbian Existence," Adrienne Rich argues that one of the primary means of perpetuating male dominance is through what she conceptualizes as the social institution of heterosexuality. The purpose of Rich's analysis is not to argue that lesbian relationships are the only means by which women can resist male domination. Rather, Rich seeks to broaden our understanding of heterosexuality as a cultural ideology and social institution that not only perpetuates traditional gender roles for women but also proscribes and devalues all forms of female friendship and community.

The last reading in this section, "Stations and Spheres," is an excerpt from Jessie Bernard's book *The Female World*. It describes the impact, during the 19th century, of the emergent gender ideology of "separate but equal" on women's relationships with each other.

"Universals" and Male Dominance Among Primates: A Critical Examination

Lila Leibowitz

The genetic basis of behavioral traits is usually argued from the claim that a behavior pattern is universal or nearly universal within a species. The notion that among humans sex roles are very standardized and certain traits are universally those of one sex or the other is not a new one. Nor is the notion that such traits are genetically programmed or "instinctive" a new one. In fact, for the century or so that anthropologists have been investigating other cultures systematically, these two intertwined notions have been tested time and again. Much evidence has accumulated about some of the behaviors that were once considered part of the genetic heritage of one sex or the other, and, as a result, the hypotheses generally have been rejected because universals have not been found. Nevertheless, there are still a few anthropologists who see in the tremendously varied sex role assignments of men and women a pervasive pattern of male dominance, and some among them who regard what they perceive as male dominance to be biologically determined. The majority of social anthropologists, however, regard sex roles and statuses among humans as varied, learned, and the product of socioeconomic and cultural forces.

It is obvious to most students of other cultures that how labor is divided differs from one society or place to another. Who sews, or cooks, or hews wood, or draws water, or engages in market bargaining, or works in the fields, or produces the greater portion of subsistence foods are matters so varied as to defy simple sexual classifications. Societies also differ as to whether a biological mother is expected to nurse her infant or

assume the major burden of caring for it, a fact which seems to surprise many Westerners who themselves belong to a tradition in which wet nurses and nannies are not long a thing of the past. Societies differ as to whether all husbands are men (West African peoples do not regard maleness as a prerequisite for husbandness). Societies differ as to whether spouses of either sex or both are taken one at a time or several at once; whether they live together or not; and whether they work with and for each other or not. More important in a discussion of sex roles and "dominance," and the degree—if any—to which they are biologically determined, are the different ways resources are controlled in different societies.

Data collected over the last hundred years show that there are quite a few variations as to who is in charge of collecting and distributing ordinary and special foods even in simple foraging societies. When women of particular kin or class or caste groups in more complex societies are in the position to allocate land or work or other valued goods to other members of their society, we are directly confronted with the problem of analyzing what sorts of control women and men exercise over the things which give people the power to negotiate decisions. Are Iroquois women who withhold the special dried foods men need for a war party exercising control over the domestic or political arena?[1] Is their veto power over men's decisions a form of dominance? Cultural variables in the control of strategic resources indicate that power relationships among humans, inter- and intra-sexual, cannot be reduced to the simple notion of "dominance" nor to its presumed biological components. As we shall see, oversimplification and vagueness as to what is meant by "dominance" are significant factors in the revival of the argument that male dominance is universal among humans, and among primate species generally.

Interestingly, the revival of the argument that sex

Reprinted from Lila Leibowitz, "'Universals' and Male Dominance Among Primates: A Critical Examination," in *Pitfalls in Research on Sex and Gender,* ed. Ethel Tobach and Betty Rosoff, Genes and Gender Series, no. 2 (Staten Island, NY: Gordian Press, 1978), by permission of the publisher and author.

roles among humans are genetically programmed was stimulated by several scientists who do not specialize in studying human behavior but who did not regard this as a drawback for the purposes of producing popular books on animal behavior and human evolution and behavior.[2] Nonscientists and social scientists then hastened to get in on their act and benefit from the rich market they uncovered among Americans.[3] After questions were raised about the scientific validity, political bias and sexist prejudice of these popularized books, the argument was moved into the arena of "serious" scientific scholarship with the publication in 1975 of E. O. Wilson's *Sociobiology,*[4] a text that received the prepublication treatment usually reserved for more readable books designed to reach general audiences.

In a major work intended to lay the scholarly foundation for a "new" and innovative *science* of social behavior that he predicts will soon replace the softness of sociology and anthropology with the hardness of more rigorous biological subdisciplines, E. O. Wilson, a noted authority on social insects, states that "aggressive dominance systems with males generally dominant over females"[5] are characteristic of the order Primates, the taxonomic order which includes monkeys, apes and humans. Coming as it does from a highly prestigious biologist in a text that addresses the issue of the evolution of social behavior, this statement has implications which are unavoidable for the conscientious student of human societies and cultures. If true, it implies that the observed range of human behavioral variability is either a departure from, or a conquest of, pre- or protohuman behavioral patterns, programs or predispositions. An important question, then, is, "Is this statement true?"

There are two ways in which I will address the question of the validity of the proposal that dominance systems and male dominance over females characterize primate social behavior. First, I will examine whether the statement represents an accurate generalization drawn from the evidence which its author cites to support it. Secondly, I will examine the concept of "dominance" on which this author's analysis is built and which allows him to underwrite "scientifically" the notion that male dominance among humans is universal, biologically determined and hence difficult to overcome at best.

The text in which the above statement appears provides extended descriptions of the social arrangements of a number of primate species. The social arrangements that are described not only fail to justify the claim of widespread or near universal male dominance but are also

somewhat confusing. Let me summarize some of the problems a reader encounters with regard to these descriptions.[6]

The mouse lemur is characterized as "an essentially solitary animal," although, we discover, mouse lemur females nest in groups. Evidently it is the *males* that are solitary. Whom or what they dominate in their solitary state is not clear. It appears that female nest groups are made up of mothers and daughters and their young who "displace" sons and brothers. "Dominant" males are characterized as those who manage to breed. Dominant males sometimes join females in their nests when the females are in estrus. Several males may join a nest when the females have passed out of estrus. The author notes, "the males evidently become more tolerant toward one another." Yet, who is becoming tolerant of whom is perhaps debatable, since all males usually are displaced to the outskirts of favored habitats.

Orangutans, the next species described, are designated as maintaining "nuclear groups," which consist of females and their young—occasionally accompanied by a usually solitary male. (In fact, the term matri-centered group seems more appropriate than "nuclear group" in this context, since the term nuclear family is used to describe the male/female/young family form among humans. But that's not the main issue just yet.) The author notes that "aggression within the society is quite rare, and nothing resembling a dominance system has been established in studies to date." Wilson cites a single instance of a female driving another female from a tree as the only clear episode of open hostility reported by observers. However, he states that males "probably do repel one another" because "a few pieces of indirect evidence suggest that such intrasexual conflict does exist." That indirect evidence consists of the fact that male orangutans are much larger than females and have vocal pouches that make their calls extremely loud. By reading from morphology to behavior, the author presumes that large noisy males win out in "intrasexual conflicts" over females, though open conflicts between males were not observed. Reading from morphology to behavior is a dangerous business, it turns out. Early on in the description of orangutans we find the statement, "As the orangs' unusual body form testifies, they are exclusively arboreal." Recent observers have learned, "The orangutan, studied in a rain forest in Indonesian Borneo, is not a tree dweller, contrary to popular belief, but does almost 100 percent of its long-distance traveling on the ground."[7] Indirect evidence of body form probably tells us very little about the nature of intrasexual conflict between males, and certainly tells us even less about whether the normally solitary males are "generally dominant over females" with whom they rarely associate.

The dusky titis of the Amazon-Orinoco region and the white-handed gibbons of Malaya and Sumatra are next discussed in sequence. Dusky titis live in small groups which consist of a female, her young and a male. These mated pairs and their young are referred to as "one of the simplest familial forms of society." The titis, it is noted, share this societal form with, among others, the white-handed gibbons whose social arrangement is described as "identical to family." In the gibbon pair "the female plays an equal role in territorial defense and in precoital sexual behavior," though it is especially, though not always, the female who emits territorial calls. While "the mother takes care of the infant . . ." a lone gibbon male who allowed a small juvenile to adopt him and thereafter "carried the smaller animal in the maternal position during much of the day," indicates that, "the male is also prepared to assume the role of the mother when she falls ill or dies."

Though it is tempting to regard the parenting capacities and pair mating arrangements of titis and gibbons in terms of the particular nuclear family form Americans have recently come to idealize, the extension of the term to nonhuman mating and nurturing arrangements violates the common practice of ethologists. It is important to note that in Wilson's descriptions the term is used with reference to a form of animal grouping which resembles only one of the many kinds of groupings that are called "family" in human societies.[8] The use of the term "family" when referring to pair bond arrangements among nonhuman primates implies a biological basis for a familiar human social convention.

The mantled howlers who are described next are "of special sociobiological interest because a high level of individual tolerance permits the formation of large multi-male societies." In addition, it is noted, they exhibit "the *unusual* circumstance of a species that appears to alternate between multimale and unimale organization and even has solitary males." The variability of howler social arrangements is clearly acknowledged. Conflict within troops is uncommon and almost never entails fighting. Not too surprisingly we learn that in this species dominance orders are "weakly defined." Despite extensive observations by the seven researchers cited, "It has not yet been established whether the troops are age-graded-male, with one dominant individual controlling younger animals, or whether the troops contain multiple high-ranking males." The possibility that there might be no hierarchy is not entertained. No mention is made in the description of behaviors that indicate that males are "dominant over females." The author simply assumes that in species where males are larger than females, as is the case among mantled howlers, the males must be dominant over the females. (The dangers of reading from morphology to behavior have already been pointed out.)

Ring-tailed lemurs also live in troops in which "fighting is rare." Yet their society is regarded as "aggressively organized." More notably we find that "adult females are dominant over males," which is "a reversal of an otherwise nearly universal primate pattern." While a linear hierarchy is observed among ring-tailed males, Wilson considers it "odd" that dominance in this hierarchy "seems to have no influence on access to estrous females." (Note that in the mouse lemur which is "solitary" and lacks a male hierarchy, "dominance" is attributed to males who have access to estrous females.)

It is hard to see on what grounds the claim for male dominance as a nearly universal primate pattern is being made, since up to this point in the argument Wilson has cited social organizations in which females seem to exclude males, social organizations in which males may or may not fight with each other, and social organizations which may or may not have male hierarchies, while no social organizations in which males determine or control female behavior have been described.

The other three primate species discussed in some detail are the hamadryas baboons, Eastern mountain gorillas, and chimpanzees. All three are treated as giving evidence of "male dominance," although consistent criteria of dominance are not established. The hamadryas males of the small "single-male" units found in Ethiopia, herd and nip at females, effectively determining what the females will do. Among the peaceful gorillas who live in multimale groups, "most dominance interactions consist of a mere acknowledgment of precedence," which is to say that an animal, male or female, who gives up space to another is regarded as subdominant. In loosely-structured groups of chimpanzees we are told that "dominance behavior is well developed." Yet dominance behavior usually involves interactions which are "subtle," again usually just giving way. "Overt threats and retreats are uncommon." Among chimpanzees we once again find that "*curiously* . . . (my emphasis) the dominance system appears to have no influence on access to females," who appear to solicit whom they please when they please. An estrous female who stopped grooming a dominant male to copulate with a subadult male exemplifies the situation.

Wilson's evidence to support the view that male dominance is universal among *all primates* is furthered with his description of the following human situation.

> *Within a small tribe of Kung bushmen can be found individuals who are acknowledged as the 'best people;' the leaders and outstanding specialists among the hunters and healers. Even with an emphasis on sharing goods, some are exceptionally able entrepreneurs and unostentatiously acquire a certain amount of wealth. Kung men no less than men in advanced industrial societies generally establish themselves by their mid-thirties or else accept a lesser status for life. There are some who never try to make it, live in rundown huts and show little pride in themselves and their work.*[9]

To set the record straight, the Kung are not tribal.[10] They live in camps of transient populations,[11] accumulate as little as possible to allow movement from camp to camp, and exchange and circulate materials and tools as well as food.[12] Camps include huts that are built — by the women, incidentally — at different times.[13] Leadership is ephemeral and task oriented, depending on who is in the camp and what has to be done.[14] There are no specialists other than shamans, some of whom are women.[15] The Kung have only recently become articulated with an entrepreneurial market economy, have no native category of "best people," and until recently, that is to say the past decade, discouraged competitiveness and pride.[16]

As we look over the evidence that's offered, it becomes pretty clear that the generalization that primate males are usually dominant over females is arrived at by treating a minority of the species described as evolutionarily important and the majority of them as unimportant. No statistical survey of the admittedly incomplete data on nonhuman primates is presented, although a series of tables summarizing some of the data on nonhuman primate social organization is offered. How reliable that data is with respect to "dominance" is another question, for clearly, there is considerable ambiguity and inconsistency just in the way the term itself is used.

Before examining the concept of dominance closely, however, let me point out that the order in which Wilson describes the social arrangements of the primates reflects his evolutionary model of "grades of sociality." Wilson explicitly rejects evolutionary models of behavior which stress either the biological relationships between primate species or focus on primate social organizational patterns as responses to ecological circumstances. Wilson's model is built on the notion that social evolution among primates involves a development from no-male, to one-male to multimale groups, but more significantly he assumes that social relationships evolve around males and male behaviors. Increases in male-to-male tolerance are at the heart of group development. That males are usually dominant over females in the no-male, one-male and multimale situations alike is expressly stated, although we've seen that this is not clearly the case. Furthermore, Wilson's notions about one-male–multimale groups are fuzzy; for example, one-male hamadryas groups are not truly comparable to the one-male groups of patas monkeys where the member male is peripheral both socially and in space.[17] Males are emphasized as central in evolution because it is commonly assumed that while all females usually have infants, not all males have the same chance to breed. The idea that "dominant" males father more offspring than subdominant ones is so pervasive that it is said to be "odd" or "curious" when evidence to the contrary is found. Yet there is no doubt "dominant" males don't have special sexual prerogatives in many, and perhaps most, species other than those Wilson regards as "curious" and "odd" (e.g., gorillas,[18] Japanese macaques,[19] cynocephalous baboons in forested areas,[20] chimps and others). Newer field studies clearly show that in many primates and in many situations social dominance is no guarantee of success with the ladies. That the text ignores such data and rejects the examination of how primate social patterns are related to ecological settings and/or vary within species, reflect the author's underlying premise that social behavior and social arrangements are genetically determined. Wilson's model of "grades of sociality" thus disregards evidence which suggests that there is an evolutionary trajectory involving increased reliance on learned and socially-transmitted behaviors in the primate order and makes more of the ill-defined notion of "dominance" than the data warrant.

To return to the uses and meaning of the term "dominance," the most thorough discussion of the concept of "dominance" and of primate behavior and social organization I have seen is that of Thelma Rowell.[21] Her review of the literature shows that whereas hierarchy and dominance-subordinance relationships have been considered the most important aspects of social behavior in animal groups, these concepts have been casually handled. Rarely have objective descriptions of social interactions been attached to statements about dominance, and predigested generalized observations make it impossible to compare studies by different observers who do not state how they define and interpret the phenomenon. Despite this obvious difficulty there is widespread agreement that hierarchical relationships occur frequently among caged animals and are less clearly discernible or absent in non-caged groups of animals. (The reasons for hierarchy in caged groups are complex. Such things as where food is placed, whether the animals were originally strange to each other, the age and prior experiences of the animals, and the nature of first encounters — all play a part in the formation and maintenance of hierarchies.) Studies which attempt to unravel the complex of factors usually associated with dominance have, therefore, been made on caged animals.

In a 1970 paper I. S. Bernstein[22] identified three dominance-related behaviors: aggression, mounting, and being groomed. For the study six species of monkeys were observed in groups living in large enclosures. Five of the six groups showed stable hierarchical relationships over several months with respect to the patterning of aggressive or agonistic encounters. In the sixth, a group of guenons, animals reversed their relationships several times during a year. Mounting relationships, and the hierarchies based on them, proved less stable than aggression hierarchies in all six species, and grooming relationships proved to be nondirectional and reciprocal. Bernstein found no correlation between the hierarchies obtained from the three kinds of relationships and concluded that they were not determined by a single social mechanism, were independent of one another, and not necessarily determined the same way in each of the groups observed. In a later study Bernstein and his associates[23] attempted to correlate aggressiveness and testosterone levels in an all-male group of rhesus monkeys and discovered that very high-ranking males — those who easily displaced all others — were neither very aggressive nor high in testosterone. A general correlation between aggressiveness and testosterone level, however, was found in lower-ranking males, who were under constant stress, leading Bernstein *et al.* to suggest that output of the hormone is determined by an animal's behavioral context, since the lowest-ranking socially active males in this study had higher testosterone levels than males living in isolation. A key issue in the dominance-aggression-hierarchy equation appears to be stress.

Rowell examines the possibility that what is often discussed as "dominance" behavior is in reality "subordinance" behavior. Ultimately, she notes, the outcome of approach-retreat interactions are decided by the behavior of the potential retreater. Animals under stress tend to avoid interactions which may have unpredictable or negative results and hesitate to initiate them. Secure animals are far less cautious. Researchers tend to attribute high rank to those who approach others, whether or not they do so in an "aggressive" or agonistic manner, especially if they displace an animal which is avoiding them. Cages induce both high levels of stress and high interaction rates which may be why dominance is so evident in the caged setting and why in these circumstances hierarchies become stabilized. In any event, "agonistic" hierarchies do not coincide with grooming or mounting hierarchies.

Rowell finds there are several reasons for asking whether the concept of dominance is a useful one in discussing the evolution of primate social behavior: 1) "Dominance hierarchies" are not consistent when determined for different types of behavior, so that the "top" animal is not the same in all situations. 2) Among primates group behavior is rarely determined by coercion, so that a "top" animal does not in fact lead or control the group. 3) Dominance has not been correlated with food-finding abilities or with danger avoidance; therefore, one cannot assume that dominance leads to significant survival advantages. 4) Dominance by some may be an expression of the subordinance of others, which results from stress. Thus it is either an ephemeral or a long-lived result of situational settings rather than an independent trait, much less a genetically determined one. 5) The males who mate are by no means always dominant. Furthermore, although Rowell does not directly address the issue of whether male dominance is universal or nearly universal among primates, it is relevant that among monkeys she finds significant variations regarding the sex of those who constitute the core of particular social groups.

Jane Lancaster[24] also has recorded some interesting observations that raise yet other questions about what is meant by male dominance. Her work on vervet monkeys shows that coalitions of females were easily formed against the top three males of the group she studied. If these offended some females by trying to monopolize a food source or by frightening an infant, even females of the lowest rank would band together to chase them. While a male's rank never changed as a result of such an encounter, his ability to bully others was curbed, and he learned to be very careful about frightening an infant. Several times Lancaster saw all the nearby adult males leave the vicinity when an infant screamed. Though they in fact were not what had frightened the infant, their behavior clearly revealed their anxiety that the females would form a coalition, directed against them.

It is hardly necessary to point out that Wilson's use of the term dominance as applied to primate societies reflects few of the caveats and cautions Rowell and Lancaster express about the behaviors subsumed under the notion of dominance. Furthermore, it is self-evident that he uses the term inconsistently: a male who breeds more than other males is defined as dominant on the basis of his breeding activities in a "solitary" species, yet in a more social arrangement a male who stands at the apex of a displacement hierarchy is called dominant though he does not breed more than other males. Such inconsistencies—as well as the inaccuracies—in the use of a term do not inspire much confidence in Wilson's claim that one of sociobiology's virtues is that it will introduce behavioral and social scientists to the analytic vigorousness of biology.

It is eminently clear that the recent contention that male dominance is universal or nearly universal among primates is unfounded. All it is is a new version of one of many pseudo-biological arguments that are used to justify social arrangements in our society. By claiming that these arrangements are found in our animal relatives, it suggests that these arrangements are the result of our genetic heritage. Now, as always, some researchers are trying to explain social traits among humans by attributing them to our innate biology. For the most part, however, such traits are no longer regarded as universal. Instead of talking about "instinctive, universal traits," researchers have been forced to talk about predilections or potentials for frequent or nearly universal traits. They therefore use vague notions such as "programmed potential" and "perceptual predisposition" to justify the conclusion that such traits are genetically determined. But like its other deterministic antecedents, this device ignores the history of changing human societies; just as it ignores the variety and variability of monkeys, it also ignores the fact that the *alternatives* to such frequent or nearly universal traits are also part of our human potential, and that "predispositions," "propensities" and "potentials" are developed in the contexts that favor them. The device of looking upon "near universals" as though they were therefore genetic seems to be a new way of minimizing the need for analyzing the social contexts in which traits have developed. This is particularly insidious if these traits reflect social privileges for some people, and result from the unequal distribution of social privileges among the different social classes, races or the sexes. Incorrectly attributing to primates in general, the male dominance which is nurtured

and relished in our own society is not science; it is political propaganda.

Endnotes

1. M. Kay Martin and Barbara Voorhies, *The Female of the Species* (New York: Columbia U. Press), 1975, pp. 225–227.
2. See, for instance, Konrad Lorenz, *On Aggression* (New York: Harcourt, Brace and World), 1966, or Desmond Morris, *The Naked Ape* (New York: McGraw-Hill), 1968.
3. Nonsocial scientist, Robert Ardrey, published *The Territorial Imperative* (New York: Atheneum) in 1966, his *African Genesis* (London: Collins) had appeared in 1961. Lionel Tiger's *Men in Groups* (New York: Vintage Books), 1920, was one of the first of the popular books by a social scientist to exploit this market.
4. E. O. Wilson, *Sociobiology: The New Synthesis* (Cambridge: The Belknap Press of Harvard University Press), 1975.
5. Ibid., p. 551.
6. In the next few paragraphs of this paper a number of words, phrases and sentences are cited verbatim from the above text. Rather than providing the reader with a long list of "Ibids" and page references, I am noting here that these citations come from pages 514–546, a chapter entitled "The Nonhuman Primates."
7. *Science News,* Vol. 113, No. 12, 1978, p. 178.
8. Lila Leibowitz, *Females, Males, Families: A Biosocial Approach* (North Scituate, MA: Duxbury Press), 1978, pp. 6–9.
9. Wilson, 1975, p. 549.
10. R. B. Lee, "The Kung Bushman of Botswana," in *Hunters and Gatherers Today,* ed., M. Bicchieri (New York: Holt, Rinehart and Winston, 1972.)
11. R. B. Lee, "What Hunters Do for a Living, or, How To Make Out on Scarce Resources," in *Man the Hunter,* eds., R. B. Lee and I. DeVore. (Chicago: Aldine, 1968.)
12. L. Marshall, "Sharing, Talking and Growing; Relief of Social Tensions among Kung Bushman of the Kalahari," *Africa,* Vol. 31, 1961.
13. F. Plog, C. J. Jolly and D. G. Bates, *Anthropology: Decisions, Adaptations and Evolution.* (New York: Alfred A. Knopf, 1976), p. 486.
14. Plog, Jolly and Bates, *Anthropology,* 1976, p. 425.
15. R. B. Lee, Personal Communication.
16. R. B. Lee, "Eating Christmas in the Kalahari," *Natural History,* Vol. 77, No. 10 (Dec.), 1969, pp. 14–19.
17. Thelma Rowell, *The Social Behavior of Monkeys*

(Harmondsworth, England: Penguin Books, Inc.), 1972, p. 63.

18. George B. Schaller, *The Mountain Gorilla: Ecology and Behavior* (Chicago: University of Chicago Press), 1963.

19. G. Gray Eaton, "The Social Order of Japanese Macaques," *Scientific American,* October, 1976, Vol. 235, No. 4, pp. 96–107.

20. Rowell, op. cit., pp. 46–66.

21. Ibid., pp. 159–164.

22. I. S. Bernstein, "Primate Status Hierarchies" in L. A. Rosenblum (ed.) *Primate Behavior,* Academic Press, 1970. Cited in Rowell, pp. 161–162.

23. R. M. Rose, J. W. Holaday and I. S. Bernstein, "Plasma Testosterone, Dominance Rank, and Aggressive Behavior in Male Rhesus Monkeys." *Nature,* Vol. 231, pp. 366–71. Cited in Rowell.

24. Jane B. Lancaster, *Primate Behavior and the Emergence of Human Culture* (New York: Holt, Rinehart and Winston), 1975.

READING 49

Housework

Nona Glazer

That the work of women has been generally ignored by social scientists is hardly a matter for wonder, when even those men dedicated to changing the roles of the sexes appear to have more trouble sustaining a conversation about "women's work" than about any other topic, including homosexuality and impotency.[1] I do not mean paid work in the labor force, which has received some attention, but the nitty-gritty of cleaning, scrubbing, grocery shopping, clothing care—the work which has been glorified as the creative responsibility of the good woman or harshly and simply judged as "shitwork."[2] Not only men, but women also—feminists because housework is *traditionally* women's work, nonfeminists because it is *only* women's work—slight the study of housework. Early in the century, when women first became interested in the scientific analysis of housework, it was (ironically, as Carol Lopate notes)[3] to rationalize the job and prepare women better to carry out their responsibilities. Taylorism, not Marxism, was the ideology.

Reprinted from Nona Y. Glazer, "Housework," in *Signs* 1 (1976): pp. 905–922, by permission of the publisher, The University of Chicago Press, and the author.

1. Warren Farrell, "Changing Men's Roles" (lecture given at Lewis and Clark College, Portland, Oreg., March 8, 1975).

2. Pat Mainardi, "The Politics of Housework," in *Woman in a Man-made World,* ed. Nona Glazer-Malbin and Helen Y. Waehrer (Chicago: Rand-McNally College Publishing Co., 1972), pp. 289–92, esp. p. 291.

3. Carol Lopate, "The Irony of the Home Economics Movement," *EdCentric: A Journal of Educational Change* 31-32 (November 1974): 40–42, 56–57. Only occasionally have sociologists looked at housework and housewives before the last several years. See Hazel Kyrk, *The Family in the American Economy* (Chicago: University of Chicago Press, 1953); and Jessie Bernard, *American Community Behavior* (New York: Henry Holt & Co., 1949). Jessie Bernard was kind enough to provide me with materials from the earlier edition of her book, since these were deleted from the revised edition (1962). The classic statement on housework is by Charlotte Perkins Gilman in *The Home: Its Work and Influence* (1903; reprint ed., Urbana: University of Illinois Press, 1972).

The invisibility of women in scholarship has evoked a good deal of commentary in recent years, but hardly anywhere has sociological acumen failed as embarrassingly as in its inability to recognize women's work — housework — as work. Ann Oakley, in her book *The Sociology of Housework,* summarizes the underlying sociological axioms which support the invisibility of women's work: (1) women belong in the family, while men belong "at work"; (2) therefore men work, while women do not work; (3) therefore housework is not a form of work.[4] Several other axioms should be added to these: (4) monetary and social rights belong to those who work — to those who are economically productive; (5) women do not work but are parasitic; (6) therefore women are not entitled to the same social and economic rights as men. Thus the invisibility of their work provides a rationale for women's second-class status in both public and private domains.

Recently, however, the study of women's work, of women as housewives, has begun to capture the attention of scholars. Recent scholarship, whether or not directed initially by feminists, centers on a discernible set of issues, each of which I shall consider: the monetary value of housework to the family and as an estimated contribution to the gross national product,[5] the social role of housewife,[6] and the integration of housework into an analysis of the organization of capitalism (with an acceptance of capitalism or from a critical perspective).[7] An issue which can be considered prefeminist (or even an antifeminist conception) is an earlier oblique approach to the subject via a study of the division of labor in the wife-husband relationship.[8] Regardless of its implicit sexism, this approach has produced some interesting data as well as some examples of what not to do. I will begin my review with some comments on this earlier research before considering the newer approaches.

Housework as the Division of Labor

Beginning with the Blood and Wolfe studies of the wife-husband relationship in the mid-1950s, sociologists have studied housework because of a concern with the effects of a wife's working outside the home,[9] with the availability of kinship networks,[10] and with the marital division of

---

4. Ann Oakley, *The Sociology of Housework* (New York: Pantheon Books, 1974), p. 9.

5. Wendyce H. Brody, "Economic Value of a Housewife," *Research and Statistics Note,* no. 9 (August 1975), pp. 1–5; Reuben Gronau, "The Measurement of Output of the Nonmarket Sector: The Evaluation of Housewives' Time," in *The Measurement of Economic and Social Performance,* ed. National Bureau of Economic Research (New York: National Bureau of Economic Research, 1973), pp. 163–90; Chong Soo Pyun, "The Monetary Value of a Housewife," in Glazer-Malbin and Waehrer, pp. 187–93; Kathryn E. Walker and William H. Gauger, *The Dollar Value of Household Work,* Cornell University Information Bulletin no. 60 (Ithaca, N.Y.: Cornell University, 1973); and Maurice Weinrobe, "Household Production and National Production: An Improvement of the Record," *Review of Income and Wealth,* ser. 20, no. 1 (March 1974): 89–102.

6. Helena Z. Lopata, *Occupation: Housewife* (New York: Oxford University Press, 1971): Oakley, *The Sociology of Housework;* Ann Oakley, *Woman's Work: A History of the Housewife* (New York: Pantheon Books, 1974). An earlier study is by Hannah Gavron, *The Captive Wife* (London: Routledge & Kegan Paul, 1966). Several pertinent studies are excluded from this review because their data are not yet available. Melvin Kohn, chief, Laboratory of Socio-Environmental Studies, National Institute of Mental Health, Washington, D.C., is currently analyzing data on housewives; Helena Z. Lopata, director,

Loyola University Center for the Comparative Study of Social Roles, Chicago, is just beginning a nationwide study of women's commitments to family and work, including housewives' commitment to their work. John Robinson of the University of Michigan Institute for Social Research has time-use data for 1974 on a representative cross section of Americans for husbands' participation in child care and household jobs. A group in the Northwestern University Sociology Department is studying the division of labor in the home in some detail, using a technique of time budgets. See Sarah Fenstermaker Berk and Catherine White Berheide, "Going Backstage: Gaining Access to Observe Household Work" (paper delivered at the Midwest Sociological meeting, Chicago, Ill., April 1975).

7. For an acceptance of capitalism, see John Kenneth Galbraith, *Economics and the Public Purpose* (Boston: Houghton Mifflin Co., 1973). The relevant writings from a critical perspective will be cited later in the review.

8. E.g., Robert O. Blood, Jr., and Donald Wolfe, *Husbands and Wives* (Glencoe, Ill.: Free Press, 1960); Elizabeth Bott, *Family and Social Network* (London: Tavistock Publications, 1957); and John P. Robinson, Philip E. Converse, and Alexander Szalai, "Everyday Life in Twelve Countries," in *The Use of Time,* ed. Alexander Szalai (The Hague: Mouton & Co., 1972).

9. For a discussion, see Rochelle Paul Wortis, "The Acceptance of the Concept of the Maternal Role by Behavioral Scientists: Its Effect on Women," in *Intimacy, Family, and Society,* ed. Arlene Skolnick and Jerome H. Skolnick (Boston: Little, Brown & Co., 1974), pp. 360–76. For a recent review of the division of labor which illustrates the conceptualization as focused on the marital relationship, see Stephen J. Bahr, "Effects on Power and the Division of Labor in the Family," in *Working Mothers,* ed. Lois Wladis Hoffman and F. Ivan Nye (San Francisco: Jossey-Bass, Inc., 1975), p. 167–85.

10. E.g., Bott; and D. M. Toomey, "Conjugal Roles and Social Networks in an Urban Working Class Sample," *Human Relations* 24, no. 5 (1971): 417–32.

labor. The main theoretical perspective used to explain the division of labor—the wife's responsibility for "feminine tasks" and the husband's responsibility for "masculine tasks"—is an assumed "rational imperative" (based, of course, on the biological differences between the sexes). Hence Blood and Wolfe write, "To a considerable extent, the idea of shared work is incompatible with the most efficient division of labor. Much of the progress of our modern economy rests upon the increasing specialization of its division of labor."[11]

This questionable theoretical framework is complemented by methodological difficulties. Studies usually have been based on the responses of wives, rather than of both spouses;[12] and the components of housework are usually left undefined, so that it is not possible to assess accurately what doing *housework* means. Are the components of grocery shopping such as a review of newspaper ads, making up a shopping list, purchasing the groceries, bringing them into the kitchen, putting away the purchases while removing uneatables from the refrigerator and empty containers from the cupboards undertaken equally by members of both sexes?[13] We do not know. In addition, some researchers have collected time-budget data, but most have relied on nonnumerical estimates of the extent of task responsibility of each mate.

A frequent interpretation of the findings of such studies is that there has been a shift toward greater participation by husbands in household tasks over the last decades and that the shift occurs in response to a wife's being in the labor force.[14] However, others conclude that the shift has been greatly exaggerated—that husbands of employed wives do very little housework, compared with their wives, and that the amount of housework done by such husbands is similar to the amount done by husbands of unemployed wives.[15]

The Monetary Value of Housework

Only the low status of women and the disparagement of housework can explain why economists have found estimating the contribution of housework to economic well-being an "insoluble problem." (In contrast, economists have proved capable of solving a similar problem, that of calculating the value of real estate occupied by owners in what was otherwise commercial property.) Theoretically, there is no justification for the exclusion of an estimated monetary value of housework by neoclassical or institutional economists for whom housework has economic utility.[16] Moreover, some economists have puzzled over the paradox (raised by Professor Pigou) that a reduction in national product would occur if a number of men decided to marry their housekeepers without any reduction occurring in actual work performed. Colin Clark calculated the estimated annual value of housework at £494 per capita in the United Kingdom for 1871 (1956 prices) and £570 per capita in 1956.[17] That housework is no minor contribution to economic well-being is shown in Clark's estimate that, if some wealthy person had paid the costs for all the housework of every family in Great Britain in 1871 at a rate earned by domestics in 1956, "the real income so earned would have exceeded the entire real income so earned in all other employment put together."[18]

In contrast to the reasons above, Marxist economists have a theoretical reason for not considering housework in estimates of national wealth, reasons which have led socialist economists in eastern Europe to exclude the value of all personal services, whether paid or unpaid, from their estimates of gross national product.[19] This issue will be discussed later in the review.

11. Blood and Wolfe, p. 48.
12. E.g., Constantina Safilios-Rothschild, "Family Sociology or Wives' Family Sociology?" *Journal of Marriage and the Family* 31 (May 1969): 290–301.
13. The concept of the division of labor is critiqued and extended in Nona Glazer-Malbin, "The Division of Labor in the Wife-Husband Relationship" (paper prepared for the Ford Foundation/Merrill-Palmer Institute Conference on Sex Roles and the Family, Detroit, Mich., November 10–12, 1975; and forthcoming in a volume edited by Constantina Safilios-Rothschild).
14. E.g., Bahr, pp. 181–84.
15. The Walker and Gauger study (n. 5 above) of 1,400 families in the Syracuse, N.Y., area shows that husband time for all families averaged 1.5 hours a day. Husbands with either employed or unemployed wives averaged more housework time when there was a baby in the home. Walker and Gauger con-

clude that husbands do *not* increase their work contribution if their wives are employed (p. 5). See also Glazer-Malbin; Joseph H. Pleck, "Men's Roles in the Family: A New Look" (paper prepared for the Ford Foundation/Merrill-Palmer Institute Conference on Sex Roles and the Family, Detroit, November 10–12, 1975; and forthcoming in a volume edited by Constantina Safilios-Rothschild); and Oakley, *Sociology of Housework,* pp. 161–65, for three statements about the exaggeration of men's housework contribution.
16. William H. Gauger, "Household Work: Can We Add It to G.N.P.?" *Journal of Home Economics* 65, no. 7 (October 1973): 12–15. Gauger noted that in the 1890s both Richard Ely and Alfred J. Marshall commented on the social utility of nonmarket labor.
17. Colin Clark, "The Economics of House-Work," *Institute of Statistics Bulletin* 20 (May 1958):209.
18. Ibid., p. 211.
19. Ibid., p. 205.

Having overlooked the time-budget studies of the 1920s for nearly forty years, economists in the United States have recently begun to calculate the estimated monetary value of housework because of demands by men.[20] A number of court suits over the loss of wives' services prompted American economists to overcome the so-called weighty problems of gathering data on the time women use to do housework and estimating the monetary value of their work. However, while the impetus for calculation came from such legal disputes, economists now examine these issues quite apart from the problem of legal equity. There are varying estimates for the monetary value of the American housewife in different years, depending on the bases for computation (e.g., age, education of the housewife and use of going-wage rates and of a discount factor): $8,200 for 1968,[21] $4,705 for 1972,[22] $13,364 for 1973.[23] Furthermore, detailed calculations computed by Kathryn Walker and William Gauger, according to the wife's employment status (and her age) and the number of children in the family (and the age of the youngest), are available based on a large sample of families in upstate New York.[24]

These estimates of a housewife's monetary value may comfort those who believe that women as housewives have been ignored and that housewives' services are as important to the national economy as they are to the individual family. However, the models used in the computation of costs (e.g., the cost of a woman leaving the labor force to care for a child) have been criticized by John Kenneth Galbraith as being aggregate-choice models, which are of limited use since they avoid consideration of individual choice by collapsing all family members into the category "household."[25] (The unit is identical to that used in the conventional sociological approach to social stratification, which, by considering the "family" to be the basic unit in the system, evades considering the individual status-creating resources of a wife; this includes ignoring the possible effect on her status-creating resources of leaving the labor force to be a housewife—evident when she returns some years later with visibly diminished earning power.)[26] In the economist's model,[27] the cost of a woman's foregoing employment to do housework is seen as affecting only her family, rather than having a potential effect also on her: for example, her willingness to remain out of the labor force and lose her employability, as when a licensed nurse forfeits her right to practice in Oregon after not being employed for five years.

The Inevitability of Domesticity

Cross-cultural data suggest that women are not inevitably domestic, responsible for housework as well as child care and excluded from power and authority. The data suggest that the cultures examined by Margaret Mead[28] and often dismissed as "exceptions" are not so rare. The scholarly works discussed here are especially welcome as cautious analyses of the twentieth-century view of women: the "man to the hunt, woman to the hearth" mythology which has dominated sociological thought. Beginning with the statements by Judith K. Brown (about women)[29] and Sharlotte N. Williams (about primates),[30] anthropologists increasingly question the universal-domestication theme. Peggy Sanday analyzes women's roles and women's status in twelve societies, contrasting those societies in which women's status in the public domain is high with those in which it is low—pointing out that it is possible to do such research *because* there are societies in which women have attained high status in the

20. Joann Vanek, "Time Spent in Housework," *Scientific American* 231, no. 5 (November 1974): 116–20. See also Hildegarde Kneeland, "Women's Economic Contribution in the Home," *American Academy of Political and Social Science, Annals* 143 (May 1929): 33–40; Maud Wilson, *Use of Time by Oregon Farm Homemakers,* Oregon Agricultural Experiment Station Bulletin no. 256 (Corvallis, Oreg., November 1929); and M. Ruth Clark and Greta Gray, *The Routine and Seasonal Work of Nebraska Farm Women,* University of Nebraska College of Agriculture Experiment Station Bulletin no. 238 (Lincoln, Nebr., January 1930).
21. Pyun, p. 192.
22. Brody, p. 5.
23. Galbraith, p. 33.
24. N. 5 above.
25. Galbraith, pp. 34–36. For an example of such a model, see Gronau.

26. Joan Acker, "Women and Social Stratification: A Case of Intellectual Sexism," *American Journal of Sociology* 78 (January 1973): 936–45.
27. E.g., Gronau. See Nona Glazer-Malbin, "The Invisible Worker: Implications for Social Stratification and Family Functions" (manuscript, September 1975).
28. Margaret Mead, *Male and Female: A Study of the Sexes in a Changing World* (New York: William Morrow & Co., 1949).
29. Judith K. Brown, "A Note on the Division of Labor by Sex," *American Anthropologist* 72, no. 5 (1970): 1073–78; and "Leisure, Busywork and Housekeeping." *Anthropos* 68, no. 5 (1973): 881–88.
30. Sharlotte Neely Williams, "The Limitations of the Male/Female Activity Distinction among Primates: An Extension of Judith K. Brown's 'A Note on the Division of Labor by Sex,'" *American Anthropologist* 73 (1971): 805–6.

public domain.[31] Ester Boserup has attacked the myth of inevitable domesticity by her examination of women's economic role in several African societies. In these societies women's power was eroded by Europeans acting on the basis of their own cultural myths about "women's place" who excluded women from significant participation and control in the political economy.[32] Ernestine Friedl reviews the position of women in hunting and gathering and in horticultural societies, concluding that childbearing and child rearing are accommodated *to* women's role in the public economy (rather than the other way around) and that it is not women's contribution to subsistence but their control over the products of their work that is crucial to their political and personal power.[33] And she suggests that the difficulties which the sexes have in interpersonal relationships — suspiciousness, female docility, aggressiveness, etc. — come from the powerlessness of women and are particularly exacerbated when the power and authority of men are challenged.

There are two especially useful discussions of women's domesticity in industrial society. M. Kay Martin and Barbara Voorhies begin with an examination of women in agricultural, pastoral societies (as well as in those examined by Friedl) and conclude with an examination of women in industrial societies.[34] Ann Oakley describes the housewife historically in a book which is equally informative to the general reader and the social scientist and which contains an excellent summary of women's labor in the home before and after industrialization.[35] Martin and Voorhies and Oakley dispel the myth that women have been confined to the household since Adam and Eve, except for instances of minor aberrations. They suggest, rather, that the development of intensive agriculture (in Europe during the Middle Ages and before) tended to increase women's relative participation in household labor (e.g., weaving, spinning directly for market and/or middlemen and/or household consumption). Women's exclusion from public life and their development into houseworkers and child caretakers

results from the separation of work and home, a characteristic of industrial capitalism. In England, for example, women were once permitted to participate in public life, taking jobs as brewers, surgeons, and traders as well as domestics, teachers, and agricultural workers — sometimes taking over from a deceased husband, but often doing the work without inheriting it from their spouses. "Women's place is in the home" is a relatively new prescription, a by-product of the transfer of production for market from the home to the factory.

Housework and Social Roles: The Housewife[36]

Helena Z. Lopata provided us with the first comprehensive study of American housewives as occupants of social roles, treating seriously and at length the varied experiences of women in the city and suburbs around Chicago during a decade that began in the late 1950s.[37] Lopata studies housework as an aspect of the housewife role,

31. Peggy R. Sanday, "Female Status in the Public Domain," in *Woman, Culture and Society,* ed. Michelle Zimbalist Rosaldo and Louise Lamphere (Stanford, Calif.: Stanford University Press, 1974). p. 192.
32. Ester Boserup, *Woman's Role in Economic Development* (London: George Allen & Unwin, 1970).
33. Ernestine Friedl, *Women and Men: An Anthropologist's View* (New York: Holt, Rinehart & Winston, 1975).
34. M. Kay Martin and Barbara Voorhies, *Female of the Species* (New York: Columbia University Press, 1975).
35. Oakley, *Woman's Work.*

36. Socialization into responsibility for housework in childhood needs systematic evaluation, including analyses of parental anxiety; see Eleanor Emmons Maccoby and Carol Nagy Jacklin, *The Psychology of Sex Differences* (Stanford, Calif.: Stanford University Press, 1974), p. 339. Analysis of sex-role models in children's books and on television suggests that girls and boys are encouraged quite early to accept female responsibility for housework. See Lenore J. Weitzman et al., "Sex Role Socialization in Picture Books for Pre-School Children" (paper delivered at the American Sociological Association meeting. Denver, Colo., September 2, 1971), p. 10; Textbook Study Group, "Sex Role Stereotyping in Ontario Primary Readers," mimeographed (Regional Municipality of York, Ont., September 1972); Women on Words and Images, *Dick and Jane as Victims: Sex Stereotyping in Children's Readers* (Princeton, N.J.: National Organization of Women Central New Jersey Chapter, 1972), pp. 18–19.
37. Lopata, no. 6 above. The inception of the book is interesting in the light of the "feminine mystique" that pervaded the initial period of her research and her interpretation of the lives of housewives. Lopata began her work when she moved to suburbia in the late 1950s, having been skeptical and uneasy about the move and then discovering that housewives were different from their portrayals in descriptions of suburbia. She completed her research about the time Betty Friedan published *The Feminine Mystique* (1963), and the volume itself was published in 1971, during the first years of the new wave of feminist criticism. (The literature on the househusband is virtually nonexistent: see Michael Weiss, "Diary of a Mad Househusband," in *Women in a Changing World,* ed. Uta West [New York: McGraw-Hill Book Co., 1975], pp. 64–67; and Mike McGrady, *The Kitchen Sink Papers* [New York: Doubleday & Co., 1975], which has also been excerpted in *Woman's Day* [September and October 1975], and in such newspapers as the Portland *Oregonian* [October 1975].)

which she examines over the life cycle rather than as a static role. Among her topics are how a woman gains the knowledge necessary to be a homemaker, who assists her with jobs—family members as well as commercial workers, the frequency with which jobs involve interaction with those in the community, the division of labor in the marital relationship, and the perceptions women have about being housewives and doing housework. She is interested in how women, fulfilling a variety of expectations with a variety of learning experiences and in a variety of social contexts (race, social class, employment status, age, presence or absence of children), carry out the jobs associated with being housewives. She suggests that the housewife role in the United States is similar to the lower-class European version of that role: the housewife is a drudge and a menial rather than, as among the European aristocracy, a manager, a coordinator, a leader of soirees, and a participant in the mainstream of the life of the times. (The former role has also been the fate of the British women studied by Ann Oakley, which suggests that we need to look at the political economy, too.) Lopata presents a multidimensional portrait of women who experience the housewife role in varied ways, so that, while some are overwhelmed by the isolation, the repetitiveness of tasks, and the double burden of the employed wife, others work out a life style which they find satisfying. Variations in the social role of housewives are presented by race, ethnicity, and social class to account for quite diverse interpretations women have of their experiences, helping to explain, for example, why working-class women may be tempted to leave the labor force—housewifery *is* creative and autonomous, compared with most jobs which women are likely to fill in the labor force. Lopata's study does not romanticize housewifery, but it stands in contrast to the denigration of housewifery that permeates the mass media and affects women's views of themselves. Lopata recognizes and details the problems with which women have to cope—with varying degrees of success—problems which include isolation from other adult contact, the disrupting effect on the marital relationship of the birth of the first child, disjointed and contradictory expectations of how women ought to be "just housewives" and yet actualizing human beings at the same time.

A somewhat contrasting view of the housewife and housework emerges from Ann Oakley's study of housework,[38] as far as I know the only full-fledged sociological study of this work and a companion volume to her

Woman's Work, discussed earlier in relation to the myth of the inevitability of domesticity. The difference between the creativity and innovativeness which characterize the women Lopata studied (though to be sure she notes enormous variations among women by social class, race, and stage in the life cycle), and the dissatisfaction with housework in the British sample results from the distinction between *doing housework* and *being a housewife.* Oakley finds women are dissatisfied with the first and yet satisfied with the second. Oakley limits her study, insofar as possible, to women's reactions to *housework* as work, discovering the fragmentation, monotony, and isolation that women dislike about the work; she examined children's influences insofar as they interfere with doing housework and as the demands of being a good mother may contradict the demands of being a good housekeeper. Lopata's conceptualization is both broader and more complex, and her resulting portrayal of housewives—not housework—is, in turn, more complex than Oakley's. American wives are shown as facing myriad problems which vary by social class, by race, and by stage in the life cycle—perhaps because Lopata was able to interview many more women than Oakley and because of her theoretical focus on the housewife as embedded in a complex set of social relationships. Oakley's treatment of housework as a job, her interest in the nature of the work and its meaning in women's lives is nevertheless extremely valuable, especially when read with its companion volume. Nobody else has given us as much detail about housework. I am not convinced that her distinction among housework, mothering, etc. as separate roles is useful theoretically; of course, it is for the purposes of doing a pilot study, as she describes her interviews with twenty working-class and twenty middle-class London women. I see the social condition of women—married women or single women with children—as significantly defined by the assignment of the housewife role to women; that is, women are socially assigned the responsibility for all the jobs that go on within the household, and housework is one of these jobs. I find it impossible to think about housework disappearing by some magic, let us say—and the housewife role not disappearing along with it.

Housework and the Political Economy

An Institutional Analysis. John Kenneth Galbraith's analysis of housework[39] is an example of an approach

---

38. Oakley, *Sociology of Housework.*

39. Galbraith, n. 7 above.

which is supportive of both a feminist perspective and the basic structure of capitalism. Galbraith sees women as exploited, as, in his words, "cryptoservants." His interpretation of women's social position is an interesting departure from conventional economics, because he is concerned with the *ease of consumption* rather than with the problem of choice of what to consume. Economic analysis usually assumes that consumption itself is problem-free, but Galbraith says that rising standards of consumption are attractive only if the consumers themselves do not have to expend a good deal of time and energy preparing the goods for final consumption. Hence an elaborate gourmet meal is desirable if the eater need not spend hours in meal preparation as well as in clean-up jobs. Women who have spent four or five hours in the kitchen preparing a family feast, only to see the food "on the table for twenty minutes and in the mouth for two minutes," may recognize in themselves a mild depression that accompanies an unusually long investment of time and a short period of enjoyment. Whether or not women become inured to this phenomenon of long, hard hours of work for quick consumption is an interesting research question. To return to Galbraith, women's role in consumption is to be responsible for household tasks related to consumption. Women "select, transport, prepare, repair, maintain, clean, service, store, protect and otherwise perform [such] tasks. . . ."[40] His concept of the convenient social virtue which "ascribes merit to any pattern of behavior, however uncomfortable or unnatural for the individual involved, that serves the comfort or well-being or is otherwise advantageous for, the more powerful members of the community" gives us a way of summarizing power relations involved in the consignment of women to the consumption-preparation role.[41] Galbraith implies that modern economies, rather than the special character of capitalism, have suborned women into this menial role, an interpretation open to argument. Since the only attempts to relieve women of housework which have met with some success appear to be in situations of privation (e.g., the People's Republic of China, the kibbutzim movement in Israel during its early years) or in short-lived communes in the United States, it is not possible to cite empirical materials to contradict Galbraith's interpretation, but there is a good deal of theoretical discussion by radical analysts. Communes are pertinent here: most of the communes in the United States have been characterized by a division of labor by sex, which assigns "inside" labor to women, and "outside" labor (farmwork, building, etc.) to men. An exception to this may be the contemporary secular communes, in which people are committed to the ideology of sex equality and which provide a structure, according to Rosabeth Kanter, to support new conceptions of gender roles.[42]

A Radical Analysis. Marxist analysts approach the question of women and housework by examining capitalism, an approach which led initially to the conclusion that women would cease being oppressed with the advent of socialism. However, reluctant to leave women on the fringes of social change in a status frozen until socialism replaces capitalism, socialist feminists have recently reexamined the situation of women. Given the dreary picture of the lack of women's relief from housework responsibilities in European socialist societies, socialist feminists now recognize that factors other than economic ones need to be considered. Juliet Mitchell, in her widely circulated statement "Women: The Longest Revolution," connects the division of labor between husband (the job outside the home) and wife (home care and child care) to the development of capitalism, arguing that women "produce" children in the home "in a sad mimicry" of the way their husbands produce commodities in their work outside the home; but she does not examine housework itself in the four structures on which she focuses (reproduction, production, sexuality, and socialization) and simply sees woman's world—the family—as embraced by man's world—production—and therefore included in that category.[43] Housework itself is considered in Margaret Benston's analysis. She uses the concepts of "exchange-value" and "use-value" to explain her conception that women's exclusion from commodity production (or their minimal participation through intermittent employment in low-paying jobs) lies at the base of their inferior position. Housework and child rearing mean that "each household constitutes an individual production unit, a preindustrial entity. . . . The rationalization of production effected by a transition to large-scale production has

40. Ibid., p. 33.
41. Ibid., p. 30.

42. Rosabeth Moss Kanter, "Sex-Role Implications of Structural Changes in Household Form: The Case of Open-ended Communal Households" (paper prepared for the Ford Foundation/Merrill-Palmer Institute Conference on Sex Roles and the Family, Detroit, Mich., November 10–12, 1975; and forthcoming in a volume edited by Constantina Safilios-Rothschild).
43. Juliet Mitchell, "Women: The Longest Revolution," *New Left Review,* no. 40 (December 1966), pp. 11–37.

not taken place in this area."[44] Benston believes that it is incorrect to see the family primarily as a unit of consumption, if by that we mean that women do not work in the home and/or that women's work is irrelevant to the economy. The former view is taken when housework is considered "leisure" or women are considered "parasitic," living off their husbands' labor. To Benston, women are an unpaid labor force, responsible for housework in both capitalist and socialist societies. Housework is not industrialized or developed into a major enterprise in the public economy but continues as a "home economy," a privatized activity. Although she suggests that the lack of industrialization of housework supports the inferior position of women, she does not believe that industrialization within capitalism would necessarily serve human, as distinct from capitalist, needs (i.e., the drive for profit) and that the inclusion of housework in the public economy would mean that all human relations would be included in the cash nexus, a condition that might be intolerable for already atomized and isolated people.[45]

Mariarosa Dalla Costa's analysis[46] is concerned with the housewife specifically, in contrast to Mitchell, who considers "women's condition" (and does not consider housework itself), and Benston, who is concerned with the nature of the work the housewife does relative to the market. Dalla Costa begins her analysis of the position of women as housewives and then moves immediately to an analysis of capitalism. (I have reached the same conclusions as Dalla Costa independently, by starting from the same point as she did: woman as housewife.)[47] Dalla Costa's analysis parallels Oakley's but concludes with an analysis of social structure, while Oakley is more concerned with social psychological phenomena.[48] Dalla

Costa begins by summarizing the effect of capitalism on women and children; they are no longer considered "productive" members of the family once they are removed from the work force by the separation of work place from home and by the enforcement of compulsory schooling. Women's work in the home isolates them from the experience of social labor and from contacts with other women doing the same work. In addition, women are only partial beneficiaries of modern capitalism: for example, while we tend to see the modern kitchen as representing the best of modern technology (especially in the United States), it is not the best that is available, given our technical sophistication.[49] Women are thus confined to the home, deprived of technical sophistication and knowledge about the social world (including how to organize and pursue their own interests); women are physically subjugated by the repression of their sexuality and by the inaccessibility of birth control methods. (These situations have been modified in the United States but by no means eliminated.) In the whole long process of the development of capitalism, women and men are pulled apart from each other as women are denied participation in work and life outside the home, made dependent upon and subordinate to men. Men are the instrument of women's oppression (not the oppressors).

Dalla Costa sees women's housework as *productive* labor in that it reproduces labor. This includes especially having and rearing children but also helping men to prepare for another day of work. At the same time, the economic dependency of women (and children) locks men into wage labor. Seeing, as she does, the problems which workers in capitalism face—boring work, low wages, cyclical unemployment—Dalla Costa does not consider the entrance of working-class women into the labor force the solution to the emancipation of women. Nor does she see paying housewives as likely to change women's status—on the contrary, it would freeze them in the home, into doing "women's work." The remainder of her discussion is a plea: for female solidarity; for women to reject the equation "housework = women's work" and to see this as part of capitalism; for women to see that the control of their reproduction and sexuality combined with

44. Margaret Benston, "The Political Economy of Women's Liberation," *Monthly Review* 21, no. 4 (September 1969): 13–27; the passage quoted is on p. 18.

45. Ibid., pp. 23–24.

46. Mariarosa Dalla Costa, "Women and the Subversion of Community," *Radical America* 6 (January–February 1972): 67–102.

47. Glazer-Malbin, "Invisible Worker."

48. Oakley, *Sociology of Housework.* In closing, Oakley states that "a major—perhaps the major—tool of feminist revolt is a comprehensive understanding of the way in which women 'internalize their own oppression.' The logic is that structures which oppress women cannot be altered unless there is a prior awareness among women of the need for change" (p. 195). This does not mean that she excludes structures, but her comments on Secombe (n. 50 below) suggest to me that, since social psychological phenomena may be prior to a person's being in a social role, these phenomena in some way are equal to, or perhaps more important than, structural features.

49. For example, household appliances are not designed for easy maintenance. I usually feel, as I clean my oven or refrigerator, that these were designed as traps, with surfaces and crevices and movable parts and fittings that demand special cleaning tools and products, endless patience, and a mechanically imaginative mind. Pieces of industrial kitchen equipment, in contrast, are designed as working tools to minimize their care and maximize efficient use.

male domination is a way of allowing working-class men especially, themselves oppressed by capitalism, to maintain an illusion of power and that this deflects these men from an awareness of their powerlessness outside of sex relations. Finally, Dalla Costa ties characteristics of women—their preoccupation with buying goods for the home, their repressive and disciplinarian tendencies, their rivalry and lack of solidarity with each other—to women's consignment to the home, to each woman's being a housewife regardless of her unique commitments, interests, and capabilities.

Some Marxists object to describing the activities of housewives as "productive" labor, reserving this term for a particular aspect of their theory of capitalism. I will consider here the discussion by Wally Secombe as an example of that position.[50] According to Marxist theory, "production" in capitalism means the creation of surplus value. The worker sells labor power to the capitalist, who extracts profit from the difference between the wage paid the worker for some of the time spent at work (which allows the worker to survive) and the remainder of the working time which creates value by the capitalist not paying the worker for it and from selling a product in the market. This is "exploitation." The housewife, in this analysis, is not exploited (another technical term) because her goods, although these have use value, do not enter the commodity market but instead are consumed in the home. But she is oppressed. She is oppressed by her own economic dependency and that of her children on her husband, whose health and well-being as well as goodwill

are crucial; her own economic situation depends on her husband being able to perform his job each day. She is oppressed by other aspects of her limited role or her complete exclusion from commodity production. She performs dull, repetitive work in the home. She is isolated from other women like herself because of her home duties, which upper-middle-class women with access to convenience foods and substitute labor may have some difficulty understanding. She is oppressed by laboring in the home to fulfill an ideal of being a good woman, while the work that she does is seen (by herself as well as by her husband and children and those outside the home) as trivial and requiring little skill, sensitivity, or intelligence, although the only difference between her husband's work and her own is that he receives a wage and she does not. But, since in capitalism only that which has a monetary value is "valued" (e.g., compare the status of volunteer work with the same work when paid for), the housewife suffers from being told that her work is worthless and that she is a parasite on her husband. Moreover, she cannot even strike, for she is in violation of the marital contract if she "neglects" her husband and children by failing to perform her domestic work.

Secombe objects to seeing housework as productive labor because the domestic worker does not relate either to the means of production or to the means of exchange, as she did in the precapitalist world. While labor in the home may add value—to the commodities being consumed—this value does not enter the marketplace, for the housewife does not create *surplus* value. Thus service which does not produce surplus value cannot be considered economically productive—which, as I noted earlier, was the reason for the decision of the eastern European socialist societies to exclude the market costs of services from their computation of national economic productivity. I am not convinced that this is a reasonable view of work in the labor force—that services cannot be considered an equivalent of commodities—or that the direct control by the capitalist of a worker's time is somehow more real than the indirect control by the capitalist of the activity of women in the household. If the labor of the domestic worker is necessary for production and necessary for the reproduction of labor (i.e., for having and rearing children, for preparing men to work each day for wages), then the monetary value attached by the capitalist seems an irrelevant criterion.

Whether the radical analysts agree on the exact meaning of the work of the housewife relative to capitalism seems of less importance than their agreement that the

---

50. Wally Secombe, "The Housewife and Her Labour under Capitalism." *New Left Review* 83 (January-February 1974): 3-24. Among the Marxists who have formulated analyses of the relation of housework to capitalism, there is a dispute about the meaning of productive labor. For brevity's sake, I am limiting my comments in this review to Dalla Costa, who—with Benston, Mitchell, Joan Landes, and Eli Zaretsky—sees housework as productive labor; and to Secombe, who—along with Lise Vogel, Ira Gerstein, and John Harrison—while agreeing with Dalla Costa and the others on many points, argues that to see housework as "productive" is inconsistent with the Marxist analysis of capitalism. See Benston; Mitchell; Joan Landes, "Wages for Housework: Subsidizing Capitalism?" *Quest* 2. no. 2 (Fall 1975): 17-30; Eli Zaretsky, "Capitalism, the Family, and Personal Life. Part 1," *Socialist Revolution* 3, nos. 1-2 (January-April 1973): 69-125; idem, *Socialist Revolution* 3, no. 3 (May-June 1973): 19-70; Lise Vogel, "The Earthly Family," *Radical America* 7, nos. 4-5 (July-October 1973): 9-50; Ira Gerstein, "Domestic Work and Capitalism." *Radical America* 7, nos. 4-5 (July-October 1973): 101-28; and John Harrison, "The Political Economy of Housework," *Bulletin of the Conference of Socialist Economists* (Winter 1973), pp. 35-51.

housewife works for the maintenance of capitalism rather than simply being a worker for her family. If housework is seen as being for the family alone, then we study the houseworker, suggesting further research questions and social policy that focus on the husband-wife relationships—as we have done. The answer to the question "Who must pay for housework?" is easy: "The husband"! Thus it has been suggested by various critics of contemporary women's position that wives be entitled to one-half of their husbands' wages or alternatively that husbands pay wives for housework on some hourly or weekly basis. This means seeing husbands and children as the only beneficiaries of the domestic work of wives—wives are indeed cryptoservants, in Galbraith's words. But this view privatizes the family, because each family is seen as a discrete, small-scale production unit. This view supports the division between the sexes—I believe Secombe deserves special attention for making this point—by posing the husband as exploiter of his wife, as he demands that she be responsible for housework (and fails to share work in the home with her to any substantial degree, regardless of his wife's status in the labor force). The demand for her housework responsibility is "in exchange for" his assuming financial responsibility for her and their children.

Many American sociologists see the family as husband and wife forming a complementary unit; the relationship is then examined using concepts such as balance and exchange. The division of labor *for* the marital couple becomes an issue of balancing the man's activities against the woman's activities, the man's interests against the woman's interests, and so on. If, in contrast, we conceptualize women's work as supporting capitalism (either considering it labor or "productive" labor), we can posit a different set of questions about the family. Our analysis shifts from exploring the relationships between the sexes in the home, from a battle of the sexes, to asking how husbands and wives are arrayed in battle by their relationship to institutions outside the home. Thus we have to deprivatize the family in our research. I believe that, as sociologists, we have often seen the family as isolated from society, somewhat in the way that family members see themselves as constructing an enclave, a private world away from the turmoil of modern industrial-urban life. In the broadest sense, Marxist analysis means expanding a "sociology of the family," relatively neglected for the past three decades or so, as a complement to the "social psychology of the family." I urge this as a complement, not a substitute.

Constructing Theory: Housework and a Sociology for Women

I want to end this review with the critique Dorothy E. Smith makes of a sociology *of* women and her model for a sociology *for* women,[51] which, she suggests, may begin with an understanding of women's position in the home as housewives. A sociology *of* women is what we have generally developed in the last half dozen years in particular, but it includes a wealth of materials predating the recent women's movement. Much writing by feminist sociologists (similar to that in other fields) is directed to the invisibility of women, to criticizing the constructed models of women as well as detailing the oppression of women in the contemporary world and revising our views of women in the past. Among these topics, the reconsideration of models comes closest to Smith's concern and this can be subsumed under the problem which she has raised repeatedly.[52]

Smith begins with the supposition that knowing includes a variety of activities—the formal organization of work places, sources of publication, systems of validation by citation and peers, and so on—that are male enterprises. The intellectual organization of the social world—sociological theory—is a product developed by men who experience the world in particular ways because of their own locations in the social structure. Their perceptions are shaped particularly by the rational, administrative structures of contemporary capitalism, and that framework is applied to all structures and experiences in the society. (For example, a direct application of the administrative model to the family can be found in the work of Rivka Bar Yosef. John Scanzoni's development of exchange theory is easily linked to the experiences of the capitalist rational world; while a more subtle linkage is in the family as an enclave, or the nomos-building model of the family, as portrayed by Peter Berger and Hansfried Kellner.)[53] Sociological "knowing" takes women as ob-

51. Dorothy E. Smith, "Some Implications of a Sociology for Women" (paper delivered at the meeting of the American Sociological Association, San Francisco, Calif., August 1975).

52. E.g., Dorothy E. Smith, "Women's Perspective as a Radical Critique of Sociology" (paper delivered at the meeting of the American Association for the Advancement of Science, Pacific Division, Eugene, Oreg. June 1972).

53. Rivka Weiss Bar Yosef, "Household Management: An Organizational Model Applied to Comparative Family Research," *Human Relations* 26, no. 5 (1973): 581–98; John Scanzoni, *Sexual Bargaining: Power Politics in American Marriage* (Englewood Cliffs, N.J.: Prentice Hall, Inc., 1972); and Peter Berger and Hansfried Kellner, "Marriage and the Construction of Social Reality," in Glazer-Malbin and Waehrer, pp. 174–82.

jects to be studied rather than as women participating in the development of the framework used for knowing reality. Having women sociologists take part in sociological activity does not mean that women cease to be objects of study, since we use the frameworks developed from the world experience of men, a world from which women are excluded or in which they participate only in marginal ways. But sociological theory proceeds from the perspective of those who are located in the center rather than on the margins of the world. To Smith, what is needed is a sociology *for* women which begins with an inquiry into how the everyday world is experienced by women, as described by women, rather than an attempt to squeeze women's experiences into preexisting models of the world, the rational, administrative framework in particular. This construction, however, is *not* the end of the analysis. What is very important (to me) is that the subsequent steps involve connecting the everyday world, as seen by women, to the larger social context, to the political economy. Women can describe their experiences of social reality—we do so a good deal of the time in what is denigrated as "women's talk"—worries about children, cooking, budgeting, house comforts, menfolk, continuing sexual attractiveness. However, we are in positions from which we cannot easily see the range of structures that impinge upon our lives—only the very clever fish knows it swims in a wet environment. A sociology *for* women would take as its task the connection of the world which women experience and describe to the less immediately apprehended world which ultimately shapes women's experiences: we have the potential to connect personal troubles with public issues.[54]

54. C. Wright Mills, *The Sociological Imagination* (New York: Oxford University Press, 1959), p. 226.

READING 50

Compulsory Heterosexuality and Lesbian Existence

Adrienne Rich

I

Biologically men have only one innate orientation—a sexual one that draws them to women,—while women have two innate orientations, sexual toward men and reproductive toward their young.[1]

Reprinted from Adrienne Rich, "Compulsory Heterosexuality and Lesbian Existence," in *Signs* 5 (Summer 1980): pp. 631-660, by permission of the publisher, The University of Chicago Press, and the author.
1. Alice Rossi, "Children and Work in the Lives of Women" (paper delivered at the University of Arizona, Tucson, February 1976).

. . . I was a woman terribly vulnerable, critical, using femaleness as a sort of standard or yardstick to measure and discard men. Yes—something like that. I was an Anna who invited defeat from men without ever being conscious of it. (But I am conscious of it. And being conscious of it means I shall leave it all behind me and become—but what?) I was stuck fast in an emotion common to women of our time, that can turn them bitter, or Lesbian, or solitary. Yes, that Anna during that time was. . .

[Another blank line across the page:][2]

The bias of compulsory heterosexuality, through which lesbian experience is perceived on a scale ranging from deviant to abhorrent, or simply rendered invisible, could be illustrated from many other texts than the two just preceding. The assumption made by Rossi, that women are "innately sexually oriented" toward men, or by Lessing, that the lesbian choice is simply an acting-out of bitterness toward men, are by no means theirs alone; they are widely current in literature and in the social sciences.

I am concerned here with two other matters as well: first, how and why women's choice of women as passionate comrades, life partners, co-workers, lovers, tribe, has been crushed, invalidated, forced into hiding and disguise; and second, the virtual or total neglect of lesbian existence in a wide range of writings, including feminist scholarship. Obviously there is a connection here. I believe that much feminist theory and criticism is stranded on this shoal.

My organizing impulse is the belief that it is not enough for feminist thought that specifically lesbian texts exist. Any theory or cultural/political creation that treats lesbian existence as a marginal or less "natural" phenomenon, as mere "sexual preference," or as the mirror image of either heterosexual or male homosexual relations, is profoundly weakened thereby, whatever its other contributions. Feminist theory can no longer afford merely to voice a toleration of "lesbianism" as an "alternative lifestyle," or make token allusion to lesbians. A feminist critique of compulsory heterosexual orientation for women is long overdue. In this exploratory paper, I shall try to show why.

I will begin by way of examples, briefly discussing four books that have appeared in the last few years, written from different viewpoints and political orientations, but all presenting themselves, and favorably reviewed, as feminist.[3] All take as a basic assumption that the social relations of the sexes are disordered and extremely problematic, if not disabling, for women; all seek paths toward change. I have learned more from some of these books than from others; but on this I am clear: each one might have been more accurate, more powerful, more truly a force for change, had the author felt impelled to deal with lesbian existence as a reality, and as a source of knowledge and power available to women; or with the institution of heterosexuality itself as a beachhead of male dominance.[4] In none of them is the question ever raised, whether in a different context, or other things being equal, women would *choose* heterosexual coupling and marriage; heterosexuality is presumed as a "sexual preference" of "most women," either implicitly or explicitly. In none of these books, which concern themselves with mothering, sex roles, relationships, and societal prescriptions for women, is compulsory heterosexuality ever examined as an institution powerfully affecting all these; or the idea of "preference" or "innate orientation" even indirectly questioned.

In *For Her Own Good: 150 Years of the Experts' Advice to Women* by Barbara Ehrenreich and Deirdre English, the authors' superb pamphlets, *Witches, Mid-*

---

2. Doris Lessing, *The Golden Notebook* (New York: Bantam Books [1962] 1977), p. 480.

3. Nancy Chodorow, *The Reproduction of Mothering* (Berkeley: University of California Press, 1978); Dorothy Dinnerstein, *The Mermaid and the Minotaur: Sexual Arrangements and the Human Malaise* (New York: Harper & Row, 1976); Barbara Ehrenreich and Deirdre English, *For Her Own Good: 150 Years of the Experts' Advice to Women* (Garden City, N.Y.: Doubleday & Co., Anchor Press, 1978); Jean Baker Miller, *Toward a New Psychology of Women* (Boston: Beacon Press, 1976).

4. *I could have chosen many other serious and influential recent books, including anthologies, which would illustrate the same point: e.g., Our Bodies, Ourselves,* the Boston Women's Health Collective's best-seller (New York: Simon & Schuster, 1976), which devotes a separate (and inadequate) chapter to lesbians, but whose message is that heterosexuality is most women's life preference; Berenice Carroll, ed., *Liberating Women's History: Theoretical and Critical Essays* (Urbana: University of Illinois Press, 1976), which does not include even a token essay on the lesbian presence in history, though an essay by Linda Gordon, Persis Hunt, et al. notes the use by male historians of "sexual deviance" as a category to discredit and dismiss Anna Howard Shaw, Jane Addams, and other feminists ("Historical Phallacies: Sexism in American Historical Writing"); and Renate Bridenthal and Claudia Koonz, eds., *Becoming Visible: Women in European History* (Boston: Houghton Mifflin Co., 1977), which contains three mentions of male homosexuality but no materials that I have been able to locate on lesbians. Gerda Lerner, ed., *The Female Experience: An American Documentary* (Indianapolis: Bobbs-Merrill Co., 1977), contains an abridgment of two lesbian/feminist position papers from the contemporary movement but no other documentation of lesbian existence. Lerner does note in her preface, however, how the charge of deviance has been used to fragment women and discourage women's resistance. Linda Gordon, in *Woman's Body, Woman's Right: A Social History of Birth Control in America* (New York: Viking Press, Grossman, 1976), notes accurately that: "It is not that feminism has produced more lesbians. There have always been many lesbians, despite high levels of repression; and most lesbians experience their sexual preference as innate . . ." (p. 410).

wives and Nurses: A History of Women Healers, and *Complaints and Disorders: The Sexual Politics of Sickness,* are developed into a provocative and complex study. Their thesis in this book is that the advice given American women by male health professionals, particularly in the areas of marital sex, maternity, and child care, has echoed the dictates of the economic marketplace and the role capitalism has needed women to play in production and/or reproduction. Women have become the consumer victims of various cures, therapies, and normative judgments in different periods (including the prescription to middle-class women to embody and preserve the sacredness of the home — the "scientific" romanticization of the home itself). None of the "experts" advice has been either particularly scientific or women-oriented; it has reflected male needs, male fantasies about women, and male interest in controlling women — particularly in the realms of sexuality and motherhood — fused with the requirements of industrial capitalism. So much of this book is so devastatingly informative and is written with such lucid feminist wit, that I kept waiting as I read for the basic prescription against lesbianism to be examined. It never was.

This can hardly be for lack of information. Jonathan Katz's *Gay American History*[5] tells us that as early as 1656 the New Haven Colony prescribed the death penalty for lesbians. Katz provides many suggestive and informative documents on the "treatment" (or torture) of lesbians by the medical profession in the nineteenth and twentieth centuries. Recent work by the historian Nancy Sahli documents the crackdown on intense female friendships among college women at the turn of the present century.[6] The ironic title, *For Her Own Good,* might have referred first and foremost to the economic imperative to heterosexuality and marriage and to the sanctions imposed against single women and widows — both of whom have been and still are viewed as deviant. Yet, in this often enlightening Marxist-feminist overview of male prescriptions for female sanity and health, the economics of prescriptive heterosexuality go unexamined.[7]

Of the three psychoanalytically based books, one, Jean Baker Miller's *Toward a New Psychology of Women,* is written as if lesbians simply do not exist, even as marginal beings. Given Miller's title I find this astonishing. However, the favorable reviews the book has received in feminist journals, including *Signs* and *Spokeswoman,* suggest that Miller's heterocentric assumptions are widely shared. In *The Mermaid and the Minotaur: Sexual Arrangements and the Human Malaise,* Dorothy Dinnerstein makes an impassioned argument for the sharing of parenting between women and men and for an end to what she perceives as the male/female symbiosis of "gender arrangements," which she feels are leading the species further and further into violence and self-extinction. Apart from other problems that I have with this book (including her silence on the institutional and random terrorism men have practiced on women — and children — throughout history, amply documented by Barry, Daly, Griffin, Russell and van de Ven, and Brownmiller,[8] and her obsession with psychology to the neglect of economic and other material realities that help to create psychological reality), I find utterly ahistorical Dinnerstein's view of the relations between women and men as "a collaboration to keep history mad." She means by this, to perpetuate social relations which are hostile, exploitive, and destructive to life itself. She sees women and men as equal partners in the making of "sexual arrangements," seemingly unaware of the repeated struggles of women to resist oppression (our own and that of others) and to change our condition. She ignores, specifically, the history of women who — as witches, *femmes seules,* marriage resisters, spinsters, autonomous widows, and/or lesbians — have managed on varying levels *not* to collaborate. It is this history, precisely, from which feminists have so much to learn and on which there is overall such blanketing silence. Dinnerstein acknowledges at the end of her book that "female separatism," though "on a large scale and in the long run wildly impractical," has something to teach us: "Separate, women could in principle set out to learn from scratch — undeflected by the opportunities to evade this task that men's presence has so far offered — what intact self-creative humanness is."[9] Phrases like "intact self-creative humanness" obscure the question of what the many forms of female separatism have actually been addressing. The fact is that

---

5. Jonathan Katz, *Gay American History* (New York: Thomas Y. Crowell Co., 1976).
6. Nancy Sahli, "Smashing: Women's Relationships before the Fall," *Chrysalis: A Magazine of Women's Culture* 8 (1979): 17-27. A version of the article was presented at the Third Berkshire Conference on the History of Women, June 11, 1976.
7. This is a book which I have publicly endorsed. I would still do so, though with the above caveat. It is only since beginning to write this article that I fully appreciated how enormous is the unasked question in Ehrenreich and English's book.

8. Susan Brownmiller, *Against Our Will: Men, Women and Rape* (New York: Simon & Schuster, 1975).
9. Dinnerstein, p. 272.

women in every culture and throughout history *have* undertaken the task of independent, nonheterosexual, woman-connected existence, to the extent made possible by their context, often in the belief that they were the "only ones" ever to have done so. They have undertaken it even though few women have been in an economic position to resist marriage altogether; and even though attacks against unmarried women have ranged from aspersion and mockery to deliberate gynocide, including the burning and torturing of millions of widows and spinsters during the witch persecutions of the fifteenth, sixteenth, and seventeenth centuries in Europe, and the practice of suttee on widows in India.[10]

Nancy Chodorow does come close to the edge of an acknowledgment of lesbian existence. Like Dinnerstein, Chodorow believes that the fact that women, and women only, are responsible for child care in the sexual division of labor has led to an entire social organization of gender inequality, and that men as well as women must become primary carers for children if that inequality is to change. In the process of examining, from a psychoanalytic perspective, how mothering-by-women affects the psychological development of girl and boy children, she offers documentation that men are "emotionally secondary" in women's lives; that "women have a richer, ongoing inner world to fall back on. . . . men do not become as emotionally important to women as women do to men."[11] This would carry into the late twentieth century Smith-Rosenberg's findings about eighteenth- and nineteenth-century women's emotional focus on women. "Emotionally important" can of course refer to anger as well as to love, or to that intense mixture of the two often found in women's relationships with women: one aspect of what I have come to call the "double-life of women" (see below). Chodorow concludes that because women have women as mothers, "The mother remains a primary internal object [*sic*] to the girl, so that heterosexual relationships are on the model of a nonexclusive, second relationship for her, whereas for the boy they recreate an exclusive, primary relationship." According to Chodorow, women "have learned to deny the limitations of masculine lovers for both psychological and practical reasons."[12]

But the practical reasons (like witch burnings, male control of law, theology, and science, or economic non-

viability within the sexual division of labor) are glossed over. Chodorow's account barely glances at the constraints and sanctions which, historically, have enforced or ensured the coupling of women with men and obstructed or penalized our coupling or allying in independent groups with other women. She dismisses lesbian existence with the comment that "lesbian relationships do tend to re-create mother-daughter emotions and connections, but most women are heterosexual" (implied: more mature, having developed beyond the mother-daughter connection). She then adds: "This heterosexual preference and taboos on homosexuality, in addition to objective economic dependence on men, make the option of primary sexual bonds with other women unlikely — though more prevalent in recent years."[13] The significance of that qualification seems irresistible — but Chodorow does not explore it further. Is she saying that lesbian existence has become more visible in recent years (in certain groups?), that economic and other pressures have changed (under capitalism, socialism, or both?), and that consequently more women are rejecting the heterosexual "choice"? She argues that women want children because their heterosexual relationships lack richness and intensity, that in having a child a woman seeks to re-create her own intense relationship with her mother. It seems to be that on the basis of her own findings, Chodorow leads us implicitly to conclude that heterosexuality is *not* a "preference" for women; that, for one thing, it fragments the erotic from the emotional in a way that women find impoverishing and painful. Yet her book participates in mandating it. Neglecting the covert socializations and the overt forces which have channelled women into marriage and heterosexual romance, pressures ranging from the selling of daughters to postindustrial economics to the silences of literature to the images of the television screen, she, like Dinnerstein, is stuck with trying to reform a man-made institution — compulsory heterosexuality — as if, despite profound emotional impulses and complementarities drawing women toward women, there is a mystical/biological heterosexual inclination, a "preference" or "choice" which draws women toward men.

Moreover, it is understood that this "preference" does not need to be explained, unless through the tortuous theory of the female Oedipus complex or the necessity for species reproduction. It is lesbian sexuality which (usually, and incorrectly, "included" under male homosexuality) is seen as requiring explanation. This

---

10. Daly, pp. 184–85; 114–33.
11. Chodorow, pp. 197–98.
12. Ibid., pp. 198–99.

13. Ibid., p. 200.

assumption of female heterosexuality seems to me in itself remarkable; it is an enormous assumption to have glided so silently into the foundations of our thought.

The extension of this assumption is the frequently heard assertion that in a world of genuine equality, where men were nonoppressive and nurturing, everyone would be bisexual. Such a notion blurs and sentimentalizes the actualities within which women have experienced sexuality; it is the old liberal leap across the tasks and struggles of here and now, the continuing process of sexual definition which will generate its own possibilities and choices. (It also assumes that women who have chosen women have done so simply because men are oppressive and emotionally unavailable; which still fails to account for women who continue to pursue relationships with oppressive and/or emotionally unsatisfying men.) I am suggesting that heterosexuality, like motherhood, needs to be recognized and studied as a *political institution* — even, or especially, by those individuals who feel they are, in their personal experience, the precursors of a new social relation between the sexes.

II

If women are the earliest sources of emotional caring and physical nurture for both female and male children, it would seem logical, from a feminist perspective at least, to pose the following questions: whether the search for love and tenderness in both sexes does not originally lead toward women; *why in fact women would ever redirect that search;* why species-survival, the means of impregnation, and emotional/erotic relationships should ever have become so rigidly identified with each other; and why such violent strictures should be found necessary to enforce women's total emotional, erotic loyalty and subservience to men. I doubt that enough feminist scholars and theorists have taken the pains to acknowledge the societal forces which wrench women's emotional and erotic energies away from themselves and other women and from woman-identified values. These forces, as I shall try to show, range from literal physical enslavement to the disguising and distorting of possible options.

I do not, myself, assume that mothering-by-women is a "sufficient cause" of lesbian existence. But the issue of mothering-by-women has been much in the air of late, usually accompanied by the view that increased parenting by men would minimize antagonism between the sexes and equalize the sexual imbalance of power of males over

females. These discussions are carried on without reference to compulsory heterosexuality as a phenomenon let alone as an ideology. I do not wish to psychologize here, but rather to identify sources of male power. I believe large numbers of men could, in fact, undertake child care on a large scale without radically altering the balance of male power in a male-identified society.

In her essay "The Origin of the Family," Kathleen Gough lists eight characteristics of male power in archaic and contemporary societies which I would like to use as a framework: "men's ability to deny women sexuality or to force it upon them; to command or exploit their labor to control their produce; to control or rob them of their children; to confine them physically and prevent their movement; to use them as objects in male transactions; to cramp their creativeness; or to withhold from them large areas of the society's knowledge and cultural attainments."[14] (Gough does not perceive these power-characteristics as specifically enforcing heterosexuality; only as producing sexual inequality.) Below, Gough's words appear in italics; the elaboration of each of her categories, in brackets, is my own.

Characteristics of male power include:

the power of men

1. *to deny women* [our own] *sexuality*
[by means of clitoridectomy and infibulation; chastity belts; punishment, including death, for female adultery; punishment, including death, for lesbian sexuality; psychoanalytic denial of the clitoris; strictures against masturbation; denial of maternal and postmenopausal sensuality; unnecessary hysterectomy; pseudolesbian images in media and literature; closing of archives and destruction of documents relating to lesbian existence];

2. *or to force it* [male sexuality] *upon them*
[by means of rape (including marital rape) and wife beating; father-daughter, brother-sister incest; the socialization of women to feel that male sexual "drive" amounts to a right;[15] idealization of heterosexual romance in art, literature, media, advertising, etc.; child marriage; arranged marriage; prostitution; the harem; psychoanalytic doctrines of frigidity and vaginal orgasm; pornographic depictions of women

---

14. Kathleen Gough, "The Origin of the Family," in *Toward an Anthropology of Women,* ed. Rayna [Rapp] Reiter (New York: Monthly Review Press, 1975), pp. 69-70.
15. Barry, pp. 216-19.

responding pleasurably to sexual violence and humiliation (a subliminal message being that sadistic heterosexuality is more "normal' than sensuality between women)];

3. *to command or exploit their labor to control their produce*
[by means of the institutions of marriage and motherhood as unpaid production; the horizontal segregation of women in paid employment; the decoy of the upwardly mobile token woman; male control of abortion, contraception, and childbirth; enforced sterilization; pimping; female infanticide, which robs mothers of daughters and contributes to generalized devaluation of women];

4. *to control or rob them of their children*
[by means of father-right and "legal kidnapping";[16] enforced sterilization; systematized infanticide; seizure of children from lesbian mothers by the courts; the malpractice of male obstetrics; use of the mother as "token torturer"[17] in genital mutilation or in binding the daughter's feet (or mind) to fit her for marriage];

5. *to confine them physically and prevent their movement*
[by means of rape as terrorism, keeping women off the streets; purdah; foot-binding; atrophying of women's athletic capabilities; haute couture, "feminine" dress codes; the veil; sexual harassment on the streets; horizontal segregation of women in employment; prescriptions for "full-time" mothering; enforced economic dependence of wives];

6. *to use them as objects in male transactions*
[use of women as "gifts"; bride-price; pimping; arranged marriage; use of women as entertainers to facilitate male deals, e.g., wife-hostess, cocktail waitress required to dress for male sexual titillation, call girls, "bunnies," geisha, *kisaeng* prostitutes, secretaries];

7. *to cramp their creativeness*
[witch persecutions as campaigns against midwives and female healers and as pogrom against independent, "unassimilated" women;[18] definition of male pursuits as more valuable than female within any

culture, so that cultural values become embodiment of male subjectivity; restriction of female self-fulfillment to marriage and motherhood; sexual exploitation of women by male artists and teachers; the social and economic disruption of women's creative aspirations;[19] erasure of female tradition];[20] and

8. *to withhold from them large areas of the society's knowledge and cultural attainments*
[by means of noneducation of females (60% of the world's illiterates are women); the "Great Silence" regarding women and particularly lesbian existence in history and culture;[21] sex-role stereotyping which deflects women from science, technology, and other "masculine" pursuits; male social/professional bonding which excludes women; discrimination against women in the professions].

These are some of the methods by which male power is manifested and maintained. Looking at the schema, what surely impresses itself is the fact that we are confronting not a simple maintenance of inequality and property possession, but a pervasive cluster of forces, ranging from physical brutality to control of consciousness, which suggests that an enormous potential counterforce is having to be restrained.

Some of the forms by which male power manifests itself are more easily recognizable as enforcing heterosexuality on women than are others. Yet each one I have listed adds to the cluster of forces within which women have been convinced that marriage, and sexual orientation toward men, are inevitable, even if unsatisfying or oppressive components of their lives. The chastity belt; child marriage; erasure of lesbian existence (except as exotic and perverse) in art, literature, film; idealization of heterosexual romance and marriage—these are some fairly obvious forms of compulsion, the first two exemplifying physical force, the second two control of consciousness. While clitoridectomy has been assailed by feminists as a form of woman-torture,[22] Kathleen Barry first pointed

16. Anna Demeter, *Legal Kidnapping* (Boston: Beacon Press, 1977), pp. xx, 126–28.
17. Daly, pp. 132, 139–41, 163–65.
18. Barbara Ehrenreich and Deirdre English, *Witches, Midwives and Nurses: A History of Women Healers* (Old Westbury, N.Y.: Feminist Press, 1973); Andrea Dworkin, *Woman Hating* (New York: E. P. Dutton, 1974), pp. 118–54; Daly, pp. 178–222.
19. See Virginia Woolf, *A Room of One's Own* (London: Hogarth Press, 1929), and *Three Guineas* (New York: Harcourt Brace & Co., [1938] 1966); Tillie Olsen, *Silences* (Boston: Delacorte Press, 1978); Michelle Cliff, "The Resonance of Interruption," *Chrysalis: A Magazine of Women's Culture* 8 (1979): 29–37.
20. Mary Daly, *Beyond God the Father* (Boston: Beacon Press, 1973), pp. 347–51; Olsen, pp. 22–46.
21. Daly, *Beyond God the Father,* p. 93.
22. Fran P. Hosken, "The Violence of Power: Genital Mutilation of Females," *Heresies: A Feminist Journal of Art and Politics* 6 (1979): 28–35; Russell and van de Ven, pp. 194–95.

out that it is not simply a way of turning the young girl into a "marriageable" woman through brutal surgery: it intends that women in the intimate proximity of polygynous marriage will not form sexual relationships with each other; that—from a male, genital-fetishist perspective—female erotic connections, even in a sex-segregated situation, will be literally excised.[23]

The function of pornography as an influence on consciousness is a major public issue of our time, when a multibillion-dollar industry has the power to disseminate increasingly sadistic, women-degrading visual images. But even so-called soft-core pornography and advertising depict women as objects of sexual appetite devoid of emotional context, without individual meaning or personality: essentially as a sexual commodity to be consumed by males. (So-called lesbian pornography, created for the male voyeuristic eye, is equally devoid of emotional context or individual personality.) The most pernicious message relayed by pornography is that women are natural sexual prey to men and love it; that sexuality and violence are congruent; and that for women sex is essentially masochistic, humiliation pleasurable, physical abuse erotic. But along with this message comes another, not always recognized: the enforced submission and the use of cruelty, if played out in heterosexual pairing, is sexually "normal," while sensuality between women, including erotic mutuality and respect, is "queer," "sick," and either pornographic in itself or not very exciting compared with the sexuality of whips and bondage.[24] Pornography does not simply create a climate in which sex and violence are interchangeable; *it widens the range of behavior considered acceptable from men in heterosexual intercourse*—behavior which reiteratively strips women of their autonomy, dignity, and sexual potential, including the potential of loving and being loved by women in mutuality and integrity.

In her brilliant study, *Sexual Harassment of Working Women: A Case of Sex Discrimination,* Catherine A. MacKinnon delineates the intersection of compulsory heterosexuality and economics. Under capitalism, women are horizontally segregated by gender and occupy a structurally inferior position in the workplace; this is hardly news, but MacKinnon raises the question why, even if

capitalism "requires some collection of individuals to occupy low-status, low-paying positions . . . such persons must be biologically female," and goes on to point out that "the fact that male employers often do not hire qualified women, *even when they could pay them less than men* suggests that more than the profit motive is implicated" [emphasis added].[25] She cites a wealth of material documenting the fact that women are not only segregated in low-paying, service jobs (as secretaries, domestics, nurses, typists, telephone operators, child-care workers, waitresses) but that "sexualization of the woman" is part of the job. Central and intrinsic to the economic realities of women's lives is the requirement that women will "market sexual attractiveness to men, who tend to hold the economic power and position to enforce their predilections." And MacKinnon exhaustively documents that "sexual harassment perpetuates the interlocked structure by which women have been kept sexually in thrall to men at the bottom of the labor market. Two forces of American society converge: men's control over women's sexuality and capital's control over employees' work lives."[26] Thus, women in the workplace are at the mercy of sex-as-power in a vicious circle. Economically disadvantaged, women—whether waitresses or professors—endure sexual harassment to keep their jobs and learn to behave in a complaisantly and ingratiatingly heterosexual manner because they discover this is their true qualification for employment, whatever the job description. And, MacKinnon notes, the woman who too decisively resists sexual overtures in the workplace is accused of being "dried-up" and sexless, or lesbian. This raises a specific difference between the experiences of lesbians and homosexual men. A lesbian, closeted on her job because of heterosexist prejudice, is not simply forced into denying the truth of her outside relationships or private life; her job depends on her pretending to be not merely heterosexual but a heterosexual *woman,* in terms of dressing and playing the feminine, deferential role required of "real" women.

MacKinnon raises radical questions as to the qualitative differences between sexual harassment, rape, and ordinary heterosexual intercourse. ("As one accused rapist put it, he hadn't used 'any more force than is usual for males during the preliminaries.'") She criticizes Susan

---

23. Barry, pp. 163–64.

24. The issue of "lesbian sadomasochism" needs to be examined in terms of the dominant cultures' teachings about the relation of sex and violence, and also of the acceptance by some lesbians of male homosexual mores. I believe this to be another example of the "double-life" of women.

25. Catharine A. MacKinnon, *Sexual Harassment of Working Women: A Case of Sex Discrimination* (New Haven, Conn.: Yale University Press, 1979), pp. 15–16.
26. Ibid., p. 174.

Brownmiller[27] for separating rape from the mainstream of daily life and for her unexamined premise that "rape is violence, intercourse is sexuality," removing rape from the sexual sphere altogether. Most crucially she argues that "taking rape from the realm of 'the sexual,' placing it in the realm of 'the violent,' allows one to be against it without raising any questions about the extent to which the institution of heterosexuality has defined force as a normal part of 'the preliminaries.'"[28] "Never is it asked whether, under conditions of male supremacy, the notion of 'consent' has any meaning."[29]

The fact is that the workplace, among other social institutions, is a place where women have learned to accept male violation of our psychic and physical boundaries as the price of survival; where women have been educated — no less than by romantic literature or by pornography — to perceive ourselves as sexual prey. A woman seeking to escape such casual violations along with economic disadvantage may well turn to marriage as a form of hoped-for-protection, while bringing into marriage neither social or economic power, thus entering that institution also from a disadvantaged position. MacKinnon finally asks:

What if inequality is built into the social conceptions of male and female sexuality, of masculinity and femininity, of sexiness and heterosexual attractiveness? Incidents of sexual harassment suggest that male sexual desire itself may be aroused by female vulnerability. . . . Men feel they can take advantage, so they want to, so they do. Examination of sexual harassment, precisely because the episodes appear commonplace, forces one to confront the fact that sexual intercourse normally occurs between economic (as well as physical) unequals . . . the apparent legal requirement that violations of women's sexuality appear out of the ordinary before they will be punished helps prevent women from defining the ordinary conditions of their own consent.[30]

Given the nature and extent of heterosexual pressures, the daily "eroticization of women's subordination" as MacKinnon phrases it,[31]   I question the more or less psychoanalytic perspective (suggested by such writers as Karen Horney, H. R. Hayes, Wolfgang Lederer, and most recently, Dorothy Dinnerstein) that the male need to control women sexually results from some primal male "fear of women" and of women's sexual insatiability. It seems more probable that men really fear, not that they will have women's sexual appetites forced on them, or that women want to smother and devour them, but that women could be indifferent to them altogether, that men could be allowed sexual and emotional — therefore economic — access to women *only* on women's terms, otherwise being left on the periphery of the matrix.

The means of assuring male sexual access to women have recently received a searching investigation by Kathleen Barry.[32] She documents extensive and appalling evidence for the existence, on a very large scale, of international female slavery, the institution once known as "white slavery" but which in fact has involved, and at this very moment involves, women of every race and class. In the theoretical analysis derived from her research, Barry makes the connection between all enforced conditions under which women live subject to men: prostitution, marital rape, father-daughter and brother-sister incest, wife-beating, pornography, bride-price, the selling of daughters, purdah, and genital mutilation. She sees the rape paradigm — where the victim of sexual assault is held responsible for her own victimization — as leading to the rationalization and acceptance of other forms of enslavement, where the woman is presumed to have "chosen" her fate, to embrace it passively, or to have courted it perversely through rash or unchaste behavior. On the contrary, Barry maintains, "female sexual slavery is present in ALL situations where women or girls cannot change the conditions of their existence; where regardless of how they got into those conditions, e.g., social pressure, economic hardship, misplaced trust or the longing for affection, they cannot get out; and where they are subject to sexual violence and exploitation."[33] She provides a spectrum of concrete examples, not only as to the existence of a widespread international traffic in women, but also as to how this operates — whether in the form of a

27. Brownmiller (n. 8 above).
28. MacKinnon, p. 219. Susan Schecter writes: "The push for heterosexual union at whatever cost is so intense that . . . it has become a cultural force of its own that creates battering. The ideology of romantic love and its jealous possession of the partner as property provide the masquerade for what can become severe abuse" *(Aegis: Magazine on Ending Violence against Women* [July–August 1979], pp. 50–51).
29. MacKinnon, p. 298.
30. Ibid., p. 220.

31. Ibid., p. 221.
32. Kathleen Barry, *Female Sexual Slavery* (see unnumbered n. above).
33. Ibid., p. 33.

"Minnesota pipeline" funneling blonde, blue-eyed mid-western runaways to Times Square, or the purchasing of young women out of rural poverty in Latin America or Southeast Asia, or the providing of *maisons d'abattage* for migrant workers in the eighteenth arrondissement of Paris. Instead of "blaming the victim" or trying to diagnose her presumed pathology, Barry turns her flood-light on the pathology of sex colonization itself, the ideology of "cultural sadism" represented by the vast industry of pornography and by the overall identification of women primarily as "sexual beings whose responsibility is the sexual service of men."[34]

Barry delineates what she names a "sexual domina-tion perspective" through whose lens, purporting objec-tivity, sexual abuse and terrorism of women by men has been rendered almost invisible by treating it as natural and inevitable. From its point of view, women are expend-able as long as the sexual and emotional needs of the male can be satisfied. To replace this perspective of domination with a universal standard of basic freedom for women from gender-specific violence, from constraints on move-ment, and from male right of sexual and emotional access is the political purpose of her book. Like Mary Daly in *Gyn/Ecology,* Barry rejects structuralist and other cultural-relativist rationalizations for sexual torture and antiwoman violence. In her opening chapter, she asks of her readers that they refuse all handy escapes into igno-rance and denial. "The only way we can come out of hiding, break through our paralyzing defenses, is to know it all—the full extent of sexual violence and domination of women. . . . In *knowing,* in facing directly, we can learn to chart our course out of this oppression, by envi-sioning and creating a world which will preclude female sexual slavery."[35]

"Until we name the practice, give conceptual defini-tion and form to it, illustrate its life over time and in space, those who are its most obvious victims will also not be able to name it or define their experience."[36]

But women are all, in different ways and to different degrees, its victims; and part of the problem with naming and conceptualizing female sexual slavery is, as Barry clearly sees, compulsory heterosexuality. Compulsory heterosexuality simplifies the task of the procurer and pimp in worldwide prostitution rings and "eros centers," while, in the privacy of the home, it leads the daughter to "accept" incest/rape by her father, the mother to deny that it is happening, the battered wife to stay on with an abusive husband. "Befriending or love" is a major tactic of the procurer whose job is to turn the runaway or the confused young girl over to the pimp for seasoning. The ideology of heterosexual romance, beamed at her from childhood out of fairy tales, television, films, advertising, popular songs, wedding pageantry, is a tool ready to the procurer's hand and one which he does not hesitate to use, as Barry amply documents. Early female indoctrina-tion in "love" as an emotion may be largely a Western concept; but a more universal ideology concerns the primacy and uncontrollability of the male sexual drive. This is one of many insights offered by Barry's work:

As sexual power is learned by adolescent boys through the social experience of their sex drive, so do girls learn that the locus of sexual power is male. Given the importance placed on the male sex drive in the socialization of girls as well as boys, early ad-olescence is probably the first significant phase of male identification in a girl's life and develop-ment. . . . As a young girl becomes aware of her own increasing sexual feelings . . . she turns away from her heretofore primary relationships with girl-friends. As they become secondary to her, recede in importance in her life, her own identity also assumes a secondary role and she grows into male identification.[37]

We still need to ask why some women never, even temporarily, "turn away from heretofore primary rela-tionships" with other females? And why does male-iden-tification—the casting of one's social, political, and intellectual allegiances with men—exist among lifelong sexual lesbians? Barry's hypothesis throws us among new questions, but it clarifies the diversity of forms in which compulsory heterosexuality presents itself. In the mys-tique of the overpowering, all-conquering male sex drive, the penis-with-a-life-of-its-own, is rooted the law of male sex-right to women, which justifies prostitution as a uni-versal cultural assumption on the one hand, while defend-ing sexual slavery within the family on the basis of "family privacy and cultural uniqueness" on the other.[38] The adolescent male sex drive, which, as both young women and men are taught, once triggered cannot take responsi-bility for itself or take no for an answer, becomes, accord-

34. Ibid., p. 103.
35. Ibid., p. 5.
36. Ibid., p. 100.

37. Ibid., p. 218.
38. Ibid., p. 140.

ing to Barry, the norm and rationale for adult male sexual behavior: a condition of *arrested sexual development.* Women learn to accept as natural the inevitability of this "drive" because we receive it as dogma. Hence marital rape, hence the Japanese wife resignedly packing her husband's suitcase for a weekend in the *kisaeng* brothels of Taiwan, hence the psychological as well as economic imbalance of power between husband and wife, male employer and female worker, father and daughter, male professor and female student.

The effect of male-identification means

> *internalizing the values of the colonizer and actively participating in carrying out the colonization of one's self and one's sex. . . . Male identification is the act whereby women place men above women, including themselves, in credibility, status, and importance in most situations, regardless of the comparative quality the women may bring to the situation. . . . Interaction with women is seen as a lesser form of relating on every level.*[39]

What deserves further exploration is the double-think many women engage in and from which no woman is permanently and utterly free: However woman-to-woman relationships, female support networks, a female and feminist value system, are relied on and cherished, indoctrination in male credibility and status can still create synapses in thought, denials of feeling, wishful thinking, a profound sexual and intellectual confusion.[40] I quote here from a letter I received the day I was writing this passage: "I have had very bad relationships with men—I am now in the midst of a very painful separation. I am trying to find my strength through women—without my friends, I could not survive." How many times a day do women speak words like these, or think them, or write them, and how often does the synapse reassert itself?

Barry summarizes her findings:

> *. . . Considering the arrested sexual development that is understood to be normal in the male population, and considering the numbers of men who are*

pimps, procurers, members of slavery gangs, corrupt officials participating in this traffic, owners, operators, employees of brothels and lodging and entertainment facilities, pornography purveyors, associated with prostitution, wife beaters, child molesters, incest perpetrators, johns (tricks) and rapists, one cannot but be momentarily stunned by the enormous male population engaging in female sexual slavery. The huge number of men engaged in these practices should be cause for declaration of an international emergency, a crisis in sexual violence. But what should be cause for alarm is instead accepted as normal sexual intercourse.*[41]*

Susan Cavin, in her rich and provocative, if highly speculative, dissertation, suggests that patriarchy becomes possible when the original female band, which includes children but ejects adolescent males, becomes invaded and outnumbered by males; that not patriarchal marriage, but the rape of the mother by the son, becomes the first act of male domination. The entering wedge, or leverage, which allows this to happen is not just a simple change in sex ratios; it is also the mother-child bond, manipulated by adolescent males in order to remain within the matrix past the age of exclusion. Maternal affection is used to establish male right of sexual access, which, however, must ever after be held by force (or through control of consciousness) since the original deep adult bonding is that of woman for woman.[42] I find this hypothesis extremely suggestive, since one form of false consciousness which serves compulsory heterosexuality is the maintenance of a mother-son relationship between women and men, including the demand that women provide maternal solace, nonjudgmental nurturing, and compassion for their harassers, rapists, and batterers (as well as for men who passively vampirize them). How many strong and assertive women accept male posturing from no one but their sons?

But whatever its origins, when we look hard and clearly at the extent and elaboration of measures designed to keep women within a male sexual purlieu, it becomes an inescapable question whether the issue we have to address as feminists is, not simple "gender inequality," nor the domination of culture by males, nor mere "taboos against homosexuality," but the enforcement of heterosexuality for women as a means of assuring male right of

---

39. Ibid., p. 172.
40. Elsewhere I have suggested that male identification has been a powerful source of white women's racism, and that it has been women who were seen as "disloyal" to male codes and systems who have actively battled against it (Adrienne Rich, "Disloyal to Civilization: Feminism, Racism, Gynephobia," in *On Lies, Secrets, and Silence: Selected Prose, 1966–1978* [New York: W. W. Norton & Co., 1979]).

41. Barry, p. 220.
42. Cavin (see unnumbered n. above), chap. 6.

physical, economical, and emotional access.[43] One of many means of enforcement is, of course, the rendering invisible of the lesbian possibility, an engulfed continent which rises fragmentedly to view from time to time only to become submerged again. Feminist research and theory that contributes to lesbian invisibility or marginality is actually working against the liberation and empowerment of woman as a group.[44]

The assumption that "most women are innately heterosexual" stands as a theoretical and political stumbling block for many women. It remains a tenable assumption, partly because lesbian existence has been written out of history or catalogued under disease; partly because it has been treated as exceptional rather than intrinsic; partly because to acknowledge that for women heterosexuality may not be a "preference" at all but something that has had to be imposed, managed, organized, propagandized, and maintained by force, is an immense step to take if you consider yourself freely and "innately" heterosexual. Yet the failure to examine heterosexuality as an institution is like failing to admit that the economic system called capitalism or the caste system of racism is maintained by a variety of forces, including both physical violence and false consciousness. To take the step of questioning heterosexuality as a "preference" or "choice" for women—and to do the intellectual and emotional work that follows—will call for a special quality of courage in heterosexually identi-

fied feminists but I think the rewards will be great: a freeing-up of thinking, the exploring of new paths, the shattering of another great silence, new clarity in personal relationships.

III

I have chosen to use the terms *lesbian existence* and *lesbian continuum* because the word *lesbianism* has a clinical and limiting ring. *Lesbian existence* suggests both the fact of the historical presence of lesbians and our continuing creation of the meaning of that existence. I mean the term *lesbian continuum* to include a range—through each woman's life and throughout history—of woman-identified experience; not simply the fact that a woman has had or consciously desired genital sexual experience with another woman. If we expand it to embrace many more forms of primary intensity between and among women, including the sharing of a rich inner life, the bonding against male tyranny, the giving and receiving of practical and political support; if we can also hear in it such associations as *marriage resistance* and the "haggard" behavior identified by Mary Daly (obsolete meanings: "intractable," "willful," "wanton," and "unchaste" . . . "a woman reluctant to yield to wooing")[45]—we begin to grasp breadths of female history and psychology which have lain out of reach as a consequence of limited, mostly clinical, definitions of "lesbianism."

Lesbian existence comprises both the breaking of a taboo and the rejection of a compulsory way of life. It is also a direct or indirect attack on male right of access to women. But it is more than these, although we may first begin to perceive it as a form of nay-saying to patriarchy, an act of resistance. It has of course included role playing, self-hatred, breakdown, alcoholism, suicide, and intra-woman violence; we romanticize at our peril what it means to love and act against the grain, and under heavy penalties; and lesbian existence has been lived (unlike, say, Jewish or Catholic existence) without access to any knowledge of a tradition, a continuity, a social underpinning. The destruction of records and memorabilia and letters documenting the realities of lesbian existence must be taken very seriously as a means of keeping heterosexuality compulsory for women, since what has been kept from our knowledge is joy, sensuality, courage, and community, as well as guilt, self-betrayal, and pain.[46]

---

43. For my perception of heterosexuality as an economic institution I am indebted to Lisa Leghorn and Katherine Parker, who allowed me to read their unpublished manuscript, "Redefining Economics" (1980). See their article: "Towards a Feminist Economics: A Global View," *Second Wave* 5, no. 3 (1979): 23–30.

44. I would suggest that lesbian existence has been most recognized and tolerated where it has resembled a "deviant" version of heterosexuality; e.g., where lesbians have, like Stein and Toklas, played heterosexual roles (or seemed to in public) and have been chiefly identified with male culture. See also Claude E. Schaeffer, "The Kuterai Female Berdache: Courier, Guide, Prophetess and Warrior," *Ethnohistory* 12, no. 3 (Summer 1965): 193–236. (Berdache: "an individual of a definite physiological sex [m. or f.] who assumes the role and status of the opposite sex and who is viewed by the community as being of one sex physiologically but as having assumed the role and status of the opposite sex" [Schaeffer, p. 231].) Lesbian existence has also been relegated to an upper-class phenomenon, an elite decadence (as in the fascination with Paris salon lesbians such as Renée Vivien and Natalie Clifford Barney), to the obscuring of such "common women" as Judy Grahn depicts in her *The Work of a Common Woman* (Oakland, Calif.: Diana Press, 1978) and *True to Life Adventure Stories* (Oakland, Calif.: Diana Press, 1978).

---

45. Daly, *Gyn/Ecology*, p. 15.

Lesbians have historically been deprived of a political existence through "inclusion" as female versions of male homosexuality. To equate lesbian existence with male homosexuality because each is stigmatized is to deny and erase female reality once again. To separate those women stigmatized as "homosexual" or "gay" from the complex continuum of female resistance to enslavement, and attach them to a male pattern, is to falsify our history. Part of the history of lesbian existence is, obviously, to be found where lesbians, lacking a coherent female community, have shared a kind of social life and common cause with homosexual men. But this has to be seen against the differences: women's lack of economic and cultural privilege relative to men; qualitative differences in female and male relationships, for example, the prevalence of anonymous sex and the justification of pederasty among male homosexuals, the pronounced ageism in male homosexual standards of sexual attractiveness, etc. In defining and describing lesbian existence I would hope to move toward a dissociation of lesbian from male homosexual values and allegiances. I perceive the lesbian experience as being, like motherhood, a profoundly *female* experience, with particular oppressions, meanings, and potentialities we cannot comprehend as long as we simply bracket it with other sexually stigmatized existences. Just as the term "parenting" serves to conceal the particular and significant reality of being a parent who is actually a mother, the term "gay" serves the purpose of blurring the very outlines we need to discern, which are of crucial value for feminism and for the freedom of women as a group.

As the term "lesbian" has been held to limiting, clinical associations in its patriarchal definition, female friendship and comradeship have been set apart from the erotic, thus limiting the erotic itself. But as we deepen and broaden the range of what we define as lesbian existence, as we delineate a lesbian continuum, we begin to discover the erotic in female terms: as that which is unconfined to any single part of the body or solely to the body itself, as an energy not only diffuse but, as Audre Lorde has described it, omnipresent in "the sharing of joy, whether physical, emotional, psychic," and in the sharing of work; as the empowering joy which "makes us less willing to accept powerlessness, or those other supplied states of being which are not native to me, such as resignation, despair, self-effacement, depression, self-denial."[47] In another context, writing of women and work, I quoted the autobiographical passage in which the poet H. D. described how her friend Bryher supported her in persisting with the visionary experience which was to shape her mature work:

> . . . I knew that this experience, this writing-on-the-wall before me, could not be shared with anyone except the girl who stood so bravely there beside me. This girl had said without hesitation, "Go on." It was she really who had the detachment and integrity of the Pythoness of Delphi. But it was I, battered and dissociated . . . who was seeing the pictures, and who was reading the writing or granted the inner vision. Or perhaps, in some sense, we were "seeing" it together, for without her, admittedly, I could not have gone on. . . .[48]

If we consider the possibility that all women—from the infant suckling her mother's breast, to the grown woman experiencing orgasmic sensations while suckling her own child, perhaps recalling her mother's milk-smell in her own; to two women, like Virginia Woolf's Chloe and Olivia, who share a laboratory;[49] to the woman dying at ninety, touched and handled by women—exist on a lesbian continuum, we can see ourselves as moving in and out of this continuum, whether we identify ourselves as lesbian or not. It allows us to connect aspects of woman-identification as diverse as the impudent, intimate girl-friendships of eight- or nine-year olds and the banding together of those women of the twelfth and fifteenth centuries known as Beguines who "shared houses, rented to one another, bequeathed houses to their room-mates . . . in cheap subdivided houses in the artisans' area of town,"

46. "In a hostile world in which women are not supposed to survive except in relation with and in service to men, entire communities of women were simply erased. History tends to bury what it seeks to reject" (Blanche W. Cook, " 'Women Alone Stir My Imagination': Lesbianism and the Cultural Tradition," *Signs: Journal of Women in Culture and Society* 4, no. 4 [Summer 1979]: 719–20). The Lesbian Herstory Archives in New York City is one attempt to preserve contemporary documents on lesbian existence—a project of enormous value and meaning, still pitted against the continuing censorship and obliteration of relationships, networks, communities, in other archives and elsewhere in the culture.

47. Audre Lorde, *Uses of the Erotic: The Erotic as Power,* Out & Out Books Pamphlet no. 3 (New York: Out & Out Books [476 2d Street, Brooklyn, New York 11215], 1979).

48. Adrienne Rich, "Conditions for Work: The Common World of Women," in *On Lies, Secrets and Silence* (p. 209); H. D., *Tribute to Freud* (Oxford: Carcanet Press, 1971), pp. 50–54.

49. Woolf, *A Room of One's Own,* p. 126.

who "practiced Christian virtue on their own, dressing and living simply and not associating with men," who earned their livings as spinners, bakers, nurses, or ran schools for young girls, and who managed—until the Church forced them to disperse—to live independent both of marriage and of conventual restrictions.[50] It allows us to connect these women with the more celebrated "Lesbians" of the women's school around Sappho of the seventh century B.C.; with the secret sororities and economic networks reported among African women; and with the Chinese marriage resistance sisterhoods—communities of women who refused marriage, or who if married often refused to consummate their marriages and soon left their husbands—the only women in China who were not footbound and who, Agnes Smedley tells us, welcomed the births of daughters and organized successful women's strikes in the silk mills.[51] It allows us to connect and compare disparate individual instances of marriage resistance: for example, the type of autonomy claimed by Emily Dickinson, a nineteenth-century white woman genius, with the strategies available to Zora Neale Hurston, a twentieth-century black woman genius. Dickinson never married, had tenuous intellectual friendships with men, lived self-convented in her genteel father's house, and wrote a lifetime of passionate letters to her sister-in-law Sue Gilbert and a smaller group of such letters to her friend Kate Scott Anthon. Hurston married twice but soon left each husband, scrambled her way from Florida to Harlem to Columbia University to Haiti and finally back to Florida, moved in and out of white patronage and poverty, professional success, and failure; her survival relationships were all with women, beginning with her mother. Both of these women in their vastly different circumstances were marriage resisters, committed

to their own work and selfhood, and were later characterized as "apolitical." Both were drawn to men of intellectual quality; for both of them women provided the on-going fascination and sustenance of life.

If we think of heterosexuality as the "natural" emotional and sensual inclination for women, lives such as these are seen as deviant, as pathological, or as emotionally and sensually deprived. Or, in more recent and permissive jargon, they are banalized as "life-styles." And the work of such women—whether merely the daily work of individual or collective survival and resistance, or the work of the writer, the activist, the reformer, the anthropologist, or the artist—the work of self-creation—is undervalued, or seen as the bitter fruit of "penis envy," or the sublimation of repressed eroticism, or the meaningless rant of a "manhater." But when we turn the lens of vision and consider the degree to which, and the methods whereby, heterosexual "preference" has actually been imposed on women, not only can we understand differently the meaning of individual lives and work, but we can begin to recognize a central fact of women's history: that women have always resisted male tyranny. A feminism of action, often, though not always, without a theory, has constantly reemerged in every culture and in every period. We can then begin to study women's struggle against powerlessness, women's radical rebellion, not just in male-defined "concrete revolutionary situations"[52] but in all the situations male ideologies have not perceived as revolutionary: for example, the refusal of some women to produce children, aided at great risk by other women; the refusal to produce a higher standard of living and leisure for men (Leghorn and Parker show how both are part of women's unacknowledged, unpaid, and ununionized economic contribution); that female antiphallic sexuality which, as Andrea Dworkin notes, has been "legendary," which, defined as "frigidity" and "puritanism," has actually been a form of subversion of male power—"an ineffectual rebellion, but . . . rebellion nonetheless."[53] We can no longer have patience with Dinnerstein's view that women have simply collaborated with men in the "sexual arrangements" of history; we begin to observe behavior, both in history and in individual biography, that has hitherto been invisible or misnamed;

50. Gracia Clark, "The Beguines: A Mediaeval Women's Community," *Quest: A Feminist Quarterly* 1, no. 4 (1975): 73–80.
51. See Denise Paulmé, ed., *Women of Tropical Africa* (Berkeley: University of California Press, 1963), pp. 7, 266–67. Some of these sororities are described as "a kind of defensive syndicate against the male element"—their aims being "to offer concerted resistance to an oppressive patriarchate," "independence in relation to one's husband and with regard to motherhood, mutual aid, satisfaction of personal revenge." See also Audre Lorde, "Scratching the Surface: Some Notes on Barriers to Women and Loving," *Black Scholar* 9, no. 7 (1978): 31–35; Marjorie Topley, "Marriage Resistance in Rural Kwangtung," in *Women in Chinese Society,* ed. M. Wolf and R. Witke (Stanford, Calif.: Stanford University Press, 1978), pp. 67–89; Agnes Smedley, *Portraits of Chinese Women in Revolution,* ed. J. MacKinnon and S. MacKinnon (Old Westbury, N.Y.: Feminist Press, 1976), pp. 103–10.

52. See Rosalind Petchesky, "Dissolving the Hyphen: A Report on Marxist-Feminist Groups 1–5," in *Capitalist Patriarchy and the Case for Socialist Feminism,* ed. Zillah Eisenstein (New York: Monthly Review Press, 1979), p. 387.
53. Andrea Dworkin, *Chains of Iran, Chains of Grief* (Garden City, N.Y.: Doubleday & Co., in press).

behavior which often constitutes, given the limits of the counterforce exerted in a given time and place, radical rebellion. And we can connect these rebellions and the necessity for them with the physical passion of woman for woman which is central to lesbian existence: the erotic sensuality which has been, precisely, the most violently erased fact of female experience.

Heterosexuality has been both forcibly and subliminally imposed on women, yet everywhere women have resisted it, often at the cost of physical torture, imprisonment, psychosurgery, social ostracism, and extreme poverty. "Compulsory heterosexuality" was named as one of the "crimes against women" by the Brussels Tribunal on Crimes against Women in 1976. Two pieces of testimony, from women from two very different cultures, suggest the degree to which persecution of lesbians is a global practice here and now. A report from Norway relates:

A lesbian in Oslo was in a heterosexual marriage that didn't work, so she started taking tranquillizers and ended up at the health sanatorium for treatment and rehabilitation. . . . The moment she said in family group therapy that she believed she was a lesbian, the doctor told her she was not. He knew from "looking into her eyes," he said. She had the eyes of a woman who wanted sexual intercourse with her husband. So she was subjected to so-called "couch therapy." She was put into a comfortably heated room, naked, on a bed, and for an hour her husband was to . . . try to excite her sexually. . . . The idea was that the touching was always to end with sexual intercourse. She felt stronger and stronger aversion. She threw up and sometimes ran out of the room to avoid this "treatment." The more strongly she asserted that she was a lesbian, the more violent the forced heterosexual intercourse became. This treatment went on for about six months. She escaped from the hospital, but she was brought back. Again she escaped. She has not been there since. In the end she realized that she had been subjected to forcible rape for six months.

(This, surely, is an example of female sexual slavery according to Barry's definition.) And from Mozambique:

I am condemned to a life of exile because I will not deny that I am a lesbian, that my primary commitments are, and will always be to other women. In the new Mozambique, lesbianism is considered a left-over from colonialism and decadent Western civilization. Lesbians are sent to rehabilitation camps to learn through self-criticism the correct line about themselves. . . . If I am forced to denounce my own love for women, if I therefore denounce myself, I could go back to Mozambique and join forces in the exciting and hard struggles of rebuilding a nation, including the struggle for the emancipation of Mozambiquan women. As it is, I either risk the rehabilitation camps, or remain in exile.[54]

Nor can it be assumed that women like those in Carroll Smith-Rosenberg's study, who married, stayed married, yet dwelt in a profoundly female emotional and passional world, "preferred" or "chose" heterosexuality. Women have married because it was necessary, in order to survive economically, in order to have children who would not suffer economic deprivation or social ostracism, in order to remain respectable, in order to do what was expected of women because coming out of "abnormal" childhoods they wanted to feel "normal," and because heterosexual romance has been represented as the great female adventure, duty, and fulfillment. We may faithfully or ambivalently have obeyed the institution, but our feelings—and our sensuality—have not been tamed or contained within it. There is no statistical documentation of the numbers of lesbians who have remained in heterosexual marriages for most of their lives. But in a letter to the early lesbian publication, *Ladder,* the playwright Lorraine Hansberry had this to say:

I suspect that the problem of the married woman who would prefer emotional-physical relationships with other women is proportionally much higher than a similar statistic for men. (A statistic surely no one will ever really have.) This because the estate of woman being what it is, how could we ever begin to guess the numbers of women who are not prepared to risk a life alien to what they have been taught all their lives to believe was their "natural" destiny—AND—their only expectation for ECONOMIC security. It seems to be that this is why the question has an immensity that it does not have for male homosexuals. . . . A woman of strength and honesty may, if she chooses, sever her marriage and marry a new male mate and society will be upset that the divorce rate is rising so—but there are few places in the United States, in any event, where she will be anything remotely akin to

---

54. Russell and van de Ven, pp. 42–43, 56–57.

an "outcast." Obviously this is not true for a woman who would end her marriage to take up life with another woman.[55]

This *double-life*—this apparent acquiescence to an institution founded on male interest and prerogative—has been characteristic of female experience: in motherhood, and in many kinds of heterosexual behavior, including the rituals of courtship; the pretense of asexuality by the nineteenth-century wife; the simulation of orgasm by the prostitute, the courtesan, the twentieth-century "sexually liberated" woman.

Meridel LeSueur's documentary novel of the Depression, *The Girl,* is arresting as a study of female double-life. The protagonist, a waitress in a St. Paul working-class speakeasy, feels herself passionately attracted to the young man Butch, but her survival relationships are with Clara, an older waitress and prostitute, with Belle, whose husband owns the bar, and with Amelia, a union activist. For Clara and Belle and the unnamed protagonist, sex with men is in one sense an escape from the bedrock misery of daily life; a flare of intensity in the grey, relentless, often brutal web of day-to-day existence:

> . . . It was like he was a magnet pulling me. It was exciting and powerful and frightening. He was after me too and when he found me I would run, or be petrified, just standing in front of him like a zany. And he told me not to be wandering with Clara to the Marigold where we danced with strangers. He said he would knock the shit out of me. Which made me shake and tremble, but it was better than being a husk full of suffering and not knowing why.[56]

Throughout the novel the theme of double-life emerges; Belle reminisces of her marriage to the bootlegger Hoinck:

> You know, when I had that black eye and said I hit it on the cupboard, well he did it the bastard, and then he says don't tell anybody. . . . He's nuts, that's what he is, nuts, and I don't see why I live with him, why I put up with him a minute on this earth. But listen kid, she said, I'm telling you something. She looked at me and her face was wonderful. She said, Jesus Christ, Goddam him I love him that's why I'm hooked like this all my life, Goddam him I love him.[57]

After the protagonist has her first sex with Butch, her women friends care for her bleeding, give her whiskey, and compare notes.

> My luck, the first time and I got into trouble. He gave me a little money and I come to St. Paul where for ten bucks they'd stick a huge vet's needle into you and you start it and then you were on your own. . . . I never had no child. I've just had Hoinck to mother, and a hell of a child he is.[58]

> Later they made me go back to Clara's room to lie down. . . . Clara lay down beside me and put her arms around me and wanted me to tell her about it but she wanted to tell about herself. She said she started it when she was twelve with a bunch of boys in an old shed. She said nobody paid any attention to her before and she became very popular. . . . They like it so much, she said, why shouldn't you give it to them and get presents and attention? I never cared anything for it and neither did my mama. But it's the only thing you got that's valuable. . . .[59]

Sex is thus equated with attention from the male, who is charismatic though brutal, infantile, or unreliable. Yet it is the women who make life endurable for each other, give physical affection without causing pain, share, advise, and stick by each other. *(I am trying to find my strength through women—without my friends, I could not survive.)* LeSueur's *The Girl* parallels Toni Morrison's remarkable *Sula,* another revelation of female double-life:

> Nel was the one person who had wanted nothing from her, who had accepted all aspects of her. . . . Nel was one of the reasons [Sula] had drifted

55. I am indebted to Jonathan Katz's *Gay American History* (n. 5 above) for bringing to my attention Hansberry's letters to *Ladder* and to Barbara Grier for supplying me with copies of relevant pages from *Ladder,* quoted here by permission of Barbara Grier. See also the reprinted series of *Ladder,* ed. Jonathan Katz et al. (New York: Arno Press); and Deirdre Carmody, "Letters by Eleanor Roosevelt Detail Friendship with Lorena Hickok," *New York Times* (October 21, 1979).

56. Meridel LeSueur, *The Girl* (Cambridge, Mass.: West End Press, 1978), pp. 10–11. LeSueur describes, in an afterword, how this book was drawn from the writings and oral narrations of women in the Workers Alliance who met as a writers' group during the Depression.

57. Ibid., p. 20.
58. Ibid., pp. 53–54.
59. Ibid., p. 55.

*back to Medallion. . . . The men . . . had
merged into one large personality: the same
language of love, the same entertainments of love,
the same cooling of love. Whenever she introduced
her private thoughts into their rubbings and goings,
they hooded their eyes. They taught her nothing
but love tricks, shared nothing but worry, gave
nothing but money. She had been looking all along
for a friend, and it took her a while to discover that
a lover was not a comrade and could never be—for
a woman.*

But Sula's last thought at the second of her death is,
"Wait'll I tell Nel." And after Sula's death, Nel looks
back on her own life:

*"All that time, all that time, I thought I was miss-
ing Jude." And the loss pressed down on her chest
and came up into her throat. "We was girls
together," she said as though explaining something.
"O Lord, Sula," she cried, "Girl, girl, girlgirlgirl!"
It was a fine cry—loud and long—but it had no
bottom and it had no top, just circles and circles of
sorrow.*[60]

The Girl and *Sula* are both novels which reveal the
lesbian continuum in contrast to the shallow or sensa-
tional "lesbian scenes" in recent commercial fiction.[61]
Each shows us woman-identification untarnished (till the
end of LeSueur's novel) by romanticism; each depicts the
competition of heterosexual compulsion for women's attention, the diffusion and frustration of female bonding
that might, in a more conscious form, reintegrate love
with power.

IV

Woman-identification is a source of energy, a potential
springhead of female power, violently curtailed and
wasted under the institution of heterosexuality. The
denial of reality and visibility to women's passion for
women, women's choice of women as allies, life companions, and community; the forcing of such relationships
into dissimulation and their disintegration under intense
pressure have meant an incalculable loss to the power of
all women *to change the social relations of the sexes, to
liberate ourselves and each other.* The lie of compulsory
female heterosexuality today afflicts not just feminist
scholarship, but every profession, every reference work,
every curriculum, every organizing attempt, every relationship or conversation over which it hovers. It creates,
specifically, a profound falseness, hypocrisy, and hysteria
in the heterosexual dialogue, for every heterosexual relationship is lived in the queasy strobelight of that lie. However we choose to identify ourselves, however we find
ourselves labeled, it flickers across and distorts our lives.[62]

The lie keeps numberless women psychologically
trapped, trying to fit mind, spirit, and sexuality into a
prescribed script because they cannot look beyond the
parameters of the acceptable. It pulls on the energy of
such women even as it drains the energy of "closeted" lesbians—the energy exhausted in the double-life. The lesbian trapped in the "closet," the woman imprisoned in
prescriptive ideas of the "normal," share the pain of
blocked options, broken connections, lost access to self-
definition freely and powerfully assumed.

The lie is many-layered. In Western tradition, one
layer—the romantic—asserts that women are inevitably,
even if rashly and tragically, drawn to men; that even
when that attraction is suicidal (e.g., *Tristan und Isolde,*
Kate Chopin's *The Awakening*) it is still an organic imperative. In the tradition of the social sciences it asserts
that primary love between the sexes is "normal," that
women *need* men as social and economic protectors, for
adult sexuality, and for psychological completion; that
the heterosexually constituted family is the basic social
unit; that women who do not attach their primary intensity to men must be, in functional terms, condemned to
an even more devastating outsiderhood than their outsiderhood as women. Small wonder that lesbians are
reported to be a more hidden population than male
homosexuals. The black lesbian/feminist critic, Lorraine
Bethel, writing on Zora Neale Hurston, remarks that for
a black woman—already twice an outsider—to choose to
assume still another "hated identity" is problematic indeed. Yet the lesbian continuum has been a lifeline for
black women both in Africa and the United States.

---

60. Toni Morrison, *Sula* (New York: Bantam Books, 1973), pp.
103-4, 149. I am indebted to Lorraine Bethel's unpublished essay
on *Sula* which first called it to my attention as a novel of woman-
identification.

61. See Maureen Brady and Judith McDaniel, "Lesbians in the
Mainstream: The Image of Lesbians in Recent Commercial Fiction." *Conditions.* vol. 6 (1979).

---

62. See Russell and van de Ven, p. 40: ". . . few heterosexual
women resent their lack of free choice about their sexuality, and
few realize how and why compulsory heterosexuality is also a
crime against them."

*Black women have a long tradition of bonding to-
gether . . . in a Black/women's community that
has been a source of vital survival information,
psychic and emotional support for us. We have a
distinct Black woman-identified folk culture based
on our experiences as Black women in this society;
symbols, language and modes of expression that
are specific to the realities of our lives.
. . . Because Black women were rarely among
those Blacks and females who gained access to
literary and other acknowledged forms of artistic
expression, this Black female bonding and Black
woman-identification has often been hidden and
unrecorded except in the individual lives of Black
women through our own memories of our particular Black female tradition.*[63]

Another layer of the lie is the frequently encountered
implication that women turn to women out of hatred for
men. Profound skepticism, caution, and righteous
paranoia about men may indeed be part of any healthy
woman's response to the woman-hatred embedded in
male-dominated culture, to the forms assumed by "normal" male sexuality, and to *the failure even of "sensitive"
or "political" men to perceive or find these troubling.* Yet
woman-hatred is so embedded in culture, so "normal"
does it seem, so profoundly is it neglected as a social
phenomenon, that many women, even feminists and lesbians, fail to identify it until it takes, in their own lives,
some permanently unmistakable and shattering form.
Lesbian existence is also represented as mere refuge from
male abuses, rather than as an electric and empowering
charge between women. I find it interesting that one of
the most frequently quoted literary passages on lesbian
relationship is that in which Colette's Renée, in *The Vaga-
bond,* describes "the melancholy and touching image of
two weak creatures who have perhaps found shelter in
each other's arms, there to sleep and weep, safe from man
who is often cruel, and there to taste *better than any
pleasure, the bitter happiness of feeling themselves akin,
frail and forgotten* [emphasis added]."[64] Colette is often

considered a lesbian writer; her popular reputation has, I
think, much to do with the fact that she writes about lesbian existence as if for a male audience; her earliest "lesbian" novels, the Claudine series, were written under
compulsion for her husband and published under both
their names. At all events, except for her writings on her
mother, Colette is a far less reliable source on lesbian existence than, I would think, Charlotte Brontë, who
understood that while women may, indeed must, be one
another's allies, mentors, and comforters in the female
struggle for survival, there is quite extraneous delight in
each other's company and attraction to each others'
minds and character, which proceeds from a recognition
of each others' strengths.

By the same token, we can say that there is a *nascent*
feminist political content in the act of choosing a woman
lover or life partner in the face of institutionalized
heterosexuality.[65] But for lesbian existence to realize this
political content in an ultimately liberating form, the
erotic choice must deepen and expand into conscious
woman-identification—into lesbian/feminism.

The work that lies ahead, of unearthing and describing what I call here "lesbian existence" is potentially
liberating for all women. It is work that must assuredly
move beyond the limits of white and middle-class Western
women's studies to examine women's lives, work, and
groupings within every racial, ethnic, and political structure. There are differences, moreover, between "lesbian
existence" and the "lesbian continuum"—differences we
can discern even in the movement of our own lives. The
lesbian continuum, I suggest, needs delineation in light of
the "double-life" of women, not only women self-
described as heterosexual but also of self-described lesbians. We need a far more exhaustive account of the
forms the double-life has assumed. Historians need to ask
at every point how heterosexuality as an institution has
been organized and maintained through the female wage
scale, the enforcement of middle-class women's "leisure,"
the glamorization of so-called sexual liberation, the withholding of education from women, the imagery of "high
art" and popular culture, the mystification of the "personal" sphere, and much else. We need an economics
which comprehends the institution of heterosexuality,
with its doubled workload for women and its sexual divisions of labor, as the most idealized of economic
relations.

63. Lorraine Bethel, "This Infinity of Conscious Pain" (see unnumbered n. above).
64. Dinnerstein, the most recent writer to quote this passage,
adds ominously: "But what has to be added to her account is that
these 'women enlaced' are sheltering each other not just from
what men want to do to them, but also from what they want to
do to each other" (Dinnerstein, p. 103). The fact is, however,
that woman-to-woman violence is a minute grain in the universe
of male-against-female violence perpetrated and rationalized in
every social institution.

65. Conversation with Blanche W. Cook, New York City,
March 1979.

The question inevitably will arise: Are we then to condemn all heterosexual relationships, including those which are least oppressive? I believe this question, though often heartfelt, is the wrong question here. We have been stalled in a maze of false dichotomies which prevents our apprehending the institution as a whole: "good" versus "bad" marriages; "marriage for love" versus arranged marriage; "liberated" sex versus prostitution; heterosexual intercourse versus rape; Liebeschmerz versus humiliation and dependency. Within the institution exist, of course, qualitative differences of experience; but the absence of choice remains the great unacknowledged reality, and in the absence of choice, women will remain dependent upon the chance or luck of particular relationships and will have no collective power to determine the meaning and place of sexuality in their lives. As we address the institution itself, moreover, we begin to perceive a history of female resistance which has never fully understood itself because it has been so fragmented, miscalled, erased. It will require a courageous grasp of the politics and economics, as well as the cultural propaganda, of heterosexuality to carry us beyond individual cases or diversified group situations into the complex kind of overview needed to undo the power men everywhere wield over women, power which has become a model for every other form of exploitation and illegitimate control.

Endnote

In its first issue (Autumn 1975), *Signs: Journal of Women in Culture and Society* published Carroll Smith-Rosenberg's now classic article, "The Female World of Love and Ritual: Relations between Women in Nineteenth-Century America." The following summer appeared Joan Kelly's "The Social Relation of the Sexes: Methodological Implications of Women's History (*Signs: Journal of Women in Culture and Society,* vol. 1, no. 4 [Summer 1976]). Among scholarly articles, these two provided, in different ways, a point of departure for my thinking in this essay. I am deeply indebted also to the growing body of lesbian research in other journals, including Blanche W. Cook's "Female Support Networks and Political Activism," *Chrysalis* 3 (1977): 43–61; and Lorraine Bethel's " 'This Infinity of Conscious Pain': Zora Neale Hurston and the Black Female Literary Tradition," lecture given at the Harlem Studio Museum, May 1978, forthcoming in *Black Women's Studies,* ed. Gloria Hull, Elaine Bell Scott, and Barbara Smith (Old Westbury, N.Y.: Feminist Press, 1980); by several books published in the last few years: Kathleen Barry, *Female Sexual Slavery* (Englewood Cliffs, N.J.: Prentice-Hall, Inc., 1979): Mary Daly, *Gyn/Ecology: The Metaethics of Radical Feminism* (Boston: Beacon Press, 1978); Susan Griffin, *Woman and Nature: The Roaring Inside Her* (New York: Harper & Row, 1978); Diana Russell and Nicole van de Ven, eds., *Proceedings of the International Tribunal on Crimes against Women* (Millbrae, Calif.: Les Femmes, 1976); and by Susan Cavin's dissertation in sociology, "Lesbian Origins: An Hystorical and Cross-cultural Analysis of Sex Ratios, Female Sexuality and Homo-sexual Segregation versus Hetero-sexual Integration Patterns in Relation to the Liberation of Women" (Ph.D. diss., Rutgers University, 1978).

Stations and Spheres

Jessie Bernard

At the end of the eighteenth century, European society consisted of a system of "positions" or "places" or "stations" or statuses, and people knew their own precise location in it. Those in lower positions "knew their place" vis-à-vis their "betters" and did not "presume." A whole array of boundary-maintaining devices—etiquette, clothes, language, vocal intonations, posture, body carriage, facial expressions—kept the several levels clearly distinguished. All, obviously, prescribed by God and necessary for social order.

The end of the eighteenth century and the beginning of the nineteenth marked a transition, a point at which local markets were beginning to give way to more complex markets and more and more work was beginning to move out of the home, separating, even segregating, the work of women from that of men. A new doctrine, a doctrine of sexual spheres, thus arose to facilitate, explain, rationalize, and justify this growing separation of women in the home from men in outside work.

Whatever the date when the concept of women's sphere was introduced, it colored people's thinking about women for well over a century. In contrast to the "station" concept, which implied an integrated system in which all positions were in well-defined and fixed status relationships with one another, the "sphere" concept denoted a separatist system. Equal in value, its apologists insisted, but nevertheless separate.

The symbolism of the sphere was, I think, significant. It conveyed the idea of a clearly bounded entity with psychological and sociological "territoriality," a kind of female "turf," with a modicum of autonomy if not complete independence. There was a hint of this in More's figure of speech describing proper women as "lawful possessors of a lesser domestic territory, rather than the turbulent usurpers of a wider foreign empire." But more importantly, it helped to deal with the psychological problem of female inferiority and subordination.

Reprinted from Jessie Bernard, "Stations and Spheres," in *The Female World* (New York: The Free Press, 1981), by permission of the publisher and the author.

Women's Sphere as Realm of the Heart

[Women's eyes] are the books, the arts, the academes,
That show, contain, and nourish all the world. . . .

Shakespeare, Love's Labor Lost,
IV, iii, 351–353

The sphere of women reflected the love-and/or-duty dynamic. It was a realm of the heart and it was duty-bound to raise the moral level of society.

It was a realm of the heart, whose "ruling purpose was to express affection, sympathies, consideration and tenderness toward others—in short, to love" (Cott, 1977, 164). Sex-role distinctions, Cott tells us, were already universal by the late eighteenth century, and "heart" was distinctly female (163).

The importance of this supportive, expressive function, or "heart," was highlighted as the brutality of the new economic system—the Gesellschaft—began to make itself increasingly felt. The home came to be seen as a protection against the harshness of the outside world. Aileen Kraditor has summarized the classic statement of the function of women's sphere as it appeared in this country: "Certain recurrent themes . . . portray the business and political world as one of strife, and the home as a peaceful refuge, where the higher values are nourished. The ugly features of the outside world are accepted as necessary for progress, but progress would be futile unless balanced and ennobled by the conservative influence of the home. Destruction of the home means destruction of the delicate balance between progress and stability, between warfare and peace, between a certain necessary brutality and an equally necessary refinement. . . . The home was the bulwark against social disorder, and woman was the creator of the home" (1968, 13).

One of the major functions of women's sphere, therefore, was "to define an oasis of non-commercial values in an otherwise acquisitive society" (Sklar, 1973, 161). It supplied the balm needed to heal the wounds inflicted by the outside world. It made life in the male world tolerable. Women were required, as Sklar notes, to "perform a kind of penance for the sins of a society they were not fully allowed to enter" (162). Although they could not participate actively in the outside world, they were indispensable to its functioning. The sphere of women undergirded both the economy and the polity. "The Queen of the Household . . . occupied a desperately necessary place as symbol and center of the one institution that prevented society from flying apart" (Kraditor, 1968, 13). It was literally an integry, and integrating force holding the whole social system together.

There was an instrumental as well as an expressive aspect to women's sphere, namely household management. Catharine Beecher paid a great deal of attention to it. Her classic work, *A Treatise on Domestic Economy,* first published in 1841 and reprinted every year until 1856, had an enormous influence among women in this country, not only on their thinking about the practice of household management but also on their thinking about women. It covered every aspect of women's sphere: planning a house, running a household, rearing children. Women, said Beecher, should take this aspect of their role seriously; they should prepare for their contribution to the national enterprise as men approached their vocations. This lesson was part of the separate-but-equal theory of women's sphere. But it was already becoming ominous.

"If on the one hand," Tocqueville wrote in 1840, "an American woman cannot escape from the quiet circle of domestic employments, on the other hand she is never forced to go beyond it" (1840, 225). The operative words are "cannot escape."

Although the female world had existed in prototypical if not in archetypical form since even before human beings appeared on the scene it was not until the eighteenth century that, in the form of women's sphere, it became the object of a cult. Almost apotheosized theologically, the belief in it became practically a tenet of religious faith, encapsulated later in the dogma that woman's place was in the home, and that, conversely, home was her place, her world (Cott, 1977, 74).

The cult of domesticity strengthened and validated the idea of women's sphere. In time almost everyone came to assume that this separate sphere was the natural—if not necessarily the divine—way of organizing society. This conceptualization of the social order became part of the received wisdom, surviving into our own day among some segments of the population—the older,

ethnic, rural enclaves—and remaining as a nostalgic image in the minds of many others.

Before the eighteenth century most women were so busy contributing to the family's subsistence income that they could not be restricted to the household. They had to go wherever their work took them. The Book of Proverbs (31, 10–27), for example, describes the formidable amount and variety of work a good woman did in those days while her husband sat at the gates, in learned disquisition, perhaps, with his cronies. A virtuous woman was almost an industrial conglomerate in and by herself. She not only cooked, spun, wove, sewed, and made candles in the household, but also planted and harvested in the field. She was active in the marketplace; she shopped for wool and flax; kept her eye on the real estate market, looked for available land, manufactured clothing and other items and sold them and fine linen to the merchants. In addition, she was wise, kind, and charitable. Nor were the generations of women who followed her any less industrious. We noted in Chapter 3 some of the many places women have had in addition to the home since biblical times. So the dogma that restricted women to the home was actually rather novel.

From a slightly different angle, it could be said not only that women had a lot of places as well as the home but also that almost everyone's place had been in the home when that was where most production of goods took place. Indeed, instead of thinking of work being taken out of the home with industrialization, it might just as well be said that the home was removed from the work site and became a relatively new phenomenon—a place increasingly specialized for consumption. For everyone, it might be added, except the women who managed it:

In the old days the home was in the shop or factory. The important things were the looms or the workbench and tools; the home itself was incidental. It was as though everyone lived in a little factory, for when the home was the industrial unit it was as much a small factory as a home. Most people prior to the Industrial Revolution did not have homes, in reality they lived in little workshops. The removal of its industrial functions to larger factories with power machinery meant that more of the home could be devoted to family living. The emergence of homes specialized for family life alone rather than for industrial purposes is a new phenomenon in our history, to which we are not accustomed even yet. . . . Thus instead of think-

ing that industrial functions have been taken out of the home, it may be equally legitimate to think of the home as splitting off from industry. . . . The home as we know it—a place where families live but do not work—is relatively new in human history (Bernard, 1942, 1973, 518–519).

A considerable amount of services continued to be supplied in the home for a long time, but even this form of work began to suffer attrition late in the nineteenth century and especially in the twentieth (Ogburn and Nimkoff, 1955). Even then the belief that woman's place is in the home persisted, now meaning primarily that her place was not in the work force.

It was not until local markets—where women, like the woman described in Proverbs, sold produce and textiles and handicrafts—gave way to more complex and distant markets and more and more work came to move out of the home, that the spheres of men and women began drastically to separate, even to segregate. In American colonial times, family members had worked as a production unit, with, to be sure, a clear-cut division of labor but not an equally clear-cut separation of "spheres." By the end of the eighteenth century, however, the domestic sphere was becoming conceptually separate (Cott, 1977, 199). At least "the shift of production and exchange away from the household, and a general tightening of functional 'spheres' [specialization] in the economy and society at large, made it seem 'separate' " (Cott, 199). That was new.

For most women, the identification of women's sphere with domesticity shrank their world, deflated it, rendered it impotent. It was, again in Tocqueville's words, like a cloister. "In the United States," he said, "the inexorable opinion of the public carefully circumscribes woman within the narrow circle of domestic interests and duties, and forbids her to step beyond it" (1840, 212). To the extent that inexorable public opinion did restrict women to such a sphere the consequences could be severely negative. If women's sphere had room only for domesticity its boundaries would be seriously restricted. A sphere thus cut off from the outer world would tend to become parochial. The moral perspective could be narrowed, become intolerant, even limited to sexual sins. Cut off from the vital issues of the day, it could make personal gossip a major preoccupation. A large number of women could, in effect, be ciphered out of the polity. Women's sphere could thus easily become a prison or a gilded cage or a doll's house. Indeed, as time went on the concept

became more and more destructive especially for the affluent, as it deprived them of work as well as of independence. The frivolity, triviality, and irresponsibility attributed to women were to a large extent a result of restrictions imposed by women's sphere.

Many women in the sphere were not happy. An enormous literature of sermons and polemics was required to keep them reconciled to the restrictions to which they were subject. Their poetry was filled with unexplained weeping. Although they were supposed to be the moral guardians of society, they were kept ignorant of moral evil, victims of "benign blindness" (Stimpson, 1979). Such topics as prostitution and homosexuality and sexual "perversions" were kept under wraps. Women's sphere might recognize the existence of fallen or lewd women; they might have run across the term "whore" in the Bible. But they were not provided with a vocabulary to talk about the world of sexuality (E.C. Parsons, 1913). Ignorance was defined as innocence. They knew about abortion, of course, but it was among the subjects spoken of only in whispers. If there were to be violations of the mores of women's sphere, they wanted to be spared the need to face them (Bernard, 1949, chap. 24). They—and everyone else—wanted women's sphere to reflect a law-abiding, God-fearing, morally pure image. Men might violate the rules of women's sphere, but the women in it preferred not to have to deal with all that. They wanted to be protected from it.

So the darker side of women's sphere was rarely known. For example, for decades, perhaps centuries, many—usually poor—women had defined physical abuse as part of the female role. They assumed that all women were in the same situation. Abuse was a fixture of their lives.

Among middle-class women, whose sphere did not define abuse as part of the female role, the solution to abuse when it could not be eliminated was secrecy. They felt unique, alone. The "skeletons in the closet" so often referred to might be relatives or ancestors who had strayed and become "family secrets." The secrets might be wife-beating, infidelity, alcoholism, all kinds of breaches of the moral code of women's sphere. The contents of such closets might be the topic of whispered rumors and gossip, but—in a world where propriety was all important—not of open discussion.

In the diaries and memoirs of women on the Overland Trail, 1842–1867, we can get a feeling for what the women's sphere with its cult of domesticity was all about. From the costs its loss incurred we get an intimate picture of what support the female networks provided women, what comfort the accoutrements of domesticity supplied. All too often both the "heart" and the "domesticity" of women's sphere were casualties of the westward movement, and women mourned their loss.

By and large, the trek to the West was a male idea: "The man usually initiated a plan to emigrate, made the final decision, and to a greater or lesser degree imposed it on his family" (Stansell, 1976, 90). Some women acquiesced; some resisted; some even mutinied. Some became reconciled; some never did. More than one woman, out of sight and sound of the wagon, threw herself onto the "unfriendly desert" and gave way to sobs, like a child, wishing herself "back home with [her] friends" (Faragher and Stansell, 1975, 156).

During the first part of the great journey, a semblance of the old division of labor between men and women could be maintained. The cult of domesticity could be preserved, albeit in a modified form. But as the going became rougher the women had to do more and more of the hard labor. Nevertheless, against great odds, they worked to preserve what the cult of domesticity had trained them to value; they tried "to maintain the standards of cleanliness and order that had prevailed in their homes back East" (Faragher and Stansell, 1975, 157). They cared for sanitation; they watched over food preparation, preventing both waste and illness, and, above all, they did what they could to support and comfort one another by preserving against almost overwhelming odds the world of the amenities, of gentleness, that constituted women's sphere (148).

At night, women often clustered together, chatting, working, or commiserating, instead of joining the men: "High teas were not popular, but tatting, knitting, crocheting, exchanging recipes for cooking beans or dried apples or swapping food for the sake of variety kept us in practice of feminine occupations and diversions." Besides using the domestic concerns of the Trail to reconstruct a female sphere, women also consciously invoked fantasy: "Mrs. Fox and her daughter are with us and everything is so still and quiet we can almost imagine ourselves at home again. We took out our Daguerrotypes and tried to live over again some of the happy days of Auld Lang Syne." Sisterly contact kept "feminine occupations" from withering away from disuse: "In the evening the young ladies came over to our house [sic] and we had a concert with both guitars. Indeed it seemed almost like a pleasant evening at home. We could none of us realize that we were almost at the summit of the Rocky Mountains." The

hostess added with somewhat strained sanguinity that her young daughter seemed "just as happy sitting on the ground playing her guitar as she was at home, although she does not love it as much as her piano." Although a guitar was no substitute for the more refined instrument, it at least kept the girl "in practice with feminine occupations and diversions; . . . no big whip would tempt her to unwomanly pleasure in the power to 'set things going' " (Faragher and Stansell, 158).

But, much as the women tried to preserve their world, to practice the domestic skills and talents, when wagon loads had to be lightened, it was the part of the load representing their sphere that had to be sacrificed.

> Books, furniture, knick-knacks, china, the daguerrotypes . . . the guitars of young musicians — the "various articles of ornament and convenience" — were among the first things discarded on the epic trash heap which trailed over the mountains. On long uphill grades and over sandy deserts, the wagons had to be lightened; any materials not essential to survival were fair game for disposal. Such commodities of woman's sphere, although functionally useless, [had] provided women with a psychological life-line to their abandoned homes and communities, as well as to elements of their [very] identities which the westward journey threatened to mutilate or entirely extinguish. Losing homely treasures and memorabilia was yet another defeat within an accelerated process of dispossession. (158).

And when the going got really rough, the last vestiges of the female world — the support women gave one another — had to be sacrificed.

Wagon trains sometimes had to break up into smaller units, so that women found themselves isolated, alone, cut off entirely from the support of other women. "Female companionship, so valued by nineteenth-century women, was unavailable to the solitary wife in a party of hired men, husband, and children that had broken away from a larger train." The women viewed their separation from other women rightly as, in effect, a death sentence (159).

Although both men and women suffered on the Overland Trail, the suffering was of a different order for the women. It occurred in a male world. The work was hard for both men and women, but it was unaccustomed work for the women, unfeminine work, a violation of their domestic role, which had been so cultivated "back home."

On the trail a women's very identity, which depended on association with others in her sphere, was dissolved. "Civilization was far more to these women than law, books, and municipal government; it was pianos, church societies, daguerrotypes, mirrors—in short, their homes" (161). And, most of all, supporting networks. All sacrificed on the trail.

Not all of the westward movement was by way of the trails. Some of the pioneers came by ship. The women were thus spared a great many hardships. They did not have to deal with Indians. They did not lose the company of women. They did not have to do hard, male-type work. Their belongings were not jettisoned. They could retain the amenities. Their husbands were business and professional men who could afford decent housing. Still, they had had to part with family and friends. And although—perhaps because—they arrived in San Francisco still "stereotypically sex-role defined" (Saxton, 1978), they were unhappy "in this masculine paradise." And, expectably, they "seldom saw their husbands." True to the kin-orientation of the female world, these women "served as family correspondents" (Saxton).

The Faragher-Stansell documents cover the years 1842 to 1867. In those years the great western plains were bypassed as too barren for cultivation; the West Coast was the destination. But in time the intervening spaces also came to be settled. And the story told in books and documents dealing with prairie settlements in the years 1865 to 1890 is even more depressing than the story of the Overland Trail. The costs to women were appalling. Life on the prairies was lethal for them, as Stansell makes painfully clear in her study of the impact on women of "this masculine imperium" (1976, 89). "The West in the years after 1840 still appeared to be masculine terrain . . . a man's country" (88). Her research shows that the severity of the cultural disruption which homesteading the Great Plains inflicted on women was unparalleled in the history of the nineteenth-century frontiers.

For the first six or seven years they lived not in houses, in which the domestic amenities—even such basic amenities as cleanliness—could be enjoyed, but in sod huts, tarpaper shacks, or dugouts which rain could reduce to a sea of mud and dry weather to a depository of dust and straw. There was no way a woman could make a home of such quarters. In winter the water froze; in summer the air stifled. "Housekeeping as a profession in the sense that Catharine Beecher promulgated it was impossible under such circumstances (Stansell, 91). When, after drought, grasshoppers, unseasonable rains, debt pay-

ments, mortgage installments, there was any profit, it went for seed, stock, farm machinery and tools. Not for labor-saving appliances for the wife. Although some farms in the 1880s had washing and sewing machines, "for the most part . . . the machine age did not greatly help woman. She continued to operate the churn, carry water, and run the washing machine—if she were fortunate enough to have one—and do her other work without the aid of horse power which her more fortunate husband began to apply in his harvesting, threshing, and planting" (92).

Nor were there churches to supply solace and companionship. Apathy and even hostility toward religion were common. "Few families read the Bible, sang hymns, or prayed together" (Stansell, 92). Except among the immigrant communities, churches and the activities that revolved around them were lacking. The observance of religious rites and activities was makeshift or absent.

Most serious of all was the deprivation these women suffered because of the lack of "the network of female friendships which had been an accustomed and sustaining part of daily life 'back home'" (92). The men could escape to the saloon in town, but not the women. There was no transportation to spare, and neighbors were too far away for walking. A young woman in Nebraska wrote in her diary: "If the country would only fill up, it there were only schools or churches or even some society. We do not see women at all. All men, single or bachelors, and one gets tired of them" (quoted in Stansell, 94).

Women were farmhands first and homemakers or mothers after. And no more than the men Tocqueville described were the farming pioneers emotionally expressive. In one case "three wives fled before [Jules Sandoz] found a woman who resigned herself to the emotionless regimen of his farm" (93). The writer Hamlin Garland, himself a son of the middle border, referred to his people as "a Spartan lot . . . who did not believe in letting our wives and children know they were an important part of our contentment" (quoted by Stansell, 94).

The prairie women were troubled by the peripheral nature of their maternal role and missed the cultural support they needed for rearing their children. "Without help from the old networks of kin and institutions, a mother could not be assured of success" (quoted in Stansell, 95). With the loss of the support of her female world, she suffered "a general attenuation of the womanliness which had been central to her own identity and sense of importance in the world" (95). Young girls, however, who had not been exposed to the old cult of domesticity and its accompanying cult of true womanhood, were better able to cope. They learned how to help their fathers, how to do male chores. They were comfortable in men's clothes. As long as "we do not degenerate mentally," said one of these girls, "it is all right" (Stansell, 94). They did not degenerate mentally. "A second generation came to maturity; some were daughters like the strong farm women of Willa Cather's novels, who managed to reclaim the land that had crushed their mothers" (96).

The price had been great. Fear, depression, mental breakdown, insanity, suicide, murder haunted the first generation of prairie women. Their lives revealed what the loss of support from their sphere had cost them.

There can be little doubt that for a great many women, east, west, north, and south, the "bonds of womanhood" were supportive and the resulting sisterhood a real, genuine basis for building their lives around. Granted that some of the evidence from letters might be mere literary conventions, the evidence from diaries and other personal documents leaves no doubt that deeply experienced "homosociality"—even, perhaps, in some cases, homosexuality—did exist as a fundamental component of women's sphere. Women who were deprived of it suffered grievously.

Reprise: Ideological Tenets of Women's Sphere

Women's sphere was an ideological construct for explaining and rationalizing the sexually separatist system that had by now crystallized in the United States. The ideology had several components: (1) a belief that although women were not intrinsically inferior to men, their sphere still had to be subordinated to that of men in the interest of national welfare; (2) a belief that women's sphere had its own contribution to make in the form of running the household competently and taking care of all its members, a female profession to be prepared for and taken as seriously as any other; (3) a belief that women's

sphere was a place for emotional sustenance and for healing the hurt inflicted by the outside world; (4) a belief that women's sphere had a duty and responsibility to uphold and transmit the moral standards of society; and (5) a belief that the home, extended to include related moral and charitable activities, was the natural, normal, and only concern of women's sphere.

Ideology, however, was one thing; living it was something else again. Human relations were not ready-made ideological artifacts. Ideology made women's sphere a realm of the heart. It was up to the women themselves to forge the "bonds of womanhood," the sisterhood, the support systems that were its essence and made it bearable in a world not always congenial or supportive to women. Excluded from partnership in the management of the economy or the polity, cut off from shared companionship with men, they sought emotional sustenance from others in their sphere, and supplied it to them in turn.

References

Bernard, Jessie. American Family Behavior. New York: Harper, 1941.

Cott, Nancy. The Bonds of Womanhood. New Haven: Yale University Press, 1977.

Faragher, John Mack. Women and Men on the Overland Trail. New Haven: Yale University Press, 1979.

Parsons, Elsie Clews. The Family. New York: Putnam, 1906.

Saxton, Ruth. "Life for Women in a Men's Paradise . . . 1840–1851." 1978. Draft.

Stansell, Christine. "Women on the Great Plains 1865–1890." Women's Studies, 4, 1976, 87–98.

Stimpson, Catherine. "The Right to Name." In Julia Sherman and Evelyn Norton Beck, eds. The Prism of Sex. Madison, Wis.: University of Wisconsin Press, 1979.

Tocqueville, Alexis de. Democracy in America, vol. 2. New York: J. and H. J. Langley, 1840.

Introduction: The Politics of Intimacy

Implicit, if not explicit, in all the preceding articles is the view that the conceptual distinction scholars have traditionally made between the private and the public domain—that is, between the domestic sphere of household, family, and kinship systems, and the extradomestic sphere of work, production, and politics—has prevented us from understanding the complex structural features of sex-based inequality. The assignment of domestic responsibilities to women and the ideology that defines this as women's proper role not only ensures women's exclusion from economic and political life, but also limits the roles women are allowed to perform outside the home. Home and work, then, and the roles women perform in each, are not insulated from each other.

When we address ourselves to the private lives or intimate relationships between women and men we perhaps see most clearly how culture, socialization, and the economic and political institutions of society interrelate to support and to perpetuate sex-based inequality. In the first article, "Men, Inexpressiveness, and Power," Jack Sattel argues that men's tendency to mask emotions such as tenderness and affection is not just a matter of inarticulateness or even a socialized inability to respond to the needs of others. Rather, he argues, it is an intentional strategy selectively used by men to gain control and advantage in both private and public spheres. The next article, "Sexuality as Consumption" by John Lippert, discusses how cultural standards of male success in the work world affect sexual interaction between men and women in ways that deprive them of meaningful erotic and affectionate relationships with each other. Arlie Hochschild's article "Attending to, Codifying, and Managing Feelings: Sex Differences in Love" illustrates how sex-based inequality is reflected even in that unique experience which would seem to involve the most private and spontaneous feelings between women and men—the experience of falling in love.

Men, Inexpressiveness, and Power

Jack W. Sattel

Another thing I learned—if you cry, the audience won't. A man can cry for his horse, for his dog, for another man, but he cannot cry for a woman. A strange thing. He can cry at the death of a friend or a pet. But where he's supposed to be boss, with his child or wife, something like that, he better hold 'em back and let them cry.

> —*John Wayne,*
> *in one of his last interviews.*

Much of the recent commentary on men and sex roles in this society has focused on the inability of males to show affection, tenderness or vulnerability in their dealings with both other men and women. John Wayne may be dead but the masculine style stressing silent strength and the masking of emotions is still very much alive. What are the origins and dynamics of such "male inexpressiveness"? How do the strictures against masculine self-disclosure connect to the other roles men and women play in this society?

In their initial thinking about American sex-roles, sociologists didn't question the social processes which gave rise to the expectations that men would be relatively unemotional and constrained in the amount of intimacy they displayed and expected from others. For example, in an influential early theoretical statement, Talcott Parsons (1951) assumed the existence of a sexual division of labor in this society whereby men largely do the work of the public sphere (the economy) and women perform the socio-emotional work of the private sphere (the family). Parsons fastened on the fact that the economy demands that action be based upon deliberative, calculated premises which are as free as possible from "contaminating" personal or emotional considerations.

Reprinted, with changes, from Jack W. Sattel, "The Inexpressive Male: Tragedy or Sexual Politics?", *Social Problems* 23 (1976): pp 469–477, by permission of the publisher and the author.

Simultaneously, in Parsons' theory, the family—women's specialized domain—serves as respite and haven from the harsh coldness of the economy. For Parsons, learning experiences which shaped men into inexpressive ways of relating to others, while reserving for women nurturant and expressive modes of relating, serve nicely to reproduce and perpetuate American institutions.

Only relatively recently, spurred by the insights of the women's and gay peoples' movements for change in American institutions, have sociologists begun to rethink the neat link Parsons postulated between what men (and women) are and do in this society. Unfortunately, much of the analysis thus far has focused so narrowly on inexpressiveness as a personality trait of men that one is left with the impression the problem's solution lies with merely re-educating individual adult men toward their (human) capacity to feel deeply or authentically. In this essay I want to criticize such analyses as fundamentally shallow—the problem, I want to argue, lies not in men's inexpressiveness *per se,* but in the power and investment men hold *as a group* in the existing institutional and social framework. I am not denying the fact of male inexpressiveness; neither would I deny the destructive consequences inexpressiveness has for individual men and for the tenor of their social relationships (Balswick & Peek, 1971; Jourard, 1971; Farrell, 1974). However, I would deny or certainly argue against an interpretation which fails to connect inexpressiveness to the social and sexual division of labor.

A 1971 article, "The Inexpressive Male: A Tragedy of American Society," typifies a line of argument which has become widespread. The authors, Balswick and Peek, conceptualize male inexpressiveness as a culturally produced personality trait which is simply learned by boys as the major characteristic of their anticipated adult masculinity. Such inexpressiveness is evidenced in two ways: first, in adult male behavior which does not indicate affection, tenderness, or emotion and second, in men's tendency to not support the affective expectations of others, especially their wives. Balswick and Peek imply that both boys and men *devalue* expressive behavior in others as non-masculine; the taunts and "put-downs" of expressive or sensitive adolescents are a ready example of how such devaluation enforces a masculine style among men. For Balswick and Peek, the "tragedy" of inexpressiveness lies in the ability of the American male to relate effectively to women in the context of the increasingly intimate American style of marriage; that is, the victim of this tragedy is the American male and the traditional American family.

I think this conceptualization of inexpressiveness has two important weaknesses. First, Balswick and Peek assume that inexpressiveness originates in, and is the simple result of two parallel and basically equal sex-role stereotypes into which male and female children are differentially socialized:

> *Children, from the time they are born both explicitly and implicitly are taught how to be a man or how to be a woman. While the girl is taught to act "feminine", . . . the boy is taught to be a man. In learning to be a man, the boy in American society comes to value expressions of masculinity . . . (such as) toughness, competitiveness, and aggressiveness. (Balswick & Peek, 1971, p. 353–4)*

Such an attempt to ground inexpressiveness in socialization overlooks the fact that masculinity is not the opposite of femininity. The starting point for understanding masculinity lies, not in its contrast with femininity, but in the asymmetrical dominance and prestige which accrues to males in this society. Male dominance takes shape in the positions of formal and informal *power* men hold in the social division of labor; greater male prestige includes and is evidenced by, the greater *reward* which attaches to male than to female activities, as well as the codification of differential prestige in our language and customs (cf. Henley, 1977). What our culture embodies, in other words, is not simply two stereotypes — one masculine, one feminine — but a set of power and prestige arrangements attached to gender. That is what is meant when we talk of this society as being "sexist."

My argument is that one reason little boys become inexpressive is not simply because our culture expects boys to be that way — but because our culture expects little boys to grow up to hold positions of power and prestige. What better way is there to exercise power than *to make it* appear — to dissemble a style — in which *all* one's behavior

seems to be the result of unemotional rationality. Being impersonal and inexpressive lends to one's decisions and position an apparent autonomy and "rightness." This is a style we quickly recognize in the recent history of American politics: Nixon guarded the assault to his position by "stone-walling" it; Gerald Ford asked us to "hang tough and bite the bullet"; while Edmund Muskie was perceived as unfit for the Presidency because he cried in public.[1]

Keeping cool, keeping distant as others challenge you or make demands upon you is a strategy for keeping the upper hand. This same norm of political office — an image of strength and fitness to rule conveyed through inexpressiveness — is not limited to the public sphere; all men in this culture have recourse to this style by virtue of their gender. The structural link usually overlooked in discussions of male inexpressiveness is between gender and *power,* rather than gender and inexpressiveness.

There is a second problem with the way Balswick and Peek conceptualize male inexpressiveness. They regard inexpressiveness as the source of communicative barriers between men and women. Balswick has particularly focused on this as *the* problem in contemporary marriages: "men who care, often very deeply, for their wives . . . cannot communicate what is really going on in their hearts." (Balswick, 1979.) Perhaps, but one of the repeated insights of my students — particularly older women students — is that male inexpressiveness in interpersonal situations has been *used against women* in a fashion Balswick's description fails to capture. Let me share a page of dialogue from Erica Jong's sketch of upper-middle class sexual etiquette, *Fear of Flying,* to suggest the use of male inexpressiveness to control a situation. The scene is the couple's honeymoon, just after they have returned from a movie:

She: "Why do you always have to do this to me? You make me feel so lonely."
He: "That comes from you."
"What do you mean it comes from me? Tonight I wanted to be happy. It's Christmas Eve. Why do you turn on me? What did I do?"
Silence.
"What did I do?"
He looks at her as if her not knowing were another injury.
"Look, let's just go to sleep now. Let's just forget it."
"Forget what?"
He says nothing.

"Forget the fact that you turned on me? Forget the fact that you're punishing me for nothing? Forget the fact that I'm lonely and cold, that it's Christmas Eve and again you've ruined it for me? Is that what you want me to forget?"

"I won't discuss it."

"Discuss what? What won't you discuss?"

"Shut up! I won't have you screaming in the hotel."

"I don't give a fuck what you won't have me do. I'd like to be treated civilly. I'd like you to at least do me the courtesy of telling me why you're in such a funk. And don't look at me that way . . ."

"What way?"

"As if my not being able to read your mind were my greatest sin. I can't read your mind. I *don't* know why you're so mad. I can't intuit your every wish. If that's what you want in a wife you don't have it in me."

"I certainly don't."

"Then what is it? Please tell me."

"I shouldn't have to."

"Good God! Do you mean to tell me I'm expected to be a mind reader? Is that the kind of mothering you want?"

"If you had any empathy for me . . ."

"But I *do*. My God, you don't give me a chance."

"You tune me out. You don't listen."

"It was something in the movie, wasn't it?"

"What, in the movie?"

"The quiz again. Do you have to quiz me like some kind of criminal. Do you have to cross-examine me? . . . It was the funeral scene . . . The little boy looking at his dead mother. Something got you there. That was when you got depressed."

Silence.

"Well, wasn't it? Oh, come on, Bennett, you're making me *furious*. Please tell me. Please."

(He gives the words singly like little gifts. Like hard little turds.) "What was it about that scene that got me?"

"Don't Quiz me. Tell me!" (She puts her arms around him. He pulls away—She falls to the floor holding onto his pajama leg. It looks less like an embrace than a rescue scene, she's sinking, he reluctantly allowing her to cling to his leg for support.)

"Get up!"

(Crying) "Only if you tell me."

(He jerks his leg away.) "I'm going to bed."

(Jong, 1973; 108-9)

The dialogue clearly indicates that inexpressiveness on the part of the male is *not* just a matter of inarticulateness or even a deeply socialized inability to respond to the needs of others—the male here is *using* inexpression to guard his own position. To not say anything in this situation is to say something very important indeed; that the battle we are engaged in is to be *fought* by my rules and when I choose to fight. Inexpressiveness signals the limits of the discussion and the tactical alignments of the participants.[2] In general, male inexpressiveness emerges as an intentional manipulation of a situation when threats to the male position occur.

I would extend this point to include the expressive quality of men's interaction with other men. In a perceptive article, "Why Men Aren't Talking," Fasteau (in Pleck and Sawyer, 1974) observes that when men talk, they almost inevitably talk of large problems—politics or art; cars or fishing—but never of anything personal. Even among equal-status peers, men seldom make themselves vulnerable to each other, for to do so may be interpreted as a sign of weakness, an opportunity for the other to secure advantage. As Fasteau puts it: men talk, but they always need a reason—and that reason often amounts to another effort at establishing who *really* is best, stronger, smarter, or ultimately, more powerful.

Those priorities run deep and are established early. In Pleck and Sawyer's (1974) collection on masculinity, there is a section dealing with men and sports. Sport activity is important because it is often held out as one area of both authentic and expressive interaction among men. I wonder. Here is an adult male reminiscing about his fourteenth year:

> I take off at full speed not knowing whether I would reach it but knowing very clearly that this is my chance. My cap flies off my head . . . and a second later I one-hand it as cool as can be . . . I hear the applause . . . I hear voices congratulating my mother for having such a good athlete for a son . . . Everybody on the team pounds my back as they come in from the field, letting me know that I've MADE IT. (Candell in Pleck and Sawyer, 1974:16)

This is a good picture of boys being drawn together in sport, of sharing almost total experience. But is it? The same person continues in the next paragraph:

> But I know enough not to blow my cool so all I do is mumble thanks under a slightly trembling upper

lip which is fighting the rest of my face, the rest of being, from exploding with laughter and tears of joy. (Candell in Pleck and Sawyer, 1974:16)

Why this silence? Again, I don't think it is just because our culture demands inexpression; silence and inexpression are the ways men learn to consolidate power, to make the effort appear as effortless, to guard against showing the real limits on one's potential and power by making it all seem easy. Even among males, one maintains control over a situation by revealing only strategic proportions of oneself.

Much of what is called "men's liberation" takes as its task the "rescuing" of expressive capacity for men, restoring to men their emotional wholeness and authenticity. To the extent such changes do not simultaneously confront the issue of power and inexpressiveness, I see such changes as a continuation rather than a repudiation of sexism. Again, let me offer a literary example. In Alan Lelchuk's (1974) novel about academic life in Cambridge, *American Mischief,* there is a male character who has gleaned something from the women's movement. The "John Wayne" equivalent of the academic male may be passé, but if one is still concerned with "scoring" sexually with as many women as possible—which this character is—male expressiveness is a good way of coming on. Lelchuk's character, in fact, tells women fifteen minutes after he meets them that he is sexually impotent, but with the clear insinuation that "maybe with you it would be different . . ." In this situation the man's skill at dissembling has less to do with handing a woman a "line" than in displaying his weakness or confidences as signs of authentic, nonexploitative male interest. Again, in a society as thoroughly sexist as ours, men may use expressiveness to continue to control a situation and to maintain their position of dominance.

I've tried to raise these points in my discussion thus far: that inexpressiveness is related to men's position of dominance, that inexpressiveness works as a method for achieving control both in male-female and in male-male interaction; and, that male *expressiveness* in the context of this society might also be used as a strategy to maintain power rather than to move toward non-sexist equality. I think my last point is most important. In 1979 Balswick wrote an article based on the conceptualization of inexpressiveness which I've criticized here. Entitled "How to get your husband to say 'I love you'," the article was published in *Family Circle,* a mass distribution women's magazine. Predictably, the article suggests *to the wife*

some techniques she might develop for drawing her husband out of his inexpressive shell. I think that kind of article—at this point in the struggle of women to define themselves—is facile and wrong-headed. Such advice burdens the wife with additional "emotional work" while simultaneously creating a new arena in which she can—and most likely will—fail.

Sexism is not significantly challenged by simply changing men's capacity to feel or express themselves. Gender relationships in this society are constructed in terms of social power and to forget that fact, as Andrew Tolson's book *The Limits of Masculinity,* (1977) so nicely points out, is to assume that men can somehow unproblematically experience "men's liberation"—as if there existed for men some directly analogous experience to the politics created by feminist and gay struggles. Men are not oppressed *as men,* and hence not in a position to be liberated *as men.* This dilemma has prevented—thus far—the creation of a theory (and a language) of liberation which speaks specifically to men. Everyday language, with its false dichotomies of masculinity–feminity/male–female, obscures the bonds of dominance of men over women; feminist theory illuminates those bonds and the experience of women within patriarchy but has little need to comprehend the experience of being male. In the absence of such formulations, masculinity seems often to be a mere negative quality, oppressive in its exercise to both women and men, indistinguishable from oppression *per se.* What would a theory look like which accounts for the many forms of being a man can take? An answer to that question poses not a "tragedy" but an opportunity.

Endnotes

1. This link is reflected in the peculiarly asymmetrical rules of socialization in our society which make it more "dangerous" for a boy than for a girl to be incompletely socialized to gender expectations (compare the greater stigma which attaches to the label "sissy" than to "tomboy"). The connection of gender to power is also apparent in data which suggest parents, as well as other adults in the child's world, exert greater social control over boys to "grow-up-male" than girls to "grow-up-female." (Parsons & Bales, 1955)

2. It would be beside the point to argue that women sometimes will also use inexpressiveness in this manner; when they do so, they are by definition acting

"unwomanly." A man acting in this fashion is *within* the culturally acceptable framework.

References

Balswick, Jack. 1979. How to get your husband to say "I love you." *Family Circle.*

Balswick, Jack and Christine Avertt. 1977. "Differences in expressiveness: Gender, interpersonal orientation, and perceived parental expressiveness as contributing factors." *Journal of Marriage and Family,* 38: 121–127.

Balswick, Jack and Charles Peek. 1971. "The inexpressive male: a tragedy of American Society," *The Family Coordinator,* 20: 363–368.

Farrell, Warren. 1974. *The Liberated Man.* New York: Random House.

Henley, Nancy. 1977. *Body Politics,* Englewood Cliffs, NJ: Prentice-Hall.

Jong, Erica. 1973. *Fear of Flying,* New York: New American Library.

Jourard, Sidney M. 1971. *Self-Disclosure,* New York: Wiley-Interscience.

Lelchuk, Alan. 1974. *American Mischief,* New York: New American Library.

Parsons, Talcott. 1951. *The Social System* (Chap VI and VII), Glencoe, Illinois: Free Press.

Parsons, Talcott and Robert Bales. 1955. "The American Family: its relation to personality and the social structure," *Family Socialization and Interaction Process,* Glencoe: Free Press.

Pleck, Joseph and Jack Sawyer. 1974. *Men and Masculinity,* Englewood Cliffs, NJ: Prentice-Hall.

Tolson, Andrew. 1977. *The Limits of Masculinity,* New York: Harper and Row.

READING 53

Sexuality as Consumption

John Lippert

I work at a Fisher Body plant over in Elyria, Ohio. And so I spend about sixty hours each week stacking bucket seats onto cars. I used to spend all my time here in Oberlin as a student. But I had to give up that life of comfort as it became financially impossible and as it became psychologically and politically a less and less satisfactory alternative. I still try to remain rigorous about my intellectual growth, though, and so I still take a few courses here at the College. Such a schizophrenic role is at times hard to

bear psychologically, and the work load is often staggering. But such a dual life-style also gives me something of a unique perspective on both Oberlin and Fisher Body. I feel this perspective is a useful contribution to this conference on men's sexuality.

One of the things that really surprised me when I went to work for Fisher Body is that it really is hard to go to work every day. I don't know why that surprised me. At first I thought that everyone around me was pretty well adjusted and that I was still an irresponsible hippie at heart. But then I found that just about everyone I know at the plant has to literally struggle to go back to work every day. Again I was surprised, but this time also encouraged, because I made the very casual assumption that

Reprinted from John Lippert, "Sexuality as Consumption," in *For Men Against Sexism,* ed. Jon Snodgrass (Albion, CA: Times Change Press, 1977), by permission of the publisher and author. Copyright 1977 by Jon Snodgrass.

I could look to the people around me for help in facing the strain of that factory. But I soon found that there is nothing "casual" about this kind of support: it is incredibly difficult to find. I have lots of friends now, from all over Northern Ohio and from all different kinds of cultural backgrounds. But most of these relationships seem based on a certain distance, on an assumption that we really do face that factory alone. At first I had to look to see if it was my fault, to see if there was something in me that made it hard to have nurturing relationships with the people I work with. I soon found out that it is my fault, but that it is part of more general phenomena. I began to explore these "phenomena" as completely as I could: this exploration became an essential part of my struggle to go to work every day.

In trying to look at these barriers between me and the people around me, I was struck immediately with the kind of role sexuality plays in mediating the relationships of people in the factory. I spend much time working with men in almost complete isolation from women. I soon found that instead of getting or giving nurture to these men that I was under intense pressure to compete with them. We don't seem to have any specific goal in this competition (such as promotions or status, etc.). Each member of the group seems concerned mainly with exhibiting sexual experience and competency through the competition. Past sexual history is described and compared in some detail: as a newcomer, I was asked to defend my sexual "know-how" within a week of joining the group. Also, we try to degrade each other's sexual competency verbally, through comments like, "Well, why don't you introduce your wife to a *real* man," or "Well, I was at your house last night and taught your wife a few things she didn't know." But it is important to note that none of what happens between men in the plant is considered "sexuality." That remains as what we do with (or to) our women when we get home. And so even though homosexuality is generally considered to be some kind of disease, most men are free to engage in what seems to be a pretty basic need for physical intimacy or reassurance. This can be expressed very simply, through putting arms around shoulders or squeezing knees, but it can also become much more intense and explicit, through stabbing between ass cheeks or pulling at nipples. But all of this physical interaction occurs within this atmosphere of competition. It takes the form of banter, horseplay, thrust and parry seemingly intended to make the need for such physical interaction seem as absurd as possible. But even through this competition, it is easy to see that many,

many men enjoy this physical interaction and that they receive a kind of physical satisfaction from it that they just don't get when they go home.

My relationships with women seem somehow equally distorted. Entry of women into the factory is still a relatively recent event, at least recent enough so that contact between men and women is still unique and very noticeable. Much occurs before words are even spoken. Like every other man there, I discuss and evaluate the physical appearance of the women around men. This analysis is at times lengthy and involved, as in "She's pretty nice but her legs are too long in proportion to the rest of her body." Of course this evaluation goes on in places other than the factory, but here it seems particularly universal and intense. Perhaps a reason for this intensity is that the factory is an ugly place to spend eight or ten hours a day, and attractive people are much nicer to look at.

I guess I really do get some sort of satisfaction from engaging in this analysis. But there is an incredible gap between the kind of pleasure I get when I sleep with someone and the kind of pleasure I get when I see someone attractive in the shop. And yet I behave as if there is some connection. Many men are completely unabashed about letting the women know they are being watched and discussed, and some men are quite open about the results of their analysis. Really attractive women have to put up with incredible harassment, from constant propositions to mindless and obscene grunts as they walk by. Men who call out these obscenities can't actually be trying to sleep with the women they are yelling at; they are simply making the women suffer for their beauty.

In this attack they are joined by some older men who just don't like the thought of working with women. Many women have been told they ought to leave the factory and get a husband, and then they are told in some detail what they have to do to get a husband! It is really difficult for women to work in that factory. In many cases women have merely added eight hours a day of boredom and frustration in the factory to eight or more hours a day of housework and childcare at home. And they have to contend with this harassment on top of all that.

But women are getting more secure in the factory. More and more now, men who are particularly offensive in this harassment are responded to in kind, with a flippant, "Up your ass, buddy!" In any case, by the time I get close enough to a woman to actually talk to her, I feel like a real entrepreneur. By that time I've already completed my analysis of the woman's physical appearance, and in the beginning of the conversation we are both trying to find out the results of the analysis. And to reinforce this feeling of entrepreneurship, when I get back to the men I'm working with, I get all kinds of comments like "Did you tap it?" or "Are you going to?"

But one thing that really amazes me about my sexuality at the factory is that it has a large effect on my sexuality at home. I first began to notice this when, in the first week, I began to feel an incredible amount of amorphous and ill-defined sexual energy at the moment I left the plant. This energy makes the drive home pretty exciting and it influences my behavior the rest of the day. I often think something like, "Well, I have two hours before I go back to work, and it would really be nice if I could get my rocks off before then." I found that dissipating this sexual energy really does make it easier to go back. Also, I began to notice that my sexuality was becoming less physically oriented (as in just being close to someone for a while) and more genitally oriented (as in making love and going to sleep). Also, as household chores were becoming more formidable while working, I began to ask people who came into my house—and for some reason, especially my sexual partners—to take more responsibility in keeping the place fixed up.

In trying to understand how my sexuality was being influenced by the factory, this relationship between sexuality at home and at work became an important clue. Working is much more than an eight-hour-a-day diversion; it influences everything I do. If I'm not actually working I'm either recuperating or getting ready to go back. Because I confront this fact every day, it's not hard for me to imagine the changes in my sexuality as essentially in response to the fact that I have to go to work every day.

Now there is an important contradiction in this "I go to work." When I'm at work, I'm not really "me" any more, at least in some very large ways. I don't work *when* I want to; I don't work *because* I want to; I don't work *at* something I'd like to be doing. I don't enjoy my job; I feel no sense of commitment to it; and I feel no satisfaction when it's completed. I'm a producer; my only significant role is that I make money for Fisher Body. Now Fisher Body values me highly for this, and at the end of each week they reward me with a paycheck which is mine to consume as I like. But notice: I have to spend a large part of that check and much of my time off in preparation for my return to my role as producer. To a large extent, I don't consume so that I can feel some satisfaction or something like that. Now I consume so that I can go back

to work and produce. And that part of my consumption which I actually do enjoy is influenced by my work in that what I enjoy has to be as completely removed from my work as possible. I build elaborate and often expensive systems (such as families, stereos, or hot rods) into which I can escape from my work each day. And this is as true of my sexuality as it is true of the music I consume for escape each day, the car I consume to get back and forth, or the soap I consume to wash the factory's dirt off me when I get home.

There is an important adjunct to this: the specifically asexual or even anti-sexual nature of the work I do. For the last three months my role as producer has consisted of stacking bucket seats on carts. That's it; nothing more and nothing less. Many parts of me are stifled by this type of work; we've all read about the monotony and so on. What is relevant here is that whatever dynamic and creative sexual energy I have is ignored for eight hours each day and at the end, is lost.

I hope that by now a picture is beginning to emerge which explains much of what is happening to me sexually as a function of this split between my role as producer and my role as consumer. What is the nature of this picture? The essential conflict is that in my role as producer, much of what is organic and natural about my sexuality is ignored for eight hours each day and at the end lost. I have to spend much of the rest of the day looking for it.

But notice: already I have lost much of what seems such a basic part of me. My sexuality is something which is no longer mine simply because I am alive. It is something which I have to look for and, tragically, something which someone else must give to me. And because my need to be sexually revitalized each day is so great, it becomes the first and most basic part of a contract I need to make in order to ensure it. The goal of this contract is stability, and it includes whatever I need to consume: sex, food, clothes, a house, perhaps children. My partner in this contract is in most cases a woman; by now she is as much a slave to my need to consume as I am a slave to Fisher Body's need to consume me. What does she produce? Again: sex, food, clothes, a house, babies. What does she consume for all this effort?—all the material wealth I can offer plus a life outside of a brutal and uncompromising labor market. Within this picture, it's easy to see why many women get bored with sex. They get bored for the same reason I get bored with stacking bucket seats on carts.

But where did this production/consumption split originate and how does it exert such a powerful influence over our lives? The essential conflict is that we really do have to go to work and we really do have to let our employers tell us what to do. There's nothing mysterious about this. People who will not or can not make a bargain similar to the one that I have made with Fisher Body are left to starve. If we are unable to convince ourselves of this by looking around this room or this College, we need only expand our observation slightly. Furthermore, Fisher Body and other employers have spent decades accumulating bureaucracies and technologies which are marvelous at producing wealth but which leave us with some awfully absurd jobs to perform. We have no say in deciding the nature of these jobs; they are designed only from the point of view of profit maximization.

But to question the economic power of Fisher Body is to question most of what is to our lives essential and leads us to an intellectual tradition which most of us find repugnant. But if we are to have an adequate look at our sexuality we must begin with these observations: that our society is largely influenced by two relationships which are universal in our society: *that as producers we are forced into roles which we cannot design and which ignore our sexuality precisely because it is an unprofitable consideration, and that as consumers our sexuality becomes a pawn in our need to escape from the work we do and our need to return to work each day refreshed and ready to begin anew.*

Now what is the power of the conclusion we have just made? It is a conclusion which was reached through the exploration of day-to-day experience, but at this point it is an intellectual abstraction which leaves much out. For instance, it doesn't consider important influences of family and school on sexuality. At this point, the conclusion is general enough to apply equally well to blue and white collar workers (the main conflict is that we really do have to go to work). The conclusion doesn't attempt to explain every detail of the life of every worker. It does, however, attempt to describe a certain dynamic to which those lives respond and certain boundaries within which those lives

occur. This conclusion is necessary for us in this conference if only from the point of view of intellectual clarity; we can hardly proceed unless we are aware that we as men and the College as an institution play a particular kind of economic role in society. Enough self-awareness to include the discussion of sexuality is a form of consumption that is simply not available to the mass of the people in our society. And it is to their time spent as producers that we owe our own extravagant consumption.

But what is the political significance of the conclusions we have reached? That is, can our discussion of sexuality affect the evolution of Fisher Body's power over us? For today, the answer seems no, that for today Fisher Body is incredibly strong because, like myself, the majority of people who work for it are basically committed to their jobs. But we need only consider individual survival for a moment to see that it can only be sought in the long run in a collective consciousness which is capable of challenging the power Fisher Body has over our lives. And this is why we need to confront our sexuality; because our sexuality is based on competition among men and at best distorted communication between men and women, it will make building that collective consciousness an incredibly difficult task.

In a short time we in the United States will feel the need for that collective consciousness much more sorely than we feel it today. The Third World is in revolt and the U.S. economy is in the midst of an economic collapse which rivals the collapse of the Thirties in proportions. As a result, we face massive unemployment in this country and the awesome prospect of battles between different groups of people fighting for the "privilege" of working for Fisher Body. If people see that it is only Fisher Body that can gain from such a battle, they may decide not to fight it. And if people see that a victory for Fisher Body means inevitably a return to a lifetime of alienation and oppression inside offices and factories, they may decide to fight instead for the right to control their own lives.

Attending To, Codifying and Managing Feelings: Sex Differences in Love

Arlie Russell Hochschild

This essay is stimulated by a finding from an exploratory study, that women are significantly more likely than men to *try* to feel or not feel in love. That is, women reflect more awareness of "feeling work" on love.[1] In the first part of this essay I discuss how people "construct" feelings and, gathering up evidence from my study and others, I posit three generalizations about how men and women construct love differently.[2] In the second part, I assume these generalizations for the moment to be true and try to explain them. There I argue that the love ideology as a cultural form is a necessary but insufficient and ultimately cyclical explanation. I turn, thus, to marriage as an institution with different meanings for men and women. For women, it is a vehicle of structural (as well as individual) mobility in a sex stratified society, much as it was for a small stratum of men in early modern France during which period courtly love developed.

Throughout I refer to *"love"* in the narrow sense of strong "interpersonal attraction" as it occurs between men and women. I also refer to it in the narrow sense of "conscious experience." Love refers here not to behavior, nor to a relationship *per se,* nor to unconscious processes (e.g., cathexsis) but to a fairly narrow plane of reality—conscious experience, as it is "constructed" by the actor. This is not all love is; it is all I am talking about when I use the word here.[3] Love is thus distinct from love ideology—a body of shared ideas about the experience of love.

General Orientation

There is a tripartite relation between ideas, social structure and self-as-architect of feeling. In the case of love, this is a relation between the ideology of love, marriage in

a sex stratified society and the self's construction of the love experience. By the ideology of love I refer to the cultural symbol system represented at large through magazines, television and especially film. Together these media make available a set of ideas and images about what love between men and women is or can be like. There are various versions of this symbol system (romantic love, conjugal love, courtly love, etc.) which highlight and shape the experiential possibilities in various ways. All express facets of the larger love ideology in American culture[4] and influence the private, apparently solitary, dialogue between self and feeling. The different meaning of marriage to men and women, in turn, influences both the ideology of love and the experience of it.

The individual in daily life is conscious of what I would posit as a "stream of raw feeling-experience,"[5] a set of cues from body and mind, inherently undifferentiated and chaotic. The individual continually performs three social acts upon this stream of raw feeling experience. These three acts are that of (a) *attending to* feelings, (b) *codifying* feelings, and (c) *managing* feelings. The love experience as a "constructed" experience is the by-product of these three acts and it is this by-product experience which, as adults, we come to think of as "natural."

The sociological study of feeling-experience is the study of these three types of social act, as they are influenced by culture and social structure. (See Hochschild 1975.) I will elaborate on each of these social acts as they bear on sex differences in the experience of love. Having done that I shall speculate about the effect of culture and social structure upon the self as it acts upon feeling-experience (hereafter referred to simply as feeling).

A. Attending to Feelings
An individual can consciously experience a feeling without attending to it. Just as the individual can consciously experience physical pain or tiredness without ac-

Reprinted from Arlie Russell Hochschild, "Attending To, Codifying and Managing Feelings: Sex Differences in Love," by permission of the author.

cording importance to that experience, so too s/he may consciously experience a feeling without attending to it. Attending to a feeling[6] involves (a) *selecting* out one constellation of mental and bodily cues from among a myriad of others and (b) *according importance* to that constellation relative to others.[7] We can do both, *whether or not* the feeling is easily defined and labelled, and whether or not we conceive of it as recognizable or understandable or as something to manage this way or that, or not at all. While, of course, we attend to the (inferred) feelings of others, I focus here on the social act of attending to one's own feelings.

This act is learned. Just as the cured deaf learn to "hear," and the blind who recover sight learn to "see," and just as we learn to listen to what we hear (e.g., classical music) or learn to observe what we see (modern art), so too we learn to feel. Suppose a child experiences those inner cues associated in adults with "falling in love." Whether or not s/he learns to attend to those cues partly depends on whether others, and especially parents, validate that attending process by attending to it themselves. Children quickly pick up the fact that there is an appropriate fit between feeling and situation, and that those feelings which occur in "wrong" situations (i.e., inappropriate feelings) are most commonly disattended. Even among children there are wide differences in attending habits and as adults we exist in full blown "emotive cultures" with elaborate attending rules.

Much of the research on love does not tell us about sex differences. The studies which do, often fail to distinguish between the social act of attending to love experiences and the acts of codifying or managing them. Further research may nonetheless be brought to bear on the proposition that: in contemporary American middle class culture, women more than men closely attend to, scan and scrutinize their experiences of love.[8] While there is little data on this, my own content analysis of descriptions of emotional experiences (N = 261) showed that women were more likely to choose to describe love experiences (58%) than were men (35%). However, it was also true that women described more anger experiences (53% women versus 30% men). From my study, it remains unclear whether (a) a tendency to select an affective sphere indicates the custom of attending to it in daily life, and (b) whether women describe many more emotions than do men, love being only one.

Lacking the proper data, I would none the less hypothesize a sex difference in the degree of attention given to the love experience for men and women. I will suggest two other ways in which men and women differ in how they act on their love experience, before theorizing about why this difference might exist.

B. Codifying Feelings

Between the stream of raw feeling-experience and the registering of part of it, I hypothesize a second social act: codification. Even if the actor disattends a feeling, s/he may "know what it is," "recognize" or understand a feeling in the sense of being able to label it as, say, love or sadness. It is the process of codification that makes this recognition possible. The two social acts of codification and attending are interrelated, but analytically separate; only by accumulating cues which have been *detected* by attention can the individual compose the cues into a unit with a label (e.g., love). On the other hand, once the individual has those compositions in mind, s/he is more likely to attend and detect certain cues.

Codification is actually a very complex process embodying several sub-processes. First of all, it involves creating *discrete compositions* from various bodily and mental cues (e.g., heart palpitations, feeling high, the image of the loved one looming large). Certain cues are separated into various groups, and divided off from other cues. The actor then learns to attend to this group of cues—or composition—simultaneously (Davitz 1969, Levy 1973). A composition is the set of indicators by which we define feeling. Many compositions together make up our inner mapping of the affective possibilities. It is a map of expectations, based on how we have arranged and categorized cues into discrete compositions. We then cast this map over the stream of raw feeling-experience. The map of compositions creates feeling*s* from inchoate feel*ing* (e.g., attraction versus affection versus euphoria versus joy). By virtue of this map we make up distinctions between "non-affective" and affective experiences defined as "pure" tiredness, "pure" sexuality, etc. We make up distinctions, too, between "naturally available" emotions (feelings which are *in the nature of* human experience) and feelings which are not. For example, in some cultures[9] homosexual attraction is thought to be unnatural or unavailable to most human beings. It is thus an experience not codified into a recognizable composition, even prior to the act of management or the imposition of external sanction.

Our experience may or may not fit the map we cast over it. When experience fails to fit the pre-established categories, the individual may experience surprise or puzzlement. S/he may conclude that s/he is experiencing an "imperfect" version of love. In my study some respondents described a search, not so much to detect, as to define already detected elements of experience—i.e., to define their feelings *relative to* a pre-existing understanding of available feelings and emotions.[10]

The individual compositions and the larger map they together form probably vary cross-culturally in ways we know little about. Levy (1973) in his study of Tahitian culture found that some feelings were, to the Western eye, well discriminated (anger, shame, fear) while others (loneliness, depression, guilt) were poorly discriminated. In a list of 301 words describing feeling in the missionary dictionary, 47 referred to anger feelings and 27 to pleasurable states, and very few referred to depressive feelings. There is, he suggests, a difference between trans-schematic experience and the cultural schema through which experience is "recognized." He found that experience which in the West might be interpreted as "falling in love" was assigned the meaning of madness; i.e., was not "recognized" as fitting into the boundaries of experience assigned to love or affection.

Even within the same culture, there may be sub-cultural differences in codification—such as that between men and women. The literature on love, though purportedly about "attitudes toward" love, hints at sex differences in codification. (Beigel 1951; Knox and Sporakowski 1968; Knox 1970; Hobart 1958; Rubin 1970; Reiss 1960; Coombs and Kenkel 1966; Banda and Hetherington 1963; Theodorson 1965.)

Like most studies on love that compare men to women, Knox and Sporakowski (1968, p. 638) found men to have a more "romantic" orientation to love, and women a more realistic or "conjugal" orientation. This study did not find nor seek to find whether or not men and women have different love experiences. But it suggests that *if* men and women have roughly similar experiences, they (a) categorize the cues of which it is composed in different ways and/or (b) arrange the cues into different compositions, associated with the same label, love. For proportionately more men than women, love is known by the following "natural" characteristics: (a) it has a strong physical component—palpitations of the heart, excitement, thrill, (b) daydreaming, preoccupation, (c) a sense of urgency and strength, (d) the absence of ambivalence, (e) exclusivity—i.e., it occurs vis à vis one "and only one" person, (f) it occurs "at first sight," immediately, and (g) it "naturally" involves jealousy of rivals, and (h) it is everlasting. Thus, if the actor experiences a mild, relatively non-physical attraction, without pre-

occupation or sense of urgency, with some ambivalence, loves more than one, and not that one "at first sight," experiences no jealousy, then the experience does not fully correspond to that composition called love.[11] Women were less likely to subscribe to this description of love. (See also Hobart 1960, p. 354; Knox 1970; Theodorson 1965; Gross 1944.)

Related to this basic finding are the findings of four other studies; in one study women were found to apply more exacting standards to the men they meet in first encounters (Coombs and Kenkel 1966).[12] A second study found that engaged males tend to seek the same qualities in a woman friend as they do in their fiancée, whereas engaged women seek different qualities in their male best friend than they do in their fiancé (Banda and Hetherington 1963). The third and fourth studies both found differences in what men and women seek in love. Rubin (1970) found that women tend to admire their male loved ones more than their boyfriends admired them. (Rubin mislabelled the scale "liking.")[13] Women were more likely to forgive or ignore faults in their loved one and to evaluate him more highly. They were also more likely, having evaluated him highly, to say, "I think that _____ and I are quite similar to each other." Men, on the other hand, evaluated their loved one less generously and less often thought themselves similar to the loved one. This assymmetry is suggested also in Reiss' pilot study (Reiss 1960) of 74 student responses to questions about the "most important needs" in their best love relationship. Twenty-two percent of the men but seventy percent of the women mentioned yes to : "I can look up to _____ very much." Thus, related to different definitional boundaries around the experience labelled "love" is a constellation of different attitudinal requirements of love for men and women—differences to which we shall return.

C. *Managing Feelings*

The third social act performed upon feelings is the management of them—the shaping, modulating, inducing, and reducing of them through feeling-work. Feeling-work is the deliberate act of trying to feel what we think we should feel in a given situation. It is the social act of trying to move experience to coincide with feeling rules. It has two sides. On the one hand, we sometimes try *not* to feel an emotion or feeling we think we ought not to feel (e.g., suppression).[14] On the other hand, we sometimes try *to* feel an emotion or feeling we think we ought to: i.e., try to fall in love.

Feeling-work is not simply the governance of expression, but of feeling itself.[15] Situations often place strains on people which are experienced as demands for emotional display of feelings we may not immediately experience. We can momentarily hold up a facade to the world and *display* the appropriate emotion. But the strain of upholding one expression with quite another underlying feeling is too much for continual daily wear. Thus, there is often a deeper effort at moving feeling itself to fit the expression thought to be appropriate to the role and occasion. Feeling-work reduces effective dissidence.

Feeling-work thus involves the active effort of bringing feelings to meet feeling rules.[16] Feeling rules, in turn, compose the inner legislature to the government of self.[17] They set up categories of "right" and "wrong" feelings for a situation and role, just as codification sets up categories of what particular feelings "are" and "are not." It is by rules of feeling that we not only feel sad at a funeral, but think we *should* feel sad; we not only feel happy at a wedding but think we *should* feel happy.

We experience these rules as guilt. The internalization of feeling rules is the setting down of guilt barriers around affect areas; they determine the range within which one has permission to feel something guiltlessly. They can be vague or clear, general or specific, contradictory or congruent, strong or weak.[18] Since feelings are often vague and ambivalent, feeling rules are often general and determine *ranges* of acceptable balance between conflicting feelings. Again, feeling rules do not determine experience but, rather, manage it. (See Hochschild 1975.)

Thomas Scheff, in his Balance of Attention Theory suggests three sorts of management relations between self and feeling. In the first, the individual "under-distances" i.e., abandons him/herself to a feeling, luxuriates in it, is passive vis à vis the feeling. Here the individual under-manages the feeling; rules are of little account. In the second, the individual over-distances (i.e., suppresses, or over-regulates the feeling). In the third, the individual achieves a balance between the controlling self and feeling.[19]

In the American understanding of love, there is cultural support for under-distance, "falling head over heels," "walking on air." However, there is data which suggests that women, if anything, actually tend to over-distance themselves from the love experience, in an attempt to control and direct it in "useful" directions. Kephart, for example, asked college men and women the following question: "If a boy (girl) had all the other qualities you desired, would you marry this person if you

were not in love with him (her)?" 64.6% of the males and 24.3% of the females said no. Less than 12% of either said yes (11.7% of males vs 4% of females). But a third of the men (23.7%) and two-thirds of the women (71.7%) were undecided. As Kephart notes, "This contrast . . . illustrates the male-female difference in romantic orientation. As one girl remarked on the questionnaire: "I'm undecided. It's rather hard to give a 'yes' or 'no' answer to this question. If a boy had all the other qualities I desired and I was not in love with him—well, I think I could talk myself into falling in love!" (Kephart, 1966, p. 473.) Kephart concludes that "contrary to popular impression, the female is not pushed hither and yon by her romantic compulsions. On the contrary, she seems to have a greater measure of rational control over her romantic inclinations than the male." (Ibid., p. 473.)

My own exploratory study of 261 student descriptions (105 males, 156 females) of emotional experience suggests the same sex difference in the management of love. The main body of the study consisted of four descriptions[20] of remembered experience from real life, each generally a page long. (Hochschild, 1975b.)[21] The data was content analyzed[22]; this essay draws on only a small part of that analysis. One code used in the content analysis was for "feeling work" (called in that study "emotion work").

Feeling work was defined as the actor's awareness of manipulating attitudes, thoughts or behaviors in the service of changing feeling. It taps a peculiar type of agentic or instrumental relation to feeling. Three requirements had to be met: (a) the individual had to know or think s/he knew what his/her feelings were, (b) the individual had to know what they "should" be, and (c) there had to be some sort of effort, some shard of volition acting on the feeling as it occurred, to close the gap between feeling and rule.[23] The coding is thus based on the acknowledgment that feeling work goes on (some flatly denied that), that one has done it or is doing it oneself. This acknowledgment is reflected in the use of self-reflective verb forms—as in "I *made myself* feel . . . ," "I *forced myself* to feel . . . ," "I *snapped myself* out of it . . . ," "I *psyched myself* up . . . ," "I *manipulated my feelings* to fit . . . ," "I *squashed my emotions down* in order to . . . ," "I *tucked my feelings in* and went back into the room."

In the majority of descriptions, there was no spontaneous mention of feeling work.[24] Rather, feelings seemed to occur "automatically," and the meaning of them, the understanding of them was the point of focus—and this, indeed, was what the questions explicitly asked for (see footnote 21). Some mentioned expression work, but this is not of concern here.

Including all feeling areas, 18% (18) of the males versus 32% (46) of the females showed awareness of feeling work. In a post hoc analysis, I reasoned that this general sex difference in feeling work might be accounted for by the large proportion of female descriptions of love — a sphere in which women might do more feeling work than men. Had the focus been on the feeling of aggression, ambition, sexuality, I might have found more men doing feeling work than women. However, when I singled out the descriptions of love, I found exactly the same sex difference there as I found in the other feeling areas, not more as I had expected. This sex difference in feeling work remained when I controlled for religion, social class, mother's occupation, age, birth order, and powerlessness.[25]

None the less, in love as in other feelings, women were more likely to record a managerial self. For example, one woman describes her attempt to make herself love another:

> Since we both were somewhat in need of a close man-woman relationship and since we were thrown together so often (we lived next door to each other and it was summertime) I think that we convinced ourselves that we loved each other. I had to try to convince myself that I loved him *in order to justify or to somehow "make right" sleeping with him. (Which I never really wanted to do.) We* ended up living together supposedly because we "loved" each other but I would say instead that we did it for other reasons which neither of us wanted to admit. What pretending I loved him when I really didn't means to me was having a "secret" nervous breakdown. . . .[26] (Emphasis here and below is mine unless otherwise noted.)

Another woman takes us closer to the experience of management, of fluctuating from one worked-on feeling to another non-worked-on feeling to which she describes herself as "reverting back."

> . . . *anyway,* I started trying to make myself like him *(a student priest 40 years her senior) and fit the whole situation. When I was with him I did like him but I would go home and write in my journal how much I couldn't stand him. I kept changing my feeling and actually thought I really liked him while I was with him but a couple of hours after he was gone, I reverted back to different feelings. . . .*

A similar situation was put differently by a woman who said, referring to her friend, "I had small doubts but I *made myself define* love as a total thing where doubts do not exist." This is in sharp contrast to those descriptions by others who take love or liking, as given, as ascribed from inside, as nothing one can *try* to feel.

At the other extreme, are examples of people trying not to love or be attracted to someone they think they do love.

> Last summer I was going out with a guy often and began to feel very strongly about him. I knew though that he had just broken up with a girl a year ago because she had gotten too serious about him. So I was afraid to show any emotion. I also was afraid of being hurt, so I attempted to change my feelings. I talked myself into not caring *about Mike . . . but I must admit it didn't work for too long. To sustain this feeling I had to almost invent bad things about him and concentrate on them or continue to tell myself he didn't care. It was a hardening of emotions I'd say. It took a lot of work and was unpleasant, because I had to concentrate on anything I could find that was irritating about him. (The story does have a happy ending — I finally, after three months, let down my wall and admitted how I felt, and to my surprise and joy, he felt the same way. Things are now going very well.)*[27]

Another woman created a social support system of friends who encouraged her feeling work; she told her friends "how terrible" her boyfriend was, and then went to them for encouragement in her attempt to disengage her feelings from him.

Although women do feeling work on love no more than on other feelings described in the study, it is my clear impression that the most elaborate examples involve women in love. There were quite a few "plain" examples *of* feeling work, as distinct from the *awareness* of feeling work suggested above; and, indeed, awareness is not always part of all the managing of feeling that people do. It is simply all that I am describing here.

Interpretation

I have said that the sociological study of feeling-experience is the study of three social acts (attending to, codifying and managing feelings) as they are influenced by culture and social structure. I have also speculated that women and men relate to love in different ways; women attend to it more (no evidence), codify it differently (considerable evidence), and manage it more (some evidence). It is now time to relate these hypotheses to each other and to the cultural and structural forces which might account for these differences.

There is, I have suggested, a close tie between attending to love and codifying love in a particular way. Men, having a more romantic notion of love, cast a different map over their experience than do women. This sets up different expectations about "what might happen" and affects how men attend to experience. The romantic rendering of love suggests a less managerial, more passive stance toward love. Romantic love is by its nature something that can not be controlled; it occurs automatically, "at first sight," and is predestined. Love feelings are in a particular way ascribed, not achieved. Indeed, the data suggest that men manage and work on love less. In romantic love we have a social mask for passivity, for abdication of the governorship of feeling. On the other hand, women understand love more as something which can, in its nature, be managed and indeed they seem to perform more feeling work upon it. By de-romanticizing love, women appear to professionalize it more. Why?

The answer, I suggest, is that young men hold hegemony over the courtship process while at the same time women, for economic reasons, need marriage more. We should inspect first the young man's control over courtship. In modern American culture, the ideology of love is a cultural invention which emancipates the young from parental control over marriage. If the decision to marry depends on love (rather than on inter-kin alliances, etc.) and if those "in love" are the best judges of that love, then they are also the most qualified to decide whether, when, and whom to marry. (Goode, 1974.) According to Goode, the love ideology is functional in societies where kin lines are relatively unimportant (also see Rosenblatt and Cozby, 1972).[28] The "young couple" is now freed of parental control, but it is the young man who, by patriarchal etiquette, has official initiation privileges: he calls, invites, pursues, proposes. The traditional woman's counter to this official patriarchal etiquette is an equally stylized but covert set of customary maneuvers to "get invited" or "proposed to." But when the woman "is courted by" men who select her and whom she does not covertly select, there is a premium on managing not only her behavior but her feelings. This is especially important given the greater importance to her of marriage.

The secondary question about the persistence of patriarchal etiquette would take another essay. Suffice it to say that the existence of the cultural support for it (e.g., in films, etc.) is not in itself a sufficient explanation. For we would then have to ask which came first, the cultural expression of that patriarchal etiquette or the real experience of members of that culture? The same problem of circularity applies to the relation between the public cultural expression of the ideology of love and sex differences in members' private experiences of love. Both culture and experience call for an explanation on the structural level.

There the question is two-fold: is marriage more important to women than to men? If so, why? Women can become social parents without marrying the father of their child but men generally can not. A man, of course, can get a woman pregnant and become the biological father, but in the usual case he has to marry the mother to become the child's *social* father. But for women the case is otherwise; it is easier for women to convert biological parenthood into social parenthood—without marriage. Men need marriage to become social fathers whereas women can become mothers, albeit socially denigrated mothers, without marrying men. But, for social reasons, women need marriage for financial security. In the long run, financial security is, to most, more important than children, and in a nutshell this is why marriage is more important to women than to men.

The economic importance of marriage to women is influenced historically by several factors; (a) women's partial displacement from the labor force during industrialization, and (b) the lack of better economic alternatives outside marriage (self support, welfare). These two factors in turn convert marriage into a means of female "structural" mobility.

Let me briefly elaborate. Before the family became differentiated from the workplace, women worked. Roughly dating from the period of industrialization, the family *as a unit* was by degrees shut out of the industrial process, women being associated with the non-productive family, men associated with the workplace. This made women dependent on men, and men "responsible for" women.[29] During this period we begin to see a new cultural emphasis on attraction and love as something which should *precede* marriage, and, as Charlotte Gilman argued long ago, preoccupy women.

Only in the last 60 years have women begun to recover their economic role by returning to the economy. There they discover a partially segregated job market in which the full-time work of women results in sixty cents for every dollar earned by a man. This has been true for single women and married women alike. Even inside marriage, women contribute only 15%–30% of total family income, and self support outside marriage has unquestionably become harder for women than men.[30]

Consequently, for women marriage takes on the function of structural mobility (see Watt, 1962). There are two kinds of social mobility through marriage for women — structural, and individual. There is one kind for men — individual mobility.[31] It is with structural mobility that I am concerned here.[32] Compared to most single women, most married women "move up" simply by the act of marrying an employed male. Evidence of this comes from data on what Jessie Bernard calls "the marriage gradient" (Bernard, 1973, p. 36). Men tend to marry down, i.e., marry women with less education and lower occupational status, while women marry men they can "look up to" — and through whom they are structurally mobile.[33] Thus, marriage is more important to women, and the process of courtship is, at the same time, out of their formal control. This results in women's more "realistic" vision of love and greater inner management of it.

A Suggestive Historical Comparison

In other eras for a certain much-smaller status group, love was also related to structural mobility — but for men, not women. Moller's discussion of the rise of courtly love in the 11th and 12th centuries in southwestern France suggests a striking parallel instance in history of the relation of love to mobility. (Moller, 1958.) During the three or so generations during which the poetry of the troubadours flourished, several social forces were operating. First, with the growth of the state, and the centralizing of the policing function, a number of knights, especially in the north, became occupationally displaced. The knights became warriors without jobs, and had skills and social orientations which became increasingly non-functional. Such knights migrated to the south where feudalism remained relatively intact. Thus, just as the much larger stratum of urban, middle class American women was occupationally displaced, so too was this smaller status group in early modern France (Bloch, 1939–40).[34]

Second, this period was one of social fluidity; the nobility was not yet a closed social class. For the unemployed knight, and others, a liaison with a noble woman could be an avenue of social mobility. In the economically backward and decentralized southwest, aspirations focused on noble or at least knightly status in the southwest, where nobles and prelates still knighted at will any person they wished. The consequent rise of men to the lower nobility and the ministeriales and to knighthood, and the existence of numerous aspirants to knighthood, involved, according to Moller, an extremely high sex ratio in the secular upper classes. Here, too, there is a structural parallel, in that a closing off of economic options in one sphere coincided with an opening up of options in another — marriage.

Third, the marriage gradient was in this particular period and place reversed. Women could easily marry beneath their status, while men, as a rule, could approach only daughters of their peers or superiors with the intention of marriage (Moller, 1958, p. 57). As Moller explains, "The usual state of things in Western Civilization where men in large proportion have been wont to marry 'simple girls,' thus was reversed during this period." (Ibid, 158.)[35] One background factor made these marriages attractive; in southwestern France and Germany, there was as yet no primogeniture. "The daughters of noblemen were included among the heirs of landed property and could succeed to fiefs in the absence of male heirs." (Ibid, p. 156). Thus, "the pursuit of heiresses was a major occupation of noblemen and a fantasy subject for indigent knights." (Ibid, p. 156)

Thus, with the occupational displacement of migrant knights, the absence of other options, and the availability of upper status women in the southwest, marriage became for a small status group of men who created the short-lived tradition of courtly love — a vehicle of structural mobility.[36]

The character of this form of love differed from that common in modern American context, but nonetheless a few suggestive similarities are striking enough to mention. In the French case there was a "ritualized public adoration of ladies in combination with servant-like actions toward them — such as granting ladies precedence, picking up their things, performing all kinds of small personal services . . . which became a badge of social superiority for men" (Ibid p. 146). In a sense this resembles the American housewife's "adoration and servant-like actions" which, too, become a badge of superiority over the pitied spinster. In both cases the lover is the dispossessed and lower status party, adapting to the presumed needs of the beloved. There is in both cases a "service orientation 'up'." The lover praises (recall Rubin's findings) the beloved.

And there is some restraint imposed on the lover; in the case of the French male courtier, it is courtois behavior, in the case of the modern American middle class woman, "feminine" behavior as defined by patriarchal etiquette. Both dispossessed and lower status parties tend to displace their former orientation and skills onto a new setting. The knight found another master to serve—the lady, and performed his warlike feats for her as a courtly lover. Perhaps in a more general way the American woman displaced her former orientation toward work onto marriage, conceptualizing her children and husband now as "products."[37]

The cultural traditions of love and the marriage market conditions underlying them differ in many ways. Courtly love was more tied to class relations, and modern love to sex-caste relations. Moreover, courtly love centers on frustration and yearning, and is disattached from marriage though not, as Moller argues, from the desire for it.[38] On the other hand, modern love is associated with marriage.

None the less, the parallel suggests that when a love attachment becomes, for one sex or the other, a means of improving one's lot in life, and when other means are unavailable, marriage takes on different meanings for the two sexes, which may in turn affect the different ways men and women construct the love experience.

Finally, love, in both cases, serves an important latent function: it obfuscates inequalities of power and status. Love defies stratification even while it is structurally generated as an ideology precisely by it. Through the romantic love complex, we attend to psychological—not economic—needs. We see the other as unique and noncomparable. Status comparisons *between* man and woman are banished from the zone of things attended to, and structural mobility is thus mystified.[39] Yet, in the American case, the evidence from Reiss suggests that women more than men want someone to look up to, or admire. Rubin (1970) suggests that structural mobility in its disguised form persists. Evidence on sex difference in the codification of love also suggests that women, to some extent and on some level are aware of this. Indeed, insofar as the mystification of inequality itself disguises the sources of inequality, the woman who codifies love as men do could be said to have "false consciousness."

Conclusions and Implications

In our inquiry into the experience of love, we see how the self acts on the stream of raw experience, through the social acts of attending to, codifying, and managing feeling. We see, too, how these social acts are shaped by culture and the structure of marriage as a vehicle of female mobility. Women do not appear to be the emotional beings, cast about by inner feelings, that we might have thought. By contrast, men seem more "irrational" than we thought by virtue of structural advantages which do not require as much rationality in love and marriage. We see here a series of possible links between the outer structure and inner constitution of emotional experience, and see in this how deep the social goes. But we catch this glimpse only when conditions have so changed as to give us modern eyes. As the condition of woman progresses, the differences in love will increasingly appear—to modern eyes—outmoded.

Endnotes

I would like to acknowledge a deep debt to Joann Costello and Joan Kaye, my research assistants in this project. They worked hard and became very involved in the exacting and often frustrating work of developing coding schema, and Joann Costello worked especially hard in helping me with computer work. The work has benefited a great deal from her sensitive and acute comments and continual supportiveness.

1. The post hoc hypothesis elaborated below will later be refined and tested against new data. In this study, women were in general more likely to show awareness of emotion work than were men: 18% (18) males vs. 32% (46) females showed awareness of emotion work out of a total of 100 male and 142 female respondents. This essay focuses on emotion work in the sphere of attraction and love.

2. The study of attraction and love is a small part of the study of that cluster of emotions and feelings associated with love relationships. These in turn form one part of the study of the self in relation to emotions and feelings—a branch of social psychology. For a broader discussion of the field of the sociology of emotions and feeling, see Hochschild, 1975-a.

3. The part of "love" that involves conscious feeling is the point of focus here. "Feeling" I define as a milder version of "emotion," which in turn I define as the individual's bodily cooperation or collaboration with an idea, an image, or concept, and the label imposed on this. To put it another way, bodily signals to the mind, and mental signals to the mind often travel separately. When they come together, in collaboration, we have emotion. Emotion is thus a bodily deepening of an idea, an image, etc. Unconscious and

behavioral indicators of emotion do not here compose the definition of love although there are other ways of usefully characterizing it.

4. Goode (1974) distinguishes between the romantic love complex (which includes ideological prescriptions that falling in love is a highly desirable basis of courtship and marriage) and the love pattern (in which love is a permissible, and expected prelude to marriage). The romantic love complex, he suggests, exists only in modern urban United States, Northwestern Europe, Polynesia and the European nobility of the 11th and 12th centuries (1974, p. 149).

5. In the Freudian perspective, this is more easily posited. According to Rapaport, for example, emotions are bodily adaptations to the environment, i.e., something, in theory, concrete. In the ethnomethodological view, however, reality resides in the account of reality, and thus, there is no raw or "actual" event apart from our account of our memory of it (Rapaport, 1942).

6. The habit of paying attention to feelings has, itself, a social history. In the early states of industrial development under capitalism women were socialized to attend more to emotion and feeling in self and others more than men. This was in part due to their closer association with the task of child rearing, and their necessity to cultivate a subterranean power base, to compensate for the lack of power in the political and economic world. During the later development of welfare capitalism, with the growth of the service sector, men have appropriated the custom of attending to emotions. Under capitalism the "usefulness" of this is associated with commercial advantage (since attending to the feelings of the client or customer is not necessarily associated with serving the best interests of the client). Under different social arrangements, attending to the feelings of others could be more closely linked to acting in the interests of others.

7. It is possible for an actor to attend to a feeling state, but misunderstand or misconstrue it. To Freud, a misunderstood or mislabeled emotion was the same as an "unconscious emotion" (see Hochschild, 1975-a). The somatic and mental cues were available to consciousness but the wrong meaning was attached to them (as when all the symptoms of anxiety are interpreted as simple fatigue). This probably happens much of the time, and as we shall see, emotion work can go on despite error in interpreting a feeling.

8. The act of attending to love experiences varies cross-culturally. Within any culture it varies by subgroup. In traditional and modern Chinese culture, for example, a young couple attracted to each other are probably likely to disattend the experience, being unprepared to "fall in love" in the American sense.

(See Yang.) In pre-industrial New England, also, a young person was likely to pick someone s/he thought s/he *could* fall in love with over time, after marriage. (Morgan, 1966.) In modern America, the process of attending to love also varies for men and women over time. Men have traditionally had to wait to fall in love until they are economically able to provide for a family; this exigency may mean that "genuine" feelings of love that precede the period of economic readiness are systematically disattended and retroactively invalidated as "mere infatuation," passing and insubstantial, until such time as the man is "ready" to attend to and validate the experience. As Broderick suggests, prepubescent children can "fall in love" but adults at least disattend this. (Broderick, 1966.)

9. One traveler to China encountered a guide who had never heard of homosexual attraction between women. It was not that she didn't sanction it; rather, she did not think that experience *existed*. For her, it did not correspond to an available or natural composition.

10. As Endnote 5 suggests, the Freudian position might deny cultural variations in the codification of affect, while the ethnomethodologist might assert that codification and attribution of meaning were all that emotion is. My position is intermediate; it posits a hypothetical raw experience which is independent of codification, and yet posits also a secondary "social act" upon that experience, which is all that we can consciously know of our emotion. Codification transforms raw experience, but raw experience is not "reduced to" the codification process.

11. "Males who had been in love once were significantly more romantic than their female counterparts, and in all classes of experience in love, males scored higher on romanticism than females." (Knox and-Sporakowski, 1968, p. 640.)

12. In a study of 734 men and women who filled out questionnaires to be the basis of an IBM computer blind date, women were more particular about their possible partner's race, religion, scholastic ability, and campus status than were men. Women were also less satisfied in the post study follow up. (Coombs and Kenkel, 1966.)

13. His "liking scale items" was composed of 13 items, 11 of which concern admiration; e.g., I think that _____ is unusually well adjusted; I would highly recommend _____ for a responsible job; I would vote for _____ in a class or group election; I feel that _____ is an extremely intelligent person, etc.

14. Emotion work is not quite the same as emotional control, if by control we mean the active preventing of

feeling. For often respondents speak of *inducing* emotion in themselves. Emotion work is also not the same as suppression, which implies the blocking of affect. Certainly when the individual has to go to some effort to induce one feeling s/he is doubtless suppressing another. However, inducing a feeling—the other side of suppression—is itself an important phenomenon and the awareness of it a sociological phenomenon, one covered by the larger concept of emotion work.

15. We might ask two questions: can we experience feeling without being aware of feeling rules? Yes. Children do much of the time, and adults do quite a bit of the time, since (a) we experience things "as they should be experienced"—i.e., we don't feel the rule because we are obeying it, and (b) rules determine only the boundaries of broad zones of affect. Second, can we do feeling work when the feeling is "unconscious"—i.e., somatic and mental cues are available to consciousness, attended to but mislabeled and misunderstood? Again yes. The feeling rule impinges on the cues, regardless of whether the label "in between" is correct or incorrect. In any event the "correctness" of fit between cues and label is measured, not by some giant psychiatrist in the sky, but by consensual agreement that certain cues go with certain labels.

16. There are also certain *rights* of feeling, e.g., "moodiness rights" of the highly qualified (prima donnas) and the disqualified (the sick, the insane, and normal people in extenuating circumstances).

17. Feeling rules are associated with role expectations (e.g., occupational roles; the cheerleader should be cheery, the nurse of a dying patient, sad and empathetic, etc.). Feeling rules in the moral sense are distinct from feeling guidelines linked to the actors' understanding of his or her own self interest (e.g., "I am better off liking my boss than disliking him."). In a larger sense, it could be said that the general moral rules serve some group interests more than others, and serve in no simple way the maintenance of some anonymous "occasion" in general.

18. When rules are ambiguous, one may not know "how to feel." When they are clear, one affectively conforms (in which case feelings are non-problematic) or deviates (i.e., the actor knows how to feel but doesn't feel that way). The affective deviant forgoes, even temporarily, a certain emotional component of membership in a social group or relationship; but his/her very inner acknowledgment of the feeling rules is itself a clue to membership.

19. In my exploratory study, I found a variety of images of feeling and emotion in the protocols which may correspond to these three sorts of relation between

feeling and the self as manager. Emotion is sometimes described with hydraulic imagery—as something that "gushes out" or gets "dammed up" or "flows." Other times it is described with fire imagery as something which "flares up," "gets ignited," or "explodes." These images of emotion imply appreciably different kinds of relation between self and feeling; the self was portrayed by some as an agent, by others as a victim and by still others as a custodian of emotion. And for each, there are various images of emotion. Agentic imagery included the vision of emotion as a resource, like food or money, something that provides energy, or fuel for production. It is something to "work on" or "work through" or "produce." For those who conceptualized themselves as victims, emotion was perceived as something that "preys on me," or "eats up my soul," or "that I am possessed by."

20. The four questions coded for emotion work were: (a) Describe as fully and completely as possible a real situation which stands out in your mind from the last year or so in which you experienced a strong emotion (any one). What did it mean to you? (b) Describe as fully and concretely as possible a real situation, important to you, in which you experienced either changing a situation to fit your feelings or changing your feelings to fit a situation. What did it mean to you? (c) Describe as fully and concretely as possible an important and real situation in which you experienced yourself as struggling. What did it mean to you? and (d) Describe as fully and concretely as possible a real situation in which you experienced feeling unequal in a relationship of real importance. How did you deal with it, and what did the experience mean to you? In addition, data was gathered on a variety of background characteristics such as age, sex, race, father's and mother's occupation, family size and birth order, as well as some attitudinal questions related to emotions.

21. The population was composed of students in two classes at University of California, Berkeley in 1974 (105 males and 156 females). This population was chosen for an exploratory study partly because it was readily available, but partly also for another good reason. Since the Free Speech Movement in 1964, the University of California, Berkeley, has become, in common parlance, a weathervane of social change for other universities across the country. This group of people is young; 45% were under 20, 48% between 20 and 25, and 7% over 25. The group was also found to be liberal on the question of sex equality: only 7% agreed that, "For all the talk, equality between the sexes isn't that important an issue." Over half (56%) agreed, "It's not just a question of economic equality. We need to overhaul the whole way boys and girls are

brought up." Thus, we reasoned, if we find sex differences of the sort studied here among this young, college-educated urban group of liberals on the question of sex equality, we might expect to find such differences *even more* among other social strata.

22. The material was coded by three coders, my research assistants Joann Costello and Joan Kaye and myself. Two coders coded 30 entire protocols independently. Our inter-coder reliability rate for those protocols on all items (over 280) was 92.5%. 7.5% of the items presented problems of difference in judgment. We continually worked on these problematic items which contributed to the 7.5% error to try to objectify our criteria. At first, I worked with the two coders, and then the two coders worked separately on the concrete coding and together on the thematic coding. This might be called the "negotiation of reality" solution to the subjectivity-of-coding problem. Needless to say, such negotiation of reality can also become a negotiation of distortion. But working together in such exacting and tiring work so reduced our clerical errors, and provided a useful comparative measure for judgment, that this method seemed far preferable.

23. In the coding of the protocols for emotion work, we had to rely on language. Some people were more articulate than others, and this may be related, as other studies suggest, to general intelligence and education. (Davitz, 1969.) However, we reasoned that among this university sample, we have a built-in control for level of education and even for a certain IQ range. We reasoned also that intelligence levels would be equally distributed between men and women, and it is the differences between the sexes which is of interest here.

24. Feeling work is not related to sensitivity to others' feelings. A content analysis of the entire protocol for "notice of another's feelings" suggests that those aware of doing feeling work are not more nor less likely to be sensitive than other respondents. On the other hand, those who do feeling work are more likely to "not want to offend or hurt the feelings of others." Theoretically one can avoid offending without doing feeling work (e.g., by controlling expression or not acting according to one's own unchanged feelings) but certainly too, feeling work can be a way of avoiding offense.

25. Especially high on feeling work are women who are: the daughters of middle class housewives (as opposed to middle class working women), Jews and Catholics (more than Protestants), middle children (more than first born or only children, or last born), and women who felt powerless to get what they want in future work (more than those who expect to get what they want in future work). Women of all these sorts were statistically more likely to acknowledge feeling work than were men.

26. A young man in a similar dilemma speaks of trying to change his feelings to accord with his conscience: "Well, I became involved with this girl—intimately. It was and still is a mere physical relationship—my guilt or conscience or whatever it is, will not allow me to just have a physical relationship *so I try to change my feelings or whatever to something romantic* so that I won't have to feel guilty . . . I do it all the time."

27. Another example of this is: "A man I met I liked a lot and spent a good deal of time with. He then decided he wanted to see me less, and although I really liked him and wanted to see him as much as possible, I had to agree and adjust myself to his decision. It made me feel helpless and angry because he was defining the relationship in his terms, and because I didn't want to lose him, I had to try to convince myself that I didn't care about his interest slacking."

28. As vertical ties to parents weaken, horizontal ties between strangers are culturally elaborated by the love ideology. Few films or songs in American culture heroize the love between parent and child; many do the love between young men and women. This particular link between kin patterns and love ideology provides a backdrop for the sex differences we seek to explain. It explains why love is relatively more important to American men and women than their counterparts in mainland China, for example. It does not explain the difference between American men and women.

29. There is little or no record of the full blown ideology of love as we know it, before the late eighteenth century in the middle class—the period in which middle class women retired to the home, and work in the growing cities was firmly established outside it. We have no evidence, either, that men and women at that time constructed love experiences in different ways.

30. This account is simplified considerably. Women's economic self-sufficiency is hindered primarily by two factors: (a) discrimination and job segregation and (b) the fact that most jobs are designed for men who can work long hours without family considerations, because they (unlike most women) have another person at home attending their family. These two factors account for women's economic vulnerability, and dependency on men through marriage.

31. Hollingshead and others have shown that love, if it is the main criterion for marriage, results in matches between men and women within similar class, racial, and religious categories. (Hollingshead, 1950.)

32. Marriage moves *some* women (and men) *further* up the social ladder than it does other women (and men). Those who move further up than others exemplify in-

dividual mobility through marriage. Here we are concerned with structural, not individual, mobility.

33. This leaves more single men at the bottom, and more single women at the top. It could be argued that the single women at the top do not have to use marriage to move up, since they are, on their own merits, already at the top. However, even the top stratum of single women does not compare in income and occupational status to the top stratum of men. Further, if all the women who marry remained single, they would not, *under present conditions,* be at the top.

34. There was also a migration of knights to this area from other areas, increasing the ratio of males to females, and creating a shortage of marriageable women.

35. "The upper nobility lost a number of their daughters to the lower nobility and *ministeriales,* these classes in turn lost some of their daughters to the urban aristocracies and also, usually for economic reasons, to the wealthier strata of the peasantry." (Ibid, p. 158.)

36. In both cases, too, the low status members of the opposite sex were considered ineligible as love partners. In the early period in France, it was lower status women who were ignored for their inability to improve the status of the knight, in the modern American case it is lower status males.

37. Moller also notes, "The symbolism of courtly love has apparently different layers of meaning, the common element of which is an anxiety regarding acceptance, which is assuaged by self-improvement and devoted service" (Ibid, 162). In the American case, too, there may well be an "anxiety regarding acceptance" on the part of women whose productive functions were taken away with industrialization and urbanization.

38. Since many men were landless, they were not eligible to marry. Thus they formed (often symbolic) adulterous liaisons with noble women, themselves locked into loveless marriages forged for financial reasons. (C. S. Lewis, 1959.)

39. In a sense love mystifies two sorts of inequality—that between the sexes and that between the generations. Men via work create status differences between the generations, whereas women via their kindling of kin ties, reduce such differences.

Bibliography

Banta, T. J. and M. Hetherington, 1963. "Relations between needs of friends and fiancees." *Journal of Abnormal and Social Psychology.* 66: 401–404.

Beigel, H. G., 1951. "Romantic Love." *American Sociological Review,* 16: 326–334.

Bernard, Jessie, 1972. *The Future of Marriage.* New York: Bantam Books.

Bloch, Marc., 1939–1940. *La Societe Foedale,* 2 vols. Paris: Michel.

Broderick, C. B., 1966. "Sexual behavior among pre-adolescents." *Journal of Social Issues,* vol: 6–21.

Coombs, Robert and W. Kenkel, 1966. "Sex differences in dating aspirations and satisfaction with computer selected partners." *Journal of Marriage and the Family.* 28: 62–66.

Davitz, Joel, 1969. *The Language of Emotion.* New York: Academic Press.

Goode, W., 1964. "The theoretical importance of love" in R. Coser (ed) *The Family, Its Structure and Function,* New York: St. Martin's Press.

Gross, Lleyellyn, 1944. "A belief pattern scale for measuring attitudes toward romanticism," *American Sociological Review,* 9: 463–72.

Hobart, Charles W., 1958. "The incidence of romanticism during courtship." *Social Forces,* 36: 362–67.

_____ 1960. "Attitude changes during courtship and marriage." *Marriage and Family Living,* 22: 352–9.

Hochschild, Arlie Russell, 1975-a. "The sociology of feeling and emotion; selected possibilities" in Marcia Millman and Rosabeth Kantor (eds) *Another Voice,* Random House, forthcoming.

_____ 1975-b. "Sex Differences in the Culture of Emotion; a Study of the Relation between Self and Feeling." Unpublished manuscript.

Hollingshead, A., 1950. "Cultural factors in the selection of marriage mates," *American Sociological Review,* 15: 619–627.

Kephart, W., 1967. "Some correlates of romantic love," *Journal of Marriage and the Family,* 29: 470–4.

Knox, David, 1970. "Attitudes toward love of high school seniors," *Adolescence,* 5: 89–100.

Knox, David H. and Michael J. Sporakowski, 1968. "Attitudes of college students towards love, *Journal of Marriage and the Family.* 30: 638–642.

Levy, R. I., 1973. *Tahitians.* Chicago: University of Chicago Press.

Lewis, C. S., 1959. *The Allegory of Love.* New York: Oxford University Press.

Moller, H., 1958. "The social causation of the courtly love complex," *International Quarterly,* 1: 137–63.

Morgan, E., 1966. *The Puritan Family.* New York: Harper and Row.

Rapaport, D., 1942. *Emotions and Memory.* Baltimore: Williams and Wilkins.

Reiss, Ira, 1960. "Toward a sociology of the heterosexual love relationship." *Journal of Marriage and Family,* May: 22: 39–44.

Rosenblatt, Paul C. and Paul C. Casby, 1972. "Courtship patterns associated with freedom of choice of spouse," *Journal of Marriage and the Family,* 34: 689–695.

Rubin, Zick, 1970. "Measurement of romantic love," *Journal of Personality and Social Psychology.* 6: 265–273.

Theodorson, George A., 1965. "Romanticism and motivation to marry in the United States, Singapore, Burma and India," *Social Forces,* 44: 17–27.

Watt, Ian, 1962. *The Rise of the Novel: Studies in Defoe, Richardson and Fielding.* Berkeley: University of California Press.

Yang, C. K. *Chinese Community and Society: The Family and the Village.*

Introduction: Occupational Inequality

The readings in Part Three so far have focused on stratification theory, and how sex-based inequality affects the personal sphere; now, we need to illustrate how the public sphere—the world of work and politics—functions to exclude women and to disparage the "feminine."

In industrialized societies one's occupation, or place in the division of labor, determines to a great degree one's probability of achieving power, prestige, and wealth. The better the occupation, the greater the opportunity to control the distribution of scarce goods and services. Not only does one's position in the occupational structure affect one's power and prestige; so too does the social organization of the work world itself. After all, work takes place within the context of a culture, and the same assumptions held by the larger culture about gender differences are also enacted in the workplace.

In the first selection, "Where Have All the Women Gone? Like the Sediment of a Good Wine, They Have Sunk to the Bottom," Rose Laub Coser reviews labor force statistics and addresses the issue of the scarcity of women in high prestige occupations, and their abundance in careers where there is a deficit in rewards. Illustrating the problems for women who enter male-dominated jobs are two selections: "Occupation/Steelworker: Sex/Female" by Mary Margaret Fonow, and "Down the Up Staircase: Male and Female University Professors' Classroom Management Strategies" by Laurel Richardson, Judith A. Cook and Ann Statham. Both studies find that women in male-dominated careers tend to be responded to in terms of their sex-status, *female*, rather than in terms of their official position or status in the workplace. To the extent that women experience status inconsistency which is not experienced by their male colleagues, women are likely to experience role-strain and pressures that men do not.

Where Have All the Women Gone?

Rose Laub Coser

Like the Sediment of a Good Wine,
They have Sunk to the Bottom[1]

The collective mental image in Western societies that associates women with home obscures the fact that the proportion of women in the labor force is just over 50 percent in the United States, and this differs but little in other Western industrialized countries. In the Soviet Union women constitute 57 percent of the population and almost 50 percent of the labor force. The idea that associates women with home and family helps to maintain the conviction that men must "make a living" and women must take care of their families; it helps to maintain the notion that, for women, work outside the home is secondary—that they ought not to strive for a career or claim the same monetary or other rewards, because they are cared for by men.

It is noteworthy that the mental image of "women at home" in the countries of the West does not accord with anybody's daily experience, for, wherever we go, we see women at work: as salesclerks and cashiers in stores and supermarkets, as tellers in banks, and recently also as postal clerks. Although they are visible physically in everyday services, they are not visible socially as workers. We think of women as being at home; the culture is geared to it, so that repair people and delivery people expect a woman to be at home at any time at which they come and do not feel that they have to plan their day to accommodate the schedule of working women. Although this seems trivial, it is symptomatic and symbolic. It keeps women in their place, at least in our mental image.

Women are typically in jobs in which there is no advancement. They are the secretaries, the nurses, the receptionists, and the sales*girls*. True, in most Western countries

Reprinted from Rose Laub Coser, "Where Have All the Women Gone?", in *Access to Power: Cross-National Studies of Women and Elites,* ed. Cynthia Fuchs Epstein and Rose Laub Coser (London: George Allen and Unwin Publishers, 1981), by permission of the publisher and the author.

they are not at the *very* bottom of the work hierarchy; they are not the errand *boys* or sewage workers, because these jobs go to the men of the underclass—often ethnic minorities—or to others considered inferior. This is not so in the Soviet Union, by the way, where women shine shoes, work on the road, or are seen paperhanging or sweeping the streets.

For Soviet women equalization takes place at the bottom, in a form of negative democratization, as Karl Mannheim (1940) has called it. But negative democratization takes place in the West as well, albeit on another level. For example, the wife of the lawyer and the daughter of the automobile worker can be seen working side by side in the secretarial pool of a hospital or business office; the nurse whose husband is a physician may well work under the authority of a head nurse who is the daughter of an Italian shoemaker or a Polish plumber. Women are the in-betweens in a class society, serving as an integrating force and making possible some marginal communication between social classes. Women from different social origins may be equals in their work positions, and yet the similarity of their positions does not lead to class action. Negative democratization helps to keep the class system going. By being allied to men through marriage, or hoping to be so allied, women do not constitute a class in itself, let alone, to use Marx's distinction, a class for itself. This helps to minimize the dangers of class conflict.

Yet, recently the new consciousness of women has helped to challenge the class system. It has helped to raise awareness to the fact that power tends to be monopolized not only by the mighty but also by upper classes of *men,* whose interest is to maintain their social and patriarchal privileges.

In all industrial societies, whether they call themselves capitalist or socialist, privileges are maintained by husbands, fathers, and grandfathers. It is mainly after marriage, and especially after the birth of a child, and increasingly as the life cycle proceeds that inequality between men and women, which is more subtle during childhood, becomes striking. For example, although women constitute 49 percent of the American student body, they constitute only slightly over 10 percent of the college professors who teach them. It is not in the formative years so much as in the later years that inequality is taken for granted. Men, especially in the middle and upper middle class, work for careers through which they realize their social identity and aspire to positions of power. Women support them in these endeavors, raising their sons to emulate fathers or surpass them and their daughters to be of service to men, whether in the family or in such sex-typed occupations as nursing or secretarial work. Not only are women held back in the development of their skills, but also they tend to be segregated into occupations that typically, as George Devereaux and Florence Winter (1950) pointed out many years ago, come under the title of "exploited." In occupations in which men are autonomous—in medicine in the United States, in academia everywhere, and in other high-prestige professions—women are outnumbered by men tenfold, and they usually remain at the bottom of the hierarchy.

I shall address myself to two issues. First, by the phenomenon that Alice Rossi (1970) has called the diminishing flow, the presence of women is inversely related to rewards within a given occupation; that is, the higher the rank, prestige, or power within an occupation or profession, the smaller is the proportion of women, with the exception of such almost uniquely female professions as nursing. Second, the presence of women is directly related to the deficit in rewards; that is, in comparing different fields or occupations we find that, where the proportion of women is higher, the deficit in rewards, as compared with those of men, increases.

Suzanne Keller (personal communication) has warned that in studying elites we must be careful to consider the size of the available pool. For example, it would make little sense methodologically to stress the fact that there were few women professors of mathematics or of the natural sciences if we did not ask how many women engaged in these studies; nor would it make sense to point to the relatively small number of Ph.D.s generally if women hardly engaged in graduate studies.

Let us take this more general point first. In the United States in 1968 women obtained only 5 percent of doctoral or first professional degrees in the physical sciences. Following Suzanne Keller's advice we must ask

whether there were few female graduate students in those fields. It turns out that there were not quite so few. Women obtained not 5 percent but 11.5 percent of the relevant master's degrees. Could we expect that there should have been more master's degrees? There could have, because they obtained 14 percent of the bachelor's degrees.

How about the social sciences, where women participate more readily? There, they obtained 12 percent of doctoral or first professional degrees; but this percentage does not reflect the available pool, because they earned 32 percent and 37 percent respectively of the bachelor's and master's degrees (Coser and Rokoff, 1971).

How about mathematics? At twenty leading universities in 1974 under 7 percent of the full-time mathematics scientists were women. Of course, it will be argued, women do not go into mathematics. Yet, they earned 32 percent of the master's degrees and 10 percent of the doctorates in 1973.

In the biological sciences in the same year 12 percent of employed Ph.D.s were women. Yet, women formed a pool of 21.5 percent of the doctorates that year, and the women's pool for the doctorate was about 30 percent of the bachelor's and master's degrees awarded (Vetter, 1975).

In sociology, in the United States during 1968–9, women comprised 12 percent of the full time faculty in 180 graduate departments, and they comprised 15 percent of all appointments. Yet, the available pool was much larger; women comprised 33 percent of the graduate student body. Everywhere, the higher the rank, the smaller is the proportion of women. Women represent one in four of the instructors and lecturers in graduate sociology departments in the United States but only one in twenty-five of the full professors (Rossi, 1970).

Academia is a masculine realm everywhere, whether in the United States, Britain, the Soviet Union, or elsewhere. Some fields attract more women than others (e.g., psychology or foreign languages in the United States). In medicine in the United States, where the proportion of women is increasing faster than in most other fields of science, women comprised 11.1 percent of the 1974 graduating class but 18 percent of the total enrollment and 22.2 percent of the first-year enrollment. However, only 7 percent of practicing physicians are women, and they are concentrated in the less prestigious and less well-paid specialties (Vetter, 1975).

The United States differs markedly from Soviet Russia in the participation of women in medicine. There,

72 percent of the physicians are women. This fact is often cited as evidence of the equal rights of women and their equal access to the professions in the USSR. Yet, we must remember that physicians in the Soviet Union do not have to obtain a doctoral degree. There also we observe a downward flow; in contrast to the large proportion of women practicing medicine, only 25 percent of doctoral degrees are held by women (Lane, 1976, ch. 7).

In Poland the percentage of women physicians has been rising steadily from 12 percent in 1921 and 20 percent in 1931 to 38.5 percent in 1960 and 50.2 percent in 1973. Yet, the inclusion of women in higher positions in medicine has not kept pace with this growth (Table 2.1). Between 1968 and 1973 the proportion of women among those physicians who obtained doctorates grew from 33 to 37 percent; yet, the proportion of women among professors of medicine declined from 14 to 12 percent (Magdalena Sokołowska, personal communication).

Let us turn our attention back to the Soviet Union. First, it is to be noted that women have made enormous strides in that country, with an ever increasing number of participants in science and education. Today, more than 49 percent of students and 28 percent of postgraduate students are women. They constitute 59 percent of those who have secondary specialized education. The number of female "scientific workers" has increased at a faster rate than the number of males, so that the proportion of women among them rose from 36.3 percent in 1950 to 39 percent in 1973 (Gvishiani, Mikulinsky, and Kubel, 1976, p. 172).

Yet, what positions do women occupy in the Soviet Union, whether in politics, the universities, or in industry?

More than one-half of the members of the Komsomol — the youth organization of the Communist Party — are women, but only one-quarter of the party's members are women. Further, 4 percent of the members of the Central Committee are women, and there is not a single woman member of the Politbureau — the body that makes the important political decisions. This is not much different from the United States, where, ever since Frances Perkins served as Secretary of Labor under Franklin Roosevelt, there have been no women in the Cabinet until recently, although there have been some women among representatives and senators.

In general, in the Soviet Union, as Sacks (1976) has shown, women are over-represented in those occupations which require the least skill (p. 90). "In industry, construction and teaching, and among scientific workers the percentage female declines very rapidly the higher the prestige and responsibility of the position. Census data show that this is also true in medicine" (p. 88). In contrast to the United States, where women comprise only 1.5 percent of the engineering profession, in the Soviet Union 30 percent of engineers are women. Yet, they comprise only 20 percent of engineering foremen, 16 percent of chief engineers, and 6 percent of factory directors.

In education more than 80 percent of the heads of primary schools are women, but women constitute less than one-third of the heads of eight-year schools and 28 percent of the heads of secondary or middle schools.[2] In the Academy of Science women form the majority among the junior scientific employees. In contrast, they constitute less than one-third of the senior scientific employees, and there is an even lower proportion of them among the scientific management personnel (following Gvishiani, Mikulinsky, and Kubel, 1976, p. 173). In academia generally, women constitute one-quarter of the associate professors but only one-tenth of the professors (Table 2.2) (Field, 1964, p. 51).[3] It seems that academia is a masculine stronghold in socialist countries as well.

Everywhere, the same pattern exists; the higher the prestige of a position, the smaller is the proportion of women. As a corollary, the higher the prestige of an occupation or profession, the more its rewards are denied to women. Alice Rossi (1970) has also shown that in sociology — and this is true in other fields as well — "an inverse relation exists between prestige standing of the university and the proportion of women on the full-time faculty at each of the top three ranks in the academic hierarchy." It is the case not only that the few women who do advance to higher positions are less well rewarded than men but also that the deficit in rewards increases with rank. The report of the Scientific Manpower Commission (1973) has shown that as late as 1971–2 not only did the proportion of women decrease with increase in rank, and not only did women in all ranks in academia receive a lower salary than men of the same rank in all eight regions of the

TABLE 2.1
Women as a Percentage of All Academia Compared With Percentage of Physicians Who Are Women: Poland.

Year	Professors	Docents	Doctors	Physicians
1968	13.8	20.8	32.7	—
1973	12.0	25.7	36.9	50.3

Sources: (1) For professors, docents, and doctors: Census of Personnel, 1968 and 1973. (2) For physicians: *Statistical Yearbooks.*

TABLE 2.2
Women Scientific Workers as a Percentage of All Higher Education Workers: Soviet Union.

Position	Oct 1, 1950	Oct 1, 1955	Oct 1, 1960
Directors and deputy directors for training and social work	4.8	5.1	5.3
Deans	6.6	8.5	8.9
Heads of departments	11.3	12.9	12.3
Professors	8.5	8.7	10.6
Associate professors	21.3	22.9	24.4
Other	42.9	41.3	41.4
All women scientists	32.7	33.1	33.6

Source: Dodge (1966), p. 207.

United States, but also in seven out of the eight regions the difference at the full professor level was greater than in the other ranks. Another way of saying this is that, in the professorial rank, over 62 percent of the men but less than 31 percent of the women made $20,000 a year or over. At the other extreme, among lecturers and instructors, over 37 percent of the men but almost 52 percent of the women made less than $10,000 (pp. 89–90).

I am limiting this discussion to academia, because it is well known, at least for the Western countries, that the diminishing flow of women applies to industry and business throughout. But academia is not only used here as a convenient example; it also serves an important — probably the most important — gatekeeper and traffic director function for the distribution of occupations and positions according to the needs of the market, as these needs are defined in the society. Academia is the gateway to positions of power and influence; to a large extent it controls mobility into these spots. Throughout, the picture is the same; the higher the position, the larger is the difference in rewards between women and men. This leads to my second point, which seems paradoxical at first but is a corollary of what has so far been shown. This is that the larger the proportion of women in a field, the more they are discriminated against. Sacks (1976) has shown that this is so for the Soviet Union, but it applies to the United States as well, where male occupations are highly remunerated even at lower educational levels. Truck drivers, auto mechanics, and delivery men (who had not even finished high school) had median earnings in 1970 of $9,640, $9,070, and $9,060 respectively; in contrast, retail sales clerks, bookkeepers, and typists, who on average had graduated from high school or had even had additional schooling, had median earnings of $6,470, $6,540,

and $7,070 respectively (Women Employed, 1977, p. 9).

With an increase in the participation of women the market value of a field seems to decrease. If the salaries of deans of school in the United States can be taken as an index of the market value of the field, it turns out that the more "feminine" the field, the lower is the market value. Deans of nursing in 1971–2 received an average salary of less than $22,500 whereas deans of pharmacy made an average of almost $26,500. Social welfare deans commanded almost $28,000, but dentistry deans received $35,000. When the proportion of women doctorates decreased from a high 80 percent in home economics to a medium 53 percent in the arts, the dean's salary rose from $24,000 to $26,500; and when the proportion of women doctorates reached only 38 percent in social welfare, the average dean's salary reached almost $28,000. In the United States the deans' salaries of $29,000 and over were all in male professions: engineering, veterinary medicine, law, dentistry, and medicine (Table 2.3).

TABLE 2.3
Salaries of Faculty Deans Compared With Percentage of Women Doctorates in Each Faculty: United States, 1971–2.

Faculty	Deans' salaries ($)	% of women doctorates	
Nursing	22,417	95.0[a]	
Home economics	24,333	79.0	
Fine arts	26,429	53.0	
Pharmacy	26,400	30.0	(1975–6)
Social welfare	27,875	30.0	(1969–75)[b]
Engineering	29,000	1.6	(of MA)
Veterinary medicine	30,750	9.4	
Law	31,071	7.2	(of LLB)
Dentistry	35,000	1.2	
Medicine	39,000	9.0	

[a]Estimate.
[b]Percentage of doctorates and expected doctorates 1969–75 in universities that are members of the Association of American Universities; in 1975 these have awarded 75 percent of all doctorates awarded to date in the United States and were currently awarding 60 percent of the yearly total.
Sources: (1) For deans' salaries: Scientific Manpower Commission (1973). (2) For percentage of women doctorates:
 (a) social welfare: McCarthy and Wolfe (1975);
 (b) pharmacy, engineering, veterinary medicine, law, dentistry, and medicine: *Chronicle of Higher Education* (October 23, 1978), p. 11, reproducing from *Degrees Awarded to Women* (National Center for Education Statistics).

TABLE 2.4

Percentage of Women in Faculty Compared With Female Salary as a Percentage of Male Salary, by Region: United States, 1971–2.

| % of women in faculty | No. of regions in which women's salary is: | |
	over 90% of male salary	under 90% of male salary
17 or less	3	1
18 or more	1	3

Source: Computed and summarized from Scientific Manpower Commission (1973), tables 98 and 99, pp. 89–90.

The inverse correlation between proportion of women and rewards holds true for geographic areas as well. If there are more women academics in a region, it is likely that the difference between the female full professors' salaries and the male full professors' salaries will be larger (Table 2.4). In three of the four regions of the United States in 1971–2 where women constituted 17 percent or less of the faculty, the salaries of women professors averaged to over 90 percent of those of males; but in three of the four regions in which women constituted 18 percent or more of the faculty, women full professors' salaries were under 90 percent of those of males (Scientific Manpower Commission, 1973, pp. 89–90).

In an empirical study at one university, Tanur and Coser (1978) have concluded from a regression analysis that women's material disadvantages were indeed related to their numbers: "Regardless of rank or time at [The State University of New York at] Stony Brook, women in

fields with a relatively high proportion of women are more likely to have lower-than-predicted salaries than do women in fields where there is a lower proportion of women."

In their comparative study of academia in Britain and the USA, Tessa Blackstone and Oliver Fulton (1974) have provided data from which this inverse correlation between participation and rewards can be deduced. Column 3 of tables 2.5 and 2.6 shows the number of women that would be on the staff of various fields if their proportion in these fields were similar to their proportion in pure science. It turns out that both in Britain and the United States, as the proportion of women graduate students becomes larger, the proportion of women on the staff becomes relatively smaller. Further, when data from this study are combined with those of another of their papers on the same subject (Blackstone and Fulton, 1975), it turns out that there is an inverse correlation in the United States (but not in the United Kingdom) between the percentage of women on the staff as a whole and the percentage of women who have attained professorial rank.

In the Soviet Union "from at least 1940 until the present, the evidence available indicates that it is in those areas where women predominate that wages have been relatively low" (Sacks, 1976, p. 91). Both economic sectors and the professions in which women predominate — light industry, trade, communications, health and culture, communal services and housing, clerical work, medicine, and teaching — are among the most poorly paid. Wage increases in these areas lag behind the national average (Lapidus, 1978, p. 190). Table 2.9 shows the high inverse correlation between female participation and wage levels.

TABLE 2.5

Percentage of Graduate Students and of Academic Staff Who Are Women: United States, 1969.

Field	Women as % of graduate students	Women as % of staff	Expected women as % of staff[a]	Difference between observed and expected (%)	Rank of women as % of graduate students	Rank of difference observed and expected
Applied science	2	1	0.8	0.2	1	3
Pure science	17	7	7	0	3.5	2
Medicine	7	10	3	7	2	5
Social science	17	9	7	2	3.5	4
Humanities	46	16	19	−3	5	1

$r_s = -0.62$
[a]Pure science was taken as the base for comparison.
Source: Blackstone and Fulton (1974), table 2.

TABLE 2.6

Percentage of Graduate Students and of Academic Staff Who Are Women: United Kingdom, 1969.

Field	Women as % of graduate students	Women as % of staff	Expected women as % of staff[a]	Difference between observed and expected (%)	Rank of women as % of graduate students	Rank of difference observed and expected
Applied science	5	2	3	−1	1	3.5
Pure science	12	8	8	0	2	5
Medicine	24	8	16	−8	5	1
Social science[b]	19	10	13	−3	3	2
Humanities	22	14	15	−1	4	3.5

$r_s = -0.67$

[a]Pure science was taken as the base for comparison.

[b]For the United Kingdom the figures for academic social science, education, and social work have not been separated by Blackstone and Fulton.

Source: Blackstone and Fulton (1974), table 2.

TABLE 2.7

Women as a Percentage of All Academic Staff Compared to Women Professors as a Percentage of All Women Teachers: United States, 1969.

Field	Women as % of all academic staff	Women professors as % of all women academic staff	Rank of women as % of all academic staff	Rank of women professors as % of all women teachers
Applied science	1	18	1	1
Pure science	7	16	2	2
Medicine	10	4	4	4
Social science	9	15	3	3
Humanities	16	11	5	5
Education	26	15	6	6
Social work	47	14	7	7

$r_s = -0.63$

Sources: (1) For women as a percentage of all academic staff: Blackstone and Fulton (1974) table 2.

(2) For women professors as a percentage of all women teachers: Blackstone and Fulton (1975), table 3.

TABLE 2.8

Women as a Percentage of All Academic Staff Compared to Women Professors, Readers, and Senior Lecturers as a Percentage of All Women Teachers: United Kingdom, 1969.

Field	Women as % of all academic staff	Women professors, readers, and senior lecturers[a] as % of all women academic staff	Rank of women as % of all academic staff	Rank of women professors as % of all
Applied science	2	18	1	1
Pure science	8	15	2	3
Medicine	9	24	3	4
Social science	10	25	4	5
Humanities	14	4	5	2

$r_s = 0.40$

[a]Blackstone and Fulton have calculated that the ranks of professor, reader, and senior lecturer in the United Kingdom correspond to the rank of professor in the United States.

Sources: (1) For women as a percentage of all academic staff: Blackstone and Fulton (1974) table 2.

(2) For women professors as a percentage of all women teachers: Blackstone and Fulton (1975), table 3.

TABLE 2.9

Distribution of Women Workers and Employees and Average Monthly Earnings, by Economic Sector: Soviet Union, 1975.

Economic sector	No. of women workers and employees	Women as % of labor force	Average monthly earnings (rubles)
Construction	3,002,000	28	176.8
Transport	2,211,000	24	173.5
Industry (production personnel)	1,662,000	49	162.0
Science and scientific services	2,015,000	50	155.4
Nationwide average	*52,539,000*	*51*	*145.8*
Credit and state insurance	423,000	82	133.8
Apparatus of government and economic administration	1,457,000	65	130.6
Education	5,904,000	73	126.9
Agriculture	4,530,000	44	126.8
Communications	1,042,000	68	123.6
Housing and municipal economy, everyday services	2,010,000	53	109.0
Trade, public catering, equipment, supply and sales	6,763,000	76	108.7
Arts	207,000	47	103.1
Public health, physical culture, social welfare	4,851,000	84	102.3
Culture	747,000	73	92.2

Source: Calculated from figures given in Tsentral'noe statisticheskoe upravlenie, *Narodnoe knoziaistro SSSR v 1975 g.* (Moscow, 1976), pp. 542–3 and 546–7.

Table 2.10 is a summary of Table 2.9. It shows clearly that, in the sectors or professions in which there is an above average proportion of women, their monthly earnings are below average; in contrast, in the sectors or professions in which the participation of women is below average, their earnings are above average two times out of three. Michael Swafford (1978) has found an inverse correlation of −0.73 between mean wages and the proportion of women in the economic sectors. Data for the Russian Republic show that since 1960 the growth in the proportion of females, particularly in science, government, and administration, has been accompanied by slow increases in wages relative to other sectors (Sacks, 1976, p.

TABLE 2.10

Summary of Table 2.9: Participation of Women in Economic Sectors, by Monthly Earnings: Soviet Union, 1975.

Women's monthly earnings	No. of sectors in which women constitute a percentage that is:	
	Above average	Below average
Above average	0	4
Below average	8	2

Source: As Table 2.9.

92). The trend in industry is similar. Decreases in the proportion of women in transportation, construction, and industry since 1945 have gone together with faster increases in wages (Sacks, 1976, pp. 91-2).

Figures for a sample of industry in Leningrad (Zdravomyslov and Iadov, 1965, p. 79), showing characteristics of different types of work, reveal a 100 percent inverse association between the proportion of women in a category and the average wage. A category in which there were only 2.3 percent women — metalwork fitters on automatic and other equipment — was paid 113.3 rubles. In contrast, where the work was 92.5 percent performed by women — semi-automated benches in the tobacco industry — the average wage was only 71.4 rubles. Between these two extremes the trends followed the same rank order (Table 2.11).

Interestingly, the Leningrad sample shows no correlation between wages and educational levels in the Leningrad industries. With the exception of the second-highest wage category — labor on control panels of automated equipment — which has a higher educational level than all of the rest, wages seem to have no relation to education. For example, the category of "manual unskilled labor requiring heavy physical work," which is at the lowest educational level, is yet relatively high on the wage scale. This contradiction becomes resolved once it is realized that this highly paid category has a low proportion of women. Similarly, the surprise in learning that workers on "semi-automated benches, e.g., in the tobacco industry," whose years of schooling are by no means the lowest, receive, however, the lowest wage — becomes dissipated when it is noted that three-quarters of these workers are women.

In summary, and briefly: women do not only stay at, or sink to, the bottom. Related to this is the fact that the more women there are in an occupation, the worse is the discrimination in the form of lower wages or denial of promotion or other rewards.

It seems that something more is going on than discrimination pure and simple. Let me mention only three factors, although there are many more at play.

One important factor is women's cultural mandate, which has remained the same in Soviet Russia as in America, Britain, and the West generally, if not in the

TABLE 2.11
Different Types of Work in Leningrad: Sample by Proportions of Women and Wage, 1965.

Occupation	% of women	Average wage (rubles)	Average years of education
Metalwork fitters on automatic and other equipment	2.3	113.5	8.3
Labor on control panels of automated equipment	8.7	110.1	9.0
Manual unskilled requiring heavy physical work, e.g. dockers	11.0	107.4	6.8
Manual work using instruments and demanding high level of training, e.g. electric fitters	16.5	96.6	8.4
Work on machines and mechanisms, requiring vocational training, e.g. joiners	20.0	89.8	8.1
Work on automated machines, e.g. in tool construction industry	44.2	78.1	8.0
Conveyer belt work on sewing machines needing high level of training, e.g. in shoe industry	86.3	87.3	7.9
Work on semi-automated benches, e.g. in tobacco industry	97.5	71.4	8.0

Source: Zdravomyslov and Iadov (1965), p. 79.

whole world. It is women's cultural mandate to care for the family. This means: first, that they do two jobs instead of one, so that they simply do not have the time or energy to do the extra work required for advancement and promotion; and second, that where women have to make a choice between career and family, it must be the career that suffers.

But perhaps more important is the fact that this leads employers or agents of promotion to use the women's cultural mandate as a basis for blocking promotions and withholding rewards. This leads to the third factor, namely, that employers and university teachers see women as prospective disturbers of the system (Coser and Rokoff, 1971). Although in fact many women work harder than men — if only to show that they deserve their status, which always seems somewhat illegitimate to others and to themselves — there is a fear that they don't produce their money's worth. I asked the President of the Sociological Association of the USSR why there were so few women professors. His answer was immediate; he said with a smirk: "Women have babies." If it will be objected that single women, or married women without children, are equally discriminated against, it must be added that they are considered a "bad risk"; they may get married or they may have children.

We must ask: what has happened in Soviet Russia, where ideology has strongly called for the equality of women for almost six decades? Also, to take another example, what has happened in the kibbutz in Israel? Why do women there remain confined to the kitchen, the laundry, and the children's house? Why don't they take part in the political decisions and in the directorship of factories or other economic units? Kibbutz women were freed of child care and housework; unlike the women of the Soviet Union, the United States, and Britain, they did not have two jobs. The answer is so simple that it sounds trivial, and yet I think it is crucial; it is that the basic stereotypes about women were not questioned on the kibbutz any more than in the outside world, a point stressed by Suzanne Keller (1973). Let me tell of a personal experience on a recent visit to two kibbutzim in Israel.

At the first kibbutz my husband and I met a couple now close to retirement. In the late 1920s they had been doctoral students, he in Vienna, she in Prague; they both had given up their studies to devote themselves to the Zionist movement. They had been equals at the time. At the time of our visit *he* was lecturing at a nearby school and doing statistical work; *she* was working in the laundry. What had happened to her? She had been "left behind," but not because she had had to spend many years raising children and cooking for the family. Her children had been raised in the children's house; the family's meals had been taken in the communal dining room. Perhaps my second story can provide the answer, for it shows that basic stereotypes about women have continued to exist even in a society ideologically based on equalitarianism.

In the second kibbutz we met a man who also had been a member for many years. We did not meet his wife, for she was in school being retrained to become a social worker. Our host prepared to be back home at 5 p.m. when his little daughter would come in from the children's house. He seemed ready enough to share in the after-hours care of the child. Yet, when he saw me take the wheel of our car on our ride with him to the nearby regional high school, he said to my husband in surprise: "How come *you* don't drive?" We explained that we both liked it better this way. When we arrived at the school, he said: "There aren't many classes going on right now, but," turning to me, "you may be interested in watching a cooking class." I suddenly understood what had happened in the kibbutz in spite of all the good intentions to the contrary.

As long as the basic stereotype is not questioned, things revert to where they were in the past after the first stage of ideological revolution. Equality is not something that can be legislated and then forgotten. It has to be watched over continuously. Rivka Bar-Yosef from the Hebrew University has called my attention to the fact that, if one is committed to bringing about equality, one has to repeatedly examine what is happening and introduce correctives into the body politic and the body social. Not having questioned the old stereotypes, people in the kibbutz were busy solving their economic problems and also trying to avoid as much as possible the development of hierarchical inequality in which expertise or other assets would lead to privileges. They forgot that a system of privileges is inherent in the traditional division of labor between the sexes.

This division of labor has a value-laden component, namely, that what women do is being valued less than what men do. As a consequence it is feared that the prestige of an occupation is being degraded with an influx of women and that male prerogatives will hence be threatened.

Hodge and Hodge (1965) have shown in a statistical study that, to the extent that women receive wages below those demanded by white males, the incomes of men will be adjusted downward by the competitive process. They suggest that discriminatory policies are due not solely to prejudice but also to attempts by white males to avoid competition.

Another consequence bears upon the attitudes of the few women who have "made it." As part of the elite they enjoy their minority status. If it is true, as I hope I have demonstrated, that increasing participation of women threatens to decrease their rewards in comparison to those of men, the exceptional woman in a male occupation must be interested in keeping women out. Her own interests would be threatened by an influx of more women, since the rewards that she now enjoys would be reduced. This explains what has been called the "queen bee syndrome"—the fact that, unless there is a strong feminist movement, many women among the happy few who "make it" refuse to stress the rights of women and, just like the men, are likely to have little interest in encouraging women to enter their field or to aspire to higher achievements within it.

It follows that it is not enough to call for increased participation of women in such elite occupations as medicine or law. If existing trends were permitted to exert themselves, women in these professions would tend to drift into lower positions—into the routine work of general practitioners, as they do in the Soviet Union, or of law firms. This would once more reaffirm male dominance. By simply swelling the ranks women would not weaken the patriarchal system. Instead, it is by making a claim to equal admission to top positions that women, or other excluded minorities, challenge the closed ranks of the system—that they challenge its institutions of exclusiveness, which are not based only on achievement, as claimed, but on monopolization of privilege. For as long as an exploited stratum is satisfied with being exploited, the elitist system is likely to be maintained. It is by giving up (to paraphrase August Bebel) the damned wantlessness of women that the elitist system can be challenged.

Equality of mobility of women can be achieved only with a complete relinquishment of existing sex stereotypes; but this means a change in the family structure. Full equality of opportunity for women is as important as it will be difficult to achieve, for it implies a change in authority structure in all of society.

Endnotes

1. The phrase was coined by Cynthia Fuchs Epstein (1970). This paper appeared in an earlier version in West Germany (Coser, 1976).

2. The figures for the Soviet Union that are not referenced were communicated to me, and translated where needed, by David Lane and Felicity O'Dell of Cambridge University.

3. In another breakdown Michael Swafford (1978) has shown that in 1970 women constituted 9 percent of the academicians, 20 percent of docents, 29 percent of senior research associates, and 48 percent of junior research associates—figures that don't differ much from the earlier figures of 1950.

References

Blackstone, Tessa and Fulton, Oliver (1974) "Sex differences, subject fields and research activity among academics in Britain and the US," *Higher Education* (April).

Blackstone, Tessa and Fulton, Oliver (1975) "Sex discrimination among university teachers: a British–American comparison," *British Journal of Sociology*, vol. 26, no. 3 (September), pp. 267–75.

Coser, Rose Laub (1976) "Das Männereich Universität: Diskriminierungen in den USA und in der Sowjetunion," *Geissener Universitätsblätter*, vol. 9 (December), pp. 38–49.

Coser, Rose Laub and Rokoff, Gerald (1971) "Women in the occupational world: social disruption and conflict," *Social Problems*, vol. 18, no. 4, pp. 535–54.

Devereaux, George and Winter, Florence R. (1950) "Occupational status of nurses," *American Sociological Review*, vol. 15, no. 5, pp. 628–34.

Dodge, Norton D. (1966) *Women in the Soviet Economy* (Baltimore: Johns Hopkins Press).

Epstein, Cynthia Fuchs (1970) *Woman's Place: Options and Limits in Professional Careers* (Los Angeles: University of California Press).

Field, Mark (1964) "Workers and mothers: Soviet women today" unpublished manuscript (Cambridge, Mass.: Russian Research Center, Harvard University).

Gvishiani, D. M., Mikulinsky, S. R., and Kubel, S. A. (eds), (1976) *The Scientific Intelligentsia in the USSR* (Moscow: Progress Publishers).

Hodge, Robert W. and Hodge, Patricia (1965) "Occupational assimilation as a competitive process," *American Journal of Sociology*, vol. 71, no. 3 (November), pp. 249–89.

Keller, Suzanne (1973) "The family in the kibbutz: what lessons for us?," Michael Curtis and Mordecai S. Chertoff (eds), in *Israel: Social Structure and Change* (New Brunswick, NJ: Transaction Books, pp. 115–44).

Lane, David (1976) *The Socialist Industrial State* (New York: Praeger).

Lapidus, Gail Warshofsky (1978) *Women in Soviet Society: Equality, Development, and Social Change* (Berkeley: University of California Press).

McCarthy, Joseph L. and Wolfe, Dael (1975) "Doctorates granted to women and minority group members," *Science,* vol. 189 (September), pp. 856–9.

Mannheim, Karl (1940) *Man and Society in an Age of Reconstruction* (London: Routledge & Kegan Paul).

Rossi, Alice S. (1970) "Status of women in graduate departments of sociology, 1968–1969," *American Sociologist,* vol. 5, no. 1, pp. 1–12.

Sacks, Michael Paul (1976) *Women's Work in Soviet Russia: Continuity in the Midst of Change* (New York: Praeger).

Scientific Manpower Commission (1973) *Summary of Salary Surveys: Salaries of Scientists, Engineers, and Technicians* (Washington, DC, August).

Swafford, Michael (1978) "Sex differences in Soviet earnings," *American Sociological Review,* vol. 43, no. 5, pp. 657–73.

Tanur, Judith M. and Coser, Rose Laub (1978) "Pockets of 'poverty' in the salaries of academic women," *American Association of University Professors Bulletin,* vol. 64, no. 1, pp. 26–30.

Vetter, Betty M. (1975) "Women and minority scientists," *Science,* vol. 189, no. 4205, p. 751. The source of data is Scientific Manpower Commission, *Professional Women and Minorities. A Manpower Data Resource Service* (Washington, DC, 1975).

Women Employed (1977) "Women in the economy: preferential mistreatment," unpublished report to the Working Women's Conference, Chicago.

Zdravomyslov, A. G. and Iadov, V. A. (1965) Personal communication, translated from Russian by Felicity O'Dell of Cambridge University.

READING 56

Occupation / Steelworker: Sex / Female

Mary Margaret Fonow

Occupations in the United States fall into two categories: The *primary sector* which is characterized by higher pay, union protection, fringe benefits, high rates of employment, high profits, and good chances for advancement and the *secondary sector* which is characterized by low pay, lack of union protection, few fringe benefits, higher rates of unemployment, few promotional opportunities and lower profits. Women in the United States have been employed in the secondary sector, and consequently, have received lower salaries and few benefits (Acker, 1980). Recent efforts to initiate an affirmative action in such basic industries as steel, communications, auto, mining, rubber, electrical, may represent an opportunity for women to break with the traditional pattern of female employment and substantially alter their socioeconomic status.

The article will examine the specific experiences of women steelworkers in their attempt to enter a male-dominated occupation. Although the primary method of

Reprinted, with changes, from Mary Margaret Fonow, "Occupation/Steelworker: Sex/Female," in the unpublished Ph.D. dissertation, *Women in Steel: A Case Study of the Participation of Women in a Trade Union,* by Mary Margaret Fonow, Ohio State University, 1977, by permission of the author.

data collection for this study was participant observation, a combination of methods was employed. First, I conducted an in-depth field study of one steel union local in a major steel-producing region of the mid-west. This local represented approximately 5,000 workers, 60 of whom were women. During the summer of 1977, I was able to make observations of the routine day-to-day activities of the union local and interview union officials. Using the snowball sampling technique, I also conducted a total of twenty-seven in-depth interviews with women steelworkers. Each interview lasted between one and one-half to two hours and all were tape recorded. I did my own transcribing. In addition, I observed the 18th Constitutional Convention of the United Steelworkers of America, August 30–September 3, 1976, Las Vegas, Nevada. At this event I conducted formal and informal interviews with twenty-three women participants (delegates, organizers and observers). I also observed informal caucus meetings and strategy sessions on women's issues.

Job Entry

On April 15, 1974 in the United States District Court in Birmingham, Alabama an industry-wide consent decree was signed by nine of the "big ten" steel companies and the union, the United Steelworkers of America. The decree required an entire restructuring of the seniority system and an affirmative action plan for the hiring and promotion of women and minorities.

The flow of information about the new policy reflected the hierarchy of the work environment. News about the hiring of women in the mill traveled downward from management and their staff, to union officials and finally to workers. Few women read about the openings in the newspaper, most relied on informal sources or "talk around town." Some of the women applied for the job despite negative publicity about the new hiring policy. A waitress applied for the job after she overhead some of the supervisors from the mill discussing the new policy in her restaurant over breakfast. "I heard them talking about it. This one was saying, ' . . . we are going to hire broads down there. The government is forcing us.'" Another woman, who had applied for a nontraditional job at the phone company, was told by the personnel director, "the steel mill is being forced to do this too." A third woman had heard about the new policy from a friend employed as a secretary by the mill. "When my friend told me about it, we all laughed. We thought it was

ridiculous. Later, I had second thoughts and put my application on file." To apply for the job in a climate of negative or hostile public opinion indicates that these women were little influenced by the normative proscriptions concerning women's work roles.

Initially, management did not believe that women would be interested in jobs as steelworkers. One supervisor remarked, "We never expected them to even apply." Another said, "I was shocked that women would even want to work in the mill. I know this might sound like prejudice, but my idea of a woman is a step above a steelworker." Many of the women steelworkers believed that management deliberately tried to discourage their employment. During the in-take interviews, personnel officials repeatedly emphasized the negative aspects of the job, particularly their perception of potential harassment from male co-workers. Typical were such remarks: "They kept stressing that men didn't want the women in there and they would be rough on me," "They kept emphasizing the harassment from men," "You are going to be working around some very vicious people." One woman reported that she was given her first assignment on a nonexistent work crew.

> I went in on a Sunday and was put on a labor gang. There is no labor gang on weekends. I didn't know what to do. It was very discouraging. At the interview I was told that I would be lifting 100 lb. bags. He wanted you to say, I can't.

I asked union officials how the men in the mill first responded to the news that women were being hired. I received a variety of responses. One category of responses reflected the idea held by some, that women would expect special privileges because of their status as females. One official told me,

> You heard things like, we are getting those broads on the gang now; broads are coming to work in the mill and they are going to have preference over us; maybe I can get a good-looking helper.

According to union officials, there was widespread fear that women would not be able to do the job and that the men would have to work twice as hard. Some of the men resented a perceived threat to a territory they had exclusively staked out for themselves. One union official said, "Some of those who are hollering the most about women are the same ones who don't appreciate the blacks and other minorities achieving goals greater than theirs." Another male official said,

*Wow, at first there was a lot of resentment. Why
don't they go home where they belong; they can't
do a man's work; they are taking a man's job; they
can't lift . . . a lot of them can't . . . A man is
often threatened by a woman who holds her own as
an individual.*

Finally there was some concern that as good paying
jobs in the region were scarce, the men would no longer
be able to secure jobs in the mills for their sons. It was not
uncommon for two or even three generations of males
from the same family to be employed in the mill. One
official said the following about the hiring of women,

*I have mixed emotions about it. Given the employ-
ment picture in this country, I feel jobs should go
first to heads of the family rather than to movements (women and blacks). The society is based on
the family.*

The Job

The early years of employment in the mill are characterized by periodic cycles of unemployment and little choice
in job assignments. Nearly all mill recruits are initially
assigned to the "labor gang." These jobs involve general
maintenance work such as: sweeping, shoveling, painting,
washing walls, cleaning track and some semi-skilled work
such as breaking up cement and laying concrete. Workers
from the labor gang are also chosen on the basis of seniority, to fill in for vacationing or disabled workers in other
departments. Most workers consider their stint on the
labor gang as temporary and once they have accumulated
enough seniority, the worker may bid on more permanent
positions. Women, particularly heads of households, are
often limited in their choices of permanent jobs because
child care responsibilities may preclude changing shifts or
working weekends. Many trade promotional opportunities for steady daylight work and weekends off. In addition affirmative action requires that women be admitted
to apprenticeship programs that lead to the skilled crafts
within the industry. While some of the women qualify for
training very few skilled jobs have opened up in recent
years.

Some women deliberately requested jobs that isolated
them from other workers as a way to minimize hostile
contacts with those male workers who do not approve of
their presence. One woman reported, "I like it best when I
work by myself or just one other person. It cuts down on

all the hassles." Another woman preferred a particular
department because it afforded her the opportunity to
work alone and because the nature of the work minimized
status distinctions.

*You see, everybody over there is in the same class.
Everybody is dirty and nobody is clean . . . so
nobody really looks down on you. Everybody on
the job over there mainly works by himself or else
has one helper but you don't get a conglomeration
of a lot of people in one department. In other
departments there are people who never get dirty
and they frown on people who do. You see those
kind of people are in a different class from us.*

Many women, in part because of low seniority,
are assigned jobs in the coke plant or blast furnace.
In general, these are the hardest, dirtiest, lowest paying
and least safe jobs in the mill. However some women cannot take advantage of transfers because of child care
responsibilities.

Work is also social and can be conceived as a network of interpersonal relationships (Richardson, 1981).
How comfortable do the women feel about interaction
with the other workers in such a male-dominated environment? Some felt it was difficult to communicate.
Understanding the rules that govern conversation became
problematic.

*If the guys talk to me, I talk to them. But I never go
out of my way to talk to the men. If you don't talk
to the guys, they say you are stuck up, conceited, a
bitch. If you do talk to them, they say you are a
whore so you can't win.*

Others simply were not interested in the kinds of
things men talk about at work: cars, sports, sex, etc. . . .
However, another woman felt that sharing in the same
work experience increased understanding between the
sexes.

*Everybody acts like men and women have never
worked together until women came into the steel
mills. All of a sudden it's a big deal . . . it's not
new. The more we work together on this basic
level, sweatin' and workin' the horrible shifts and
going through all the suffering you go through, you
really begin to understand each other.*

Black workers do not always feel that they can be
honest in their social relations with white workers in the
mill. Attempting to converse across sex and race lines,

poses special problems for black women. One woman said,

I prefer to work with another black person cause it is hard to talk to a white person all day. You are afraid to say what you are doing . . . like fixing up your house or buying a new car. If it looks like you are getting on your feet, the white resents it. They think you are getting too far ahead of yourself. Black and white workers get along fine as long as the black person lets a white person feel as though they are still on top. There are times you would like to say something but you don't. The mill is not as bad as other places I've worked.

Although over time the relationship between men and women and black and white becomes easier to establish, for the most part getting along meant the absence of any overt hostility or conflict. Although they seldom had the opportunity, women preferred working with other women in the mill.

Sexism took a variety of forms within the plant. Job placement, job training, and promotional opportunities were cited as features of sex discrimination. One woman believed that the company deliberately tried to ensure the failure of women, by placing unqualified women in difficult positions.

They pick women for certain jobs that they know in advance will wash-out. Placement is not done according to ability or aptitude. In order to fill the quotas, they pick women off the street rather than a woman already in the mill who has a little experience. They build-in failure.

Another woman believed that the testing procedure for apprenticeships was biased and successfully argued the case with her employer.

I placed a bid for an apprenticeship program. I failed the mechanical aspect of the aptitude test that would qualify me for the job. I had to convince the company that failure on the aptitude test did not necessarily disqualify me for the apprenticeship. I explained that women are not given the opportunity to become familiar with mechanical principles. I threatened that I felt I was being discriminated against. They let me into the program. My work on the job was termed "above average" by my supervisors and my average in my school work is 89 (70 is passing).

Job evaluation also drew criticism from some of the women. Some believed that women were fired more quickly for mistakes or that the rules governing the performance of tasks were more strictly applied. When the rules were more narrowly interpreted the men became more hostile and resentful of the presence of women. One woman related the following:

The rules were tightened specifically for women and the men lost some of the informal privileges won over the years. There was an informal agreement between the men working the blast furnace that they could exchange assignments, if they didn't want to work a specific job that day. They traded jobs and took turns. In the rush to prove that women can't do the job the company came down hard and stopped allowing the workers to take turns. They showed us the rules from the book. This caused a lot of resentment toward the women. I think the company knew it would.

Some women even felt that they were assigned to departments where the men were particularly hostile and that men were assigned women helpers as punishment for work infractions.

In addition to the structural features of sexism, there is the tension and psychological strain associated with being the first women to cross occupational barriers. Because of their high visibility as "ground-breakers," the women faced incredible pressures to do an exemplary job. A sampling of comments reveals: "I put in two parts to their one," "you have to prove yourself over and over," "you are constantly being watched." Sometimes they feel the pressure to be the standard bearer for the entire population of women. One woman explained:

While I was working on the lids (coke ovens) I was told to move these 100 lb. lead boxes. I wanted to prove that I could do it. That all women could do it. After the third lift, I ripped open my intestines and had to be rushed to the hospital. It took surgery and a three-month recovery period. What I didn't know at the time was that no man would have lifted that much weight. They would have asked for a helper or simply refused.

There is also the constant pressure of interpreting male reaction to your presence. Women often hear the men say, "The mill is no place for a woman," "You are taking a job away from a man who needs the money to raise a family," "Women don't do their share," "Women get the easy jobs because they flirt with the foreman." Sometimes their sexuality is called into question. One woman remarked, "If you are too nice, you are a whore, if you aren't nice enough, you're a bitch." Even accepting help from male co-workers becomes problematic.

> *You are under so much pressure. If you walk out of the shanty and you are carrying this heavy bucket, the other workers come along and say, how come you let her carry all that? You should be carrying that for her. But if you let them help you, someone else says, see that, you're doing all her work.*

One dimension of sexism in the mill is sexual harassment. According to Farley, sexual harassment is unsolicited nonreciprocal male behavior that values a woman's sex role over her function as worker and can include a wide range of behavior from propositions for dates, to touching to actual rape (1978: 33). The practice of sexual harassment is not limited to steel mills or to male-dominated occupations in general. Rather it occurs across the lines of age, marital status, physical appearance, race, class, occupation, pay range (MacKinnon, 1979: 28). Sexual harassment is rarely about sex. According to Farley (1978) the issue is power or dominance, and sexual harassment is one form of general dominance aimed at keeping women subordinate at work. Steel mill supervisors, who hold the power to reward or punish, are more likely to be perpetrators of sexual harassment. More often than not it is the implicit or explicit promise of a better job assignment or the threat of a worse one. One woman explained, "One foreman used to say, come work for my crew. You can sit in the office all day. Sure I thought, but what would I have to give in return?" Another woman believed that she was given a particularly hard job because she refused to go out with her supervisor. In addition, the job was deliberately left for her to finish after her days off.

> *Last summer this foreman kept bugging me to go out with him. I refused. He stuck me in some of the dirtiest jobs. He put me in the oil pits. They had to lower me in this narrow hole. I was scared to death. I was new in the mill and I was petrified. I had to remove the oil with buckets. It must have been 110° down there. I came up crying; I was really scared. I was off the next two days but when I came back, he put me on the same job. Usually when you start a job the next crew on the next shift finishes it. You see, he saved it for me to finish after my days off.*

Direct physical contact of a sexual nature was not prevalent but such incidents did happen.

> *Once a foreman grabbed my boob, under eight layers of thermal underwear. It scared the shit out of me, 'cause the doors on the trailers aren't locked. What do you do? When it happens, it's a strange thing. At first you think, he doesn't know he is doing it or he didn't mean it . . . but he knew.*

Sexual coercion or harassment was not limited solely to supervisory personnel. Some cases were reported between women workers and their male co-workers. However, this type of harassment most often took the form of gossip, verbal remarks, graffiti, or persistent requests for dates.

Despite the hassles, women steelworkers were satisfied with their jobs because the alternatives were less desirable. During the interviews I asked women to compare their present job with previous jobs. Working in the mill is substantially more attractive than jobs that have been traditionally available to women such as clerical, waitress, or sales. Better pay, greater job security, health care benefits, degree of supervision, union protection, pace of work were cited again and again as the difference between working in steel and previous jobs. Caught between strict supervision and customer demand, former sales clerks were the most dissatisfied with previous jobs.

> *It was tougher being a salesgirl. The stores have a strict dress code and for the money they pay, it's just not worth it. There is all this pressure to get a quota of sales. The customers don't understand this. Some would boss you around . . . "get me this, get me that." They feel as if you are their servant. I am the same as the person that comes in and I don't want to be treated like I am below them.*

Another former sales clerk responded:

> *It sounds funny but sales was more difficult. I was hassled constantly, if not by my employer, then by the customers. We had to attack them when they come in and this makes some people belligerent. They treated you like you weren't there.*

A factory worker from a non-union shop compared her old work with her job in the mill.

> *On my old job, I had to stand on one foot all day. We worked a constant eight-hour day. It was like production but we got a straight hourly wage, no*

incentive rate. In the mill you can work at your own speed. At the factory they pushed you and pushed you. They didn't care if you lost your fingers in the press; they just wanted that production. I am now making double what I used to and the pressure is a lot less.

Overall the majority of women were much more satisfied with their jobs in the mill than with previous jobs. It seemed nobody wanted to return to the "pink-collar ghetto."

The Union

One way to cope with the problems associated with entering a traditional male occupation is union participation. The women in the mill, while often critical of union performance, were overwhelmingly in favor of unions. I asked one woman employed in the mill since 1934 to tell me what the mill was like before the union was established.

Before the union came, they worked you harder and they treated you like you weren't human. They never called you by name, they just sissed *at you like you were a cat.*

She also reported that you never knew from one day to the next if you would even have a job. Workers were often forced to bribe mill supervisors in order to keep the jobs.

At that time the ladies bought gifts so they could hold their jobs and the forelady treats them good. I did not go for that. At $2.44 a day I couldn't afford it.

Most of the women in the mill did not have to reach back in their memories to 1934 in order to recall what life was like without a union. Most had been employed in the nonunionized sector of the labor market prior to their employment in steel and most could make comparisons between the two. In fact, the number one response to the question, "What surprised you the most about your new job?" was union protection and union benefits.

Although the number of women who are unionized and the percent who participate in union affairs is small, their potential influence is far greater than their numbers suggest. In the case of women steelworkers, women are 8 percent of the union members covered by the basic steel

agreement, and 15% of the total membership, yet their impact can be felt on all levels. On the local level women are a source of new ideas and energy needed to revitalize the labor movement. In fact, they participate on the local level in greater numbers than their proportion of the steel work force. At the district level women have formed networks, some publishing newsletters that lobby for the concerns of women steelworkers, the same concerns facing all working women. Their efforts to include child care, maternity leave and other health and safety issues in the collective bargaining agreement can become a model for other unions. In fact, the steel contract in general is often the model for other industries. On the national level women in the United Steelworkers of America can place pressure on the AFL–CIO to organize the vast number of unorganized women workers. The potential to shape national policy on such work issues as flextime, job sharing, affirmative action, job training, CETA, insurance benefits and retirement is unprecedented.

Another avenue for change is the Coalition of Labor Union Women (CLUW), a national organization of women trade unionists. Working women from a variety of industries have formed their own network to lobby the unions to promote the rights of women in the workplace and to help to organize the vast number of unorganized women workers in the United States. CLUW is also training women for leadership roles in the trade union movement. The efforts of women to make their unions more responsive to the concerns of working women is very likely to have an impact on the quality of work life for both men and women in the workplace.

References

Acker, Joan
  1980 "Women and Stratification: A Review of Recent Literature." *Contemporary Sociology* 9:25–35.
Farley, Lin
  1979 *Sexual Shakedown: The Sexual Harassment of Women on the Job*. New York, New York: Warner Books.
MacKinnon, Catherine A.
  1979 *Sexual Harassment of Working Women*. New Haven, Conn.: Yale University Press.
Richardson, Laurel Walum
  1981 *The Dynamics of Sex and Gender: A Sociological Perspective*. Boston, Mass.: Houghton-Mifflin.

Down the Up Staircase:
Male and Female University Professors'
Classroom Management Strategies

Laurel Richardson, Judith A. Cook, and Anne Statham

In Classroom 315, a male full professor, noticing a pair of conversing students, stops his lecture and says to the duo, "Hey, you two. If you want to talk, *leave!*" Across the corridor, his female colleague, an assistant professor, is plagued by another set of side-talkers. She, however, continues her lecture, albeit at a raised volume, and then faced with looks of approbation from the rest of the class, turns to the offenders and says lightly, "Excuse me. I know you are interested in this material, and we will get to the discussion soon." She hopes they will be more courteous the next time the class meets.

In classrooms all over the university, students are sleeping, reading newspapers, writing letters or in other ways *being inattentive;* they are interrupting the professor and other students, monopolizing class discussion, coming in late, leaving early or in other ways *disrupting the classroom;* they are *challenging the competency of their professors;* and they are *not participating* in class discussion or responding to the professor's favorite question, "Any questions?"

Each of these—being inattentive, disrupting the classroom, challenging the competency of the professor and not participating—presents a potential problem that requires solution for the university professor who is charged, after all, with *teaching.* And, for each of these classroom management problems, the professor must derive a strategy so that teaching can be accomplished, the problem minimized or eradicated.

Reprinted, with changes, from Laurel Richardson, Judith A. Cook, and Anne Statham, "Down the Up Staircase: Male and Female University Professors' Classroom Management Strategies," in *Sex-Typed Teaching Styles of University Professors and Student Reactions,* #NIE-G-78-20208, by permission of the authors.

This paper examines whether these classroom problems are handled differently by male and female professors. That is, it asks the questions: Are there sex differences in the strategies used for management of classroom problems? Does the fact that there are different expectations for males and females affect teaching styles? If such be the case, then sex differences are relevant not only for understanding differential strains on male and female professors, but more generally on the strains and conflicts that women may experience as they enter professional roles which have been sex-typed male.

We hypothesize that male and female professors will use different strategies to manage their classrooms. We base this on the literature on gender, role strain, and status inconsistency.

Everyone enjoys many statuses simultaneously. For example, a person has an age status, a racial status, an ethnic status, occupational status, marital status, etc. Assigned to each status are particular expectations and a relative esteem or prestige rating. Thus, for example, in this society a woman is (still) expected to be warm, nurturant, passive, and dependent, whereas a man is expected to be strong, assertive, definitive, and active. (Walum, 1977:Chapter One). And, in this society (as in every other known society), the sex-status, male, has higher prestige than the sex-status, female. Moreover, the expectations for a university professor are more congruent with the expectations for males than for females, and the prestige granted to university professors (cf. Hodge, *et al.,* 1964) is high and more congruent with the esteem granted men (Hartley, 1969; Pheterson, 1971). Consequently, a woman who becomes a university professor is likely to experience *both* role conflict (her role expectations as a female conflict with those of professor) and status inconsistency (her status as a female is inconsistent with her status as a professor). On the other hand, neither role conflict nor status inconsistency is likely to be experienced by the male university professor.

Consequently, women professors may experience a chain of double-binds. First, since they are likely to be responded to in terms of their lesser status, female, they will not be viewed as *legitimate* holders of authority. To be viewed as legitimate, however, may require adopting masculine sex-typed styles of interaction which in turn may lead to resentment and punishment (cf. Kanter, 1977). To reduce the resentment, then, she may have to increase her feminine sex-typed behaviors. However, by so doing, she may be judged incompetent (cf. Eskilson and Wiley, 1976; Meeker and Weitzel-O'Neill, 1976), and once again, not legitimately in authority.

Therefore, there are two primary issues which women university professors face. First, the establishment of their *legitimacy* as an authority; and second, the reduction of their *appearance* as an authority. These are issues which structurally and situationally are not conflicts which would be experienced by male professors.

Male professors, in contrast, will enter a position which is consistent with their status as male. However, they are entering a university culture with norms regarding what constitutes "good teaching." Some of those norms are that professors should be accessible to students, not be "too authoritarian," and establish a classroom atmosphere in which interaction between student and professor is encouraged (Macke, Richardson, Cook, 1980). To the extent that a male professor accepts those ideas about teaching, he may find that the authority granted him because of his status, male, may hamper his attempts to generate an interactive classroom atmosphere. Consequently, he may experience a conflict between his incorporated cultural norms of "good teaching" and his authority. In order to reduce his conflict, he may develop strategies that *reduce* his appearance of authority. However, this conflict is fundamentally different from that experienced by females because it is a qualitatively different experience to operate from a position of legitimated authority—to have the authority to choose to reduce it—than it is to not have that authority.

Procedures

To explore whether male and female professors do differ in management strategies, fifteen (full-time, regular) female professors at a large state university were selected and matched to fifteen male professors on rank (assistant,

associate, full),[1] academic discipline (humanities, social science, natural sciences), and sex-ratio (proportion of females to males) of department. The sample was selected so that we could discover whether women professors, regardless of rank, disciplinary orientation or sex-ratio of department had a different set of strategies for managing common classroom problems than men did.

Each of the faculty members in the sample was interviewed using an open-ended format. The interviews, which lasted from one to two hours, were tape-recorded, transcribed and subjected to a content analysis by two of the researchers (one a professor, the other a graduate student), each working independently and cross-checking their work with the other.

Two primary conceptual categories were employed: (1) strategies to increase the legitimacy of authority and (2) strategies to reduce the appearance of authority. Following the logic of content analysis, the particular indicators and examples were derived directly from the interview materials. Four commonly discussed management problems were analyzed, namely (1) being inattentive, (2) disrupting the classroom, (3) challenging the competency of the professor, and (4) not participating in class.

Classroom Management Problems

Inattentiveness

A common problem discussed in the interview concerned students not paying attention, e.g., reading the newspaper, writing letters, falling asleep. Reactions to this problem varied primarily by rank, and sex, although disciplinary orientation or sex-ratio of department did not apparently affect the professor's strategy.

Women assistant professors dealt with inattentiveness from their students by ignoring it because "it did not disturb other students" or by approaching it indirectly such as by asking the offending student his/her opinion on the subject under discussion. Men assistant professors

---

1 Professors are both "in rank" and ranked in universities based on their length of experience, their teaching excellence, service to the university and community, and their scholarship and publications. Assistant professors are in a probation period for six years (normally) before they achieve tenure (or are "let go") and (usually) the rank of Associate Professor. Full Professorship, or simply *Professor,* is the highest rank possible, is not always achieved, and is rarely attained before another six years of university service has elapsed.

were likely to report reprimanding the student in public or private, explaining how inattentiveness would hurt their grade or confronting students about their rudeness, as in the following example:

If a student is reading the newspaper and not pay-
ing attention I will sometimes actually physically
take the paper away and either demand an apology
from the student or else tell him that attendance is
not required, that it is an insult for him to be doing
this.

At the associate level, males and females ignored inattentiveness ("I care but it doesn't disrupt the lecture") while others relayed disapproval through eye contact. At this level, moreover, women were as likely as men to directly reprimand the student, although the women's reprimands tended to be less harsh than the men's. One woman associate professor in the hard sciences stated:

I would just stop the student after class and confess
to him that it is a bother to me, *and that unless*
there is some overriding reason, I would suggest
that if there is no way he can be attentive to the
class to not come (emphasis ours).

A different tone was apparent in the comments of male associates. As one Humanities professor explained:

I tell them to take a little NoDoz before class. 'Why
do you give me your sleepy hours and give the
damn bar your awake ones'.

Another reported:

They yawn. They read newspapers until you tell
them not to. You say: 'You are welcome to read
the newspaper but not in my classroom'.

At the full professor level both men and women reported little concern over inattentiveness. Several professors noted that they themselves had spent time as students writing letters or reading newspapers in class. Overall, the attitude among the senior faculty was that students, not professors, were responsible for maintaining interest in the classroom.

In summary, then, there are both sex and rank differences in the management of inattentiveness. Female assistants ignore the infractions or indirectly solve it by involving the student in the classroom discussion. Male assistants reprimand. At the associate level, although both males and females reprimand the offending student, the approaches are qualitatively different. Whereas the

women will gently correct the student, privately, for bothering *her,* the males are more harsh, directive and public in their comments. At the full professor level, no sex-differences appear since none of the professors viewed inattentiveness as a problem.

Disruptions

The second problem discussed by the professors involved situations in which students disrupted the classroom atmosphere through behavior such as talking with other students during a lecture, side-talking during discussions, and monopolizing class time with constant questions or comments.

Talking during a lecture and side-talking were approached directly by assistant professors. Women were more likely to reprimand the student in an informal, off-handed, humorous way seemingly designed to reduce feelings of embarrassment.

Male assistant professors, however, were more likely to use public humiliation. They saw "making a big scene" in class as an effective method for stopping the offending behavior as well as preventing future incidents. Statements such as "It was enough social embarrassment to stop it" indicated that these professors felt that embarrassing students was a legitimate strategy.

At the associate level, professors also dealt with the problem by reprimanding students. Women's reprimands involved the theme that they, as professors, were disturbed by the behavior. One woman in the hard sciences explained: "I can't stand idle conversation in a large lecture and I have stopped a lecture and explained to them that I must require that they be involved in what we are doing." Another related an incident in which she required two students to sit apart during classes to prevent further disturbances to her teaching. The men associate professors' reprimands emphasized that the talking was disruptive to the other students in the class, as illustrated by the following excerpts: "It's difficult for other people"; "It's causing us a problem if there is a second conversation going on"; and "You are probably disturbing other students."

Full professors dealt with disruptive talking directly by simply telling the student to either stop or leave. Absent from their reprimands were justifications for delivering them, e.g., you are bothering me, you are bothering other students. The following are some examples:

I told the person in class that if they want to come
to class they shouldn't carry on private conversa-
tions. (man–humanities)

(I say) 'If you want to talk to each other go out in the hall and talk. You are welcome to leave any time you want'. (woman–social sciences)

Disruptions of the classroom atmosphere, according to the professors, also occurred when a student monopolized teacher/student interaction. As one associate male in the social sciences explained, "Sometimes you get a student who has to answer every question." Or, as another in the humanities stated, (Sometimes you get) "a pest," a student whose "questions do not pertain to whatever we are dealing with that day or that week or whatever." All the professors handled the "hyper" student in a similar manner. They would speak to him/her privately after several weeks had passed asking that questions or comments be saved for after class. None of the professors reported feeling wholly satisfied with their resolution of the problem, however, because an "out of control" student can destroy the classroom atmosphere and no matter what the professor does about it the other students hold the professor accountable for being either too lenient (letting the monopolizer monopolize) or too authoritarian (shutting the student off).

Handling disruptions involving side-talking, then, differed by rank and sex. Female assistant professors reprimanded students in a friendly, conciliatory way whereas male assistant professors publicly embarrassed the disrupter. Associate women discussed the disruption with the student as personally problematic for her whereas male associates told the student s/he was bothering the other students. Only at the full professor level is there a convergence: both males and females publicly stop the disrupting student(s) and do not, apparently, soft-pedal or justify their responses to disruptive behavior. However, there were no differences in how professors handled the classroom monopolizer. They discussed the issue with him/her after class after the problem had become habitual and entrenched.

Challenges to Competency

The third management problem involved dealing with students who verbally challenged a professor's competency. Responses to this situation revealed sex and rank-related differences, although no disciplinary or sex-ratio difference emerged.

Verbal challenges reported by women assistant professors were usually viewed positively. One woman explained, "I guess I'd like to see more of that. To me it says that they are thinking, they are moving, they are questioning." Another woman in the humanities felt that,

"To me, the best thing that could happen in a class would be for them to disagree entirely with me and open the book and try to prove to me that I'm wrong." However, there were some nonverbal student behaviors that were seen as negative by assistant women. One gave the following example: "Every once in a while you get what I call a 'smirker,' somebody who just sits in the back of the room and has this wide smirking expression on his face. I've had women, but more often men doing this." The women handled this problem by ignoring it.

Men at the assistant level perceived they were being verbally challenged more frequently than the female assistants. Their response was to divert the challenge to another time and place, usually a later discussion in their office, as illustrated by the following:

I had one student, very bright, very nice fellow. But he kept attacking me for being anti-Soviet. I said, 'OK. That's fair if you want to attack me from that point of view. Why don't you read this? Come in and we'll discuss it and see what happens.' (man–humanities)

Both women and men associates reported verbal challenges. Women report handling this in class with a considerable patience, even when they felt the student was clearly wrong, as the following exemplifies: "I thought that this course would never get off the ground. I dialogued with him every day, not all period, but once every day for three weeks . . . It was a hassle." (social sciences).

On the other hand, men associates were more likely to handle challenges by explaining how the student was wrong or inaccurate. This usually involved responding to the challenge with a defense of their own position:

He challenged things like the dates. I said, 'I know they are the dates because I just put this lecture together.' He said, 'No, you're wrong.' I said, 'Well, I don't think I'm wrong.' It went on like this so I finally said, 'Look, I know I'm right . . . if you'd like to come to my office I'll show you books and articles that I used to draw up my lectures.' (humanities)

I try to explain why it is that certain opinions are inadequate or incorrect, and that there are all different levels of interpretation, and at certain levels you can say that this is right and this is wrong. (humanities)

Full professors encountered verbal challenges less frequently but a few instances were mentioned by women. In these cases the challenges came during the first few days of classes and were responded to directly and immediately. The women interpreted these challenges as minor testing behaviors that they dealt with routinely and quickly.

Challenges to competency, therefore, were experienced by women at all ranks. Female assistant professors welcomed these challenges as long as they were verbal and direct; however, even though they were concerned about the indirect ones, they handled them by ignoring them. Associate women used class time to discuss the issues with the students and full professors quickly stopped the challenges.

Male professors at the assistant and associate ranks, but not at the full rank, reported challenges to their competency. Assistant males would divert the challenger and request s/he come to his office later to discuss the differences. Associates, on the other hand, would *tell* the student in class why his/her ideas were inadequate or wrong.

Lack of Student Participation

The fourth management problem involved the reluctance of students to participate in class discussions, to ask questions, or to make comments concerning the class material. Since all of the professors described their teaching styles as involving student participation, the potential for this problem was present for all the professors. Analysis of the interviews indicates that there are sex and rank differences, although no sex-ratio or disciplinary differences.

At the assistant professor level none of the women reported problems with eliciting student interaction in the classroom. In fact, several felt that their female status encouraged student input. As one woman in the social sciences explained, "I really do think that one of the reasons students are more open to asking questions . . . (is) because I'm a woman." Another in the humanities commented, "I'm very concerned about how my students are feeling, how they're reacting with each other and me. I think that's very much because women are taught to think about it and worry about it and men aren't as much."

Men assistant professors tended to describe the opposite situation. They felt that their status as male hindered professor/student interaction and mentioned several strategies designed to de-emphasize their authoritativeness. These strategies included joking with the students ("I use a little humor to break the ice"), using relaxed body language ("To promote class discussion . . . my usual style is to sit on top of the desk cross-legged or lotus position or legs hanging"), and dressing informally ("I don't wear coats and ties"). Some of the men articulated the conflict they felt between expectations that they be authoritative but at the same time open to students' ideas and questions.

At the associate level, women professors were unanimous in their enthusiasm for the interactive classroom teaching style. Absent from these women's comments were mentions of special techniques used to "break the ice" or problems getting students to talk in class. In addition, all the women mentioned that they enjoyed the "give and take" of classroom interaction.

Men associate professors also elicited student interaction, but their attitude toward it differed from their female counterparts. The men were more likely to view class discussions and student comments as something they *should* encourage rather than something they enjoyed and wanted to encourage. In the words of one chemistry professor, "It's worth *wasting* ten minutes out of an hour lecture to get feedback from the students." (Emphasis ours.) In addition, associate males, like the assistant males, felt that their position as an authority restrained student/professor interaction, and they devised strategies to "loosen up" the classroom. One humanities professor, for example, purposefully dressed informally and allowed a great amount of time for student input. Another in the social sciences explained, "I try to get to class early and try to talk with different students before class begins, just to be there . . . introduce elements of informal exchange."

Full professors mentioned few difficulties in eliciting student participation. Two of the women said they only experienced this problem when students were unprepared, and most of the men did not mention this issue. However, two of the men did note that it had become harder for *them* to relate to students rather than vice versa, although they tried to do so. One man explained, "When I came here as a young instructor I had a much easier rapport with students . . . (now) the students sort of detect that what I really want to do is get home into my study and write."

Females, regardless of rank, disciplinary orientation or sex-ratio report no problem in involving students in discussion. Assistant and associate professor males view their status as *males* and authority figures as having a dampening effect on classroom interactions, and some full male professors no longer much cared about student participation anyway.

Discussion

According to theoretical expectations, females rather than males should devise strategies for classroom management through which they can simultaneously increase the legitimacy of their authority and reduce its appearance, whereas males will have greater latitude in devising strategies since they operate from a position of granted authority.

Sex differences did emerge at the assistant and associate levels. At these ranks, females were less harsh, more accepting, more likely to interpret challenges as an "awakening" of the student, and more likely to engage in the give and take of free discussion than their male counterparts. In effect, then, a junior female faculty member *does* use strategies that draw upon societal expectations of how *females* should behave. She is demonstrating her authority, but softening it at the same time; she reduces the appearance of authority as she displays it.

Male assistants and associates, on the other hand, reprimand students publicly and harshly, directly correct student's misconceptions, "point-prove" outside of class, and have difficulty in getting students to partake in classroom discussions. That is, these males were less hesitant to display their legitimacy as authorities and used strategies that, even when similar to the females were more direct and potentially humiliating to the students. Ironically, although males saw that their authority had a dampening effect on students, they nevertheless *used* it to maintain classroom control.

Strategies employed by males and females at the lower ranks are, indeed, different, and they are consistent with our theoretical conceptualization. Sex does have saliency for the performance of the university professor role at the junior ranks. However, that saliency disappears once full professorship is attained. Males and females at that level report very similar strategies. Why should this be? Why do male and female full professors have more similar styles than their junior colleagues? Why does sex status become less relevant?

Chronological age, in the case of this sample, will not explain the differences since some of the full professors were younger than the assistants and associates. Even amount of teaching experience is not an apparent explanatory variable, for again, some senior faculty had taught less than some assistants and associates. Further, faculty member's reports that most students do not know the differences in academic ranks suggests that our results are not attributable to differential prestige ratings.

Rather, it is suggested that what the full professors share in common is that they, as indicated even by the connotation of their title, have been *fully* accepted as members of the academic community. That is, they have achieved the highest position possible within the academic ranking system. Saying that, of course, raises new questions for further research, namely: What is there about the *structure* of the university that allows males and females to experience the classroom similarly *only* when full professorship has been obtained? What is there about the *experience* of being a full professor that contributes to these similarities? Since so few women obtain this status, are there some invisible barriers that only a few women see and leap over? Or, are there some demands that one foregoes one's *style* as a woman in order to become a full professor?

References

Burchard, W. W.
  1954 "Role Conflicts of Military Chaplains," *American Sociological Review,* 19:528–35.
Eskilson, Arlene and Mary Glenn Wiley
  1974 *The Study of Teaching,* New York: Holt, Rinehart and Winston, Inc.
Goffman, Irving W.
  1957 "Status Consistency and Preference for Change in Power Distribution," *American Sociological Review,* 22:275–88.
Goode, William J.
  1960 "A Theory of Role Strain," *American Sociological Review,* 25:483–496.
Gross, Neal, W. S. Mason, and A. W. McEachern
  1966 *Explorations in Role Analysis: Studies of the School Superintendency Role,* New York: John Wiley and Sons.
Hartley, Ruth E.
  1969 "Sex-role Pressures and the Socialization of the Male Child," *Psychological Reports,* 5:457–468.
Hodge, Robert W., Paul M. Siegel, and Peter H. Rossi
  1964 "Occupational Prestige in the United States, 1925–1963." *American Journal of Sociology,* 70:290–93.
Jackson, Elton F.
  1962 "Status Consistency and Symptoms of Stress," *American Sociological Review,* 27:469–80.
Kanter, Rosabeth Moss
  1977 *Men and Women of the Corporation,* New York: Basic Books, Inc.
Lensky, Gerard E.
  1954 "Status Crystallization: A Non-Vertical Dimension of Status," *American Sociological Review,* 19:405–13.

Lewis, Michael

1972   "Parents and Children's Sex-Role Development," *School Review,* 80:229–40.

McKee, John P.

1959   "Man's and Woman's Beliefs, Ideals and Self-Concepts," *American Journal of Sociology,* 54:346–363.

Meeker, B. F. and P. A. Weitzel-O'Neill

1977   "Sex Roles and Interpersonal Behavior in Task-Oriented Groups," *American Sociological Review,* 42:91–105.

Merton, Robert K. and Elinor Barber

1963   "Sociological Ambivalence," in Edward A. Tiryakian (ed.) *Sociological Theory, Values,* *and Socio-culture Change,* New York: The Free Press of Glencoe.

Pheterson, Gail, Sara B. Kiesler, and Philip Goldberg

1971   "Evaluation of the Performance of Women as a Function of Their Sex, Achievement, and Personal History," *Journal of Personality and Social Psychology,* 19:144–48.

Sherriffs, A. C. and R. F. Farrett

1953   "Sex Differences in Attitudes About Sex Differences," *Journal of Psychology,* 35:161–68.

Walum, Laurel

1977   *The Dynamics of Sex and Gender: A Sociological Perspective,* Chicago: Rand McNally.

Introduction: Political Inequality

Not only are males more likely to hold occupational positions that provide greater rewards, they are also more likely to have access to power in the political sphere. In her article "Women and Power: The Roles of Women in Politics in the United States," Cynthia Fuchs Epstein analyzes why women rarely govern, addresses some of the myths about women and politics and suggests alternative ways for women to gain political strength. How ideas about women and politics are perpetuated is illustrated by two brief selections—a letter to Ann Landers from a "Cuckoo Candidate" and a spoof, "What Does a Well-Dressed 'Male Mayor' Wear," from the Dallas *Morning News*. In "They Dress Like Girls and Tell Dirty Jokes," Ellen Goodman provides a humorous but rather shocking insight into what really goes on in those all-male secret clubs which forge the bonds of the old-boy network in American politics.

Finally, lest we forget that the state has that most awesome power of determining why and when and who should engage in warfare, we conclude with a selection which illustrates that—when it serves the interests of the politically powerful—women have not only been allowed to participate in activities ordinarily reserved for men, but have been pressured to do so. Leila J. Rupp in "Woman's Place Is in the War: Propaganda and Public Opinion in the United States and Germany, 1939–45" finds that during World War Two both governments appealed for women's participation in the war effort. This appeal was based on women's traditional roles as wives and mothers, rather than on their own economic interests; thereby making it easier for industry to discharge women from their employ at the close of the war.

Women and Power: The Roles of Women in Politics in the United States

Cynthia Fuchs Epstein

In the United States, as in other countries, women rarely govern. They have not been regarded as part of the political arena, and until recent times this was considered to be normal. Politics at every level of participation was considered to be the province of men. The reasons offered for this phenomenon were: women's disinterest in politics, originating in their early socialization; their incapacity to assume political leadership roles; and their family responsibilities, which precluded political activity. These views have been held both by the popular culture and by social scientists,[1] although millions of women have participated as voters and as workers in political campaigns and although women formed and led one of the most effective political mobilizations in American history—the women's suffrage movement.[2] Perceiving women as "outside" politics is as curious a matter of "pluralistic ignorance"[3] or "selective inattention" as can be found in history.

The reality of women's poor representation as political leaders and the fiction that they are not political actors are related issues. This paper will show how cultural myths and the ways in which women are located in the social structure interact to underplay and undermine women's access to and participation in, politics, particularly in decision-making roles. The paper will indicate that, although on the whole women participate less than men in political life, there is probably a far greater pool of interested and qualified women who would take on more political responsibility if they could than is commonly believed. It will show how a combination of prejudices against women's leadership roles and their differential placement in the tracking system makes it difficult for them to have political "careers." It will also examine how women who do have political careers achieve them

Reprinted from Cynthia Fuchs Epstein, "Women and Power: The Roles of Women in Politics in the United States," in *Access to Power: Cross-National Studies of Women and Elites,* ed. Cynthia Fuchs Epstein and Rose Laub Coser (London: George Allen and Unwin Publishers, 1981), by permission of the publisher and the author.

by routes that are alternative to those followed by men—routes that are more limited and more difficult for a political aspirant to follow and situated to minimize competition with men. Finally, it will explore indicators of changes in American society that suggest the opening of opportunities to women to participate more freely and more "normally" in political life.

Myths About Women and Politics

Myths about women and political activity abound at both factual and interpretive levels. They especially center on women's supposed political disinterest, ignorance, and inattention.

Myths About Socialization

Some political scientists who have sought to explain the participation of men and women in politics have suggested that political habits are formed early (Githens and Prestage, 1977); further, boys are socialized to believe that they should be interested in political affairs, and girls are socialized to believe that they should not. These conclusions have been reached by Herbert Hyman (1959), by Fred Greenstein (1961), and more recently by Dean Jaros (1973), who found boys to be invariably more "political" than girls. The documentation of differences between male and female youngsters was considered evidence of different male and female tracks of development in political interest. The findings of these social scientists have recently been challenged both methodologically and theoretically by a group of sociologists at the University of Illinois. There, Orum and his associates (1974) found no sex differences among boys and girls in a large sample of Illinois schoolchildren, probing their views on a number of political dimensions. The discrepancy between earlier studies and the 1974 study, even considering the possible effects of social change in the society, raised questions about the limits of method in the earlier studies and led to challenge of the assumption that differences between the sexes in adult life are explained by childhood socialization. Orum *et al.* have suggested that a better explanation of male–female differences in adult political participation is a structural or situational view, explaining, for example, that fewer women than men go into public life because they are confined to their homes, whereas men are more active because of the demands of their jobs' ancillary activities. This latter view was offered earlier by Lipset (1960) and other political scientists who considered women's roles as wives and mothers to have a priority precluding the assumption of other roles. Lipset has written that "the position of the married woman illustrates the problem of available time or dispensability as a determinant of political activity. The sheer demands on a housewife and mother mean that she has little opportunity or need to gain politically relevant experiences" (p. 204).

Although I agree with Lipset that housewives with young children may have difficulty replacing themselves in the home, "having time" for politics is clearly related to cultural views about how people *should* spend their time. This leads directly to the other myths that explain that women are "outside politics" because political behavior demands time that they must spend in performing family roles.

The Myth of Role Conflict and the Myth of Political Participation

Probably the most frequently offered explanation for the absence of women from high office, as well as their lack of political participation, is the one holding that women's roles as wives and mothers conflict with political roles in the same ways as they do with work roles. As Lipset (1963) has noted, meeting the demands of child care, when fathers do not share these tasks, often makes political activity impossible and may even depress levels of interest and self-confidence. From the local to the national level politics includes evening and weekend activities. The woman whose family claims her time may not be free to attend the meetings and social and other events that are necessary to make contacts and build a power base. Many people feel that motherhood precludes activity outside the home, where continuous time commitment is involved, and mothers of small children seem to share this view. A study by Lynn and Flora (1973) of women's attitudes and activities in the 1968 US elections has shown that mothers feel less politically effective than non-mothers.

Obviously, many women interested in politics face role conflict. But the problem stems not only from actual time pressures on women but also from the normative realm—from beliefs about how women *should* spend their time. Thus, it is commonly expected, not only that women *will* feel role conflict in such cases, but also that they *ought* to and that this should deter them from political activity that is more than intermittent and casual. The electorate may deny that a woman candidate for office has found personal solutions to role demands or that political activity is her first choice, with priority above family demands. Women who do manage to marshal their energies and support from their families often face hostile and condescending attitudes from voters because they must withdraw from family responsibilities, as men do, during a campaign.

Although male candidates usually try to show that they have strong family ties and the support of wives and children, they seldom face questioning from the electorate as to the quality or extent of the care that they give their children or the affection that they give their wives.[4] A woman is caught in what has been described as a "double bind": if she campaigns vigorously, she is apt to be criticized as a neglectful wife and mother; if she claims to be an attentive mother, her ability to devote time and energy to public office is questioned.

This confluence of factors may account for the fact that in the United States few women in top public office have family responsibilities, because they are either single, widowed, or old enough to have grown-up children. Of the eighteen women representatives in the Congress elected in 1976, ten were married and eight were single, divorced, or widowed. At state and local levels of government women tend to conform to the profile of the average American woman; that is, more are married, and a greater proportion are widowed than divorced (Johnson and Stanwick, 1976).

Although few women officeholders have young children, it is interesting to note that those who do are as active, if no more active, in outside organizations than those who do not have young children. There also appears to be little relationship between motherhood and the amount of time that women officeholders report they devote to their office (Johnson and Stanwick, 1976, p. xliv). Those with children seem to work as hard as those without children.

That women's political activities are subject to cultural imperatives and mechanisms of exclusion is demonstrated by a case deviant from the general pattern—that of women who are active in school district politics.

Although the presence of young children in the home does seem to affect women's political activity at a national level, even as voters, research by Kent Jennings (1977) has indicated that young mothers are more active in local school politics than young fathers in their age cohort and more active than young nonmothers. These women attend late night meetings and raise money to campaign and run for office. They do all the things that it once was believed mothers of young children couldn't do and didn't want to do and that were thought to be reasons why they did not participate in politics.

It is not difficult to account for this. School board elections are considered legitimate activities for women, and men don't stand in the way of their participation; nor are school boards tied into networks of political patronage and economic benefit, as are other political offices. There is less at stake here in terms of power that men may wish to hold exclusively.

The fact of women's extensive activity in voluntary organizations, whether political, educational, or social contradicts the explanation that role conflict is at the root of their non-participation in public life.

Women have long been active participants in political campaigns. An estimated 6 million women did some sort of volunteer work in the Kennedy–Nixon presidential campaign of 1960 (Gruberg, 1968). In fact the percentages of women engaging in these activities are generally close to those of men.[5] Of course, much of this work was ringing doorbells, stuffing envelopes, and phoning. Yet, women's work as political "footsoldiers" has also been explained by the fact that "women have more time to give" (Gruberg, 1968, p. 52).[6] Of course, most women work within the boundaries of community, travelling little. But many have gone on the campaign trail as paid staff and volunteer workers.

Women have also been important disseminators of political information as members of the League of Women Voters and have engaged in lobbying efforts on matters of social legislation through such "non-politically" oriented organizations as the National Council of Women, the American Association of University Women, the National Federation of Business and Professional Women's Clubs, and, more recently, the National Organization of Women—organizations whose memberships each run to the hundreds of thousands. Not all members of these clubs are active or interested in politics, but until recently most women who sought political office came from the ranks of voluntary workers in non-partisan or non-political organizations.

A study conducted by the Center for American Women and Politics at Rutgers University established a profile of the typical woman who runs for and wins public office in the United States. She is married, has two or more children, and holds a job in addition to running her home. She is a joiner; she belongs to more organizations than male officials on average (Johnson and Carroll, 1978). She is also politically ambitious, aspiring to one or more other offices in the future.

Clearly, not all women have time for politics, nor the inclination. But there appear to be sizable numbers of women who can circumvent those obstacles and wish to do so.

The Myths About Voting Behavior

It has been documented that women voted less than men in the past (Lane, 1959, p. 209; Lipset, 1960). Their proportionately poorer turnout at the polls has precipitated the indictment that women are not responsible citizens. In the past some political scientists have attributed their behavior to cultural views of voting as unladylike, undesirable, or not permitted in their families (Lane, 1959, p. 211; Gruberg, 1968). But it has been noted that women voted less than men only among certain groups (e.g., in poor and rural areas and among recent immigrants), with male–female differences diminishing as social class, education, and occupational rank increased (Lane, 1959; Lipset, 1960). However, Shanley and Schuck (1974) have pointed out that over the broad spectrum women always voted *nearly* as often as men and that the differences have diminished with time. These political scientists have also stressed that women have expressed the same degree of party loyalty, shared men's sense of civil responsibility, and discussed politics in the home as much as men (citing the studies of Campbell *et al.*, 1964).

There is another aspect to myths about women's voting behavior—the differing interpretations of the reasons why women vote as they do.

We know that family members vote alike. The influence of male members of the family is assumed to be dominant, and it is believed that women vote for candidates favored by their husbands and fathers.

However, similar husband–wife voting patterns may come from the fact that most people marry homogamously. Most spouses come from similar backgrounds, and their common values bring them together in the first place. Where there are differences between spouses it has been assumed that women change and adopt men's opinions. But at various times proportions of men and women's votes differ, and political scientists have explained that husbands and wives are voting differently, along sex-linked lines rather than family lines.

Do the men (i.e., fathers) always influence children politically? Several studies have found that children of both sexes more often model or agree with the mother in political behavior and attitudes, when mother and father differ (Nogee and Levin, 1958; Jennings and Langton, 1969; Thomas, 1971). One study cited by Goot and Reid (1975) has shown that, where there is disagreement in the family between mother and father, some children vote the mother's preference. This is one of many studies that they have referred to in a monograph that disputes many popular and "scientific" assumptions about male influence over women by taking a critical look at the classic studies of voting and political participation.

Critical analysis of the "reasoning" offered by political scientists to indicate women's derivative decisions about voting has also been made by McCormack (1975). She has noted that when women vote as their husbands do it is assumed that their husbands are influencing them, but that when they vote differently, which occurs with some frequency, they are often damned as parochial, conservative, or politically unimaginative. McCormack has cited the findings of Lipset (1960) and Tingsten (1963), which show (1) that women do not always vote as their husbands do and (2) that when they do not their political sentiments are sometimes more conservative and sometimes less authoritarian: "Among working class voters in Italy, wives do not share their husbands' pro-Communist sympathies; in France, they did not share their husbands' Poujadist support; and in Germany, they did not initially support National Socialism" (p. 21).

The studies cited provide sufficient contradictory evidence to make us wary about the ways in which causality is inferred in looking at men's and women's voting behavior and political participation.

Myths are created and perpetuated by the aggregation of all women or all men. It is misleading to aggregate all women in posing gender differences on such mass phenomena as voting behavior. For example, M. Kent Jennings (1977) has pointed out that whether women work or not affects their political participation; those who work full time participate more actively. He has also suggested that a staging process may exist, whereby higher-status working women become more politically active and are followed later by lower-status women. There are the impacts of education and age as well. Youth and higher education increase the political participation of women (Jennings, 1977; Lipset, 1960) and cancel out the effect of sex status.

Yet, sex status is often theoretically linked to women's access to, and participation in, leadership roles. This is also questionable.

Politics and the Personality Myth

Many political studies have led us to believe that women do not possess the needs and other traits of the males who opt for political careers and succeed in them. One school of literature has reasoned that people with certain kinds of personalities choose occupations and careers that are consonant with their emotional make-up. Costantini and Craik (1972), for example, "found" women not to have male traits and took this to explain (1) their poor representation in political life and (2) the failure of those who do participate. Yet, later evidence (Kohn, 1977; Kanter, 1977) suggests that personality is often flexible and situational and is likely to change in the direction evoked by the role demands of social structures. Hence, *exclusion* from certain social structures may explain the differences in "traits" found by personality studies.

Interpretations, perceptions, and judgments of motivating factors may be affected by cultural bias. For example, Costantini and Craik (1972), from their analysis of political activists in California, have reported that "If the male leader appears to be motivated by self-serving considerations, the female leader appears to be motivated by public-serving considerations" (p. 235). Further, female leaders tend to express a "forceful, effective and socially ascendant style in an earnest, sobersided and ambivalent manner," whereas male leaders tend to express the same personal style in a more "easy-going, direct and uncomplicated way" (p. 217).

Social Structure: Statuses and Situations

The previous section of this paper has questioned the notions that women are not socialized to be interested in politics, that they lack the time to engage in politics, and that too few women play roles as political actors to constitute a pool of candidates for political office.

This section will explore how women's position in the social structure creates conditions that make it difficult for them to ascend political hierarchies. It will look at the ways in which women's status sets tend to exclude the acquisition of political statuses and at how the status sequences that lead to political office follow tracks from which women are excluded.[7]

Status Sets and Role Integration

Although "role conflict" may be challenged as a major explanation for women's poor representation in political roles, it is a fact that some combinations of statuses (i.e., status sets) are integrative and that others tend to create conflict.

Meeting the norms attached to one status can be facilitated by holding another status with complementary role expectations. For example, Max Weber in 1919 (in Gerth and Mills, 1946) pointed out that proportionately more lawyers than other professional men went into politics because their law careers would be enhanced by political connections. Politics makes lawyers more visible to potential clients and gives them knowledge that they can use in their legal practices. Physicians, on the other hand, would suffer professionally from political activity that prevented them from keeping up with developments in their fields.

Thus, in the course of their occupational activity men may find not only that it serves them to be political but also that they *must* be political. Many need to be aware of the politics of the community in which they work, to calculate what to do about tax policy or legislation that will affect their businesses. They need information about how contracts are given out by municipal agencies, they have to be aware of new regulations, and they need to know those administering them.

Because women are not working in positions that demand such knowledge, they are not propelled toward attaining certain kinds of political knowledge or becoming political themselves. Not all women have occupational roles, and rarely do they have decision-making roles that put them into community politics integrated with work. But when it is necessary for them to be political to carry out their roles, they are political, as has been shown by M. Kent Jennings's (1977) observations on women's activity in school board politics. Involvement in political life is usually situational and role specific.

Status Sequences and Background: Tracking and Political Leadership Roles

Although cultural norms support women's behavior as voters and their contribution as political workers during campaigns, it is far more difficult for women to win cultural approval as candidates for office or for serious political ambitions. The society's norms support women as political amateurs but not as "professionals." This means that women do not choose to run for office and that party leaders do not choose them to be candidates.

Women face difficulties wherever they are clearly in competition with men. In addition to the general cultural view that women ought not to win, they are handicapped because they cannot travel the same routes as men to legitimacy and competency. If they do, they have a chance. Johnson's studies have shown that, once women become candidates, they win in about the same proportion as men (1978, pp. 311–12; and note 13). The problems of women entering politics can best be conceptualized by examining whether and how they can acquire the same status sequences and the same status sets as males and can deal with the problems caused when their sex status is inappropriately focused upon in political and professional settings.

Passage through certain status sequences is characteristic of men in political life. Attending certain schools and having careers as lawyers or businessmen are important preparations for political activity. Women, underrepresented in business and especially in the practice of law,[8] have been unable to develop networks and accumulate the resources that are necessary for building careers in politics.

Education. Women holding political office have tended to have both less education than their male counterparts (Jennings and Thomas, 1968; Costantini and Craik, 1972) and a different kind of education. Even now, women in public office include fewer graduates than men in public office.

In the past even women who had elite educations experienced segregated schooling. Until recently they were barred from attending Harvard, Columbia, Yale, and Princeton, especially their schools of law and business, and they were thus seriously limited in access to the "eastern establishment" and the political jobs that drew from those networks (Putnam, 1976). Attending the "sister" institutions of Wellesley, Barnard, or Vassar was a separate and unequal experience that did not prepare women for later careers as the male colleges did. Of course, elite education was not typical for men elsewhere in the country, and the opportunity structure differed for them too.

To the extent that they were differently or less educated than men, women could not make friendships that would become politically useful and did not have colleagues who could be drawn on as a political constituency. This means that women rarely could travel the status sequence that led to careers, except at the lowest levels. Channels to political opportunity were usually closed to women. Jennings and Thomas (1968) have pointed out how discouraged women were in seeking a range of political offices when they were viewed as clearly unattainable.

Further, women often view their current political careers not as steps up the ladder but as completed achievements (Costantini and Craik, 1972). Kirkpatrick (1974, p. 73) has also shown that most women think of election to a state legislature as a last rather than a first step of a political career. This is true for most men (Wahlke *et al.,* 1972), but many more men than women consider it as only a first step. However, Marilyn Johnson (private communication) has pointed out that these studies are not of matched samples and that, when men and women holding the same public office are compared, patterns of gender differences are often mitigated or reversed regarding political ambitions.

Widow's Succession and Voluntary Associations. Women who go into politics at most levels necessarily come by different routes from men. The most important of these leading to high office has often been characterized as "widow's succession."

Such women usually have come to office as appointed replacements on the death of a prominent husband or father with whom they served the functional equivalent of apprenticeship. Although these are idiosyncratic events, in sum they constitute a pattern, because a large proportion of women have followed this path. Werner (1966, 1968) found that, of the seventy women who served in Congress between 1917 and 1964, about one-half had relatives in Congress and more than one-half were either appointed or elected to fill a vacancy, often one caused by the death of a husband. This is still a pattern. The two women senators serving in the 95th Congress were filling seats vacated by the deaths of their husbands. The first two (of five) women governors came to office this way.[9] The third woman elected as a governor was widely acknowledged to be a figurehead for her husband, and it wasn't until 1974 that a woman governor—Ella Grasso of Connecticut—was elected in her own right. She was followed by Dixie Lee Ray in the state of Washington. All women in the US Senate were widows of senators or succeeded their still living husbands until Nancy Landon Kassebaum was elected in 1978, and even she too was related to a prominent political figure, Alf Landon—a presidential candidate in 1936.

It is probable that most of these "successors" were supported because they were viewed as compliant persons causing no threat to the men in the political cliques created by the deceased male incumbents. In spite of this some of these women showed or are showing skill in wielding power for a time.

Another route to elective office is by way of participation in voluntary organizations—a path that is largely unique to the United States. Women in state legislatures and other elective bodies below the level of Congress have tended to come from the ranks of voluntary organizations. Jeane Kirkpatrick (1974)—author of the first in-depth study of women in state office—found that until recently the typical female officeholder came from a background of voluntary service, chiefly in church and school organizations. The women surveyed were older on average than their male counterparts and usually had first run for office after the age of 40; women in office through widow's succession are also on average older than their male colleagues. In contrast, 90 percent of a matching group of male legislators had made their first attempt at public office before the age of 40.

Consequences of Conforming to Status Set Typing[10]

We have seen that most women come to political office by routes that disadvantage their long term careers. Yet, some women do follow more traditional routes, matching male patterns more closely, to the benefit of their future careers.

The Salience of the Lawyer Status. The most useful route to political office for women, although not the most typical, seems to be through law, and their growing participation in the legal profession appears to be women's best hope for more political involvement in the future.

Kirkpatrick's (1974) study of women state legislators, for example, found distinct differences between lawyers and non-lawyers. Women lawyers were definitely younger than the median for non-lawyers who were candidates; four of the six studied were under 40 when they first ran for the legislature, and the only one under 30 was a lawyer. Kirkpatrick has noted that a woman who is a lawyer can win nomination and be elected to a legislature without the years of party or community service that characterize most other women's careers. "If you are a woman and a lawyer," one state legislator pointed out, "you have an instant credibility that most women do not have." This legitimacy created by the status of lawyer operates throughout the political hierarchy.

Women who are lawyers can more legitimately "hang out" as men do at local political clubs. "Clubhouse lawyers" are regarded as present for the purpose of doing business, and women's lawyer status helps to define their presence in these terms. In this context particularly, following the prescribed status sequences en route to political office serves to legitimate a candidate not only by providing the appropriate credentials but also by permitting the playing out of a set of dynamics associated with political roles.

All five of the new congresswomen elected in 1972 were lawyers (Diamond, 1977).[11] In spite of the fact that women constituted only 1-3 percent of the legal profession during 1917-70—the period studied by Bullock and Heys (1972)—20 percent of the regularly elected women congresswomen were lawyers.

Characteristics of Women Officeholders. Status sequences that conform to the "preferred" and "ideal" are extremely important for women, even when most men fall short of the ideal. During the fifty-three-year period studied by Bullock and Heys (1972) 69 percent of the regularly elected women but only 10 percent of the widows had held public office before entering Congress; 57 percent of the regularly elected women but only 20 percent of all freshmen listed party activities. These data suggest that certain kinds of political experience are more crucial for women than for men who wish to be elected to Congress.

Ideology and Opportunity Structure. Status sequences and opportunity structure can also explain patterns in women's ideology and partisanship as political actors.

As mentioned earlier, studies in the United States and western Europe have provided data said to show that women tend to vote more conservatively than men (Jacquette, 1974). This may be explained by their lesser education and workforce participation. Seymour Martin Lipset (personal communication, 1978) has pointed out that:

> . . . *women's conservative voting (by large margins) in much of Europe is related to the fact that women are more religious than men, and that in many countries religious people are more conservative than irreligious ones. Hence, in France, Italy, etc., women vote much more for right parties, while men vote left. In the U.S., religion versus irreligion does not exist as a factor related to voting. The more religious (females) are, however, more moralistic here. Hence women do show up as more anti-gambling, more anti-corruption, more*

> *opposed to liberal divorce laws, more favorable to prohibition in the past, less liberal with respect to homosexual rights, more peace oriented.*

Here we see that the variables that explain voting behavior are not necessarily sex role linked, except in so far as what women do is interpreted differently from what men do. In American society women are not religious to a greater extent than men. But in the United States the assumption is made that women are more moralistic than men (Lipset, 1960; Gruberg, 1968). I suggest that women are as rational or irrational as men in voting their self-interest as well as their ideologies. For example, many women voted for prohibition because drunken husbands were poor providers and physically abused women and children in the home. Thus, it was not "moralism" but self-interest that determined their decision in some cases, and social awareness in others. This same reasoning may be applied to their opposition to more liberal divorce laws, which have been seen as threatening to women's economic interests. Furthermore, the "moral" positions said to be taken by women (e.g., being peace oriented) are often conceptualized as "liberal" when applied to men's political behavior.

We must be wary in accepting the view that women are more conservative than men even by a "male standard." As mentioned earlier, women in Europe have been less favorable to authoritarian candidates than men at various times.

It has also been pointed out that the proportion of women voting conservatively, by classic measures, varies and is often very close to the figure for men. In the United States Campbell *et al.* (1964, p. 641) have reported that in 1948 and 1952 somewhat fewer women than men (2 percent and 4 percent respectively) supported the Republicans, and this again seemed to be the case in 1958 (Steinem, 1972, p. 51). And, in 1964, 1968, and 1972 more women voted Democratic. The proposition has been offered that women are more "right wing than men" by a "small but sizable proportion" (Blondel, 1965, p. 60). But counterindications have been cited by Goot and Reid (1975), notably from later studies, which show that more women than men opposed conscription, the Vietnam war, nuclear weapons, racial discrimination, and capital punishment and that more women than men were sympathetic to a wide range of social welfare programs (pp. 20-1). American women's acquisition of other statuses may account for this change, or their growing sense of political efficacy because of the women's movement. Historically, American women involved in politics have supported reform movements and voted liberally.[12] As indicated by Table 8.1, women Democrats outnumbered women Republicans at every level of public office in 1977.

Note that the proportion of women Democrats rose as the level of office rose, from 51 percent among municipal councilors to 73 percent among state executive officeholders and to an overwhelming 73 percent (thirteen out of eighteen) in the US Congress.

When women party leaders[13] were compared to male party leaders by Costantini and Craik (1972), Republican women were not different from men with regard to public policy issues, but among the Democrats women were considerably more liberal. A 1976 analysis of the voting records of women members of Congress indicated that women officeholders of both parties tended more than men to oppose increased military spending and a hardline foreign policy (*New York Times,* April 11, 1976).

Women officeholders also consider themselves more liberal than their male counterparts. In a study by the Center for the American Woman and Politics (Johnson and Carroll, 1978), among the women 30 percent considered themselves to be liberal, 36 percent middle of the road, and 35 percent conservative. Among the men 22 percent considered themselves to be liberal, 33 percent middle of the road, and 45 percent conservative.

The fact that women in politics tend to be more liberal than men, assuming that these findings hold, may be due to women's greater opportunity to be elected by parties that are more committed to ideologies of elite turnover and equality and whose appeal is to the underprivileged and to minority groups. However, in those parties they must also face the resistance of working class men, who tend to be conservative on issues of sex role equality.

Reform Movements as a Track for Women. Some women have been able to gain footholds in political life because their involvement in social or political protest movements and as members of reform political insurgent groups—these activities often overlap—has helped them to accumulate political and organizational expertise. But this pattern has had its negative as well as its positive consequences for women's attainment of political office. Reform movements often develop as a response to crisis on a temporary basis; they may not always become institutionalized. Therefore, reform activity has been only an occasional means of entry for women into mainstream politics. It should be noted, however, that women seem to have more chance to be elected in times of social crisis (Lipman-Blumen, 1973) and that many prominent women in leadership positions today have come from insurgent political clubs. Bella Abzug is one of the latter.

Reform and insurgent political groups may become a more important road for women into political life. In the early 1970s women moved into law in increasing numbers, and a good proportion of them were interested in, and confident about, assuming political roles. Many of them chose law careers because of their backgrounds in recent social-protest movements and their feeling that men could not and would not represent women effectively on such issues as abortion, sex discrimination in employment, and rape. They were politicized and eager to learn, to gain the political credentials conferred by the law, and to grasp the levers of power.

Women pursuing political office in the 1970s have been somewhat more likely to come from the left than from the right. Many have developed political ties with men through activities in the antiwar movement. For example, Carol Bellamy, who won the city council presidency in New York in 1977, went to work for one of the

TABLE 8.1
Party Affiliation of Women Officeholders, 1977.

Party	US House (no.)	State Executive (%)	State Senate (%)	State House (%)	County Commission (%)	Mayor (%)	Municipal Council (%)
Democratic	(13)	73	71	60	59	50	51
Republican	(5)	16	26	36	30	33	33
Independent	(0)	11	3	4	10	17	15
Other	(0)	0	0	0	1	—	1
Total	(18)	(56)	(68)	(281)	(281)	(290)	(2,172)

Source: Johnson and Carroll (1978), p. 21A.

largest Wall Street law firms—Cravath, Swaine, and Moore—and was a principal organizer of Wall Street Lawyers Against the Vietnam War; Patricia Schroeder, Congresswoman from Colorado, ran on a campaign stressing opposition to the Vietnam War and other social issues (Schroeder, 1977).

A Matter of Integrity. Of the various attributes that women are expected to bring to office, integrity is one of the most curiously double-edged. On the one hand, Americans like their political leaders to be honest. On the other hand, within the structure of the political system, where norms permit and encourage political actors to bargain and deal, people of too resolute integrity are suspect. Their role partners may believe that they are poor members of the "club" and not amenable to trading.

Are women so pure? Are they pure "naturally"? To some extent women's integrity has been demonstrated. They played no decision-making roles in the Watergate scandals, for example. However, their relative purity may stem only from the fact that they have not been part of the party machines or of the established political order. If they have played cleaner politics than men, it may relate less to their superior morality than to the structure of their political positions. Where women hold public office, it appears that they are concentrated in positions not on the route to the top leadership and that they experience less pressure toward corruption. Whether in the legislative or the executive branch, women tend to receive assignments in the fields of health, education, and welfare. In other countries the division of labor is similar, with the addition of the "cultural" ministries. In the past they have been virtually absent from departments or committees dealing with business regulation, public utilities, economic and industrial development, public safety, and public works, although there is some change in this pattern. They are found only marginally in positions dealing with natural resources, transportation, labor and manpower, justice, foreign policy, and environmental protection.

To some extent women's political assignments reflect a society-wide division of labor along sex status lines; except for those in national or state political office their work is low paid and low in prestige and power. They are *expected* to be pure and not self-serving. But in countries where women have held high executive office, they have engaged in the same machinations, legal or extralegal, that men have. This has been true of Indira Gandhi in India, Golda Meir in Israel, Sirimavo Bandaranaike in Sri Lanka, and both Eva Peron and Isabel Peron in Argentina.

The Dynamics of Sexual Status. The processes that result in women's focus on moral issues and their relative success as reform candidates make them vulnerable to some structural constraints on career. Furthermore, a cultural view that defines "good women" as being pure, both ideologically and sexually, is a constraint on their access to the political opportunity structure.

One of the problems that women faced in the past came with the end of each political campaign. When the campaign crisis ended, it was difficult for women to maintain political relationships by "hanging out" in the clubhouse as male party members did.

Regular party activity flourishes and expands during political campaigns in election years. But in interim periods—this is particularly true in city politics—clubs manage to attract a corps of workers chiefly by offering services to constituents and social activities. But the clubhouse atmosphere often discourages women's participation except as spouses or companions. The woman political aspirant is often isolated from the club's social life—a problem for those attempting to travel either the "regular" or the "reform" road to political power.

Allegations of sexual impropriety are a continuing problem for women who seek entry to a political leadership. When women are sponsored by male leaders—an important way to advancement for both men and women—others may assume that a sexual relationship exists. There is also a great deal of sexual joking and innuendo in the political clubhouse.[14] Women who find such behavior embarrassing or offensive often stay away, unless there are specific tasks to be done or they are specially protected. Embarrassment and sexual harassment reduce or channel women's political participation, so that it is available when needed but structured so that it will not become a political threat.

A presumption of sexual availability undermines the legitimacy of the woman's status and makes for discomfort. Sexual liaisons by women with members of political leaderships can have varied results. The sexually connected woman may gain an insider's access to contacts and information, but she may be considered as merely an appendage, without autonomy or political importance. On balance, sexual liaisons have not politically benefited women.

The Effect of Numbers of Eligibles on the Political Opportunity Structure.[15]   The number of women engaging in political activities above the local level has been relatively small. This has had consequences both for the cultural view of the appropriateness of women's quest for political office and for the resultant stereotype of the "proper" candidate and officeholder. The women's movement, however, has encouraged women to think of themselves as appropriate candidates. As a result, in the 1970s more women have presented themselves for party positions in a serious way, and more have been qualified (e.g., as lawyers). Party leaders now feel it important to consider women as nominees and to consider their candidacies, even if they do not give them full support.

It seems to be true now, as studies have shown in the past, that parties tend to put up women candidates in districts where they have little chance of winning (Hightower, 1974; Diamond, 1977). In a study of all women candidates running for office in 1976, Carroll (1977) found that, in approximately half of the cases in which party leaders sought out and encouraged women to run for office, it appeared that they were recruiting candidates as "sacrificial lambs." Yet, even if most of these races were lost, both the parties and the electorate were getting used to the idea of women candidates, and the women were gaining campaign experience. Again, proper credentials were important to winning. In Hightower's sample (1974, p. 21) there were seven lawyers and one third-year law student among the forty-six women candidates running for office in New York; five of the seven elected were lawyers.

The number of women candidates for federal office increased by 38 percent between 1972 and 1974. During this same period similar increases occurred at the state level, where the number of women candidates increased by 71.4 percent and the number elected rose by 35 percent (US Department of Commerce, 1976).

Campaigning. American political campaigning, grueling for anyone, requires days and nights of meetings and speeches. Usually, male politicians have the support of their political club, family, and friends. Wives of politicians are expected to meet the public and often give speeches for their husbands. Judith Stiehm (1977) has suggested that a two-person investment in a political career is typical in American politics. Women candidates, however, usually cannot depend on active support from the party organization. Therefore, they tend to rely on a personal rather than an organizational following for fund raising, publicity, and telephone and door-to-door canvassing.

Funding. Financial backing is unusually difficult to ob-

tain for aspiring female officeholders, and every study of women candidates attests to this.[16] Women do not ordinarily have access to large sums for campaigning, even if they are from wealthy families—Judith Stiehm (1977) has estimated that it costs $400,000 to win a $40,000-a-year job in her study of state elections in California—nor do they have the contacts to tap outside financial resources, lacking access to the "old-boy" networks that donate a great deal of primary campaign money. Since they are not able to make the kinds of contributions that men make, women do not get political backing in return. Backing a woman for election to even a moderately important office is usually considered a poor investment. Party leaders raise funds and acquire power by supporting winning candidates and then brokering their obligations through patronage. Since women have not been viewed as winners who are capable of producing a return on a backer's investment, few political bosses have been willing to sponsor them, except where they can make a gesture of support without fear that it will be costly. Women also do not get corporate contributions as do male candidates. But this may change; as women make more money in professional and business careers, they may feel free to contribute to causes and candidates who will advance their interests and careers.

Discrimination. Women officeholders reported in a 1977 study (Johnson and Carroll, 1978) that their access to political leadership was hindered by discrimination and prejudice, especially from party leaders. Between 68 and 86 percent of women in every office polled agreed that men in party organizations tried to keep women out of leadership roles. In contrast, male officeholders identified the sources of women's difficulties as stemming from their own problems as family members or from their deficiencies of background or training.

The opposition of men and their view that they are not in opposition remain difficult constraints on women's political careers.

Social Change and Access of Women to the Political Opportunity Structure

Women's Political and Legal Networks

One of the most serious problems that women faced in developing political careers was the refusal of support by political groups with male leaderships, coupled with the fact that there were no comparable women's political groups with which they might seek alliance. But the activities of the women's movement and of women lawyers both in the law schools and in the political sphere (Epstein, forthcoming) have been important in moving women into politics in greater numbers.

In 1971 women activists formed the National Women's Political Caucus (NWPC) to promote the development of women's political potential and to generate political action on the issues raised by the women's movement.

The NWPC is active in nearly every state in the union, raising campaign funds for aspiring women candidates. It has become powerful enough symbolically for women candidates to seek NWPC endorsement, but the amounts of money that it has been able to raise are small. Since its founding it has played a significant role in the presidential nominating process. It was instrumental in bringing about rules changes to allow the seating of large numbers of women delegates at the party conventions. In 1972, 40 percent of the Democratic National Convention delegates were women, compared with 13 percent in 1968; and women comprised 30 percent of the Republican delegates in 1972, compared with 17 percent in 1968. In 1976, however, these figures declined somewhat.

Although it is not as strong and pervasive as major party organizations, the NWPC has been important as a symbol of women's growing political consciousness and frustration and represents a new source of political pressure. Not since the suffrage movement have women's political associations acted so cohesively to lobby Congress and the Executive on "women's issues."

Women also are uniting as officeholders to press for issues concerning them that often cut across party lines. Caucuses promoting the interests of special groups arose in the late 1960s and 1970s within many organizations, and now in the Congress there is a Congresswoman's Caucus, as there are Black and Hispanic Caucuses. The Congresswoman's Caucus, for example, in 1977 exacted a promise from the Secretary of Health, Education, and Welfare that he would conduct a thorough study of social security to identify any discrimination against women that could be corrected through legislation (*New York Times,* November 27, 1977, p. 65).

The mutual support of women candidates has been striking. In particular, there is a group of women politicians who are lawyers and Democrats that travels widely and has women's movement connections. They have formed a professional and personal network and assist each other with funds, endorsements, and planning. They also assist women who are newcomers to politics. In this way women running for local political office often achieve national visibility because the media tend to focus on women candidates because they are uncommon.

There is also anecdotal evidence to indicate that women politicians defer to their female colleagues' rights and status. It is now a commonly told tale that, when Bella Abzug was offered the post of chair of the Equal Economic Opportunities Commission (EEOC) by President Carter, she informed him that the EEOC rightfully belonged to the New York City Human Rights Commissioner, Eleanor Holmes Norton. Norton got the appointment. On the other hand, when Abzug sought the US Senate nomination in New York, although she lost the primary, she had national visibility and a great deal of support from women far from her state (Stein, 1978).

Women Officeholders: An Accounting

It will be remembered that until about 1972 most women who attained high political posts were usually appointed to fill vacancies left by husbands or fathers. Some of these women then sought election. By 1974, however, women were beginning to be elected to important posts in their own right, although their numbers remained small. In the 95th Congress, elected in 1976, only three of the eighteen Congresswomen held the seats of their late husbands; before 1949, 45 percent of the women in Congress had succeeded their husbands; and in 1949–71, 29 percent had (*New York Times,* January 30, 1978). All the women who have served in the US Senate until 1978 came to it by the route of widowhood or family affiliation.[17] As already noted, Ella Grasso was the first woman to "make it on her own" to any governorship, and she was followed shortly by Dixie Lee Ray of Washington state. Two women were named to the Carter Cabinet, and women held 12 percent of all presidential appointments in 1978 (Stein, 1978). Johnson (personal communication) has said that estimates ran as high as 18 percent in 1979. There were six women lieutenant governors in the USA in 1979. The year 1979 showed no great increase of women in Congress (seventeen). In fact this was less than in 1978, when there were eighteen, or in the "record" year 1962, when there were twenty. Women constituted 9.3 percent of state legislators in October 1978 — 702 out of 7,561 members (*Wall Street Journal,* October 11, 1978). After the November 1978 elections women were 10.2 percent of state legislators (National Women's Education Fund, 1979). In 1970 they numbered 334 or 4.4 percent of the total. Irene Diamond (1977) has reported that, following the 1974 elections, women constituted 9.1 percent of the state legislators in the lower houses and 5 percent of the legislators in the upper houses. She has further reported that, except for the election year immediately following the winning of women's suffrage, no change of this magnitude has ever occurred in such a short time (p. 26).

Outlook for Women in Poltics.   It is difficult to envisage that sex status will ever become irrelevant to politics. Since government is the arena of highest power in society, it is guarded closely, and the interlocking networks of economic position, political patronage, informal associations, and entrenched party machinery all act as barriers to outsiders. For women to become insiders they will have to progress in political careers by all the routes that men take and by some new routes of their own in concert with all women.

Endnotes

1. This view has been noted by a number of political scientists in recent times. But Martin Gruberg (1968) has noted in his preface to *Women in American Politics:*

   In politics, American women have been virtually invisible. Political scientists, mostly male, have tended to overlook this major group. For example, the standard work on party and pressure politics, V. O. Key's Politics, Parties and Pressure Groups, *ignores women completely except for a few pages about suffragettes. A basic book on pressure groups, Harmon Zeigler's* Interest Groups in American Society, *also omits mention of women; and most textbooks about American government make no reference to female political activity. The same is true of books on state and local government. (p. v)*

2. Although the suffrage movement has been characterized as an isolated phenomenon, not predictive of women's future political behavior.

3. The term "pluralistic ignorance" is used here to characterize collective misperception of actual facts, whether by genuine ignorance or by failure to "register" what has been seen to occur. An extreme example of this phenomenon was the ignorance or inattention of Germans to the Nazi extermination camps. This is a somewhat different way of using the term than that of Robert K. Merton (1968), who, summarizing the work of Floyd Allport and others on "pluralistic ignorance," has offered his own interpretation that the phenomenon occurs when one's own

attitudes and expectations are not shared and one nevertheless assumes that they are uniformly shared (p. 431).

4. The memoirs of prominent national political figures show that, whatever their public stance as family men, as a rule they have rarely permitted their families to interfere with their work or careers. See Myra MacPherson (1975).

5. Marilyn Johnson (private communication) has reported that the Michigan election studies show this.

6. Shanley and Schuck (1974) have observed that, because *what men do* is used as a standard for political behavior, female political activities are often regarded as nonpolitical. For instance, when a woman hosts a party for a candidate, she is said to be engaging in a social activity; but when men socialize at the clubhouse, they are said to be engaging in political behavior. Women workers are also seen as "contributors" by their husbands. In research on New York City political clubs Moran (1978) has noted that male leaders often thank the unpolitically involved husbands of women political workers for contributing their wives' time and energy to the campaign. These "redefinition" procedures are functional for underplaying women's political efforts and acquisition of expertise. I have discussed elsewhere (Epstein, 1970b) how the "mechanism of redefinition" is used by a person to redefine a role to make it more compatible with cultural views of what a person of that status—age, sex, etc.—should be doing. For example, my study of women lawyers in practice with their husbands has shown that they say not that they are engaging in legal work but that they are "helping their husbands" (Epstein, 1971). Thus, they shift focus from doing a socially disapproved activity (i.e., engaging in a male occupational activity) to a socially approved activity (i.e., engaging in the approved female role of being a good wife).

7. I rely now, as I have before (Epstein, 1970a, 1970b), on the theoretical framework devised by Robert K. Merton's (1957, 1968) theoretical framework for the dynamics of status sets as enunciated in *Social Theory and Social Structure* and by "oral publication" (again his concept) in lectures at Columbia University.

8. The salience of a career in law as a characteristic background of political leaders has been pointed out by many prominent social scientists, among them Eulau and Sprague (1964), Schlesinger (1957), and Putnam (1976).

9. They were Nellie Taylor Ross, elected in 1924 in Wyoming—the first state to give women the vote and the first to elect a woman to Congress. The second was Miriam Ferguson, elected in Texas in the same year but inaugurated sixteen days after Ross. Lurleen

Wallace of Alabama served as governor in 1967–8, succeeding her husband George Wallace, who was prohibited by law from running for office for the third consecutive time.

10. As defined before (Epstein, 1970a, p. 166), status set typing refers to the phenomenon that exists when a class of persons who share a key status (e.g., lawyer) also share other matching statuses (e.g., white, Protestant) and it is considered appropriate that this be so.

11. Unfortunately for my theory, new Congresswomen elected in 1974 and 1976 were not lawyers, but one of three new Congresswomen elected in 1978 was an attorney. However, I still predict a mounting trend as the numbers of women lawyers increase in the pool of eligibles.

12. Women's special participation in reform politics, noted by Leon Epstein (1967), has been referred to in the study by Kirkpatrick (1976, p. 9) of the presidential election of 1972. She has reported that "the new political breed of the 1970s" was said to contain large numbers of women who differed from traditional women even more sharply than the men differed from their traditional male counterparts. The new woman was said to be distinguished especially by her demand for a more equal share of power and by willingness to compete with men for it. See also Wilson (1962), Leader (1977), Diamond (1977), Frankovic (1977), and Mezey (1977).

13. Party leaders studied include: Congress members and state legislators holding office in 1965; members of the state delegations (i.e., delegates and alternates) to the Republican and Democratic National Conventions of 1960 and 1964; members of the delegation slate pledged to Nelson Rockefeller, which lost to the Goldwater slate in California's 1964 presidential primary; and 1964 county committee chairs of the two major parties.

14. I am indebted for this material to the preliminary report of her research on political clubs by Eileen Moran of the Graduate Center, City University of New York.

15. I am indebted to the work of Robert Merton on the social consequences of relative and absolute numbers. See also Rosabeth Moss Kanter's (1977) discussion on the impact of numbers for women managers. See also Blau (1977).

16. The most recent was done by an organization called the Center for the Study of Congress (reported through the Associated Press in the New York Times, March 4, 1978).

17. Maurine Neuberger was not appointed to fill the seat left vacant by her husband Richard Neuberger, but she ran for his seat and won.

References

Alexander, Dolores (1978) "It's November: why are these women running?," Working Woman (November), pp. 65–6.

Blau, Peter (1977) Inequality and Heterogeneity (New York: Free Press).

Blondel, J. (1965) Voters, Parties and Leaders, rev. ed. (Harmondsworth: Penguin books).

Bullock III, Charles S. and Heys, Patricia Lee Lindley (1972) "Recruitment of women for Congress: a research note," The Western Political Quarterly, vol. 25, no. 3 (September), pp. 416–23.

Campbell, Angus, Converse, Philip E., Miller, Warren E. and Stokes, Donald E. (1964) The American Voter (New York: Wiley).

Carroll, Susan (1977) "Women candidates and state legislative elections, 1976: limitations in the political opportunity structure and their effects on electoral participation and success," unpublished paper presented at the American Political Science Association, Annual Meeting, Washington, DC.

Citizens' Advisory Council on the Status of Women (1976) Women in 1975 (Washington, DC: US Government Printing Office).

Costantini, Edmond and Craik, Kenneth H. (1972) "Women as politicians: the social background, personality, and political careers of female party leaders," Journal of Social Issues, vol. 28, no. 2, pp. 217–36.

Diamond, Irene (1977) Sex Roles in the State House (New Haven and London: Yale University Press).

Epstein, Cynthia Fuchs (1970a) "Encountering the male establishment: sex-status limits on women's careers in the professions," American Journal of Sociology, vol. 75, no. 6, pp. 965–82.

Epstein, Cynthia Fuchs (1970b) Woman's Place: Options and Limits in Professional Careers (Berkeley: University of California Press).

Epstein, Cynthia Fuchs (1971) "Law partners and marital partners: strains and solutions in the dual-career family enterprise," Human Relations, vol. 24, no. 6, pp. 549–64.

Epstein, Cynthia Fuchs (1975) "Positive effects of the double negative," American Journal of Sociology, vol. 78, no. 4, pp. 912–35.

Epstein, Cynthia Fuchs (forthcoming) Women Lawyers (New York: Basic Books).

Epstein, Leon D. (1967) Political Parties in Western Democracies (New York: Praeger).

Eulau, Heinz and Sprague, John D. (1964) Lawyers and Politics (Indianapolis and New York: Bobbs-Merrill).

Fichter, Joseph H. (1964) Graduates of Predominantly Negro Colleges: Class of 1964, Public Health Services

Publication No. 1571 (Washington, DC: US Government Printing Office).

Fichter, Joseph H. (1971) "Career expectations of Negro women graduates," in Athena Theodore (ed.), *The Professional Woman* (Cambridge, Mass.: Schenkmann), pp. 429–48. Originally in *Monthly Labor Review,* vol. 90, no. 11 (1967), pp. 36–42.

Frankovic, Kathleen A. (1977) "Sex and voting in the US House of Representatives: 1961–1975," *American Politics Quarterly,* vol. 5, no. 3, pp. 315–30.

Gerth, Hans H. and Mills, C. Wright (1946) *From Max Weber: Essays in Sociology* (New York: Oxford University Press).

Githens, Marianne and Prestage, Jewel L. (1977) *A Portrait of Marginality: The Political Behavior of the American Woman* (New York: David McKay Co.).

Goot, Murray and Reid, Elizabeth (1975) *Women and Voting Studies: Mindless Matrons or Sexist Scientism?* (London and Beverly Hills: Sage Publications).

Greenstein, Fred I. (1961) "Sex-related political differences in childhood," *Journal of Politics,* vol. 23, no. 2, pp. 353–71.

Gruberg, Martin (1968) *Women in American Politics* (Oshkosh, Wisc.: Academia).

Hightower, Nikki Van (1974) "The politics of female socialization," unpublished Ph.D. dissertation (New York: New York University, Department of Political Science).

Hyman, Herbert (1959) *Political Socialization* (Glencoe, Ill.: Free Press).

Jacquette, Jane (ed.) (1974) *Women in Politics* (New York: Wiley-Interscience).

Jaros, Dean (1973) *Socialization to Politics* (New York: Praeger).

Jennings, M. Kent (1977) *Another Look at the Life Cycle and Political Participation* (Ann Arbor: University of Michigan).

Jennings, M. Kent and Langton, K. P. (1969) "Mothers versus fathers: the formation of political orientations among young Americans," *Journal of Politics,* vol. 31, no. 2, pp. 329–58.

Jennings, M. Kent and Thomas, Norman (1968) "Men and women in the party elites: social roles and political resources," *The Midwest Journal of Political Science,* vol. 12, no. 4 (November), pp. 469–93.

Johnson, Marilyn (1978) "Broadening elective and appointive political participation," in Ann Foote Cahn (ed.), *Women in Midlife: Security and Fulfillment, Part I,* a compendium of papers submitted to the Select Committee on Aging and the Subcommittee on Retirement Income and Employment, US House of Representatives, Ninety-Fifth Congress, Second Session (Washington, DC: US Government Printing Office), pp. 299–319.

Johnson, Marilyn and Stanwick, Kathy (1976) *Profile of Women Holding Office* (New Brunswick, NJ: Center for the American Woman and Politics, Eagleton Institute of Politics, Rutgers — The State University).

Johnson, Marilyn and Carroll, Susan (1978), in association with Kathy Stanwick and Lynn Korenblit *Profile of Women Holding Office, II* (New Brunswick, NJ: Center for the American Woman and Politics, Eagleton Institute of Politics, Rutgers — The State University). Originally published in Center for the American Woman and Politics, *Women in Public Office: A Biographical Directory and Statistical Analysis,* 2nd ed. (Metuchen, NJ: Scarecrow Press, 1978).

Kanter, Rosabeth Moss (1977) *Men and Women of the Corporation* (New York: Basic Books).

Kirkpatrick, Jeane (1974) *Political Woman* (New York: Basic Books).

Kirkpatrick, Jeane (1976) *The New Presidential Elite* (New York: Russell Sage Foundation and the Twentieth Century Fund).

Kohn, Melvin L. (1977) *Class and Conformity: A Study in Values,* 2nd ed. (Chicago: University of Chicago Press).

Lane, Robert E. (1959) *Political Life: Why People Get Involved in Politics* (Glencoe, Ill.: Free Press).

Leader, Shelah Gilbert (1977) "The policy impact of elected women officials," in *The Impact of the Electoral Process, Sage Electoral Studies Yearbook, Vol. III,* ed. Louis Maisel and Joseph Cooper (Beverly Hills, Calif.: Sage Publications, 1977).

Lipman-Blumen, Jean (1973) "Role de-differentiations as a system response to crisis: occupational and political roles of women," *Sociological Inquiry,* vol. 43, no. 2, pp. 105–29.

Lipset, Seymour M. (1963) *Political Man* (New York: Doubleday; London: Heinemann).

Lynn, Naomi B. and Flora, Cornelia Butler (1973) "Motherhood and political participation: a changing sense of self," *Journal of Political and Military Sociology,* vol. 1 (March), pp. 91–103.

MacPherson, Myra (1975) *The Power Lovers: An Intimate Look at Politicians and their Marriages* (New York: G. P. Putnam's Sons).

McCormack, Thelma (1975) "Toward a nonsexist perspective on social and political change," in Marcia Millman and Rosabeth Moss Kanter (eds), *Another Voice: Feminist Perspectives on Social Life and Social Science* (Garden City, NY: Anchor Books), pp. 1–33.

Merton, Robert K. (1957, 1968) *Social Theory and Social Structure* (New York: Free Press).

Merton, Robert K. and Nisbet, Robert (1976) *Contemporary Social Problems,* 4th ed. (New York: Harcourt Brace Jovanovich), pp. 432–40.

Mezey, Susan Gluck (1977) "Local representatives in Connecticut: sex differences in attitudes towards women's rights policy," unpublished paper presented at the Annual Meeting of the American Political Science Association.

Moran, Eileen (1978) "The sexual division of labor in American political parties," unpublished paper presented at the New York Women's Anthropological Conference.

National Women's Education Fund (1979) *Roster of Women State Legislators as of January 1979* (Washington, DC: US Government Printing Office).

New York Times (New York, 1976–8).

Nogee, Philip and Levin, Murray B. (1958) "Some determinants of political attitudes among college voters," *Public Opinion Quarterly,* vol. 22, no. 4, pp. 449–63.

Orum, Anthony M., Cohen, Roberta S., Grasmuck, Sherri and Orum, Amy W. (1977) "Sex, socialization and politics," in Marianne Githens and Jewel L. Prestage (eds), *A Portrait of Marginality: The Political Behavior of the American Woman* (New York: David McKay Co.), pp. 17–37.

Putnam, Robert D. (1976) *The Comparative Study of Political Elites* (Englewood Cliffs, NJ: Prentice-Hall).

Sanders, Marion K. (1956) *The Lady and the Vote* (Boston, Mass.: Houghton Mifflin).

Schlesinger, Joseph A. (1957) "Lawyers and American politics: a clarified view," *Midwest Journal of Political Science,* vol. 1, no. 1 (May), pp. 26–39.

Schroeder, Patricia (1977) "Explorations of external barriers to women's happiness and success," unpublished paper presented at the Conference on Mental Health for Women: Challenges and Choices, Rochester, New York, November 12.

Schwindt, Helen Demos (1978) "All the President's women," *Ms, vol. 6, no. 7 (January), pp. 51*–4 and 91–2.

Seligman, Lester (1971) *Recruiting Political Elites* (New York: General Learning Press).

Shanley, Mary L. and Schuck, Victoria (1974) "In search of political women," *Social Science Quarterly,* vol. 55, no. 3, pp. 632–44.

Stiehm, Judith (1977) "Ideology and participation: the first will remain last," (unpublished paper presented to the Western Political Science Association, March 31).

Stein, Nancy (1978) "Uphill all the way," *Newsbrief* (New York: Women's Center for Community Leadership, Hunter College), p. 4.

Steinem, Gloria (1972) "Women voters can't be trusted," *Ms,* vol. 1, no. 1 (July), pp. 47–51 and 131.

Thomas, L. Eugene (1971) "Political attitude congruence between politically active parents and college-age children: an inquiry into family political socialization," *Journal of Marriage and the Family,* vol. 33, no. 2, pp. 375–86.

Tingsten, Herbert (1963) *Political Behavior* (Totowa, NJ: Bedminster Press).

US Department of Commerce, Bureau of the Census (1976) *A Statistical Portrait of Women in the US,* Current Population Reports, Special Studies Series P-23, No. 58 (Washington, DC: US Government Printing Office), pp. 55–6.

Wahlke, John C., Eulau, Heinz, Buchanan, William and Ferguson, Leroy C. (1962) *The Legislative System: Explorations in Legislative Behavior* (New York: Wiley).

Wall Street Journal (New York, 1978).

Werner, Emmy E. (1966) "Women in Congress, 1917–1964," *Western Political Quarterly,* vol. 19, no. 1 (March), pp. 16–30.

Werner, Emmy E. (1968) "Women in the state legislatures," *Western Political Quarterly,* vol. 21, no. 1 (March), pp. 40–50.

Wilson, James Q. (1962) *The Amateur Democrat: Club Politics in Three Cities* (Chicago: University of Chicago Press).

Cuckoo Candidate

Ann Landers

DEAR ANN LANDERS: I'm a middle-aged man who has the courage to state that males have more brain power than females and there is plenty of proof. In the first place a man's brain is physically larger than a woman's.

Second: Women are shallower. They stress unimportant details and have trouble getting to the point. Also their feelings get in the way of their intellect.

I am not signing this letter because I plan to run for public office and unfortunately the mentally inferior species possesses the vote. — A MAN WITH COURAGE

DEAR MAN: You're going to need your courage — also a crash helmet, should your identity become known. There's not a shred of validity to your theory, but I'm printing it because there are others who believe as you do, and you are all cuckoo.

The Columbus *Dispatch,* 22 April 1979.

What Does a Well-Dressed "Male Mayor" Wear?

The Dallas *Morning News*

DALLAS — Female politicians long have complained about sexism in news coverage. Reporters have described Kathy Whitmire as "the petite mayor of Houston." Yet, no one would dream of calling John Tower "the petite senator from Texas."

Reporters want to know how much the newly elected Houston mayor weighs. The only person who asks how much Gov. Bill Clements weighs is his doctor.

So, in the interest of fair play, this seems a good time to turn the tables and write about a male politician the kind of story some reporters like to write about "lady" politicians.

Dallas Mayor Jack Evans, a tall, willowy man, was interviewed last week in his fifth-floor office at City Hall. The scene was striking. The natural tones of the office furniture perfectly matched his camel sports coat.

The interview began with a question about the change in city managers — George Schrader has been replaced recently by his assistant, Charles Anderson. The mayor was asked to compare the two men.

As the mayor pondered, he flicked a thread from his light-blue designer shirt. His jewelry was gold and understated.

Reprinted from "What Does a Well-Dressed 'Male Mayor' Wear?", The Dallas *Morning News,* as it appeared in the Columbus *Citizen-Journal,* 11 December 1981.

"Are you interested in their different approaches to city government or the differences in their policies?" he asked boyishly.

What about the differences in the way the two managers dress? What kind of fashion statement do they make?

"George Schrader is more formal. He was always in three-piece suits," said the husband of North Dallas home-maker Gene Evans.

"Charles Anderson is a lot more casual. His clothes are, too."

The mayor shyly drew the conversation back to City Hall issues. He explained there was a tough zoning case in the council meeting the day before.

But how does he know what to wear to face a challenge like that? Does he have a favorite outfit that cheers him up and keeps him going?

"I love clothes, but I'm a casual clothes man myself," said the leggy mayor, who was sporting a pair of brown slacks. "But for council meeting days, I usually wear a gray, pin-striped suit. There's always one in my closet."

What does he consider his worst fashion mistake?

"It's this cashmere coat that looks like a horse blanket. There just aren't very many places I can wear it. I would never bring it to City Hall."

It's 10 a.m. and the mayor's schedule for the day was jammed. There were mass transit issues, visiting dignitaries, decisions on urban planning. Time was at a premium.

That's why it's so important for him to have the kind of hair style he can do himself. He ran a well-manicured finger through his mane of gray-frosted hair. The pompadour was full and shining. He confided he's been going to the same barber for 20 years.

"Is the frosting natural, or do you touch it up?"

"It's all natural," he said vivaciously. "And I want you to print that. I do not use any hair dressing. People are always teasing me about putting on greasy kid stuff. It just isn't true."

He didn't even blush at the next question: Do the council members expect him to make them coffee?

"Not yet," he said demurely.

Now, about his lifestyle. Has it changed since he's been mayor? What does he do for fun?

"Oh, I like to socialize, I love meeting people. I do a lot of socializing on the job. There are lots of luncheons and dinners. Of course, I have to watch what I eat. I don't like to put on weight. I like to keep in shape."

He struck a lithesome pose.

Will he share his secrets of keeping trim?

"I use the stairs instead of the elevator. I eat small portions."

The mayor smiled disarmingly and said he had to excuse himself. He was due to make a speech in the council chambers.

He made a graceful exit.

But the scent of his after-shave still lingered. It's Lagerfeld from Neiman-Marcus.

They Dress Like Girls and Tell Dirty Jokes

Ellen Goodman

BOSTON—In every female life there is an inevitable confrontation with something called the secret all-male club.

For most of us, the big moment comes in fourth grade when the boys who can say no more about the opposite sex than "Girls are Yucky!" suddenly hang a notice on some door or other that rules: NO GIRLS ALLOWED.

That is the crucial bylaw of every male club.

For a time, fourth-grade boys succeed in making their female classmates mad and little sisters sad. But one day the girls find out what is going on inside the club.

What is going on inside is that fourth-grade boys are sitting around, giggling, and telling stupid dirty jokes.

That discovery prepares women for the future. From then on, whenever they are faced with all-male societies, they are equipped with two crucial pieces of information:

- The most important word in the expression "old boys club" is "boys."
- What they probably are doing inside is sitting around, giggling, and telling dirty jokes.

The old boys who moved into power last week also have their club. It appears that the president, the vice president, the attorney general and the secretary of defense all belong to an exclusive male society in San Francisco known as the Bohemian Club.

The Bohemian Club is so all-male that its members do not hire women to work at their 2,700-acre redwood retreat. They are so all-male that they are being sued for sex discrimination. They admit it—with nary a blush.

Their defense rests on the idea that club members would be "inhibited by the presence of women." Inhibited from what, you ask?

It appears that one of the fun things the upper-crust bohemians do is produce dramatic events where members dress up as women and—you've got it—tell dirty jokes.

The club's attorney, for example, a distinguished silver-haired fellow, recalled in detail his artistic triumph as a wood nymph. "We wore wings and body stockings." That, he maintains, he could not have done comfortably in front of women.

Do not be alarmed. As far as I know, none of the august members of the Cabinet have donned the old tutu and taken to the kick line. At least there are no photographs extant.

They are merely following tradition. The truth is the more upper crust, top drawer, preppy and elite a man is in America, the more likely he is to belong to a club whose basic ritual is cross-dressing and telling dirty jokes.

In my town, which drips with ivy, the exclusive Tavern Club holds theatricals during which assorted sober souls who turn the financial wheels of the Northeast can be seen in what they do not call drag.

At Harvard, the exclusive Hasty Pudding Club has existed for years on the single joke of all-male and relatively blue-blooded chorus lines. In such places, the future leaders of America kick up their legs and let down their hair, so to speak.

No less an expert than John Spooner, stockbroker, author and Duchess of Woppery in the Hasty Pudding production of 1959, described this male activity as a throwback to dubious prep-school practices.

I am more inclined to pathos; it occurs to me that the elite are so self-controlled that their female side can only burst out into these hysterical rituals of release.

But I don't want to suggest that all men do when they get together in their clubs is play dress-up.

They also play sports, and sports fans. For many years the big event of the season at the Harvard Club of Boston was an all-male boxing night.

On that evening, some of the most highly respected

professionals in Boston—men who transplant our kidneys, transform our laws and translate our finances—would don black tie, and sit down to dinner while two less-fortunate souls beat each other up in the center ring.

Boys, as they say, will be boys.

Out of those places and out of that mind set, the chains of the old-boy network are forged. It is no surprise that those chains reach all the way to Washington. But the cast may never have come in such numbers.

If the boys from the Bohemian are true to their society, keep your eyes on center stage. This Cabinet may put on quite a show.

READING 62

Woman's Place Is in the War: Propaganda and Public Opinion in the U.S. and Germany, 1939–1945

Leila J. Rupp

" . . . [M]en are apt to wake up some day and stop wars on the ground that women win them," editor Anne O'Hare McCormick wrote optimistically in 1943.[1] She expressed a conviction as widely held in our time as in hers, that women benefit from wars because they are drawn into areas of activity previously closed to them. The Second World War, in particular, brought an unprecedented number of women into such areas, including heavy industry and the armed forces.

But the temporary lowering of barriers made no permanent impact on women's opportunities or status in society. In both the United States and Nazi Germany, recruitment propaganda urged women to participate in the war effort but did not challenge traditional conceptions of women's nature and roles. The appeals addressed to women in both countries reveal an insistence that

women function primarily as wives and mothers. Despite the fact that both governments collected information on public opinion suggesting that women responded in greater numbers to economic motivation, recruitment campaigns seldom appealed to women on this basis. Instead, propaganda urged women to protect and care for their sons and husbands by taking up war work. An examination of the content of propaganda directed at women and of women's attitudes toward employment indicates that women could be and were mobilized in wartime without challenging traditional ideas or bringing about permanent changes in the status of women. This essay concentrates on the American experience during the war and considers briefly the similarities of the German case in order to suggest that women do not necessarily "win" modern wars regardless of the political or economic system under which they live.

American and German Propaganda for the Mobilization of Women

The government of Franklin Roosevelt and the Nazi regime of Adolf Hitler differed in ideological founda-

Reprinted from Leila J. Rupp, "Women's Place Is in the War: Propaganda and Public Opinion in the United States and Germany, 1939-1945," in *Women of America! A History,* ed. Carol. R. Berkin and Mary B. Norton, (Boston: Houghton Mifflin, 1979), by permission of the publisher and the author.
1. *The New York Times,* March 8, 1943, p. 8.

tions, ultimate objectives, and methods of social control.[2] Nevertheless, both handled the problem of mobilizing women in similar ways, a fact that suggests that women have been assigned similar roles in modern Western societies and that these roles are subject to manipulation in response to the needs of highly industrialized economies in wartime. Women constituted the largest available labor reserve in both countries. The American government debated but did not institute labor conscription, choosing to rely instead on intensive propaganda campaigns designed to "sell" war work to women. The Nazis, hampered by a chaotic bureaucratic structure and Hitler's conviction until mid-war that Germany could win in a state of partial mobilization, passed but did not systematically enforce the registration of women for civilian labor. In lieu of effective conscription, Nazi propaganda urged women to participate in the war effort. Although the Nazi effort pales beside the massive American campaigns, both governments relied on propaganda rather than conscription to mobilize women for war.

The United States succeeded in mobilizing women, but Germany did not. The American female labor force increased by 32 percent from 1941 to 1945; the German increased by only 1 percent from 1939 to 1944. In spite of the fact that preparations for war began in Germany before 1939, the insignificant increase in the German female labor force does not reflect an advanced stage of mobilization. American women assumed the places of men called into military service, but German women did not respond to the increasingly serious labor shortages that even the importation of foreign workers and prisoners of war could not solve.

The Office of War Information (OWI), in conjunction with the War Manpower Commission, designed the American campaigns responsible for, in its own words, "selling" the war to women. Even after a Congressional attack on the Domestic Branch of the OWI in 1943 resulted in a severe budget cut, the Office continued to act as a coordinating agency for promotional campaigns. It issued monthly guides to magazine and newspaper writers, editors, and radio commentators, suggesting approaches to war topics and recommending allocation of time and space so that the various media would empha-

size the same themes at the same time; supervised and distributed films; maintained a close relationship with the advertising industry through the War Advertising Council; and planned major national campaigns designed to recruit women for war work. Four campaigns, launched in December 1942, March 1943, September 1943, and March 1944, combined national information efforts with intensive local campaigns in areas of labor shortage.[3]

All of these campaigns used similar media techniques. Newspapers and magazines publicized the need for women workers and featured stories about women who were already at work. The OWI urged magazines to picture women workers on their front covers in September 1943 and arranged a competition for the best cover, with prizes awarded during a special exhibition at the Museum of Modern Art in New York. Posters and billboards appealed to women to take war jobs. The OWI distributed announcements and recordings prepared by famous radio personalities in order to encourage stations to devote spot announcements, special features, and entire shows to the campaigns. Theaters across the country showed special womanpower shorts such as *Glamour Girls of 1943*. A Retailers War Campaign Committee published a calendar that suggested advertising techniques such as displays of work clothes and included a schedule to coordinate war advertising. The War Advertising Council encouraged advertisers of all kinds of products to tie in war themes with their ads. The War Manpower Commission prompted Boy Scouts to paint recruitment slogans on sidewalks and suggested that officials in labor shortage areas ceremoniously inscribe the names of new women war workers on a roster in the city hall.

In contrast to American campaigns, the German propaganda effort seems minor.[4] Propaganda emanating from both a Nazi Party and a state propaganda agency spread throughout Germany by means of regional and local offices. Newspapers, pamphlets, posters, films, slide shows, exhibitions, and community bulletin boards reached the most isolated areas. But such propaganda was never a top priority for the Nazis. Responsibility for

---

2. Much of this essay is based on my book, *Mobilizing Women for War: German and American Propaganda, 1939–1945* (Princeton: Princeton University Press, 1978). Full documentation is available in the book.

3. Copies of OWI publications and information about its activities can be found in the Records of the OWI (RG 208), Washington National Records Center, Suitland, Maryland.

4. Information on the dissemination of propaganda urging women to participate in the war effort can be found in the Records of the NSDAP (T-81), National Archives Microcopy, Washington, D.C. T-81 includes directives from the Propaganda Ministry (roll 24), the Party propaganda agency (roll 117), and the women's organization (roll 75).

much of it devolved upon the Nazi women's organization, indicating the relative unimportance of the propaganda, for the organization was neither important nor powerful in the Nazi hierarchy. Only one major campaign, launched in 1941, matched the American ones in planning and intensity. Despite the lack of concerted campaigns, however, German propaganda continued to call for sacrifice for the good of the state, a theme much in evidence in prewar propaganda aimed at both women and men.

The Patriotic Approach

The appeals to American women recommended by the OWI campaign plans and those actually used in the recruitment efforts reveal a great deal about attitudes toward women in the United States. Although some of the campaign plans suggested an appeal to women on the basis of high wages—"There's a good job, at war wages, that are the same as men's wages, waiting"—this was never the major emphasis of a campaign plan and was rarely mentioned in actual recruitment. Even as the government recommended such an appeal, it cautioned that wages should not be stressed too much or increased spending and inflation might result. But more complex, although perhaps not entirely conscious, reasons underlay American reluctance to appeal to women as economic beings interested in earning good money. Most of the campaign plans emphasized the importance of reaching women through emotion rather than reason: "The copy should be pitched on a *highly emotional, patriotic appeal.*" The cherished notion that women are ruled by their emotions set the tone and determined the content of most of the recruitment efforts.

American propaganda developed a special form of emotional appeal in addressing women. Assuming that women responded to personalized patriotism rather than any abstract ideal, the government noted: "The 'shorten-the-war' theme is obviously the one which appeals most deeply to women. Mothers, grandmothers, sisters, wives, sweethearts—there isn't one who doesn't want her man back as fast as possible. Working will speed the day—and will help make the waiting easier."

Such personalized patriotism took two forms. Women were promised that their contributions could help to bring their men back sooner, or were threatened with responsibility for the death of a soldier if they refused to cooperate. One plan stated: "It should be made clear that by working on a war job (war production or civilian) a

woman is protecting her own loved ones from death on the battlefield. . . ." An announcer in one radio spot told women: "You *can* do something—you can shorten the war, make your son or husband's chances of coming home better!" A second spot illustrates the guilt approach: "Certain women in [city] are unintentionally prolonging the war. They have *not* taken war jobs. The need for them is critical. *Are you one*?" Likewise, a special booklet for critical labor shortage areas warned: "Unless local women like yourself apply for war jobs now, our soldiers on the war fronts may die needlessly."

This appeal to personalized patriotism dominated actual mobilization propaganda. A War Manpower Commission recruitment poster pictured an obviously nonemployed woman sadly clutching a letter from her husband in the service. The caption read: "Longing won't bring him back sooner . . . GET A WAR JOB!" Another poster, taking up the government's suggestion that men needed to be persuaded to let their wives take jobs, showed a woman worker and her husband in front of an American flag, and proclaimed: "I'm proud . . . my husband *wants* me to do my part." An advertisement for DuBarry Beauty Preparations promised that "One woman can shorten this war!" Making perfectly explicit the personalized appeal, a newspaperwoman wrote of the "deep satisfaction which a woman of today knows who has made a rubber boat which may save the life of her aviator husband, or helped to fashion a bullet which may avenge her son!"[5]

These selected examples of personalized patriotism are typical of the primary appeal used in propaganda addressed to women, although recruitment efforts used other approaches as well, including the glamorization and the domestication of factory work.

Glamour became an integral part of much of the propaganda. One woman newspaper-reporter-turned-factory-worker complained that there were "too many pictures of beautiful girls posed on the wings of planes with a glowing caption to make you think that war is glamorous."[6] *Life* featured a two-page spread of models in work clothes entitled "Flying Fortress Fashions." *Woman's Home Companion* proved that women war workers could be beautiful by taking four of them to Hollywood to be

5. Mrs. William Brown Meloney, "Foreward," in *American Women at War, by 7 Newspaper Women* (N.Y.: National Association of Manufacturers, 1942), p. 6.
6. Nell Giles, *Punch In, Susie! A Woman's War Factory Diary* (N.Y.: Harper, 1943), pp. 1–2.

dressed and made up as starlets. An advertisement for Woodbury Facial Soap enticed women with the caption: "She turned her back on the Social Scene and is finding Romance at work!" Such propaganda promised women that they could be glamorous and desirable as war workers in industry, despite overalls and smudged noses.

The appeal to glamour revealed an underlying assumption that women are frivolous and concerned with their appearance above all else. Another secondary appeal assumed that women were naturally suited to housework but not other types of work. Campaign plans constantly recommended that recruitment liken war work to "women's work": "Millions of women find war work pleasant and as easy as running a sewing machine, or using a vacuum cleaner." Following this suggestion, one writer reported that women took to industrial machines "as easily as to electric cake-mixers and vacuum cleaners."[7] A top official at the Aberdeen Proving Ground found that women workers "justified his hunch

that a determined gal can be just as handy on a firing range as over the kitchen stove."[8]

Similarities in German propaganda make clear that the concept of woman as wife and mother is pervasive in Western culture. Because Nazi ideology had called on women as well as men to sacrifice their individual interests to the good of the state even before the war, the Nazi image of women (as opposed to Nazi policy toward women) had to change less than the American image. But in spite of the emphasis on abstract patriotism, the Nazi propagandists utilized a concept of extended motherhood similar to that of the Americans.

The American woman who avenged her son by producing a bullet had her counterpart in the German factory

7. Mary Hornaday, "Factory Housekeeping," in *American Women at War,* p. 35.
8. Quoted in Peggy McEvoy, "Gun Molls," *Reader's Digest,* 42 (March 1943), p. 48.

worker who reportedly spoke of her devotion to her soldier son in this way: "Earlier I buttered bread for him, now I paint grenades and think, this is for him."[9] Nazi propaganda did not glamorize war work, but at least one writer used an approach identical to the American domestication of factory work, arguing that women could master industrial jobs because they were experienced at running sewing machines and using typewriters.

These various appeals reveal the way in which propaganda in both countries exhorted women to take up jobs in areas previously reserved for men without challenging traditional ideas about women's nature and roles. War work for women threatened to upset the social order by breaking down sex roles, a threat symbolized by the furor, especially in the United States, over women appearing in public in pants. But the danger could be neutralized by presenting war work as an extension of a woman's traditional role as wife and mother. The concept of personalized patriotism assumed that women took war jobs in order to bring their men home sooner. The glamorization of war work and women workers in the United States assured the public that the wearing of overalls wrought no permanent changes, while the domestication of factory work, intended to persuade women that they could handle industrial jobs, also assured the public that such jobs would not transform women.

In the United States and Germany, contrary to the intentions of its disseminators, propaganda was more important in adapting public images to the wartime situation without disrupting the social order than it was in mobilizing women.

The relationship between propaganda and the success or failure of mobilization is a complex one. Propaganda may operate in conjunction with a number of objective factors, such as financial incentive, by stressing or ignoring appeals that touch on women's actual concerns. This relationship does not assume that women are simply manipulated into and out of the labor force. Although it would be difficult to recover women's motivations in seeking or not seeking employment during the war, even with exhaustive interview data, the information on public attitudes toward employment of women collected by both the American and German governments sheds some light on the question of women's motives and sets in perspective the propaganda campaigns in both countries.

Governmental Neglect of Public Attitudes

Propagandists in both countries assumed that patriotism would be the strongest factor motivating women to take war jobs and, at a more basic level, that women accepted the current idea of their "place." The information on public attitudes collected by the governments suggests that both assumptions were wrong. While the German material is somewhat sketchy on these points, the information gathered by the United States government gives a good indication of public attitudes.

The idea that woman's "place" was in the home except in the war emergency maintained a strong following in the United States during the war, but among men more than women. Real obstacles such as childcare and domestic responsibilities, rather than their own attitudes, kept most nonemployed American women from seeking employment. Despite the lack of conclusive material on the motives of women who did work during the war years, evidence indicates that the women to whom the propaganda was addressed believed financial incentive, rather than patriotism, brought women into the labor force. The American and German governments collected information on public opinion in order to improve the effectiveness of their recruitment efforts, but they failed to act on their knowledge. This seeming paradox strengthens the argument that a major function of propaganda was the adaptation of public images of women in a nonthreatening way.

In the United States, the Office of War Information collected two basic types of information. The first included surveys of representative samples of the population, undertaken in conjunction with the National Opinion Research Center at the University of Denver, and weekly intelligence reports on public attitudes.[10] The second, more interesting, type of information consists of letters solicited from volunteer correspondents.[11]

The OWI compiled lists of possible "able and unbiased observers" in several major categories: editors, labor editors, clergymen, businessmen, social workers, and housewives. The head of the Correspondence Panels Section asked these individuals to write a confidential

9. "Munition für die Söhne," in Magda Menzerath, *Kampffeld Heimat: Deutsche Frauenleistung im Kriege* (Stuttgart: Allemannen Verlag Albert Jauss, 1944), p. 49.

10. The OWI reports of poll data and weekly intelligence reports can be found in the Records of the Office of Government Reports (RG 44), boxes 1798, 1802, 1803, 1805, 1806, Washington National Records Center, Suitland, Maryland.
11. The Correspondence Panels materials can be found in the Records of the Office of Government Reports (RG 44), boxes 1733–1761, WNRC, Suitland, Maryland.

monthly report on public opinion among the people with whom they came into contact. The records of the Correspondence Panels Section include the letters of hundreds of individuals from urban and rural locations throughout the country, recruited throughout the war years. While the panels are by no means representative of the population as a whole, they do consist of a fairly wide range of mostly middle class respondents in the selected occupational categories. The choice of categories precluded women war workers; most of the 139 women correspondents were housewives (51.8 percent) or social workers (36.7 percent). This material cannot reconstruct the motivations of women who chose to take up war work, but the letters of the women correspondents, and especially their responses to a March 1944 questionnaire on the employment of women, provide valuable evidence on the attitudes of women toward mobilization and propaganda. After all, these women, especially the housewives, were the ones at whom the recruitment propaganda was aimed.

The OWI surveys and reports, designed to guide the officials in charge of the recruitment campaigns, tended to stress the reluctance of nonemployed women to take up war work. A report dated May 6, 1942 noted that two-thirds of the country's women had "given little thought as yet to undertaking such employment." In August of the same year, a special report indicated that the most important obstacle to the employment of women was their reluctance to enter the labor market. Asked in January 1943 how they felt they could best contribute to the war effort, a large majority (77 percent) of nonemployed women replied that they could continue to do just what they were doing. By June 1943, the OWI still reported widespread resistance among nonemployed women to taking up war work. A survey undertaken late in 1943 showed that a majority of American women were aware of the need for labor and thought more women should enter the labor force, but that 73 percent of the nonemployed women were unwilling to take a full-time war job. The OWI continued to report resistance among nonemployed women into 1944.

Such results spurred the OWI to investigate the reasons why women avoided employment. Most women, when asked, expressed concern over home responsibilities. A June 1943 survey reported that women with children overwhelmingly opposed the idea of employment, and noted that this fact had serious consequences for the recruitment effort, since five out of six nonemployed young women were mothers.

Women with young children often faced real problems in taking a job, and many of the intelligence reports took seriously the obstacles women felt prevented them from participating in the war effort. While some of these reports called for the provision of services, especially childcare, which would make possible the employment of women, the OWI concluded that the attitudes of the women themselves were extremely important in keeping women out of the labor force. One report commented: "Not all of these reasons [i.e., domestic responsibilities] are to be taken at face value. . . . There are strong prejudices in some social groups against married women working, and the feeling that woman's place is in the home has a deep appeal for most women." This statement, however, reflects attitudes of government officials more faithfully than those of women themselves.

A poll taken in 1944 on attitudes toward the registration of women found that of the 36 percent of the women surveyed who opposed registration, only 27 percent gave as a reason their belief that "woman's place is in the home." Despite the fact that this was the reason women gave most often, it still represents less than 10 percent of all the women surveyed, hardly the basis for the statement that most women believed that their place is in the home. Another 1944 survey reported that only 1 percent of the women and men who thought that the demand for women workers had decreased in the last months believed that women should stay at home and take care of their children.

Male Fears and Female Attitudes

If attitudes did in fact stop women from seeking employment, the OWI's information suggests that men's attitudes, rather than women's, were responsible. Men often expressed fears that women might replace them in the labor force or depress wages or that the employment of women might destroy family life. Such fears prompted the OWI to address men specifically in the campaigns designed to recruit women. One survey investigated the attitudes of both women and men and reported: "Women are more prone than men to favor the use of married women in war industries; and, as might be expected, women who are now working approve the idea more frequently than housewives and unemployed women."

The letters of male correspondents strengthen the impression created by the surveys and polls that men, rather than women, believed in the old adage about woman's place. An OWI report based on letters written in September and October 1943 expressed fear that women would want to remain in the labor force after the war. One man summed up this attitude well: "We should immediately start planning to get these women back where they belong, amid the environment of homelife, where they can raise their children in normal, healthy happy conditions, free from demoralizing influences." Women correspondents, too, reported male fears that women would not be satisfied to return to housekeeping after the war. An Ohio farm woman warned: "And be very careful about how many women you men push into industry. Post-war days will come bye and bye and women in industry will be a head-ache for someone." Several women reported that husbands prevented their wives from taking jobs.

A social worker with personal experience saw the problem as more subtle than overcoming the objections of men who flatly refused to permit their wives to work:

Here is the difference between a man working & a woman as seen in our home—while I prepare the evening meal, my husband reads the evening paper. We then do the dishes together after which he reads his medical journals or cogitates over some lecture he is to give or some problem at his lab. I have to make up grocery lists, mend, straighten up a drawer, clean out the ice box, press clothes, put away anything strewn about the house, wash bric a brac, or do several hundreds of small "woman's work is never done stuff." . . . All this while my husband is relaxing & resting. When I worked full time, we tried doing the housecleaning together but it just didn't click.

This woman put into words a classic problem: how can women manage paid employment and the domestic responsibilities society assigns them at the same time? Her dismissal of full sharing of household duties with her husband as an attempt that "just didn't click" indicates the difficulties of changing long-established patterns in the sexual division of labor.

Significantly, the women correspondents, and even the housewives, did not express the conviction that women belonged at home. Yet of all the housewife correspondents, not one seems to have taken a job in the course of the war. Only two women even noticed the irony of their reporting on the effectiveness of recruitment campaigns. An Indiana housewife wrote: "My own personal suggestion is that woman power (especially me) be drafted before breaking up any more families." Yet she appeared to be waiting to be drafted rather than volun-

tarily taking a war job. A woman from Iowa apologetically noted that the care of her two young children kept her from taking employment. Her comment prompted a marginal note penned by an OWI staff member to the effect that she was "about the only HW [housewife] who seems to have considered taking a job." That seems to be true.

In fact, a number of correspondents actually quit jobs, or reported that women were leaving employment, because of increased household responsibilities. A Philadelphia woman with the Amalgamated Clothing Workers Union, recruited as a member of the labor editors panel in 1943, married and quit her job, resulting in a transfer to the housewives panel. She noted:

Too bad you didn't want a comment on manpower this week because I am a victim of the m-p-shortage, and have had to give up my own job in order to come home and keep house for lack of an adequate housekeeper at any price. I think I detect a trend in this direction with a majority of my married friends caught in the same predicament.

Other correspondents complained about the "servant problem" or reported that many women were doing their own housework for the first time. Statistics show that most women did not leave their jobs for lack of domestic help, but the letters indicate the social confusion that must have resulted as women employed in domestic service responded to the opportunity of better employment.

The letters of the correspondents show that the OWI was wrong in assuming that women avoided employment out of a belief that they belonged at home. The Office was also wrong in believing that women sought jobs out of personalized patriotism. The attitudes of the women correspondents on the issue of women's motives in taking up war work are extremely interesting in light of the government's insistence on using an emotional patriotic approach in recruitment propaganda. Although many correspondents mentioned patriotism as a factor influencing women to seek employment, most believed that money was the primary motive. One housewife summed up what many others expressed:

The main inducement is money! So-called patriotism plays a minor part. It's only in newsreels and in write-ups or on propaganda radio programs that a noble femme takes over a greasemonkey's job, or rivets or welds because her husband or sweetheart is a Jap prisoner—or something! I've never met up with any such noble motive. It's more apt to be a fur coat.

Only one correspondent supported the government's interpretation of why women worked, reporting that women took jobs out of a "[f]eeling of identification with beloved member of family attached to fighting forces and personal stake in each additional shell manufactured."

More surprising than the correspondent's reports that women, like men, took employment for the income is the frequent expression of the belief that women sought jobs out of dissatisfaction with housewifery. A social worker in Utah wrote: "Many women thoroughly enjoy working & getting away from the home. They seem to get much more satisfaction out of it than out of housework or bringing up children." A Baltimore housewife agreed: "Women like to be out taking a part in the world. They feel a grateful sense of freedom, an aliveness, a personal satisfaction. They forget their own small lives." One unusually articulate correspondent, a social worker from Houston, summed up the feelings of several of the women:

> To many, it affords an opportunity to escape the responsibilities of housekeeping and caring for children which was never really accepted in the first place. Employment, particularly at a job ordinarily filled by a man, is to some a legitimate channel for the expression of aggressive drives in women. I have talked with quite a number of women who seemed to me to be rather obviously competing with their husbands and at least one who was watching her husband who was employed in the same plant.

Such opinions suggest that the war may have provided an eagerly awaited opportunity for some women to take up paid employment in a socially approved fashion. One letter makes this point explicitly: "For some women the war situation has made work acceptable whereas heretofore they were inhibited against paid employment." A glimpse of the women the government ignored, women who had worked before the war, is provided in the comments of a Pittsburgh housewife:

> I have talked to women that are working in big plants doing men's work that say "Boy, have the men been getting away with murder all these years. Why I worked twice as hard selling in a department store and got half the pay." Grandmothers are working out in the real heavy stuff and are jolly and like it.

Thus, the letters of the women correspondents offer an extraordinary opportunity to examine the views of ordinary—if mostly white middle class—women on the issue of wartime employment. These letters provide the first indication in the OWI records that women might enjoy the economic independence and satisfaction of a job. That the correspondents, most of them housewives, believed that women sought employment for financial gain and often preferred employment to full-time housework suggests that the OWI staff overemphasized the reluctance of women to take employment.

Public opinion generally accepted the wartime employment of women, yet fears that women might want to linger on in the labor force after the war indicate little change in basic attitudes. Home responsibilities and lack of institutional arrangements to lighten women's load kept some women out of the labor force, but the government failed to act on this information in order to make possible the employment of more women. The OWI continued to attempt to persuade women that their place was in the war, despite indications that men's attitudes were more significant in erecting barriers to women's participation.

Women in the Labor Force

Despite the obstacles, however, millions of American women moved into war industry or took jobs for the first time. Germany presents a sharp contrast, even though the Nazi government, like the American, anxiously kept an eye on public opinion. The Security Service of the SS collected and compiled reports on the attitudes of the population, circulating these reports to government agencies every few days.[12] But the Nazi regime failed to make use of this information to improve the recruitment effort. As the war continued, German women complained about low wages, suggesting that they too were interested in working for money. Their complaints about receiving less pay than men doing the same work led the Security Service to recommend an equal pay policy to encourage women to seek employment, but the policy was never implemented. And so, as in the United States, heavy household responsibilities and lack of institutional

---

12. The Security Service reports on the German population can be found in the Records of the Reich Leader of the SS and Chief of the German Police (T-175), rolls 258–266, National Archives Microcopy, Washington, D.C.

arrangements to alleviate the burden combined to keep women out of the labor force.

The German government, like the American, viewed women's participation in the labor force as a temporary arrangement. One report stressed that "the main task of every woman lies in the performance of her domestic and maternal duties, and that if in exceptional times the woman must to a great extent be brought into industry for reasons of state, her nature should be taken into account as much as possible." It then went on to emphasize the importance of suiting the conditions of work to woman's nature and of convincing "the woman through propaganda of the necessity of her voluntary participation in the labor force."

One important factor in explaining the reluctance of German women to take employment was unique to the Nazi state. The Security Service reports make clear that German women feared the imposition of controls by the regime should they take jobs. This led to enormous resentment on the part of employed women, who were subject to such controls, against nonemployed women who avoided registering with the employment offices. Women often criticized the "so-called better circles" and the wives and daughters of Nazi Party leaders for avoiding employment. Employed women could not understand why the government did not conscript the nonemployed for war work. Since women already in the labor force could be punished by law for infractions of work discipline, they believed that other women too should be subject to legal sanctions. A February 1942 report noted that employed women were willing to make sacrifices but could not understand why the burden of war should be so unequally distributed. In particular, workers in armaments industries favored the conscription of women in the interests of social justice.

When a registration decree ordering women to report to the employment offices went into effect in January 1943, the working population greeted it enthusiastically, wondering only why it had not been passed earlier. In the weeks that followed, the Security Service noted first that women were reporting to employment offices that were often unprepared to place them, later that the willingness of women to take war work had not increased. The working class believed that not all women covered by the order had registered, a conviction that the statistics bear out. The complaint that leading personalities used their influence to keep women out of the labor force surfaced in a December 1943 report. In April 1944, women were still complaining that many had not registered, that those

who had registered had not been employed, and that middle and upper class women were not cooperating.

The fear of German women that employment would subject them to greater control by the government indicates that women were not the fanatical supporters of the regime pictured in Nazi propaganda. Although the Security Service reported that women stood resolutely behind Hitler, they in fact avoided registering with the employment offices, complained about wages and working conditions, and criticized Party measures and even Party leaders. For purposes of comparison, however, the indications that women were not moved by appeals to patriotism are most important. The German government, like the American, paid little attention to its own information about public opinion when designing recruitment campaigns.

Conclusion

The divergence between Nazi propaganda and the realities of the Third Reich is clear. Although the American case was less extreme, it also shows propaganda diverging from reality. Nazi propaganda portrayed the German woman joyfully sacrificing her personal interests for the good of the people, but in reality German women avoided employment. The American woman, according to propaganda, took a war job in order to bring her man home sooner, but the OWI's own survey material suggested that women in fact responded predominantly to the high wages offered in war industry.

In light of the OWI's information on the importance of financial incentive to American women, one would expect propaganda that emphasized wages to succeed in encouraging women to enter the labor force. The Nazi government, in a situation of low wages for women, could not use such an appeal and would not raise wages, but the United States faced no such difficulties. American wages were attractively high, and the OWI's correspondents indicated that they believed that women took employment because of high wages.

Early on in the propaganda effort, the OWI recommended an appeal based on high wages, but only hesitantly, fearful of encouraging inflation. But the appeal based on wages was never central or even prominent in the campaign plans, and rarely if ever appeared at all in actual mobilization propaganda. The OWI concentrated on an emotional patriotic appeal in disregard of both women's motives and the very real obstacles preventing women from seeking employment. The lack of appeals to women's needs or desires to earn money, in spite of information suggesting that women would respond to such appeals, strengthens the impression that wartime propaganda avoided challenging traditional assumptions about women. By ignoring or downplaying economic motivation, women could be viewed as wives and mothers responding to the needs of the country rather than as workers.

An examination of propaganda and public opinion shows that both the United States and Germany urged women to move into new areas of activity without changing basic attitudes about women. The wartime changes expanded the options of women in a way intended by the propagandists and understood by the population as temporary. The way in which public images of women adapted to the needs of recruitment propaganda—by presenting women's participation in the war effort as an extension of traditional maternal roles, particularly in the American case—helped to assure that the wartime range of options would contract once again in peacetime. The German experience was complicated by defeat and occupation, but the postwar situation in the United States shows that the image of women did not have to make tremendous adjustments after the war. The American public perceived the war as an extraordinary situation and accepted many temporary changes it would not tolerate in peacetime.

The OWI material on public opinion suggests that the public accepted the employment of women in war industry without revising traditional attitudes. Many men feared permanent changes, but the postwar situation assured them that little had changed. The proportion of employed women in the female population continued to increase after the immediate postwar layoffs, as it had throughout the twentieth century, but the war itself had no permanent impact on this trend. Women who had found their first opportunity to work during the war and women who moved from poorly paying jobs into more desirable factory jobs were no doubt affected by the experience, yet the impact of the war on public attitudes toward women was negligible. The seeming paradox of the intensely domestic 1950s following on the heels of a supposedly liberating war dissolves if one considers the form in which war participation was presented to the public.

Thus, in two very different but highly industrialized societies women were recruited for war work without challenging traditional attitudes or bringing about permanent changes. The form of recruitment propaganda reveals how tenacious the image of woman as wife and mother is, even in crisis situations. Such evidence indicates that modern war is a factor of dubious value in the struggle of women for status and power in society. Despite the fact that millions of women experienced the male world of heavy industry and high wages for the first time, Anne O'Hare McCormick was wrong. The case of the Second World War suggests that in wartime women are not necessarily the winners.

PART FOUR

Social Change

INTRODUCTION

We have seen how socialization, authority structures, and political, economic and domestic institutions converge to produce and maintain a social order in which males and females are differentially valued and differentially rewarded. Those forces are so powerful, pervasive, and intricately interwoven that to effect social change is beyond the power of the individual, no matter how well-intentioned that individual might be.

Yet, societies can and do change. In democratic and quasi-democratic societies, the most effective avenue to social change is the social movement. Social movements originate in collective discontent, establish linkages between individuals and groups who share the same discontent, develop leadership and establish goals and means. Social movements and the strategies they employ (e.g., marches, boycotts, strikes and demonstrations) are a legitimate and regular part of the democratic process—so much so that, for example, in American society today's established social institution is likely to have been yesterday's social movement.

Since we are concerned with social movement activity directed toward altering sex-based inequalities, most of our attention in this section must be addressed to the women's movement—for it is this movement that has been the primary force in altering sex-based inequalities. And, although the media have presented the women's movement as a modern phenomenon, its roots are well grounded historically. Indeed the continuity between the contemporary movement and the Suffrage Movement which culminated in the enfranchisement of women in 1920 is remarkable. More than two hundred years ago, for example, Abigail Adams gave this warning to her husband John, when he was fashioning the constitution of the United States:

In the new code of laws which I suppose will be necessary for you to make, I desire you would remember the ladies and be more generous and favorable to them than your ancestors. Do not put such unlimited power in the hands of husbands. Remember, all men would be tyrants if they could. If particular care and attention is not paid to the ladies, we are determined to foment a

317

rebellion, and will not hold ourselves bound by any laws in which we have no voice or representation. (Adams, 1776: 149–150)

John Adams nonetheless failed to take his wife's warning seriously; he urged her to be patient, noting that there were more important issues than "ladies'" rights.

It is important to recognize, however, that although the goals of women activists have repeatedly been debased and branded as "only women's issues," those issues are ones that threaten the quality of life—as well as life itself—not only of women, but also of men and children of all classes and ethnic heritages.

Through the years, as women formed groups and organized to promote a cause—whether to free Black slaves and to ensure their enfranchisement, to obtain passage of temperance laws, to obtain their own right to vote, to pass laws outlawing child labor, to organize labor unions, to work for peace, to establish schools for Black children, to obtain safe methods of birth control, to pass the Equal Rights Amendment, or to shut down unsafe nuclear power plants—they have reiterated the same themes. Among these are concern for the pain that people have suffered by having their physical, emotional and intellectual development thwarted; concern for the injustice that powerless persons have experienced through having had their rights and opportunities denied in the political and economic spheres, and their contributions to society ignored by history; commitment to the humanitarian treatment of the young, the old, the sick, and the disenfranchised; and concern for finding peace in a world of war and aggression.

We have, then, a long history in this society of feminist activism and antifeminist backlash. The contemporary women's movement and the backlash against it must be viewed, therefore, in the context of a long progressive struggle to redress inequality and to reduce the impact of "masculinist" values.

During the 1960s, when the contemporary women's movement emerged, the country was witnessing a flourish of social movement activities around a variety of issues: civil rights, the Vietnam War, and student rights in higher education. The women's movement of this period grew from the discontent of two distinct groups of women: older, college-educated professional women who experienced intense discrimination in employment and dissatisfaction with traditional family roles; and younger women, enrolled in college and/or immersed in the university community, who found themselves cast into the traditional roles of "chicks," secretaries, dishwashers, and cooks by the male leadership of the anti-war, civil rights, and student movements of the day. Not surprisingly, these two social bases created and built different forms and styles of movement organizations, and developed different goals and strategies. The older professional women moved towards a more moderate ideology and traditional organizational form, establishing groups such as the National Organization for Women (NOW), the Women's Equity Action League (WEAL), and the National Women's Political Caucus. The younger women claimed a more radical vision and organized smaller collectivities, based on consciousness-raising and geared toward political activism around a variety of issues. These included women's health, abortion, the media portrayal of women, lesbian ideology and activism, racism and other issues affecting women of color; nuclear proliferation; and violence against women in the form of rape, incest, sexual harassment, pornography and wife-battering. They established alternative structures within which a distinctively feminist women's culture could flourish, such as women's recording companies, bookstores, theatre groups, restaurants, poetry groups, women's spirituality groups, publishing companies, etc.

The women's movement of today, like all other general social movements, continues to be comprised of many separate and diverse movement organizations; each with its own strategies, style, membership base, leadership, and specific goals. Holding ideologies that may be moderate, radical, socialist, or Marxist, these smaller movement organizations are held together by overlapping membership and occasional participation in common political activities around a particular issue, such as the Equal Rights Amendment. Conflicts and disputes over ideology and strategy are sometimes bitter among various branches of the women's movement, but this is in no way unique to this particular movement. To some extent, all social movements thrive when they are heterogeneous and diverse in their goals and ideologies; any social movement, whatever its focus, needs radicals to define its ultimate political utopia and, in some sense, to demonstrate to society how moderate are the reforms sought by liberals.

Although the Equal Rights Amendment has mobilized women, the ultimate vision of many women's groups is so broad as to include a fundamental restructuring of all institutions in society that perpetuate and sustain male dominance. Interestingly, then, the fact that feminist groups can be found within every major institution of society—in the professions, in academia, in labor, in religion, and in the worlds of art, music and literature—and are mobilized around practically every issue imaginable, from pornography, prostitution, abortion, health, child care, women's sexuality and lesbian concerns, to Black, Native American, Jewish, and Hispanic women's concerns, and nuclear power—suggests not that the movement is about to end for lack of unity. Rather, that because it permeates every facet of social life, feminist thought is having a major impact not only on the economic and political institutions of society, but on the lives of individuals as well.

In Part Four we shall examine the contemporary feminist movement and its relationship to other organized interests. We turn our attention to the power and strength of the feminist challenge to the established institutions. We do this by first describing the diversity of the movement and some of the issues confronting it today, and then examining the impact feminism has had on individual consciousness and interpersonal relationships. We conclude with a look to the future and the feminist vision.

Introduction: The Feminist Movement

The contemporary women's movement, like all other general and broad-based social movements, is comprised of heterogeneous organizations, each having its unique and distinctive ideology, identity, style, and membership base. We shall begin our examination of the contemporary women's movement with the article "Political Philosophies of Women's Liberation," by Alison Jaggar. Although this article was written in 1972, it is still relevant in that Jaggar identifies and distinguishes between the major feminist ideologies—Liberal Feminism, Classical Marxist Feminism and Radical Feminism—which continue to inform the feminist movement. Potential divisiveness within the movement is the issue addressed by Gay Hadley in her poem, "Sistersong."

Social movements do not consist only of formal collectivities, organizations, and well-defined groups; they also include more amorphous networks and unorganized aggregates of sympathizers. Thus, the women's movement, like any other social movement, has far more followers or sympathizers than it does active members of movement organizations. For example, a Harris poll conducted in 1976 found that although 65% of U.S. women support "most of the efforts to strengthen and change women's status in society," only 17% have a positive image of the women's movement and its major organizations. Identification with and participation in a social movement requires, then, more than mere agreement with its goals; even more than a person's realization that s/he is in an objectively unjust and difficult situation. The individual must also identify the link between her/his own circumstances and the ideals and goals of the feminist movement.

In her article "Ambiguities in Identity Transformation: From Sugar and Spice to Professor," Joan Huber describes the social events and experiences in her life which led to her own identity transformation as a feminist. Huber provides insight into the general social conditions which affected women of her generation and set the stage for the rise of what has been termed the moderate branch of the women's movement of the late 1960s. In "Collective Work and Self-Identity: The Effect of Working in a Feminist Illegal Abortion Collective," Melinda Bart Schlesinger and Pauline Bart describe another pathway to becoming a feminist. This, in the late 1960s, was the route typically followed by younger women who affiliated with the more loosely organized radical branch of the movement. The reader may also want to review "The Woman Who Talked Back to God—And Didn't Get Zapped" by Sonia Johnson, as this article shows how the escalation of anti-feminism witnessed in recent years has actually served to increase, and even to precipitate, feminist activism.

In addition to underlying ideologies and membership concerns, social movements coalesce around specific issues. One issue that has propelled the women's movement is the right of women to control their own bodies, including the right to decide whether to carry a baby to term or to seek an abortion. Marge Piercy in her poem, "Right to Life," usurps the anti-abortionist slogan and eloquently defends the "right to life" of women: the right to control their own bodies.

Over a decade ago, violence toward women in the form of rape became the issue, perhaps more than any other issue, that unified the feminist movement. Out of women's grassroots efforts to define the nature and causes of rape, and strategies to stop rape, crisis centers began to emerge around the country, and most were established and run by feminist collectives. Other forms of violence against women—wife-beating, incest, and sexual harassment— have since become public issues as well, largely as a result of feminist activism. In confronting the various forms of violence encountered by women, feminists argue that none of these issues can be understood and dealt with as an isolated "social problem." Rather, the society itself—in which all these forms of sexually-based violence thrive—must be questioned.

Recently, that confrontation has focused on the violence perpetrated on women through pornography. Although feminists are divided on the First Amendment (freedom of the press) consequences of demanding censorship of pornography, they agree that pornography in and of itself is violence, and therefore it is a feminist issue. Around the country, feminists are organizing collectively to confront pornography, using methods which range from public educa-tion—through the use of media presentations—to civil disobedience. The latter includes conduct-ing raids on adult bookstores and "snuff" films (where the woman is *actually* murdered at the end of the movie) and "kiddie porn" (where young children are filmed having intercourse, contact fellatio, or sodomy with adult men). In the article "Pornography and the Women's Liberation Movement," Diana E. H. Russell, sociologist and one of the founders of Women Against Violence in Pornography and Media, outlines the reasons why pornography is a feminist issue and proposes actions to confront it.

The feminist movement, then, is composed of a diversity of beliefs, members, organizations and issues. Despite that diversity, there is considerable unity. That unity, moreover, is partially built and maintained through the sharing of work, and, most importantly, the sharing of play and humor. There is a light-bulb joke about feminists that goes: "How many feminists does it take to change a light-bulb?" The answer is: "That's not funny!" The joke is rooted in the belief that feminists have "no sense of humor." The reality is that what has been culturally defined as "funny" very often has women, and other oppressed groups, as the brunt of the joke; and it is true that feminists sees no humor in jokes that demean women. This does not mean that feminists lack a sense of humor. Rather, it means that feminists recognize the *power* of humor to keep people in their place and/or to advance a cause. Drawing upon this power, feminists have been using humor for political purposes: raising the esteem of women, deprecating patriarchal in-stitutions, and creating solidarity amongst women. We conclude this section with a few examples of feminist humor, and invite you to collect more. The first two selections are about "biological" phenomena. Gloria Steinem in "If Men Could Menstruate," fantasizes how men, if they did menstruate, would turn their monthly periods into a "macho-competitive activity. Catherine Tucker in her poem "Decades," faces a different and "hairy" problem. Cartoons by Nicole Hollander, Brian Campbell, Frank Baginski and Reynolds Dodson, ridicule sexist propositions. And finally, "Specism: The Dialectics of Doghood,"—"pawed" by Jessica Celiasister, the "pet" dog of an anonymous Women's Studies Professor—is both a feminist "spoof" and a feminist reminder that too much complacency too soon is ill-advised.

Political Philosophies of Women's Liberation

Alison Jaggar

Feminists are united by a belief that the unequal and inferior social status of women is unjust and needs to be changed. but they are deeply divided about what changes are required. The deepest divisions are not differences about strategy or the kinds of tactics that will best serve women's interests; instead, they are differences about what *are* women's interests, what constitutes women's liberation.

Within the women's liberation movement, several distinct ideologies can be discerned. All[1] believe that justice requires freedom and equality for women, but they differ on such basic philosophical questions as the proper account of freedom and equality, the functions of the state, and the notion of what constitutes human, and especially female, nature. In what follows, I shall outline the feminist ideologies which are currently most influential and show how these give rise to differences on some particular issues. Doing this will indicate why specific debates over feminist questions cannot be settled in isolation but can only be resolved in the context of a theoretical framework derived from reflection on the fundamental issues of social and political philosophy.

The Conservative View

This is the position against which all feminists are in reaction. In brief, it is the view that the differential treatment of women, as a group, is not unjust. Conservatives admit, of course, that some individual women do suffer hardships, but they do not see this suffering as part of the systematic social oppression of women. Instead, the clear differences between women's and men's social roles are rationalized in one of two ways. Conservatives either claim that the female role is not inferior to that of the male, or they argue that women are inherently better adapted than men to the traditional female sex role. The former claim advocates a kind of sexual apartheid, typically described by such phrases as "complementary but equal"; the latter postulates an inherent inequality between the sexes.[2]

All feminists reject the first claim, and most feminists, historically, have rejected the second. However, it is interesting to note that, as we shall see later, some modern feminists have revived the latter claim.

Conservative views come in different varieties, but they all have certain fundamentals in common. All claim that men and women should fulfill different social functions, that these differences should be enforced by law where opinion and custom are insufficient, and that such action may be justified by reference to innate differences between men and women. Thus all sexual conservatives presuppose that men and women are inherently unequal in abilities, that the alleged difference in ability implies a difference in social function and that one of the main tasks of the state is to ensure that the individual perform his or her proper social function. Thus, they argue, social differentiation between the sexes is not unjust, since justice not only allows but requires us to treat unequals unequally.

Liberal Feminism

In speaking of liberal feminism, I am referring to that tradition which received its classic expression in J. S. Mill's *The Subjection of Women* and which is alive today in various "moderate" groups, such as the National Organization for Women, which agitate for legal reform to improve the status of women.

The main thrust of the liberal feminist's argument is that an individual woman should be able to determine her social role with as great freedom as does a man. Though women now have the vote, the liberal sees that we are still subject to many constraints, legal as well as customary, which hinder us from success in the public worlds of politics, business and the professions. Consequently the liberal views women's liberation as the elimination of those constraints and the achievement of equal civil rights.

Underlying the liberal argument is the belief that justice requires that the criteria for allocating individuals to perform a particular social function should be grounded in the individual's ability to perform the tasks in question. The use of criteria such as "race, sex, religion, national origin or ancestry"[3] will normally not be directly relevant to most tasks. Moreover, in conformity with the traditional liberal stress on individual rights, the liberal feminist insists that each person should be considered separately in order that an outstanding individual should not be penalized for deficiencies that her sex as a whole might possess.[4]

This argument is buttressed by the classic liberal belief that there should be a minimum of state intervention in the affairs of the individual. Such a belief entails rejection of the paternalistic view that women's weakness requires that we be specially protected.[5] Even if relevant differences between women and men in general could be demonstrated, the existence of those differences still would not constitute a sufficient reason for allowing legal restrictions on women as a group. Even apart from the possibility of penalizing an outstanding individual, the liberal holds that women's own good sense or, in the last resort, our incapacity to do the job will render legal prohibitions unnecessary.[6]

From this sketch it is clear that the liberal feminist interprets equality to mean that each individual, regardless of sex, should have an equal opportunity to seek whatever social position she or he wishes. Freedom is primarily the absence of legal constraints to hinder women in this enterprise. However, the modern liberal feminist recognizes that equality and freedom, construed in the liberal way, may not always be compatible. Hence, the modern liberal feminist differs from the traditional one in believing not only that laws should not discriminate against women, but that they should be used to make discrimination illegal. Thus she would outlaw unequal pay scales, prejudice in the admission of women to job-training programs and professional schools, and discrimination by employers in hiring practices. She would also outlaw such things as discrimination by finance companies in the granting of loans, mortgages, and insurance to women.

In certain areas, the modern liberal even appears to advocate laws which discriminate in favor of women. For instance, she may support the preferential hiring of women over men, or alimony for women unqualified to work outside the home. She is likely to justify her apparent inconsistency by claiming that such differential treatment is necessary to remedy past inequalities—but that it is only a temporary measure. With regard to (possibly paid) maternity leaves and the employer's obligation to reemploy a woman after such a leave, the liberal argues that the bearing of children has at least as good a claim to be regarded as a social service as does a man's military or jury obligation, and that childbearing should therefore carry corresponding rights to protection. The liberal also usually advocates the repeal of laws restricting contraception and abortion, and may demand measures to encourage the establishment of private daycare centers. However, she points out that none of these demands, nor the father's payment of child support, should really be regarded as discrimination in favor of women. It is only the customary assignment of responsibility for children to their mothers which it makes it possible to overlook the fact that fathers have an equal obligation to provide and care for their children. Women's traditional responsibility for child care is culturally determined, not biologically inevitable—except for breast-feeding, which is now optional. Thus the liberal argues that if women are to participate in the world outside the home on equal terms with men, not only must our reproductive capacity come under our own control but, if we have children, we must be able to share the responsibility for raising them. In return, as an extension of the same principle of equal responsibility, the modern liberal supports compulsory military service for women so long as it is obligatory for men.

Rather than assuming that every apparent difference in interests and abilities between the sexes is innate, the liberal recognizes that such differences, if they do not result entirely from our education, are at least greatly exaggerated by it. By giving both sexes the same education, whether it be cooking or carpentry, the liberal claims that she is providing the only environment in which individual potentialities (and, indeed, genuine sexual differences) can emerge. She gives little weight to the possible charge that in doing this she is not liberating women but only imposing a different kind of conditioning. At the root of the liberal tradition is a deep faith in the autonomy of the individual which is incapable of being challenged within that framework.

In summary, then, the liberal views liberation for women as the freedom to determine our own social role and to compete with men on terms that are as equal as possible. She sees every individual as being engaged in constant competition with every other in order to maximize her or his own self-interest, and she claims that the function of the state is to see that such competition is fair by enforcing "equality of opportunity." The liberal does not believe that it is necessary to change the whole existing social structure in order to achieve women's liberation. Nor does she see it as being achieved simultaneously for all women; she believes that individual women may liberate themselves long before their condition is attained by all. Finally, the liberal claims that her concept of women's liberation also involves liberation for men, since men are not only removed from a privileged position but they are also freed from having to accept the entire responsibility for such things as the support of their families and the defense of their country.

Classical Marxist Feminism

On the classical Marxist view, the oppression of women is, historically and currently, a direct result of the institution of private property; therefore, it can only be ended by the abolition of that institution. Consequently, feminism must be seen as part of a broader struggle to achieve a communist society. Feminism is one reason for communism. The long-term interests of women are those of the working class.

For Marxists, everyone is oppressed by living in a society where a small class of individuals owns the means of production and hence is enabled to dominate the lives of the majority who are forced to sell their labor power in order to survive. Women have an equal interest with men in eliminating such a class society. However, Marxists also recognize that women suffer special forms of oppression to which men are *not* subject, and hence, insofar as this oppression is rooted in capitalism, women have additional reasons for the overthrow of that economic system.

Classical Marxists believe that the special oppression of women results primarily from our traditional position in the family. This excludes women from participation in "public" production and relegates us to domestic work in the "private" world of the home. From its inception right up to the present day, monogamous marriage was designed to perpetuate the consolidation of wealth in the hands of a few. Those few are men. Thus, for Marxists,

an analysis of the family brings out the inseparability of class society from male supremacy. From the very beginning of surplus production, "the sole exclusive aims of monogamous marriage were to make the man supreme in the family, and to propagate, as the future heirs to his wealth, children indisputably his own."[7] Such marriage is "founded on the open or concealed domestic slavery of the wife,"[8] and is characterized by the familiar double standard which requires sexual fidelity from the woman but not from the man.

Marxists do not claim, of course, that women's oppression is a creation of capitalism. But they do argue that the advent of capitalism intensified the degradation of women and that the continuation of capitalism requires the perpetuation of this degradation. Capitalism and male supremacy each reinforce the other. Among the ways in which sexism benefits the capitalist system are: by providing a supply of cheap labor for industry and hence exerting a downward pressure on all wages; by increasing the demand for the consumption goods on which women are conditioned to depend; and by allocating to women, for no direct pay, the performance of such socially necessary but unprofitable tasks as food preparation, domestic maintenance and the care of the children, the sick and the old.[9]

This analysis indicates the directions in which classical Marxists believe that women must move. "The first condition for the liberation of the wife is to bring the whole female sex back into public industry."[10] Only then will a wife cease to be economically dependent on her husband. But for woman's entry into public industry to be possible, fundamental social changes are necessary: all the work which women presently do—food preparation, child care, nursing, etc.—must come within the sphere of public production. Thus, whereas the liberal feminist advocates an egalitarian marriage, with each spouse shouldering equal responsibility for domestic work and economic support, the classical Marxist feminist believes that the liberation of women requires a more radical change in the family. Primarily, women's liberation requires that the economic functions performed by the family should be undertaken by the state. Thus the state should provide child care centers, public eating places, hospital facilities, etc. But all this, of course, could happen only under socialism. Hence it is only under socialism that married women will be able to participate fully in public life and end the situation where "within the family [the husband] is the bourgeois and the wife represents the proletariat."[11]

It should be noted that "the abolition of the

monogamous family as the economic unit of society"[12] does not necessitate its disappearance as a social unit. Since "sexual love is by its nature exclusive,"[13] marriage will continue, but now it will no longer resemble an economic contract, as it has done hitherto in the property-owning classes. Instead, it will be based solely on "mutual inclination"[14] between a woman and a man who are now in reality, and not just formally, free and equal.

It is clear that classical Marxist feminism is based on very different philosophical presuppositions from those of liberal feminism. Freedom is viewed not just as the absence of discrimination against women but rather as freedom from the coercion of economic necessity. Similarly, equality demands not mere equality of opportunity to compete against other individuals but rather approximate equality in the satisfaction of material needs. Hence, the classical Marxist feminist's view of the function of the state is very different from the view of the liberal feminist. Ultimately, the Marxist pays at least lip service to the belief that the state is an instrument of class oppression which eventually will wither away. In the meantime, she believes that it should undertake far more than the minimal liberal function of setting up fair rules for the economic race. Instead, it should take over the means of production and also assume those economic responsibilities that capitalism assigned to the individual family and that placed the woman in a position of dependence on the man. This view of the state presupposes a very different account of human nature from that held by the liberal. Instead of seeing the individual as fundamentally concerned with the maximization of her or his own self-interest, the classical Marxist feminist believes that the selfish and competitive aspects of our natures are the result of their systematic perversion in an acquisitive society. Viewing human nature as flexible and as reflecting the economic organization of society, she argues that it is necessary for women (indeed for everybody) to be comprehensively reeducated, and to learn that ultimately individuals have common rather than competing goals and interests.

Since she sees women's oppression as a function of the larger socioeconomic system, the classical Marxist feminist denies the possibility, envisaged by the liberal, of liberation for a few women on an individual level. However, she does agree with the liberal that women's liberation would bring liberation for men, too. Men's liberation would now be enlarged to include freedom from class oppression and from the man's traditional responsibility to "provide" for his family, a burden that under liberalism the man merely lightens by sharing it with his wife.

Radical Feminism

Radical feminism is a recent attempt to create a new conceptual model for understanding the many different forms of the social phenomenon of oppression in terms of the basic concept of sexual oppression. It is formulated by such writers as Ti-Grace Atkinson and Shulamith Firestone.[15]

Radical feminism denies the liberal claim that the basis of women's oppression consists in our lack of political or civil rights; similarly, it rejects the classical Marxist belief that basically women are oppressed because they live in a class society. Instead, in what seems to be a startling regression to conservatism, the radical feminist claims that the roots of women's oppression are biological. She believes that the origin of women's subjection lies in the fact that, as a result of the weakness caused by childbearing, we became dependent on men for physical survival. Thus she speaks of the origin of the family in apparently conservative terms as being primarily a biological rather than a social or economic organization.[16] The radical feminist believes that the physical subjection of women by men was historically the most basic form of oppression, prior rather than secondary to the institution of private property and its corollary, class oppression.[17] Moreover, she believes that the power relationships which develop within the biological family provide a model for understanding all other types of oppression such as racism and class society. Thus she reverses the emphasis of the classical Marxist feminist by explaining the development of class society in terms of the biological family rather than explaining the development of the family in terms of class society. She believes that the battles against capitalism and against racism are both subsidiary to the more fundamental struggle against sexism.

Since she believes that the oppression of women is basically biological, the radical feminist concludes that our liberation requires a biological revolution. She believes that only now, for the first time in history, is technology making it possible for women to be liberated from the "fundamental inequality of the bearing and raising of children." It is achieving this through the development of techniques of artificial reproduction and the consequent possibility of diffusing the childbearing and child-raising role throughout society as a whole. Such a biological revolution is basic to the achievement of those important but secondary changes in our political, social and economic systems which will make possible the other prerequisites for women's liberation. As the radical feminist sees them, those other prerequisites are: the full self-determination, including economic independence, of women (and children); the total integration of women (and children) into all aspects of the larger society; and the freedom of all women (and children) to do whatever they wish to do sexually.[18]

Not only will technology snap the link between sex and reproduction and thus liberate women from our childbearing and child-raising function; the radical feminist believes that ultimately technology will liberate both sexes from the necessity to work. Individual economic burdens and dependencies will thereby be eliminated, along with the justification for compelling children to attend school. So both the biological and economic bases of the family will be removed by technology. The family's consequent disappearance will abolish the prototype of the social "role system,"[19] the most basic form, both historically and conceptually, of oppressive and authoritarian relationships. Thus, the radical feminist does not claim that women should be free to determine their own social roles: she believes instead that the whole "role system" must be abolished, even in its biological aspects.

The end of the biological family will also eliminate the need for sexual repression. Male homosexuality, lesbianism, and extramarital sexual intercourse will no longer be viewed in the liberal way as alternative options, outside the range of state regulation, in which the individual may or may not choose to participate. Nor will they be viewed, in the classical Marxist way, as unnatural vices, perversions resulting from the degrading influence of capitalist society.[20] Instead, even the categories of homosexuality and heterosexuality will be abandoned; the very "institution of sexual intercourse," where male and female each play a well-defined role, will disappear.[21] "Humanity could finally revert to its natural 'polymorphously perverse' sexuality."[22]

For the radical feminist, as for other feminists, justice requires freedom and equality for women. But for the radical feminist "equality" means not just equality under the law nor even equality in satisfaction of basic needs: rather, it means that women, like men, should not have to bear children. Correspondingly, the radical feminist conception of freedom requires not just that women should be free to compete, nor even that we

should be free from material want and economic dependence on men; rather, freedom for women means that any woman is free to have close relationships with children without having to give birth to them. Politically, the radical feminist envisions an eventual "communistic anarchy,"[23] an ultimate abolition of the state. This will be achieved gradually, through an intermediate state of "cybernetic socialism" with household licenses to raise children and a guaranteed income for all. Perhaps surprisingly, in view of Freud's reputation among many feminists, the radical feminist conception of human nature is neo-Freudian. Firestone believes, with Freud, that "the crucial problem of modern life [is] sexuality."[24] Individuals are psychologically formed through their experience in the family, a family whose power relationships reflect the underlying biological realities of female (and childhood) dependence. But technology will smash the universality of Freudian psychology. The destruction of the biological family, never envisioned by Freud, will allow the emergence of new women and men, different from any people who have previously existed.

The radical feminist theory contains many interesting claims. Some of these look almost factual in character: they include the belief that pregnancy and childbirth are painful and unpleasant experiences, that sexuality is not naturally genital and heterosexual, and that technology may be controlled by men and women without leading to totalitarianism. Other presuppositions are more clearly normative: among them are the beliefs that technology should be used to eliminate all kinds of pain, that hard work is not in itself a virtue, that sexuality ought not to be institutionalized and, perhaps most controversial of all, that children have the same rights to self-determination as adults.

Like the other theories we have considered, radical feminism believes that women's liberation will bring benefits for men. According to this concept of women's liberation, not only will men be freed from the role of provider, but they will also participate on a completely equal basis in childbearing as well as child-rearing. Radical feminism, however, is the only theory which argues explicitly that women's liberation also necessitates children's liberation. Firestone explains that this is because "The heart of woman's oppression is her childbearing and child-rearing roles. And in turn children are defined in relation to this role and are psychologically formed by it; what they become as adults and the sorts of relationships they are able to form determine the society they will ultimately build."[25]

New Directions

Although the wave of excitement about women's liberation which arose in the late '60's has now subsided, the theoretical activity of feminists has continued. Since about 1970, it has advanced in two main directions: lesbian separatism and socialist feminism.

Lesbian separatism is less a coherent and developed ideology than an emerging movement, like the broader feminist movement, within which different ideological strains can be detected. All lesbian separatists believe that the present situation of male supremacy requires that women should refrain from heterosexual relationships. But for some lesbian separatists, this is just a temporary necessity, whereas for others, lesbianism will always be required.

Needless to say, all lesbian separatists reject the liberal and the classical Marxist beliefs about sexual preferences; but some accept the radical feminist contention that ultimately it is unimportant whether one's sexual partner be male or female.[26] However, in the immediate context of a male-supremacist society, the lesbian separatist believes that one's sexual choice attains tremendous political significance. Lesbianism becomes a way of combating the overwhelming heterosexual ideology that perpetuates male supremacy.

> *Women . . . become defined as appendages to men so that there is a coherent ideological framework which says it is natural for women to create the surplus to take care of men and that men will do other things. Reproduction itself did not have to determine that. The fact that male supremacy developed the way it has and was institutionalized is an ideological creation. The ideology of heterosexuality, not the simple act of intercourse, is the whole set of assumptions which maintains the ideological power of men over women.[27]*

Although this writer favors an ultimate de-institutionalization of sexual activity, her rejection of the claim that reproduction as such does not determine the inferior status of women clearly places her outside the radical feminist framework; indeed, she would identify her methodological approach as broadly Marxist. Some lesbian separatists are more radical, however. They argue explicitly for a matriarchal society which is "an affirmation of the power of female consciousness of the Mother.[28] Such matriarchists talk longingly about ancient matriarchal societies where women were supposed to have been physi-

cally strong, adept at self-defense, and the originators of such cultural advances as: the wheel, pottery, industry, leather working, metal working, fire, agriculture, animal husbandry, architecture, cities, decorative art, music, weaving, medicine, communal child care, dance, poetry, song, etc.[29] They claim that men were virtually excluded from these societies. Women's culture is compared favorably with later patriarchal cultures as being peaceful, egalitarian, vegetarian, and intellectually advanced. Matriarchal lesbian separatists would like to re-create a similar culture which would probably imitate the earlier ones in its exclusion of men as full members. Matriarchal lesbian separatists do not claim unequivocally that "men are genetically predisposed towards destruction and dominance,"[30] but, especially given the present research on the behavioral effects of the male hormone testosterone,[31] they think it is a possibility that lesbians must keep in mind.

Socialist feminists believe that classical Marxism and radical feminism each have both insights and deficiencies. The task of socialist feminism is to construct a theory that avoids the weaknesses of each but incorporates its (and other) insights. There is space here for only a brief account of some of the main points of this developing theory.

Socialist feminists reject the basic radical feminist contention that liberation for women requires the abolition of childbirth. Firestone's view is criticized as ahistorical, anti-dialectical, and utopian. Instead, socialist feminists accept the classical Marxist contention that socialism is the main precondition for women's liberation. But though socialism is necessary, socialist feminists do not believe that it is sufficient. Sexism can continue to exist despite public ownership of the means of production. The conclusion that socialist feminists draw is that it is necessary to resort to direct cultural action in order to develop a specifically feminist consciousness in addition to transforming the economic base. Thus their vision is totalistic, requiring "transformation of the entire fabric of social relationships."[32]

In rejecting the radical feminist view that the family is based on biological conditions, socialist feminists turn toward the classical Marxist account of monogamy as being based "not on natural but on economic conditions."[33] But they view the classical Marxist account as inadequate, overly simple. Juliet Mitchell[34] argues that the family should be analyzed in a more detailed, sophisticated, and historically specific way in terms of the separate, though interrelated, functions that women perform within it:

production, reproduction, sexuality, and the socialization of the young.

Socialist feminists agree with classical Marxists that women's liberation requires the entry of women into public production. But this in itself is not sufficient. It is also necessary that women have access to the more prestigious and less deadening jobs and to supervisory and administrative positions. There should be no "women's work" within public industry.[35]

In classical Marxist theory, "productive labor" is viewed as the production of goods and services within the market economy. Some socialist feminists believe that this account of productiveness obscures the socially vital character of the labor that women perform in the home. They argue that, since it is clearly impossible under capitalism to bring all women into public production, individuals (at least as an interim measure) should be paid a wage for domestic work. This reform would dignify the position of housewives, reduce their dependence on their husbands and make plain their objective position, minimized by classical Marxists, as an integral part of the working class.[36] Not all socialist feminists accept this position, however, and the issue is extremely controversial at the time of this writing.

One of the main insights of the feminist movement has been that "the personal is political." Socialist feminists are sensitive to the power relations involved in male/female interaction and believe that it is both possible and necessary to begin changing these, even before the occurrence of a revolution in the ownership of the means of production. Thus, socialist feminists recognize the importance of a "subjective factor" in revolutionary change and reject the rigid economic determinism that has characterized many classical Marxists. They are sympathetic to attempts by individuals to change their life styles and to share responsibility for each other's lives, even though they recognize that such attempts can never be entirely successful within a capitalist context. They also reject the sexual puritanism inherent in classical Marxism, moving closer to the radical feminist position in this regard.

Clearly there are sharp differences between socialist feminism and most forms of lesbian separatism. The two have been dealt with together in this section only because each is still a developing theory and because it is not yet clear how far either represents the creation of a new ideology and how far it is simply an extension of an existing ideology. One suspects that at least the matriarchal version of lesbian separatism may be viewed as a new ideology: after all, the interpretation of "freedom" to mean "freedom from men" is certainly new, as is the suggestion that women are innately superior to men. Socialist feminism, however, should probably be seen as an extension of classical Marxism, using essentially similar notions of human nature, of freedom and equality, and of the role of the state, but attempting to show that women's situation and the sphere of personal relations in general need more careful analysis by Marxists.[37]

This sketch of some new directions in feminism completes my outline of the main contemporary positions on women's liberation. I hope that I have made clearer the ideological presuppositions at the root of many feminist claims and also shed some light on the philosophical problems that one needs to resolve in order to formulate one's own position and decide on a basis for action. Many of these philosophical questions, such as the nature of the just society, the proper account of freedom and equality, the functions of the state and the relation between the individual and society, are traditional problems which now arise in a new context; others, such as the role of technology in human liberation, are of more recent origin. In either case, feminism adds a fresh dimension to our discussion of the issues and points to the need for the so-called philosophy of man to be transformed into a comprehensive philosophy of women and men and their social relations.

Endnotes

1. All except one: as we shall see later, lesbian separatism is evasive on the question whether men should, even ultimately, be equal with women.
2. The inequalities between the sexes are said to be both physical and psychological. Alleged psychological differences between the sexes include women's emotional instability, greater tolerance for boring detail, incapacity for abstract thought, and less aggression. Writers who have made such claims range from Rousseau (*Emile, or Education* [1762; translation, London: J.M. Dent, 1911]; see especially Book 5 concerning the education of "Sophie, or Woman"), through Schopenhauer (*The World As Will and Idea* and his essay "On Women"), Fichte (*The Science of Rights*), Nietzsche (*Thus Spake Zarathustra*), and Freud down to, in our own times, Steven Goldberg with *The Inevitability of Patriarchy* (New York: William Morrow, 1973–74).
3. This is the language used by Title VII of the Civil Rights Act with Executive Order 11246, 1965, and Title IX.

4. J. S. Mill, *The Subjection of Women* (1869; reprint ed., London: J. M. Dent, 1965), p. 236.

5. Ibid., p. 243.

6. Ibid., p. 235.

7. Friedrich Engels, *The Origin of the Family, Private Property and the State* (1884; reprint ed., New York: International Publishers, 1942), pp. 57–58.

8. Ibid., p. 65.

9. This is, of course, very far from being a complete account of the ways in which Marxists believe that capitalism benefits from sexism.

10. Engels, op. cit., p. 66.

11. Ibid., pp. 65–66.

12. Ibid., p. 66.

13. Ibid., p. 72.

14. Ibid.

15. Ti-Grace Atkinson, "Radical Feminism" and "The Institution of Sexual Intercourse" in *Notes from the Second Year: Major Writings of the Radical Feminists,* ed. S. Firestone (N.Y., 1970); and Shulamith Firestone, *The Dialectic of Sex: The Case for Feminist Revolution* (N.Y.: Bantam Books; 1970).

16. Engels recognizes that early forms of the family were based on what he calls "natural" conditions, which presumably included the biological, but he claims that monogamy "was the first form of the family to be based, not on natural, but on economic conditions — on the victory of private property over primitive, natural communal property." Engels, op. cit., p. 57.

17. Atkinson and Firestone do talk of women as a "political class," but not in Marx's classic sense where the criterion of an individual's class membership is her/his relationship to the means of production. Atkinson defines a class more broadly as a group treated in some special manner by other groups: in the case of women, the radical feminists believe that women are defined as a "class" in virtue of our child-bearing capacity. "Radical Feminism," op. cit., p. 24.

18. These conditions are listed and explained in *The Dialectic of Sex,* pp. 206–9.

19. "Radical Feminism," op. cit., p. 36.

20. Engels often expresses an extreme sexual puritanism in *The Origin of the Family, Private Property and the State.* We have already seen his claim that "sexual love is by its nature exclusive." Elsewhere (p. 57) he talks about "the abominable practice of sodomy." Lenin is well known for the expression of similar views.

21. "The Institution of Sexual Intercourse," op. cit.

22. *The Dialectic of Sex,* p. 209.

23. Ibid., final chart, pp. 244–45.

24. Ibid., p. 43.

25. Ibid., p. 72.

26. "In a world devoid of male power and, therefore, sex roles, who you lived with, loved, slept with and were committed to would be irrelevant. All of us would be equal and have equal determination over the society and how it met our needs. Until this happens, how we use our sexuality and our bodies is just as relevant to our liberation as how we use our minds and time." Coletta Reid, "Coming Out in the Women's Movement," in *Lesbianism and the Women's Movement,* ed. Nancy Myron and Charlotte Buch (Baltimore: Diana Press, 1975), p. 103.

27. Margaret Small, "Lesbians and the Class Position of Women," in *Lesbianism and the Women's Movement,* p. 58.

28. Jane Alpert, "Mother Right: A New Feminist Theory," *Ms.,* August 1973, p. 94.

29. Alice, Gordon, Debbie, and Mary, *Lesbian Separatism: An Amazon Analysis,* typescript, 1973, p. 5. (To be published by Diana Press, Baltimore.)

30. Ibid., p. 23.

31. It is interesting that this is the same research on which Steven Goldberg grounds his thesis of "the inevitability of patriarchy"; see note 2 above.

32. Barbara Ehrenreich, "Socialist/Feminism and Revolution" (unpublished paper presented to the National Socialist-Feminist Conference, Antioch College, Ohio, July 1975), p. 1.

33. Engels, op. cit., p. 57.

34. Juliet Mitchell, *Woman's Estate* (New York: Random House, 1971). Lively discussion of Mitchell's work continues among socialist feminists.

35. For one socialist feminist account of women's work in public industry see Sheila Rowbotham, *Woman's Consciousness, Man's World* (Baltimore: Penguin Books, 1973), chap. 6, "Sitting Next to Nellie."

36. One influential exponent of wages for housework is Mariarosa Dalla Costa, *The Power of Women and the Subversion of Community* (Bristol, England: Falling Wall Press, 1973).

37. Since I wrote this section, I have learned of some recent work by socialist feminists which seems to provide an excitingly new theoretical underpinning for much socialist feminist practice. An excellent account of these ideas is given by Gayle Rubin in "The Traffic in Women: Notes on the 'Political Economy' of Sex." This paper appears in *Toward an Anthropology of Women,* ed. Rayna R. Reiter (New York: Monthly Review Press, 1975). If something like Rubin's account is accepted by socialist feminists, it will be a difficult and important question to work out just how far they have moved from traditional Marxism and how much they still share with it.

Sistersong

Gay Hadley

If we should turn against each other now
If we should turn
        to little wars of envy
        seizing castoffs
        cutting patterns from old cloths

satisfied with remnants from the sun
If we should turn against each other now
If we should turn
        from our own stars
        our primal energy
        pale moonbeams vying
        for a sunken light
What will there be left for us if we should turn
Save one more endless, separated night?

Ambiguities in Identity Transformation: From Sugar and Spice to Professor

Joan Huber

A person who maintains a self-definition with no social support is mad; with minimum support, a pioneer; and with broad support, a lemming. Most of us are lemmings. We accept or change our ideas of our own rights and duties only when we perceive social support for doing so.

In the United States, social and occupational identities are closely related; a person is what he or she does.

Occupations are ranked in order of their prestige and pay and this ranking becomes part of our identity. To explain and justify the wide variation in occupational income and prestige, the ideology of equal opportunity holds that, with free public education, the rewards a person gets are deserved because hard work and brains determine the outcome. But the gap between the ideal and the real is great: black men and white women earn about half to two-thirds the pay of white men, and black women earn only about a quarter of it. Systematic discrimination accounts for most of the variation. Sometimes the subordinated claim that they see no discrimination and this fact is occasionally used as evidence that none exists. Social scientists are not surprised, however, when those who are discriminated against accept dominant social definitions and explanations. To see the givens of one's own society as a structure of illusions is a lonely business and only those who have the courage of pioneers can face up to it. I am no pioneer. My self-definition has been largely a response to events of my own time. This essay briefly recounts an attempt to redefine social rights and duties, supported by social conditions which made traditional work roles so uncomfortable that the search for alternatives became necessary.

Let us briefly examine broad technological and demographic changes which have made traditional roles obsolete and then focus on the specific events of the last 50 years which have affected the social identity of women of my generation who grew up in the Depression years. Although as an academic I am a statistical rarity, a woman in a male occupation, this account will stress aspects of self-definition common to many women by linking biographical and historical events.

In traditional societies most labor is domestic or agricultural and people work where they live. Industrialization requires wage labor away from the home but the wages are typically so low that both women and children work in order to provide for the family. By the late 19th century, the dramatic rise in real income enabled families to subsist on the wages of only one earner and women stayed home to perform unpaid labor. In the transition from rural to urban society, however, the birthrate fell and in the 20th century, birth control methods became so reliable that rational child-spacing was possible. At about the same time, the growth of large organizations required an enormous pool of educated labor. Women could be induced to work for about half the wages of men with a similar level of education; hence the clerical segment of the work force became predominantly female. The 20th century thus brought a high demand for female labor along with an increasing ability to control pregnancy, and a decreasing desire for large families. These technological and demographic facts set the stage for the women's movement.

Specific events of the last 50 years affecting women's roles include the depression of the thirties. As expected in hard times, the birthrate fell sharply. At the same time, married women were often fired because they did not "need" the money. Thus women were discouraged both from working and from having large families. Meanwhile, the influence of Freudian psychology made women feel responsible for taking care of their children's egos and cleaning up their ids. Women were caught in a double bind: if they didn't stay home, they were bad mothers; if they did, their children were likely to become victims of pernicious momism.

World War II had an apparently opposite effect: women swarmed into the work force and even into the armed services. But not for long. The birthrate usually rises after all wars and World War II was no exception. For the first time in history the inverse relation between family income and number of children was reversed when the upper middle class took to procreation with a vengeance. A better demonstration of lemming-like behavior would be hard to find. Family togetherness was, as the popular magazines asserted, a way of life for the sophisticated moderns of the postwar world. In practice, this meant that mommy, after spending all week with the kids, could spend the weekend with the kids and daddy. The experience was alleged to be richly rewarding and to have a cement-like effect on family relationships. Doing fun things with daddy and the kids gave the ultimate substance and meaning to a woman's life.

As the togetherness generation grew up, an alarming fact appeared: a nasty generation gap separated the mommies and the daddies from the kids who, contrary to expectation, showed signs of laziness, ingratitude, and total irresponsibility as indicated by the way they picked up their rooms, wore their hair, and spent their parents' money. Moreover, the availability of liquor and pot gave many middle-class parents a degree of contact with their friendly local police that they had not anticipated. Parents of the depression generation nervously asked themselves what had gone wrong and almost unanimously described the situation with one word: permissiveness.

For adult white males, the decade of the sixties was a real loser: blacks, teenagers, and women got out of hand at the same time; not all of them, but enough to make the decade very noisy. The assorted demands were of 28 varieties but common themes included a fundamental questioning of basic institutions like the system of social stratification and the family, and a strong desire for social change. By the end of the decade pollution was an additional problem that threatened not only the organization of the American economy but possibly the future of life on the planet. The importance of this fact to female identity problems can hardly be overestimated. A large family becomes a sign of social and moral irresponsibility rather than a monument to the energy and endurance of a selfless woman. Although this country is rich and can (if one ignores obligations to the rest of the world) afford to keep a class of persons whose main function is to do domestic service for males, the traditional maternal aspects of the role are so changed that the ancient arguments for keeping women at home do not apply. New role definitions are evolving, new ideas of appropriate occupations and life-styles for men and women, new personal and family relations, and new modes of socializing children. Stimulated by the larger events sketched in here, my own identity has changed considerably in the last quarter century and I shall trace the changes here: a short history of a lemming.

With a twin sister I was born in 1925 in a small town in the Midwest. My grandparents had lived on farms but in my parents' generation the dominant occupation was teaching. My parents always expected me to go to college so I cannot claim to have chosen, inspired by the Protestant ethic, to live the austere life of a college student, thus deferring the riotous gratification which characterizes the life of a dropout. My mother had been a dedicated fifth-grade teacher with total recall for the songs, stories, and projects of her childhood and teaching days and she enriched our minds with great energy. In other respects our rearing was similar to that of girls of our parental occupational and income level. The most impressive aspect of this socialization is the capacity to sweep unpleasant facts about a girl's future under the rug.

Girls are socialized with double-talk because no one has ever demonstrated the relationship of doing well in school to domestic service. Since housewives' activities are not inherently interesting, a lot of fast talking is required to convince little girls that they face a great future. I should like to report that at an early age I noticed the vast discrepancies between what people said and what they did, and reacted in moral outrage; but I climbed no infant barricade. Far from it. I liked being a girl. I liked pretty clothes and I liked playing with dolls. Boys led a dull and colorless life, in brown corduroy knickers and grey sweaters, always hitting things.

On the other hand, while my father went off to a roll-top desk in an office with an interesting smell of formaldehyde, my mother's activities did not inspire emulation. On Mondays she disappeared into the basement, wearing an old pair of rubber galoshes and a slightly raveled sweater, to do the family wash. Dirty clothes were first boiled in a big copper tub, stirred with a stick worn smooth. Sometimes the tub would boil dry and you could smell charred underwear all over the house. Handker-

chiefs were put in a crock with some Clorox and swished around to remove the mucous. I thought that cleaning the mucous off a dirty handkerchief was unpleasant, especially when the user had a heavy cold. When I told my mother this, she replied that Kleenex was too expensive. Putting clothes through the wringer was most exciting because the newspapers constantly carried tales of an unwary child who had caught fingers or an arm with hideous consequences. But the job took all day and the basement was damp and dark, with spiders on the beams. Tuesdays she would stand all day long in the kitchen, alone, doing the ironing, with time off to get lunch and dinner and wash up. Some jobs were fun, like decorating Christmas cookies and Easter eggs. Others were bad: when the cat threw up and you could see the worms crawling in the vomit; she sent us off to scrub our hands while she cleaned up the mess.

Clearly, all those jobs had to be done and neither my mother nor anyone else questioned that it was her responsibility to do them. But the value of the work was measured when my sister and I found that we could get out of practically any job by claiming that we needed to practice the piano, cello, violin, or do homework. Schoolwork obviously outranked housework. I have always been grateful to my mother that she ignored my messy room (most of the time) and let me get my work done.

The same ambivalence about the value of present activity for future life-style was apparent in high school. As captain of the debate team and editor of the school paper, I demonstrated that Susan B. Anthony and all those brave ladies had not lived in vain. But the occupations most frequently mentioned to me were teacher and librarian. No one told me outright that to aspire to the diplomatic corps was fatuous, but I was thoroughly exposed to the view that, as a girl, you should have a realistic occupation because your husband might die and you might need to work; and you could always find a job teaching no matter where you lived. In grade school I had liked the idea of being a teacher but by the time I was in fifth grade, I noticed that the perfect grade to teach was always the one I was in. By the time I was in high school, simple extrapolation led me to conclude that teaching would be attractive only if the students were grown up and interested in assorted ideas. But college teaching was not what my advisors had in mind.

In college the ambivalence about the future permeated the women's lives. Most of the young women expected to marry. A few spoke seriously and sincerely of the joys of homemaking, especially if they were in home economics and had devoted great energy to learning to scrub carrots and pare apples to make Waldorf salad and other delicacies. A more common response was wry resignation; occasional cracks could be heard about the utility of a college education for a career in the kitchen. We were told that our education would make us better mothers although no one explained how knowing anything about the Icelandic Eddas or the Duino Elegies would improve the ability to communicate with a five-year-old. Most of us regarded the pious pronouncements about our civilizing influence on the next generation as pure treacle designed to give everyone the good feeling that ours was the best of all possible worlds.

I was ambivalent but I played the game. I finished college at 19 and married at 20. Admitted to a top graduate school, I didn't go because it seemed sensible to defer a Ph.D. till after the children I wanted were somewhat grown. Although my name had come to represent the fact that I was able to manage my life as an adult, I changed it without thinking much about it because there was no choice. This was the way things were. I began to act out the role of housewife, confronted by a spate of low-level technological problems.

An example will help the reader who has never learnt a semi-skilled trade to understand what housewives do, hence what is involved in a change of identities. A pressing problem in the cotton age was to learn to iron a shirt without scorching the collar. Like flying an airplane, the procedure is easy once you have mastered it although it is less exhilarating. To do the job properly requires about 20 minutes. The more damp and heavily starched the shirt, the more likely that you will scorch it. Moreover, if the shirt is too damp, ironing it may require up to an hour for if you fail to get it completely dry, it will relax limply the moment you have ceased paying any attention to it. And an overstarched shirt will not only abrade the skin right off the wearer's neck but give him the look of a martial character in a comic opera. But if you iron it when it is too dry, it will remain gullied with wrinkles and advertise to the world that your unfortunate husband has an incompetent wife. Furthermore, proper starch should be heavy for the collar, lighter for the cuffs, and lighter still for the body of the shirt. Making the starch is tricky because unless it is stirred vigorously at just the right moment, ineradicable lumps appear and you must throw it out and start over. If you decide that a clean shirt every day is more than a man needs, then you must learn how to remove the extra accumulation of dirt from the collar;

that is, you must learn to use Clorox. If you don't use enough, the collar will remain an earthy shade of yellowish-grey but if you use too much, it will disintegrate. This is why shirts sent out to the laundry are always white but don't last very long. What a housewife is actually learning to do is to find minimax solutions to a wide variety of problems. Even women of modest intelligence become extraordinarily adept at rapid solutions involving a host of variables. Unfortunately, the problems themselves are trivial.

I had plenty of company. The pressure on women to devote themselves to domestic concerns was enormous at that time because, first, during the depression and the war many families had deferred having children until times were better. The sudden release of pent-up demand isolated the young woman who couldn't discuss the number of stitches her episiotomy had required, or what should be done if the baby's b.m. was green. (If you are sure he hasn't eaten any crayons — the consequences are colorful but harmless — call the doctor right away.) Second, the depression that many economists had expected in the transition to a peacetime economy didn't occur and, for the middle classes, job security was high with real income growing at a steady rate. Many women found that they were being kept in a style to which they were not accustomed and hence they expanded their activities to include gracious living, a concept extolled by the women's magazines. A three-color layout would show a willowy creature in a velvet hostess gown in a spotless kitchen putting the finishing touches on a six-course dinner for eight. In practice, gracious living meant that, with the aid of a mix-master and a dishwasher, you were supposed to emulate the life-style of a middle-class Victorian English woman who had a nanny, a tweenie, a cook, and a parlor maid to help her. Gracious living could, however, keep a woman fully occupied at home, for an unlimited number of hours can be spent preparing excellent food, keeping the table linens spotless and the silver gleaming, arranging a stunning centerpiece, and choosing an amusing little rosé. The message was clear: no woman ever need be bored at home. Something is wrong with a woman who is not gloriously happy performing these delightful functions.

Nowhere at that time do I recall reading an honest statement about what it meant to be a housewife. Women were told that they played warm, motherly, nurturant, friendly, companionable roles — but they were never advised of the price. The fact is that a married woman has little control over her own future because in industrial societies so much depends on the occupational performance of her husband. A married woman must either remain passive and hope that things will turn out all right or attempt to control the outcome by influencing her husband's performance; in plainer terms, she must do nothing or try to control another person to attain the ends she seeks. Either choice is profoundly unsatisfactory. In most marriages, the important life decisions are either made by the husband or occur as a consequence of his occupational performance: which job to take, which city to live in, what kind of house or neighborhood to live in, in short, just about everything that matters. In such circumstances to speak of an equal marriage of partners is fatuous. A career as a homemaker means that a woman, even if she is very bright and works very hard, will spend about 20 years at a semi-skilled blue-collar job in preparation for another 30 years of domestic service with a little amateur social work on the side. Her job performance will have little influence on her share of income, prestige, and influence. The marriage and family texts do not put the matter in these words because the situation might sound a little like a system of forced labor. However, the discrepancy between what people say and what they mean is even greater in the role which is chosen or foisted upon the great majority of women: motherhood, the most important job in the world.

Mothers are important because they take care of children, the hope of the future. Or so people say. I agreed and, as the months of my first pregnancy passed, I had no doubts about the rightness of having or adopting a baby, nor about the fact that the job of rearing them devolved mainly on women. But I was curious to know how I would feel, home alone all day with a baby. Almost a quarter of a century later I still hold the maternal role in such esteem that to admit that I was sometimes bored and lonely is hard to do. Nevertheless, spending almost all one's waking hours in the company of preschool children requires sound nerves, a good imagination and — what many women do not have — the desire to spend almost all one's waking hours in the company of preschool children.

In the fifties, as today, the middle-class woman who left her preschoolers and went off to school or work was suspected of sacrificing their psyches to her own needs. Women who stayed home with their babies would declare with a hint of piety that they wouldn't have anyone else bringing up their babies, no indeed; their educations weren't wasted one bit because a child needed an educated mother who could guide its growth intelligently and teach it to be creative and outgoing. In fact, colleges offer almost no training in child rearing for either men or women, and the enrichment of children's lives usually excludes a discussion of Edward Albee or existentialism. Actually, the idea that mamma should stay home with the kiddies changing diapers and dishing out the applesauce lest they feel rejected and come to a bad end is a myth designed to keep women out of the labor market, using guilt as a mechanism of social control. No one really cares who wipes up the spilt milk. Other persons perform this service for the children of the Queen of England and no one worries about how her children will turn out. Indeed, the diapers of almost all upper-class children are changed by someone other than the mother and no evidence shows that these children turn out worse than others nor does one hear an outcry about maternal neglect.

Society appears to care little whether poor women can stay home and take care of their babies for in most states the ADC grants are so small that the mother cannot buy adequate food, let alone the other things that children need. Indeed, ADC grants are much lower than welfare grants to the blind, the disabled, and the elderly although no evidence explains why ADC families need less than others. Unfortunately, many Americans seem less moved by a systematic concern for the needs of children than by a fear that educated women may get uppity and try to compete in the job market.

Although the role of mother may be emotionally rewarding, it is not very rewarding economically. The value of the unpaid services is less than the wage of an unskilled male laborer. Indeed, should a mother be out of commission and have to be replaced, anyone with a good disposition and a strong back will do. In a tight labor market, a strong back is a sufficient qualification. Substitutes for mothers receive almost the lowest wages in this society. Economists have a theory to explain, *pari passu,* why things are the way they are, but the theory requires the assumption that no systematic discrimination exists and is therefore not helpful. One may, of course, argue that a mother's real worth is in personal terms — that she cannot be emotionally replaced. This argument is unanswerable. Neither can a father. Still, the knowledge that one's economic contribution is worth less than the minimum wage does not enhance self-esteem.

The next stage in the development of my identity involved unpaid labor but in a larger arena, the community. Volunteer work may be loosely defined as white-collar busywork that no one cares enough to pay for. This fact is a tautology whose implications are never clearly spelled out to the women who do the work. Going to one's neighbors with a packet of official receipts, collecting for heart, cancer, and polio can give you a real sense of fulfillment, especially if you ignore the fact that the richest nation on earth could easily afford to support research on such diseases without sending volunteers around with tin cans. I shall illustrate the good works one could do in those days in order to clarify the effect of such activity on one's identity.

My first invitation to serve as a volunteer came from the ladies' auxiliary at the local hospital. They asked me to serve as a pink lady, so-called because they wore crisp, coral-colored cotton jumpers. The job specs called for sorting mail twice a day before carrying it to the patients and fending off visitors who, unless closely watched, would herd themselves in quantity into the room of the hapless patient. The job attracted wives of prominent businessmen who felt a need to help suffering humanity. I found that the nurses disliked tripping over us, and I quit with the discovery that 80 percent of the time there was nothing to do.

As a Den Mother for the Cub Scouts, I agreed to inculcate a set of virtues — I can no longer remember which ones — into a group of young males who otherwise would have been outdoors playing by themselves. A certain latitude was permitted the Mother in choice of activity and my Den went for an inordinate number of nature walks in the hills back of town because (a) it kept them from wrecking the living room and (b) I liked messing around in ponds hunting frogs as much as they did. Some days it rained and we had to do something indoors but the memory is blocked. Three meetings were occupied taking them to the home of a woman who made ceramics and charged almost nothing to teach the Den to make clever ashtrays as Christmas gifts for their parents. As my charges galloped down her cellar steps and elbowed their way among the pottery, her soft voice and sweet smile demonstrated that saints still walk this earth. The boys broke only three items.

A very different sort of activity was the American Association of University Women whose purpose, focusing on significant issues, was to study and then act. The difficulty was that women who really liked to study and act were out in the real world, studying and acting. The national leadership tried to involve the branches with a host of issues but the local ladies preferred the study and practice of gourmet cooking which was basically intellectual because some of the recipes were French. As a vehicle for even a modest degree of action at the local level, the AAUW was not very satisfactory, leading one of my

friends to formulate the drip-drip theory of social change: if you drip water on a rock long enough, one day it will be eroded. The theory provided little emotional comfort but it was intellectually satisfying.

To attend a meeting of the Parent-Teacher Association always gave you a warm glow because it showed that you were really interested in your child's progress and were the right kind of parent; besides, it could temporarily allay your anxiety about what was going on at school. The real function of the PTA was to provide a captive audience to be coopted by the superintendent and the principal to legitimate the school's need for more money. Since the schools, because of the increasing number of children to be processed, always needed money desperately, school administrators were very gracious to parents who worked for the PTA. It made us feel good to be told that our participation was crucial to the cognitive and emotional development of our children because, after all, you can't have a good school unless the parents are really interested. At one point in my career as a volunteer, I rose to dizzying heights of local power as president of both the AAUW and the PTA. My name often appeared on the Women's Page of the local newspaper, amidst reports of engagements, golden wedding anniversaries, and really exciting new cookie recipes.

Churches are financed mainly by pledges but a common way of raising additional funds is through women's guilds which hold rummage sales and bazaars. The rummage is provided by members who clean out their closets once or twice a year, give the really good things to friends and relatives, and the rest to the church to sell to people who can pay only a low price and will hence seek out the castoffs of higher income strata: aging underwear, dresses, frayed shirts, a cracked object of art, and a kitchen pot with a loose handle. One might suppose that working at a rummage would gratify the ego because one must play lady bountiful, politely dispensing items to the poor. In fact, the experience is corrosive because it increases the awareness that, by any standard of Christian decency, our society is not very moral; and worse, that the socks one is selling to the poor at five cents a pair have huge holes in the heels.

The bazaar was fun. Groups of women met several times a month to make pretty little things to sell to other women who wanted to buy pretty little things. Some of the items were handsome but others were latter-day versions of the antimacassar. I contributed my share. With common pins I stuck sequins into styrofoam balls to make tree ornaments; made Christmas wreaths out of pine cones; arrangements of weeds, lacquered and gilded; and knitted hats for skiers. My prize contribution sold very well: argyle socks for babies, in pink and blue. As everyone said, they were just darling. They were also useless because any healthy baby would kick them off in two minutes. Once I computed the return on the time we spent making our wares and found that we worked for about four cents an hour. The money would be sent to the vestry, earmarked for a special item such as a dishwasher for the church kitchen. But the work generated a feeling of togetherness which could hardly be measured in dollars.

When the children entered junior high and stopped coming home for lunch, I asked myself at the end of one year what had been accomplished. The answer reminded me that graduate school was now or never. I dropped most of the volunteer activities and began driving to the nearest university, a round trip of about 150 miles. Driving improved one's alertness, especially when it snowed. I changed universities for the Ph.D. and the round trip was 200 miles. After more than 100,000 miles of driving and some other activities, I earned the degree. In those five years my social identity was transformed.

I lived on the far edges of two worlds separated not only by miles but by social definitions. The professors were naive about the lives that business and corporation people lead and the corporate types had no idea that in graduate school you work seven days a week or else. Both worlds defined me as pleasant but eccentric. The professors felt that taking courses was, on the whole, a worthy enterprise and one kindly man informed me that he had had a housewife in a course a year earlier and she even got an A. The local people were sympathetic too. "Aren't you finished *yet*?" they would inquire in concerned tones after I had been commuting about a year. "Well, I guess it's just hard trying to keep house and go to school." Yet marginality has an enormous advantage: one becomes aware of the social givens that other people take for granted. I was forced to become aware of institutionalized sexism.

Even in graduate school the future had to be swept under the rug when a woman thought about finding a job. Many women were stymied by the nepotism rule and, if this didn't stop them, by the rule that the university will not hire its own graduates. A married man can find a job and move his family. A married woman has different options: she may obtain a post outside her department in an obscure corner of the university; she may become part of a labor reserve, called upon when the department is shorthanded or needs someone to teach the large introductory sections, with low wages; worse, she may be called often to teach, but not given tenure, retirement, and other rights; she may commute to another town, especially if she loves driving; she may have another baby and go back to the PTA for another 10 years; or she may end the marriage and hunt for a job. I was lucky and found a job 100 miles away in a different direction. I commuted for two years, employed part-time because I couldn't make the trip every day. Then my marriage ended and I became a full-time worker.

I like my new identity because I no longer have to pretend that everything is all right when I know that it is not. At times I feel a little like a house-nigger when my colleagues anxiously ask if everything isn't really all right. My colleagues like to think of themselves as kindly creatures who certainly don't want to do women in. Many of them grasp the idea of sexism quite easily although others have difficulty with it. A number of my male colleagues were uneasy when I remarried and retained my maiden name, for example. Many find it hard to apply their sociological insights to concrete problems; that is, they do not see the relation between what they say and what they do. The discrepancy is especially obvious in radicals whose desire to press for the total transformation of society stops abruptly at the kitchen door.

Once when I was about 18 I told my father that I really didn't want to spend the rest of my life doing housework. As a long-time follower of Norman Thomas, he replied that I was snobbish: if poor women had to do such work, on what grounds did I consider myself to be above it? I reminded him that he did not feel obliged to be a ditchdigger because he was a man; why did I have to do housework all my life because I was a woman? He looked quite surprised. Then he said slowly, "I don't know."

The old answers won't do. Social arrangements can be devised where no person—black, poor, female— automatically inherits the dirtiest jobs at the lowest wages. Furthermore, the fact that the dirtiest jobs have the lowest wages is a man-made situation and can be changed. The social and technological changes that spawned the women's movement will continue to be felt. Increasingly, women will find their lives trivialized if the old institutions deny them full identity as grown human beings. Both men and women can devise new institutions to create new options for all humans.

Collective Work and Self-Identity: The Effect of Working in a Feminist Illegal Abortion Collective

Melinda Bart Schlesinger and Pauline B. Bart

This paper is an attempt to illustrate some of the ways in which people change when they participate in a democratically structured group that performs a vitally needed service.

In 1969 abortion was still illegal, although the need to terminate unwanted pregnancies was great. The right to abortion on demand was one of the key principles of the emergent Women's Liberation Movement, a demand later expanded to the right of women to control their bodies. There were semiformal and informal referral systems where women were given names of abortionists. One of these volunteer informal referral services was operated by a University of Chicago student from her dormitory, and she wanted a group to take it over. There was a group of women living in the Hyde Park community near the University of Chicago who had begun to develop feminist consciousness. Many of them had been in the peace and civil rights movements, and when the Chicago Women's Liberation Union was organized, it seemed logical to them to counsel women and help them to obtain illegal abortions. Thus, they took over the task as well as the pseudonym Jane from the student. At that time, no one thought that eventually they would be performing the abortions. Moreover, they made the assumption, which was later dispelled, that the abortionists to whom they were referring the women were M.D.s.

Because the group could provide a steady supply of "customers," they were in a better bargaining position than were individual women who needed abortion. Thus, they were able to negotiate with the abortionists, who had to lower their rates and agree to perform some free abortions. The Jane women also lent the clients up to $50.00 to help them pay the fees, funds which were taken from the fees of women who paid the full amount.

Once the women in Jane learned that the abortionists were not M.D.s, they realized that lay persons could perform competent abortions; they knew the abortions were competent because of the feedback from the clients. Thus, when one abortionist taught one of the women how to perform the procedures, she taught the rest, and they fired the professional abortionists. The hierarchy of the group flattened because the abortionist could no longer choose which women would assist at the procedures, and any woman at any stage of her pregnancy with or without money could obtain a humane, demystified abortion from this group of women whose safety record for first-trimester abortions equalled that of New York state when that state legalized abortions. At first, because of the relatively high fees paid to the illegal abortionists, the clients were more likely to be students since they could afford those fees. However, in the winter of 1971 when the women took over and made it possible to lower or eliminate fees so that any woman at any stage of her pregnancy could obtain an abortion, the abortions were done primarily *with* (their word) poor black women from the "projects." The clients did not constitute a homogenous group, however. They ranged in age from 11 to 50, and in occupation from policewoman to weatherwoman.

During its four years of operation, from 1969 to 1973, Jane proved that abortions could be performed safely, humanely and very inexpensively by non-professional "paramedics" working in apartments.

The following roles existed in Jane when the women assumed control:

First-trimester abortionist

Long-term abortionist — Sometimes called midwife. Long terms were for abortions that took place after the first three months of conception.

Reprinted from Melinda Bart Schlesinger and Pauline B. Bart, "Collective Work and Self-Identity: The Effect of Working in a Feminist Illegal Abortion Collective," in *Workplace Democracy and Social Change,* ed. Frank Lindenfeld and Joyce Rothschild Whitt (Boston: Porter-Sargent, 1981), by permission of the authors.

Big Jane	The administrator
Call Back Jane	Also an administrator who returned the calls the women wanting abortions left on the answering tape
Driver	Transported the women from "the Front" to the place where the procedures were done and back to "the Front," the place from which the women and their significant others left.
Worker at the Front	(Called "working the Front.") One woman described the responsibilities of this position as being a stewardess with radical feminist consciousness.
Assistants	Gave shots, inserted speculums, dilated cervixes.
Counsellor	Everyone was supposed to counsel. The process consisted primarily of demystifying the abortion procedure. It was done either with individuals or with groups.

While everyone had to counsel, ideally all women were expected to try to perform every task. Not all women wanted to assist and fewer wanted to do abortions, either because of lack of time, commitment, interest or skill. The ideology was that everyone *could* do everything, rather than an ideology supporting a division of labor and specialization. It was thought that the women they were doing the procedures *with* (their term) would benefit by seeing the Jane women change jobs, since it demonstrated that the skills were easily transferable and not mystical. Rothschild-Whitt (1979) in her paper which seeks "to identify some of the structural commonalities which link these new collective organizations and to develop a theoretical framework for understanding them," lists nine principles which contrast such organizations with bureaucratic organizations. The principles relevant to the chart above, and which the informants agreed were applicable to Jane are that equality of status was attempted through task sharing, that differentiation was minimized to "eliminate bureaucratic

division of labor," and role rotation, teamwork and task sharing resulted in the above as well as in "demystification of specialized knowledge." Women in Jane learned through the apprenticeship system and work roles were holistic. Because everyone counselled, grounding their work in the experience of women needing abortions, understanding why that woman chose not to have that child at that time, they did not experience the alienation that medical personnel sometimes report when involved in abortions (e.g., Denes, 1976).

While in the nineteenth century, before physicians attained hegemony, women did perform abortions for other women (Mohr, 1978), there is no current sociological literature on lay abortions. Standard sociological organization theory does not accurately predict the behavior of collectives, as Rothschild-Whitt notes (1976), since these "movement organizations" (Zald and Ash, 1964) neither transform means into ends in the quest for survival, nor bureaucratize charisma. Radical alternative and self-help health clinics have been studied, however. Peterson (1976) found that a feminist health clinic did not achieve its goal of providing real alternatives because "by remaining within the model of delivering medical services, the clinic's structure . . . [was an] extension of the regular delivery system" making "paramedical workers out of non-professionals" in spite of their countervailing ideology. Moreover, inequality between client and practitioner remained since the practitioners controlled the definitions of services because of their greater knowledge and access to scarce resources. Taylor (1976) gives another example of an alternative health service which did not meet its goals. However, Kleiber and Light (1978) describe a successful alternative structure for women's health care, and Marieskind (1976) found that a self-help clinic "was a potential resource of value, particularly for dealing with shortages of health personnel and changing sexist medical practices" (1976). Marieskind notes that the value of a self-help model, whether it be Parents Without Partners or AA "lies in the fact that it efficiently utilizes an untapped medical resource — the cooperation and participation of the patient." However, none of these studies has addressed the social psychological issues which this paper focuses on: the effect of participating in such organizations on the participants.

Method

Obtaining the women's permission to be interviewed about the Service, or Jane, was difficult. They considered it ironic for a group that was anti-professional and anti-academic to be studied by an academic, although they were not concerned (with one exception) about their illegal activities becoming known. Seven of them had been arrested, but after the Supreme Court decision legalizing abortion, the charges were dismissed.

But some of the key women decided to trust Bart because she had been active in the Women's Movement, her self-presentation was not "professional," and she did not have a grant, which was considered proof of her not having been coopted. They told the other members that she could be trusted, and, for the most part, there was no difficulty obtaining interviews. Some women even called asking to be interviewed. Everyone contacted, including women who were originally reluctant, ultimately agreed to be interviewed. They were promised input into the study and, indeed, this and other papers have benefited from their cooperation.

Light and Kleiber, who studied the Vancouver Women's Health Collective, also received feedback from the collective members (1978, 17), but, unlike Light and Kleiber, Bart could not observe the collective at work. However, she has observed and received health care services from other feminist clinics, one of which was partially staffed by former Jane members.

The interviews were unstructured at first, and became semi-structured when the important issues emerged. Sometimes this resulted in interviewing members more than once. The interviews were then coded, and this paper deals with answers coded in the following areas: career goals, personal task competency, personal growth, political growth, increase in feminist orientation, and demystification of the medical profession (N = 34). Thus, the various aspects of personal change could be recorded. Such changes will be discussed including the negative experiences some women experienced. (Table 1)

Findings

Personal Growth and Increased Competency

The categories of personal competency and personal growth were collapsed because they overlapped. Seventeen women reported changes in categories, with some women reporting change in both categories. Frequently, personal growth was perceived as a result of their increased sense of competency. For example, one woman said: "I entered the group as a real quiet, shy person, hardly able to articulate anything at all. By the time I left I was the strong person in the group. I had learned all the skills that were available to me. I developed a great deal. Now I am a functional, happy, normal person." The second reported: "I would make dumb jokes and try to put them [the women coming for abortions] at ease. Before that I was real shy and would never talk to anybody. It made me come out of my shell." (Table 2)

Fifteen of the women expressly mentioned competency and its effect on their self-concept. The following quotes illustrate two examples of this change:

> I could learn and I could pick up skills. It made a whole lot of sense the way people learned through the Service . . . There was a whole thing of responsibility and respect that I don't think I've really had a whole experience with before. What it did was give me a whole different sense of myself and what I was capable of doing.

> I had a real good feeling about myself and I was real confident. I was able to do a lot of things at one time and I knew that I was doing them well. That felt good and I was real happy with myself.

The Service made it possible for these women to experience a new sense of competency. It has been found

TABLE 1
Effect of the Service on the Members

Number	Direction of Change
22	positive
3	both positive and negative
2	negative
7*	no change
34	

*Many of these women already were politicized and/or considered themselves competent.

TABLE 2
Kinds of Changes the Women Experienced

Number	Kind of Change
17	personal "growth" and increased sense of competence
16	political "growth" and increased feminist orientation
5	changed career goals
8	changed attitudes toward doctors
46*	

*The sum is more than 27 because some women changed in more than one way.

that women perceive themselves as less competent than men in achievement related areas (Frieze et al., p. 59). Moreover, the literature both popular and empirical suggests that housewives are particularly vulnerable in this area (which is expressed in the phrase "I'm just a housewife"). These women are, in fact, not married to their houses, but Parsons has called a housewife a "pseudo occupation" (1942) and Ferree has found that working class housewives have lower self-esteem and feelings of competence than a comparison group of women who were employed either part or full time (1976). Several of the key members who started Jane were housewives.

This increased sense of competence had political overtones for several of the women, one of whom maintained in a statement which is the essence of the Jane philosophy, indeed of the self-help philosophy:

> I had achieved something . . . I can do things that I never felt I could do. I think the important thing about the Service is that people really learn that if it's necessary you can take the tools of the world in your own hands. All that crap about how you have to be an expert . . . it's just a ruse to make you feel incompetent in your own life. One thing we all learned is that if you want to do something you can learn how to do it.

Specifically with regard to the tasks in the Service she remarked:

> You think you could never stick your hand into a toilet bowl full of blood and vomit and pull out a placenta and look at it. You think you could never put a needle into somebody's ass. But if you have to do it and you're the only person who can do it— you do it. And once you've done it, you say, my God, I can do this. It's not terrible. You wouldn't want to do it every day but you can do it. You're not going to be weak. You can be responsible for yourselves and your brothers and sisters.

Another woman whose comment had political overtones maintained, "I could take a taboo apart and learn the skill involved. This reduced the power things had over me and increased my own sense of self as a person who could do this." Thus, we see that these women's experience in a democratically structured organization gave them the feeling of regaining control of their lives.

Finally, there were some changes with regard to personal growth that did not involve feelings of increased competency per se. One woman maintained, "my participation in the Service grew me into the person I was meant to be." A second woman remarked, "I can't remember a time in my life when I felt so good about doing something. It was such an incredible experience when it came to helping people." The second statement supports the work of Reissman (1965) and Braeger (1965) on the beneficial effects of helping on the helper.

Political Growth and Feminist Orientation

Originally, the categories of political growth and feminist orientation were to be analyzed separately. Upon examining the data, it appears that almost everyone who recognized political growth connected it to or also recognized feminist growth. Some of the women did not mention feminist growth explicitly, but implied it from their discussion of issues such as health care. Sixteen women felt some type of change in the feminist/political arena as a result of participation in the Service. While all of them recognized that at least some aspect of their feminist politics had developed, six of these also mentioned more general types of political growth. Some of these six felt that their politics became more anarchist. One woman maintained, "We found that working without a set of rules is a very efficient thing to do. If we had to label ourselves we would call ourselves anarchists." Evidently, for some of the women, working in a democratically structured group caused them to reject any type of authoritarianism. Another group of women maintained that the Service caused them to become more radical. One woman remarked, "By the time I was finished with the Service I was more and more frustrated and convinced that I didn't want to be part of the political, economic, or medical systems . . . I felt that we had to do it ourselves. I was more a radical than a reformist."

One type of increasing feminism resulting from participation in Jane was that many women felt a change in their relationships to other women. Some examples of this change are illustrated by the following quotes: "I am constantly amazed at the process and relationships I had with women (in the Service). These became a source of power with me. I then describe that as feminism."

> I may be more friendly towards women . . . I think before I would have some women friends but not many. Suddenly I had almost exclusively women friends. I guess it (the Service) changed my attitude about women . . . I do know them better.

> . . . being involved in Jane, especially in the counselling part where one has to talk to many

women and being up at the Front, I found that under the skin it didn't matter if you were big or black or white or green or small or fat or rich or poor. Women had to deal with the same problems and it radicalized me in that respect. I feel that tremendous kinship to women and I find that I seek out women . . .

Such increased positive feelings — indeed, one might call it female bonding — were probably most effected by the female world in which they participated (See Carroll Smith Rosenberg, 1975, for a description of this world in the nineteenth century) for both the women's co-workers and the clients were women.

The second type of feminist growth involves a more general type of orientation toward women's issues. The following quotes are examples of this type of change:

"I wanted to be a person who did things but I wasn't. The Service was the first thing I ever did and I've been active ever since in feminist things."

"I didn't really have a direction that I was going in — I didn't know what I wanted to do with myself. What Jane did for me was radicalize me and get me involved in women's issues."

[Before the Service] abortion interested me as an issue particularly. Feminism didn't interest me at all . . . I discovered I could get them an abortion but there were all these other things wrong with their lives . . . I got more into thinking that what's wrong with a woman's situation is that she is a woman . . . Then there was a way of looking at what was going on in their lives and that made sense to me. There was an instrument they could use to make their lives better. The Service was a very politicizing thing.

Career Goals

Working in the Service influenced the career goals of five women. All of them are in health-related areas. Two are in nursing school (one is a nurse midwife), two are doing women's self-help courses and speaking engagements, and one is in medical school. All of them maintain that the Service had a major impact on what they are doing now. (It should be noted that the number of women who fit this category is very small, because it was often unclear if Jane had been the primary influence on their career goals.) The student in nurse midwifery, noting that some people find it contradictory that a woman who was involved in "kill-

ing babies" should be helping women to have them, remarked, "It's all part of the same thing. It's all part of letting women do what they want to do."

Demystification of Medicine

The "Medical Mystique" refers to the deification of physicians and things associated with them. It involves a perception of physicians as super people with a quasimystical power which may not be questioned by lay people who could not possibly know as much. Eight women recognized change in their attitudes toward the medical profession. All of the women in this category realized the absurdity of the medical mystique and questioned what doctors could do and did. With the exception of one woman, all of those who fell into this category also recognized an increase in their task-related competency. Furthermore, change in this area was also highly associated with feminist/political growth (five out of seven). The following quotes are examples of this type of change:

I guess before the Service I was locked up into thinking about how I should act, especially with doctors. If they said something to me it was like law. If a doctor said something to me then of course I would do it. The Service made me question and the more I found out about what they tell people the more skeptical of them I got. At this point I wouldn't like to go to a doctor for anything.

As a result of Jane I know that people who have an intelligence of ninety or above can learn to do anything that the doctor does. I think that the doctor was cut down to size . . . He's just about as big as I am, no more or less. He's a technician who has learned a trade. He's not some fantastic creature. He's as fallible as I am.

Another woman told how her experience as an abortionist in Jane resulted in better treatment for her child when he was seriously cut and had to be taken to the emergency room. The staff refused her entry, claiming she would become upset or faint at the procedure. Needless to say she knew she would not and was able to successfully insist that she be in the room and holding her child's hand. When she was told that she would have to bring him in several times a week for the dressings to be changed, she insisted that she could do it herself, persuaded them to teach her how, and saved herself time, particularly important because she was employed. Her son was saved the additional alienating experience of hospital care. One could note the irony of a woman's training in abortion helping her be a more competent mother, saving her son from the exacerbation of distress that is a frequent response to hospital treatment because of separation from parents. Thus, by learning the skills involved (or seeing others learn the skills) the women realized that almost anyone has the ability to do some of the things that doctors maintain only they can do.

Negative Cases

There were five people whose experiences in the Service were less than positive. Two of the women were in Jane for a relatively short time and one admits that had she been in it longer she may have had a more positive experience. One saw the Service as being very hierarchical and resistant to change. She felt she cared more about women than other women in the Service. She maintained, "It was probably the first experience that made me cynical . . . for the sake of the good that people see they really do ignore some of the other crap that goes on." This was a time when males were running the Service. Thus, it was more hierarchical.

As Rothschild-Whitt (1979) notes, participation in collective organizations is time-consuming because of the democratic process which attempts to achieve consensus. The Jane informants agreed that this was the case with Jane. One woman especially resented giving her time. Other women could not meet this and other demands of the organization and for them the experience became a negative one.

Three of the women did not perform medical procedures. Performing such tasks often led to a positive experience. One of these women wanted to but was not allowed. Another was considered too slow. The third one thought it "icky." The fourth person wouldn't counsel and the fifth was seen as an incompetent abortionist. Thus, none had good experiences doing procedures and such good experiences were associated with an overall positive experience in the Service.

Rothschild-Whitt (1979) notes that because of the emotional intensity of collective organizations, an intensity which is both threatening and satisfying, criticism is concealed or softened. This observation is true for Jane since the issue of how to deal with incompetence caused interpersonal conflicts. It was difficult to "fire" incompetent workers. Frequently, they were isolated socially in the hope that they would get the message that they were not wanted. One abortionist was "fired" and the woman firing her reported that it was the hardest thing she ever did in the Service. Dealing with incompetency was particularly difficult for another reason. When mistakes are made in clinics or hospitals, not only is there back-up equipment and personnel, but an informal system is available to cover up such errors. Because Jane was illegal, their resources for dealing with mistakes were limited. They did have arrangements with sympathetic physicians so that seriously ill patients could be cared for at some hospitals. In addition, they had the necessary self-presentation skills to see to it that women with serious problems would be admitted to hospitals in any event. Moreover, they coached women on how to manage such experiences. However, women told me that even though competence was extremely important, they felt that if any one person could be "fired" they themselves were at risk.

General Changes

One section of this paper was going to deal with general types of change (those who mainly changed politically, those who changed personally and those who changed in both respects). Political/feminist and medical profession attitudes were to be seen as political, while personal growth/competency and career goals would be viewed as personal. Upon review of the data however, it appears that all categories are so closely entwined that to distinguish between them in such a manner would be arbitrary. For example, often personal competency is related to self-help and the "we can do it ourselves" attitude, which is very political. This finding is also consistent with the tenet of the Women's Movement that "the personal is the political." The following quote illustrates this. "The whole aspect of self-help and self-determination was important. Having breached this by learning medical skills I began to really feel that I had power . . . It was such a good feeling of overcoming some of my own taboos that I began to see that as a real important thing for all women." Only four of the women who mentioned more than one category of change stayed exclusively within either the personal or political category. Perhaps the only trend to be found is that all those who expressed positive change in any category were very involved in the Service. That is, they were in it for at least a year, learned some of the medical skills involved, or had strong social ties to the women in the Service. It should be mentioned at this point that perhaps the number of women who changed was no larger because some of the women came into the Service with some of the ideas discussed. Thus, while their attitudes may have been reinforced, they were not changed by participation in the Service.

Although there was no "party line" on most issues, the basis for belonging to Jane was a commitment to the ideal of women maintaining control of their bodies. In fact some members claimed that the lack of such a line was one factor accounting for Jane's success. Because large segments of the membership were relatively homogenous (Bart, 1977) social control could for the most part be based on "personalistic and moralistic appeals rather than direct supervision" (Rothschild-Whitt, 1979). But the informants disagreed that the members were selected because of their sharing of "basic values and world view"; such sharing, they claimed, was true only on the issue of abortion. However, we would conjecture that a vocal proponent of the war in Vietnam would have had difficulty participating no matter how much she was committed to a woman's right to abortion. The diversity was among various liberal and left positions, with feminist anarchism becoming the major emergent philosophy.

Zald and Ash (1964) note that movement organizations differ from full-blown bureaucratic organizations since they want to change society rather than provide it with a regular service. This position is supported by Jane's disbanding after the Supreme Court decision legalizing abortion.

Since the organization was committed to the ideal of women maintaining control over their bodies, this control was more fully realized when the women learned they could gain control by learning the procedures and becoming independent of the male abortionists. The democratic structure that the women introduced appears to be much more conducive to the ideal of controlling their lives, and was, in fact, an example of it. As the women gained control, the hierarchy flattened and more women could do more things. Thus, more members of the organization had the opportunity to experience the feeling of self-determination. The virtues of a democratically structured organization can be clearly seen in terms of the numbers of women who were able to become fully involved and committed. As King-Janus (1956) and Pearl (1964) maintain, commitment to an ideal is an important aspect in determining to what extent the "helping person" will change.

It should be pointed out that the democratic structure was not the only aspect of the Service that was conducive to growth. The fact that the problem was so immediate and the results so concrete caused many women to feel their experience with Jane to be especially meaningful. One might think that the illegality aspect would be detrimental to some women's self-concept. It is interesting to note that this did not occur. Rather, the illegality added to the immediacy of the problem and caused the women to really feel that they were providing an essential service. The fact that they were providing an essential service was one of the reasons the women gave for the success of the Service (Bart, 1977). As Rothschild-Whitt notes (1976): "It is unlikely that members of a collectivist-democratic organization would be able to maintain their self-conscious resistance to more cost-efficient models of organization if they were in the business of producing goods or services which were similar to and competing with those produced by bureaucratic organizations."

Through their direct involvement with a medical procedure, the women learned more about their bodies. The importance of learning skills and gaining information about certain medical procedures cannot be over-stressed in terms of the beneficial effects it appears to have. This educational and informational aspect would seem to be quite essential for any group. Again, a democratic organization, which allows more members to receive more information, would certainly be more conducive to this outcome.

Thus, any organization which desires its members to grow in positive ways would probably be most effective if it allows as many members as possible to become actively involved in learning skills, gaining information and participating in decision-making activities. It should be mentioned, however, that if this organization demands the level of competency and commitment that characterized the Service, some members may have negative experiences because of their inability to meet these high standards.

Conclusion

This paper described the changes in women participating in an illegal feminist abortion collective. Their sense of competence and autonomy increased, they became more radicalized and more feminist, notably increasing their identification and bonding with other women. In addition, their experience in providing health care led to a demystification of medicine generally.

This study not only demonstrates that the belief that only physicians can perform safe abortions is incorrect, it also shows the limits of the current ideology promoted by the "human potential movement" that people "grow" by taking care of themselves, by being their own best friends — in short, by focusing on their own needs rather than on other people and their needs.

One of us (Bart) calls this ideology "the growth-spaceautonomy approach" and has pointed out that it can function as a legitimization of psychopathy. After all, cancer is also growth. The dichotomy between taking care of oneself and taking care of others is demonstrably false. It was, indeed, by taking care of *others* that the Jane women fulfilled their own potential.

We will close with a statement from one of the women exemplifying this process:

> *You can do some of them (medical skills) and it's all right and you can do them well. It makes you feel like you can do anything in the world.*

References

Bart, Pauline B. 1977. "Seizing the Means of Reproduction: A Feminist Illegal Abortion Collective — How and Why It Worked." Paper presented at the Meetings of the American Sociological Association, Chicago.

———. 1978. Review of *In Necessity and Sorrow* by Magda Denes. *Sociology and Social Research* 63, 1 (October).

Denes, Magda. 1976. *In Necessity and Sorrow: Life and Death in an Abortion Hospital.* New York: Penguin.

Ferree, Marx. 1976. "Working-Class Jobs: Housework and Paid Work as Sources of Satisfaction." *Social Problems* 23, 4 (April): 431–441.

Frieze, Irene H., Jacquelynne E. Parsons, Paula B. Johnson, Diane N. Ruble, and Gail L. Zellman. 1978. *Women and Sex Roles.* New York: W. W. Norton.

Kleiber, Nancy and Linda Light. 1978. *Caring for Ourselves.* Vancouver: School of Nursing, University of British Columbia.

Mohr, James C. 1978. *Abortion in America.* New York: Oxford University Press.

Parsons, Talcott. 1942. "Age and Sex in the Social Structure of the U.S." *American Sociological Review:* 604–606.

Rothschild-Whitt, Joyce. 1976. "Conditions Facilitating Participatory-Democratic Organizations." *Sociological Inquiry* 46, 2: 75–86.

———. 1979. "Collective Democracy: An Alternative to Rational-Bureaucratic Models of Organization." *American Sociological Review.*

Smith-Rosenberg, Carroll. 1975. "The Female World of Love and Ritual: Relations Between Women in Nineteenth-Century America." *Signs* 1, 1 (Autumn): 1–29.

Zald, Mayer N. and Roberta Ash. 1964. "Social Movement Organizations: Growth Decay and Change." *Social Forces* 44 (May): 327–341.

Right To Life

Marge Piercy

SAILLE

A woman is not a pear tree
thrusting her fruit in mindless fecundity
into the world. Even pear trees bear
heavily one year and rest and grow the next.
An orchard gone wild drops few warm rotting
fruit in the grass but the trees stretch
high and wiry gifting the birds forty
feet up among inch long thorns
broken atavistically from the smooth wood.

A woman is not a basket you place
your buns in to keep them warm. Not a brood
hen you can slip duck eggs under.
Not the purse holding the coins of your
descendants till you spend them in wars.
Not a bank where your genes gather interest
and interesting mutations in the tainted
rain, any more than you are.

You plant corn and you harvest
it to eat or sell. You put the lamb
in the pasture to fatten and haul it in
to butcher for chops. You slice
the mountain in two for a road and gouge
the high plains for coal and the waters
run muddy for miles and years.
Fish die but you do not call them yours
unless you wished to eat them.

Now you legislate mineral rights in a woman.
You lay claim to her pastures for grazing,
fields for growing babies like iceberg
lettuce. You value children so dearly
that none ever go hungry, none weep
with no one to tend them when mothers

work, none lack fresh fruit,
none chew lead or cough to death and your
orphanages are empty. Every noon the best
restaurants serve poor children steaks.

At this moment at nine o'clock a partera
is performing a table top abortion on an
unwed mother in Texas who can't get Medicaid
any longer. In five days she will die
of tetanus and her little daughter will cry
and be taken away. Next door a husband
and wife are sticking pins in the son
they did not want. They will explain
for hours how wicked he is,
how he wants discipline.

We are all born of woman, in the rose
of the womb we suckled our mother's blood
and every baby born has a right to love
like a seedling to sun. Every baby born
unloved, unwanted is a bill that will come
due in twenty years with interest, an anger
that must find a target, a pain that will
beget pain. A decade downstream a child
screams, a woman falls, a synagogue is torched,
a firing squad is summoned, a button
is pushed and the world burns.

I will choose what enters me, what becomes
flesh of my flesh. Without choice, no politics,
no ethics lives. I am not your cornfield,
not your uranium mine, not your calf
for fattening, not your cow for milking.
You may not use me as your factory.
Priests and legislators do not hold
shares in my womb or my mind.
This is my body. If I give it to you
I want it back. My life
is a non-negotiable demand.

Reprinted from Marge Piercy, "SAILLE: Right to Life," in *The Moon is Always Female,* (New York: Random House, 1980), by permission of the publisher and the author.

345

Pornography and the Women's Liberation Movement

Diana E. H. Russell

Why have most women in the Women's Movement shied away from pornography as a woman's issue for so long? This is an important question. Until a greater portion of the Women's Movement is with us on this, we aren't going to get very far. The fact is that an incredible, scary, hate campaign against women has been escalating in the last eight years with scarcely a peep of protest from most feminists. Only with the "snuff" movies can we talk of the movement taking action. But after the "snuff" movies left town—temporarily—so did most of the action.

Why?

I believe there are many reasons. First, because we have observed that the anti-pornography forces have almost always been conservative, homophobic, antisex, and pro the traditional family. They have equated nudity and explicit sex with pornography. They are often against abortion, the Equal Rights Amendment, and the Women's Liberation Movement. We have been so put off by the politics of these people, that our knee-jerk response is that we must be *for* whatever they are *against*.

But we don't have to ally ourselves with them. We haven't yet. And we won't! The women amongst them can relate to our focus on the abuse of women by pornography better than we can relate to the "sin" approach. They can come to us if they can accept the rest of our politics too.

The second reason why most feminists have so far ignored the issue of pornography is that most of us bought the male liberal and radical line that being against any aspect of the so-called sexual revolution meant being a reactionary, unliberated prude. Men were seen as the sexually liberated sex, women the sexually repressed sex. To be liberated, women at least had to tolerate and accept male sex trips, including pornography, and sometimes try to imitate them, as in *Playgirl* magazine. But all this assumes that there can be a sexual revolution without a sex-*role* revolution too, and that change means women changing to be more like men. No thank you!

The third reason for neglecting this issue is that most of us have refused to look at pornography ourselves. It is painful to face the hatred of women so evident in it. While we resent what we are *forced* to see in our newspaper ads, in the grocery stores, in the red-light-district posters and neon signs, few of us follow through and say, "My Goddess! This stuff is hateful. I need to check out what is going on *inside* some of these places!" Like some Jews in Germany early on in the Nazi period who didn't want to read the writing on the wall, many women prefer not to know the depth and dangerousness of misogyny. Heterosexual women in particular have a hard time facing this aspect of male culture, since they don't want to see this side of the men they relate to. But most lesbians haven't made an issue out of it either, and a few have even confused male abuse of lesbians in pornography with lesbian pornography. Far more disturbing yet, some actually argue that sadomasochistic sex is fun and healthy for lesbians. Sadly, few of us have been immune to the liberal-radical line on pornography.

A fourth reason is that we have been deceived like everybody else by the male scientists and so-called experts who claim that there is no evidence showing that pornography is harmful. We are told that pornography helped diminish the problem of rape and other sex crimes in Denmark, that this is a fact, and that any feelings we may have to the contrary about pornography are irrational. But new research and a more thorough analysis of the existing research has revealed that this was an irresponsible conclusion of the Commission on Obscenity

Reprinted from Diana E. H. Russell, "Pornography and the Women's Liberation Movement," in *Take Back The Night,* ed. Laura Lederer, (New York: William Morrow, 1980), pp. 301–396, by permission of the author.
This article was first presented as the concluding speech at the Feminist Perspectives on Pornography conference in 1978, where Diana E. H. Russell, a founding member of Women Against Violence in Pornography and Media, gave her views on how the Women's Movement should proceed to fight pornography.

and Pornography, as well as of many other almost exclusively male scientists who have done similar research.

A fifth reason why so few feminists have confronted pornography is that we have often, for practical and strategic reasons, taken a piecemeal approach to problems. We focus on battered women, or rape, or the molestation of female children, or whatever. But all these crimes against women are linked. How can we stop rape and woman-battering by staffing rape-crisis centers and refuges when there are thousands of movie houses, millions of publications, a multibillion-dollar business that promote the idea that violence and the rape of women is sexually exciting to men, and that *we* like it too?

Sixth, as with prostitution, many of us get confused by the argument that it is an issue of survival (money) for some women. This is true, and I think it's important to recognize that women's role in pornography is not the primary problem. It is the men who profit most from it, and who are its consumers, who must be attacked and exposed. But beyond that, we cannot automatically support every institution which happens to provide some money for some women. The German concentration camps did that too. We *have* to consider whether the institution is operating in such a way as to be destructive to women as a *class*. Money aside, many women including ex-pornography models, have made a strong case for the destructive effect on the women involved.

Seventh, there is a fear that being anti-pornography means we are necessarily pro-censorship. For people who have worked through all the other reasons, this one often still bothers them. So I'd like to spend a little more time on it.

With few exceptions, most feminists, as well as liberal and radical nonfeminists, have been so hung up on the censorship issue that they have refused to allow themselves to recognize pornography as a problem for women, refused to analyze what is going on in pornography and why, and refused even to allow themselves to *feel* outraged by it. We have largely remained silent while this ever more conspicuous and vicious campaign against us has been mounted—even though it is impossible to open our newspapers to the entertainment section and not see something of what is going on, at least in this city.

I wish we could end this short-circuiting in our thinking and feeling. It seems to me there are four distinct and important steps in dealing with a social problem.

1. First, we need to *recognize* it. Many problems are never recognized as such. The murder of women, for example, is still hidden by the word homicide. There are very few murders of women by women—when we are murdered it is almost always by men. We have to recognize *fem*icide before we can consider why the problem exists and what can be done about it.

2. The second step involves *feeling* about the problem once it is recognized. To simply acknowledge rape, woman-battering, woman-hatred in pornography, and not *feel* outraged is another kind of unhealthy short-circuiting that goes on.

3. Third, we need to try to understand the *cause* of the problem, to analyze it, before we can take action. If, for example, our analysis of rape is that it happens rarely and a few crazy men are responsible, clearly it has very different implications than if we see rape as an extreme acting out of the socially sanctioned male role.

4. And, finally, there is the question of what to do about it. In the case of pornography it is only at step four that the issue of the pros and cons of censorship or banning comes up, and it is only one of many, many questions. Equally important are questions on the pros and cons of civil disobedience, demonstrations, boycotts, education, petitions, legal suits, or the use of more militant tactics.

In the case of pornography many people, including feminists, don't allow themselves to contemplate the first three steps—is pornography a problem, is it a woman's problem, and if so, what do I *feel* about this problem? Why does this problem exist? They simply say, "I'm against censorship of any kind!" And the meaning of the First Amendment becomes the topic of discussion. In this way the freedom of speech issue has been used, not always consciously, to freeze us into saying and doing nothing against pornography.

I would hope that whatever your particular view is on the First Amendment in relation to pornography, *you* will avoid this short-circuiting process, and you will point out to others when they are doing it. I believe that to act together we have to be in agreement regarding the first steps of recognition, feeling, and analysis. We also have to be able to agree on some actions we think are worth doing. But we don't have to agree on the banning issue.

I personally believe that portraying women being bound, raped, beaten, tortured, and killed for so-called sexual stimulation and pleasure should be banned, because I believe these portrayals encourage and condone these crimes against women in the real world. People seem to have forgotten that many individual liberties are curtailed by all societies for the perceived welfare of the whole society. Examples in the United States are polygamy, marriage or sex with individuals below a certain age, incest, cannibalism, slavery, rape, homicide, assault, and, absurdly, homosexuality. The point is that all societies have found it necessary to outlaw many forms of violent and exploitive behavior, and thereby deny individuals the right to act out certain impulses. Sometimes, of course, prejudice and ignorance are behind these restrictions, as in the case of homosexuality. But it is clear that pornography is not such a case. I do not see myself as unconcerned about free speech and the First Amendment. And I am quite happy to work with other feminists who disagree with my position on banning pornography.

However, working to obtain laws to bar violent pornography does not seem to me to be a *priority* strategy at this time. Not that I believe in any one strategy to the exclusion of others. I think a multistrategy approach is appropriate, with women choosing tactics in keeping with their politics, their skills, and their circumstances. However I do believe action is necessary—lots of it—and soon! Change is not brought about by magic spells or ardent wishes.

I want to say more about civil disobedience, a strategy that I believe would be particularly effective for women in this country at this time.

I believe this strategy has lost some of its appeal as an effective tool because its victories for Black people in this country seemed very short-lived and insufficient. But women as a caste are obviously in a very different situation from Blacks as a caste, and I believe some of these differences would make civil disobedience much more effective for women.

The depth of concern about an issue is sometimes measured by willingness to pay a price of some kind, e.g., the inconvenience and indignity of arrest. The suffragette's fight is a case in point. But if the tactics used scare and threaten the public, as happened with the Weathermen or the SLA (Symbionese Liberation Army), for example, then they are likely to backfire. Civil disobedience shows commitment and concern in a very dramatic way without making people feel so threatened.

When a minority group engages in civil disobedience, it ultimately depends on the often nonexistent goodwill of the majority whether demands are met or not. Women are not only a majority but are so integrated into the male world, particularly in the family, that we cannot be isolated and ghettoized in the same way that members of minority groups have been. If wives and girl friends are being arrested for actions against pornography, husbands and lovers are going to have to deal with it. First, they will have to take care of children and/or the household—itself a consciousness-raiser. They will be *made* to care about pornography, at least in this indirect way, because it will affect them negatively in a way they can recognize.

Another way in which civil disobedience is a particularly suitable tactic is that most of us don't relish being violent. Civil disobedience is therefore much easier for us to practice than for men.

Hence, a factor that is often a *strategic* weakness for us—our integration with the male population—becomes a strength. A factor that is often a *tactical* weakness for us—a common unwillingness to meet violence with violence—becomes a strength. And to the extent that we are badly treated by the police in this situation, we will gain all the more support for our cause. This is not to say that those of us who are less integrated into the male world—particularly lesbians—don't have an important place in this struggle. We have the advantage of not having to deal with male resistance in our homes, which is why we have played and continue to play such a key role in the Women's Movement. This also means we would probably be among the first to take the risks necessary to show how powerful civil disobedience can be as a strategy for women on this and other issues.

Women have been taking life-and-death risks for centuries. Simply by being women, we risk being raped. Many of us are hassled at work or beaten at home because we are women. Some of these risks we cannot avoid. Some risks perhaps we can. Continuing to live with a violent husband or lover, for example, is very, very risky. Indeed, marrying someone we barely know, or even someone we know very well, can be very risky in a society that does not recognize rape within marriage, and in which the interests of males are so entrenched both legally and socially. I would like to urge all of us to examine our lives and see if there isn't a way to take fewer personal risks and more political risks.

The time has surely come for us to face the viciously sexist nature of pornography; to confront this form of the male backlash; and to spread the word to other women that we will have to organize to take action, to stop this dangerous anti-women propaganda. By taking more political risks where necessary, women may need to take fewer personal risks later on.

If Men Could Menstruate—

Gloria Steinem

A white minority of the world has spent centuries conning us into thinking that a white skin makes people superior — even though the only thing it really does is make them more subject to ultraviolet rays and to wrinkles. Male human beings have built whole cultures around the idea that penis-envy is "natural" to women—though having such an unprotected organ might be said to make men vulnerable, and the power to give birth makes womb-envy at least as logical.

In short, the characteristics of the powerful, whatever they may be, are thought to be better than the characteristics of the powerless — and logic has nothing to do with it.

What would happen, for instance, if suddenly, magically, men could menstruate and women could not?

The answer is clear — menstruation would become an enviable, boast-worthy, masculine event:

Men would brag about how long and how much.

Boys would mark the onset of menses, that longed-for proof of manhood, with religious ritual and stag parties.

Congress would fund a National Institute of Dysmenorrhea to help stamp out monthly discomforts.

Sanitary supplies would be federally funded and free. (Of course, some men would still pay for the prestige of commercial brands such as John Wayne Tampons, Muhammad Ali's Rope-a-dope Pads, Joe Namath Jock Shields—"For Those Light Bachelor Days," and Robert "Baretta" Blake Maxi-Pads.)

Military men, right-wing politicians, and religious fundamentalists would cite menstruation ("men-struation") as proof that only men could serve in the Army ("you have to give blood to take blood"), occupy political office ("can women be aggressive without that steadfast cycle governed by the planet Mars?"), be priests and ministers ("how could a woman give her blood for

our sins?"), or rabbis ("without the monthly loss of impurities, women remain unclean").

Male radicals, left-wing politicians, and mystics, however, would insist that women are equal, just different; and that any woman could enter their ranks if only she were willing to self-inflict a major wound every month ("you *must* give blood for the revolution"), recognize the preeminence of menstrual issues, or subordinate her selfness to all men in their Cycle of Enlightenment.

Street guys would brag ("I'm a three-pad man") or answer praise from a buddy ("Man, you lookin' *good*!") by giving fives and saying, "Yeah, man, I'm on the rag!"

TV shows would treat the subject at length. ("Happy Days": Richie and Potsie try to convince Fonzie that he is still "The Fonz," though he has missed two periods in a row.) So would newspapers. (SHARK SCARE THREATENS MENSTRUATING MEN. JUDGE CITES MONTHLY STRESS IN PARDONING RAPIST.) And movies. (Newman and Redford in "Blood Brothers"!)

Men would convince women that intercourse was *more* pleasurable at "that time of the month." Lesbians would be said to fear blood and therefore life itself — though probably only because they needed a good menstruating man.

Of course, male intellectuals would offer the most moral and logical arguments. How could a woman master any discipline that demanded a sense of time, space, mathematics, or measurement, for instance, without that in-built gift for measuring the cycles of the moon and planets — and thus for measuring anything at all? In the rarefied fields of philosophy and religion, could women compensate for missing the rhythm of the universe? Or for their lack of symbolic death-and-resurrection every month?

Liberal males in every field would try to be kind: the fact that "these people" have no gift for measuring life or connecting to the universe, the liberals would explain, should be punishment enough.

Reprinted from Gloria Steinem, "If Men Could Menstruate," with permission.

And how would women be trained to react? One can imagine traditional women agreeing to all these arguments with a staunch and smiling masochism. ("The ERA would force housewives to wound themselves every month": Phyllis Schlafly. "Your husband's blood is as sacred as that of Jesus—and so sexy, too!": Marabel Morgan.) Reformers and Queen Bees would try to imitate men, and *pretend* to have a monthly cycle. All feminists would explain endlessly that men, too, needed to be liberated from the false idea of Martian aggressiveness, just as women needed to escape the bonds of menses-

envy. Radical feminists would add that the oppression of the nonmenstrual was the pattern for all other oppressions. ("Vampires were our first freedom fighters!") Cultural feminists would develop a bloodless imagery in art and literature. Socialist feminists would insist that only under capitalism would men be able to monopolize menstrual blood. . . .

In fact, if men could menstruate, the power justifications could probably go on forever.

If we let them.

READING 70

Decades

Catherine P. Tucker

in my thirties
my mustache became
more evident

i could
remove it
bleach it
or leave it be

as it was
in my thirties
i decided
to leave it be

as part of my growth
but bleach it
being somewhere
between wo and man

in my forties
i'm going for
blond handlebars

in my fifties
a silver goatee

and in my sixties
a Claus-like beard
that flows
across deserts.

All About Men

Nicole Hollander

Reprinted from Nicole Hollander, *Mercy, It's the Revolution and I'm in My Bathrobe,* (New York: St. Martin's Press, 1982), by permission of the publisher. Copyright 1982 by Field Enterprises, Inc.

Skin Tight Armor

Brian Campbell

"IT'S JUST NOT FAIR, I TELL YOU! SHE WEARS THAT SKIN TIGHT ARMOR AND HAS THE NERVE TO ACCUSE ME OF SEXUAL HARASSMENT!"

Reprinted from Brian Campbell, "Skin Tight Armor," in The Ohio State University *Lantern,* by permission of the cartoonist.

"Splitsville"

Frank Baginski and Reynolds Dodson

Specism: The Dialectics of Doghood

Jessica Celiasister

(This article was "pawed" by the "pet" dog of an anonymous Women's Studies professor.)

The liberation movements of the 1960s brought the problems of racism, classism, and sexism out into the open, and the 1970s added awareness of heterosexism. As we enter the 1980s under the cloud of Reagan's election and the commercial exploitation of Benji, the time for a thorough and dialectical analysis of specism has arrived. As every door at The Ohio State University points out, "Every dog has his day." Need I point out either the sexism or the specism embodied in this infamous quotation? The bane of my and every other dogs' life is that oft-heard refrain: "No dogs allowed." Is it any wonder that every small town and city sprouts "Beware of the Dog" signs? Every oppressed group responds in whatever manner possible in an exploited situation: in the 1960s, Black people rioted in the cities, women throughout history have earned the reputation of poisoners of the men who oppress them, and dogs bite. Oppression breeds violence. But that is not my point.

Think for the moment of a dog's life. (Even the language is tainted: "It's a dog's life," "dog-eared," "dogged," "cur," "bitch," etc.) Let me hasten to add here that I do not mean to downplay the oppression of my sister cats, birds, hamsters, rabbits, and whatever other sisters have been brought into human homes occupying the status of "pets." If I have learned anything at all from the women's movement, and I pride myself on having learned quite a lot, it is that we must do our own work, while always supporting the struggles of other oppressed sisters. It is my hope that some interested cat sister will take up the flag of cat liberation, that my work will be of theoretical use, and that we can work together in the common

Reprinted from Jessica Celiasister, "Specism: The Dialectics of Doghood," by permission of the author.

cause of liberation from the oppression of specism.

I would like to focus in this essay on the interaction among all the different forms of oppression: sexism, racism, classism, heterosexism, specism. Developing a model for understanding the relationships among all these oppressions—a model that will prove useful in developing goals and strategies for the revolution—is my eventual aim. This paper is meant only as an introduction to the problem.

We know ever so much about class-based oppression. And we know that traditional stratification models have little relevance for women. A woman takes her class not only from her relationship to the means of production, but also from her father's or husband's relationship to the means of production. Dogs have no relationship to the means of production. Even Benji and Lassie (a male dog passing as female) and Rin Tin Tin, who no doubt earned and earn enormous sums for their "masters," own none of their wealth. Any one of them, found in Kroger's parking lot, would go straight to the pound like anyone else, and curtains it would be after five days. Their work, their art, their wealth would mean nothing. Just as any woman can be raped, regardless of class, so too can any dog be snatched by the dog catcher.

Racism interacts with specism in an interesting way. Eugenics, once the backbone of both the American nativist movement and Nazi racism, is no longer respectable in liberal circles. But just go to the home of an ACLU member who breeds dogs and you will hear blood-curdling statements about pedigree, stock, studs, papers, and so on. Breedism is the form racism takes in specist oppression. It determines a dog's class and a dog's worth (bought and sold on the slave block), it determines whether a dog can enter a dog show (shades of the Miss

America Pageant protest of 1968!), it determines whether a dog in the pound will be adopted, it determines a dog's reproductive life. "Pedigreed" dogs are ruthlessly "bred" in response to the demand of the capitalist market, with disastrous health consequences—congenital hip displacement, bad backs, and so on. While we "mutts" avoid forced breeding and the dangers of excessive over-breeding, life for us is, as they say, no bed of roses. Charges are hurled against those of us in the movement to the effect that we are unsatisfied because we are ugly, neurotic, unloved. It is true that many of us are "misfits," according to society's standards, outcasts because of our lack of "breed," but we want to liberate all of our sisters, even the poodles with red toe-nail polish and pink ribbons who feel pampered and protected. False consciousness must be done away with. We must stop being petted.

I am getting awfully tired right now, so let me finish quickly. The sexist elements of our oppression are obvious. Ponder, if you will, the connection between the confinement of women in the domestic sphere and the "domestication" of the dog. We have no control over our reproductive powers. I myself had a hysterectomy at six months; as it happened, it was what I preferred, but I could not have stopped it if I had felt otherwise. As a matter of fact, people who get their dogs from the "pound" must sign an agreement to the effect that they will have their dog "spayed" (distasteful word!). The institution of heterosexism is pervasive in the dog world as well. Sexuality is totally out of a dog's control. We do not own our bodies. Furthermore, we are isolated in private homes and, if we are valuable commodities, subjected to forced heterosexual relations.

Let me just say in conclusion that the theoretical connections between and among the different forms of oppression seem clear. They need to be developed and worked into a comprehensive theory that will take account of all aspects of oppression, including sizism. It is my hope that our movement, which is yet young, will move quickly, since we have the distinct disadvantage of a short lifespan. Socialism is not the answer: look at the situation of dogs in China. Radical feminism still has a ways to go: note the request in a local newsletter that dogs not be brought to meetings since they are "disruptive." We must seek alliances but we must do our work ourselves. Dogs of the world unite! We have nothing to lose but our leashes!

Introduction: Racism and Sexual Politics in the Movement

The American women's movement, historically, has been comprised largely of white middle-class married women; its goals, style, and strategies have tended to reflect the interests of its membership base. By the mid-1970s the most crucial question facing the movement was whether or not it could speak to the concerns of the mass of women in American society; that is, not only to white middle-class married women, but also to women of color, lesbians, and working-class women. In addition, men who were interested in altering the social arrangements between the sexes began to ask what they might do to redress the political wrongs articulated by feminists, and what role they might play in the movement. In this section, we shall examine crucial internal issues facing the feminist movement. We shall be asking whether the movement is capable of developing a membership base diverse enough, and an ideology and politics broad enough, to transform all of the social institutions which sustain and perpetuate sex-based inequality.

In the first article, "Notes for Yet Another Paper on Black Feminism, or Will the Real Enemy Please Stand Up?", Barbara Smith analyzes what she calls the "triple oppressions"—racism, sexism, and capitalism—and demonstrates how these systems function together to oppress Black and Third World women. She argues that in order for women of color to join ranks with the largely white middle-class women's movement, the movement must begin to understand and to address issues of racism and classism both within its own ranks and in the society as a whole. From the perspective of Black and Third World women, the most controversial argument advanced by Smith is that an analysis of Black women's oppression must take into account that Black women are oppressed not only by racism and classism, but also by Black men. Mirtha Quintanales, in the selection "I Paid Very Hard for My Immigrant Ignorance," raises the issues of race, ethnicity, class and affectional preferences, the conceptual and pragmatic difficulties of the category "Third World women" and "women of color," and shares some of her own personal struggles as a Latina Feminist. "The Bridge Poem," by Donna Kate Rushin, describes how it feels—as a woman of color— to be torn between various groups and social identities, and to have to be all things to all people.

356

In the next selection, "Not for Lesbians Only," Charlotte Bunch discusses yet another issue which has divided women in the movement and which has often led lesbian women to believe that there is no place for them in the feminist movement: the gay–straight split. Bunch argues that lesbian-feminism should not be viewed as a political analysis and struggle "for lesbians only," but rather as a fight to be engaged in by all women against heterosexual domination as one of the major institutions of all women's oppression.

The last two selections focus on the role that the men's movement can/should/is playing in altering the social world we have inherited. Susan Griffin's poem, "An Answer to a Man's Question: What Can I Do About Women's Liberation?,"suggests that if a man were to experience, himself, the physical and emotional constraints of existence as a woman in America, he would not have to ask that question. More sociologically, Joseph H. Pleck in his article "Men's Power with Women, Other Men, and Society: A Men's Movement Analysis" analyzes the contribution which a men's movement analysis makes to a feminist understanding both of men and power, and of the existing power relations between women and men.

Notes for Yet Another Paper on Black Feminism, or Will the Real Enemy Please Stand Up?

Barbara Smith

This paper was initially written in order to clarify some ideas for myself, as a result of attending an International Women's Day Program in 1976, sponsored by a Third World mixed-left sectarian group. That day the analysis of feminism was constantly rejected, the reality of patriarchy denied, and the phrase "men are not the enemy" repeated many times.

I do not consider the following to be anything but notes which have contributed to my own political thought and may contribute to the making of a more comprehensive analysis at another time. It is not high-level theory but it is based upon a Black feminist evaluation of facts.

Black and other Third World women's relationships to the systems of oppression in this society are, by definition, different from those of other oppressed groups who do not experience both racial and sexual oppression at the same time. The effect of this double, actually triple oppression because of class, is not merely arithmetic—one plus one plus one—but geometric.* There is such a thing as racial-sexual oppression which is neither solely racial nor solely sexual. A good example is forced sterilization of Third World women: racism and imperialism determine the racial or nationality group to be oppressed and sexism and misogyny determine that women are the appropriate targets for abuse.

The fact that we, as Third World women, face oppression specific to our combined racial, sexual, and class status means that we will also develop specific theory and practice in order to fight our oppression. Inherent in

Black feminist analysis is the assumption that the white segments of the women's movement must also address, understand, and fight racism inside their ranks and in the society as a whole.

* * * *

Feminism is potentially the most threatening of movements to Black and other Third World people because it makes it absolutely essential that we examine the way we live, how we treat each other and what we believe. It calls into question the most basic assumption about our existence and this is the idea that biological, i.e., sexual identity determines all, that it is the rationale for power relationships as well as all other levels of human identity and action. An irony is that among Third World people biological determinism is rejected and fought against when it is applied to race, but generally unquestioned when it applies to sex.

Rigid sex roles, sexism, and violence towards women seem entrenched in Black society and culture, perhaps even more deeply than in white society and culture as indicated by the fact that there has been so much resistance to the examination of our oppression until this point. Black and other Third World women are sexually oppressed every day of our lives, but because we are also oppressed racially and economically, sexual oppression has not been considered a priority. It has been rendered falsely invisible.

By naming sexual oppression as a problem it would appear that we would have to identify as threatening a group we have heretofore assumed to be our allies—Black men. This seems to be one of the major stumbling blocks to beginning to analyze the sexual relationships/sexual politics of our lives. The phrase "men are not the enemy" dismisses feminism and the reality of patriarchy in one breath and also overlooks some major realities. If we cannot entertain the idea that some men *are* the enemy,

Reprinted from Barbara Smith, "Notes for Yet Another Paper on Black Feminism, or Will the Real Enemy Please Stand Up?" in *Conditions, Five: The Black Women's Issue,* ed. Lorraine Bethel and Barbara Smith, and in *Conditions, Two,* Autumn 1979, Box 56, Van Brunt Station, Brooklyn, NY 11215, by permission of the author.

*I would now also include Lesbian oppression as a force in Black women's lives. Not integrating an analysis of heterosexism into this paper when I wrote it in 1976 is a major drawback.

especially white men and in a different sense Black men too, then we will never be able to figure out all the reasons why, for example, we are being beaten up every day, why we are sterilized against our wills, why we are being raped by our neighbors, why we are pregnant at age twelve and why we are at home on welfare with more children than we can support or care for. Acknowledging the sexism of Black men does not mean that we become "man-haters" or necessarily eliminate them from our lives. What it does mean is that we must struggle for a different basis of interaction with them. That if we care about them and ourselves we will not permit ourselves to be degraded or manipulated.

I think there are many problems inherent in trying to reach a viable Black feminist analysis of what goes on in Black women's lives. I want to briefly discuss two of them here.

The first is economics. I am in essential agreement with the Marxist analysis that it is our material conditions which most clearly affect what we are able to do in our lives. These determine to a huge extent the content and quality of our lives: for example, the amount of access we have to the basic necessities of food, clothing, housing and health care as well as what we are able to think, what we are taught to believe and what we are allowed to do. If, for example, a poor Black woman were no longer poor, she probably would no longer be a welfare mother. She would still, however, be a mother, suffering the sole responsibility for the care of her children, the isolation and overwork inherent in that role under patriarchy. She also might very well still be raped, beaten, sterilized, or pregnant against her will since these kinds of oppression are not solely motivated by economic causes. She would also still be Black whatever else occurred. Sexism and racism are inherently part of all that happens to Black women, indeed are just as central to our material conditions as class oppression.

I realize that little will change in our lives until capitalism is destroyed and economic conditions and relationships radically changed. I also realize that while struggling for survival we cannot always examine and fight all the forces that make our lives intolerable. But this does not mean that these forces do not exist. Therefore those of us who try to examine and fight these forces must not hesitate to do so merely in order to maintain political "correctness" and a false sense of solidarity. I do not believe that socialism will resolve political conflicts that do not spring solely from an economic root. It may provide an atmosphere in which these situations can be criticized and worked upon, but it does not appear to contain the answers to nor an analysis of phenomena which are based more directly in realms other than the economic. I think it is essential to struggle against sexism and racism just as we struggle against economic oppression. These are not trivial oppressions but very real ones which pre-date capitalism and therefore will not necessarily disappear when capitalism disappears.

The second major problem is how we think about men. White males are the primary oppressor group in American society. They oppress Black people, they oppress working people, they oppress women, they oppress Black women. They also oppress each other. To say that men are not the enemy, that it is instead the ruling class is sophistry. In this country, white men *are* the ruling class, the ruling class *are* white men. It is true that not all white men are capitalists or possess extreme class privilege, but it is safe to assume that 99 44/100% of them are racists and sexists. It is not just rich and powerful capitalists who inhibit and destroy life. Rapists, murderers, lynchers, and ordinary bigots do too and exercise very real and violent power because of their white-male privilege.

One can endlessly make fine distinctions about who the oppressors really are. For me a workable and general definition of an oppressor is the person(s) who takes away your freedom. This means the person may be of the same class as you (your husband, your parents, your neighbors, strangers); the same race as you (your husband, your parents, your neighbors, strangers); and even the same sex as you (a racist or class exploiter). The identity of the oppressors we face in our day-to-day lives is fluid and constantly changes. We may all oppress someone. Refusing to name persons as oppressors but instead using a remote concept means that people do not really have to be responsible for what they do, that any negative action is excusable because it's really the system's fault anyway. When your working-class white husband beats you, he is your direct oppressor. Your body is not being mutilated by the "ruling class." The ruling class of course gives full approval and support to what your husband is doing, because among other reasons they are at home beating their wives, "girlfriends," mothers, sisters and daughters too. When the poor Black man on your block rapes you, he is your direct oppressor. You are not being raped by the "ruling class." The ruling class again approves of your rape because they are in every sense raping Black and white women too, but it is not the ruling class who is negating your freedom and brutalizing you at that moment. When your white employer mistreats you as you clean up her home, it is not the ruling class who is oppressing you, it's her. Of course the white man who pays you your inadequate wages, i.e., her husband, may be a member of the ruling class, but it is more likely that he is an ordinary middle-income racist male who also mistreats his wife. Your own Black sister who stays at home with her children is not getting paid anything for doing the same kind of work you do, i.e., housework.

White males are the group who most often have the opportunity to oppress everybody, but Black and other Third World men can oppress women too and do so quite effectively and cruelly. One thing that Black feminism does is to be quite specific about naming the oppressor/enemy. This is another way of saying that the personal is political, a reality that many people do not want to accept. It is much less threatening on a gut level to call the oppressor the "Ruling Class" and to ignore everything and everyone else who is making your life intolerable and unfree. Talking about the ruling class is in many ways a male construct. For Third World working-class men it may be more nearly accurate to say that it is the ruling class who exploit and dominate their lives. For Third World women who do not experience the same reality or suffer the same oppression as men, this concept is incomplete and until this is acknowledged women will continue to be exploited. The man who beats you is a member of the ruling class in your own home.

Let me make clear that I am not saying that feminism will solve everything, that it is the only road to "salvation." Black feminism, if it is to provide sound analysis of Black women's situation, must incorporate an understanding of economic oppression and racism as well as of sexism and heterosexism. What I am saying is that a deeply serious analysis of sexual oppression cannot be left out of revolutionary politics, that to ignore the pervasive and killing results of sexism as a trivial concern of Black and other Third World women is naive and false. As women all of us know how our lives have been undermined and broken because we are women, whether we consciously acknowledge it or not. This is why those of us who are Black and feminists must be committed to struggle and to learn with each other so that we can better understand the nature of the triple oppression we face. Only when we begin to understand and to practice the politics that come out of this understanding will we have a hope of becoming truly free.

March 8, 1976

Author's Postscript
I wanted to share with readers how I feel and have always felt about ". . . Will the Real Enemy Please Stand Up?" Saying what I've said and having it in print scares me. This is because the essay so specifically addresses in a critical way the reality of violence against Black women by Black men. This has been a deeply taboo subject judged politically "incorrect" in different historical eras and by people of many different political persuasions. Even with the murders of twelve Black women in my own community (Boston) in a four-month period this year, I still fear that what I've said here will be misunderstood and dismissed by those who most need to hear it. Yet, I stand by the accuracy and integrity of my analysis and have always felt that it belonged in a Black feminist publication. I wanted readers to know that writing this and having it published were difficult and challenging decisions for me.

I Paid Very Hard for My Immigrant Ignorance

Mirtha Quintanales

Columbus, Ohio
January, 1980

Dear Barbara (Smith),

Thanks for your letter. I can appreciate your taking the time to write. It can get *so* difficult for busy people to keep up with correspondence . . . I only hope that you have taken some time to rest, gather your energies. I'm just beginning to emerge from a several-week period of semi-hermitdom myself. I, too, was exhausted. Too much work too many responsibilities—often the worry of not moving fast enough, or too fast to have any kind of an impact. After a brief peaceful interlude, the pressures are beginning to build again, Oh well . . .

I wanted to tell you about my visit to San Francisco, about coming together with my Latina lesbian/feminist sisters. The joy and the pain of finding each other, of realizing how long we've "done without," of how difficult it's going to be to heal ourselves, to find our voices . . . But how perfectly wonderful to finally have a family, a community. Yet I find that there is too much to tell. Cannot easily compress it all in a letter. How I wish that we could meet and talk! So much of the Black lesbian/feminist experience speaks to our own . . . I passed around all the literature you'd handed out at conferences—including Conditions 5. And the Latina sisters were amazed. Lorraine Bethel's "What Chou Mean *We* White Girl?" was especially telling . . . Many of our feelings given form, meaning. Please let her know that her work has been very helpful to us—particularly in sorting out what we want and don't want in our relationships with white, mainstream American feminists. Yes, there is a lot we can learn from each other.

Reprinted from Mirtha Quintanales, "I Paid Very Hard for My Immigrant Ignorance," in *This Bridge Called My Back: Writings by Radical Women of Color,* ed. Gloria Auzaldua and Cherrie Moraga (Watertown, MA: Persephone Press, 1981), by permission of the author.

But Barbara, I am worried. At the moment I am in the process of organizing a roundtable for the NWSA* conference, on the topic of racial and ethnic minority lesbians in the U.S. There are two other women involved—a Greek friend of mine from Berkeley, and a Black woman from San Francisco. And I feel the tension building. The Greek woman's many attempts to "connect" with the Third World lesbians and "Women of Color" (most poignantly at last year's conference) have been met with outright rejection. Unfortunately, being loud, aggressive and very Greek-identified, she has found a great deal of rejection in white, mainstream lesbian/feminist circles as well. Clearly she does not fit there either.

The Black woman's commitments, from what I can gather, are understandably with Third World women, women of color. And I am quite uncomfortably in the middle. As a Third World, Caribbean woman I understand what it means to have grown up "colonized" in a society built on slavery and the oppression of imperialist forces. As an immigrant and a cultural minority woman who happens to be white-skinned, I empathize with the pain of ethnic invisibility and the perils of passing (always a very tenuous situation—since acknowledgment of ethnic ties is inevitably accompanied by stereotyping, prejudice *and* various kinds of discrimination—the problem is not just personal, but "systemic," "political"—one more reality of American "life"). How to reconcile these different kinds of "primary emergencies": race and culture? Of course this kind of conflict tends to obscure the issue of *class* and its relationship to race and ethnicity so important for the understanding of the dilemma.

*National Women's Studies Association

Not all Third World women are "women of color"—if by this concept we mean exclusively "non-white." I am only one example. And not all women of color are really Third World—if this term is only used in reference to underdeveloped or developing societies (especially those not allied with any superpower). Clearly then it would be difficult to justify referring to Japanese women, who are women of color, as Third World women. Yet, if we extend the concept of Third World to include internally "colonized" racial and ethnic minority groups in this country, so many different kinds of groups could be conceivably included, that the crucial issue of social and institutional racism and its historic tie to slavery in the U.S. could get diluted, lost in the shuffle. The same thing would likely happen if we extended the meaning of "women of color" to include all those women in this country who are victims of prejudice and discrimination (in many respects), but who nevertheless hold racial privileges and may even be racists.

I don't know what to think anymore. Things begin to get even more complicated when I begin to consider that many of us who identify as "Third World" or "Women of Color", have grown up as or are fast becoming "middle-class" and highly educated, and therefore more privileged than many of our white, poor and working-class sisters. Sometimes I get angry at my lover because she does not seem to relate to my being a "Cuban" lesbian. And yet, can I really relate to the fact that she grew up in a very small town, in a working-class family—with little money, few other resources, little encouragement to get an education, etc.? Yes . . . and no. There have been times in my life when my family had little money or food. There have been times in my life when I lived from day to day not knowing if I would be alive "tomorrow"—not knowing really how it felt to plan for "next month," or "next year."

Yet, even though I grew up having to heat my bathwater and sleep in a very lumpy bed, even though I grew up often being ashamed of bringing my friends home because our furniture was old and dilapidated, I went to private schools, spent summers at the beach, traveled, had plenty of toys and books to read; took music and dancing lessons, went horseback riding—my parents being very conscious of, and being very *able* to give us the best (if not always in terms of material comforts) that their middle-class resources gave them access to—including the services of a long string of nurse-maids (my mother worked, and in Cuba often the *maids* had maids—even if it meant putting little girls to work as servants and baby-tenders—economic exploitation galore!).

Yes, I have suffered in this country. I have been the victim of blatant prejudice and institutional discrimination. As an ethnic minority woman and a lesbian I have lived in the margins, in fear, isolated, disconnected, silent and in pain. Nevertheless, those early years of relatively "blissful" middle-class childhood (although I have to say that after age 7 it was *hell*—political violence and death always lurking) in my own country where I was simply part of the "mainstream" if not a little better off because of my father's professional status, have served me as a "cushion" throughout my life. Even in the United States, as an essentially middle-class (and white-skinned) woman, I have had "opportunities" (or have known how to make them for myself), that my very white, working-class American lover has never had. Having managed to graduate from college (one out of three in her graduating high school class who managed to make it *to* college) against tremendous odds, she is still struggling with the fact that she may never really learn the ropes of surviving well in mainstream, middle-class American society. And need I add that mainstream white, middle-class American feminism is as insensitive to her needs as it is to mine?

I realize that I cannot fight everybody's battles. But need I create false enemies in order to wage my own? I am a bit concerned when a Latina lesbian sister generalizes about/puts down the "white woman"—especially if she herself has white skin. In the midst of this labeling, might she not dismiss the fact of her own white privileges—regardless of her identification with Black, Native American, and other Third World women of color? Might she not dismiss the fact that she may often be far better off than many white women? I cannot presume to know what it is really like to be a Black woman in America, to be racially oppressed. I cannot presume to know what it is really like to grow up American "White Trash" and destitute.

But I am also a bit concerned when a Black sister generalizes about/dismisses all non-black women, or all women who are not strict "women of color" or strictly "Third World." If you are not WASP in this country, if you or your family have known the immigrant experience or ghetto life, you are likely to be very much acquainted with the social, economic, political reality of internal colonization. Yes, racism is a BIG MONSTER we all need to contend with—regardless of our skin color and ethnic affiliation. But I think we need to keep in mind that in this country, in this world, racism is used *both* to create false differences among us *and* to mask very very significant ones—cultural economic, political . . . And yes, those who have been racially oppressed must create separatist spaces to explore the meaning of their experiences—to heal themselves, to gather their energies, their strength, to develop their own voices, to build their armies. And yes, those of us who have not been victims of racial oppression must come to terms with our own racism, our own complicity with this system that discriminates and oppresses on the basis of skin color and body features. And of course it would be irresponsible liberal folly to propose that social and institutional racism could be eliminated by simply "becoming" personally non-racist, by becoming "integrated" in our private lives . . . How ridiculous for white folk to think that a long history of slavery and every other kind of oppression, that an *ongoing* and *insidious* reality of social, economic, political exploitation could be magically transcended through a few individual choices . . . And even if everybody's skin should suddenly turn black, it would be quite impossible to truly know what it means to have grown up—generation after generation—Black and female in America. Of course our skin is not likely to "turn," and so regardless of how "conscious" we claim to be of the "Black experience" in America, we shall always be limited by our own history and the reality of our white skin and the privileges it automatically confers on us.

Ironically, when a Black American sister (or anyone for that matter) puts me, or other ethnic women of this society in the same category with the socially dominant White American Woman on the basis of lighter-than-black skin color, she is in fact denying my history, my culture, my identity, my very being, my pain and my struggle. She too is being *personally* racist. When she fails to recognize that the "social privileges" of lighter-than-black ethnic-minority lesbians in this society are almost totally dependent on our denial of who we are, on our *ethnic death,* she also falls prey to the racist mythology that color differences are the end-all indications of social inequality. That those who happen to have the "right" skin color are not only all alike but all hold the same social privileges. Yes, lighter-than-black skin color *may* confer on some ethnic minority women the option of becoming "assimilated," "integrated" in mainstream American society. But is this really a privilege when it always means having to become invisible, ghost-like, identity-less, community-less, totally alienated? The perils of "passing" as white American are perils indeed. It should be easy enough at least for *lesbians* to understand the meaning of being and yet not being, of "merging" and yet remaining utterly alone and in the margins of our society.

And while it is true that a lesbian/feminist community and culture have emerged, while it is true that Black, Latina and other Third World/lesbians "of color" have begun to speak up, it is not true that we have yet engaged in a truly un-biased, un-prejudiced *dialogue.* We are still measuring each other by the yardstick of the White, Capitalist, Imperialist, Racist American Patriarch. We are still seeing radical differences when they don't exist and not seeing them when they are critical. And most disastrously, we are failing to recognize much of what we *share.* Is it not possible for us to recognize, respect and settle our differences; to validate our various groups' struggles and need for separate spaces, and yet to open our eyes to the fact that divided we are only likely to succeed at defeat?

It is pure folly to think that a small group of Latina or Black or Chinese American lesbians can, on its own, create a feminist revolution. It is pure folly to think that middle-class wasp feminists can do so . . .

Barbara, I ache to live with and love with my Latina lesbian/feminist sisters—to speak "Spanglish," to eat arroz con frijoles, to dance to the salsa, to openly talk sex and flirt with one another; to secretly pray to Yemayá, Chango, Oshun, and the Virgen de Guadalupe. I run to them for refuge, for dear life!

But when I meet you and other Black lesbian sisters—and am moved by what we seem to share, I ache for you also. I spend time with Stacy (Anastasia) and other Southern European/North African/Mediterranean lesbian sisters—and am stirred by what we seem to have in common, I feel deep yearning for them . . . I read the words of other ethnic American lesbian sisters and I find that I understand them and want to share in these women's lives. And I live, love and work with working-class sisters. Have lived, loved and worked in the poor urban ghettos of Chicago and Boston. Have spent some time in the poor, rural, isolated mountains of New Mexico. Have traveled to Latin American countries, to India, Thailand, Taiwan, Hong-Kong, Japan—feeling the pain of my poor and hard-working sisters—struggling against all odds to stay alive, to live with dignity. I cannot sleep sometimes—haunted by the memories of such all-encompassing poverty—the kind of poverty that even poor Americans could not begin to conceive. India. India was the unraveling. How insignificant our troubles seem in the United States . . . How ridiculously small my own struggles . . . I don't feel guilt or shame, but this nausea . . . To find us squabbling over who may or may not be called a feminist, who may or may not join or take part in this or that particular political group, etc, etc. The privilege of having feminist "groups"—most women in the world just eat shit. And lesbians—who really knows the fate of most lesbians in the world, especially the Third World?

Is it not possible for all of us here in America to turn *right now* to *all* the sisters of the world—to form a common, human-woman-lesbian bond?

I have lost some sleep lately pondering over this race/culture/class problem . . . We've got to do *something*! Many of us Latinas are non-white—as a matter of fact, most of us are racially mixed to various degrees. Ask a Black or "mulatto" Puerto Rican woman what her identity is though, and most likely she will tell you "Puerto Rican." All Chinese American women are non-white. But ask any of them what her identity is. She will not tell you "yellow," she will tell you Chinese, or Chinese American. Many African peoples are "Black," but ask a Nigerian, an Ethiopian, etc. what her identity is, and she will tell you "Nigerian," or "Ethiopian," or whatever . . . Obviously "Black Culture" is an American phenomenon. Many of us don't really understand this. I know I didn't for a long time. When I first came to this country I just assumed that Black people were simply American (for that matter I just assumed *all* Americans shared the same "American Culture"). I grew up with people of all kinds of skin-color—but we were all *Cuban* and understood each other, even though we *could* recognize the most minute "color differences," even though we could recognize class differences. How was I supposed to know—given the propaganda—that there was no such thing as a "melting pot"? How was I supposed to know that racism was so

widespread and so deeply ingrained in American society? I was *shocked* in my sophomore year in college when several Black women implied that I was a racist when I said I could not figure out what was different about being Black or Yellow, or White, or Red in the United States. I could understand not knowing about a "culture," but not knowing about a "race"? Was "race" per se so important? Was it really linked to a "culture"? This was a weird notion to me indeed!

Well I paid very hard for my immigrant ignorance. I'm still paying—even though I have learned a great deal since then about American sub-cultures and about American racism. Many of my Latina sisters have had similar experiences, and the big question is always there—Will we ever really be accepted by our Black American sisters? I cannot really convey the pain—especially in those of us who *are* Afro-Hispanic-American but light skinned—of seeing so much of ourselves in, of being so drawn to African-American women, and yet feeling that we are likely to be denied a connection, to be rejected. The fucking irony of it! Racism. It has so thoroughly poisoned Americans of all colors that many of us can simply not see beyond it. I'm sorry about this long letter Barbara—especially this last part. But I have not been able to get over this pain. I used to have this recurrent dream (for years) that I would alternately become black and white and black and white over and over and over again . . . It felt really good. But I've never quite figured out all of what it meant . . . Well, take care Barbara.

In sisterhood,
Mirtha

The Bridge Poem

Donna Kate Rushin

I've had enough
I'm sick of seeing and touching
Both sides of things
Sick of being the damn bridge for everybody

Nobody
Can talk to anybody
Without me
Right?

I explain my mother to my father my father to my
 little sister
My little sister to my brother my brother to the
 white feminists
The white feminists to the Black church folks the
 Black church folks
To the ex-hippies the ex-hippies to the Black
 separatists the
Black separatists to the artists the artists to my
 friends' parents . . .

Then
I've got to explain myself
To everybody

I do more translating
Than the Gawdamn U.N.

Forget it
I'm sick of it

I'm sick of filling in your gaps

Sick of being your insurance against
The isolation of your self-imposed limitations

Sick of being the crazy at your holiday dinners
Sick of being the odd one at your Sunday Brunches
Sick of being the sole Black friend to 34 individual
 white people

Find another connection to the rest of the world
Find something else to make you legitimate
Find some other way to be political and hip

I will not be the bridge to your womanhood
Your manhood
Your human-ness

I'm sick of reminding you not to
Close off too tight for too long

I'm sick of mediating with your worst self
On behalf of your better selves

I am sick
Of having to remind you
To breathe
Before you suffocate
Your own fool self

Forget it
Stretch or drown
Evolve or die

The bridge I must be
Is the bridge to my own power
I must translate
My own fears
Mediate
My own weaknesses

I must be the bridge to nowhere
But my true self
And then
I will be useful

Reprinted from Donna Kate Rushin, "The Bridge Poem," in *This Bridge Called My Back: Writings by Radical Women of Color,* ed. Gloria Auzaldua and Cherrie Moraga (Watertown, MA: Persephone Press, 1981), by permission of the author.

Not for Lesbians Only

Charlotte Bunch

*The following is an expanded and revised version
of a speech given at the Socialist Feminist Conference, Antioch College, Yellow Springs, Ohio,
July 5, 1975. Many of the ideas expressed here
about lesbian feminist politics were first developed
several years ago in The Furies. Nevertheless, I am
continually discovering that most feminists, including many lesbians, have little idea what lesbian
feminist politics is. This speech takes those basic
political ideas and develops them further, particularly as they relate to socialist feminism.*

I am listed in your program as Charlotte Bunch-Weeks, a
rather ominous slip of the tongue (or slip in historical
timing) that reflects a subject so far avoided at this conference that I, for one, want to talk about.

Five years ago, when I *was* Charlotte Bunch-Weeks,
and straight, and married to a man, I was also a socialist
feminist. When I left the man and the marriage, I also
left the newly developing socialist feminist movement — because, for one reason, my politics then, as now,
were inextricably joined with the way I lived my personal,
my daily life. With men, with male politics, I was a
socialist; with women, engaged in the articulation of
women's politics, I became a lesbian feminist — and, in the
gay–straight split, a lesbian feminist separatist.

It's that gay–straight split that no one here seems to
want to remember — and I bring it up now, not because I
want to relive a past painful to all concerned, but because
it is an essential part of our political history which, if ignored, will eventually force lesbians to withdraw again
from other political women. There were important
political reasons for that split, reasons explicitly related to
the survival of lesbians — and those reasons and the problems causing them are still with us. It is important —
especially for political groups who wish to give credence

and priority to lesbian issues — to remember why
separatism happened, why it is not a historical relic but
still vital to the ongoing debate over lesbianism and
feminism.

In my own personal experience, I, and the other
women of The Furies collective, left the women's movement because it had been made clear to us that there was
no space to develop a lesbian feminist politics and life
style without constant and nonproductive conflict with
heterosexual fear, antagonism, and insensitivity. This was
essentially the same experience shared by many other lesbian feminists at about the same time around the country.
What the women's movement could not accept then — and
still finds it difficult to accept — is that lesbianism is
political: this is the essence of lesbian feminist politics.
Sounds simple. Yet most feminists still view lesbianism as
a personal decision or, at best, as a civil rights concern or
a cultural phenomenon. Lesbianism is more than a question of civil rights and culture, although the daily
discrimination against lesbians is real and its alleviation
through civil libertarian reforms is important. Similarly,
although lesbianism is a primary force in the emergence
of a dynamic women's culture, it is much more. Lesbian
feminist politics is a political critique of the institution
and ideology of heterosexuality as a cornerstone of male
supremacy. It is an extension of the analysis of sexual
politics to an analysis of sexuality itself as an institution.
It is a commitment to women as a political group, which
is the basis of a political/economic strategy leading to
power for women, not just an "alternative community."

There are many lesbians still who feel that there is no
place in socialist feminist organizations in particular, or
the women's movement in general, for them to develop
that politics or live that life. Because of this, I am still, in
part, a separatist; but I don't want to be a total separatist
again; few who have experienced that kind of isolation
believe it is the ultimate goal of liberation. Since unity and
coalition seem necessary, the question for me is unity on
what terms? with whom? and around what politics? For
instance, to unify the lesbian feminist politics developed

---

within the past four years with socialist feminism requires more than token reference to queers. It requires an acknowledgement of lesbian feminist analysis as central to understanding and ending woman's oppression.

The heart of lesbian feminist politics, let me repeat, is a recognition that heterosexuality as an institution and an ideology is a cornerstone of male supremacy. Therefore, women interested in destroying male supremacy, patriarchy, and capitalism must, equally with lesbians, fight heterosexual domination—or we will never end female oppression. This is what I call "the heterosexual question"—it is *not* the lesbian question.

Although lesbians have been the quickest to see the challenge to heterosexuality as a necessity for feminists' survival, straight feminists are not precluded from examining and fighting against heterosexuality. The problem is that few have done so. This perpetuates lesbian fears that women remaining tied to men prevents them from seeing the function of heterosexuality and acting to end it. It is not lesbianism (women's ties to women) but heterosexuality (women's ties to men), and thus men themselves, which divides women politically and personally. This is the "divisiveness" of the lesbian issue to the women's movement. We won't get beyond it by demanding that lesbians retreat, politics in hand, back into the closet. We will only get beyond it by struggling over the institutional and ideological analysis of lesbian feminism. We need to discover what lesbian consciousness means for any woman, just as we struggle to understand what class or race consciousness means for women of any race or class. And we must develop strategies that will destroy the political institutions that oppress us.

It is particularly important for those at this conference to understand that heterosexuality—as an ideology and as an institution—upholds all those aspects of female oppression discussed here. For example, heterosexuality is basic to our oppression in the workplace. When we look at how women are defined and exploited as secondary, marginal workers, we recognize that this definition assumes that all women are tied to men. I mention the workplace because it upset me yesterday at the economics panel that no one made that connection; and further, no one recognized that a high percentage of women workers are lesbians and therefore their relationship to, and attitudes toward, work are fundamentally different from those assumed by straight workers. It is obvious that heterosexuality upholds the home, housework, the family as both a personal and economic unit. It is apparently not

so obvious that the whole framework of heterosexuality defines our lives, that it is fundamental to the negative self-image and self-hatred of women in this society. Lesbian feminism is based on a rejection of male definitions of our lives and is therefore crucial to the development of a positive woman-identified identity, of redefining who we are supposed to be in every situation, including the workplace.

What is that definition? Basically, heterosexuality means men first. That's what it's all about. It assumes that every woman is heterosexual; that every woman is defined by and is the property of men. Her body, her services, her children belong to men. If you don't accept that definition, you're a queer—no matter who you sleep with; if you do not accept that definition in this society, you're queer. The original imperialist assumption of the right of men to the bodies and services of women has been translated into a whole variety of forms of domination throughout this society. And as long as people accept that initial assumption—and question everything *but* that assumption—it is impossible to challenge the other forms of domination.

What makes heterosexuality work is heterosexual privilege—and if you don't have a sense of what that privilege is, I suggest that you go home and announce to everybody that you know—a roommate, your family, the people you work with—everywhere you go—that you're a queer. Try being a queer for a week. Do not walk out on the street with men; walk only with women, especially at night, for example. For a whole week, experience life as if you were a lesbian, and I think you will know what heterosexual privilege is very quickly. And, hopefully, you will also learn that heterosexual privilege is the method by which women are given a stake in male supremacy—and that is therefore the method by which women are given a stake in their own oppression. Simply stated, a woman who stays in line—by staying straight or by refusing to resist straight privileges—receives some of the benefits of male privilege indirectly and is thus given a stake in continuing those privileges and maintaining their source—male supremacy.

Heterosexual women must realize—no matter what their personal connection to men—that the benefits they receive from men will always be in diluted form and will ultimately result in their own self-destruction. When a woman's individual survival is tied to men, she is at some intrinsic place separated from other women and from the survival needs of those other women. The question arises not because of rhetorical necessity—whether a woman is personally loyal to other women—but because we must examine what state each of us has in the continuation of male supremacy. For example, if you are receiving heterosexual benefits through a man (or through his social, cultural, or political systems), are you clear about what those benefits are doing to you, both personally and in terms of other women? I have known women who are very strong in fighting against female job discrimination, but when the battle closes in on their man's job, they desert that position. In universities, specifically, when a husband's job is threatened by feminist hiring demands, I have seen feminists abandon their political positions in order to keep the privileges they receive from their man's job.

This analysis of the function of heterosexuality in women's oppression is available to any woman, lesbian or straight. Lesbian feminism is not a political analysis "for lesbians only." It is a political perspective and fight against one of the major institutions of our oppression—a fight that heterosexual women can engage in. The problem is that few do. Since lesbians are materially oppressed by heterosexuality daily, it is not surprising that we have seen and understood its impact first—not because we are more moral, but because our reality is different—and it is a *materially* different reality. We are trying to convey this fact of our oppression to you because, whether you feel it directly or not, it also oppresses you; and because if we are going to change society and survive, we must all attack heterosexual domination.

ERA

Ed Stein

Reprinted from Ed Stein, "ERA," in the *Rocky Mountain News,* Denver, Colorado, with permission.

An Answer to a Man's Question, "What Can I Do About Women's Liberation?"

Susan Griffin

Wear a dress.
Wear a dress that you made yourself, or bought
* in a dress store.*
Wear a dress and underneath the dress wear
* elastic, around your hips, and underneath your*
* nipples.*
Wear a dress and underneath the dress wear a
* sanitary napkin.*
Wear a dress and wear sling back, high heeled
* shoes.*
Wear a dress, with elastic and a sanitary napkin
* underneath, and sling back shoes on your feet,*
* and walk down Telegraph Avenue.*
Wear a dress, with elastic and a sanitary napkin
* and sling back shoes on Telegraph Avenue and*
* try to run.*

Find a man.
Find a nice man who you would like to ask you
* for a date.*
Find a nice man who will ask you for a date.
Keep your dress on.
Ask the nice man who asks you for a date to
* come to dinner.*
Cook the nice man a nice dinner so the dinner is
* ready before he comes and your dress is nice*
* and clean and wear a smile.*
Tell the nice man you're a virgin, or you don't

have birth control, or you would like to get to
* know him better.*
Keep your dress on.
Go to the movies by yourself.

Find a job.
Iron your dress.
Wear your ironed dress and promise the boss you
* won't get pregnant (which in your case is pre-*
* dictable) and you like to type, and be sincere*
* and wear your smile.*
Find a job or get on welfare.
Borrow a child and get on welfare.
Borrow a child and stay in the house all day with
* the child, or go to the public park with the*
* child, and take the child to the welfare office*
* and cry and say your man left you and be*
* humble and wear your dress and your smile,*
* and don't talk back, keep your dress on, cook*
* more nice dinners, stay away from Telegraph*
* Avenue, and still, you won't know the half of*
* it, not in a million years.*

Reprinted from Susan Griffin, "An Answer to a Man's Question, 'What Can I Do About Women's Liberation?'" in *Like the Iris of An Eye* (New York: Harper & Row, 1976), by permission of the author.

Men's Power with Women, Other Men, and Society: A Men's Movement Analysis

Joseph H. Pleck

My aim in this paper is to analyze men's power from the perspective afforded by the emerging anti-sexist men's movement. In the last several years, an anti-sexist men's movement has appeared in North America and in the Western European countries. While it is not so widely known as the women's movement, the men's movement has generated a variety of books, publications, and organizations,[1] and is now an established presence on the sex role scene. The present and future political relationship between the women's movement and the men's movement raises complex questions which I do not deal with here, through they are clearly important ones. Instead, here I present my own view of the contribution which the men's movement and the men's analysis make to a feminist understanding of men and power, and of power relations between the sexes. First, I will analyze men's power over women, particularly in relation to the power that men often perceive women have over them. Then I will analyze two other relationships men are implicated in—men's power with other men, and men's power in society more generally—and suggest how these two other power relationships interact with men's power over women.

Men's Power over Women, and Women's Power over Men

It is becoming increasingly recognized that one of the most fundamental questions raised by the women's movement is not a question about women at all, but rather a question about men: why do men oppress women? There are two general kinds of answers to this question. The first

is that men want power over women because it is in their rational self-interest to do so, to have the concrete benefits and privileges that power over women provides them. Having power, it is rational to want to keep it. The second kind of answer is that men want to have power over women because of deep-lying psychological needs in male personality. These two views are not mutually exclusive, and there is certainly ample evidence for both. The final analysis of men's oppression of women will have to give attention equally to its rational and irrational sources.

I will concentrate my attention here on the psychological sources of men's needs for power over women. Let us consider first the most common and common-sense psychological analysis of men's need to dominate women, which takes as its starting point the male child's early experience with women. The male child, the argument goes, perceives his mother and his predominantly female elementary school teachers as dominating and controlling. These relationships *do* in reality contain elements of domination and control, probably exacerbated by the restriction of women's opportunities to exercise power in most other areas. As a result, men feel a lifelong psychological need to free themselves from or prevent their domination by women. The argument is, in effect, that men oppress women as adults because they experience women as oppressing them as children.

According to this analysis, the process operates in a vicious circle. In each generation, adult men restrict women from having power in almost all domains of social life except child-rearing. As a result, male children feel powerless and dominated, grow up needing to restrict women's power, and thus the cycle repeats itself. It follows from this analysis that the way to break the vicious circle is to make it possible for women to exercise power outside of parenting and parent-like roles and to get men to do their half share of parenting.

There may be a kernel of truth in this "mother domination" theory of sexism for some men, and the social changes in the organization of child care that this theory suggests are certainly desirable. As a general explanation of men's needs to dominate women, however, this theory has been quite overworked. This theory holds women themselves, rather than men, ultimately responsible for the oppression of women—in William Ryan's phrase, "blaming the victim" of oppression for her own oppression.[2] The recent film *One Flew over the Cuckoo's Nest* presents an extreme example of how women's supposed domination of men is used to justify sexism. This film portrays the archetypal struggle between a female figure depicted as domineering and castrating, and a rebellious male hero (played by Jack Nicholson) who refuses to be emasculated by her. This struggle escalates to a climactic scene in which Nicholson throws her on the floor and nearly strangles her to death—a scene that was accompanied by wild cheering from the audience when I saw the film. For this performance, Jack Nicholson won the Academy Award as the best actor of the year, an indication of how successful the film is in seducing its audience to accept this act of sexual violence as legitimate and even heroic. The hidden moral message of the film is that because women dominate men, the most extreme forms of sexual violence are not only permissible for men, but indeed are morally obligatory.

To account for men's needs for power over women, it is ultimately more useful to examine some other ways that men feel women have power over them than fear of maternal domination.[3] There are two forms of power that men perceive women as holding over them which derive more directly from traditional definitions of adult male and female roles, and have implications which are far more compatible with a feminist perspective.

The first power that men perceive women having over them is *expressive power,* the power to express emotions. It is well known that in traditional male–female relationships, women are supposed to express their needs for achievement only vicariously through the achievements of men. It is not so widely recognized, however, that this dependency of women on men's achievement has a converse. In traditional male–female relationships, men experience their emotions vicariously through women. Many men have learned to depend on women to help them express their emotions, indeed, to express their emotions for them. At an ultimate level, many men are unable to feel emotionally alive except through relationships with women. A particularly dramatic example oc-

curs in an earlier Jack Nicholson film *Carnal Knowledge.* Art Garfunkel, at one point early in his romance with Candy Bergen, tells Nicholson that she makes him aware of thoughts he "never even knew he had." Although Nicholson is sleeping with Bergen and Garfunkel is not, Nicholson feels tremendously deprived in comparison when he hears this. In a dramatic scene, Nicholson then goes to her and demands: "you tell him his thoughts, now you tell me *my* thoughts!" When women withhold and refuse to exercise this expressive power for men's benefit, many men, like Nicholson, feel abject and try all the harder to get women to play their traditional expressive role.

A second form of power that men attribute to women is *masculinity-validating* power. In traditional masculinity, to experience oneself as masculine requires that women play their prescribed role of doing the things that make men feel masculine. Another scene from *Carnal Knowledge* provides a pointed illustration. In the closing scene of the movie, Nicholson has hired a call girl whom he has rehearsed and coached in a script telling him how strong and manly he is, in order to get him sexually aroused. Nicholson seems to be in control, but when she makes a mistake in her role, his desperate reprimands show just how dependent he is on her playing out the masculinity-validating script he has created. It is clear that what he is looking for in this encounter is not so much sexual gratification as it is validation of himself as a man—which only women can give him. As with women's expressive power, when women refuse to exercise their masculinity-validating power for men, many men feel lost and bereft and frantically attempt to force women back into their accustomed role.

As I suggested before, men's need for power over women derives both from men's pragmatic self-interest and from men's psychological needs. It would be a mistake to overemphasize men's psychological needs as the sources of their needs to control women, in comparison with simple rational self-interest. But if we are looking for the psychological sources of men's needs for power over women, their perception that women have expressive power and masculinity-validating power over them are critical to analyze. These are the two powers men perceive women as having, which they fear women will no longer exercise in their favor. These are the two resources women possess which men fear women will withhold, and whose threatened or actual loss leads men to such frantic attempts to reassert power over women.

Men's dependence on women's power to express

men's emotions and to validate men's masculinity have placed heavy burdens on women. By and large, these are not powers over men that women have wanted to hold. These are powers that men have themselves handed over to women, by defining the male role as being emotionally cool and inexpressive, and as being ultimately validated by heterosexual success.

There is reason to think that over the course of recent history—as male-male friendship has declined, and as dating and marriage have occurred more universally and at younger ages—the demands on men to be emotionally inexpressive and to prove masculinity through relating to women have become stronger. As a result, men have given women increasingly more expressive power and more masculinity-validating power over them, and have become increasingly dependent on women for emotional and sex role validation. In the context of this increased dependency on women's power, the emergence of the women's movement now, with women asserting their right not to play these roles for men, has hit men with special force.

It is in this context that the men's movement and men's groups place so much emphasis on men learning to express and experience their emotions with each other, and learning how to validate themselves and each other as persons, instead of needing women to validate them emotionally and as men. When men realize that they can develop themselves the power to experience themselves emotionally and to validate themselves as persons, they will not feel the dependency on women for these essential needs which has led in the past to so much male fear, resentment, and need to control women. Then men will be emotionally more free to negotiate the pragmatic realignment of power between the sexes that is underway in our society.

Men's Power with Other Men

After considering men's power over women in relation to the power men perceive women having over them, let us consider men's power over women in a second context: the context of men's power relationships with other men. In recent years, we have come to understand that relations between men and women are governed by a sexual politics that exists outside individual men's and women's needs and choices. It has taken us much longer to recognize that there is a systematic sexual politics of male-male relationships as well. Under patriarchy, men's relationships with other men cannot help but be shaped and patterned by

patriarchal norms, though they are less obvious than the norms governing male-female relationships. A society could not have the kinds of power dynamics that exist between women and men in our society without certain kinds of systematic power dynamics operating among men as well.

One dramatic example illustrating this connection occurs in Marge Piercy's recent novel *Small Changes*. In a flashback scene, a male character goes along with several friends to gang-rape a woman. When his turn comes, he is impotent; whereupon the other men grab him, pulling his pants down to rape *him*. This scene powerfully conveys one form of the relationship between male-female and male-male sexual politics. The point is that men do not just happily bond together to oppress women. In addition to hierarchy over women, men create hierarchies and rankings among themselves according to criteria of "masculinity." Men at each rank of masculinity compete with each other, with whatever resources they have, for the differential payoffs that patriarchy allows men.

Men in different societies choose different grounds on which to rank each other. Many societies use the simple facts of age and physical strength to stratify men. The most bizarre and extreme form of patriarchal stratification occurs in those societies which have literally created a class of eunuchs. Our society, reflecting its own particular preoccupations, stratifies men according to physical strength and athletic ability in the early years, but later in life focuses on success with women and ability to make money.

In our society, one of the most critical rankings among men deriving from patriarchal sexual politics is the division between gay and straight men. This division has powerful negative consequences for gay men and gives straight men privilege. But in addition, this division has a larger symbolic meaning. Our society uses the male heterosexual-homosexual dichotomy as a central symbol for *all* the rankings of masculinity, for the division on *any* grounds between males who are "real men" and have power and males who are not. Any kind of powerlessness or refusal to compete becomes imbued with the imagery of homosexuality. In the men's movement documentary film *Men's Lives*,[4] a high school male who studies modern dance says that others often think he is gay because he is a dancer. When asked why, he gives three reasons: because dancers are "free and loose," because they are "not big like football players," and because "you're not trying to kill anybody." The patriarchal connection: if you are not trying to kill other men, you must be gay.

Another dramatic example of men's use of homosexual derogations as weapons in their power struggle with each other comes from a document which provides one of the richest case studies of the politics of male–male relationships to yet appear: Woodward and Bernstein's *The Final Days.* Ehrlichman jokes that Kissinger is queer, Kissinger calls an unnamed colleague a psychopathic homosexual, and Haig jokes that Nixon and Rebozo are having a homosexual relationship. From the highest ranks of male power to the lowest, the gay–straight division is a central symbol of all the forms of ranking and power relationships which men put on each other.

The relationships between the patriarchal stratification and competition which men experience with each other and men's patriarchal domination of women are complex. Let us briefly consider several points of interconnection between them. First, women are used as *symbols of success* in men's competition with each other. It is sometimes thought that competition for women is the ultimate source of men's competition with each other. For example, in *Totem and Taboo* Freud presented a mythical reconstruction of the origin of society based on sons' sexual competition with the father, leading to their murdering the father. In this view, if women did not exist, men would not have anything to compete for with each other. There is considerable reason, however, to see women not as the ultimate source of male–male competition, but rather as only symbols in a male contest where real roots lie much deeper.

The recent film *Paper Chase* provides an interesting example. This film combines the story of a small group of male law students in their first year of law school with a heterosexual love story between one of the students (played by Timothy Bottoms) and the professor's daughter. As the film develops, it becomes clear that the real business is the struggle within the group of male law students for survival, success, and the professor's blessing—patriarchal struggle in which several of the less successful are driven out of school and one even attempts suicide. When Timothy Bottoms gets the professor's daughter at the end, she is simply another one of the rewards he has won by doing better than the other males in her father's class. Indeed, she appears to be a direct part of the patriarchal blessing her father has bestowed on Bottoms.

Second, women often play a *mediating* role in the patriarchal struggle among men. Women get together with each other, and provide the social lubrication necessary to smooth over men's inability to relate to each other non-competitively. This function has been expressed in many myths, for example, the folk tales included in the Grimms' collection about groups of brothers whose younger sister reunites and reconciles them with their king-father, who had previously banished and tried to kill them. A more modern myth, James Dickey's *Deliverance,* portrays what happens when men's relationships with each other are not mediated by women. According to Carolyn Heilbrun,[5] the central message of *Deliverance* is that when men get beyond the bounds of civilization, which really means beyond the bounds of the civilizing effects of women, men rape and murder each other.

A third function women play in male–male sexual politics is that relationships with women provide men a *refuge* from the dangers and stresses of relating to other males. Traditional relationships with women have provided men a safe place in which they can recuperate from the stresses they have absorbed in their daily struggle with other men, and in which they can express their needs without fearing that these needs will be used against them. If women begin to compete with men and have power in their own right, men are threatened by the loss of this refuge.

Finally, a fourth function of women in males' patriarchal competition with each other is to reduce the stress of competition by serving as an *underclass.* As Elizabeth Janeway has written in *Between Myth and Morning,*[6] under patriarchy women represent the lowest status, a status to which men can fall only under the most exceptional circumstances, if at all. Competition among men is serious, but its intensity is mitigated by the fact that there is a lowest possible level to which men cannot fall. One reason men fear women's liberation, writes Janeway, is that the liberation of women will take away this unique underclass status of women. Men will not risk falling lower than ever before, into a new underclass composed of the weak of both sexes. Thus, women's liberation means that the stakes of patriarchal failure for men are higher than they have been before, and that it is even more important for men not to lose.

Thus, men's patriarchal competition with each other makes use of women as symbols of success, as mediators, as refuges, and as an underclass. In each of these roles, women are dominated by men in ways that derive directly from men's struggle with each other. Men need to deal with the sexual politics of their relationships with each other if they are to deal fully with the sexual politics of their relationships with women.

Ultimately, we have to understand that patriarchy has two halves which are intimately related to each other. Patriarchy is a *dual* system, a system in which men oppress women, and in which men oppress themselves and each other. At one level, challenging one part of patriarchy inherently leads to challenging the other. This is one way to interpret why the idea of women's liberation so soon led to the idea of men's liberation, which in my view ultimately means freeing men from the patriarchal sexual dynamics they now experience with each other. But because the patriarchal sexual dynamics of male–male relationships are less obvious than those of male–female relationships, men face a real danger: while the patriarchal oppression of women may be lessened as a result of the women's movement, the patriarchal oppression of men may be untouched. The real danger for men posed by the attack that the women's movement is making on patriarchy is not that this attack will go too far, but that it will not go far enough. Ultimately, men cannot go any further in relating to women as equals than they have been able to go in relating to other men as equals—an equality which has been so deeply disturbing, which has generated so many psychological as well as literal casualties, and which has left so many unresolved issues of competition and frustrated love.

Men's Power in Society

Let us now consider men's power over women in a third and final context, the context of men's power in the larger society. At one level, men's social identity is defined by the power they have over women and the power they can compete for against other men. But at another level, most men have very little over their own lives. How can we understand this paradox?

The major demand to which men must accede in contemporary society is that they play their required role in the economy. But this role is not intrinsically satisfying. The social researcher Daniel Yankelovich[7] has suggested that about 80% of U.S. male workers experience their jobs as intrinsically meaningless and onerous. They experience their jobs and themselves as worthwhile only through priding themselves on the hard work and personal sacrifice they are making to be breadwinners for their families. Accepting these hardships reaffirms their role as family providers and therefore as true men.

Linking the breadwinner role to masculinity in this way has several consequences for men. Men can get psychological payoffs from their jobs which these jobs never provide in themselves. By training men to accept payment for their work in feelings of masculinity rather than in feelings of satisfaction, men will not demand that their jobs be made more meaningful, and as a result jobs can be designed for the more important goal of generating profits. Further, the connection between work and masculinity makes men accept unemployment as their personal failing as males, rather than analyze and change the profit-based economy whose inevitable dislocations make them unemployed or unemployable.

Most critical for our analysis here, men's role in the economy and the ways men are motivated to play it have at least two negative effects on women. First, the husband's job makes many direct and indirect demands on wives. In fact, it is often hard to distinguish whether the wife is dominated more by the husband or by the husband's job. Sociologist Ralph Turner writes: "Because the husband must adjust to the demands of his occupation and the family in turn must accommodate to his demands on behalf of his occupational obligations, the husband appears to dominate his wife and children. But as an agent of economic institutions, he perceives himself as controlled rather than as controlling."[8]

Second, linking the breadwinner role to masculinity in order to motivate men to work means that women must not be allowed to hold paid work. For the large majority of men who accept dehumanizing jobs only because having a job validates their role as family breadwinner, their wives' taking paid work takes away from them the major and often only way they have of experiencing themselves as having worth. Yankelovich suggests that the frustration and discontent of this group of men, whose wives are increasingly joining the paid labor force, is emerging as a major social problem. What these men do to sabotage women's paid work is deplorable, but I believe that it is quite within the bounds of a feminist analysis of contemporary society to see these men as victims as well as victimizers.

One long-range perspective on the historical evolution of the family is that from an earlier stage in which both wife and husband were directly economically productive in the household economic unit, the husband's economic role has evolved so that now it is under the control of forces entirely outside the family. In order to increase productivity, the goal in the design of this new male work role is to increase men's commitment and loyalty to work and to reduce those ties to the family that might compete with it. Men's jobs are increasingly structured as if men had no direct roles or responsibilities in the family—indeed, as if they did not have families at all. But paradoxically, at the same time that men's responsibilities in the family are reduced to facilitate more efficient performance of their work role, the increasing dehumanization of work means that the satisfaction which jobs give men is, to an increasing degree, *only* the satisfaction of fulfilling the family breadwinner role. That is, on the one hand, men's ties to the family have to be broken down to facilitate industrial work discipline; but on the other hand, men's sense of responsibility to the family has to be increased, but shaped into a purely economic form, to provide the motivation for men to work at all. Essential to this process is the transformation of the wife's economic role to providing supportive services, both physical and psychological, to keep him on the job, and to take over the family responsibilities which his expanded work role will no longer allow him to fulfill himself. The wife is then bound to her husband by her economic dependency on him, and the husband in turn is bound to his job by his family's economic dependence on him.

A final example from the film *Men's Lives* illustrates some of these points. In one of the most powerful scenes in the film, a worker in a rubber plant resignedly describes how his bosses are concerned, in his words, with "pacifying" him to get the maximum output from him, not with satisfying his needs. He then takes back this analysis, saying that he is only a worker and therefore cannot really understand what is happening to him. Next, he is asked whether he wants his wife to take a paid job to reduce the pressure he feels in trying to support his family. In marked contrast to his earlier passive resignation, he proudly asserts that he will never allow her to work, and that in particular he will never scrub the floors after he comes home from his own job. (He correctly perceives that if his wife did take a paid job, he would be under pressure to do some housework.) In this scene, the man expresses and then denies an awareness of his exploitation as a worker. Central to his coping with and repressing his incipient awareness of his exploitation is his false consciousness of his superiority and privilege over women. Not scrubbing floors is a real privilege, and deciding whether or not his wife will have paid work is a real power, but the consciousness of power over his own life that such privilege and power give this man is false. The relative privilege that men get from sexism, and more importantly the false consciousness of privilege men get from sexism, play a critical role in reconciling men to their subordination in

the larger political economy. This analysis does not imply that men's sexism will go away if they gain control over their own lives, or that men do not have to deal with their sexism until they gain this control. I disagree with both. Rather, my point is that we cannot fully understand men's sexism or men's subordination in the larger society unless we understand how deeply they are related.

To summarize, a feminist understanding of men's power over women, when men have needed it, and what is involved in changing it, is enriched by examining men's power in a broader context. To understand men's power over women, we have to understand the ways in which men feel women have power over them, men's power relationships with other men, and the powerlessness of most men in the larger society. Rectifying men's power relationship with women will inevitably both stimulate and benefit from the rectification of these other power relationships.

Endnotes

1. See, for example, Deborah David and Robert Brannon, eds., *The Forty-Nine Percent Majority: Readings on the Male Role* (Reading, Mass.: Addison-Wesley, 1975); Warren Farrell, *The Liberated Man* (New York: Bantam Books, 1975); Marc Feigen Fasteau, *The Male Machine* (New York: McGraw-Hill, 1974); Jack Nichols, *Men's Liberation: A New Definition of Masculinity* (Baltimore: Penguin, 1975); John Petras, ed., *Sex: Male/Gender: Masculine* (Port Washington, N.J.: Alfred, 1975); Joseph H. Pleck and Jack Sawyer, eds., *Men and Masculinity* (Englewood Cliffs, N.J.: Prentice-Hall, 1974). See also the *Man's Awareness Network (M.A.N.) Newsletter,* a regularly updated directory of men's movement activities, organizations, and publications, prepared by a rotating group of men's centers (c/o Knoxville Men's Resource Center, P.O. Box 8060, U.T. Station, Knoxville, Tenn. 37916); the Men's Studies Collection, Charles Hayden Humanities Library, Massachusetts Institute of Technology, Cambridge, Mass. 02139.

2. William Ryan, *Blaming the Victim* (New York: Pantheon, 1970).

3. In addition to the mother domination theory, there are two other psychological theories relating aspects of the early mother–child relationship in men's sexism. The first can be called the "mother identification" theory, which holds that men develop a "feminine" psychological identification because of their early attachment to their mothers and that men fear this in-

ternal feminine part of themselves, seeking to control it by controlling those who actually are feminine, i.e., women. The second can be called the "mother socialization" theory, holding that since boys' fathers are relatively absent as sex role models, the major route by which boys learn masculinity is through their mothers' rewarding masculine behavior, and especially through their mothers' punishing feminine behavior. Thus, males associate women with punishment and pressure to be masculine. Interestingly, these two theories are in direct contradiction, since the former holds that men fear women because women make men feminine, and the latter holds that men fear women because women make men masculine. These theories are discussed at greater length in Joseph H. Pleck, "Men's Traditional Attitudes toward Women: Conceptual Issues in Research," in

The Psychology of Women: New Directions in Research, ed. Julia Sherman and Florence Denmark (New York: Psychological Dimensions, in press).

4. Available from New Day Films, P.O. Box 315, Franklin Lakes, N.J. 07417.

5. Carolyn G. Heilbrun, "The Masculine Wilderness of the American Novel," *Saturday Review* 41 (January 29, 1972), 41–44.

6. Elizabeth Janeway, *Between Myth and Morning* (Boston: Little, Brown, 1975); see also Elizabeth Janeway, "The Weak are the Second Sex," *Atlantic Monthly* (December, 1973), 91–104.

7. Daniel Yankelovich, "The Meaning of Work," in *The Worker and the Job,* ed. Jerome Rosow (Englewood Cliffs, N.J.: 1974).

8. Ralph Turner, *Family Interaction* (New York: Wiley, 1968), p. 282.

Introduction: Spiritual Politics

Presently, religion is one of the institutions which is being scrutinized and challenged by feminists who maintain that Judeo-Christian principles and practices constitute, in Western societies, a formidable social force in the perpetuation of culturally prescribed gender roles. Some feminists have rejected all forms of religion, arguing that religious worship is simply another means of diverting women's attention from the political action needed to change existing political and economic institutions. Other feminists are not turning away from spiritual concerns, but are attempting instead to create new religious visions and forms of worship consistent with feminist principles. Adherents to new theological visions and spiritual experiences as a means of creating and sustaining feminism can be considered as either *reformists* or *revolutionaries*. Reformists believe that although major changes must be made in the patriarchal doctrine and structure of established religions, the existent Judeo-Christian tradition is, nevertheless, salvageable. By contrast, the revolutionary point of view holds that the only way to be free of the male imagery which permeates Judeo-Christian teachings and practices is to create fundamentally new and feminist spiritual visions and forms of worship. In this section, we shall examine some of the visions and transformations proposed by both reformists and revolutionaries in their attempt to alter one of the most powerful institutions preserving and justifying the status quo.

In the first selection, "Feminist Spirituality: The Politics of the Psyche," Judith Antonelli discusses the relationships among patriarchal religion, patriarchal society, feminist political action and spiritual growth. The next two selections illustrate some of the reforms sought by feminists within the context of existing religious doctrine and practices. The first is a "Feminist Shabbat Service" designed for and by Jewish feminists from Hillel's Women's Programming in Columbus, Ohio; the second is a feminist interpretation of a much-ignored biblical story, "The Coming of Lilith" by Judith Plaskow.

Not only are feminists finding new ways to visualize their spirituality within the contexts of Judeo-Christianity, they are also discovering affinities with other spiritual traditions. Ellin Carter alludes to an historical spiritual affinity of women with nature and patriarchal religion under more lasting phenomena in her poem, "Encounter." In the selection "Woman Who Races Birds," Connie Gaib provides visual illustrations and gives a brief account of the effect of Native American Indian beliefs on her own spiritual quest. Finally, Margo Adler discusses the beliefs and rituals of contemporary witches in "Women, Feminism, and the Craft," an excerpt from her book *Drawing Down the Moon*, and argues that feminist witchcraft is a revolutionary spiritual and political force for challenging patriarchal ideas and structures.

Feminist Spirituality: The Politics of the Psyche

Judith Antonelli

There is a great deal of doubt expressed in various segments of the women's movement as to the relevance of feminist spirituality to politics. The strongest critics of spirituality see it as escapist, as focusing on inner subjective reality as opposed to external objective conditions — thus taking away from the "real" political work that needs to be done. Those who have written in defense of spirituality have mostly emphasized the necessity to work on *both* the inner and outer aspects of reality, refusing to reduce feminism to a choice of either/or. However, this in itself does not challenge the notion that spirituality and politics are two separate categories.

One of the reasons why spirituality is viewed as apolitical by some women is that up until the feminist movement, radical politics have been materialist — i.e., dealing only with visible, physical reality. Whether communist, socialist, leftist, or anarchist, radical politics have focused on *control of the means of production* as the central issue in freeing ourselves from oppression. The women's movement, while expanding on this to include other issues such as reproduction, has generally aligned itself with the materialist view of reality. For an issue to be considered "political" by materialists, it must be analyzed from this perspective; unseen forces are not acknowledged as having any influence. Spirituality is seen simply as "an opiate of the people" — i.e., as a way of diverting people's attention from their oppression in the here and now. While this can be said of patriarchal religion, it is not necessarily the essence of spirituality itself.

Spirituality is a world view based on energy, a perception which includes the nonvisible and nonmaterial. It deals with the collective psyche (soul) of humanity. Ritual, astrology, tarot, dreams, and mythology are sym-

Reprinted from Judith Antonelli, "Feminist Spirituality: The Politics of the Psyche," adapted from the original *Chrysallis* article, by permission of the author. Copyright 1978 by Judith Antonelli.

bolic languages emerging from the unconscious. Psychic energy (Life Force, Creative Principle) is inherently Female, and this realization is the essence of *feminist* spirituality.

Materialist revolutions do not work to dig out oppression by its roots. They change social structures from the top down; "benevolent dictators" have decreed that equality in wealth and sexual roles shall be the norm. The difference between socialist and capitalist fascism (that is, authoritarianism or state power based on repression) is that at least the socialist fascists want everyone to be fed. That's worth something — but not enough. In fact, it may be more insidious, since when you're starving amidst wealth, oppression is an obvious fact.

Nonrational, spiritual reality is not acknowledged in socialist societies. Religion is condemned, although the reverence for Mao and Fidel certainly resembles the worship of God the father in capitalist countries. Mental illness is also still present, which indicates some kind of suppression of the nonrational, unconscious mind. Competition, nationalism and patriotism, imperialism, an emphasis on industrialized production, and technological control of Nature continue after "revolution": China is working on the bomb; Cuba has political prisoners. Moreover, heterosexual, monogamous marriage and thus the patrilineal nuclear family are the only sanctioned form of sexuality. The repression of the varied forms of sexual expression indicates the suppression of sexual, or life, energy — i.e., the Female principle. Materialist (or socialist) revolutions are, therefore, still patriarchal.

Materialist politics are much like behaviorist psychology in that underlying causes, usually unseen, are dismissed as impossible, for all that exists is the visible. Human behavior is viewed as completely conditioned by the external environment, and people are thus treated as abstractions, machines, or white rats. Karl Marx and B. F. Skinner are truly brothers under the skin. Therefore, materialist politics take the symptom — that most people in the world are denied the right to a comfortable material existence—and treat it as the problem. Clearly, destruction of the world by a small group of white men in order to achieve more wealth than they can ever possibly use does not make sense. We are talking here about a drive for power, a need for domination, that must be examined in psychological, motivational terms if we are to truly understand it and dismantle it. Although motivational psychology has generally been used by the patriarchy to discredit political struggle, feminists can now use it as a tool to explain oppression.

The Female principle is primary in Nature. Woman possesses a power that no man can every have: the capacity to give birth to new life, as well as the ability to experience an unlimited amount of pleasure in the sexual act. She is the creator of life, while his role in conception is, at best, a secondary one. Patriarchy is based on the "phallacy" that the male is creator. Man's original awe and envy of woman becomes, under patriarchy, resentment and hostility. The only way man can possess Female power is through woman, and so he colonizes her, suppressing her sexuality so that it serves him rather than being the source of her power.

Patriarchy creates a split in consciousness. When body and mind are split, one must confront the fact that woman can create with her body *and* her mind, while man can create only with his mind. In compensation, to cover his own lack of completeness, to make himself feel superior, man claims all rational-intellectual processes as his own, devaluing all bodily, emotional, and intuitive functions, while simultaneously saying that these functions are *all* that women are capable of. Patriarchy is based on fear of the Female and the suppression of all "female" qualities: woman, nature, the body, feelings and emotion, instinct, intuition, and, finally, life itself.

Patriarchy is indeed a male neurosis. Every social institution under male dominance is an expression of man's womb envy, designed to take woman's power away from her and place it in the hands of men. In squelching Female energy, patriarchy creates a culture that is destructive and death-oriented. If man denies his dependence on the Female and tries to usurp her, making himself primary, he can only be the destroyer of life; he is not able to create life. While woman sheds the Blood of Life each moon at menstruation, man can only shed the blood of death through warfare and killing. Imperialism can be seen as the logical extension of rape; invasion of a people's homeland, as well as ecological destruction, is psychically analogous to the rape and invasion of a woman's body. Now that man has all but conquered Woman, Nature, and Earth, he is already beginning colonization of the Moon, another symbol of the Female principle!

The essence of a spiritual view of politics lies in the perception that matter is a manifestation of energy, that material reality reflects and symbolizes psychic reality. An obvious example is that emotional conflicts often emerge in the form of physical illness. This is not to deny that material reality also gives rise to energy patterns—for life is a cyclical process, not a linear one, and therefore *both* can be true. However, I am here focusing on just *one* aspect of the cycle—the fact that the spiritual gives rise to the material—in order to make my point that spirituality is indeed political (i.e., that it deals with the distribution of power).

There are many political examples of how material reality is symbolic of psychic reality. The torture of animals (instinctual beings) and the predominance of right-handedness (dominance by the brain's left hemisphere) are indicative of the hyper-rationalism of our society. One of the most glaring examples, however, is in racism: the oppression of people of color by the white race. Black and white have a very strong psychological significance in terms of the intuitive/rational split. Blackness, darkness, the New Moon, and the night have all been symbols of the unconscious, instinct, inner-directed energy, the void from which all creation begins. Whiteness, brightness, the Full Moon, and the daytime symbolize conscious awareness, ego, rational intellect, outward energy. It is no accident that as our world grows more rational and more ego-dominated, white supremacy over dark-skinned peoples increases also. Fear of blackness and what it represents psychically is one of the roots of racism, as well as of the notion (especially prevalent in allopathic medicine) that white is clean, sterile, and pure—while black is seen as a symbol of sadness and death.

Symbolic language, then, is very important for us to decipher. There is a wealth of information in mythology, for example, which tells us about the transition from matriarchy to patriarchy. Myth *is* hystory,* but in allegorical, not literal, form. The predominance of a Mother Goddess represents matriarchy: the predominance of the Female principle, a society in which women

---

*I prefer this spelling to the term "herstory" because it indicates the linguistic connection to "womb" (from the Greek word). Both are "where we come from."

control the means of production and reproduction, and where Female clans are the basic social unit. Patriarchy, the institution of laws which break the mother–child bond and assure men of knowledge of their paternity, begins when the son kills his mother and paves the way for the ascendance of a father god, who represents the predominance of male power. Women today who are trying to bring back Goddess worship are not worshipping idols, escaping through mysticism, or revering an external god-substitute. The Goddess represents nothing less than Female power and woman's deification of her own essence. It is external only to the extent that this power is contained within the cycles of Nature as well as within ourselves.

Every oppressed people needs a sense of its hystory; therefore, researching our matriarchal past is not escapist, but a very important political act. We must develop an analysis of history from the perspective of the balance between the Female and male principles. Knowledge of our past shapes and clarifies our vision of the future. We can gain much of this knowledge intuitively, for the collective unconscious contains our memories of matriarchy.

Developing our psychic power is also political. To think that we can rely only on physical techniques of self-defense is naïve in light of the fact that men have the military weapons and the technology to wipe us out instantly as soon as they recognize the threat we pose. We *must* develop psychic power as a means of self-defense. Living in the country must also not be seen as privileged and escapist. It is imperative that women learn survival skills such as living off the land, growing food, and healing with herbs. We must begin to put good nurturing energy into the Earth in order to counteract man's manipulation of her. Who knows how many "natural catastrophes" have been the retaliation of Mother Nature for all the damage that has been done to her?

If we are to survive the massive destruction that is the inevitable outcome of male supremacy, we *must* attune ourselves to psychic reality. Dismissing spirituality as apolitical, relegating it to a different sphere than the material, is short-sighted and feeds right into the rationalist fears that work to maintain the patriarchy.

READING 83

Feminist Shabbat Service

Sigrid Ehrenberg, Jane E. Lesley, Deirdre B. Mandzuch, and Sora Newman

A condensed version of this Service follows

Introduction

After the Hillel Women's Programming Committee decided to sponsor a Feminist Sabbath celebration, four of us met to plan a dinner and write a Sabbath service.

Reprinted from Sigrid Ehrenberg, Jane E. Lesley, Deirdre B. Mandzuch, and Sora Newman, "Feminist Shabbat Service," by permission of the authors.

None of us had ever written a Sabbath service before, but we were inspired by the Women's Seder sponsored by Women's Programming the previous Passover, by an impromptu Sabbath celebration at the Michigan Women's Music Festival last August, and by the efforts of our Jewish sisters around the country to create a Jewish religious and cultural experience meaningful to feminists.

Our service tonight is a combination of traditional works, new feminist versions of some traditional material, as well as our own thoughts. We have used excerpts from the *Women's Shabbat* written by the Jewish Feminist Collective (UCLA Hillel), *The Hebrew Goddess* by Raphael Patai (Avon Books, 1978), and *Ancient Mirrors of Womanhood* by Merlin Stone (New Sibylline Books, 1979).

Blessing the Sabbath Candles

Tonight we light these candles in the hope they will shed new light on our traditions, inspire us to learn about our foremothers and share their stories with each other; to illuminate our heritage from darkness. And let the flame of this light give us warmth with one another as we share this evening of celebration (Women's Seder, L.A., 1976).

The traditional Sabbath is not merely a day of rest, a negative refraining from work, but a time of joy, a day of spirit, of creative leisure. For centuries it was the only bright day in a week of poverty and persecution, a time for celebration of peace, human freedom, study, the enjoyment of good food and drink.

As feminists, our days are often intensely busy, filled with struggle, conflict, and a tendency to exhaust our energies. Let us turn to the Sabbath for a time of rest and renewal, a time to reaffirm our faith in life, to share joy with our sisters.

For many of us the traditional faith is no longer sustaining, and may even feel like a destructive influence in our lives. Those of us with working mothers remember the hectic pace and tension as they prepared for the day of rest. Being an observant Jewish woman often seemed oppressive. Still there was a richness in our celebrations, and now a vacancy in their absence. What are our strong and revitalizing memories? How can we reclaim or create the meaning of our heritage?

Sharing

(Women may feel free to share their experiences and thoughts on the meaning of the Sabbath).

Blessing the Wine (Kiddish) and the Bread

Praised be thou, Shekhina, Queen of the Universe, who has created the fruit of the vine.

Praised be thou, Shekhina, Queen of the Universe, who has created the bread of the earth.

Dinner

After Dinner

A time for remembering and telling.

Lilith

Accounts of the mythical character Lilith appear both in the Talmud (a sixty-three volume explanation of the Torah, and collection of Jewish law) and in the Kabalah (a system based on a mystical method of interpreting the scriptures to unravel sacred mysteries and foretell the future).

According to these sources Lilith was the first wife of Adam, who refused to be sexually submissive, saying, "Why must I lie beneath you? I also was made from dust, and am therefore your equal."[1] Adam tried forcing Lilith into obedience, and it was in a rage that she uttered God's name and vanished. The rest of the myth continues even today . . . Adam was lonely, so God created another being . . . this time from Adam's rib. Thus Eve was born. It is interesting to note that while Lilith first appears in the Talmud and Kabalah as Adam's first wife, she later appears in these works as the name of a demon of the night, Lilit. It is Lilith who supposedly encourages men to "Spill their sperm defying their ideas of the legitimacy of each child born."[2] Today Jewish women look at Lilith as a figure of strength, and a re-affirmation of their religion and culture, not as a passive human being shadowing and reacting to one man's whims and actions.

Shekhina

Praised are You, Queen of the Universe, who with a word bring on evening. With wisdom You open the gates of heaven and with purposeful intelligence You cycle time and switch the seasons and order the orbits of a sky full of stars. You create each day and each night afresh. You roll light in front of darkness and darkness in front of light so gradually that no moment is quite like the one before or after it. Second by second You make day pass into night, and You alone know the boundary point which divides one from the other. Unifier of all beings is Your name. Timeless, changeless Creator, may You rule over us forever and ever in constant watchfulness. Praised are You,

1. Women in Judaism: The Status of Women in Formative Judaism, Leonard Swidler, Scarecrow Press, N.J., 1976, p. 128.
2. Ancient Mirrors of Womanhood: Our Goddess and Heroine Heritage, Merlin Stone, New Sybilline Books, Inc., N.Y., 1979, p. 127.

Queen of the Universe, who brings the evening in (Women's Shabbat Service, L.A.; 1976).

Ruth

Tonight we turn back to a recognition of our foremothers such as Deborah, Leah and Rachel. Our list would not be complete unless we look at the timeless and beautiful story of Ruth; the story of a deep abiding love between two women.

And it came to pass in the days when the judges judged, that there was a famine in the land. And Elimelech, his wife Naomi and their two sons went into the land of Moab. And Naomi's husband died and her sons took Orpah and Ruth, women of Moab as wives. Ten years later Naomi's sons died and Naomi and her two daughters-in-law started to return to the land of Judah. Naomi said unto her two daughters-in-law: "Go, return each of you to her mother's house; the Lord deal kindly with you, as ye have dealt with the dead, and with me." But her daughters-in-law refused to go and Naomi said: "Turn back, my daughters; why will ye go with me? Have I yet sons in my womb, that they may be your husbands? Turn back, my daughters, go your way." And Orpah went back to her mother's house but Ruth cleaved unto Naomi and said: "Entreat me not to leave thee, and to return from following after thee; for whither thou goest, I will go; and where thou lodgest, I will lodge; thy people shall be my people, and thy God my God; where thou

diest, will I die, and there will I be buried; the Lord do so to me, and more also, if aught but death part thee and me." So Naomi returned with Ruth to the land of Judah.

Kaddish

Kaddish is the prayer of mourning. It is the prayer of consolation and loss. Although death is the most tragic loss we can suffer, there are other significant losses that cause us pain and suffering. Often there is no channel to express our grief. Frequently we may not even recognize our need for mourning and letting go.

There are few rituals to celebrate or recognize the milestones in our adult lives, and there are few rituals to help us mourn the passing away of meaningful phases and relationships. The *Kaddish* is a prayer to affirm life. We can turn to it for all forms of mourning, and we can create new words and rituals for both affirmation and comfort in times of grief.

Conclusion

Tonight has been a special experience for us. As we rediscover our identity as Jewish feminist women and collectively create new expression of our traditions, we feel strength and solidarity. Let this tradition continue.

The Coming of Lilith

Judith Plaskow

In the beginning the Lord God formed Adam and Lilith from the dust of the ground and breathed into their nostrils the breath of life. Created from the same source, both having been formed from the ground, they were equal in all ways. Adam, man that he was, didn't like this situation, and he looked for ways to change it. He said, "I'll have my figs now, Lilith," ordering her to wait on him, and he tried to leave to her the daily tasks of life in the garden. But Lilith wasn't one to take any nonsense; she picked herself up, uttered God's holy name, and flew away. "Well, now, Lord," complained Adam, "that uppity woman you sent me has gone and deserted me." The Lord, inclined to be sympathetic, sent his messengers after Lilith, telling her to shape up and return to Adam or face dire punishment. She, however, preferring anything to living with Adam, decided to stay right where she was. And so God, after more careful consideration this time, caused a deep sleep to fall upon Adam, and out of one of his ribs created for him a second companion, Eve.

For a time Eve and Adam had quite a good thing going. Adam was happy now, and Eve, though she occasionally sensed capacities within herself that remained undeveloped, was basically satisfied with the role of Adam's wife and helper. The only thing that really disturbed her was the excluding closeness of the relationship between Adam and God. Adam and God just seemed to have more in common, being both men, and Adam came to identify with God more and more. After a while that made God a bit uncomfortable too, and he started going over in his mind whether he might not have made a mistake in letting Adam talk him into banishing Lilith and creating Eve, in light of the power that God had given Adam.

Meanwhile Lilith, all alone, attempted from time to time to rejoin the human community in the garden. After her first fruitless attempt to breach its walls, Adam worked

hard to build them stronger, even getting Eve to help him. He told her fearsome stories of the demon Lilith who threatens women in childbirth and steals children from their cradles in the middle of the night. The second time Lilith came she stormed the garden's main gate, and a great battle between her and Adam ensued, in which she was finally defeated. This time, however, before Lilith got away, Eve got a glimpse of her and saw she was a woman like herself.

After this encounter, seeds of curiosity and doubt began to grow in Eve's mind. Was Lilith indeed just another woman? Adam had said she was a demon. Another woman! The very idea attracted Eve. She had never seen another creature like herself before. And how beautiful and strong Lilith had looked! How bravely she had fought! Slowly, slowly, Eve began to think about the limits of her own life within the garden.

One day, after many months of strange and disturbing thoughts, Eve, wandering around the edge of the garden, noticed a young apple tree she and Adam had planted, and saw that one of its branches stretched over the garden wall. Spontaneously she tried to climb it, and struggling to the top, swung herself over the wall.

She had not wandered long on the other side before she met the one she had come to find, for Lilith was waiting. At first sight of her, Eve remembered the tales of Adam and was frightened, but Lilith understood and greeted her kindly. "Who are you?" they asked each other, "What is your story?" And they sat and spoke together, of the past and then of the future. They talked not once, but many times, and for many hours. They taught each other many things, and told each other stories, and laughed together, and cried, over and over, till the bond of sisterhood grew between them.

Meanwhile, back in the garden, Adam was puzzled by Eve's comings and goings, and disturbed by what he sensed to be her new attitude toward him. He talked to God about it, and God, having his own problems with Adam and a somewhat broader perspective, was able to help him out a little—but he, too, was confused. Something had failed to go according to plan. As in the days of

Abraham, he needed counsel from his children. "I am who I am," thought God, "but I must become who I will become."

And God and Adam were expectant and afraid the day Eve and Lilith returned to the garden, bursting with possibilities, ready to rebuild it together.

READING 85

Encounter

Ellin Carter

Here he comes again
God Almighty
with his thunderbolt
burning chariot
spears and commandments
briefcases ballpoints
and meataxes

He would like to pin me down
confine me
call me a witch if I wriggle
hang me burn me or
set me to saying
    "Just wait till your
    Father gets home"

Centuries come and go
civilizations rise and fall
I have seen them
they are not my concern
mine are the seasons shifting
the old earth turning
slower than four billion years ago
but still revolving
tides moonrise
the chirp of crickets
a bee on honeysuckle

As he scurries near
I dance spirals around him
and spread my arms
to take him in

Woman Who Races Birds

Connie Gaib

Developing a personal spirituality, I have found, is a quest to unite forces one feels inside and outside of the self to construct a reality perception of life as meaningful. Religious systems also provide reality constructions for their specific spiritualities, but, the beliefs of Roman Catholicism which determined my initial orientation had me ignoring internal forces (i.e., ego awarenesses like sexuality) for the most part because they were considered evil. Instead, I was taught to look mainly to external forces. I believed that this Christian God ruled above all else and life's meaning centered around pleasing this entity. Good was generated from this entity and opposed evil, dividing the world (or cosmos) and creating a tension among the outside forces. This kind of orientation creates tensions and dichotomies within believers because what is located outside the self is thought superior, and that inside, inferior.

Native American Indian spiritualities, on the other hand, provided me with guidelines to construct a reality orientation uniting all internal and external forces as part of an integrated whole, all of equal importance. The essence of this reality orientation is a force of life which pervades everything that exists in all realms known to Native American believers. To them, the Great Spirit pervades the sky (stars, wind, rain), the forces of the earth (mountains, rivers), the forces of beings (animals and humans), the forces of nature (trees, plants), and the forces of events (earthquakes). Adopting this kind of orientation allowed me the opportunity to feel myself as part of a greater whole, equal in importance to all in reality rather than inferior to a superior force.

The following excerpt from a paper I wrote detailing the transformation process from a Catholic/Christian reality orientation to my current personal spirituality portrays the impact of studying Native American spiritualities. The orientation shifts from relying on external forces

to define life's meaning, to uniting internal forces with external ones.

*   *   *   *

I had been away from the Catholic Church as a practitioner for quite some time, just kind of tabling the beliefs, not really knowing what to do with them. This led me very early in my undergraduate career to start searching for new perspectives in which to understand all the beliefs I had held. It was fascinating one day as I was driving in the countryside. For a part of the drive I thought about the man Jesus who I was raised to believe in. I realized for the first time that this could very well have been an historical person who was seen by society as someone very different, someone who had some ideas to share about the plight of what it meant to be human. When I could relate to this dominating force that I have encountered in Christianity as human, the system lost much of its control on my being.

This experience led me to seek understanding of other kinds of ideas for what it meant to be human and different realms of reality for comprehending that humanity. Drug experimentation "stopped my world"; it allowed me to see into myself and relate to others in a way that was undefined by standard norms and I could feel that there were other forces of being to be explored. In essence, internal and external awareness increased. This led me to feel connections within my emerging self-defined reality — I was not just a human here to exploit the remainder of what the Catholic God had provided, rather I would be in harmonious existence.

I then did some coursework on Native American Indians focusing research on their specific spiritual systems, what happened to their systems when Christians invaded America and the resulting cultural/spiritual combinations of the two systems. Native American spirituality was to help solidify this new developing perspective of being human, basically human, in conjunction with how humans fit in the larger world perspective with the trees, the flowers, the animals, the earth and the entities that could not be seen. There were internal and external forces of being to Native Americans rather than the single ruling force of authority in Christianity, and this conceptualization has helped me to change how I perceived reality. There was no longer a dichotomized cosmos of good and evil, rather all took place and united in one harmonious cosmos. I could relate to this wholeness, I wanted to be this wholeness, and for a couple of years I felt I would only be satisfied if I were to go and join Native Americans in their environment.

I was particularly moved by a book called *Seven Arrows* which contained a detailed path explaining Plains Indians' philosophy on how to attain the wholeness. The Medicine Way of the Sioux, the Comanches, the Crow and the Blackfeet has definitely left a deep imprint on my eclectic spirituality. It is an internal path on which one embarks to grow in Trust, Introspection, Wisdom and Illumination. This book is such an internal, integrated part of my peace. I feel it. And whenever I read it I see parts of myself on the pages.

Reading this book also led me to acquire a new name. Native American children receive their names when adults notice a distinguishing characteristic or through events that occur around the child to be named. A person can receive several names throughout life, in line with personality transformations and one's modes of being. When I read this book I was inspired to claim a name in line with my personality and modes of being. Since my being thrives in the morning sun, I am at my peak at that time, and since my spirit is so moved by mountains and feels so at peace in that environment, I chose the name Morning Sun Mountain Woman. Here is my visual image.

Another event which helped me to understand my spirit and personality occurred one day as I was riding my bicycle out in the country. I was soaring swiftly down a long hill, enjoying the speed in the open air. I looked over toward the morning sun and I had a companion; a bird had joined me and we were racing onward down the hill. We went for about a mile and the bird turned off, the race was a draw. That same summer I was riding again, feeling so free on my self-propelled machine, and the next thing I knew I was surrounded by a flock of birds who raced me down the path. After two experiences of joining our feathered friends in motion, and after experiencing the speed with which my spirit and personality had been growing, I knew I was Woman Who Races Birds. I had acquired yet another name in the Native American tradition.

In making these spiritual transformations, then, I changed my reality orientation from a construction which was almost totally outside of my being to one which could feel the interconnectedness of outside forces to my inside forces. This union is evident in having named my being within the context of a total reality and the result of these changes is harmonious peace instead of a tension-ridden existence.

Women, Feminism, and the Craft

Margot Adler

There are few moments in life, for most of us, when one feels as if one has stepped into a Minoan fresco or into the life of a wall painting from an Etruscan tomb. But on a full-moon summery night, in the unlikely borough of Staten Island, I entered such a moment.

Nineteen women, including a visiting Italian feminist and a well-known writer, sat nude in a circle in a darkened room. Molded candles of yellow hung by thongs from a loft bed. The small, bright flames cast a pattern of light and shadow. The room seemed powered by the muted oranges and reds of the bed coverings, and by the sweet scent of damiana mixed with marijuana, and by the pungent incenses that permeated the air, incenses with names like Vesta and Priestess.

A bathtub was filled with cool water, scented with musk and flower petals. A flutist played soft music while the women, one by one, entered the water, bathed, and were towel-dried by the others. There was laughter and a sense of ease.

After a short ritual a goblet was filled to the brim with wine and passed sunwise around the circle. The most powerful moment was yet to come: the pouring of libations to the goddesses and heroines of old. Each woman took a sip, then dipped her fingers into the wine and sprinkled a few drops into the air and onto the floor. As she did so, she invoked a particular goddess, gave thanks, or expressed a personal or collective desire. The well-known writer asked for the inspiration of Sappho to aid her in the work on her new book. The Roman Goddess Flora was thanked for the coming of spring and summer. Laverna—Roman goddess of thieves—was invoked to help a woman gain acquittal in a court case. Laverna was invoked again by a woman who had been caught using

"slugs" instead of tokens in the New York subways.[1] Demeter, Isis, Hecate, Diana—the names continued. The goblet passed to each woman three times and the requests became more and more collective. Concerns were expressed for the coven as a whole, for women in struggle everywhere, for women in prison and in mental wards, for the feminist movement. And great hopes for the future were expressed by all. The ritual ended with the music of drums and flutes.

Fruit was brought out and shared—a large bowl carved from a watermelon, filled with blueberries and pieces of honeydew and cantaloupe. There were plates filled with olives and dates. There was a foamy strawberry drink and a huge block of ice cream covered with berries, and one large spoon. It was easy to feel transported to another age, some great festival, perhaps, an ancient college of priestesses on a remote island somewhere in the Aegean. . . .

This meeting was not unique. Such rituals have been taking place in many parts of the country. Feminist covens are springing up all over the United States, some of them showing more creativity, more energy, and more spontaneity than many of the more "traditional" groups that have been in existence for years. I have had personal contact with nine of these covens, located in Texas, California, New York, Oregon, Florida, and Massachusetts. There are others in Missouri, Illinois, Pennsylvania, and, almost certainly, many other states.

The presence of the feminist movement as a force that connects with Neo-Paganism and modern Witchcraft has had many ramifications. Links have been forged between these groups and new strains have been created. Many men (and some women) in the more mainstream Craft groups are upset by the growth of feminist covens, since many feminist Witches have purposely rejected some principles, norms, and structures of the modern Craft. Moreover, a number of feminists have stated that women are Witches by right of the fact that they are women, that nothing else is needed, and feminist Witch Z Budapest has at times declared the Craft to be "Wimmins Religion," a religion not open to men. In addition, feminist Witches have stated that Witchcraft is not incompatible with politics, and further that the Craft is a religion historically conceived in rebellion and can therefore be true to its nature only when it continues its ancient fight against oppression.

In most of what we still may call the "counterculture," the split between the political and the spiritual seems to be widening. In contrast, portions of the feminist movement seem to be combining political and spiritual concerns as if they were two streams of a single river. In the past four years there have been a number of feminist conferences on questions of spirituality; several have attracted more than a thousand participants. On the same agenda with discussions of Witchcraft, matriarchies, and amazons and workshops on the psychic arts, such as tarot, astrology, massage, psychic healing, and meditation, are discussions and workshops on the relationship between political, economic, and spiritual concerns.[2] It has become clear at these conferences that many women regard political struggles and spiritual development as interdependent, and feel that both are needed to create a society and culture that would be meaningful to them.

Linking feminist politics with spirituality and, in particular, with Witchcraft is not a new idea; the connection, which may be very ancient, was noticed in 1968 by the founders of WITCH, a group of women who engaged in political and surrealist protest actions. In its first manifesto WITCH stated that the link between women, Witchcraft, and politics is very old:

WITCH is an all-woman Everything. It's theater, revolution, magic, terror, joy, garlic flowers, spells. It's an awareness that witches and gypsies were the original guerillas and resistance fighters against oppression—particularly the oppression of women— down through the ages. Witches have always been women who dared to be: groovy, courageous, aggressive, intelligent, nonconformist, explorative, curious, independent, sexually liberated, revolutionary. (This possibly explains why nine million of them have been burned.) Witches were the first Friendly Heads and Dealers, the first birth-control practitioners and abortionists, the first alchemists (turn dross into gold and you devalue the whole idea of money!). They bowed to no man, being the living remnants of the oldest culture of all—one in

which men and women were equal sharers in a truly cooperative society, before the death-dealing sexual, economic, and spiritual repression of the Imperialist Phallic Society took over and began to destroy nature and human society.[3]

The organization came into existence on All Hallows Eve 1968. The original name of the group was Women's International Terrorist Conspiracy from Hell, a name that certainly ruffled the feathers of conservative members of the Craft. But actually, only the letters were fixed; the name kept changing to suit particular needs. At a demonstration against the policies of Bell Telephone the group emerged as Women Incensed at Telephone Company Harassment. This kind of change happened a number of times.

At the time WITCH was founded it was considered a fringe phenomenon by the women's movement. Today its sentiments would be accepted by a much larger number of feminists, albeit still a minority.

Up to now we have seen the Neo-Pagan revival as a movement of men and women attempting to live a way of life and uphold values that have been a minority vision in Western culture. In general, Neo-Pagans embrace the values of spontaneity, nonauthoritarianism, anarchism, pluralism, polytheism, animism, sensuality, passion, a belief in the goodness of pleasure, in religious ecstasy, and in the goodness of *this* world, as well as the possibility of many others. They have abandoned the "single vision" for a view that upholds the richness of myth and symbol, and that brings nourishment to repressed spiritual needs as well as repressed sensual needs. "Neo-Pagans," one priestess told me, "may differ in regard to tradition, concept of deity, and ritual forms. But all view the earth as the Great Mother who has been raped, pillaged, and plundered, who must once again be exalted and celebrated if we are to survive."

Most women and men who have entered Neo-Paganism have done so because the basic tenets or the actual practices of one or another Neo-Pagan group came close to feelings and beliefs they already held. It "felt like home." It provided a spiritual and religious framework for celebration, for psychic and magical exploration, and for ecological concern and love of nature.

But in the last few years many women have taken a different path to Neo-Paganism. These feminists have a history of political action. They view all human concerns as both spiritual and political, and they regard the separation between the two as a false idea born of "patriarchy," an idea unknown before classical times and one that has produced much bitter fruit—the splitting of human beings into "minds" and "bodies." In this country, as we shall see, the writings of Native Americans often make this same point: that there is a relationship between the political and the spiritual. What is the nature of this understanding? How have feminists come to it? And how has this led to an identification with Witches and Witchcraft?

The two women who edited the *New Woman's Survival Sourcebook*[4] describe what they found on a cross-country journey:

> . . . we found wherever there are feminist communities, women are exploring psychic and non-material phenomena; reinterpreting astrology; creating and celebrating feminist rituals around birth, death, menstruation; reading the Tarot; studying pre-patriarchal forms of religion; reviving and exploring esoteric goddess-centered philosophies such as Wicce. . . . When we encountered this trend on our first stops, our initial reaction was indifference bordering on uneasiness and apprehension, a frequent reaction among feminists who are intellectually oriented or who are political activists.

Susan Rennie and Kirsten Grimstad said that they began to feel that their early impressions stemmed from a conditioning that had led them to suspect and ridicule anything that could not be "scientifically validated" and that they had always associated things spiritual with reactionary politics. They soon changed their view. As they traveled, they came to feel that women were becoming sensitized to "the psychic potential inherent in human nature," that women are "the repository of powers and capabilities that have been suppressed, that have been casualties of Western *man's* drive to technological control over nature." They put forth the idea that women have an even deeper source of alienation than that which comes from the imposition of sex roles; that, in fact, patriarchy has created the erroneous idea of a split between mind and body and that women's exploration of spirituality is "in effect striving for a total integration and wholeness," an act that takes the feminist struggle into an entirely new dimension. "It amounts," they said, "to a redefinition of reality," a reality that challenges mechanistic views of science and religion as well as masculine politics.

As we listened to women (these were the long night sessions) telling about their discoveries, explora-

tions, experiences of the spiritual, nonmaterial in their lives, our conviction grew that this trend is not reactionary, not authoritarian, not mystical, not solipsistic. The effect we observed was that this reaching out for a broader conception of our natural powers, a larger vision of wholeness, is energizing, restorative, regenerative.[5]

Morgan McFarland, feminist and Witch, told me that for years she had kept her feminist politics and her Witchcraft separate. She said that when she first "blew her cover" and told her feminist friends that she was a Witch, she did so because she wanted to share with women a perspective that was broader than political action.

"I felt they were standing on a spiritual abyss and looking for something. And also, that I was looking for strong, self-defined, balanced women who were capable of perpetuating something that is beautiful and vital to the planet. Within my own tradition it is the women who preserve the lore and the knowledge and pass it on from one to another. I have begun to see a resurgence of women returning to the Goddess, seeing themselves as Her daughters, finding Paganism on their own within a very feminist context. Feminism implies equality, self-identification, and individual strength for women. Paganism has been, for all practical purposes, antiestablishment spirituality. Feminists and Pagans are both coming from the same source without realizing it, and heading toward the same goal without realizing it, and the two are now beginning to interlace."

The journey of feminist women toward a spirituality that does not compromise political concerns took less than five years. It probably began with the consciousness-raising group, which gave women a chance to talk about their seemingly private, personal experiences and find them validated by thousands of other women. The great lesson of CR was that personal feelings were to be trusted and acted upon, and that the personal was political. The step from the CR group to the coven was not long. Both are small groups that meet regularly and are involved in deeply personal questions. Only the focus differs.

Consciousness-raising provided an opportunity for women (some of them for the first time) to talk about their lives, make decisions, and act upon them, without the presence of men. Women used such groups to explore their relations with women, men, work, motherhood and children, their own sexuality, lesbianism, their past youth, and the coming of old age. Many women began to explore their dreams and fantasies; sometimes they tentatively began individual and collective psychic experiments.

Most of the original CR groups no longer exist. Most of the women have moved on into political action or, in many cases, into the exploration of women's history, which has led a number of them into research on matriarchy. This research has turned up legends of the amazons and the myth cycles involving ancient goddesses and heroines; it has led women to the Great Mother Goddess in all her aspects. It has also led many women into magic and psychic work. Jean Mountaingrove, a coordinator of *WomanSpirit,* talked with me about this process.

"Feminism tells us to trust ourselves. So feminists began experiencing something. We began to believe that, yes indeed, we *were* discriminated against on the job; we began to see that motherhood was not all it was advertised to be. We began to trust our own feelings, we began to believe in our own orgasms. These were the first things. Now we are beginning to have spiritual experiences and, for the first time in thousands of years, we trust it. We say, 'Oh, this is an experience of mine, and feminism tells me there must be something to this, because it's all right to trust myself!' So women began to trust what they were experiencing. For example, a woman has a dream about stones and she goes to the library to see what there is about stones. Then she finds Stonehenge. Then she gets interested in the Druids and discovers that people do ceremonies and that this is often called Witchcraft. Then this woman becomes interested in Witches, and goes to them to find out what's going on. I think that's how connections are made."

Enter one of the many feminist bookstores in this country and look at the titles of poetry and literary magazines with names like *Hecate, 13th Moon, Dykes and Gorgons, Hera, Wicce,* and *Sinister Wisdom,* and you will have an idea of the connection between Witchcraft and goddess worship and the women's movement. Almost all these magazines identify women with the Goddess and with Witches. The Witch, after all, is an extraordinary symbol—independent, antiestablishment, strong, and proud. She is political, yet spiritual and magical. The Witch is woman as martyr; she is persecuted by the ignorant; she is the woman who lives outside society and outside society's definition of woman.

In a society that has traditionally oppressed women there are few positive images of female power. Some of the most potent of these are the Witches, the ancient healers, and the powerful women of preclassical Aegean civilizations and Celtic myth. Many women entering on

an exploration of spirituality have begun to create *experiences,* through ritual and dreams, whereby they can *become* these women and act with that kind of power and strength, waiting to see what changes occur in their day-to-day lives. After all, if for thousands of years the image of woman has been tainted, we must either go back to when untainted images exist or create new images from within ourselves. Women are doing both. Whether the images exist in a kind of atavistic memory thousands of years old (as many women believe) or are simply powerful models that can be internalized, women are beginning to create ritual situations in which these images become real. Priestess McFarland writes:

> We are each Virgin Huntresses, we are each Great Mothers, we are Death Dealers who hold out the promise of rebirth and regeneration. We are no longer afraid to see ourselves as her daughters, nor are we afraid to refuse to be victims of this subtle Burning Time. The Wicce is Revolutionary.

Some writers, such as Sally Gearhart, have maintained the division between spiritual and political, arguing strongly against the effectiveness of most present-day political action. Gearhart has written, in the pages of *WomanSpirit,* that the three known strategies of political action—political revolution, seizing power within the system, and setting up alternative structures—have failed, and that only a fourth strategy, "re-sourcement," finding a "deeper," "prior" source as powerful as the system itself, can threaten it and lead to change. She has noted that thousands of women have separated themselves from society and the world of men to lead isolated lives with other women, and she has called upon women who choose to remain in the mainstream of society, or women who have no choice, to set up a buffer state to protect the separatist women until they can gain the strength to create a new women's culture.[6]

But other women and most feminist witches such as Z Budapest, believe in the firm, continuing connection between spirituality and day-to-day political action. As an exile from Hungary, feminist, Witch, and leader of the Susan B. Anthony Coven in Los Angeles, Z has made her life a vivid example of this connection. We have seen how she left Hungary in 1956, but soon found her oppression as a woman in the United States equal to her oppression in Hungary. Z brought the status of Witchcraft as a religion to public attention with her trial in 1975 on the charge of violating a Los Angeles statute against fortune-telling. This law is one of the countless vague antioccult laws that exist in almost all cities and states. Ostensibly they exist to prevent "fraud," but they ban divination of all kinds, not merely divination for money. The Los Angeles law forbids the practice of "magic," clairvoyance, palmistry, and so forth. Since Z does tarot readings professionally, she was "set up" by a woman police agent who telephoned for a reading. Z was brought to trial, convicted, and fined. Many witnesses, ranging from anthropologists to Witches, came to her defense.

Z told me that "religion" was "the supreme politics." "Religion is where you can reach people in their mysteries, in the parts of their being that have been neglected, but that have been so important and painful; and you can soothe and heal, because self-images can be repaired through knowledge, but only experience can truly teach. The experience is to allow us these conditions again. Let us be priestesses again. Let us feel what that feels like, how that serves the community."

Z's vision for the future is a socialist matriarchy. Like many feminist Witches, she has a vision of a past matriarchal age, during which "the Earth was treated as Mother and wimmin were treated as Her priestesses." The manifesto accepts many of the theses proposed by Elizabeth Gould Davis in *The First Sex:* that women were once supreme and lost that supremacy when men, exiled from the matriarchies, formed into bands and overthrew the matriarchies, inventing rape and other forms of violence.

Ritual

Theorists of politics, religion, and nature have often viewed the universe in a strangely similar way. Many have noted the interconnectedness of everything in the universe and also the fact that most people do not perceive these connections. Spiritual philosophers have often called this lack of perception "estrangement" or "lack of attunement"; materialists have often called it "alienation" or, in some cases, "false consciousness." Perhaps theory, analysis, and the changing of society can end our experience of alienation on the conscious level. Ritual and magical practice aim to end it on the unconscious level of the deep mind.

By ritual, of course, we do not mean the continuation of those dry, formalized, repetitive experiences that most of us have suffered through; these may once have produced powerful experiences, but in most cases they have been taken over by some form of "the state" for purposes not conducive to human liberation. We are talking about the rituals that people create to get in touch with those powerful parts of themselves that cannot be experienced on a verbal level. These are parts of our being that have often been scorned and suppressed. Rituals are also created to acknowledge on this deeper level the movements of the seasons and the natural world, and to celebrate life and its processes.

Many strong priestesses in the Craft have talked about the primacy and importance of ritual.

Sharon Devlin: "Ritual is a sacred drama in which you are both audience and participant. The purpose of it is to activate those parts of the mind that are not activated by everyday activity, the psychokinetic and telekinetic abilities, the connection between the eternal power and ourselves. . . . We need to re-create ecstatic states where generation of energy occurs."

Z Budapest: "The purpose of ritual is to wake up the old mind in us, to put it to work. The old ones inside us, the collective consciousness, the many lives, the divine eternal parts, the senses and parts of the brain that have been ignored. Those parts do not speak English. They do not care about television. But they do understand candlelight and colors. They do understand nature.

Alison Harlow: "It is a conciousness-altering technique, the best there is. Through ritual one can alter one's state of consciousness so that one can become perceptive to nonmaterial life forms, whatever you choose to call them, and through this perception one can practice subjective sciences."

In what additional ways do feminists think about ritual? Jean Mountaingrove began by telling me that, since dreams seem to speak from our unconscious mind to our conscious mind, perhaps ritual is the way our conscious mind speaks to our unconscious mind. She and Ruth would occasionally share water from a stream, she said, to symbolize the sharing of the waters of life. She added, "If I want my unconscious mind to understand that I love Ruth and that she is my partner, then we engage in a ritual together and the connection is very deep. All the words we say to each other may not do that. Ritual makes the connection on another level."

Jean observed that ritual has a particular and radical relevance for feminists. "Since our culture—the one we share with men— is so contaminated, often when a group of women get together we only have words to use, and these words are all conditioned. Often we can argue and use words to divide. But our actions have not been so limited by men's definitions. So we need to find actions that have clearness about them, that do not have hierarchical connotations . . . because some of our symbolic behavior has also been contaminated. If I pat someone on the head, it may mean that I am bigger and better than she is; it may be condescending . . . but if we can find ways, like washing each other's hands, actions that we do mutually and that have not been contaminated, we can use such actions as a kind of vocabulary that cuts underneath all the divisiveness and unites us."

Women are creating this new language. They are developing psychic skills in workshops with names such as "Womancraft" and "Womanshare"; they are reinterpreting events related to women in a new light and using these insights to create new ritual forms. For example, a number of women are using "Moon Huts" for retreats during menstruation. In doing this, they are re-creating an experience common to women in ancient times and in many tribal societies today. These women are convinced that, contrary to popular scholarly assumption, such retreats were not forced on women because of "uncleanliness" but were introduced by women themselves to celebrate their mysteries and to have a time of collective interchange. It has also been theorized that before artificial light and modern forms of contraception all the women of a tribe often menstruated at the same time.

Some women have begun to work with their dreams. In one instance, twelve women spent a weekend in the wilderness together. They slept in a circle with their heads together, facing inward, their bodies like spokes of a wheel. They wove "dream nets" from wool and fibers and sewed "dream pillows" filled with mugwort and psyllium seeds. A woman who experienced this weekend told about her dream:

> I am with a mass of chanting women under the deck of an old ship which we are rowing across the sea. All the women are looking for their city. We have come to this land and see a man standing on the shore. He asks, "Why have you come here?" We say, "We came here to find our city." He says, "Go back. Your city is not here." We pay no attention to him but start through this forest right at the edge of the water and walk down an inward-turning spiral road which leads us down to a city in its center. At the bottom is an old woman. We say, "We have come to find our city." She says, "This is an old city. This is not your city. Your city is not here. You have to look further." The women then disperse to look for our city.

WomanSpirit commented:

> Margaret's dream tells me that we will not find our culture in the men's world, but neither will we find it in our ancient woman culture. It is still to be found.[7]

One example of a simple and powerful ritual is described in an early issue of WomanSpirit: an attempt to come to terms with the concept of Eve. Feminists and Neo-Pagans naturally feel that the story of Adam and Eve, as commonly interpreted, has probably done more to debase and subjugate women than any other such tale in Western history. In addition, the story has been used to inculcate demeaning attitudes toward mind, body, sensuality, and the pursuit of knowledge. WomanSpirit suggests that only by turning over biblical tradition and regarding Eve positively, as the bringer of knowledge and consciousness, can we end permanently the split between mind and body and the hatred of both that was foisted upon us by Christianity and much of the classical and Judaic traditions from which Christianity sprang. In an article titled "Eve and Us" a woman leading a class in theology speaks of coming to acknowledge Eve. She presents a counterthesis: Eve was "the original creator of civilization." The Fall was really "the dawn of the awakening of the human consciousness." The class notes that it is Adam who is passive. Eve is persuaded logically and rationally to become "as the gods." "Eve and the serpent were right," said the leader of the discussion. She opened up "a whole new world of consciousness. Every advance in literature, science, the arts can be traced mythically back to this event and in this light it is indeed Eve who is the original creator of civilization . . . and we women have the right and the responsibility to claim her as our own."

At this point in the class a spontaneous ritual occurred. Unlike many rituals in the Craft, which are learned carefully, this came from an immediate need to affirm women's being. A woman produced an apple and "the apple was ceremoniously passed around the circle and each woman took a bite, symbolizing her acceptance of and willingness to claim Eve as her own and recognize our mutual oneness with her."[8]

Women have also begun to create lunar rituals. The association of women with the moon is, of course, an ancient association.

> Last night [one woman writes] we hung out of the east windows and howled at the moon, incredible orb gliding up over the eastern hills . . . and made

up a song to her. During the night I fell into a dream that enabled me to undersee the belly of death, as the giver of life. . . .[9]

Another wrote of a celebration of the New Moon in June 1974:

Women seemed to be coming up the hill for hours. I hear voices and flutes in the distance. . . . We sit in a large circle in front of the cabin. We join hands and follow each other down to the meadow, down into the darkness. We tell stories of darkness. Ruth tells the myth of Persephone being abducted by the lord of the dark underworld. . . . We begin a free word and sound association from the word "darkness." This is very moving. Words and sounds come fast and flowing and die down again. There are images of fear as well as power and strength expressed, a lot of images of calm, warmth and rest. A large candle is lit. . . . [Billie] has made ten small bags with drawstrings, each from a different material. Each has a black bead attached to the drawstrings, signifying the dark moon. She gives them to us to keep. We are very pleased as the bags are passed around the circle. . . . We find seeds inside the bags. Seeds, the small beginning, the New Moon. . . . We stand for a farewell of Robin Morgan's 'Monster,' ending with us all shouting, 'I am a monster!'[10]

Confronting the "Goddess"

It is not surprising that women involved with these rituals and perceptions should begin to confront the idea of a feminine deity. They have found the Goddess, or have been led to the Goddess, and the idea of "Goddess" is fraught with problems and potentialities for feminists.

No matter how diverse Neo-Pagans' ideas about deities, almost all of them have some kind of "Thou Art God/dess" concept, even though a few whom I have met would say that such a concept as articulated by the Church of All Worlds contains a bit of hubris. Nevertheless, most would agree that the goal of Neo-Paganism is, in part, to become what we potentially are, to become "as the gods," or, if we *are* God/dess, to recognize it, to make our God/dess-hood count for something. This is a far different notion from the common conception of deity in Western thought as something "exclusive," "above," "apart," and "outside." Tim Zell has said that in Neo-

Paganism deity is *immanent,* not *transcendent.* Others have said that it is *both* immanent and transcendent.

But whatever "deity" is for Neo-Pagans, there is no getting around the fact that the popular conception of deity is *male.* And this is so, despite the countless esoteric Christian and Jewish teachings that say otherwise. The elderly Neo-Pagan author W. Holman Keith, whose little-noticed book *Divinity as the Eternal Feminine* came out in 1960, noted:

In spite of all that Christians say to the contrary, they conceive of deity as male. They will protest that they do not believe in anthropomorphism, that God is spirit, etc. But these protestations do not completely dispose of the above contention.[11]

More recently Mary Daly has written extensively on the idea that all the major religions today function to legitimate patriarchy and that since "God is male, then the male is God," and that "God the father" legitimates all earthly Godfathers, including Vito Corleone, Pope Paul, and Richard Nixon.[12] Since this image called "God" is the image beyond ourselves, greater than ourselves, it becomes the image of power and authority, even for most of those who profess atheism. It functions as a powerful oppressive image, whether or not we believe in "him"; it can also affect one's self-image. And this remains true whether "man" created "God" in "his" own image or the other way around. As many occultists would say: There is a continuing relationship between the human mind and its creations, and those creations affect all other human minds.

Western women have been excluded from the deity quest for thousands of years, since the end of Goddess worship in the West. The small exception is the veneration paid by Catholics to the Virgin Mary, a pale remnant of the Great Goddess. So, if one purpose of deity is to give us an image we can *become,* it is obvious that women have been left out of the quest, or at least have been forced to strive for an oppressive and unobtainable masculine image. Mary Daly has proposed to answer this problem with the idea of "God as a verb," but many women find this too abstract and prefer to look to the ancient goddesses.

A female deity conceived of as all-powerful and all-encompassing can create contradictions and other problems in an anarchistic feminist community that emphasizes the value of self. But the attractiveness of the Goddess to women was inevitable. She touched a deep chord and has been celebrated in the music of Kay Gardner and in a number of feminist songs, ranging from Cassie Culver's humorous "Good Old Dora" to Alex Dobkin's extraordinary hymn to the Goddess and the Goddess within all women, "Her Precious Love."[13]

Many women have had powerful experiences with deity as feminine. "It never occurred to me to create my own religion," wrote one woman, "or more importantly, that god was female. Discovering that femaleness gave me a tremendous sense of relief. I felt her blessing touch me for the first time. I felt a great weight drop from me. I could actually feel my last prejudices against my own female mind and body falling away."[14]

Jean Mountaingrove, who spent twenty years as a practicing Quaker, told me of her first experience of deity as feminine.

"There was this Quaker meeting at Pendle Hill, a Quaker retreat center outside of Philadelphia. We used to have meetings every morning and lots of weighty Quakers came to these meetings. And I sat in the back row, morning after morning, listening to all these messages coming through about 'the fatherhood of God' and 'the brotherhood of Man' and 'he' and 'him.' And one morning, after about thirty minutes, that feeling inside of me that I have always learned to trust as guidance just swelled and swelled until I was shaking, a feeling that I should say something. And I felt if I didn't say it, I would be betraying something I had learned to trust. All I said was, 'Mother. Sister. Daughter.' And it fell like a rock through this still pool of fatherhood and brotherhood. But then, everyone in the stillness could reflect on what that might mean. I had declared myself. I had declared myself as being—what shall I say?—on the fringe. My feminism was considered 'in poor taste.' But several women came up to me afterwards and hugged me, and that meant a lot."

Jean told me that years later, at a commune in Oregon, she began getting impressions from a special grove of trees. "I had a scientific background which makes fun of this sort of thing," she said. "I thought it was pretty kooky. But Ruth had a background in Jungian psychology and had read *The White Goddess,* so she watched all of this happening with a lot of understanding which I myself did not have. I was drawn to the tallest tree in the grove and I would come to it and just cry; and it was tears of joy and relief; and I would feel that I was whole and perfect; my own judgment of myself was that I was very inadequate, but the spirit of the tree, which I called Mother, seemed to think I was all right."

Some of the women I met had an easy and long-term relationship with the Goddess. One woman told me that she would go hunting with her father and brother as a child, and would call upon Diana as mistress of the hunt. This recalled my own invocations to Artemis and Athena when I was twelve.

Other women had a problem with the idea of "Goddess." "It's amazing," one wrote, "how much the basis of my life now has to do with the things I was raised not to believe in and to some extent still don't . . . that goddess business makes me very antsy too. I would like to know more about how spirituality ties in (or doesn't tie in) with what I call 'real life'—going to work, having relationships, getting sick, doing or not doing politics."[15]

In another example the editors of *WomanSpirit* described the results of a discussion among a group of women:

> *Many of us had a real difficulty with the concept of a goddess. Who was this goddess and why was she created? We felt she represented different forms of energy and light to different people. Even though we had trouble with the words, we felt that the force of the goddess was inevitable, she was flowing through us all by whatever name, she was the feeling of the presence of life. Goddess was a new name for our spiritual journey, the experience of life.*[16]

The obvious criticism is that the idea of a single Goddess, conceived of as transcendent and apart, creates as many problems as the male "God." Trading "Daddy" for "Mommy" is not a liberation. A woman takes up this question.

> *I have been thinking for days and weeks about Goddess. The word, the concept, the idea, the projection, the experience. For many months I have been experimenting with the word, using it freely, reverently, longingly. That is my strongest experience in regard to it, one of longing—oh that there were a Goddess to pray to, to trust in, to believe in. But I do not believe in a Goddess.*
>
> *Not a Goddess who exists as a being or person. Yes, the goddess who is each of us, the one within. . . . She is the inner strength, the light, the conscious woman who knows her own perfection, her own perfect harmony with the cosmos. . . .*
>
> *This common existence of all things is holiness to me. . . . I understand that the word "Goddess" is used to express this unity reality in a symbolic way. So too is "God" used. There is no one called*

"Goddess" to seek outside of ourselves or to enter into us. There is only in each our own center of unity energy which is connected to all. . . .

But I do not believe that changing the sex of that concept does away with its problems. Not at all. To say Goddess instead of God still continues the separation of power, the division between person and the power "out there!". . .[17]

I doubt this dilemma exists as forcibly for women in the Craft, perhaps because some of them have never considered these ideas. But, more importantly, as priestesses, they are taught that within the circle they *are* the Goddess incarnate. And they have been taught to draw that power into themselves through the ritual of Drawing Down the Moon. Women who have come to the Goddess outside the channels of Neo-Paganism and the Craft are beginning to find rituals and concepts that allow for the same idea. They are finding the Goddess within themselves and within all women. And, as might be expected, those feminists who have found joy in ritual, and who have discovered that the concept of "Goddess" feels right inside, are often drawn into the Craft.

The Streams Converge

On a Friday night in Boston, April 23, 1976, some one thousand women sat down on the benches and pews of the old Arlington Street Church. The benches filled up and the women spilled over onto the floor and into the aisles, and became silent as the flute music of Kay Gardner created a sense of peace. The lights were dimmed and Morgan McFarland, Dianic High Priestess, came to the front, wearing a long white robe, accompanied by four members of her women's coven, the same coven that we have seen mentioned in *The New Broom*. The occasion was a ritual: "Declaring and Affirming Our Birth," to mark the beginning of a three-day women's spirituality conference, with the unusual name "Through the Looking Glass: A Gynergenetic Experience." The conference was attended by over thirteen hundred women, and besides an address by feminist theologian Mary Daly, the conference was most noteworthy for the large number of Witch priestesses who attended from as far away as Texas and California.

This relationship between feminist spirituality and the Craft is complex. Perhaps, if we had to choose one instant to catch all the qualities, problems, strains, and enormous potentialities in that uneasy relationship, this ritual could be such a prism. There are Morgan and the women in the coven standing in the church, looking a bit apart, somewhat too elegantly dressed, too stereotypically "feminine." I remembered how much more at ease they were working a ritual in a Dallas living room, where none of us wore anything except a string of beads. But here they are, standing in front of the altar of a church, holding candles, while a thousand women watch and wait. Most of these women are taking it in for the first time, realizing that they are all here to begin the creation of a new culture. Morgan steps out in front and speaks.

"In the infinite moment before all Time began, the Goddess arose from Chaos and gave birth to Herself . . . before anything else had been born . . . not even Herself. And when She had separated the Skies from the Waters and had danced upon them, the Goddess in Her ecstasy created everything that is. Her movements made the wind, and the Element Air was born and did breathe."

A candle is lit in the East. Morgan speaks.

"And the Goddess named Herself: Arianrhod — Cardea — Astarte. And sparks were struck from Her dancing feet so that She shone forth as the Sun, and the stars were caught in Her hair, and comets raced about Her, and Element Fire was born."

A candle is lit in the South.

"And the Goddess named Herself: Sunna — Vesta — Pele. About her feet swirled the waters in tidal wave and river and streaming tide, and Element Water did flow."

A candle is lit in the West.

"And She named Herself: Binah — Mari Morgaine — Lakshmi. And She sought to rest Her feet from their dance, and She brought forth the Earth so that the shores were Her footstool, the fertile lands Her womb, the mountains Her full breasts, and Her streaming hair the growing things."

A candle is lit in the North.

"And the Goddess named Herself: Cerridwen — Demeter — the Corn Mother. She saw that which was and is and will be, born of Her sacred dance and cosmic delight and infinite joy. She laughed: and the Goddess created Woman in her own image . . . to be the Priestess of the Great Mother. The Goddess spoke to Her daughters, saying, 'I am the Moon to light your path and to speak to your rhythms. I am the Sun who gives you warmth in which to stretch and grow. I am the Wind to blow at your call and the sparkling Air that offers joy. I give to all my priestesses three aspects that are Mine: I am Artemis, the Maiden of the Animals, the Virgin of the Hunt. I am Isis, the Great Mother. I am Ngame, the

Ancient One who winds the shroud. And I shall be called a million names. Call unto me, daughters, and know that I am Nemesis.'"

Later, the cauldron is filled with fire and the chanting begins, at first very softly: "The Goddess is alive, magic is afoot, the Goddess is alive, magic is afoot." Then it becomes louder and louder until it turns into shouts and cries and primeval sounds. Morgan speaks for the last time.

"We are Virgins, Mothers, Old Ones—All. We offer our created energy: to the Spirit of Women Past, to the Spirit of Women yet to come, to womanspirit present and growing. Behold, we move forward together."

At the end of the ritual the women in the church begin to dance and chant, their voices rise and rise and rise until they shake the roof.

Later, a few women said they didn't want priestesses standing apart on pedestals and altars; they did not want to see energy sent "upward"; they wanted it aimed "at the oppressor." Despite this, acknowledging this, the uneasy, explosive, potentially powerful alliance between feminism and the Craft was apparent for all to feel, during this conference where many women said they felt, for the first time, that a new "women's culture" was a reality.

Endnotes

1. Where did feminist Witches get Laverna from, you may ask? From Charles Godfrey Leland's *Aradia, or the Gospel of the Witches* (London: David Nutt, 1899), reprinted (New York: Samuel Weiser, 1974), pp. 89–98: Leland writes that Laverna is mentioned in Horace, *Epistles,* I, xvi, 59–62.
2. Two examples of conferences on feminist spirituality: Through the Looking Glass, a Gynergenetic Experience, in Boston, April 23–25, 1976; A Celebration of the Beguines, in New York City, October 30–31, 1976.
3. I originally saw this manifesto in mimeographed form, but it has been published, thanks to Robin Morgan, in *Sisterhood Is Powerful,* ed. Robin Morgan (New York: Random House, 1970), pp. 539–43. Quotation on p. 539.
4. Kirsten Grimstad and Susan Rennie, eds., *The New Woman's Survival Sourcebook* (New York: Alfred A. Knopf, 1975).

5. Kirsten Grimstad and Susan Rennie, "Spiritual Explorations Cross-country," *Quest,* Vol. 1, No. 4 (Spring 1975), 49–51.
6. Sally Gearhart, "Womanpower: Energy Re-sourcement," *WomanSpirit,* Vol. 2, No. 7 (Spring Equinox 1976), 19–23.
7. Ruth Mountaingrove, "Clues to Our Women's Culture," *WomanSpirit,* Vol. 2, No. 6 (Fall Equinox 1975), 45.
8. Jude Michaels, "Eve & Us," *WomanSpirit,* Vol. 1, No. 1 (Autumn Equinox 1974), 5–6. In connection with this, I am reminded of the words of the fourth-century Emperor Julian, who observed that the doctrine of Adam and Eve was unfit for any enlightened mind: "What could be more foolish than a being unable to distinguish good from bad? . . . In short, God refused to let man taste of wisdom, than which there could be nothing of more value . . . so that the serpent was a benefactor rather than a destroyer of the human race." *The Works of the Emperor Julian.* trans. Wilmer Cave Wright, 3 vols. (Cambridge: Harvard University Press, 1961), III, 327.
9. "Voices," *WomanSpirit,* Vol. 1, No. 1 (Autumn Equinox 1974), 38.
10. Carol, Patti, and Billie, "Moon Over the Mountain: Creating Our Own Rituals," *WomanSpirit,* Vol. 1, No. 1 (Autumn Equinox 1974), 30. Robin Morgan's poem appears in *Monster* (New York: Vintage Books, 1972), pp. 81–86.
11. W. Holman Keith, *Divinity as the Eternal Feminine* (New York: Pageant Press, 1960), p. 14.
12. Mary Daly, *Beyond God the Father* (Boston: Beacon Press, 1973), pp. 16–19.
13. Records: Alix Dobkin, Kay Gardner, et al., "Her Precious Love," on *Lavender Jane Loves Women* (1975), Alix Dobkin Project 1, 210 W. 10 St., New York, N.Y. 10014; Cassie Culver, "Good Old Dora," on *3 Gypsies* (1976), Urana Records—ST-WWE-81; Kay Gardner, *Mooncircles* (1975), Urana Records, a division of Wise Women Enterprises, Inc., P.O. Box 297, Village Station, New York, N.Y. 10014—ST-WWE-80.
14. Fran Winnant, "Our Religious Heritage," *WomanSpirit,* Vol. 1, No. 3 (Spring Equinox 1975), 51.
15. Monica, letter to *WomanSpirit,* Vol. 2, No. 7 (Spring Equinox 1976), 62.
16. *WomanSpirit,* Vol. 2, No. 6 (Fall Equinox 1975), 64.
17. Fran Rominsky, "goddess with a small g," *Woman-Spirit,* Vol. 1, No. 1 (Autumn Equinox 1974), 48.

Introduction: Consequences for Intimate Lives

The feminist movement has had an impact not only on the institutional and individual levels; it has also helped to create new ways through which intimate relationships can be made more egalitarian. However, because there are few institutional and legal supports for alternative relationships, it is a struggle to forge a life in which both partners can have equal access to career fulfillment and domestic "bliss." The readings in this section will explore some of the new kinds of relationships being constructed by those who want a more egalitarian and meaningful life together.

One attempted solution, although by no means the typical one, has been "role-reversal"—the male takes over the traditionally defined woman's place in the home, while the female becomes the primary breadwinner. How role-reversal deepened one man's sense of both the meaning of marriage and the pervasiveness of sexism is described by Joel Roache in "Confessions of a Househusband." More common than role-reversal is the attempt to make a success of the "two-career" marriage. Increasingly, couples are finding that in order for each partner to achieve career success, they may have to reside in different cities. The complexity and problems of such arrangements, including the ever-present conflict with the normative social order, is analyzed by Harriet Engel Gross in her article "Couples Who Live Apart: Time/Place Disjunctions and Their Consequences."

Not only has the feminist movement influenced normatively defined and socially sanctioned relationships, it also has had an impact on those which are not publicly condoned. Letitia Anne Peplau, Susan Cochran, Karen Rook and Christine Padesky, in "Loving Women: Attachment and Autonomy in Lesbian Relationships," describe the impact of feminism on lesbian couples. The authors find that feminist-identified lesbian couples are likely to construct relationships that are both personally intimate and egalitarian, granting each member considerable independence and autonomy. This article suggests that personal independence and deep commitment to one another are not mutually exclusive orientations, and that they are more likely to occur if both partners are committed to a feminist ideology.

Confessions of a Househusband

Joel Roache

Many men are coming to realize that sex-role privilege inflicts enormous damage on them, turning half of humanity into their subordinates and the other half into their rivals, isolating them and making fear and loneliness the norm of their existence. That ponderous abstraction became real for me in what many men consider a trivial realm: housework.

Every movement produces its truisms, assumptions that very soon are scarcely open to argument. The Women's Movement is no exception, and one of its truisms is that the home is a prison for women, trapping them in housework and child care, frustrating and distorting their need for fulfillment as whole persons. Whatever reality lies behind many situation comedy stereotypes— the nag, the clinging wife, the telephone gossip—is rooted in this distortion. Only after I had assumed the role of househusband, and was myself caught in the "trap of domesticity," did I realize that the reality behind those stereotypes is a function of the role, not the person.

Two years ago, my wife Jan and I tried to change (at least within our own lives) society's imposed pattern of dependent servant and responsible master by deciding to share equally the responsibility of housework. We made no specific arrangement (a mistake from which I was to learn a great deal); it was simply understood that I was going to take on roughly half of the domestic chores so that she could do the other work she needed to do.

There was something of a shock for me in discovering the sheer quantity of the housework, and my standards of acceptable cleanliness fell rapidly. It became much easier to see my insistence on neatness as an inherited middle-class hang-up now that I had to do so much of the work myself. One of the long-standing sources of tension between Jan and me was almost immediately understood

and resolved. What's more, I enjoyed it, at first. When not interrupted by the children I could, on a good day, do the kitchen and a bedroom, a load of laundry, and a meal in a little over two hours. Then I'd clean up after the meal and relax for a while with considerable satisfaction. So I approached the work with some enthusiasm, looking forward to seeing it all put right by my own hand, and for a while I wondered what all the fuss was about.

But within a few weeks that satisfaction and that enthusiasm began to erode a little more each time I woke up or walked into the house, only to find it all needed to be done again. Finally, the image of the finished job, the image that encouraged me to start, was crowded out of my head by the image of the job to do all over again. I became lethargic, with the result that I worked less efficiently, so that even when I did "finish," it took longer and was done less well, rendering still less satisfaction. At first I had intellectual energy to spare, thinking about my teaching while washing dishes; pausing in the middle of a load of laundry to jot down a note. But those pauses soon became passive daydreams, fantasies from which I would have to snap myself back to the grind, until finally it was all I could do to keep going at all. I became more and more irritable and resentful.

Something similar happened even sooner and more dramatically to my relationship with our three children. I soon found myself angry with them most of the time, and I almost never enjoyed them. Then I watched myself for a couple of days and realized what was going on. They were constantly interrupting. I had tried simply to be available to them in case they needed me while I went on reading, writing, cleaning, or watching television. But of course with a six-year-old, a four-year-old, and a one-year-old, someone would need me every five to 15 minutes. Just enough time to get into something, and up Jay would come with a toy to be fixed, or Matthew would spill his juice, or Eric would get stuck between the playpen bars and scream. In everything I tried to do, I was frustrated

Reprinted from Joel Roache, "Confessions of a Househusband," in *Ms.,* 1 (November 1972): pp. 25–27, by permission of the author. Copyright 1972 by Joel Roache.

by their constant demands and soon came, quite simply, to hate them; and to hate myself for hating them; and at some level, I suspect, to hate Jan for getting me into this mess. My home life became a study in frustration and resentment.

I soon reached the conclusion that if I was going to keep house and take care of the children, I might as well give up doing anything else at the same time if I hoped to maintain any equilibrium at all. So I deliberately went through my housekeeping paces in a daze, keeping alert for the children but otherwise concentrating on whatever was before me, closing down all circuits not relevant to the work at hand. I maintained my sanity, I think, and I ceased to scream at the children so much, but neither they nor anyone else got the benefit of any creative energy; there just wasn't any. In half a day I could feel my mind turning into oatmeal, cold oatmeal, and it took the other half to get it bubbling again, and by then it was bedtime, and out of physical exhaustion I would have to go to sleep on whatever coherent ideas I might have got together in my few hours of free time.

Things went on this way for quite some time, partly because I couldn't think of an acceptable alternative, and partly because I was on a kind of guilt trip, possessed by the suicidal notion that somehow I had to pay for all those years Jan was oppressed. After a while I began to "adjust"; even cold oatmeal has a certain resilience. I began to perceive my condition as normal, and I didn't notice that my professional work was at a standstill. Then Jan became involved in community organizing, which took up more and more of her time and began to eat into mine, until finally I found myself doing housekeeping and child care from eight to 16 hours a day, and this went on for about eight weeks. The astonishing thing now is that I let this masochistic work load go on so long. I suppose my guilt trip had become almost equivalent to a woman's normal conditioning, in reducing my ability to resist effectively the demands of Jan's organizing. And the excitement of her newly discovered self-sufficiency and independence (after eight years of her struggle to make me recognize what I was doing to her) functioned in the same way as the normal assumption of the superior importance of a male's work as provider.

I can pinpoint the place in time when we saw the necessity for a more careful adjustment of responsibilities, defining duties and scheduling hours more precisely and adhering to them more faithfully. It was at a moment when it became clear that Jan's work was beginning to pay off and her group scored a definite and ap-

parently unqualified success. I went around the house for a full day feeling very self-satisfied, proud of her achievement, *as if it were my own,* which was fine until I realized, somewhere near the end of the day, that much of that sense of achievement resulted from the fact that I had no achievement of my own. I was getting my sense of fulfillment, of self-esteem, *through her,* while she was getting it *through her work.* It had happened: I was a full-fledged househusband.

A similar moment of illumination occurred at about the same time. Jan had spent the afternoon with a friend while I took care of the children and typed a revision of the bibliography for the book I was trying to finish at the time, the kind of drudgery more prosperous authors underpay some woman to do. By the time Jan got home I was in a state of benumbed introversion, and when she began to talk about the substance of her afternoon's conversation, I was at first bored and finally irritated. Before long I was snapping at her viciously. She sat there looking first puzzled, then bewildered, and finally withdrawn. In a kind of reflexive self-defense she cut me off emotionally and went on thinking about whatever was on her mind. As I began to run down, I realized that what she had been trying to talk about would normally be interesting and important to me, yet I had driven her away. Then I looked at her and suddenly had the really weird sensation of seeing myself, my own isolation and frustration when I used to come home and try to talk to her. I realized that I was in her traditional position and felt a much fuller understanding of what that was. In that moment, on the verge of anger, an important part of what we had been doing to each other for all those years became clearer than it had ever been to either of us.

Another problem was suddenly clear to me also. The loneliness and helplessness I had felt before we traded responsibilities had been a function of my own privilege. My socially defined and reinforced role as *the* responsible party to the marriage had cut me off from Jan's experience; had made inevitably futile our attempts to communicate with each other from two very different worlds. Since she has a strong sense of herself as a responsible adult, Jan was bound to resist the limits of her role as dependent and (though we would never have said it) subordinate. When I found myself muttering and bitching, refusing to listen, refusing to provide any positive feedback on her experience in the outside world, I realized that her preoccupation, her nagging and complaining, her virtual absence from my psychic world, had not been neurotic symptoms but expressions of resistance to my privilege and to the power over her life that it conferred.

Jan's failure to force a real change in our life together for so long is a grim tribute to the power of socialization, and to my ability to exploit that power in order to protect myself from reality. When Jan realized how really minimal were the satisfactions of housework, there was also a voice within her (as well as mine without) suggesting that perhaps she was just lazy. If she began to hate the children, she knew that it was because they were helping to prevent her meeting real and legitimate personal needs, but the voices were always there hinting that the real trouble was that she was basically a hateful person and thus a poor mother. If her mind became sluggish, she knew at some level that she was making an adaptive adjustment to her situation, but those voices whispered in a thousand ways that she might be going crazy, or perhaps she was just stupid. And when she became sullen and resentful toward me, the voices were always there to obscure her perception that I had it coming. They even encouraged her to feel guilty, finally, when she did not feel my success as her reward, the payoff for all her drudgery. They kept her from realizing that such a payoff cost her a sense of her independent selfhood; that it was at best the pittance of exploitation: shit wages for shit work.

Those voices, within and without, kept reminding us both that Jan's real destiny was to keep me comfortable and productive and to raise "our" children. The feelings I'd come to experience in a few months had for years made Jan feel lazy, selfish, and egotistic; unable to empathize with the needs of the family (read: my need for success). Just as importantly, her knowledge that the sources of her troubles were not all within herself could not have received any reinforcement in the social world. I was her only link with that world; my affection and "respect" were her only source of assurance that she was real. To the extent that identity depends on recognition by others, she depended on me for that as surely as she depended on me for grocery money. The result was that she was afraid to share with me huge areas of her life, any areas which might threaten my regard for her. She could not afford, psychologically or economically, to challenge me overtly. And when she managed to make any suggestion that her discontent was a function of what was being done to her, it was battered down, by my recriminations, into a quagmire of guilt.

I had had some inkling of all this before I ever committed myself to cooking a meal or washing a single pair of socks (as my responsibility, rather than a favor to her). But at every stage of our experiment in role reversal (or rather our attempt to escape roles) my understanding of her position became more real. I had got a lot of domestic services but I had been denied real contact with a whole human being, and hard upon my guilt came anger, rage at what had been done to us both.

I don't have space here to go on and extend our experience into the world outside the family. It is enough to say that when someone has concrete power over your life, you are going to keep a part of yourself hidden and therefore undeveloped, or developed only in fantasy. Your identity becomes bound up in other people's expectations of you—and that is the definition of alienation. It did not take long for me to make connections between the alienating ways in which Jan had to deal with me in the early years of our marriage and the way that I was dealing with my "senior colleagues," the men and women who had power to fire me and did.

Our experience also helped me to understand the distortions of perception and personality that result from being the "superior" in a hierarchical structure. The nuclear family as we know it is one such structure, perhaps the crucial one. But the alienation which results from privilege pervades all our experience in a society which values human beings on the basis of sex, race, and class and which structures those standards into all its institutions. Housework is only a tip of that iceberg, but for Jan and me it has helped to make the need to fundamentally transform those institutions a gut reality.

Couples Who Live Apart: Time/Place Disjunctions and Their Consequences

Harriet Engel Gross

The cultural premium on voluntarism coupled with the presumed uniqueness of intimate interpersonal relations prevents most people from reflecting upon ways in which larger social forces permeate such relationships. Social scientists, to be sure, enjoy a corrective to this popular view in the heritage from Simmel (1950, 1971) to Goffman (e.g., 1967) which affirms the social structural undergirding of even our seemingly most subjective personal responses. Among our theoretical forefathers it was Simmel particularly, who underscored the ways in which time and space coordinates of social interaction create and maintain subjective realities. His analysis of the stranger, for example, illustrates this spatial/social focus. The stranger, he said, is both physically among us, "near," and yet "far" in that he is socially remote—a conflation which renders problematic his incorporation into the social fabric. (Simmel, 1950: 402–408) My own research with spouses who live apart—who maintain separate residences and who thereby alter the spatial and the temporal underpinnings of "typical" marital relations—also illustrates the effects of structural variables on subjective reactions. We shall see that marriage as we define it, presumes temporal and spatial constitutive elements, which when altered, threaten the relationship's ability to "make sense" to its participants.[1]

Sample

The data reported here are based on open-ended interviews (about 1½ hours) with 37 spouses (one of whom lived within the Chicago Metropolitan area) representing members of 21 couples who were legally married; who had been living apart for at least 4 days at a time, for a period of six months or longer. The following demographic profile is based on 37 of our 50 respondents who are members of dual-career variants of such couples. (As a second stage of this research we are now interviewing non-dual-career spouses who live apart in an attempt to isolate independent effects of separate residences from dual career contingencies.)

The mean age for husbands is 37, for wives it is 36. Consistent with Gerstel's (1977) findings, these are relatively affluent couples, with family income greater than $35,000 for about half (48%) of the marriages. This high family income reflects the high educational and occupational attainment of these individuals: 93% of husbands and 90% of wives have completed some graduate work. Equally high percentages of both groups (husbands 85% and wives 86%) are currently working in professions or are completing advanced degrees to enable them to. For the most part, too, these are not newlyweds: 38% have been married from 2–9 years; 62% for longer than 9 years. Typically, they have maintained two residences for a relatively short period: in 57% of the marriages the spouses have lived apart less than 18 months (14% have lived apart for 3 years or longer). The frequency with which they see each other seems to be bimodal: 43% are apart less than 1 week, 10% from one week to a month, and 48% for longer than a month. This suggests that the life-style is adopted under two sets of conditions: the spouses will see each other often enough (i.e., within a week) to make the separation reasonably tolerable, or the fact of being too far apart to regroup frequently is accepted as a necessary consequence of an unavoidable obstacle: e.g., only one medical school accepted the wife, and it is 1,000 miles from the husband's job location.

Reprinted from Harriet Engel Gross, "Couples Who Live Apart: Time/Place Disjunctions and Their Consequences," by permission of the author.

Of Time and Place

Berger and Kellner (1964) have called attention to the order-bestowing function of marriage—to the fact that marriage is a relationship that creates for the individual ". . . the sort of order in which he can experience his life as making sense." Since, as these authors argue, the reality-making force of social relationships like marriage hinges on the proximity of partners to the relationship, we should expect marriages which separate spouses to render this reality or sense-making function more problematic. Gerstel's (1977) findings and Kirschner's (1976) as well as our own, confirm this point, since we all find among these couples a sense that something is missing when they are apart. A wife's response put it this way:

> I miss the opportunity to share everyday routine things, like 'What did you have for lunch today?'

A husband said that he missed:

> the lack of interpersonal communication—that sharing of little things, like trying to tell some of the neat little things that happened since you last talked to her, but after twenty-four hours, they're more trivial than they were to start with. There was a loss of that facet of our relationship.

What they call attention to as they amplify this point is not a substantive interest in such minutiae, but rather that such exchanges between spouses cement their intimacy, their sense of involvement with each other. Small talk, like the more weighty exchanges (what Gerstel calls "real" communication, 1977:360) between partners in intimate relationships, provides confirmation of—indeed, constructs the familiar web of meanings—which helps produce the ordered (and ordering) world that is their relationship. And since costly long-distance telephone conversation constrains against such small talk (visual cues are missing as well) there is no easy way to replace or compensate for this marital interaction component (Gerstel, 1977:361).

I would suggest, however, that it is more than such face-to-face communication that builds the shared experience base on which marriage's sense-making function depends; and that, therefore, the marriages of couples who live apart lack something beyond Berger and Kellner's (1964:3) point about the diminution of meaning-sustaining conversation. In co-residence marriages, couples have a common base (*their* home) and co-ordinated time schedules around which they join their ordered worlds. Such time and place (or space) com-

monalities are constitutive dimensions of social relationships which ground or situate the partners to such relationships. Couples who live apart, by contrast, do not build their daily schedules around each other's time constraints to the same degree, nor do they have one common base which is theirs together and their only "home." To the extent that two-residence marriages alter the time and space dimensions of traditional marriage, they dislocate the partners in such relationships. The time and place dislocations that result from these two features of living apart are experienced as time/place dissonance that jeopardizes the sense-making function of their marriage over and above the threat that conversational diminution produces. I will begin the discussion of these issues with ways in which time dislocations undermine the order-providing function of these marriages.

Time

Co-resident couples who typically separate each workday morning to regroup each evening have a daily regimen obviously different from these couples who live apart. For two-residence couples, one consequence of not needing to fit one's daily schedule and work periods around a mate's schedule is the freedom from constraint that such dovetailing of schedules imposes. This freedom is a decided advantage, the benefits of which both spouses, but particularly wives, articulate. For career-committed individuals, the increased productivity that follows from concentrated, uninterrupted work is highly valued. (Gerstel, 1977: 363.)

> I have so much more time, I am able to do what I want, when I want.

Yet, there is a concomitant response, usually subjectively unconnected to this one, a response that notices a diminished capacity to work as concertedly or purposefully as they might like.

> I find I waste a lot of time.
> I don't get down to business the way I'd like to.
> I'm not as focused as I'd like to be all the time.

Our analysis of such responses indicates that they occur most often in the context of discussions about how time is spent when mates would normally be together. One husband told of how he noticed that he had completed only four pages of a report he was reading during the whole evening. He could not concentrate and his mind kept wandering away from what he was reading. I think of these statements about diminished concentration capacity as evidence for a feeling of being unmoored in a meaning-giving relationship. The fact that members of such couples are not around to sustain realities for each other results in a kind of unhinging, as if they literally felt detached from a meaning-giving unit.

Such responses seem to confirm the thesis that intimate relationships provide the moorings that facilitate purposeful action. It is not surprising then that such purposefulness might be particularly jeopardized at those times when mates would be together as intimates. However, there is also some suggestion that separation influences capacity to focus attention and work productively during regular working hours. Especially for those couples who do not come together on a regular basis, e.g., every weekend, an awareness develops that "it is time" to get back together. One husband, whose work depended on what he called creative bursts, said he knew it was time to visit his wife when his creativity seemed to be waning.

After about four weeks of this sort of pagan lifestyle, I get less motivated.

For professionals, whose careers demand heavy intellectual and emotional outlays, any such threat to ability to concentrate or work concertedly could become prohibitively costly. The increased productivity that these spouses connect to their freedom from the constraints of their mates' schedules could be counteracted by this diminished capacity to work purposefully.

What such responses about inability to work productively may mean is that a partner to an intimate relationship may be missing the feeling of being situated in a relationship that gives meaning and purpose to one's life, precisely because one spends an important life-ordering commodity—time—in that relationship. "Being situated" here means being time-bounded, which is to say—having one's own time expenditures connected into the time expenditures of someone else with whom, as a consequence of this coordination, one builds a common sense of purpose and meaning. Joined-time then would be a constitutive dimension of the relationship—a quality that defines the relationship and allows it to provide the sense of ordering that it does.

If joined time is a dimension of relationship that, when missing threatens the meaning-giving potential of that relationship, the question becomes—how much and what kind of time must be spent in the relationship in

order for it to provide its benefits? Though we cannot answer the question about amount of time definitively, these couples' responses do suggest that the pattern of their separation and regrouping affects the quality of the relationship. Irregular regrouping, that is getting together when either one's schedule permits them to do so, challenges the relationship's taken-for-granted quality in ways that a regular regrouping pattern (e.g., every weekend) does not. Couples who see each other every weekend have the obvious advantage of being separated for shorter time periods compared to couples who cannot get together every weekend. They also have a pattern of separating and regrouping that roughly parallels the work–leisure pattern for most of the culture, that is, they are away from each other when others are working and together for the weekend which they, like other couples, are then able to devote to activities they can do together. The "weekends-together" pattern, then, is least discrepant from the work–leisure rhythm of their co-resident dual-career counterparts. It is the pattern of separation relative to other patterns that is least likely to threaten their sense of what marriage "is." Spouses who spend weekends together do not report feeling "awkward" when they come together, but spouses separated for longer periods do use this and similar terms. The latter say such things as the situations feel "unreal" when they get back together or "artificial." One woman told of feeling that she was having an affair when she visited her husband.

When I get there it takes a day or so to decide that nothing has changed and to feel comfortable about it. There's always that worry when you first get back together.

Another put it this way:

It's usually sort of strange. There's a 'What do we talk about first?'—a distance. It's weird.

There is also significance to meeting every weekend consistently because a weekend visit after a longer separation may be too short and too compressed a period to accomplish everything their expectations build up for their time together.

If you are together for a short time, say a weekend, the first day revolves around arriving, the second day is sandwiched in between with shopping and stuff that needs to be done, and the third day focuses on leaving.

Several spouses registered complaints similar to the one quoted below—acknowledging that the time together was not what they had hoped for. They seemed perplexed by this fact, as if they could not quite understand how something they had so looked forward to could disappoint them.

> *I've noticed with my husband now, there's a period of strangeness. We're glad to see one another, but we haven't got anything to say. It takes several days for that to break down and for us to begin chattering in detail—to really feel comfortable. And when you have only a couple of days, you never get it, so there's that strangeness, that let-down like—'Why aren't I enjoying this more?'*

By contrast, couples who are together each weekend seem to accommodate themselves to the routine of this pattern and take comfort in its regularity. They tell of taking a specific train, arriving at a fixed time, and a schedule of events throughout the weekend which seems to function as a new joined time that somewhat fortifies their relationship.

Yet, even for couples who meet each weekend and who seem to have reconstituted their relationship around their new time together, there are strains related to time management. Couples who live apart are very much aware of their need to use their time together constructively. (Kirschner and Walum, 1978) In this respect, they are like other dual-career couples (Rapoport and Rapoport, 1976:302) but time considerations are even more vital to them because the separation increases their time apart. They tell how they protect their time together from potential depletion and incursion of visits from friends and relatives. They allocate their time together in recognition of the fact they must spend what they have together wisely if the relationship is to withstand the injury to it that limited and nonnormative time periods together impose. Though regularity of contact can mitigate the disappointments referred to above (when the visit is not all they had hoped for), such disappointment is not uncommon. Even for those who see each other relatively often, such unfulfilled expectations mar the satisfaction of coming together. Because time together is so clearly bracketed off from "other time," this very distinctiveness makes their period together more vulnerable. They are cognizant of "spoiled time" together in ways, I suspect, co-resident couples are not. It is as if their period together suffers from overload. Since time together is a limited commodity, there is an urgency to their respective needs to draw from it the sustenance that this very urgency undermines. They need more from their relationship at the same time that they can draw less from it.

Duration and pattern of separation, then, are important contingencies that affect the degree to which such marriages are able to provide the personal mooring expected from marriage in our culture, and, in turn, this capability is related to the degree of strain associated with the life-style. No doubt the effect of any of these variables (e.g., pattern of separation) interacts with others (e.g., duration of separation) to mitigate or increase the challenge to the marriage's capacity to order their lives, but it is difficult to isolate such interactions. Two obvious interaction effects, we and the others who have studied this lifestyle (Kirschner and Walum, 1978; Gerstel, 1977) have found, have to do with length of marriage and financial wherewithal: having an account calibrated in years together is as important as a bank account on which to draw to pay for the emotional as well as considerable ensuing financial costs (e.g., telephone bills, traveling, and two-household expenses).

Understandably, the longer they have been married, the greater their ability to withstand the ravages of missed time together. One younger husband, with access to a WATS line (such access so frequently figures into this lifestyle as to constitute an enabling condition), spoke to his wife every night, yet he reported that neither of them felt this was satisfactory. He stressed how they both missed the ability to talk to each other regularly. He readily agreed to the term "corrosive" when I used it to summarize what he had been saying about the effect of separation on their relationship. But an older wife, married more than fifteen years who was less negative about the effects of separation, said in response to my question about how often she and her husband kept in touch:

> *Oh, we get a chance to speak to each other quite often, as often as we like. We talk on the phone about once a week.*

The ability to cope with and manage the threat to their sense of the marriages' stability, to the "intactness" of their relationship, then, is sensitive not only to how much time they now spend together, but how much time together they have behind them as well. To be sure, time together does not ensure meaningfulness—witness the many psychologically distant couples who live together—but a certain irreducible minimum seems to be fundamental to the feeling that there is "enough time together" for there to be a meaningful relationship.

Place

The discussion of time dislocations centered on ways in which not spending time together on a routine, joined basis, jeopardizes the taken-for-granted quality of the relationship so that it does not feel right or make sense. This is what terms such as "artificial," "awkward," and "weird" signify. In similar and interconnected ways (difficult to distinguish because time and place variations occur simultaneously) the place irregularities of these marriages contribute to the awareness that something is awry—out of order. These mates report reactions they recognize to be inappropriate, and they are puzzled by these responses. The puzzlement, I would argue, indicates that the taken-for-granted quality of the relationship is challenged and the challenge is unsettling, unhinging. A husband reported that his wife felt as if they were doing something illicit when he stayed with her in the dormitory room in which she lived.

> She kind of felt, at least early in the year, kind of immoral when she had a man staying in her room. It was a weird situation.

Despite the fact that her own moral view did not condemn sexual liaisons among others who lived in the dorm and, though it was a co-educational residence, she felt "nervous" with her own husband in that place. Another husband said that he had to consciously avoid the feeling that he should "play host" when his wife visited him in his apartment. He knew the response was inappropriate, but it was something he apparently associated with someone "visiting" his place. Inappropriate reactions like these are evidence of the disturbed nomos (Berger and Kellner's (1964) term for sense of order) that variation from co-residence produces. The "nervousness" and "weirdness" they associated with these situations are the strain they feel as a consequence of having the sense-making function of their relationship undermined.

These spouses use terms such as "turf" and "re-entry problems" to communicate their place-related incongruities. Not unexpectedly, the place dislocations are most obvious for the partner who sets-up a new residence and for both of them when they are together in that residence, away from their shared base. As the following excerpt indicates, "a new place" can add novelty to their relationship but it is not *their* place ('this isn't my place, my turf'). The passage is in response to a question about different reactions when this wife and her husband come together in their previous home (where he remains) as compared to when he visits her, in her apartment.

> Oh yes, it's not nearly so good here because he's not so comfortable here. This isn't my beat, this isn't my turf. And that's O.K., we do things together, we explore. It's fun, it's an adventure, but what I like for total relaxation and happiness is to go home.

Here, "total relaxation," that is, feeling more comfortable, attests to the order-sustaining value that shared space produces.

The re-entry problems they talk about are evidence that they miss the familiarity, the sense of being "in place" that living together provides. Feeling ill at ease in "his" or "her" place is further indication that the sense-making function of relationships inheres in spatial interconnectedness. To the extent that they feel "out of place," they are acknowledging that feeling "in place" gives the relationship the order-constructing quality they expect from it. Feeling like a guest in the company of the mate, seeming to intrude, are additional reactions that bespeak the dislocation they feel. That such feelings attach to the awareness of not being a part of, not sharing the space that is identified as "his" or "hers" (as distinct from "theirs") comes through in the following quote.

> She had her own little world here that I was definitely not a part of. I got the feeling that she kind of—resented is perhaps too strong—but thought, I was intruding into her sphere.

The dislocations of space coordination are especially pronounced when both move into new residences as a result of the decision to live apart. This can occur for a variety of reasons: because they may want to reduce expenses and, therefore, each takes a less costly apartment, or because the job changes put them in two new locations. In such instances, neither one of them has a shared based to retreat to and they both have "turfs" alien to the other. A husband recognized this awareness, but thought it affected his wife even more than it did him.

> It's kind of interesting, the fact that I moved out of what had been our apartment gave her a greater sense of being cut-off. She didn't have a home to go to, she never really felt at home here.

Having made the point that time/place variations render marital relations and the meaning one can draw from them more problematic, I should not leave the impression that only negative consequences flow from these variations. Significant satisfactions do result from successfully managing a difficult life-style and being able to devote unfettered time to work obligations. For some spouses there may also be heightened appreciation of the relationship because their time together is so scarce.

> *When you do get together, it's something special. I prefer always to have not enough time. Our relationship has become more efficient in the use of time.*

There is also the compensating novelty that non-routine interaction brings — the feeling of adventure from having new places to explore mentioned by the wife quoted above. But my impression of the interviews as a whole suggests that for the majority of these spouses such responses are viewed as island benefits in a sea of costs. For the most part these "benefits" are compensatory afterthoughts, much more than dominant reactions. In another paper (Gross, 1978) I discuss additional factors which constrain toward dissatisfaction and add to the burdensomeness of this life-style.

Conclusions

What I have termed time/space dissonance presumes implicit comparison with co-residence living. That is, the discrepancies these spouses register, reflect the contrast they are making with time and place reactions of intimates who do not live apart. Saying, "I have *more* time" and "I feel like a guest" means relative to how one would or should feel, if he/she did not live apart. So part of the strain results from discrepancies one senses from what is normative, what "should be." But in addition to this discrepancy, I think there is also some absolute minimum time/place coordination that might be necessary for the relationship to provide a sense of well-being and orderliness. That is, even if such relationships could become common and prevalent enough to eliminate the feeling that they are nonnormative, there might be limits to the reduction of time and place coordination that intimate relationships could tolerate, without breaking down.[2] Such limits would influence judgments about the life-style's prognosis: perhaps no amount of normalization can completely neutralize its disabling effects.

Beyond this prognosis, what I think this study reaffirms is that intimate relationships, like all social arrangements, are quite sensitive to variation in their time/place coordinates. Intimate relationships make sense of experience because partners to such relationships occupy time and place together and fashion a sense of order from these commonalities. To the extent that part-

ners alter these commonalities, they disturb that sense of order and disorient themselves as a consequence. Relationships apparently need time and place constancies which can only be tampered with so far, before these disorientations become disabling. As one wife's poignant paraphase put it: "You know the old issue: if a tree falls in the forest, does it make a noise if nobody's there to hear it? Does a relationship exist if you don't spend time in it?"

Endnotes

1. A version of this paper was first presented to the Sociology of Family section of the 1978 (September) Annual Meetings of the American Sociological Association Meetings in San Francisco.
2. Simmel's (1950:123-4) point about the inherent vulnerability of dyadic relationships — their sensitivity to partner withdrawal — also suggests that sustained separation cannot bode well for the intimate dyad.

References

Berger, Peter and Hansfield Kellner
  1964 "Marriage and the Construction of Reality: an Exercise in the Microsociology of Knowledge." Diogenes 46:1-25.
Gerstel, Naomi R.
  1977 "The Feasibility of Commuter Marriage." Pp. 357-67 in Peter J. Stein, Judith Richman, and Natalie Hannon (eds.) The Family: Functions and Conflicts and Symbols. Reading, Ma: Addison-Wesley.
Gross, Harriet Engel
  1978 "Couples Who Live Apart: The Dual-Career Variant." Paper presented at the Annual Meetings of the American Sociological Association, San Francisco Hilton Hotel, San Francisco, California, September.
Goffman, Erving
  1967 Interaction Ritual. Garden City, New Jersey: Anchor.
Kirschner, Betty Frankle
  1976 "The Two-location Family: Some Preliminary Ideas." Paper presented at Women in Mid-Life Crisis Conference. Cornell University. October 30.

Kirschner, Betty Frankle and Laurel Richardson Walum
  1978   Two-location Families: Married Singles. Alternative Lifestyles. 1 (November):513–525.
Rapoport, Rhoda and Robert Rapoport
  1976   Dual-career Families Revisited. New York: Harper.

Simmel, Georg
  1971   On Individuality and Social Forms. Chicago: University of Chicago Press.
  1950   The Sociology of Georg Simmel. Glencoe: Free Press.

READING 90

Loving Women: Attachment and Autonomy in Lesbian Relationships

Letitia Anne Peplau, Susan Cochran, Karen Rook, and Christine Padesky

Virtually no empirical research exists concerning the romantic and sexual relationships of lesbians. Investigators interested in interpersonal attraction and close relationships (see review by Huston & Levinger, in press) have focused exclusively on heterosexual relationships. Research on homosexuals (see review by Morin, 1977) has typically studied gay men, and has primarily been concerned with issues of etiology and personal adjustment. Heterosexual women can readily find information about the joys and problems of relationships with men in advice columns, scholarly books, and even college courses on marriage and the family. Lesbians have no comparable sources of accurate information about the nature of love relationships between women. Unfortunately, clinicians and others interested in understanding lesbian lifestyles are also forced to rely on speculation and common sense, rather than on documented evidence.

The available literature on lesbians suggests two distinct value orientations that may influence lesbian relationships. The first, *dyadic attachment,* concerns an

emphasis on establishing emotionally close and relatively secure love relationships. The second, *personal autonomy,* concerns an emphasis on independence and self-actualization that may lead to a questioning of traditional patterns of love relationships. It seems likely that all close relationships require a balancing of the desire for intimacy and the desire for independence. As Levinger (1977) suggests, individuals must somehow "walk the path between counterdependency and overdependency . . . between interpersonal enmeshment and personal isolation" (p. 155). According to Hess and Handel (1959), the effort to achieve a satisfactory pattern of separateness and connectedness is a fundamental task of family life. To understand contemporary lesbian relationships, it is important to consider each of these themes and their social origins. At the same time, an analysis of attachment and autonomy in lesbian relationships may also shed light on basic issues relevant to all close relationships.

Dyadic Attachment

Lesbians have typically been depicted as emphasizing the emotional quality of love relationships. According to Chafetz (1974), lesbians "develop more meaningful emotional attachments to other females than to males" (p. 189) and find it easier to achieve open communication and

Reprinted from Letitia Anne Peplau, Susan Cochman, Karen Rood, and Christine Padesky, "Loving Women: Attachment and Autonomy in Lesbian Relationships," in *Journal of Social Issues,* vol. 34, no. 3, 1978, pp. 2–27, by permission of the publisher and the author.

emotional expression in same-sex relationships. Gagnon and Simon (1973) observe that for most lesbians, "the pursuit of sexual gratification as something separate from emotional or romantic involvement is not particularly attractive" (p. 182). Such views suggest that lesbians desire relatively permanent, sexually exclusive, and emotionally close relationships.

A desire for intimacy in close relationships undoubtedly reflects many factors, ranging from psychologically based affiliative needs (e.g., Sullivan, 1953; Weiss, 1974) to culturally based norms concerning love and personal relationships (Rubin, 1973). Of particular importance for women, however, is the impact of sex-role socialization. Young women have been taught to value emotionally close and relatively permanent relationships. The traditional message has clearly indicated that close relationships should be based on love and romance, rather than on sex (Peplau, Rubin, & Hill, 1977). Sexual fidelity and commitment have been emphasized. It seems likely that all American women, both lesbian and heterosexual, are exposed in some measure to socialization pressures encouraging strong dyadic attachments. Several researchers have noted the continuities between the sex-role socialization of lesbian and heterosexual women in our culture. According to Strom, "much of the sexual and courtship behavior of lesbians closely resembles that of heterosexual women and differs from that of gay men" (Note 1, p. 1). Gagnon and Simon (1973) argue that the lesbian "follows conventional feminine patterns in developing her commitment to sexuality and in conducting not only her sexual career but her nonsexual career as well" (p. 178). This view suggests that sex-role prescriptions concerning women's orientation towards love are a major influence on lesbian relationships.

Personal Autonomy

A second theme in descriptions of lesbians concerns personal autonomy. Abbott and Love (1972) suggest that lesbians, unlike heterosexual women, are not afraid to develop qualities of independence, self-actualization, strength, and intelligence; and that in preferring a same-sex partner, lesbians choose personal autonomy over culturally prescribed female roles. Cassell (1977) postulates that women who become lesbians "seek autonomy and independence, and define the self by activity rather than relationships" (p. 75). An emphasis on autonomy may lead women to prefer relationships that are less exclusive and that last only so long as they remain personally satisfying. Autonomy concerns might also lead women to emphasize the importance of having separate interests and friends outside a primary love relationship.

Within contemporary American society, a desire for personal autonomy may be fostered by such diverse factors as a psychologically based concern with ego identity or self-actualization, and recent social criticisms of the constraints imposed by the institution of monogamous marriage (e.g., Smith & Smith, 1974). For lesbians, however, a concern with autonomy is probably most closely tied to feminism. The modern feminist movement espouses an ideology with clear implications for women's personal lives: Sex-role change requires modification not only in legal and political institutions but also in personal relationships (Abbott & Love, 1972; Millett, 1970).

The impact of feminism on lesbian relationships may be to temper a desire for exclusive dyadic relationships with a broader commitment to personal goals or to the lesbian feminist community (Barnhart, 1975; Strom, Note 1). We expect lesbian feminists to value equal-power relationships and to minimize the importance of sexual exclusivity or temporal permanence in relationships. Barnhart's research on one radical lesbian feminist community indicated that "applied to pair relations, equality means a woman need not limit her emotional and sexual involvement to only one other woman" (1975, p. 106). Feminism encourages women to develop personal interests and commitments apart from love relationships.

Variations in Orientations towards Relationships

We propose that lesbians' orientations towards love relationships vary along two primary dimensions concerning the value placed on dyadic attachment and on personal autonomy. These two sets of values are not necessarily mutually exclusive. Ramey (1976) suggests that greater attention to personal growth can convert lopsided "pair bonds" into more egalitarian "peer bonds" that can foster self-actualization for both partners. Raush (1977) explicitly rejects the notion that autonomy and intimacy are polar opposites. He argues instead that autonomy may be a developmental prerequisite for adult intimacy, and he further observes that relationships provide a means for individuals to transcend their own personal limitations. We expect individual differences in the importance given to attachment and to autonomy, with some persons giving equal emphasis to both.

Variations among lesbians in the importance given to attachment and autonomy are affected by many factors. Historically, there may be a trend towards increased emphasis on personal independence and self-actualization, fostered in part by the women's movement. This historical trend may be mirrored in the life histories of individual women who as adults are re-examining traditional attachment values learned in childhood, and are considering new values of personal independence that may be more compatible with their current life-styles. Some women may reconcile strong desires for independence and for intimacy with relative ease. Other women, however, may experience conflict in combining these two sets of relationship values. A radical lesbian feminist interviewed by Barnhart illustrates this possible conflict: "In spite of the ideal that a pair ought to have separate interests and that polygamy is desirable, Tina felt cheated in her relationship because she had expected to have someone with whom she could share all her activities and time" (1975, p. 110).

Lesbians' social characteristics, including their attitudes, socioeconomic status, and membership in various groups, may have important effects on relationship values. In this study, we were centrally concerned with the impact on feminism on orientations towards love relationships. We predicted that personal autonomy would be most important to women who view themselves as feminists and who are actively involved in feminist groups. Since the contemporary women's movement is a relatively new phenomenon, it might be expected to have its greatest impact on women who are younger and more highly educated. In contrast, we predicted that dyadic attachment would be most important to women who are least involved with the women's movement and who are relatively conservative in other aspects of life, such as religion.

Implicit in our approach to studying lesbian relationships is a hypothetical model which posits that social characteristics of women influence their relationship values, which in turn influence the nature of their actual relationships. This model is analogous to Reiss's (1967) work on sexual permissiveness, which suggested that people's position in the social structure influences their sexual standards, which in turn affect their sexual behavior. This causal model is quite useful in organizing information about lesbian relationships and presenting the results of our research. It is important to keep in mind, however, that such models are necessarily oversimplifications. Other causal links undoubtedly occur. For instance, the nature of a woman's close relationships can shape and change her values. In all close relationships, causal connections among social characteristics, values, and behavior are likely to be complex and reciprocal.

Method

The present study had three major objectives. First, it was designed to examine lesbians' values about love relationships and to determine whether separate orientations towards dyadic attachment and personal autonomy could be identified. Second, the study investigated social characteristics of women, including feminist involvement, that might be associated with particular relationship values. Finally, the study explored links between these value orientations and various aspects of an on-going relationship, including love and satisfaction, future commitment, sexual behavior, problems, and the balance of power.

Women were recruited for a study of "Lesbian Relationships" by ads placed in a university newspaper, a feminist student publication, and a gay community newsletter. Leaflets were distributed at a university campus and at the Los Angeles Women's Building. Contacts were also made with a community feminist center, the Los Angeles Gay Community Services Center, and a church-related lesbian rap group.

Participants spent approximately one hour filling out a detailed questionnaire. Most women completed the questionnaire in a group setting, either at UCLA or at one of five meetings scheduled at community locations; other participants were scheduled individually. Responses were anonymous. All data were collected in 1976.

Participants

The 127 women in our sample ranged in age from 18 to 59 with a median of 26 years. All but two women were white. The sample was fairly equally divided between women who worked full-time for pay (46%) and women who were students in college or graduate school (41%). The majority of women (88%) either held a BA degree or were currently college students. Over 25% of the women had some graduate training.

Participants had diverse religious backgrounds: 38% were raised as Protestants, 35% as Catholics, and 17% as Jews. Most indicated that they were currently not very religious (means 3.6 on 9-point scale of religiosity.) Only 13% said they attended religious services weekly, and 63% said they went to religious services less than once a year.

At the time of our study, 61% of the women reported being in an on-going "romantic/sexual relationship" with a woman, and the remaining women had previously had at least one "romantic/sexual relationship" with a woman. Most women in our sample reported having had several lesbian relationships: 17% had had only one relationship, 46% had had two to five relationships, and 37% had had six or more. The length of the women's longest lesbian relationship ranged from one month to 25 years, with a median of 2.5 years. The women's age when their first lesbian relationship began ranged from 13 to 47, with a median of just over 20 years.

Most of the women indicated that they had had relationships with men at some point in their lives. Over 95% of the women had "dated" a man; 84% had been in a "romantic/sexual relationship" with a man. The median number of such relationships was four. About 80% of the women had had sexual intercourse with a man; of these, the median number of heterosexual partners was five.

It is important to emphasize that our sample is not representative of lesbians, either in Los Angeles or elsewhere. As Morin (1977) has observed, there is no such thing as a representative sample of members of a hidden population such as lesbians. While our sample is fairly diverse in religion, occupation, and income, it does not include a full spectrum of lesbians. Women in our sample were relatively young, well-educated, middle-class whites. Our sample probably overrepresents women involved in lesbian and/or feminist groups, and women who are relatively open about being lesbian. The women who volunteered may well have been more interested in psychological research or more trusting of psychologists than other lesbians.

The Questionnaire

Participants completed a 23-page questionnaire. Development of the questionnaire was based on extensive two-hour interviews with 12 lesbians about their relationships and on group discussions with lesbian students. The questionnaire benefited from previous research with heterosexual couples (Hill, Rubin, & Peplau, 1976; Peplau, Rubin, & Hill, 1977; Peplau, in press; Rubin, Peplau, & Hill, Note 2).

The first part of the questionnaire concerned participants' background and involvement in lesbian and feminist activities. Questions probed attitudes toward lesbian relationships, as well as more general beliefs about romantic relationships and about women's roles. The second part of the questionnaire focused on a specific "romantic/sexual relationship." For women who were currently in a relationship, questions assessed love and commitment, sexual behavior, living arrangements, and problems. Women who were not currently in a relationship answered similar questions about their most recent past relationship.

Results and Discussion

A major goal of this research was to investigate characteristics that lesbians value in love relationships. The questionnaire asked women to rate on a 9-point scale the importance for them personally of 20 statements relevant to a romantic/sexual relationship. This set included statements about self-disclosure, joint activities, similarity of attitudes, sexual compatibility and exclusivity, permanence of the relationship, power and the division of tasks, and interests and friends outside the relationship.

We predicted that the patterning of responses to these statements would indicate distinct dimensions of dyadic attachment and personal autonomy. A factor analysis of the 20 items provided strong support for this prediction. The best fit to our data was obtained by an orthogonal two-factor solution. Table 1 presents the eight statements that loaded most highly (> .35) on each factor.

The first factor clearly reflected dyadic-attachment concerns with having a close-knit, exclusive, and relatively permanent relationship. Emphasis was given to spending time together, sharing activities, sexual fidelity, and knowing that the relationship will last a long time. We anticipated that two other items about emotional expressiveness would form part of this factor: "being able to talk about my most intimate feelings" and "being able to laugh easily with each other." However, these statements were both endorsed strongly by virtually all women (means 8.2 on 9-point scale) and so did not differentiate between the two factors.

The second factor reflected personal-autonomy concerns with independence and equality. Included were statements about having friends and interests outside the relationship, and not insisting on a future commitment. For the women in this sample, personal autonomy was strongly linked to concerns that both partners have similar attitudes about women's issues and about politics. This pattern is consistent with our expectation that, for lesbians, personal autonomy is associated with feminism. Not surprisingly, the set of attitudes comprising this factor is quite similar to values espoused by lesbian feminists studied by Barnhart (1975) and Strom (Note 1), and discussed in articles appearing in the Los Angeles-based, feminist newspaper, *Lesbian Tide*. Although personal-autonomy values may have diverse roots for the general

TABLE 1
The Dyadic Attachment and Personal Autonomy Scales

Scale Item	Loadings
Dyadic Attachment (Factor 1)	
1. Sharing as many activities with my partner as possible	.76
2. Living together	.72
3. Spending as much time together as possible	.70
4. Knowing that the relationship will endure for a long time	.69
5. Sexual fidelity in the relationship	.68
6. Knowing that my partner depends on me	.54
7. Sexual compatibility	.47
8. Working together on tasks like shopping, cooking or cleaning, rather than dividing such tasks between us	.43
Personal Autonomy (Factor 2)	
1. Having similar attitudes about women's issues	.74
2. That we both have similar political attitudes	.63
3. Having a supportive group of friends as well as my romantic/ sexual partner	.63
4. Having an egalitarian (equal-power) relationship	.49
5. Being able to have sexual relations with people other than my partner	.41
6. Trying new sexual activities or techniques with my partner	.38
7. Having major interests of my own outside the relationship	.37
8. Enjoying our relationship now without insisting on a future commitment	.37

Note: Items on the Dyadic Attachment scale loaded below .35 on Personal Autonomy, and vice versa. Individual scale scores were estimated by computing mean responses for the 8 items on each scale.

population, for lesbians such values are tied to contemporary feminist ideology.

On the basis of the factor analysis, separate Dyadic Attachment and Personal Autonomy scales were constructed. Each woman was assigned a dyadic attachment score based on the average of her responses to the eight items in this scale listed in Table 1; similarly, each woman received a personal autonomy score based on the average of her responses to the eight items included in that scale.

For the 127 women in our sample, there was a small negative correlation between scores on these two scales, $r = -.26, p < .001$. Women who gave great importance to one orientation tended to de-emphasize the other, but this tendency was quite small in magnitude, and some women endorsed both sets of values equally strongly. About 20% of the women scored above the median on both scales; another 18% scored below the median on both. These data provide empirical support for the con-

tention of Rausch (1977) and others that an emphasis on attachment is not necessarily incompatible with an emphasis on autonomy; the two are not mutually exclusive.

Relationship Values and Social Characteristics
Further analyses examined the links between relationship values and such social characteristics of women as their background, attitudes, and involvement in feminist and lesbian activities.

Demographic characteristics. No relationship was found between attachment scores and the woman's age, education, employment status, income, or parental education. Consistent with the notion that strong proponents of dyadic attachment are more conservative, it was found that women who scored high on attachment reported being significantly more religious than other women. In contrast, women who scored high on personal autonomy were significantly younger, better educated, less religious, and had more highly educated parents than women who scored low on personal autonomy. These results suggest that whereas a concern with dyadic attachment may cut across different demographic groups, an emphasis on personal autonomy tends to be concentrated among younger lesbians with higher levels of education.

Romanticism.   To examine the possibility that dyadic attachment is associated with more traditional attitudes about love relationships, a 6-item general romanticism scale (adapted from Rubin, 1969) was included in the questionnaire. Items assessed such beliefs as that true love lasts forever or that love can overcome barriers of race, religion, and economics. The wording of items was modified so as to be appropriate for same-sex relationships. As we expected, scores on this romanticism scale were significantly correlated with scores on the dyadic attachment scale, $r = .50, p < .001$. Women who valued exclusivity and permanence in their love relationships were likely to believe in traditionally romantic conceptions of love. In contrast, the relationship between romanticism and personal autonomy scores was weaker and in the opposite direction, $r = -.27, p < .001$.

Sex-role traditionalism scale.   We have suggested that traditional sex-role socialization may contribute to an emphasis on dyadic attachment, whereas feminist ideology may contribute to an emphasis on personal autonomy. The questionnaire included a 10-item sex-role traditionalism scale (Peplau, 1973), assessing general attitudes about proper roles for women and men. Although women in the sample tended to reject traditional attitudes about sex roles, significant relationships were found between scores on the sex-role scale and scores on dyadic attachment, $r = .32, p < .001$, and on personal autonomy, $r = -.38, p < .001$. Women who wanted a relatively secure and permanent love relationship held somewhat more conservative attitudes about sex roles, whereas women who desired autonomy and equality in love relationships tended to reject traditional sex roles to a greater degree. Thus it appears that women's relationship values are to some extent tied to more general beliefs about sex roles.

Feminist involvement.   It was predicted that personal autonomy would be valued most strongly by lesbians actively involved in feminism. The questionnaire included an 8-item index of involvement in feminist activities. Questions concerned the frequency of participation in feminist groups, attendance at feminist social and political events, and self-rated involvement in feminist activities. Slightly over half the women (58%) in our sample currently belonged to a feminist group or organization, and 42% had participated in a feminist consciousness-raising group at some time. As expected, active feminists scored significantly higher on personal autonomy, $r = .52, p < .001$, and lower on dyadic attachment, $r = -.50, p < .001$.

Lesbian activism.   Finally, we examined links between relationship values and women's involvement in the lesbian community in Los Angeles. While all of the women in our sample were self-defined lesbians, they varied considerably in their participation in gay political and community activities. A measure of lesbian activism was developed based on the number and types of lesbian activities a woman had attended during the past year and on the term she preferred in describing herself. On this basis, women were divided into three groups. *Apolitical women* did not participate in lesbian rap groups, collectives, or other gay organizations. While they might attend gay bars or private parties, they were not involved in other activities of the gay community. These women often described themselves as "a person" or "a human being." *Political moderates* had some involvement in the gay community other than bars and parties. They participated in such activities as rap groups, concerts, the local gay church, lesbian athletic groups, or the Gay Community Services Center, but they did not consider themselves to be radical. These women were likely to describe themselves as "gay" or "lesbian." Finally, a group of *politically radical women* were highly active in lesbian feminist activities. For example, they might participate in a radical women's center, in lesbian work collectives, in lesbian publications, or in radical therapy groups for women. Their self descriptions often included such terms as "radicalesbian," "lesbian feminist," or "dyke." This latter group is the most similar to the lesbian feminists studied by Barnhart (1975) and Strom (Note 1). For the women in our sample, lesbian activism was virtually synonymous with feminist involvement. Consequently, we predicted that the radical lesbians in our sample would give relatively greater importance to autonomy and lesser importance to attachment than other women. Data presented in Table 2 confirm both predictions. Radical lesbians scored significantly higher on personal autonomy and lower on dyadic attachment than other women ($p < .001$ in both instances). Apoliticals and political moderates had similar scores on both scales.

TABLE 2
Relationship Values and Lesbian Political Activism
(Mean Scores)

	Apoliticals	Political Moderates	Radicals
Dyadic Attachment	6.6	6.3	5.2
Personal Autonomy	5.9	6.0	6.9
(N)	(28)	(53)	(46)

Current Relationships

A major objective of this research was to investigate characteristics of women's actual relationships, and the impact that dyadic attachment and personal autonomy values may have on relationships. To avoid problems associated with retrospective reports, we limited our analyses to the 77 women in the sample who were currently in a relationship at the time of our study.

History of the relationship. Women were asked how they and their partner had first met. About a quarter of the women reported meeting "through friends," and another quarter met through school (16%) or work (10%). Although 18% of the women indicated having met "through a lesbian activity (e.g., dance, meeting, encounter group)," only one woman had met her partner "at a lesbian bar." About 12% met "through a feminist (not specifically lesbian) activity." High and low scorers on both attachment and autonomy were equally likely to have met their partner through school, work, or lesbian activities. But relationship values were associated with two other ways of meeting a partner. Since high-autonomy women tended to be active feminists, it was not surprising that they were significantly more likely than low-autonomy women to have met through a feminist activity. In fact, all the women who met a partner in this way scored above the median on autonomy. Women who scored high on attachment were significantly more likely than low scorers to have met their partner through friends.

The length of current relationships among women in this subsample varied from one month to 11 years, with a median of 13 months. Women who scored high on personal autonomy tended to have begun their current relationship more recently, $r = -.50, p < .001$. This may reflect the facts that high-autonomy women were significantly younger than other women and that they gave less importance to having long-term relationships. In con-

trast, scores on dyadic attachment were unrelated to the length of the current relationship.

About 62% of the women in our sample lived with their partner. Among those not living together, 80% of the women saw their partner three or more times a week. Since the dyadic attachment scale emphasized the importance of partners' spending time together, we expected that attachment scores would be related to how often respondents saw their partner. Significant support was found for this prediction. Among women scoring above the median on attachment, 82% lived together, compared to only 44% of low scorers. Among those who were not living together, 63% of high-attachment women saw their partner daily, compared to only 20% of low-attachment women. Scores on personal autonomy were inversely related to frequency of contact; high-autonomy women were significantly less likely than low-autonomy women to live with their partner or to see her daily.

These results indicate that women's values were significantly related to characteristics of their current love relationship. A strong emphasis on personal autonomy was associated with spending less time with one's partner, having a shorter-term relationship, and having met through a feminist activity. A somewhat different pattern was found for dyadic attachment. An emphasis on attachment was not associated with the length of the women's relationship, but was related to seeing one's partner frequently and having met through friends.

Intimacy and satisfaction. Most of the women reported being in a close, loving relationship. About 75% indicated that they and their current partner were "in love"; only 17% said they were not in love, and 8% were undecided. Women reported considerable closeness in the relationship (mean 7.7 on 9-point scale) and a high degree of satisfaction (mean 7.1 on 9-point scale). It is possible that such high levels of satisfaction among the women in our sample may in part reflect a sampling bias; women may have been less likely to volunteer for the research if their current relationship was unhappy. Nonetheless, these data clearly indicate that lesbian relationships can be highly satisfying.

We expected women who gave importance to dyadic-attachment values to report greater intimacy and closeness in their relationship. Clear support was found for this prediction. Among women scoring above the median on attachment, 87% reported being "in love" compared to only 57% of women scoring below the median on attachment, $p < .01$. The questionnaire also included Rubin's (1973) "love scale" and "liking scale." Although these two measures were developed on heterosexual samples, their content appeared to be potentially appropriate for lesbian relationships. The 9-item love scale assesses elements of attachment, caring, and intimacy; it includes such items as "I feel I can confide in __ about virtually everything" and "It would be hard for me to get along without __." A moderately high correlation was found between scores on dyadic attachment and on Rubin's love scale, $r = .54, p < .001$. Scores on the 9-item liking scale, a measure of respect and affection for the partner, were also correlated with dyadic attachment, $r = .40, p < .001$. Finally, significant correlations of a lower order were also found between dyadic attachment and ratings of closeness and of satisfaction in the relationship, both $rs = .20, p < .05$.

These data indicate that a general emphasis on the importance of having emotionally close and relatively secure dyadic relationships is associated with greater intimacy in current relationships. Two processes may underlie this association between dyadic attachment and intimacy. First, women who emphasize attachment values may be more likely to idealize their partner and the relationship. At the same time the experience of being in a very close, satisfying relationship may reinforce a belief in the importance of attachment concerns.

No relationship was found between personal autonomy and any measure of love or closeness. Although women who placed importance on personal autonomy and activities outside the relationship reported seeing their partner less often, they were not less satisfied with their relationship. This suggests that the lower frequency of interaction among high-autonomy women is a desired pattern, not an indication of lesser intimacy or happiness in the relationship.

Future expectations. The women were asked to estimate the likelihood that their current relationship would exist in six months, one year, and five years. Most women expressed at least moderate confidence that their present relationship would continue into the future. About 44% of the women were certain (7 on 7-point scale) that their relationship would continue for six months, 37% were certain it would last a year, and 26% were certain it would exist in five years. Answers to these questions were related to measures of satisfaction with the relationship. For example, estimates of the likelihood of the relationship enduring for one year were correlated with self-reported closeness, $r = .74$, with satisfaction, $r = .74$, and with scores on both the love scale, $r = .58$, and liking scale, $r = .51$ (all r's at $p < .001$). There was also a tendency for women in longer term relationships to give higher estimates of the longevity of their relationships, $r = .24$, $p < .05$.

Additional questions assessed women's willingness to make major changes in their own lives in order to preserve their relationship. On one item, women were asked to imagine that their partner had decided to move to another city to pursue an attractive job or educational opportunity, and were then asked how likely it was that they would move with their partner. Less than half of the women said they definitely (28%) or probably (13%) would move in order to continue the relationship. About 30% reported being uncertain what they would do, and about 30% indicated that they probably or definitely would not move. Responses to a parallel question gauging the probability that the partner would move with the respondent followed a similar pattern. These results suggest considerable variation in women's relative commitment to their relationship versus their work or education.

Further analyses examined the links between these measures of commitment to the relationship and women's relationship values. Women who scored high on dyadic attachment were significantly more likely than low scorers to expect their relationship to continue into the future, and were more likely to say that both partners would move to preserve the relationship (all t-tests significant at $p < .01$). In other words, women who valued permanence in relationships expressed greater optimism about the future of their own current relationship, and said that they were more willing to make a major change such as moving in order to preserve the relationship. In contrast, women who valued personal autonomy showed an opposite pattern. Women who scored above the median on autonomy were significantly less likely than low scorers to indicate that either partner would move, and expressed less confidence in the future continuation of their current relationship (all *t*-tests significant at $p <$ .01).

Sexual behavior. The women in our sample were generally quite satisfied with the sexual aspects of their relationship (mean 5.9 on 7-point scale of overall sexual satisfaction). Nearly three quarters of the women indicated that they found sex extremely satisfying, and only 4% reported that sex was not at all satisfying. One factor contributing to satisfaction was the high frequency with which women experienced orgasm when having sex with their current partner. Over 70% of the women said they "almost always" experienced orgasm; 14% said they "usually" did. Only one woman in ten said that she experienced orgasms "occasionally" and only 4% said "never." Another factor contributing to satisfaction was the reported lack of guilt among our respondents. About 80% said they never felt guilty about their sexual activity with their partner; 16% said they did occasionally, and only 4% reported usually or always feeling guilty.

Perhaps as a consequence of high sexual satisfaction, many women expressed a desire to have sex somewhat more frequently than they had recently. While 50% of the women were satisfied with the actual frequency of sex in their relationship, 45% desired to have sex more often and 5% preferred a lower frequency of sex. When asked how often they and their partner "had engaged in sexual activity that included genital stimulation" during the past month, most women reported having had sex about once a week. Specifically, 8% of the women said they had not had sex during the past month; 21% had had sex once or twice during the month; and 33% had had sex "once a week." A third of the women (29%) reported having sex two to three times a week, and 8% said they had sex four or more times a week. There was a positive correlation between reported frequency of sex and sexual satisfaction, $r = .46, p < .001$, and between frequency of sex and frequency of orgasm, $r = .32, p < .01$. There was also a tendency for sexual frequency to be lower in longer-term relationships, $r = -.31, p < .01$, and among older respondents, $r = -.31, p < .01$.

Two predictions were made concerning the relationship of dyadic attachment and personal autonomy values to sexual behavior. First, we anticipated that there would be a greater emphasis on love as a basis for sex among women with strong attachment values. Our questionnaire inquired whether the woman had been "in love" with her current partner when they first had sex with each other. While the proportion of women who were in love was

greater among women scoring above rather than below the median on attachment (68% versus 52%), this difference was not statistically significant. Scores on attachment were, however, related to self-rated sexual satisfaction, $r = .20, p < .05$. Scores on personal autonomy were not related to any measure of sexual satisfaction.

A second prediction was that sexual exclusivity would be associated with low scores on personal autonomy. Only 13% of the women in our sample said they had had sex with someone else during the past two months. Furthermore, only 28% had had sex with another person since their current relationship began. Analyses indicated that having sex outside the relationship was not related to the woman's sexual satisfaction with her primary partner, nor with her frequency of having orgasms with her primary partner. This suggests that women do not seek new sexual partners because of dissatisfaction with their primary relationship. Rather some women may positively value non-exclusivity. Consistent with this notion was the finding that women who scored above the median on personal autonomy were more likely than low scorers to have had sex with another person during the past two months, 22% versus 5%, $p < .07$. No relationship was found between scores on dyadic attachment and sexual exclusivity.

The problem of independence versus dependence. Based on clinical experience, Sang (Note 3) suggested that an emphasis on emotional closeness in lesbian relationships might create problems concerning independence and dependence. "By far the most frequent theme in lesbian couple relationships has to do with time together and time alone. Many lesbians feel that if they are in a committed relationship they will not have time to be themselves" (p. 5). Our questionnaire examined women's perceptions of potential problems in their relationship, including concerns related to independence and dependence.

The questionnaire included a list of 17 "factors that may cause difficulties in close relationships" (adapted from Hill, Rubin, & Peplau, 1976). Women indicated whether each factor was likely to lead to major difficulties, minor difficulties, or none at all in their relationship during the next year. Many women expressed some concern about independence. For example, "my desire to be independent" was cited as a major problem by 17% of women, and as a minor problem by 37%. In a similar vein, "my partner's dependence on me" was cited as a major problem by 11% of women, and as a minor problem by 29%. We expected that dyadic attachment and personal autonomy would be associated with different concerns about independence/dependence. As anticipated, women who scored above the median on attachment were significantly less likely than low scorers to see their own desire for independence as a problem, $t = 2.6, p < .01$. While only 6% of high-attachment women thought their own independence might be a major problem, 32% of low-attachment women listed this as a possible major problem. Presumably, women who value a close, secure relationship are less likely to have strong desires for personal independence. In contrast, scores on personal autonomy were significantly associated with concerns about "my partner's dependence on me," $t = 2.5, p < .01$, presumably because high-autonomy women want to guard their own independence from an overly dependent partner.

Of the 17 problems listed on the questionnaire, four others were cited fairly often as a source of potential difficulty. Some women indicated that major problems might be created by "living too far apart" (20%), "jealousy" (17%), "differences in interests" (13%) and "conflicting attitudes about sex" (11%). All other problems, including differences in attitudes and backgrounds, pressure from parents, and feelings about being a lesbian were cited infrequently. It should be emphasized, however, that most women anticipated few problems in their relationship. Women typically cited only one factor as a possible major problem.

The balance of power.   A final aspect of lesbian relationships considered in this study concerned women's perceptions of the balance of power in their relationship. It was predicted that women who strongly valued personal autonomy might be more likely than other women to have egalitarian relationships. This would be consistent with the finding that high-autonomy women were more likely to be active feminists, and the fact that the personal autonomy scale included an item concerning the importance of having an equal-power relationship.

Women were asked to indicate which partner "has more of a say about what you and (__) do together." Responses were on a 5-point scale from "I have much more say" to "(__) has much more say." A later question asked which partner should have more say in the relationship. (For details about these measures and data from a heterosexual sample, see Peplau, in press.)

Results indicated that virtually all women (97%) believed that ideally both partners should have "exactly equal say" in the relationship. Not all women attained this ideal, however. Only 64% of the women in our sample reported that their current relationship actually was "exactly equal." Contrary to our prediction, no relationship was found between the balance of power and scores on either personal autonomy or dyadic attachment (see Peplau & Caldwell, Note 4).

Summary and Implications

Our investigation of lesbian relationships supports several conclusions. First, most of the women in our sample reported a high degree of closeness and satisfaction in their current relationship. While we do not know how representative this finding is of all lesbians, it does provide a clear empirical demonstration that a high degree of intimacy is possible in lesbian relationships. The majority of women in our sample also indicated that they and their current partner shared equally in power.

Second, evidence was found linking women's values concerning relationships to characteristics of their current love relationship. Women who endorsed attachment values of togetherness and security differed significantly from women who de-emphasized these values. An emphasis on attachment was associated with spending more time with the current partner, reporting greater closeness and satisfaction with the relationship, expressing greater confidence that the relationship would continue in the future, and worrying less that personal independence would create difficulties for the relationship. Women who endorsed autonomy themes of equality, having personal interests outside the relationship, and de-emphasizing future commitment differed significantly from women who gave less importance to these values. In particular, a strong emphasis on autonomy was associated with spending less time with the partner, being less willing to maintain the relationship at the expense of work or education, being more likely to have a sexually open relationship, and worrying about having an overly dependent partner.

Third, support for our contention that autonomy and attachment are distinct but not mutually exclusive orientations was provided by evidence that the two had different correlates. For example, reports of closeness and satisfaction in the relationship were related to attachment values but not to autonomy values. Whether or not a woman was a strong proponent of equality and personal independence had no impact on her happiness with her current relationship. In addition, sexual exclusivity was related to autonomy values but not to attachment values. A woman was more likely to have sex outside her primary relationship if she valued personal independence strongly rather than weakly, but the degree to which a woman valued dyadic attachment was unrelated to sexual openness.

The results of this study are pertinent to social-psychological research on close relationships in several ways. Our study provides an empirical demonstration of the importance of dimensions of autonomy and attachment in love relationships, and suggests a methodology for studying these relationship values. The study also provides empirical support for the theoretical view of Raush (1977) and others that autonomy and intimacy are not polar opposites, but rather are independent dimensions. It is possible for individuals to be strongly oriented towards both ideals. Finally, the study documents interrelationships among social characteristics, relationship values, and features of actual dyadic relationships (see Reiss, 1967). We can speculate that comparable research on gay men and heterosexuals would also find autonomy and attachment to be important value dimensions. Further, we imagine that while the relationship correlates of autonomy and attachment might be the same across samples, the social origins of these value orientations would be different for lesbians, gay men, and heterosexuals.

This study also contributes to a growing body of empirical research concerning lesbians and their life-styles. In a recent critique of research on homosexuality, Morin (1977) urged that higher priority be given to studies concerning the diversity of homosexual life-styles and the dynamics of gay relationships. Our research represents a first step in that direction. A few major similarities were found among the lesbians we studied. Virtually all women viewed intimate self-disclosure as essential to a good relationship. The majority of women said their current relationship was extremely close and personally satisfying, and most reported equal power in the relationship. While we do not know how representative these findings are of all lesbians, they clearly indicate that lesbians can establish personally rewarding and egalitarian love relationships.

Around these areas of commonality, wide variations were found in womens' values about relationships, and the characteristics of their own current relationships. The patterning of these values and experiences reflected dimensions of dyadic attachment and personal autonomy, and were strongly related to womens' involvement in feminism. In their love relationships as in other aspects of their lives, lesbians are a diverse group. As lesbians continue to evaluate the sorts of personal relationships they prefer, the importance given to attachment and autonomy concerns may shift. It seems likely however, that the need to reconcile basic desires for intimacy and for independence will continue.

Reference Notes

1. Strom, D. *Ideology and identity within a community of lesbian feminists.* Paper presented at the meeting of the American Sociological Association, Chicago, September 1977.
2. Rubin, Z., Peplau, L. A., & Hill, C. T. *Loving and leaving: Sex differences in romantic attachments.* Unpublished manuscript, Brandeis University, 1978.
3. Sang, B. E. *Lesbian relationships: A struggle towards couple equality.* Paper presented at the meeting of the American Psychological Association, San Francisco, August 1977.
4. Peplau, L. A., & Caldwell, M. A. *Power in lesbian relationships.* Unpublished manuscript, University of California, Los Angeles, 1978.

References

Abbott, S., & Love, B. *Sappho was a right-on woman: A liberated view of lesbianism.* New York: Stein & Day, 1972.

Barnhart, E. Friends and lovers in a lesbian counterculture community. In N. N. Glazer-Malbin (Ed.), *Old family, new family.* New York: Van Nostrand, 1975.

Cassell, J. *A group called women: Sisterhood and symbolism in the feminist movement.* New York: David McKay, 1977.

Chafetz, J. S. *Masculine/feminine or human? An overview of the sociology of sex roles.* Itasca, IL: Peacock, 1974.

Gagnon, J. H., & Simon, W. *Sexual conduct: The social sources of human sexuality.* Chicago: Aldine, 1973.

Hess, R. D., & Handel, G. *Family worlds: A psychosocial approach to family life.* Chicago: The University of Chicago Press, 1959.

Hill, C. T., Rubin, Z., & Peplau, L. A. Breakups before marriage: The end of 103 affairs. *Journal of Social Issues,* 1976, *32* (1), 147–168.

Huston, T. L., & Levinger, G. Interpersonal attraction and relationships. *Annual Review of Psychology,* in press.

Levinger, G. Re-viewing the close relationship. In G. Levinger & H. Rausch (Eds.), *Close relationships: Perspectives on the meaning of intimacy.* Amherst, MA: University of Massachusetts Press, 1977.

Millett, K. *Sexual politics.* Garden City, NY: Doubleday, 1970.

Morin, S. F. Heterosexual bias in psychological research on lesbianism and male homosexuality. *American Psychologist,* 1977, *32,* 629–637.

Peplau, L. A. *The impact of fear of success, sex-role attitudes and opposite-sex relationships on women's intellectual performance.* Unpublished doctoral dissertation. Harvard University, 1973.

Peplau, L. A. Power in dating relationships. In J. Freeman (Ed.), *Women: A feminist perspective* (2nd ed.). Palo Alto, CA: Mayfield, in press.

Peplau, L. A., Rubin, Z., & Hill, C. T. Sexual intimacy in dating couples. *Journal of Social Issues,* 1977, *33* (2), 86–109.

Ramey, J. W. *Intimate friendships.* Englewood Cliffs, NJ: Prentice-Hall, 1976.

Raush, H. L. Orientation to close relationships. In G. Levinger & H. L. Raush (Eds.), *Close relationships: Perspectives on the meaning of intimacy.* Amherst, MA: University of Massachusetts Press, 1977.

Reiss, I. L. *The social context of premarital sexual permissiveness.* New York: Holt, Rinehart & Winston, 1967.

Rubin, Z. *The social psychology of romantic love.* (Doctoral dissertation, University of Michigan, 1969). (University Microfilms No. 70-4179)

Rubin, Z. *Liking and loving: An invitation to social psychology.* New York: Holt, Rinehart & Winston, 1973.

Smith, J. R., & Smith, L. G. *Beyond monogamy: Recent studies of sexual alternatives in marriage.* Baltimore, MD: Johns Hopkins University Press, 1974.

Sullivan, H. S. *The interpersonal theory of psychiatry.* New York: W. W. Norton, 1953.

Weiss, R. S. The provisions of social relationships. In Z. Rubin (Ed.), *Doing unto others.* Englewood Cliffs, NJ: Prentice-Hall, 1974.

Introduction:
Feminism in the Future

We have learned from the previous selections that the feminist movement has had a decided influence on institutions, individual consciousness, and intimate relationships. Yet, the movement has still not attained its ultimate objective: the creation of a society in which the "double standard" in all its forms has been eradicated. The principles upon which the movement is based require fundamental and major restructuring of all our established institutions. It is partly because the ultimate goals are based on a *revision* of society, and partly because the movement has been relatively successful in mobilizing activists and achieving some of its lesser goals (e.g., passage of credit bills, homemaker bills, abortion rights, women's studies curricula, text book revisions, etc.), that the feminist movement continues to meet powerful and sustained opposition.

It is fitting, then, that we end our analysis by examining the serious challenges confronting feminism. Recognizing the importance of having the power to name, identify, and construct a world-view, we include the article "Toward a Feminist Aesthetic" by Julia Penelope and Susan J. Wolfe (Robbins). Recognizing the multiplicity of issues at stake in the coming decade, including the conservative backlash unfolding in American society, we include Verta Taylor's article "The Future of Feminism in the 1980s." As history has taught us, patriarchy will not "wither away;" rather, as Taylor argues, it is only through the feminist struggle that society will be transformed. We end our study not by mourning the death of feminism, but by celebrating the resiliency of those who continue even in the face of strong opposition to build a movement committed to establishing a just and nonsexist society. Such is the theme of the song "The Rock Will Wear Away," written in 1976 by feminist composers Meg Christian and Holly Near. Sung by women in the movement throughout the decade of the 1970s, the theme of its chorus—many small, weak entities joining together to defeat a larger, stronger one—still stands as the challenge of feminists in the future.

Toward a Feminist Aesthetic

Julia Penelope and Susan J. Wolfe (Robbins)

This is not the first paper or article tentatively titled "Toward a Feminist Aesthetic," or to reflect a growing awareness that something called a "feminist aesthetic" is not only possible but necessary. Feminist critics have begun to see the bare outlines of such an aesthetic, and indications suggest that the basis of this aesthetic will be linguistic. The phrase "women's style" seems to imply that women use language rules in some ways that differ significantly from the ways men do, or that women use a different set of rules.

Neither purely literary nor linguistic discussions of "women's style" have isolated features that are clearly unique to women's uses of language.[1] In our study we have chosen to restrict our attention to women's prose in order to avoid many of the problems posed by the social context of speech. In literature, the writer has relatively more control over the speech act as a complete unit of discourse. Although a piece of fiction may contain situations in which men function as speakers or in which both women and men are depicted as speakers, the writer — for our purposes the female writer — nevertheless defines the entire universe of discourse in which these situations occur. As feminist critics and historians continue to reclaim the writings of women lost through neglect and ignorance, we have increasing access to the chronological development of a tradition available to us in the printed word. On the other hand, the novel itself has a tradition of providing an open-ended universe of discourse in which the writer has maximum control of life, language, and point of view within the novel.

Discussions of women's literature are apt to emphasize the fact that the "content" of women's literature is different from that written by men because women bring a "different sensibility" to literature. As Lillian Robinson, a feminist literary critic, has observed: "Women speak for women — for our experience and the viewpoint it shapes,

if not necessarily in our common interest. No man, however sincerely our partisan, is able to speak with our authority about the lives, the feelings, or the consciousness of women." As women, we are taught to be quiet, passive, docile, tame. But the writer must be active, articulate, independent, wild. Only a woman can understand the effects in our lives of that inherent conflict. Our understanding, as Patricia Meyer Spacks has described it, is discernible "Through all literary genres — criticism as well as poetry, fiction, autobiography — . . . The same consciousness of difficulty presents itself over and over" (p. 41). The conflict between our experience of ourselves and the ways in which we have learned to structure our experience is the subject of an entry (October 1912) in anthropologist Ruth Benedict's diary. The effort to resolve this conflict and grasp the flux of our lives is here her central concern:

> *The trouble is not that we are never happy — it is that happiness is so episodical. A morning in the library, an afternoon with someone I really care about, a day in the mountains, a good-night-time with the babies* [her sister's children] *can almost frighten me with happiness. But then it is gone and I cannot see what holds it all together. What is worthwhile? What is the purpose? What do I want? . . .*
> *What is it that holds these episodes together? Much as I have rebelled against it, I cannot hit on any answer but the old one of self development. Perhaps my trouble comes from thinking of the end as my present self, not as a possible and very different future self. . . .*

(Quoted in Moffatt and Painter, p. 152).

Such discussions, emphasizing that the difference between women's and men's writing derives from a difference in life experience and perspective, may imply that there is no such thing as "woman's style." Or they may assume that there are differences, accept the male literary standard, and condemn women's writing on that basis.

Reprinted from Julia Penelope and Susan J. Wolfe, "Toward a Feminist Aesthetic," in *Chrysalis 6* (1978), by permission of the authors.

This has been the case with two well-known books that have appeared in the past two years, *Flying*, by Kate Millett, and *Of Woman Born*, by Adrienne Rich—one a novel, the other an analytical exploration.

Elinor Langer's attack on *Flying* is justified (to her mind, at any rate) by the title of her attack, "Confessing." In her opening paragraph, she summarizes her views on the differences between women's and men's writing:

> *Men repress; women confess. The stiff upper lip versus the quavering one. There are occasions when too much of the latter makes the former seem attractive, and for me reading Kate Millett's* Flying *was one of them. After it, I would cheerfully have settled down with the* Principia. *As it was, I reached for the Kleenex, my sorrow not only for the author of this modern pilgrim's regress, but for its readers.*

According to Langer, "Confession, under the auspices of the Women's Movement, is getting to be a messy business." Her concern for the "Mess" of confessional writing provides her with a respectable façade, and she comments that "*Flying* should not have to bear the weight of the entire confessional genre." Langer interweaves two separate issues: the legitimacy of the so-called confessional genre and the purported "absence of a genuinely critical tradition in the Women's Movement." Langer doesn't say that there is no "feminist critical tradition." She specifically says that there is no critical tradition in the feminist movement, which implies that if there were such a criticism, it would reject *Flying* as typical women's literature and value books that reflect traditional literary values. As Langer observes, Millett "made criticism of the book's content nearly impossible," because "everything one might think of to say about it, she has said herself."

> *How does one criticize the sad, true, tragic-comic and egocentric material that is the heart of most private journals? What is a reader to say? Where is the opportunity for discussing either style or values? It is not so different in the case of a published work like* Flying *. . . The critic is silenced or hypocritical.*

Because Langer is looking specifically for something negative to say, Millett has written Langer out of her universe of discourse. When she is debating writing the "book," Millett says:

> *I cannot write that book. It would have to say that I'm what? And what am I anyway? I hate confes-*

sionals. Bless me father for I have sinned. A whining form. . . . (p. 23)

> *Though I like to imagine this is my first book, I seemed, at thirty-six, to be past the age of the obligatory autobiographical novel. . . . The confessional should wait upon one's ripe old age. . . .*

> *You may well ask how I expect to assert my privacy by resorting to the outrageous publicity of being one's actual self on paper. There's a possibility of working it if one chooses the terms. . . . outshouting image-gimmick America through a quietly desperate search for self. And being honest enough. Of course it is impossible to tell the truth. For example, how does one know it? I will not belabor the difficulty by telling you how hard I have tried. And if compulsion forces me to tell the truth, it may also lead me into error, or invention. (p. 83)*

The controlling consciousness of *Flying* is so uncompromising that even the honesty of dishonesty is explicitly dealt with. Langer, left to her own devices, must either abandon her values and seek a new method of criticism, or she must remain silent. Instead, she chooses to complain that she has nothing to do. She cannot discuss the values of *Flying* because its values exist in a new universe of discourse she refuses to enter; she can't discuss the book's content because it explores its own content; she cannot discuss its style because she doesn't know how.

Langer's outrage has since been repeated in the hostile reviews of Rich's *Of Woman Born*. By refusing to read the book on its own terms, and in its own language, the reviewers try to avoid or disguise the meaning of the work. Adrienne Rich is called "schoolgirl Rich," and her prose "awkward," "cliché-ridden," "muddled polemics," and "the sloppy rhetoric of revolution." Helen Vendler, borrowing two catchy phrases from Octavio Paz, calls Rich's language both the "rhetoric of violence" and the "rhetoric of sentimentality." Neither of these labels, however, can be substantiated from the book itself, and they suggest the refusal of these reviewers to read the book on its own terms. In fact, the reviewers tell us that they are "vexed," "disturbed," and "troubled" by the book, adjectives that indicate that their reactions are more reflex than reflection, knee-jerk responses to what they regard as an "illegitimate" use of language.

In each of these situations, women writers have been attacked for exploratory and highly personal uses of language. It is "women's language" that immediately calls into question the value of their observations and interpretations of reality. In spite of the efforts of critics, women among them, to exclude women's perspectives in the novel by condemning our style, we would maintain with Spacks that the sensibility that women bring to our interpretation of the world *is* reflected in the language we choose for expressing our perceptions.

We would go further, however, and claim that the unique perceptions and interpretations of women require a style that reflects, captures, and embodies the quality of our thought. That the thinking of women has traditionally been regarded as a marginal activity has justified trivializing our uses of language. What emerges clearly from the writing of women is dissatisfaction, a conscious malaise, with language as men have defined it through the centuries. Male language is insufficient, ill-suited, as an expressive mode for women's sensibility. Mary Daly, in *Beyond God the Father,* points out that linguistic structures formulated by man "serve the purposes of patriarchal social arrangements" (p. 22). Another feminist, Peggy Allegro, contrasting women's relationship to language within the patriarchy and in our changing lives, defines the possibilities for women: "Our goal as I see it might be to constantly be open to new language, new ways of making the strange familiar, new ego images, and new ways of synthesizing our private languages with each other. Our success will be in direct proportion to our ability to say no to Daddy, to resist the rigidly enforced male language (way of perceiving the strange), and our ability to prevent ourselves from, like Daddy, imposing our private language on each other" (p. 184). As Barbara Starrett says, "Women have the ability, despite our programming, to think in ways that negate dualities" (p. 113). Susan Griffin, speaking of the interconnectedness of feminists' writing and their lives, describes how new images create new space:

> Why we write, as feminists, is not separable from our lives. We have woven together a kind of textured echo chamber, a flexible moving acoustical system, the new sounds we utter changing the space even before we hear each syllable. Our writing, our talking, our living, our images have created another world than the man-made one we were born to, and continuously in this weaving we move, at one and the same time, toward each other, and outward, expanding the limits of the possible. (p. 7)

Even typographical conventions and punctuation have political implications; they can be altered to transform old meanings or they can confine meaning and hinder expression. In her Afterword to *Woman Hating,* "The Great Punctuation Typography Struggle," Andrea Dworkin recounts her battle to determine how her text would be punctuated and which words would or would not be capitalized, and her defeat at the hands of establishment editors:

> this text has been altered in one very serious way. I wanted it to be printed the way it was written — lower case letters, no apostrophes, contractions. . . .
>
> my publisher, in his corporate wisdom, filled the pages with garbage: standard punctuation. he knew his purposes; he knew what was necessary. our purposes differed; mine, to achieve clarity; his, to sell books. . . .
>
> there is a great deal at stake here. many writers fight this battle and most lose it. what is at stake for the writer? freedom of invention. freedom to tell the truth, in all its particulars. freedom to imagine new structures. (pp. 197–201).

Barbara Starrett, in "I Dream in Female," comments on her use of quotation marks at the bottom of a page: "The thought occurs: as my consciousness level rises, will I finally put the entire world-as-it-is in quotes?" Rich, in *Of Woman Born,* found in the course of her research and analysis that the subject of motherhood is "hedged by taboos, mined with false-namings" (p. 15).

As women begin to occupy ourselves as writers, we discover that English does not easily suit itself to the ideas we wish to express; the structure of the language has been made to fit a way of knowing not ours. One way of exposing the patriarchal understanding of "knowledge" is to examine some of the etymological developments of the word *science,* since patriarchal culture esteems the kinds of knowledge denoted by this term. The word *science,* of course, is derived from the Latin *scīre,* "to know." What is rarely, if ever, pointed out is that the semantic development of the verb *scīre* shows that it originally meant "to separate one thing from another." The Proto-Indo-European root from which *scīre* evolved was **skei-,* which meant "to cut, split." Science, our culture's prevailing way of "knowing," developed out of the method of analysis that systematically splits things apart, separates one thing from another. Barbara Starrett writes (p. 112), "Male structures are dependent on the concept of duality. . . . We are sometimes told that dualism helps us to make distinctions and aids clarity of thought. This is not true. Dualism always poses an ethical choice, an either/or; one opposite is always preferable to the other. There is no room for gradations and levels, for complexities, for multi-focusing. Dualities reinforce linear, cause-and-effect, hierarchical thinking. Aristotelian logic, for example, is a series of linear regressions of the true/false binary."[2] Adrienne Rich, discussing the polarities of "inner" and "outer" as Freud described them in his essay "On Negation," has this to say:

> As the inhabitant of a female body, this description gives me pause. The boundaries of the ego seem to me much less crudely definable than the words "inner" and "outer" suggest. I do not perceive myself as a walled city into which certain emissaries are received and from which others are excluded. . . . The child that I carry for nine months can be defined neither as me nor as not-me. Far from existing in the mode of "inner space," women are powerfully and vulnerably attuned both to "inner" and "outer" because for us the two are continuous, not polar. (pp. 63-4).

Feminist writers are acutely aware of the inadequacy of the English language as males have shaped it over the past centuries. Andrea Dworkin, the author of *Woman Hating* and *Our Blood*, comments on her problems as a writer in confronting the English language: "I write however with a broken tool, a language which is sexist and discriminatory to its core. I try to make the distinctions, not 'history' as the whole human story, not 'man' as the generic term for the species, not 'manhood' as the synonym for courage, dignity, and strength. But I have not been successful in reinventing the language" (*Woman Hating*, p. 26). Jill Johnston analyzes her own style in her introductory "Remarks" and contrasts the prevalent style of her book *Lesbian Nation: The Feminist Solution* with "the old academic style" she uses elsewhere (pp. 139-40). Other feminist writers (e.g., Mary Daly, Kate Millett, Bertha Harris) employ women's style quite consciously, stating within their works the principles which underlie their attempts to extend the limits of English to encompass women's sensibilities and perceptions.

The most obvious and striking evidence of women's concern for language and its role as a naming process is the frequency with which women are choosing new names for ourselves. There are several ways that are particularly common. Women are changing patronymic endings; one woman recently lost a lawsuit in New York where she attempted to change her name from *Cooperman* to *Cooperperson* (she has won her case since we first wrote

this!), and the novelist *Elana Dykewoman* was formerly *Elana Nachman*. Women choose from nature names that appeal to them, such as *Chocolate Waters* and *Woodwoman*, or select goddesses and heroic women, such as *Morgan* and *Artemis March*.

But women are experimenting with larger units of English than naming: We are replacing names and abstract nouns with active, process verbs and concrete nouns; we are using specific organic verbs in place of more general, abstract verbs. In a short story by Maud Haimson, "Hands," the characters lack names as labels. Instead, the naming of the women is itself a process, and the references to them change as their situations alter with respect to their environment, their relation to each other, and their understanding of these relationships:

> She waited a moment until this little woman came in. She wasn't regular little, smaller than that even. At first, the little woman didn't pay attention to the other woman, instead she moved her looks toward the rocks as though they were a matter of now importance. The new-to-the-cave woman nodded and waited. The cave woman picked up a small rock, touched it all around, and brought it to the older woman. The older outside woman took it, touched it and holding it asked the inside woman if she'd been outside. The stone woman shook her head and taking a look at her stove picked up some rocks and put them in her many pocketed cloth-like thing going to the ground, pockets in the back too with bulges from stones. She followed the other woman out. (p. 60)

In addition to the shifting labeling process, which changes as the women shift identity in relation to each other, the noun modifiers provide us with new information about the women. For example, the cave/stone woman later becomes the "new-to-the-outside woman" with respect to her shift in position in her environment. The little woman doesn't "look" at the rocks, she "moves her looks toward" them. The stone woman doesn't put her rocks in a "coat"; it is a "many pocketed cloth-like thing going to the ground" (it has characteristics, but it, too, is engaged in the processes connected with its being and functions). Other phrases in the passage seem to have been adapted from patriarchal language. "The little woman," for example, is a phrase which men use to refer jocularly to their wives, a phrase by which they indicate paternal amusement for the women they possess. Haimson, however, has shown that the term merely denotes the relative size of one of the women: She "wasn't regular little, smaller than that even." In wrenching such phrases from their patriarchal meanings and contexts, Haimson creates a new language without creating new words. As Mary Daly has stated in *Beyond God the Father* (pp. 22–23), women need not create new combinations of sounds or of letters on paper:

> *Rather, words which, materially speaking, are identical with the old become new in a semantic context that arises from qualitatively new experience. The word* exodus *as applied to the community of women is stripped of its patriarchal, biblical context, while at the same time speaking to and beyond that context. So also the word* sisterhood *no longer means a subordinate mini-brotherhood, but an authentic bonding of women on a wide scale for our own liberation.*
>
> *Moreover, this liberation of language from its old context implies a breakthrough to new semantic fields. The new context has its source and its verification in the rising consciousness women have of ourselves and of our situation. Since this consciousness contradicts the established sense of reality which is reflected in the prevailing social and linguistic structures, its verbal expressions sometimes involve apparent contradictions. The words of women's becoming function in such a way that they raise questions and problems and at the same time give clues to the resolution of those problems.*

In reclaiming the naming process, feminist authors are taking a crucial step toward liberating women from the value system that patriarchal labels embody and perpetuate.

In Marge Piercy's *Woman on the Edge of Time,* the English language is projected into a non-sexist future. Some of her changes in the language are the sort one might expect: *For sure,* a contemporary slang interjection signaling assent, is *fasure; criticized* has lost its Latinate final syllable and has become *critted.* Other changes reflect conceptual structures:

> *"Luciente and Bolivar have not been communing. Meshing badly. Sparks and bumps. Tonight we try to comprehend that hostility and see if we can defuse it."*
>
> *"Aren't people allowed to dislike each other?"*
>
> *"Not good when they're in the same core. Jackrabbit is close to both. Such bumping strains per. They compete for Jackrabbit's attent. They are*

picky toward each other's ways. We have critted them for it before, but matters lift only briefly. When they crit each other, it does not hold up under scrutiny as honest—but self-serving." Parra smiled wryly.

> *"Suppose after worming they still can't stand each other?"* (p. 199)

In this excerpted passage, the language used to speak of the qualities of human relationships has become more concrete, less abstract. When two people cannot get along with each other, they are said to "mesh badly." The unpleasantly descriptive term "worming" refers to a group session similar to, but more evolved than, either consciousness-raising or group therapy.

"Women's style," in a time when we have at last gained some degree of access to the benefits of mass media distribution, reveals that women's use of English has a long, if unfamiliar, development. As Moffat and Painter speak of their experience in editing selections from women's diaries: "What united these disparate lives for us is what we heard as an unconscious call by the women for a redefinition of these concepts [love, work, and power] into a less divisive, more organic pattern for existence. . . ." (p. 4). The consciousness, if not the public right to language, has been with us for some time. The women of the 20th century who write speak out of a tradition of invisibility, a tradition of the closely guarded, personal, revelatory language of diaries and journals. Our style, therefore, does not conform to the male style we have been taught to regard as "literary" and "correct." Use of the term "confessional" to automatically condemn any work of art reflects the literary tradition of a male-dominated culture which perpetuates a false dichotomy between our lives and our art. The so-called "confessional style," the voice of women for centuries, is only said to be non-literature when written by women, because we are said to be using it emotionally, not artistically. When, however, an Augustine or a Rousseau writes what he calls "confessions," he is said to be exploring the profundities of the "human condition." Such is the critical universe of discourse created within patriarchal culture.

For centuries, women have written in the confessional style, using it for describing our own lives in private; now we are bringing it forth as a dynamic public affirmation of our newly acquired identities as whole women. Our style, which reflects its heritage, is outside the literary world, "on the periphery" in Mary Daly's terms. That the style *is* outside is now its strength, however, rather than its weakness. From this boundary, new visions are evolving, "a new species which redefines sexuality and reproduction; the production and exchange of use values; and all the languages of the conscious and subconscious" (Harriet Desmoines, p. 70). Women are constantly challenging and shifting the boundaries of English in ways most often associated with poetic consciousness. As a result, many of the works by women, those that have reached us, are described as "poetic prose" or "prose poetry," that twilight genre. Our tradition has its sources in the unspoken lives of women, although it didn't emerge as a public style until Gertrude Stein and Virginia Woolf began to publish and gain recognition as "literary" writers. Our language is in struggle with externally imposed silence.

> "I began to write," the dancer said, "to allow the words which had accumulated in my throat to spill onto the page. They came in strange grunts, shapes, grimaces, at first, which I am just coming to recognize. The important thing," she hoarsely whispered, "is to speak. Is to speak. Don't be afraid to speak. Silence is death," she said. (Deena Metzger, p. 13)

Even in the study of language, women are choosing to focus on features we share with each other. This approach suits the communal quality of the emerging aesthetic, an aesthetic that contrasts sharply with the patriarchal one that Lillian Robinson terms the "bourgeois aesthetic":

> It is a fundamental precept—indeed, an axiom—of bourgeois aesthetics that good art, although probably adhering and contributing to a tradition, is art that celebrates what is unique and even eccentric in human experience or human personality. Achievement, from this perspective, reflects individual heroism. Isolation is an individual condition. This is the norm, whether the achievement and the isolation be that of the artist or the character. It seems to me that this is a far from universal way for people to be or to be perceived, but one that is intimately connected to relationships and values perpetuated by capitalism. For this reason, I would seriously question any aesthetic that not only fails to call that individualism into question, but that does so intentionally, in the name of feminism.

She later asks "whether the best role for the arts or for criticism is to celebrate that which is basic or that which is marginal, what is common or what is exceptional." The "best" criticism is that which draws on the shared experiences, the common life experiences of women, rather than the unique, or individual, experience.[3]

Robinson examines writing by women that continues to be ignored because it does not meet traditional "literary" standards, but, as she observes, "Certain writings by women who are acknowledged 'official' writers do partake of the impulse towards wholeness that characterizes the movement itself." It is this "impulse towards wholeness" that we believe describes the evolving feminist aesthetic.

There can be little doubt that women writing in the 20th century are intensely conscious of the many ways in which we wrestle with English in our efforts to remake a language that suits our conceptual processes. The previously separated strands of this remaking finally begin to weave themselves into a discernible whole. From Virginia Woolf and Gertrude Stein to Kate Millett and Elana Dykewoman, the relationship between consciousness and linguistic choice is confronted and articulated as the self expressing itself in and through a language remade, reordered: the feminist aesthetic.

> What sort of diary should I like mine to be? Something loose knit and yet not slovenly, so elastic that it will embrace anything, solemn, slight or beautiful that comes into my mind. I should like it to resemble some deep old desk, or capacious holdall, in which one flings a mass of odds and ends without looking them through. I should like to come back, after a year or two, and find that the collection had sorted itself and refined itself and coalesced, as such deposits so mysteriously do, into a mould, transparent enough to reflect the light of our life, and yet steady, tranquil compounds with the aloofness of a work of art. The main requisite, I think on rereading my old volumes, is not to play the part of censor, but to write as the mood comes or of anything whatever; since I was curious to find how I went for things put in haphazard, and found the significance to lie where I never saw it at the time. —Virginia Woolf, Easter Sunday, April 20th [1919] (Quoted in Moffatt and Painter)

Woolf goes on to comment that the "looseness" of diary writing may quickly become "slovenly," and we see here that she held always before her the established values of male writers. Yet her consciousness of the expressive possibilities for diary writing, her ruminations on its potential as a literary form, and her concept of its style as a mold capable of accommodating a random assortment of ideas, impressions, "odds and ends"—a catch-all within which such a mass might sort itself into patterns and meanings previously unimagined—all these possibilities are being realized in the writing of contemporary women.

In 1935 or thereabouts, Stein contributed her observations on the relationships between the categories of English and the genres of prose and poetry in "Poetry and Grammar," which appeared as one of the essays in *Lectures in America*. In this particular essay, Stein explains how the function of nouns as permanent "names" gives rise to her syntactic style:

One of the things that is a very interesting thing to know is how you are feeling inside you to the words that are coming out to be outside you.

Do you always have the same kind of feeling in relation to the sounds as the words come out of you or do you not. All this has so much to do with grammar and with poetry and with prose.

Words have to do with everything in poetry and prose and some writers write more in articles and prepositions and some say you should write in nouns, and of course one has to think of everything.

A noun is a name of anything, why after a thing is named write about it. A name is adequate or it is not. If it is adequate then why go on calling it, if it is not then calling it by its name does no good.

. . . but generally speaking, things once they are named the name does not go on doing anything to them and so why write in nouns. Nouns are the name of anything and just naming names is alright when you want to call a roll but is it any good for anything else. . . .

As I say a noun is a name of a thing, and therefore slowly if you feel what is inside that thing you do not call it by the name by which it is known. . . .

. . . I like the feeling of the everlasting feeling of sentences as they diagram themselves.

In that way one is completely possessing something and incidentally one's self. Now in that diagraming of the sentences of course there are articles and prepositions and as I say there are nouns but nouns as I say even by definition are completely not interesting, the same thing is true of adjectives.

Adjectives are not really and truly interesting. In a way anybody can know always has known that, because after all adjectives effect nouns and as nouns are not really interesting the thing that effects a not too interesting thing is of necessity not interesting. . . .

Besides the nouns and the adjectives there are verbs and adverbs. Verbs and adverbs are more interesting. In the first place they have one very nice quality and that is that they can be so mistaken. It is wonderful the number of mistakes a verb can make and that is equally true of its adverb. Nouns and adjectives never can make mistakes can never be mistaken but verbs can be so endlessly, both as to what they do and how they agree or disagree with whatever they do. . . .

. . . But nouns still have to be mentioned because in coming to avoid nouns a great deal happens and has happened. It was one of the things that happened in a book I called Tender Buttons.

In the Making of Americans a long a very long prose book made up of sentences and paragraphs and the new thing that was something neither the sentences nor the paragraph each one alone or in combination had ever done. I said I had gotten rid of nouns and adjectives as much as possible by the method of living in adverbs in verbs in pronouns, in adverbial clauses written or implied and in conjunctions.

But after I had gone as far as I could in these long sentences and paragraphs that had come to do something else I then began very short things and in doing very short things I resolutely realized nouns and decided not to get around them but to meet them, to handle in short to refuse them by using them and in that way my real acquaintance with poetry was begun. (pp. 209–28)

For Stein, then, nouns as labels do not point to reality. In her view of language there can be no easy separation of artist from language, or from the perceptions that her language must learn to bring forth. Robinson observes, with respect to trying to deal with art as "product": ". . . according to the prevailing view of the process, one is still supposed to act as if it is an *it*. . . . The expression cannot be arbitrarily divided from the feelings that give rise to it, nor either of these from the lived reality at the base" (p. 7). This refusal to split oneself from one's creation is perhaps one of the reasons so many readers have trouble reading Gertrude Stein: She is always Present in her language, There before the reader as creator, as the controlling consciousness. There are no ambiguous silences in Stein, no unfilled spaces through which the reader can avoid or escape her meanings. She rarely deletes even redundant words from her sentences. Her writing reveals the process of the act of writing, not an art object or a "product," but the *process* of creation itself, with its ambiguities, its backtrackings, and the stumblings of which Woolf was so conscious.

In the early 1970s, Jill Johnston began to take up the implications of Stein's approach to language and carry it in a different direction than Stein herself had. As Johnston observed to her readers in her prefatory "Remarks" to *Lesbian Nation:*

> All repetitions of thoughts ideas material projections plans reflections reveries fantasies in the same or varied phrases in different contexts constitute my way of working circles within circles, . . . Every departure from a point of origin carries within it a renewed approach to it. Each return to the point of origin completes the cycle of one existence and begins another. The style and the object are the same: the return to the harmony of statehood and biology through the remembered majesties of women.

At one point in *Gullible's Travels,* Johnston mentions a woman who has accused her of ripping off the women's movement:

> I had a letter from a woman saying that . . . my writing style shows my middle class self indulgence which I try to pass off as women's language or beginnings of a new women's culture.[4]

Yet Johnston's debt to Gertrude Stein is apparent in the following quotation, in which she refers to the relationship between her syntax and her involvement with reality:

> I meant to lie so I could present the confusing non-sequitur of two such unhappy products in shock over ghastly disclosures blundering beautifully on to destruction by filling themselves inside as well as up against as spherical bodies all parts orientating themselves in an infinite number of positions in a rectangular space like sentences not too abruptly rotating their angular facets as cut stones or the multi-colored ball we lost to the tide in the harbor waiting for the ferry playing volley catch . . .
> (p. 130)

A few pages later, Johnston, like Woolf, points to the world as a "mass of odds and ends"; her sentences, which may aspire to nonsense but never attain it, make sense of the world in which she writes:

> i've made innumerable efforts to make words write without sense and found it impossible. but if we line things up as lists and images we could have a sense of the world as a tremendous clutter of things about which we do nothing but talk constantly, then if you happen to be broke you can just go flying around some interior full of people holding them all up with a phony gun which they know is your hand, . . . (p, 143)

For Johnston, like Stein, the sentence must capture the processes of reality as the writer perceives it; each returning of the sentence is another view of the interpretive creative process, making something of this "drifting material of life." Like Woolf's imagined rider, Johnston goes at such a pace that she "must make the most direct and instant shots at [her] object," choosing and shooting words without pause.

The intimate awareness and self-consciousness of the woman struggling with her impulse to create bleeds through the syntax of her prose, the struggle to live becoming the struggle to create, becoming the struggle in language. Elana Nachman makes explicit the physical act of typing her manuscript and summoning her characters as Inez Riverfinger:

> Moments have passed, and I will make Abby reappear. It is as easy as this, a voice squeezed from black plastic keys, telling stories in bed. The hammering of myself into the background will seem to be over. This hammering, this background—the language of our getting older, the time of our being no longer children but young women, that is to say, forming into identifiable shapes, it is not simple. From time to time you will hear that faint tackety-tackety-tackety, like kids at summercamp, making bronze name plates in relief dot by dot:
> these are our lives, these are our lives, these are our lives. (p. 7)

Again, we become aware of life moving and drifting around us, from the past of children earnestly engraving their names in bronze to Inez, creating Abby from her typewriter, in some future that is the present.

Like the essays of Johnston, Kate Millet's *Flying* is an ongoing book "with its own revision" (*Gullible's Travels,* pp. 127, 131). Quick changes, instant revisions, force themselves into a new syntax. Millett works her way toward the sentences that will accommodate swift changes, life reviewed as it is being lived, the constant and sweeping shifts of perception:

> *What is old, gray, dreary to me, is new to them, what they have to hear. While I go on, loathing the pompous lecture language, its cold abstraction the very antithesis of that vital hurt coming now, living it.* (p. 95)

Where the event as memory and the living of it as remembrance fuse in the immediate consciousness of the writer, the dichotomies of past/present, here/there, fact/fiction fall away. For Johnston, leaving herself "behind for a fiction,"

> *Words are very very heavy magic. So everything you say is true. The necessities of style distort both fact and fiction. . . . In the universal unstable compound of fable and fact that passes for our lives. (Gullible's Travels,* pp. 127–9)

In the act of creation, living in creation, where the language explores the coherence of what has been split into fact and fable, truth and fiction, in which the only belief is in living, that living itself necessitates a language in which all are simultaneously possible. If language calls truth into question, then self-consciousness remakes language and presses it beyond its proscribed limitations.

The writer is her audience is her critic. The risk lies in the possibility that she may be talking only to herself, as many women have been doing all their lives for centuries. The "talking-to-oneself" of the diaries and journals becomes the prose of revelation and revolution, the turning around in consciousness, vulnerability. Elana Dykewoman, talking to herself, talks to all women. She would like to internalize the emptiness of her male contemporaries, to acquire the blankness which others might admire. But she cannot assume the fashionable profundity of nothingness; instead, like women before her, she finds a fullness of words exploding into rich chaos, the unordered chaos of experience. She notes that others call her inward speech "talking to yourself." Looking into herself, the woman writer finds a profusion of words, and, if she *is* talking to herself, well and good.

A feminist aesthetic, as it emerges out of women's evolution, grounds itself in female consciousness and in the unrelenting language of process and change. A feminist aesthetic will encompass the exposure of cultural and social attempts to cripple women, to bind us, to strip us of our self-awareness, and it will also trace the unwinding of the patriarchal bonds that have limited our perceptions and descriptions of our experience. Such an aesthetic may incorporate the "truth criterion" suggested by Marcia Holly (in Donovan, pp. 38–47), but must also record the progressive development of a female culture. Although it may be "premature to say what such an aesthetic may entail," Donovan is aware that "Radical feminists and lesbians have been in the forefront of the women's movement in seeking the patterns that identify women as a separate cultural group" (p. 77). As she also observes, ". . . aesthetic judgments are rooted in epistemology: one cannot understand why someone thinks something is beautiful or significant until one understands the way s/he *sees,* knows the world" (p. 78). What had been perceived as boundaries melt; categories become shape-changers; and sentences are never "complete" because the perceiving is the movement itself.

As women strain to break through the limits of English, certain patterns begin to emerge, recurrences of similar syntactic ways of ordering perception that is always moving and often contradictory. One observation may negate another. The natural imagery of growth, proliferation, and evolution replaces nature as object and product. Flux, not stasis, characterizes experience. Labels and abstract nouns as viable perceptive categories give way to active, process verbs and concrete nouns, the language of touch; verbs of specific action replace the abstract, more general verbs. On the discourse level, we find a discursive, conjunctive style instead of the complex, subordinating, linear style of classification and distinction.[5] It is not that there is no classification taking place, but rather that the syntactic structure must accommodate itself to the shifting perspectives of the writer's observing mind. As she attempts to order her perceptions, the clauses are juxtaposed to express the relationships as they suggest themselves, in contrast to a subordinate syntax in which the complexity of experience is embedded in dependent clauses, reflecting experience already categorized, qualified, detached from its happening.

Mary Daly, in the essentially expository prose of *Beyond God the Father,* exemplifies the frequently organic, natural, concrete style. Her use of language, although often violent, is always direct and specific when she speaks of women's experience:

> *. . . clinging to these [symbols] as fixed and ultimate is self-destructive and idolatrous.* (p. 15)

. . . symbols grow out of a changing *communal situation and experience.* (p. 15)

. . . the becoming *of women cannot be understood merely conceptually and abstractly but through active* participating *in the* overcoming *of servitude. Both activism and creative thought* flow from *and* feed into *the* evolving *woman-consciousness. The cumulative effect is a* surge *of awareness. . . .* (p. 16)

The process of cutting away *the Supreme Phallus can hardly be a merely "rational" affair.* (p. 19)

. . . The woman-consciousness is being wrenched *free . . .* (p. 18)

Yet the liberating *potential of these elements is* choked off *in the* surrounding *atmosphere of the images, ideas, values, and structures of patriarchy. (p. 18)*

Jill Johnston's prose in *Lesbian Nation,* which works through the process of her identification with lesbian feminism, is "an interlocking web of personal experience and history and events of the world forming a picture of an evolving political revolutionary consciousness of one who was female who emerged from straight middle unconscious postwar amerika." She repeats her observations is slightly altered forms, rephrasing them, shifting their meanings, "working circles within circles" such that "every departure from a point of origin carries with it a renewed approach to it." Her sentences run on unmarked by conventional punctuation; her puns restore the naming function of language, reclaiming the phrases and the literary conventions of patriarchal language and turning them to feminist phrases:

. . . the 350 years of Abraham inter-sample Abraham lived for 350 years because the bible ages are only a succession of sons and fathers and grandfathers intensely identifying with their ancestors their son so identified naturely with the father that he believed he was the father and of course he was as was Abraham and Isaac and Jacob and Esau and Reuben and Simeon and Levi and Judah and Joseph each one lived for 350 years, but who are the daughters of Rachel and Ruth and Sarah and Rebekah the rest we do not know the daughters never had any daughters they had only sons who begat more sons and sons so we have very little sense, from that particular book, of the

lineage and ligaments and legacies and identities of mothers and daughters and their mothers and mothers and daughters and sisters who were naturally not lesbians if they had nothing of each other save sons so now we must say Verily Verily, I say unto thee, except a woman be born again she cannot see the kingdom of Goddess a woman must be born again to be herself her own eminence and grace the queen queen-self whose mother has pressed upon her mouth innumerable passionate kisses so sigh us. . . . (pp. 266–7)

Johnston's style of ever-widening circles manifests her changing perspectives as her consciousness evolves, returning to themes as her narrative moves forward in historical time.

The syntactic structure and the punctuation found in the novels of Bertha Harris appear to be more "conventional" than Johnston's. There are no page-long, run-on sentences, and most of the conventions of punctuation are observed. Harris violates the rules of traditional grammar only by her sentence fragments, which accentuate the humorous content of the paragraphs that contain them. When we examine whole paragraphs, however, we discover the parallel structures, short simple sentences, frequent repetitions, and conjoined phrases and clauses characteristic of cumulative style:

Like all painters in this women's group of women painters, she is engrossed in the preparation and eating of food. Mushes of lentils and Spanish onion. Haute Chinese. Arcane Hungarian. Elaborate; cheap. It always tastes wonderful; and Flynn, when they invite her to their long weekly dinner parties, eats the most. In her thirties, she is filling out. She has buttocks. Her breasts are wonderful. (lover, p. 88)

Some call the woman I love silver, and some call her gold. Before I got to be her lover, she painted a painting and presented it to me. It is entitled "One Hundred and Forty-Seven Cunts." Much of it she painted with her fingers. It is still rolled up, the three panels of it, and wrapped in plastic at the bottom of a cardboard box. I still don't have a wall of my own. The painter's frequent headaches intimidate me — I believe them a superior manifestation of cognizance of all that is horrible; they are a function of mighty brain power. Her wondrous hair sprouts from those headaches. It is like those flowers whose petals grow backwards, yearning towards the stem. Like chrysanthemums, I remember now. Except when she takes up the scissors and cuts it all off; and then none of it is any longer than a clipped fingernail all over her skull; and then there is nothing that will hide the machinery of the headache: it shows. I use the word "love" when I speak to her, and she uses my name. . . . (lover, pp. 137–8)

Even these brief excerpts illustrate what might be called a "simultaneous novel." All events—different pasts, present, and future—tend to be narrated in the "historic present" or simple present tense, and Harris even includes her random thoughts during the creative process as part of the narrative ("like chrysanthemums, I remember now"), addressing the reader, making herself and her reader part of the narrative as she addresses her in an offhand, conversational manner.

She switches to the past tense, however, to recount actual historical events. Each section of the novel begins with a short, italicized passage describing one event; this is frequently a tale of the undeserved torture and martyr-dom of women, and is occasionally related ironically.

Kate Millett, too, has broken through the boundaries of linear time in *Flying*. Utilizing words as though they were the frames of an autobiographical film, flashing back and forward in her paragraphs, Millett is able to capture and fuse events at different points in time. She creates portraits through the photographic use of sentence fragments which lack verbs, and she uses the simple pres-ent and the progressive aspect to lend immediacy to past events and to convey a sense of movement in and between time:

I look across the pond now as my mind's eye drinks that moment in color—and matches it against the black and white a Pentax saw, saw and held last summer at Brookfield and the sun fell in scatters through sycamore leaves. Celia, her hair uncombed after breakfast, played the lute for us in the open air. Now only these portraits remain: my mind's version in motion and sound, and the still shot upon paper. Celia bending then upon her lute, playing it in sunlight one fine morning our summer of delight, her straight hair merely braided, not dressed as now in five choirs upon her head for concert. A figure outlined against a white New England wall, wearing the yellow jersey that with the true cheekiness of an aristocrat she never seemed to change, and a pair of faded jeans I

bought her on the Bowery. Celia a profile leaning over the great pear-shaped lute. Strange instru-ment, only its face showing in the photo, its back hidden against her body, the wonderfully carved facets of polished wood filetted together in perfect laminations, the very shape of craft and song. Ex-amining again her tomboy succulence that Connect-icut June day, the extravagant delicacy of her face, something even of her eyes' fine beauty captured one forever time ago to pierce me now as they did that muddled September night I scrawled on yellow paper, cursing her good-bye. Eyes light a light through the tunnel of loss. And now the music rises, sound in air expanding as the lyrics come crisp and Elizabethan. . . . superior art of song defeating mere prose in its finer medium. Time, and again in time recurring. Sound once lost in space, now miraculously reassembled here within the same stones' echoes as it echoes in the mind while I sit again, this moment erasing the bird's chatter about the pond a hundred miles upriver from where the sound now echoes to their miracle performed. (pp. 114–7)

Millett's command of the conjunctive style is evident when she describes her lovemaking in sentences which are at once fragmented and fused. Questions and imperatives flow into statements, unmarked by standard terminal punctuation. Phrases and clauses are juxtaposed, stacked upon one another, and frequently run together without conjunction. There are fragments which lack subjects and which contain progressives without auxiliary verbs, fragments and sentences in the simple present and future. Millett also shifts her point of view, addressing her lover and herself in the second person, addressing her lover in both second and third person:

. . . I must doubt it, even this, her hand on my breast will she touch the nipple with exquisite care, feels like it connects to the clitoris begins to heat be-tween my legs. . . . What sick thought is this, or is it that final safety with her, bewildered at the joy in her hand searching me, opening to her fingers upon the lips of my other mouth wet making little noises, silence to be filled with her tongue while she sifts me, reams, files, selects, and plays upon the nerve like a button pressed all heat flooding out I open wider to receive her will split myself take her whole up to the elbow, straining in hope. I love the way you move as I move dancing under your hand's

power deep in me shaking when you press hard fast against the wall deep like a storm in me. I must stop breathing, so fierce you are. So powerful. (p. 481)

Millett, like Woolf, Stein, Johnston, and Harris, requires the run-on, infinite syntax in which words explode, collide, brush, and fuse. It is the syntax of woman's consciousness, the rush of perception, the speech that tells all as it emerges. It is the syntax that charges through time/space, taking into itself the urgency of speed; the trick is not to get "caught in time."

Finally there comes the terror of the sentence written even as it is lived, the risk of confronting one's experience *as* meaning, the fear that such knowledge itself must be lived with. In such risk, control sustains.

Having claimed that the prose style of 20th-century feminist writers inheres in a woman's perspective, having described some linguistic characteristics shared by several of these writers—their mutual concern with consciousness and language, their refusal to accept patriarchal segmentations of perceptual phenomena—have we provided some grounding for a feminist aesthetic? Do we have an epistemological framework that encompasses women's perspectives? We would say yes.

Those perspectives change. Jill Johnston, after nearly two years of silence, now writes essays again for the *Village Voice.* Her topics have changed and so has her prose style. In one recent *VV* article, for example, Johnston writes with praise of Steve Gaskin's farm in Tennessee, a commune renowned for promulgating the dogma that women should be "barefoot and pregnant." In an article entitled "Pick It Cover It or Kiss It Goodbye," Johnston discusses her maturity:

> *The subject of the george burns christmas special was a search for a good opening number. We're always doing something to get into a position to do something. This subject is yourself reading. Now imagine anything else. If you find yourself at a loss then lose yourself in it. Finding a loss is a good find. The subject is the feeling of loss. This year I lost all the leaves on my butternut tree again.* (p. 31)

There is still the feeling of movement from one sentence to the next. She still plays with clichés, but she no longer makes their buried meanings backfire. Gone are the multiple meanings and directions created by yanking old saws out of their cultural context. Now the clichés are accepted on their own terms, teased a little, but largely left as they came to her. Nor do the sentences run from page to page; her statements are direct, almost terse. Johnston says she has "matured." If our hypothesis has any validity to it, she has, in fact, abandoned her exploration of her woman's perspective, and her style no longer pushes at the limitations of English. Her style and her subject are still the same, but neither aspires to "a return to the harmony of statehood and biology through the remembered majesties of women." Now, "the subject is the feeling of loss," a subject inspired by her search for a suitable topic for her column. She compares her writing and its purpose to the opening lines of a television variety show. Such a subject does not require a new language for its expression.

Endnotes

1. Jesperson, for example, claimed that women use more emotive adjectives than men, especially those that make fine color distinctions, and Lakoff was apparently intuitively satisfied with his assertion and incorporated it without serious thought in her cataloguing of the features of women's language.

2. Our discussion here, and throughout the body of the paper, makes a distinction between female and male modes of thinking, which might suggest that we have introduced our own dichotomy and, thereby, an internal contradiction to our thesis. This problem derives, like so many others in recent criticism, from male control of our understanding of reality. Thus, for example, thought processes which do not follow the traditionally endorsed patterns (such as Aristotelian "logic") have been defined as *non-thought;* what does not fall within the boundaries of the male universe of discourse—i.e., the "rational"—is "irrational." Once otherness has been identified and excluded, the dichotomies proliferate. What is not "logical" is "illogical"; what is not "sane" is "insane"; what is not "order" is, by definition, "chaos." Because this dualistic terminology excludes those forms of thought that it has defined as "illegitimate," we are concerned here with establishing that such processes have their own expressive modes and constitute that perceptual complex which has been labeled "feminine." The dichotomy is not even ours, although we remain trapped by its consequences in our discussion. For this reason, it would be easy to show that some males have also written in the style we are describing: e.g., Whitman, Emerson, cummings, to name only three. We would suggest that such male writers are relatively few in number when compared to the great number of male writers for whom there is a long history of publication and criticism. Further,

those male writers who have "discovered" expressive modes similar to those being used by women in the 20th century found such modes comfortable because they, too, were dissatisfied with the linear, dualistic language of classification and cause-and-effect favored within the larger patriarchal tradition of thought. (See note 5.)

3. In speaking of distinguishing between those experiences which are "basic" and those which are "marginal," Robinson explains that she is "not proposing a crude quantitative game," that, although most women are "heterosexual," Lesbianism is a basic experience "because it puts women in direct touch with the social forces that define a sexist society."

4. We have quoted this passage from Johnston for two reasons. First, although she has occasionally claimed that she was inventing a new language for women, her style clearly derives from that of Stein. Second, the letter written to Johnston raises the important issue of class, addressed more directly by Lillian Robinson. Most, but not all, of the writers we examine in this paper have had access to the privileges and benefits of their connections to white males. Most of them have had at least some education beyond the high-school level. Johnston is only one example. She has had the time to experiment with English. She knows the "rules" of standard English because she has had the opportunity to learn them. Therefore, because she does know "the rules," she not only knows *how* to break them in ways that will work for her, but she also, to some extent, is thereby freed from the constraint of having to constantly demonstrate to others that she does know them. Women who are not so economically or educationally advantaged, on the other hand, either steadfastly adhere to the language of their class and/or region, or they endeavor to imitate the language of power — i.e., standard English — in order to prove their competence to those who have economic power. In contrast to women like Johnston, Woolf, and Stein, such women cannot "afford" to experiment with a language with which they are unfamiliar and which, for them, may be a second dialect. Given such a social reality, the claims of Johnston do partake of "middle class self indulgence." We see no way to avoid these issues. As long as there is a "prestige dialect" that everyone aspiring to status is expected to acquire, and as long as publishers, editors, and reviewers sanction only those works written in the prestige dialect, there will be no way to resolve this conflict in possibilities. (See, for example, Andrea Dworkin's discussion of the politics of punctuation in *Woman Hating*.) To argue, however, that the conflict results only from class differences is oversimplification. The present class structure in our society defines only male class and access to power within that hierarchical structure. In most cases, women belong to a specific class only through their fathers or husbands, not through their own economic status as individuals within the system.

5. As we pointed out in note 3, some males have also found the nonlinear style more congenial than the linear, subordinating style. We are referring here to the syntactic style taught in our schools as expository prose. It is also the prose style used by most male novelists. Hemingway, influenced by Stein's ideas about language and art, managed to combine the assertiveness of the conjunctive style with the cause-effect structure of simple declaratives, an essentially linear style that incorporates the dichotomies of subordination.

Bibliography

Allegro, Peggy, "The Strange and the Familiar: The Evolutionary Potential of Lesbianism," *The Lesbian Reader,* Oakland, Calif.: Amazon Press, 1975.

The Carpenter (June Arnold), *the Cook and the Carpenter,* Plainfield, Vt.: Daughters, Inc., 1973.

Covina, Gina, and Laurel Galana, eds., *The Lesbian Reader,* Oakland, Calif.: Amazon Press, 1975.

Crouch, Isabel M., and Betty Lou Dubois, "Features of Female/Male Undergraduates' Language Behavior," manuscript, 1976, to appear.

Daly, Mary, *Beyond God the Father,* Boston: Beacon Press, 1973.

Desmoines, Harriet, "Go Tell Aunt Rhody," *Sinister Wisdom,* I,1.

Donovan, Josephine, ed., *Feminist Literary Criticism,* Louisville, Ky.: University of Kentucky Press, 1975.

Dubois, Betty Lou, and Isabel M. Crouch, "The question of tag questions in women's speech: they don't really use more of them, do they?", *Language in Society,* 4, 289–94.

Dworkin, Andrea, *Woman Hating,* New York: E. P. Dutton & Co., Inc., 1974.

Dykewoman, Elana, *They Will Know Me by My Teeth,* Northampton, Mass.: Magaera Press, 1976.

Goulianos, Joan, *by a Woman writt,* Baltimore: Penguin Books, 1973.

Griffin, Susan, "Transformations," *Sinister Wisdom,* I, 2 (December 1976), 6–10.

Haimson, Maud, "Hands," *The Lesbian Reader,* Oakland, Calif.: Amazon Press, 1975.

Harris, Bertha, *Catching Saradove,* New York: Harcourt, Brace and World, 1969.

_____, *The Confessions of Cherubino,* Harcourt, Brace, Jovanovich, 1972.

_____, *lover,* Plainfield, Vt.: Daughters, Inc., 1976.

Jesperson, Otto, *Language, Its Nature, Development and Origin,* New York: 1964.

Johnston, Jill, *Gullible's Travels,* New York: Links Books, 1974.

_____, *Lesbian Nation: The Feminist Solution,* New York: Simon & Schuster, 1973.

_____, "Pick It Cover It or Kiss It Goodbye," *Village Voice,* January 17, 1978.

Lakoff, Robin, *Language and Woman's Place,* New York: Harper & Row, 1975.

Langer, Elinor, "Confession," *Ms.* (December 1974), 69–71.

Metzger, Deena, "Transformations," *Sinister Wisdom,* I, 2 (December 1976), 10–17.

Millett, Kate, *Flying,* New York: Alfred A. Knopf, 1974.

Moffat, Mary Jane, and Charlotte Painter, *Revelations: Diaries of Women,* New York: Vintage Books, 1975.

Nachman, Elana, *Riverfinger Women,* Plainfield, Vt.: Daughters, Inc., 1974.

Piercy, Marge, *Woman on the Edge of Time,* New York: Alfred A. Knopf, 1976.

Rich, Adrienne, *Of Woman Born,* New York: W. W. Norton, 1976.

Robinson, Lillian, "Who Speaks for Women—And Is It Poetry?," paper delivered at Modern Language Association, New York City, December 1976.

Smith-Rosenberg, Carroll, "The Female World of Love and Ritual: Relations Between Women in Nineteenth-Century America," *Signs,* I, 1 (Autumn 1975), 1–29.

Spacks, Patricia Meyer, *The Female Imagination,* New York: Avon Books, 1975.

Stanley, Julia P., "Fear of *Flying?*," *Sinister Wisdom,* I, 1 (December 1976), 52–62.

_____, "The Rhetoric of Denial: Delusion, Distortion, and Deception," *Sinister Wisdom,* I, 3 (April 1977).

Starrett, Barbara, "I Dream in Female: The Metaphors of Evolution," *The Lesbian Reader,* Oakland, Calif.: Amazon Press, 1975, p. 113.

Stein, Gertrude, *3 Lives,* New York: Vintage Books, 1936.

_____, *Everybody's Autobiography,* New York: Vintage Books, 1973.

_____, *Lectures in America,* Boston: Beacon Press, 1957.

Steinberg, Danny D., "Chomsky: From Formalism to Mentalism and Psychological Invalidity," *glossa,* 9, 2 (1975), 218–52.

Thorne, Barrie, and Nancy Henley, eds., *Language and Sex: Difference and Dominance,* Rowley, Mass.: Newbury House, 1975.

READING 92

The Future of Feminism in the 1980s: A Social Movement Analysis

Verta Taylor

All social movements originate in some contradiction or conflict in the larger social order (Useem, 1975). When a social movement persists throughout modern history, as the American feminist movement has, we can only assume that the injustices, grievances, and oppression on

Reprinted from Verta Taylor, "The Future of Feminism in the 1980s: A Social Movement Analysis," by permission of the author. Copyright 1981 by Verta Taylor.

I gratefully acknowledge Leila Rupp for her extensive comments, criticism, editorial assistance, and encouragement in the creation of this paper. I also thank Laurel Richardson for a careful reading of the manuscript and for inspiring me to write this paper.

which it is based are deeply rooted in society. The long and arduous struggle of women to gain equality and the frequency with which this struggle has risen to become a massive social movement compels us to recognize that the more central a social pattern is to the perpetuation of a way of life, the more difficult will be the process of altering that pattern. Feminism owes its existence to the universality of misogyny, androcentrism, gynophobia, and heterosexism. Feminism exists and expresses itself throughout history as a collective struggle to transform society because women are, and have been, everywhere oppressed at every level of social exchange, from the simplest social encounter to the most complex and elaborate traditions and institutional forms on which societies rest. From a social movement perspective, then, the general conditions that create the context for feminist activity were always present in American society. Indeed, instances of collective action on the part of women abound in women's history, especially if one includes female reform societies, women's church groups, alternative religious societies, and women's clubs. However, it seems that collective activity on the part of women directed specifically toward improving their own status has flourished only in periods of generalized social upheaval, when sensitivity to moral injustice, discrimination, and social inequality was widespread in the society as a whole (Chafe, 1977).

The first wave of feminism in this country grew out of the abolitionist struggle of the 1830s; the second developed out of the social reform ethos of the 1890s; and the contemporary movement emerged out of the general social discontent of the 1960s and carried forward into the 1970s with vigor. It is significant that of all of the manifestations of social activism in the 1960s, feminism is one of the few movements that still flourished in the 1970s.

In the 1980s, American society still confronts the feminist challenge. At the same time, political and social trends in this country reflect a turning away from the values of equality, human rights, and social justice. Many observers have even argued that the swing toward political and social conservatism that culminated in the election of Ronald Reagan to the presidency is, in fact, a deliberate backlash against the feminist momentum of the 1970s and the gains women have spent decades inching toward in this country (O'Reilly, 1980; Yankelovich, 1981). Even those recently won rights which, according to major public opinion polls, have been applauded not only by feminist activists but by the majority of Americans—all

the way from equal pay for equal work to legal abortion—are presently under siege. In response to the growing attack on women's rights on every front, one woman was quoted by syndicated columnist Ellen Goodman as saying, "all I know is that I am in the same movement for the second time in my life and I'm not even 40" (*Citizen's Journal,* 1981). Although this woman was talking specifically about women's rights, she also might have been talking about peace, poverty, civil rights, or the environment. Put bluntly, feminism in the 1980s will confront a social milieu which is inhospitable to all those who seek fundamental change in society. What then might we expect of feminism as a social movement in the 1980s?

The purpose of this paper is to examine the ways in which the contemporary anti-feminist backlash is likely to affect the nature and direction of organized feminist activity in the coming decade. The analysis will be organized around three major topics. First, I shall describe the contemporary women's movement and the ways in which it will continue to grow out of and build upon the feminism of the past two decades. The second section of the paper examines the relationship between feminism as a social movement and the Right as a countermovement in the context of the conservative social and political trends developing in society at the outset of the 1980s. Finally, the third section concludes by exploring the potential impact of feminist/anti-feminist conflict on the existence and spread of feminist activism in the decade ahead.

Characteristics of the Contemporary Women's Movement: Feminism as a Movement of Social Transformation

The contemporary women's movement, like its predecessor movements in this country, was influenced by women's past efforts to gain equality in American society, and grew out of and remains closely tied to other social movements which seek to alter various aspects of society. However, the feminist movement of today differs from its forerunners in at least three important ways: it has developed a diverse membership and decentralized organizational base; it is pursuing through diverse strategies a wide range of objectives that strike at the root causes of sex-based inequality; and it has developed an ideology and politics directed at transforming other oppressive social institutions which perpetuate and sustain patriarchy, such as capitalism, racism, and heterosexism (Chafe,

1977). No feminist movement over the course of American history has attempted so much. In this section, I shall examine the ideology and the structure of the contemporary feminist movement in order to demonstrate the legacy that the activism of the 1960s and 1970s passes on to the movement of the 1980s.

Ideology

While ideas do not necessarily cause social movements, ideology is one part of the study of the nature and dynamics of any social movement. Feminist ideology today is a mix of several different orientations which differ in the scope of change sought and the extent to which they link women's inequality to other basic social institutions such as capitalism, racism, and heterosexism (Jaggar and Struhl, 1978; Eisenstein, 1981). I will not attempt to describe systematically values and beliefs of the contemporary feminist movement here, but will focus instead on identifying and examining the relationship between two general strands of contemporary feminist thought: liberal feminism and radical feminism.

All feminist politics today is predicated on the belief that women disproportionately occupy *peripheral* positions in society, that is, roles that are subordinate to, deemed less important than, and accorded lesser rewards than, those held by men. Men, at the same time, are more frequently found in *core* positions, those that command higher social prestige, power, and wealth (Richardson, 1981). From a feminist perspective, two major strategies for change follow from this analysis, and both historically have been reflected in the ideology and actions of the feminist movement in this country (Giele, 1978). The first strategy for change, what has traditionally been termed the liberal feminist approach, holds that society should make a greater effort to *redistribute persons* (women and men) between the core and the periphery, for example, through affirmative action. The second, and the more radical approach, is for society to *redistribute rewards* between the core and the periphery, that is, to replace the present hierarchical relations between them with an egalitarian structure, which ultimately means transforming all the existing forms of hierarchy and stratification that sustain and perpetuate patriarchy, in other words, fundamentally changing the whole social system.

What these two strategies of change reflect are the difference between what is traditionally conceptualized in the social movement literature as a reform versus a revolutionary movement. As far as ideology is concerned, the basic difference between a reform and a revolutionary movement is in the scope or amount of social change sought, that is, whether its objectives are restricted or comprehensive (Killian, 1973). A reform movement accepts the basic social order and seeks to change only some limited part of it, such as a law or a specific institution. A revolutionary movement, by contrast, has the purpose of introducing an entirely new set of values to replace prevailing ones and thus advocates change in a society's most basic and important institutions. Of course, the dichotomy drawn between a reform and a revolutionary movement is not always clear. As we shall see, neither of these conceptualizations characterizes adequately the nature of the contemporary feminist movement. Furthermore, if we look more closely at these two strategies for change and the ideology and actions associated with each, the differences between the contemporary women's movement and earlier waves of feminist activism in this country are apparent.

The American women's rights movement of the 18th and 19th centuries was essentially a liberal feminist reform movement. It asked for equality within the existing social structure and, indeed, in many ways can be considered to have been, like all reform movements, a reaffirmation of existing values within the society. Feminists believed that if they obtained the right to an education, the right to own property, marriage rights, the right to vote, employment rights, in other words, equal civil rights under the law, they would attain equality with men.

The basic ideas identified today as liberal feminist have changed very little since their formulation in the 18th and 19th century women's rights movements when they seemed progressive, even radical, in their historical context (Eisenstein, 1981). However, in their contemporary context, liberal feminist ideas are best understood, as "mainstream" feminism. Liberal feminist ideology holds that women lack power simply because they are not as women allowed equal opportunity to compete and to succeed in the male public world, but are, instead, relegated to the subordinate private world of home, domestic labor, motherhood, and family. Feminism becomes but one wave of the larger human rights movement whose objective is to bring women into the mainstream, that is, into full participation in public life. The major strategy for accomplishing this is through gaining formal legal equalities for women while, at the same time, making up for the fact that women's starting place in the "race of life" is unequal to men's (Eisenstein, 1981). This is why liberal feminists often place as much emphasis, if not more, on changing individual women as they do on changing society. To use the popular jargon of the day, women are urged to "dress for success," to "play games mother never taught them," become more "assertive," and to "open up their own options" by choosing freely whether to work or not to work, to become a mother or to have an abortion, to marry or to remain single. Liberal feminists, likewise, tend to define patriarchy in individualist, rather than structural, terms; for example, as a problem of certain men oppressing certain women (Friedan, 1963). In sum, the liberal conception of equality involves equality within government, law, and the economic sphere, or more generally, in the public arena, and fails to recognize how women's inequality is rooted in rearing children, performing domestic responsibilities and dependence on men in the context of traditional heterosexual marriage—in other words, in the complex interplay between the public and private spheres of social life. Liberal feminism is, in essence, a reform movement. It asks for equality for women within a structure that is patriarchal.

Contemporary radical feminist ideology began to emerge in the early 1950s with Simone de Beauvoir's theory of "sex class," developed further out of women's activism of the late 1960s, and flourished and took root in the feminist movement of the 1970s. Today it is emerging as the dominant ideology, although often implicitly, behind organized feminist activism. The radical approach, in contrast to the liberal perspective, recognizes women's identity and subordination as a "sex class," which means that the distribution of all of society's scarce goods, services, and privileges is profoundly related to, if not determined by, whether one is female or male (de Beauvoir, 1952; Firestone, 1970; Millett, 1971; Atkinson, 1974; Rubin, 1975; Rich, 1976; Griffin, 1978; Daly, 1978; Eisenstein, 1978). Once women are viewed as a "sex class," the structural and social nature of partriarchy cannot be simply ignored by treating patriarchy merely in individual terms. Rather, sex-based inequality derives from the fact that all the institutions of society are constructed so as to create and perpetuate a social world in which males are dominant and females are subordinate and, furthermore, are linked to one another in such a way that male superiority becomes, in fact, dependent upon female subordination (Acker, 1980; Richardson, 1981). For example, in American society, as in most other industrialized societies, power, prestige, and wealth belong to those who control the distribution of resources outside the home, in the extradomestic spheres of work and politics. The assignment of domestic responsibilities to women, or the

ideology that woman's place is in the home, is therefore one of the primary ways by which sex-based inequality is maintained not only in the home, but in political and economic institutions as well.

Radical feminism, unlike the liberal position, does not deny that men are privileged as men and that they benefit as a group from their privilege—not just in the public arena, that is in the labor force and in politics, but also in relation to housework, sexual reproduction, sexuality, and marriage. Rather, patriarchy is a system of power which structures and sustains male privilege and female subordination in every sphere of life, in the nature and dynamics of the economic, political, and domestic institutions of society as well as in all its authority structures—religion, the law, and the sciences (Richardson, 1981). To unravel the complex structural base of sex-based inequality requires, from a radical feminist perspective, a fundamental transformation of all institutions in society and the existing relations between them.

Radical feminism, is, therefore, a transformational politics. Its ultimate vision is revolutionary in its scope: to construct a fundamentally new social order that alters all the established patriarchal ways of seeing, defining, thinking about, structuring, and experiencing the world.

Although contemporary feminist ideology is diverse and complex, the most important trend taking place in feminist ideology today is the increased radicalization of the contemporary movement. This shift is evident at both the *individual* and the *organizational* levels.

The feminist movement of the late 1960s and 1970s sought to alter not only the larger society, but also its individual participants. Central to the movement was the objective of "raising women's consciousness." Consciousness raising is an identity-altering experience after which a woman inhabits a transformed world in which her identity, biography, beliefs, behavior, and relationships have fundamentally changed (Cassell, 1977). What is particularly interesting is the extent to which participation in liberal feminist reform organizations and in working on "women's issues" such as rape or battered women in the context of established organizations has raised women's consciousness, increased their feminist activism, and contributed to their radicalization (Schlesinger and Bart, 1983; Sparks, 1979). Women have also become radicalized in working through their own personal experiences such as sexual harassment, divorce, abortion, employment discrimination, incest, and rape; they have become aware of the political rather than the personal nature of these experiences (Huber, 1973; Keuck, 1980b).

Radicalization is evident at the group level also. By the end of the 1970s, liberal feminist organizations, such as the National Organization for Women, the Women's Equity Action League, the Women's Legal Defense Fund, the National Abortion Rights Action League, that had been pursuing women's equality within the law, began to adopt objectives and strategies consistent with a more radical stance. Many of these groups do not explicitly identify the radical bases of their actions. For instance, in 1979 NOW included in its objectives not only the Equal Rights Amendment (ERA) and reproductive choice, but also the following issues as priorities for the future: examining the threat of nuclear energy to the survival of the species, lesbian and gay rights, homemakers' rights, the exploitation of women in the home, the sexual segregation of women in the workplace, and examining the influence of corporate, patriarchal, and hierarchical models of organization on the activities and strategies of NOW (Eisenstein, 1981). If there is a single objective of the women's movement that reflects the extent to which the dichotomy between liberal reform and revolutionary change is blurred, it is the Equal Rights Amendment. Although the ERA asks for equality for women within the existing legal and economic structure, it is based on the fact that women are discriminated against as a "sex class" and therefore has radical feminist implications.

Thus, despite the fact that contemporary feminist thought encompasses diverse beliefs and is by no means a monolithic perspective, as an ideology feminism generally is far more comprehensive in its analysis of the institutions which perpetuate and sustain patriarchy than in any other period of history. As feminist activist and writer Charlotte Bunch puts it, the feminism of the 1980s is not, as it has been in past periods of history, just a "laundry list of women's issues" or areas for social reform—for example, abortion, rape, wife-beating, equal pay. Neither is feminism merely a constituency of women, that is, it is not just "what women want." There are and will always be a large number of women organized against feminism (Bunch, 1981). Instead, feminism in its contemporary context is a transformational politics, a comprehensive ideology which addresses nearly every issue in the world from international peace to the economic policy of the United States. It is precisely because feminist ideology has become a tool for linking various social issues that it has become so threatening to the established patriarchal society. For example, the belief in a woman's right to control her body, once applied to other issues, raises the questions not only of rape, sexual harassment, and incest, but also of job safety, the destruction of life through starvation, poverty, chemical dumping, nuclear proliferation, and the exporting of unsafe drugs banned in this country to the Third World (Bunch, 1981).

In some ways, then, as an ideology, feminism in the 1980s appears to have come full circle; it is renewing its alliance with other movements for human rights from which it emerged in this country and around the world. The difference between this wave of feminism and earlier ones is that this time the fundamental base or analysis of human injustice originates in a distinctively feminist analysis which envisions a world guided by feminist egalitarian principles. Feminist sociologist Jessie Bernard describes "the current restructuring of sex roles as no less epochal than the restructuring of the class system which was one of the first consequences of the industrial revolution" (Bernard, 1975). Thus, while the "woman problem" of the last decade was viewed by feminists primarily from the perspective of what wrongs have been done to women, and what discrimination they have borne, feminists now are asking a much larger question: How can American society be changed according to feminist principles so that it is a just and fair society for all people regardless of sex, race, class, sexual politics, or any other social characteristic?

Although the contemporary feminist movement appears to be moving toward an increasingly radical ideological position, ideology alone is an incomplete explanation of either the dynamics or the consequences for social change of a social movement (Marx and Wood, 1975; McCarthy and Zald, 1977; Useem, 1975). We turn now to an examination of the structure of the contemporary women's movement to demonstrate further the radical nature and potential of contemporary feminist activity.

Structure

There is a tendency in sociology and in American society generally to think of social movements as having well-defined membership, clear-cut leadership, and being centrally directed in a hierarchical-like fashion. This conceptualization is neither a valid nor useful model from which to depict or to analyze organized feminist activity in the United States today. A more useful conceptualization is the multigroup model, developed by Gerlach and Hine (1970) and recently applied to the women's movement by Cassell (1977). It views any general and broad-based social movement as comprised of a number of relatively independent movement organizations that differ in ideology, goals, and tactics, are characterized by a decentralized leadership, and are loosely connected by multiple and overlapping membership, friendship networks, and cooperation in working for common goals. As Jo Freeman found in her analysis of the women's movement of the late 1960s, the most recent wave of feminist activism in this country has, from its beginnings, conformed to this kind of structural model (Freeman, 1975). Freeman further pointed out that it was not so much differing feminist ideology that accounted for the emergence of multiple relatively independent, and strategically diverse branches of the movement; to a large extent, the movement actually began without an ideology. Rather, it was the diversity of its membership base; for example, factors such as differences in members' prior organizational expertise, experience in other movements, expectations, social status, and relations with different kinds of target groups that created a decentralized structure (Freeman, 1979). Not surprisingly, too, the necessity for a decentralized structure found its way into movement ideology, specifically as the belief that large hierarchical organizations were a part of the problem, rather than the solution.

The spread of the feminist movement in the United States in the 1970s resulted in the further formation of uncounted numbers of independent feminist groups. In this decade there are feminist groups engaged in promoting a wide range of objectives that strike at the root causes of sex-based inequality; for example, reintroducing the ERA, displaced homemaker concerns, women's health, abortion, home birth, media portrayal of women, lesbian rights, racism and anti-Semitism, job training for welfare women, the organization of clerical workers, violence against women in the form of rape, incest, sexual harassment, wife-battering, pornography, nuclear proliferation, and chemical dumping. Alternative structures guided by a distinctively feminist women's culture have also flourished in the 1970s, such as women's bookstores, theatre groups, music collectives, poetry groups, art collectives, publishing and recording companies, women's spirituality groups, women's vacation resorts, and other feminist-run businesses. Very often, these separate segments or branches of the women's movement recruit from different sectors of the population, develop their own organizational styles, and have their own specific goals and means; each, in other words, "does its own thing" (Freeman, 1979).

Because the structure of the contemporary women's movement is so amorphous, it is sometimes easy to be misled into thinking that there is no movement, only a series of unrelated efforts. Its amorphous noncentralized structure is, however, a major source of the movement's strength. Sociologically speaking, the movement can be described as segmentary, that is, made up of many groups of varying sizes and scope; polycephalous, that is, having many and competing leaders among its diverse groups or branches; and reticulate, that is, its various branches are woven together to form a loosely held network (Gerlach and Hine, 1970). Segmentation and proliferation occur within any movement, according to Gerlach and Hine (1970), when the movement's ideology stresses a belief in personal access to power, as well as because of ideological, strategic, and social cleavages (e.g., age, class, racial and ethnic background). The women's movement of course has sought to transform women as much as society. Participants have, therefore, been encouraged to initiate new directions of feminist activity by launching new projects and groups. For instance, many women involved in the early anti-rape movement are presently organizing child-assault, incest, and anti-pornography groups. In this type of movement structure, leadership is ephemeral, since it is weakly developed and exists primarily at the local level. But such kinds of movements produce multiple leaders who build a name and establish a wide following on the basis of personal qualities and relationships. Nevertheless, despite the fact that separate groups under their own leadership tend to "do their own thing," they intersect at both the personal and organizational levels to form a reticulate macrostructure. Cohesion between segments of the movement is obtained primarily through overlapping friendship networks, including ties between members and group leaders, by sharing basic ideological themes (e.g., as Cassell terms it, the belief in "women's way versus men's way"), by sharing a common culture (e.g., social events, conferences, ingatherings, and publications), by common operations (e.g., national marches, demonstrations and letter-writing campaigns), by travelling spokespersons from the movement (often sponsored by local feminist collectives and women's studies programs in major universities). An illustration of the extent to which feminist in-gatherings had proliferated by the end of the 1970s is found in events such as the annual meetings of the Women and the Law Conference, the National and Regional Women's Studies Association, and the Association for Feminist Psychologists, not to mention numerous other annual cultural events, such as the Michigan Womyns' Music Festival attended by over 4,000 women and local events such as "Take Back the Night" (anti-rape) marches, feminist concerts, lesbian writers workshops, and clinics on substance abuse among women.

This type of movement structure is highly adaptive in affecting social change and in helping a movement to survive in the face of strong opposition. Because it permeates every institution of society, operates in multiple localities, and recruits from different socio-cultural and socio-economic groupings, it becomes difficult to suppress. It also maximizes innovation in strategy and ideology through its diversity and is a functional structure by which to recruit new membership. New feminists are made not by membership drives or official recruitment campaigns, but through individual proselytyzing, through women's becoming radicalized by working on reform-oriented issues, through taking women's studies classes, through being a rape or incest survivor (Keuck, 1980b), and through a method of feminist recruitment that has always been important to the women's movement in this country, the transmission of feminism from mothers to daughters, sometimes even to sons, husbands, and fathers. In short, there is no such thing as a "card-carrying" feminist.

This type of movement structure gains strength also from its extramovement linkages, two especially: its linkages to other movements; and to organizations and persons in the established order. Feminists very often have ties to other social movements, for example, socialist feminists to other leftist and radical movements, feminists working in women's health to the anti-nuclear movement, women of color to Black, Hispanic, American Indian, Asian American, and other liberation movements, lesbians to the gay rights movement, and liberal feminists to the various established institutions in which they work. A participant in any one movement branch may prevail upon her extramovement friends to aid the women's movement indirectly by, for example, providing funds to support a rape project or produce a feminist play; or even directly by, for example, picketing a pornographic movie or by instigating the creation of a sexual harassment policy at their place of employment. Thus, nonparticipants become influenced to support the movement by word or deed.

Finally, there is another potential for social change which the women's movement has that others do not. Women frequently live with their "oppressors" or, if not, they have men as fathers, brothers, and sons. To the extent that feminism changes women's own lives, it also has an impact on the lives of intimate others (Litewka, 1978). No such movement holds so much potential power over its oppressor class.

Despite the fact that the contemporary women's movement today is increasingly diverse, decentralized, and loosely held together, at the beginning of the 1980s efforts were being made to set aside internal ideological disputes in order to mobilize momentum in response to the growing backlash from the New Right. Around the country national, regional, and local conferences were formed and held by feminists to define strategies for the 1980s and to build a unified feminist front. At one such recent conference, "Advancing Feminism: Strategies for the '80s," held in Columbus, Ohio and attended by over 300 women from a five-state area, feminist activist and writer Charlotte Bunch, once a proclaimed feminist separatist, suggested that the organizational task of the women's movement in the 1980s is not to build a "purer" feminism as was the case in the 1970s, but to build a broad base by forming coalitions among feminist groups and other human rights movements. In the same vein, feminist songwriter Holly Near in a song, "You Are Not My Enemy" on her 1981 album "Fire in the Rain," urges radical feminist politics to be more warm-hearted, stressing that the essential feature of the revolutionary process should be to bring people together, not to make enemies of compatriots. One example of women "coming together" was a joint statement issued in March 1981 by 24 ideologically diverse women's groups, ranging from the League of Women Voters to the Women's Equity Action League, charging that the Reagan Administration's budget cuts were inimical to women's interests.

The women's movement, then, remained a vital force in American society at the outset of the 1980s, pursuing revolutionary objectives through an increased coalitional politics. Many would argue that it is presumptuous to use the term "revolution" for the activities of the contemporary feminist movement. The term "revolution" in Western social thought is usually reserved for sudden radical change in the political or economic order by means of a violent rebellion or overthrow (Paynton and Blackey, 1971). From a feminist perspective, however, much of what has been termed "revolutionary" change has been for women, at best, mere variation on the same patriarchal theme, and, at worst, no change at all. For example, in revolutionary socialist societies, women still are subordinate to men (Dallin and Lapidus, 1977; Yedlin, 1980). Just because American women are not employing traditional social movement tactics, such as marching in the streets, as they did so often in the late 1960s and early 1970s, or arming themselves for the defeat of the established political order, as male-led revolutionary movements have traditionally done, does not necessarily mean that feminism has been coopted by the established order, that it is not, in other words, a strong revolutionary force in contemporary society.

Feminism is revolutionary, first, because conversion to it involves fundamental change in a woman's identity and way of life. Second, feminism is revolutionary in terms of the effects it has had on established institutions, for it has confronted them not only with fundamentally new questions but new ways of defining and solving a broad range of old problems, all the way from divorce to sexual harassment in the workplace. Third, the women's movement, in seeking ways to remedy the generating conditions that gave rise to women's activism, has had major effects on all our social, economic, and political institutions. Contemporary feminist ideology and activism, therefore, has developed a more comprehensive analysis of the institutions which perpetuate and sustain patriarchy than it has at any other point in history.

The fact that collective action geared toward equality for women can be found within practically every major institution of society, and has given rise to so many new and emergent institutions, suggests that the feminist challenge today is having a major impact on every facet of social life and on the lives of many individuals as well. Indeed, this appears to be the means by which feminism is likely to dismantle the complex structural base of patriarchy and ultimately to transform society. If this is the case, then the organization and the strategies of the contemporary feminist movement would seem to be highly adaptive in helping the movement to survive and to reach its ultimate objectives. At the same time, however, this kind of movement generates countermovement activity structured in a way similar to the movement itself—that is, activity of a segmentary, polycephalous, and reticulate nature (Gerlach and Hine, 1970). We turn now to a brief examination of the actions and activities directed against feminist activism in the early 1980s, actions which can be viewed as a direct response to the momentum achieved by feminism in the decade of the 1970s.

The Social Context of Contemporary Feminism: Political Conservatism, Anti-Feminism, and the New Right

The life and direction of any social movement is influenced not only by its own internal dynamics, but also by factors external to the movement itself; that is, the larger social environment in which it exists. In his analysis of the American women's movement, William Chafe (1977) found that the continued existence and spread of feminist activism historically has been related to whether or not the demands of feminists were consistent with—that is, drew upon and reinforced—larger social trends taking place in the society. This question can be approached from two vantage points. I shall ask first whether the feminist vision actually speaks to the daily lives or the situation in which most women find themselves, since this clearly affects the potential support that can be mobilized for the movement (Oberschall, 1973). I shall then ask how contemporary feminist concerns relate to the direction of larger social and political trends developing in American society today, specifically, how the rise and spread of anti-feminism is likely to affect the existence and the direction of the women's movement in the 1980s.

Social Trends Affecting Feminist Support

According to Chafe, the women's movement of the late 1960s and early 1970s spoke more directly to the daily experiences of women than feminism had in any other period of American history. This was true even when women did not explicitly identify as feminists. For example, a 1976 Harris poll found that 65 percent of women supported "most of the efforts to strengthen and change women's status in society," although only 17 percent had a positive image of the women's movement per se. Feminist concerns and objectives, according to many scholars, were at the outset of the 1980s more comprehensive of women's experiences, the movement's decentralized structure more inclusive, and its membership base more diverse in terms of age, class, race, and ethnicity than at any other period in the movement's history (Arrington and Kyle, 1978; Charlton, 1981). However, the feminist movement is not the only group in society attempting to influence women's perceptions of their experiences and the changing circumstances of their lives. Perhaps as important an influence on women has been the popular image of woman that emerged by the late 1970s, particularly the effect that this image has had on women's feminist participation.

Ellen Goodman in one of her syndicated columns (1978) describes what she calls today's "new improved ideal American woman." In short, she is a superwoman. She is a gourmet cook, wears designer suits, and earns at least 25,000 dollars a year doing creative, interesting, and socially useful work; a supermom who spends little, but "high quality," time with her 2.6 children; and, finally, a superwife who enjoys a "meaningful" relationship with her husband which means, of course, that she ends each day being multiorgasmic until midnight. This image of women flooded the popular media by the end of the 1970s and is the dominant one of the early 1980s. Two new magazines, *Savvy* and *Working Woman,* appeal solely to the new liberated superwoman, and hundreds of seminars, books, consulting firms, and weekend and evening programs sponsored by major universities exist simply to profit from the "needs" of the new liberated professional woman. This image of woman served well the interests of a capitalist society that required a majority of women to be "working mothers," not only to meet the society's labor force needs, but in order to provide the second paycheck necessary to sustain a middle-class way of life for most families. By 1978 over 50 percent of women worked outside the home; since they made up 43 percent of the total work force, it was therefore becoming difficult to consider working women as atypical (Blau, 1975). Furthermore, by publicly reinforcing the idea of the "working mother," dominant groups were able to coopt and legitimize at least a narrow conception of women's equality which not only weakened liberal feminism as a protest movement but also demobilized the relatively more radical and subversive demands of feminists, such as passage of the ERA. After all, if women have already attained equality with men, what is there for "serious" and "virtuous" women to protest about anyway?

The consequence of this propaganda was, therefore, exactly what was intended, to reduce the mass support base of the feminist movement. By the end of the 1970s, the readiness of a large number of potential supporters of feminism to become actual supporters of the movement had declined. Many of the early feminists who had been active in the late 1960s, although still sympathetic to feminist concerns, were by the early 1980s complacent or, as Beverly Stephen, a reporter for the New York *Daily News* describes it, too many of those who marched for women's rights in the 1960s decided it was safe to exchange their pants and sturdy shoes for dress-for-success suits and high-heeled shoes (*Savvy,* 1980). At the same time, many younger women have never known that the women's movement was about anything other than getting ahead. As Stephen puts it, "they are so busy learning to play games mother never taught them that they are not aware that only a decade ago they would not have been allowed to play."

Those women who remain committed to the movement in the 1980s recognize, of course, that the popular image of woman bears little relationship to the world in which most women find themselves. For example, 80 percent of women remain in segregated low-paying women's jobs with only 7 percent of women earning 15,000 dollars or more a year, while 46 percent of men do; women earn, on the average, only 59 cents to every dollar earned by men. Women with four years of college earn less, in fact, than men who have completed only the eighth grade (English, 1981; Richardson, 1981). Not only do a disproportionate number of poor families consist of a woman with her children, but female-headed families make up the largest group of recipients of welfare payments (Giele, 1978).

The attempt by the established order to coopt or legitimate the least threatening and consequential elements of feminism through the glamorous image of the "working mother," in effect, served to further radicalize and to broaden the objectives and membership base of organized feminist activity. Some of the newer issues raised by feminists are particularly relevant to women of color who had turned away from white middle-class feminism in the 1960s and early 1970s in favor of participation in other, male-led liberation movements serving primarily racial and ethnic interests. One, for example, is the increasing level and acceptability of violence against women in society today (Smith, 1979). According to 1980 FBI statistics, one out of every two women in this country experiences battering at least once in her lifetime, one of every four experiences incest, one of every four is raped and 97 percent of all violence between men and women occurs against women, with 26 percent of all murders being women by their husbands (Henry, April 1981). Feminism at the outset of the 1980s speaks also to the concerns of other diverse constituencies, such as lesbians, older women, disabled women, displaced homemakers, Jewish women, mothers concerned about chemical dumping, unsafe drugs, and nuclear proliferation, working women of all occupations through the issue of sexual harassment, unemployed women, and to those concerned about pornography as a method of debasing women.

There is, however, another group of women who have been influenced by the public image of woman and the dominant ideology behind it. But for them it has been an extremely effective means of discouraging participation in and support of the feminist movement. Interestingly, these women, responding to the same set of experiences and changing circumstances of their lives that feminists are responding to, have fashioned a rather different sort of response. They have become anti-feminists, active members of anti-ERA, anti-abortion, and other groups of the New Right. Ironically, too, many of these women are even engaged in a battle that feminists are fighting, the New Right's crusade against pornography. According to Deirdre English's research on the anti-abortion movement, the women of the Right are mostly white, middle-class older homemakers with few employment options, married to men whose salaries are no longer adequate to support their families (*Mother Jones,* 1981). English argues that in joining the New Right, these anti-feminist women, like feminist activists, are responding to the weight of their own oppression as women. In other words, the issues that face them are the same ones that confront feminists: a worsening economy, the fear of going to war, and, most important, a lack of commitment from men. Like feminists, they, for example, fear the fact that a man can no longer support a family without his wife going to work, the widespread incidence of divorce, the fact that 50 percent of men default on child support in the first year after a divorce and a single woman cannot support her children on her own, the fact that legalized abortion has often meant the abdication of any male responsibility for pregnancy. Put bluntly, English suggests that these women quite accurately sense that feminism has freed men and may never get around to actually freeing women.

The popular image of feminism promised a woman a glamorous career, a happy marriage, *and* motherhood—that is, two, if not three, full-time jobs; or, it promised her a glamorous career if she gave up marriage. Instead, more often than not what she got was not either of these two choices but still another not too glamorous one, a divorce and a dead-end job in the pink collar ghetto. The difference, then, between these women of the Right and feminists is not in the problems they face but in their approach to these problems. Anti-feminism is reactionary, expressed in the desire to return to the simple solutions of the past. It blames feminists for the new complexities and hardships of women's lives. Because in a patriarchal society marriage ultimately remains for women the major means of upward mobility, the anti-feminist turns to the past, to the safety, security, and protection of men. She recognizes, at least, that a woman alone has little chance for economic gain, or even to achieve any status on her own.

Ironically, as English points out, participation in the anti-feminist movement actually offers women opportunities that once were provided by the feminist movement. For displaced or discontented homemakers who yearn for a more satisfying life, it is an opportunity to organize and to work collectively in a female, almost sisterly, setting to affirm their own political power. Unlike in the feminist movement, however, leadership in the Right is almost entirely male.

In the 1980s, then, we find the larger community of women who might become potential supporters of feminism divided, on the one hand, and complacent, on the other. There are, however, signs that the complacent are awakening to the threat of the anti-feminist backlash. Interestingly, too, even noted anti-feminist Phyllis Schlafly has recently begun to offer feminist-like objections, although never in feminist terms, to Reagan's lack of women appointees in the executive branch (Mann, 1981); and anti-feminist and anti-gay activist Anita Bryant, when confronted with the breakup of her own marriage, admits that not only feminists, but perhaps even lesbians, have a point (Jahr, 1980).

If, as I have suggested, the feminist vision of the 1980s does speak to the broad concerns of the mass of women in society, why are so many potential supporters of feminism complacent or organized to work against feminist objectives and concerns? The explanation lies in how the feminist vision relates to larger social and political trends taking place in the society today. We turn now to examine those trends.

Anti-Feminism as a Political Force

The growth and direction of any social movement is always affected by the ebb and flow of sentiments in society toward it, particularly the extent to which its goals and means are viewed as consistent with or counter to larger political activities, trends, and social norms in the society (Zald and Ash, 1964; Turner and Killian, 1972). Of course, all social movements will encounter some resistance, since any effort to transform society inherently challenges the prevailing distribution of power and privilege in some way. The feminist movement today exists in a political climate that is inhospitable to social reform movements generally and to feminism specifically. Indeed, so powerful are anti-feminist sentiments and forces in American society that members of a major political party, the Republican party, were elected in 1980 on a platform developed explicitly to "put women back in their place." For instance, the Republican party, after forty years of faithful support of the ERA, dropped it from its platform, called for a constitutional amendment to ban abortion, and aligned itself with the economic and social policies of a coalition of conservative organizations referred to as the "New Right."

Most observers agree that Reagan's 1980 victory over Carter and the Republican sweep of Congress reflects, along with economic discontent and concern over foreign policy, a decisive swing in American society away from liberalism toward social and political conservatism. My purpose here is to analyze how this political trend has affected contemporary American feminism and feminist concerns. I shall begin by describing briefly the New Right in order to demonstrate that conservative and New Right politics is not simply unconcerned about women's equality, but is explicitly anti-feminist.

The overall structure of the New Right movement is quite similar to that of the contemporary feminist movement. It is decentralized, comprised of a loosely connected network of groups having diverse objectives and separate but overlapping membership and leadership. Unlike the women's movement, however, member groups of the New Right tend to be hierarchically run, or "top-down" rather than grass roots organizations (Gordon and Hunter, 1977; English, 1981). Included in the New Right movement, although this list is by no means comprehensive, are such explicitly anti-feminist groups as Stop-ERA, the National Pro-Life Political Action Committee, the National Right to Life Committee, the Phyllis Schlafly Report, along with other groups such as the Moral Majority, Fund for a Conservative Majority, American Conservative Union, Young Americans for Freedom, National Right to Work Committee, National Rifle Association, God Bless America, Inc., the Conservative Caucus, the Heritage Foundation, the new Ku Klux Klan and John Birch Society, and the recently organized central political wing of the Right, the National Conservative Political Action Committee (Bendell, 1981).

The separate and diverse organizations are held together by overlapping membership, travelling spokespersons and media figures, national, regional and local conferences (for example, the National Conservative Political Conference), and by working for common goals. Although the Right contains within it considerable potential for ideological schisms and factionalism—for example, over the issues of nuclear power, U.S. support of Israel in the Middle East conflict, religious ideology, especially between its Catholic and fundamentalist Protestant groups, and social class—along certain lines it is unified. Interestingly, the issues which essentially propel and unify the Right, around which there is fundamental consensus, are anti-feminist ones. Its chief goals at present are three: to pressure networks and advertisers to end "sex and immorality" on television, to pass the Family Protection Act, and to adopt the Human Life Amendment. The Family Protection Act is a package that outlaws everything from school books that portray the sexes in untraditional roles, sex education, and the intermingling of the sexes in sports to gay rights and federal funding for programs serving incest victims, battered women, and divorced women. At the same time, it would permit prayer in public schools, federal funding for Christian schools, student spankings by teachers, and tax benefits to married couples and to those who support elderly parents in the home. The Human Life Amendment would declare the fetus a legal person from the moment of conception, thus outlawing not only abortion, even in the case of incest or rape and even if a woman's life is endangered by giving birth, but also would ban some forms of birth control, such as the intrauterine device. A woman who had an abortion and the doctor who performed it would be defined as murderers. The Human Life Amendment is proposed as a constitutional amendment, is supported by Reagan, and out of the 34 states needed to convene a constitutional convention to pass the HLA, by 1981 19 had passed resolutions.

To achieve its goals, the Right employs strategies as diverse as the groups comprising it. Many are geared toward legal reform through the use of legitimate strategies such as baking cakes or sending roses to state legislators on the day of a vote on the ERA, door-to-door canvassing, phone campaigns, and expensive television campaigns and other propaganda directed against liberal and pro-choice senators. In 33 states, a sophisticated voter identification program was launched by pro-life groups to survey voter opinion and sell or give the results to anti-abortion and anti-ERA candidates to use in mail campaigns for fund raising. Pro-life advocates have also undertaken massive anti-abortion and anti-ERA mailings to elected officials. The clear message of these mailings, in the words of a CBS reporter, is "vote our way, or we'll get you." Other New Right strategies are less legitimate, consistent with the counterrevolutionary nature of New Right politics. These include such tactics as bombing abortion clinics, infiltrating state delegations to the Houston International Women's Year Conference, disseminating life-threatening anti-gay propaganda, and establishing alternative institutions, such as organizations that "front" as abortion clinics but whose real purpose is to intimidate abortion seekers through showing slides of aborted fetuses and giving women false information about the dangers of abortion. In addition, training camps have been established by the Ku Klux Klan to train explorer scouts in guerilla warfare to "battle with communists and homosexuals" (*News,* 1981).

Perhaps one of the most powerful tactics used by the New Right to advance its cause has been the deceptive use of labels which signify traditionally acceptable American values and beliefs to lend legitimacy and credibility to the movement and its cause. For example, Vice President Bush, at a national meeting of the Conservative Political Action Conference, a coalition of New Right groups, characterized the conservative platform as "progressive," stating that conservatives, not liberals, have the *new* ideas. The Moral Majority which, in fact, appears to represent a small but highly organized minority opinion (Yankelovich, 1981), makes everyone else the "immoral minority." Words such as "freedom," "family," "choice," "human life," "work," and "peace" ring out in speeches at right-wing gatherings and flood their printed literature. However, as Jane O'Reilly (1980) points out in an insightful analysis of New Right language, what the Right really means by "freedom" is free enterprise, that is, business free from environmental and other governmental regulation and taxes. "Family" means a working father, mother at home, and two children, in other words, 7 percent of all American households at the present time. "Choice" really means denying other women's right to choose an abortion by imposing one view of morality on society. "Human life" means saving an unborn fetus at the expense of an adult woman if necessary, but, ironically, taking the life of a criminal through capital punishment to preserve the life and moral fabric of society. By "work," the Right means maintenance of right-to-work, or anti-union, laws; a crackdown on "welfare chiselers" who do not work, and ending affirmative action "quotas." And, finally, "peace" refers to male leadership and machismo, that is, as Reverend Jerry Falwell, leader of the Moral Majority, puts it, a foreign policy no longer "under the complete control of avid supporters of the women's movement" (O'Reilly, 1980). At the same time, negative labels are used to stigmatize and to blame the opposition for the decay of society. Groups whose concerns are as broad as health care, the environment, poverty, world peace, and human rights; not to mention groups such as Blacks, Jews, women, Hispanics, and gays, are termed "special interest groups" and are held responsible for the loss of morality and true Christian values.

Women and their demand for equality have become for the Right the scapegoat for all the problems confronting American society today. Whether it is the increase in divorce, the rise in teenage pregnancy, the loss of jobs by white men, the decline of Christian morality, the increased acceptability of homosexuality, the failure of American business, the lack of a "tough" foreign policy, or the humiliations and defeats the U.S. has suffered both at home and abroad, women and the women's movement are blamed. Political liberalism, too, is linked with women. In fact, liberalism is characterized by the Right as having the same kinds of subordinate traits ascribed to females and disparaged by the larger society. It is "soft" on Communism, "passive" in its exercise of military power, "permissive" with the poor, "submits" to domination by small Third World countries, and has developed policies guided by "emotion"—by the "bleeding-heart" rather than the rational approach.

For the Right, the answer to the decadence, permissiveness, and naivete of political liberalism, then, is a return to masculine values and to the glorification of maleness and male bonding and the hatred of femaleness. In short, the warrior and the all-male group are the essence of New Right conservative politics. In the face of the broad changes brought about by the women's movement and the increasing emphasis in society on traditionally feminine as opposed to masculine values— egalitarianism rather than hierarchy, cooperation rather than competition, nurturance rather than rugged individualism, peace rather than conflict—masculinity and maleness rears its head and reasserts patriarchal forms. The fundamental purpose of the New Right and of right-wing politics is to preserve male interest, to protect male domination and all that is male, in other words, to ensure the continuation of patriarchy (Rupp, 1981).

From a social change perspective, what is significant is not the strong disagreement between feminists and anti-feminists about how to solve the major problems facing society today. Rather it is the sharp rise in political activism around the same set of central issues that compels us to take a closer look at the similar nature and origins of both feminist and anti-feminist activity. The New Right, much like the movements to which it is responding, is a movement of self-affirmation. In the 1960s and 1970s, a variety of oppressed, devalued, and "deviant" groups in society "came out"—for example, gays, Blacks, Hispanics, women, the disabled, the aged, fat people— and organized collectively to demand recognition from the larger moral order, redress for inequities they had suffered in the past, and equal access to institutional resources. These movements set into motion at least the beginnings of a redistribution of societal rewards, not only of power and prestige, but access to economic benefits as well. To some extent, the New Right movement can be viewed as the collective efforts of a new set of "deviants" who perceive that the attempts of other populations to claim the legitimacy of their cultural values has forced upon conservatives a new kind of "deviant" status (Kitsuse, 1981). The Right has even developed its own "oppression mentality." Thus, like other movements of "oppressed groups" in society, the New Right is, in part, a movement of self-affirmation which seeks to reclaim the moral superiority of its own values and interests by, so to speak, "coming out of the family room." However, the solution to its grievances is to "bring things back to normal," which means to restore the legitimacy of its own cultural values and lifestyles by rolling back the social and political changes that have already happened, many of which they attribute to the success of the feminist movement. The Right, then, is reacting to what it perceives as a cultural revolution already in progress which threatens its own social and economic advantage. The ability to mobilize disparate groups around the single issue of the importance of women's role as homemaker and childbearer in the family illustrates, in fact, the success, not the failure, of feminists to make inroads toward change in American society (Yankelovich, 1981).

What then will be the effect of such well-organized opposition to feminism on the nature and direction of the women's movement in the 1980s? Will the reassertion of patriarchal values by conservatives and the New Right reverse the gains women have struggled so long to achieve? Or, given the momentum of the feminist movement of the past decade, can there *ever* be a return to the previous status quo between women and men? We turn now to these questions in order to make some general concluding observations about what the future holds for the feminist movement.

The Outcome of Movement-Countermovement Conflict

Our analysis all along has assumed that movements and countermovements are a part of a common dialectical process of collective action centered around changing women's place in society. Feminist protest arose out of certain social conditions and, in turn, gave rise to antifeminist counterprotest which, ironically, developed out of some of the same injustices that gave rise to feminism. I have also argued that feminism today is no longer a liberal social reform movement as it was in prior periods of American history but, taken as a whole, has funda-

mentally radical implications for restructuring the social order. The women's movement of the 1980s has a diverse membership base, has established deep roots in society both in established institutions and through the creation of new institutions, and has developed a comprehensive ideology directed at changing all institutions that perpetuate patriarchy and other forms of social injustice. In short, the contemporary feminist movement has passed beyond the lift-off stage and has acquired a momentum of its own, almost independent of the generating conditions that gave rise to it. As we have seen, anti-feminist opposition is also a powerful political force both within the ranks of the established political system, as well as outside of it in the form of a highly organized countermovement. However, the membership base of the anti-feminist movement is less diverse than that of the feminist movement (Huber et al., 1976; Tedin, 1977; Arrington and Kyle, 1978) and its goals and ideology are more particularistic, since they are, in essence, a reaction to feminist successes. Our task here is to examine the effect of movement and countermovement interaction.

It should be emphasized that opposition from the established order is a natural and expected part of any social movement. Ironically, one of the most effective ways to squelch a movement is for the established order, especially the media, to ignore it entirely (Molotch, 1979). By contrast, overt opposition can facilitate both the spread of a movement and the radicalization of its ideology and actions. Without opposition from dominant groups there is, after all, no risk or bridge-burning associated with joining a movement and thus no firm basis for establishing commitment to its goals and ideals (Turner, 1972).

Strong and overt opposition was, in part, what the feminist movement lacked in the mid- to late 1970s. Politically liberal dominant groups, including the popular media, gave the appearance of supporting feminist concerns through ineffectual affirmative action programs, the appointment of women to government, and the construction of the popular image of the "working mother." The effect was to reduce mass support for the movement. The more radical branches of the movement managed, however, to broaden and to maintain a perception of opposition that was useful in promoting movement growth and radicalizing its members. Among more politically radical feminists, conversion to feminism entailed risks, ranging all the way from being shunned by family, friends, and male lovers to losing a marriage, job, one's children, or even the threat of physical violence. For example, the director of a women's studies program at a major university was raped after appearing on a local television station to talk about women's studies. In the same community, five NOW members were arrested, convicted, and fined for writing pro-ERA and anti-rape slogans on a cement wall already covered with four-letter words and misogynist graffitti. The established media, of course, rarely acknowledge the persecution of feminists. Such events are, however, a major topic of discussion in the feminist network. If opposition is an important factor in movement growth, then it can be argued that the ability to maintain a "psychology of persecution" explains, in part, why radical feminism continued to flourish in the 1970s at the same time that liberal feminism declined. Contrary to what might seem to be the case, then, the escalation of opposition against feminism, as long as it falls short of complete suppression of the movement, may actually serve to increase commitment to feminist activism.

Effective suppression of a movement can be accomplished in two principal ways: by force, or by controlling interaction at the grass roots level to prevent recruitment. Although rarely reported by the media, both of these strategies have been and are being used against the more radical branch of the movement. For example, force was used in 1979 by U.S. immigration officials to deny some women entry into the country to attend the Michigan Womyns' Music Festival. Others were allowed entry, but "Sexual Perversion" was stamped on their visas (Gillespie-Woltemade, 1980). At a national NOW conference in Houston in 1979, the Ku Klux Klan threatened the lives of women attending the conference. Feminist collectives around the country report taps on their phones, especially in communities where right-wing groups have set fire to pornographic bookstores and theatres. Attempts to squelch feminist interaction are also occurring. Some universities have refused to establish women's studies programs, have dismantled existing ones in response to campaigns by New Right groups, and have denied feminist groups use of their facilities. For example, the University of San Francisco refused to host the 1982 annual conference of the National Women's Studies Association on its campus because of the association's lesbian contingent. Ironically, this is the same university which housed the founding convention of the NWSA in 1977. This latter method of suppression is, in many ways, a more effective means of suppression than the application of outright physical force and violence, since it prevents movement interaction and recruitment of new

feminist converts and does not evoke public attention.

Recruitment, of course, is essential to the growth of the movement. According to Lofland (1966), the conversion process to a social movement can be accounted for by two general types of factors. The first are *predisposing factors* that operate to produce a pool of potential converts to a movement. As we have seen, the circumstances and experiences of feminists are not qualitatively distinct from those of non-feminists. The second stage in the conversion process, which Lofland terms *situational contingencies,* develops largely from face-to-face interaction between potential converts and movement activists. Since women have available a number of alternative and competing ways of defining and solving their problems, for example, religious, psychiatric, and secular ones, then feminist recruitment will depend on gaining access to potential converts. To acquire a feminist understanding and world view, a woman must have her feminist consciousness raised. In the 1980s, feminist conversion will, perhaps more than ever before, depend on preserving networks of feminist interaction, both in the form of published media and face-to-face contact through community and women's studies programs. But it will also depend on how feminists go about persuading women. To establish the legitimacy of feminist claims, the movement must minimize the differences between its members and those they hope to reach, while at the same time setting themselves apart as those who are committed to the larger feminist cause (Thorne, 1975).

If escalation of opposition often leads to the escalation of a movement, we can conclude, then, that as antifeminist opposition becomes more intense and overt, feminist recruitment and activism might flourish. Indeed, complacent women are already beginning to swell the ranks of the movement. The president of the National Organization for Women, Eleanor Smeal, reports, for example, that after the election of the Reagan administration new memberships began to run at about 9000 or 10,000 a month—two to three times the average in previous years (Charlton, 1981). By the end of the unsuccessful ERA campaign in June 1982, NOW alone had raised approximately 8 million dollars, more than any political action committee spent in the 1982 congressional elections, and built a giant political machine with a trained staff of 300. Furthermore, liberal and radical feminist groups are joining forces with each other and with other minority groups, even male-led ones, to block the efforts of the Right to end abortion and to eliminate social programs that largely serve women and other minority groups. Women ran for political office in record numbers in 1982, many on a feminist platform expressing anger over the defeat of the ERA. Strong and visible opposition seems also to have provoked greater public sympathy in society for feminist concerns. Even the established media, all the way from *Time Magazine* and *New York Magazine* to major television news commentators have begun to express alarm over the growing anti-feminist backlash. As social movement scholar Ralph Turner (1968) suggests, in American society for a movement to be defined as a legitimate protest, rather than simply deviant or non-conforming individual behavior, it must give the appearance of being a truly powerless group that has suffered real injustices. In the late 1970s, dominant groups managed to deny that women were disadvantaged by emphasizing the so-called privileges of life "on the pedestal." Should the Right succeed not only in blocking the passage of the ERA as it already has done, but also in rolling back some of the other gains made by women, especially those which a large number of women who are not explicitly feminist support, it is likely that more women, and perhaps even more men, might come to accept women's claims of injustice and develop greater sympathy for feminist demands.

The actions of countermovements affect not only the spread and direction of the initial movement, but also have outcomes for the changes the movement seeks to bring about. From her study of countermovements, Mottl (1980) suggests three general types of consequences of movement-countermovement conflict. First, since the aim of a countermovement is to preserve the status quo, it may be successful in at least reversing some of the changes set into motion by the initial movement. Already this outcome is taking place. Government support for women's issues has decreased sharply through policy changes such as cuts in funds for Title IX, which guarantees equal opportunity in education; cuts in grants for women-oriented programs such as nurses' training; cuts in Small Business Administration funding for women's programs; and the elimination of women-in-science program. However, when a movement has gained as much momentum as the contemporary feminist movement has, countermovement successes are not likely to terminate the process of change, but are likely, instead, to serve as precipitating events to escalate future protest by the movement. Second, if countermovements do manage at least to stabilize the process of change brought about by the initial movement, the outcome is likely to be an increase in political pluralism among the community of women, rather than the squelching of the initial movement. In short, both feminist and anti-feminist interests would coexist as major forces in society. Indeed, the fact that Reagan has appointed the first woman justice of the Supreme Court, whether she is a feminist or not, suggests that the new administration recognizes that women are by no means a political monolith. The third effect of strong countermovement activities is that they provide justification for dominant groups to shore up and to consolidate their defenses against the demands of the original movement, to "come out," so to speak, as specifically "anti-feminist." Already we are seeing this trend in budget reductions for affirmative action and women's studies programs, in the denial of welfare payments for abortions, and in the reduction of aid to families with dependent children. At still another level, a noted and widely published scholar in gender studies reports having recently had both a book manuscript and an article rejected for publication simply for being "too feminist," a charge that has never been made previously in such blatant terms against her work. This third outcome, however, only serves to make anti-feminist opposition move visible and could serve to precipitate increased feminist activism.

At the end of the 1970s, many feminists mourned the passing of the "good old days" of the late 1960s and early 1970s when opposition forced women to "stand up and be counted" as feminists. If the beginning of the 1980s is any sign of what is to come in the next decade, feminists will confront challenges as, if not more, difficult than those they faced when they constructed the last wave of the feminist movement. Already the movement has begun to organize and to form coalitions to meet the challenge of the Right, following the advice of an earlier feminist, Mother Jones, who urged: "Don't mourn, organize!" In this phrase lies the future of feminism in the 1980s, only this time women will come to the movement with far more political sophistication and organizing experience than they have had at any other period in the history of women's struggle to gain equality. And the demands they will make on society will be far more radical than their feminist foremothers might ever have dreamed possible.

References

Acker, Joan R.
  1980   "Women and stratification: a review of recent literature." Contemporary Sociology 9: 25–35.

Arrington, Theodore S. and Patricia A. Kyle
1978   "Equal Rights Amendment activists in North Carolina." Signs (Spring): 666–680.

Atkinson, Ti Grace
1974   Amazon Odyssey. New York: Links.

Bendell, Ben
1981   "The new right sets its agenda." The Guardian, April 1.

Bernard, Jessie
1975   Women, Wives, Mothers. Chicago: Aldine.

Blau, Francine D.
1975   "Women in the labor force: an overview." Pp. 211–226 in Jo Freeman (ed.), Women: A Feminist Perspective. Palo Alto, California: Mayfield.

Bunch, Charlotte
1981   "Feminism's future." Paper presented at a Conference, Advancing Feminism: Strategies for the '80s, February, Columbus, Ohio.

Cassell, Joan
1977   A Group Called Women: Sisterhood and Symbolism in the Feminist Movement. New York: David McKay.

Chafe, William Henry
1972   The American Woman: Her Changing Social, Economic, and Political Roles, 1920–1970. New York: Oxford University Press.
1977   Women and Equality: Changing Patterns in American Culture. New York: Oxford University Press.

Charlton, Linda
1981   "Sisterhood is braced for the Reagonautes." New York Times, June 1.

Dallin, Dorothy A. A. and Gail W. Lapidus (eds.)
1977   Women in Russia. Stanford: Stanford University Press.

Daly, Mary
1978   Gyn/Ecology. Boston: Beacon.

deBeauvoir, Simone
1952   The Second Sex. New York: Bantam.

Eisenstein, Zillah
1978   Capitalist Patriarchy and the Case for Socialist Feminism. New York: Monthly Review Press.
1981   The Radical Future of Liberal Feminism. New York: Longman.

English, Deirdre
1981   "The war against choice." Mother Jones Magazine, February/March.

Freeman Jo
1975   The Politics of Women's Liberation. New York: David McKay.
1979   "Resource mobilization and strategy: a model for analyzing social movement organization actions." Pp. 167–189 in M. N. Zald and J. D. McCarthy (eds.), The Dynamics of Social Movements. Cambridge Massachusetts: Winthrop.

Gerlach, Luther P. and Virginia H. Hine
1970   People, Power, Change: Movements of Social Transformation. Indianapolis: Bobbs-Merrill.

Giele, Janet Zollinger
1978   Women and the Future. New York: Free Press.

Gillespie-Woltemade, Nellice
1980   "Feminism as an international metaculture." Paper presented at the Annual Meeting of the American Sociological Association, August, New York.

Goodman, Ellen
1978   "Excerpts from a speech given at the Association of National Advertisers." Ms. Magazine, March: 54.
1981   "Struggle of the 1960's starts all over again." Citizen Journal, March 12, Columbus, Ohio.

Gordon, Linda and Allen Hunter
1977   "Sex, family, and the new right: anti-feminism as a political force." Radical America 12(1): 9–25.

Griffin, Susan
1978   Woman and Nature. New York: Harper and Row.

Henry, Susan
1981   "Commonwoman." In What She Wants, a women's newspaper, April, Cleveland, Ohio.

Huber, Joan
1973   "From sugar and spice to professor." In Alice S. Rossi and Ann Calderwood (eds.), Academic Women on the Move. New York: Russell Sage Foundation.

Huber, Joan, Cynthia Rexroat and Glenna Spitze
1976   "E.R.A. in Illinois: a crucible of opinion on women's status." Unpublished paper, University of Illinois, Urbana-Champaign.

Jaggar, Alison M. and Paula Rothenberg Struhl
1978   Feminist Frameworks. New York: McGraw Hill.

Jahr, Cliff
1980   "Anita Bryant's startling reversal." Ladies Home Journal, December.

Keuck, Donna
1980a   "Feminist issues in Japan." A panel presentation at the Annual Meetings of the North Central Sociological Association, April, Dayton, Ohio.
1980b   "Community action to prevent Rape." A class presentation in Sociology of Women course, Ohio State University, Columbus.

Killian, Lewis M.
1973   "Social movements: a review of the field." Pp. 9–53 in L. M. Killian (ed.), Social Movements. Chicago: Rand McNally.

Kitsuse, John
  1981   "Coming out all over: deviants and the politics of social problems." Social Problems 28(1): 1–13.

Knedler, Brian
  1981   "Klan to battle homosexuals." News, February.

Litewka, Jack
  1979   "The socialized penis." Pp. 63–73 in Alison Jaggar and Paula Rothenberg Struhl (eds.), Feminist Frameworks. New York: McGraw-Hill.

Lofland, J.
  1966   Doomsday Cult. Englewood Cliffs, New Jersey: Prentice-Hall.

Mann, Judy
  1981   "G.O.P. women are getting their act together." The Washington Post, February 13.

Marx, Gary T. and James L. Wood
  1975   "Strands of theory and research in collective behavior." Pp. 363–428 in Alex Inkles, James Coleman, and Neil Smelser (eds.), Annual Review of Sociology, Vol. I. Palo Alto: Annual Reviews, Inc.

McCarthy, J. D. and M. N. Zald
  1973   The Trend of Social Movements in America: Professionalization and Resource Mobilization. Morristown, New Jersey: General Learning Corp.
  1977   "Resources mobilization and social movements: a partial theory." American Journal of Sociology 82(May): 1212–1239.

Millett, Kate
  1971   Sexual Politics. New York: Avon.

Molotch, Harvey
  1979   "Media and movements." Pp. 71–93 in M. N. Zald and J. D. McCarthy (eds.), The Dynamics of Social Movements. Cambridge, Massachusetts: Winthrop.

Morgan, Robin
  1980   "The first feminist exiles from the U.S.S.R." Ms. Magazine, November.

Mottl, Tahi L.
  1980   "The analysis of countermovements." Social Problems 27(5): 620–635.

Oberschall, Anthony
  1973   Social Conflict and Social Movements. Englewood Cliffs, New Jersey: Prentice-Hall.

O'Reilly, Jane
  1980   "To fight them, we've got to understand what they're saying." Savvy Magazine, October.

Paynton, Clifford T. and Robert Blackey
  1971   Why Revolution: Theories and Analyses. Cambridge, Massachusetts: Schenkman.

Rich, Adrienne
  1976   Of Woman Born. New York: Norton.

Richardson, Laurel
  1981   The Dynamics of Sex and Gender. Boston: Houghton-Mifflin.

Rubin Gayle
  1975   "The traffic in women: notes on the political economy of sex." In Rayna Reiter (ed.), Toward an Anthropology of Women. New York: Monthly Review Press.

Rupp, Leila J.
  1981   "Can it happen here? Nazi Germany, homosexuality, and the right." Unpublished Paper, Ohio State University, Columbus.

Russell, Diana, with Laura Lederer
  1981   "What is pornography? Pp. 21–29 in Laura Lederer (ed.), Take Back the Night. New York: William Morrow.

Schlesinger, Melinda Bart, and Pauline Bart
  1983   "Collective work and self-identity: the effect of working in a feminist illegal abortion collective." In Laurel Richardson and Verta Taylor (eds.), Feminist Frontiers. Reading, MA: Addison-Wesley.

Smith, Barbara
  1979   "Notes for yet another paper on black feminism, or Will the real enemy please stand up?" Conditions: Five 2(2).

Sparks, Caroline Heyward
  1979   Program evaluation of a community rape prevention program. Doctoral dissertation, Ohio State University, Columbus.

Stephen, Beverly
  1980   "This couldn't be happening to us." Savvy Magazine, October.

Tedin, K. L., David W. Brady, Mary E. Buxton, Barbara W. Gorman and Judy L. Thompson
  1977   "Social Background and Political Differences Between Pro-E.R.A. and Anti-E.R.A. Activists." American Politics Quarterly 5(3): 395–408.

Thorne, Barrie
  1975   "Protest and the problem of credibility: uses and knowledge and risk-taking in the draft resistance movement of the 1960's." Social Problems 23(2): 111–123.

Turner, Ralph
  1969   "The Public Perception of Protest." American Sociological Review 34: 815–831.

Turner, Ralph H. and Lewis M. Killian
  1972   Collective Behavior. Englewood Cliffs, New Jersey: Prentice-Hall.

Useem, Michael
    1975   Protest Movements in America. Indianapolis,
            Indiana: Bobbs-Merrill.
Yankelovich, Daniel
    1981   New Rules. New York: Random House.

Yedlin, Tova
    1980   Conference on Women in Eastern Europe and
            the Soviet Union. New York: Praeger.
Zald, Mayer and Roberta Ash
    1966   "Social movement organizations, decay and
            change." Social Forces 44: 327–341.

READING 93

The Rock Will Wear Away

Meg Christian and Holly Near

For someone who usually composes in total isolation, never uttering a public peep until every note,
every word is perfectly polished and practiced, the
experience of co-writing a song was fairly traumatic. But it was real wonderful to learn to share
creative processes, and then to even like the result!

The theme of the chorus is a common one:
many small, weak entities joining together to defeat
a larger, stronger one. Holly heard the rock-water
imagery in a Vietnamese poem, while I fondly
recall the flies in the elephant's nose in Judy
Grahn's poem. You haven't really heard this song
until you've sung it yourself with a whole roomful
of women. For me, that experience is one of those
moments when I feel our growing collective
strength and purpose, and I know we can win.

Sixteen-year-old virgin
Springtime takes her to the park
Where the moon shines down like the future
    calling her out of the dark
But her nightmare finds her freedom
And leaves her lying wounded, worn from
    invasion

Light as a feather floating by
Landing, then covered with soot
Waiting now, watching now for rain
To wash clean her pain

CHORUS:
Can we be like drops of water falling on the
    stone
Splashing, breaking, dispersing in air
Weaker than the stone by far
But be aware that as time goes by
The rock will wear away
And the water comes again

Thirty-year-old mother
Autumn finds her pregnant once more
And the leaves like gold and copper
    reminding her that she is poor
And her children often are hungry
And she hungers too, for knowledge,
    time and choices

CHORUS:
Eighty-year-old poet
Winter keeps her home and alone
Where she freezes and darkness keeps her
    from writing her final wisdom
But she lights her last red candle
And as it is melting, tilting it, writing now